Joomla! E-Commerce with VirtueMart

Build feature-rich online stores with Joomla! 1.0/1.5 and VirtueMart 1.1.x

Suhreed Sarkar

BIRMINGHAM - MUMBAI

Joomla! E-Commerce with VirtueMart

First published: March 2009

Production Reference: 1200309

Published by Packt Publishing Ltd.
32 Lincoln Road
Olton
Birmingham, B27 6PA, UK.

ISBN 978-1-847196-74-3

www.packtpub.com

Cover Image by Prasad Hamine (hamine_p@hotmail.com)

Credits

Author
Suhreed Sarkar

Reviewers
Niko Kotiniemi
Tom Canavan

Acquisition Editor
David Barnes

Development Editor
Usha Iyer

Technical Editor
Bhupali Khule

Indexer
Monica Ajmera

Production Editorial Manager
Abhijeet Deobhakta

Editorial Team Leader
Akshara Aware

Project Team Leader
Lata Basantani

Project Coordinator
Rajashree Hamine

Proofreader
Joel T. Johnson

Production Coordinator
Shantanu Zagade

Cover Work
Shantanu Zagade

About the author

Suhreed Sarkar is an IT consultant, trainer, and technical writer. He studied Marine engineering, served on board for two years, and then started his journey into the IT world with MCSE in Windows NT 4.0 track. Later, he studied business administration and earned an MBA from the University of Dhaka. He has many BrainBench certifications on various topics including PHP4, Project Management, RDBMS Concepts, E-commerce, Web Server Administration, Internet Security, Training Development, Training Delivery and Evaluation, and Technical Writing.

He has taught courses on System Administration, Web Development, E-commerce, and MIS. He has consulted for several national and international organizations including United Nations, and helped clients build and adopt their web portals, large scale databases, and management information systems. At present, he is working on building a framework for the education sector in MIS, and promoting use of ICTs in education.

Suhreed is a renowned technical author in Bengali—having a dozen book published on subjects covering web development, LAMP, networking, and system administration. He authored *Zen Cart: E-commerce Application Development*, published by Packt Publishing.

When not busy with hacking some apps, blogging on his blog (`http://www.suhreedsarkar.com`), reading the philosophy of Bertrand Russell or the management thoughts of Peter F Drucker—he likes to spend some special moments with his family.

I would like to thank the Packt team for their excellent, professional support, and a special thanks to David Barnes without whose support this book would not have been started and got into shape. I would also like to thank Usha Iyer, Bhupali Khule, and Rajashree Hamine who have helped me throughout the whole process. I express my heartiest gratitude to the reviewers, Niko Kotiniemi and Tom Canavan, for providing insightful comments on the first drafts of this book.

About the reviewers

Niko Kotiniemi is a freelance web-developer and a web/mobile technology enthusiast living in Jyväskylä, in central Finland. He has worked with developing and maintaining web sites as a freelancer for approximately three years and lately, he has also reviewed two Joomla! books for Packt Publishing: Joomla! Accessibility and Joomla! Cash.

Niko Kotiniemi also works part-time at Federation of Special Service and Clerical employees, ERTO, a labor union whose membership among others includes those that work in the IT-service industry on the private sector. Last, but not least, he studies a Bachelor's degree in software and telecommunications engineering at the Jyväskylä University of Applied Sciences, JAMK.

In the spare time that he gets, he enjoys the outdoors, with his family and friends, or delving into that next ultimate solution or API that will allow applications and websites to interlink and share information.

Tom Canavan has been in the Computer and IT industry throughout his career. Currently, he is the Chief Information Officer of a very large `.com`. He has worked in this industry for twenty-four years in various capacities.

He authored the book *Dodging the Bullets: A Disaster Preparation Guide for Joomla! Web Sites* and is very active in the Joomlasphere.

He and Kathy Strickland of `raptorservices.com.au` are the co-hosts of the popular podcast `REBELCMS.COM`.

I appreciate Packt for giving me the opportunity to review this book. I thoroughly enjoyed the material.

I dedicate this book to all open source activists in Bangladesh.

Table of Contents

Preface

Joomla! is an award-winning content management system, which can be used to build multiple types of websites including, but not limited to, e-commerce sites. Joomla!'s power comes from its extensibility through different types of extensions, namely components, modules, plug-ins, and templates. There is a vast repository of over 4,500 Joomla! extensions, most of which are available free of cost and comes with open source licensing. VirtueMart is one such extension which helps to build an online shop in conjunction with Joomla!. Being an extension of Joomla!, VirtueMart provides seamless integration with a Joomla! site, using the same security, look and feel, and convenient framework for extending the e-commerce application. Web developers can easily build a Joomla! and VirtueMart-based e-commerce website without the need for custom coding. Even ordinary people, with little knowledge in HTML, CSS, and PHP, can build a functional online store using Joomla! and VirtueMart. This book teaches how to build a Joomla! and VirtueMart online shop without delving into extensive coding.

What this book covers

Chapter 1, Introduction to Joomla! and E-Commerce, introduces Joomla! and VirtueMart along with some other components similar to VirtueMart. This chapter describes Joomla!, its main features, and the e-commerce options in Joomla!. It also elaborates on VirtueMart and its features, and lists alternatives to VirtueMart and the other shopping carts that can be used with Joomla!

Chapter 2, Installation and Basic Configuration of Joomla! and VirtueMart, explains the installation of Joomla! and Virtuemart. First, it shows the basic requirements for installing Joomla! and VirtueMart. It then proceeds to show the installation procedures for Joomla! and VirtueMart. This chapter also describes installing and uninstalling Joomla! components, plug-ins, modules, and templates. It also explains setting up the basic configurations for a Joomla! site, installing the VirtueMart component and modules, and configuring the basic options for a VirtueMart shop. At the end of this chapter, you will get a Joomla! site with the VirtueMart shopping cart installed.

Chapter 3, Configuring the VirtueMart Store, explains how to configure a VirtueMart shop. First, this chapter explains configuring the shop, creating and using appropriate zones, currencies, and locales, installing and uninstalling appropriate modules, and configuring those followed by configuring the payment methods, shipping methods, and taxes for the shop. The configuration options discussed in this chapter are specific to VirtueMart which gives basis for further configuring and customizing the shop.

Chapter 4, Managing the Product Catalogue, explains details about building a product catalogue and managing the catalogue for a VirtueMart store. This chapter teaches managing manufacturers and vendors, managing the product categories and products, creating and using product attributes, and creating and using product types. In this chapter, you are going to add and edit a lot of information about manufacturers, vendors, product categories, and products. In this chapter, the VirtueMart shop will take shape with the products you want to sell.

Chapter 5, Managing Customers and Orders, discusses managing customers and orders. Specifically, it teaches configuring the user registration settings for VirtueMart, managing users for the VirtueMart shop, creating and managing fields for the customer registration form, creating and managing user groups, and creating and using order status types. This is followed by viewing order statistics, viewing details of an order, updating an order, and managing inventory. The skills taught in this chapter are invaluable for any shop administrator.

Chapter 6, Customizing the Look and Feel, discusses customizing the look and feel of the shop. This chapter teaches installing and applying a new Joomla! template to the site. It then shows how to customize the look and feel of the VirtueMart store. It also explains VirtueMart theming and layouts. Later, this chapter shows how to customize the look and feel of the VirtueMart store as a whole, and how to use search engine friendly (SEF) URLs for your shop.

Chapter 7, Promotion and Public Relations, describes the promotion and public relations tools available in VirtueMart. This chapter teaches you to use Joomla!'s and VirtueMart's promotional tools like banner ads, specials, and featured products, and also how to use coupons to attract more customers. Later, this chapter explains how to use newsletters and product notifications to keep continuous communication with your customers. You will also learn how to use VirtueMart's product review feature to express customer experiences.

Chapter 8, Localization of VirtueMart, deals with the localization of VirtueMart. This chapter enables you to understand the need for, and importance of localization. It then shows you how to use different regions and region-specific taxes for the shop. This chapter also shows how to use multiple currencies for the shop. In addition to taxes and multiple currencies, this chapter also shows how to install new languages for the Joomla! site and VirtueMart shop. Later, it teaches how to translate the interface as well as website's contents into your desired language.

Chapter 9, Extending VirtueMart's Functionalities, deals with third-party extensions to extend VirtueMart's functionalities and tweaking some extensions to suit your needs. This chapter teaches you to use the appropriate extension for bulk import and export of products to your VirtueMart shop catalogue and to use product tag clouds. In addition to bulk import and export of product information, you will also learn to update multiple product information at the same time using AJAX. This is followed by using testimonials and commenting to improve product reviews and using wholesaling. In this chapter, you will also learn to use social networks and bookmarking sites to spread news about your site. This chapter also shows how to spice up your shop by using the new visual cart module, display slideshows with product images, and include modules in the content items.

Chapter 10, Maintenance and Troubleshooting, teaches you the necessary maintenance tasks and common problems that can occur. You will learn to move the shop to your server after building it on your local computer, back up and restore files and databases, and handle the security of your site. This is followed by identifying common problems, troubleshooting them, and finding solutions from online forums.

Appendix A, Configuration Options, lists detailed configuration options for some of the shipping and payment modules for VirtueMart. This works as a reference point for using all shipping and payment modules with your Joomla! and VirtueMart online shop.

Appendix B, Resources for Joomla! and VirtueMart, mainly shows how to set up a development environment on your local computer and where to get the resources for Joomla! and VirtueMart. First, it shows you how to setup a WAMP Server on your local computer for getting started with building the Joomla! and VirtueMart shop. Later, you get a list of sites from where you can get software, tutorials and support, for both Joomla! and VirtueMart.

What you need for this book

First of all, you will need an Apache, MySQL, and PHP environment to run Joomla! and VirtueMart. We have used Joomla! 1.5.9 and VirtueMart 1.1.2 for this book. All descriptions and screenshots are based on these versions. For some activities in this book (for example, relocating the site to remote server), you need a hosting account on a Linux server with *cPanel* access. If you do not have access to any webhosting service, you can still use Joomla! and VirtueMart, and learn by using your own computer. In that case, you need to set up a development environment by installing WAMP on a Windows machine. For more information on setting up development environment on your Windows computer, please see the *Appendix* B. To get the exact results, instructions in this book should be followed from the beginning to the end, and you should perform the tasks as described.

In addition to an Apache, MySQL, and PHP environment, Joomla! and VirtueMart, familiarity with HTML, CSS, and PHP will be of added advantage, especially for tweaking the extensions as described in Chapter 9. Basic skill in creating MySQL databases through phpMyAdmin will also be necessary.

Who this book is for

Are you a Joomla! user who wants to build an e-commerce store? Do you have a Joomla! site and want to add e-commerce to it to sell products? Then this book is for you! The pre-requisites are simple. You should already know how to build a site with Joomla!, have a smattering of CSS and HTML and perhaps some PHP.

Conventions

In this book, you will find a number of styles of text that distinguish between different kinds of information. Here are some examples of these styles, and an explanation of their meaning.

Code words in text are shown as follows: "In second line, we have mentioned the version of Joomla!. `client = 'site'` means this translation pack is for Joomla! site."

A block of code will be set as follows:

```
var $log_path = './public_html/bdosn/logs';
var $tmp_path = './public_html/bdosn/tmp';
```

When we wish to draw your attention to a particular part of a code block, the relevant lines or items will be shown in bold:

```
var $dbtype = 'mysql';
var $host = 'localhost';
var $user = 'root';
var $db = 'bdosn';
var $dbprefix = 'jos_';
```

Any command-line input or output is written as follows:

```
wget --max-redirect=1000 "http://www.yourserver.com/index2.php?option=
com_joomlapack&view=backup&key=yoursecretkey&format=raw"
```

New terms and **important words** are shown in bold. Words that you see on the screen, in menus or dialog boxes for example, appear in our text like this: "You need to check **Yes** in the **Enabled** field, and configure the parameters".

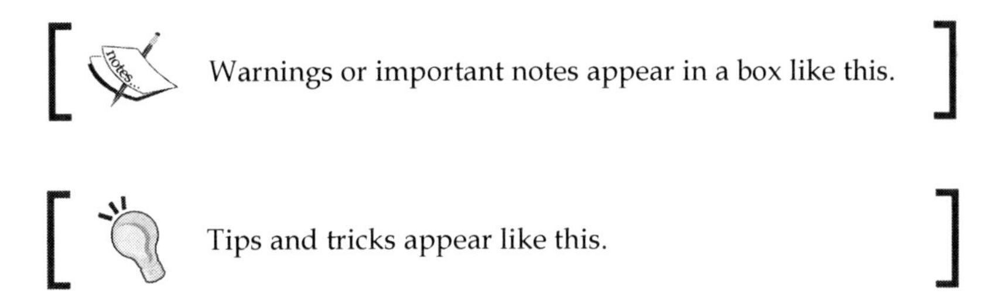

Warnings or important notes appear in a box like this.
Tips and tricks appear like this.

Reader feedback

Feedback from our readers is always welcome. Let us know what you think about this book—what you liked or may have disliked. Reader feedback is important for us to develop titles that you really get the most out of.

To send us general feedback, simply drop an email to `feedback@packtpub.com`, and mention the book title in the subject of your message.

If there is a book that you need and would like to see us publish, please send us a note in the **SUGGEST A TITLE** form on `www.packtpub.com` or email `suggest@packtpub.com`.

If there is a topic that you have expertise in and you are interested in either writing or contributing to a book, see our author guide on `www.packtpub.com/authors`.

Customer support

Now that you are the proud owner of a Packt book, we have a number of things to help you to get the most from your purchase.

Errata

Although we have taken every care to ensure the accuracy of our contents, mistakes do happen. If you find a mistake in one of our books—maybe a mistake in text or code—we would be grateful if you would report this to us. By doing so, you can save other readers from frustration, and help us to improve subsequent versions of this book. If you find any errata, please report them by visiting `http://www.packtpub.com/support`, selecting your book, clicking on the **let us know** link, and entering the details of your errata. Once your errata are verified, your submission will be accepted and the errata added to any list of existing errata. Any existing errata can be viewed by selecting your title from `http://www.packtpub.com/support`.

Piracy

Piracy of copyright material on the Internet is an ongoing problem across all media. At Packt, we take the protection of our copyright and licenses very seriously. If you come across any illegal copies of our works in any form on the Internet, please provide us with the location address or website name immediately so that we can pursue a remedy.

Please contact us at `copyright@packtpub.com` with a link to the suspected pirated material.

We appreciate your help in protecting our authors, and our ability to bring you valuable content.

Questions

You can contact us at `questions@packtpub.com` if you are having a problem with any aspect of the book, and we will do our best to address it.

1
Introduction to Joomla! and E-Commerce

Joomla! is an award winning **Content Management System (CMS)** used for building multiple types of web sites, including e-commerce sites. Joomla!'s base functionalities are extended through the use of components, plugins, and modules. There are several components for adding e-commerce functionalities to a Joomla! site. The VirtueMart is one of the widely used components for building a multipurpose online shop. This chapter is going to introduce Joomla! and VirtueMart, along with some other such components. On completion of this chapter, you will be able to:

- Describe what Joomla! is
- Describe the main features of Joomla!
- Describe e-commerce options in Joomla!
- Describe VirtueMart and its features
- List alternatives to VirtueMart
- List which other shopping carts can be used with Joomla!

What is Joomla!?

You have picked up this book to implement e-commerce functionalities in Joomla!. This means you are already familiar with Joomla! and you already know what Joomla! is. However, to be clear, some of us may need to know what Joomla! is. Let us see how Joomla! is defined on its web site `http://www.joomla.org`:

> *Joomla! is an award-winning CMS that will help you build web sites and other powerful online applications. Best of all, Joomla! is an open source solution that is freely available to everybody.*

The definition above briefly describes what Joomla! is. However, it is still far from listing its power and features. Joomla! is one of the best open source content management systems, which can be used for almost any purpose. Its robust architecture and extensibility make it popular among site builders, designers, and developers.

Joomla! is a fork of Mambo, another PHP-MySQL-based content management system. In August 2005, the OpenSourceMatters, Inc. (OSM), a not-for-profit formed under United States law, and exists to provide organizational, legal, and financial support for the Joomla open-source project. The word 'Joomla' originated from Swahili word *jumla*, which means "all together" or "as a whole". The name appropriately reflects the community spirit.

Joomla! 1.0.x was released at the end of the year 2005, with a revamped Joomla! 1.5.x being released in 2007. Joomla! 1.5 has many changes from its earlier codebase and application framework. However, there is still a mechanism to run extensions designed for Joomla! 1.0.x in Joomla! 1.5.x versions by enabling a plugin. This is better known as "legacy mode" in Joomla! 1.5.x. In the Joomla! Extensions directory, all components, modules, and plugins are marked as either Joomla! 1.5 Native, Joomla! 1.0, or Joomla! 1.5 Legacy, from which the developers know whether that extension will be compatible with their version of Joomla! or not.

For more information on the Joomla! project and its history, please visit `http://www.joomla.org`. You will find detailed information about Joomla! and its functionalities. This book's scope is limited to implementing e-commerce functionalities in Joomla!. For a basic understanding of Joomla! administration, customization, and extension development, please consult other books published in Joomla! series by Packt Publishing listed at `http://www.packtpub.com/joomla-books`.

Main features of Joomla!

Joomla! is a very powerful, and probably the most popular, CMS. Its popularity is due to powerful features which enable users to easily and rapidly build and manage a rich web site. Following are some of the major features of Joomla!:

- **Easy installation and administration**: Joomla! is easy to install and configure. Its web-based installer allows Joomla! CMS to be installed through a few steps. It has a rich graphical user interface for configuring and administering the site.
- **Separation between frontend and backend**: The frontend and backend are clearly separated and protected with security authentication. The web site's user interface is presented as frontend, whereas all administrative and management tasks remain in the backend. Some of the common management tasks, such as editing owned articles, submitting articles, and so on, are also accessible from the frontend.
- **Access control**: Joomla! uses authentication for management and administration tasks. There are different types of groups, with different set of access rights. For example, members of the *Author* group can have access to some components, submit their contents, and edit their own articles. Similarly, members of the *Publishers* group can edit, delete, or publish articles submitted by authors. Access rights can also be set while creating content items, menu items, and so on.
- **Easy templating system**: Joomla! has an easy templating system which enables designers and developers to develop and customize Joomla! templates using some basic HTML, CSS, and PHP. The Joomla! templating system can apply separate templates for different sections and categories.
- **Easy extensibility through components, plugins, and modules**: One of the greatest features of Joomla! is its extensibility. Joomla! has a large number of components, plugins, and modules which allow users to add functionalities appropriate for them. Joomla!'s application framework allows developers to build applications which can run as Joomla! components. At present, there are more than 4,200 extensions available for Joomla!, and these can be downloaded from a single source `http://extensions.joomla.org`.
- **Search Engine Friendly URLs**: Joomla! can generate search engine friendly URLs from its core components. There are also some third party extensions for generating and managing SEF URLs in Joomla!.

There are many other features of Joomla! and with every release, the list of features continues to grow.

Use of Joomla!

Joomla! is used for multipurpose web sites ranging from personal blogs to enterprise portals. It has almost every functionality needed for building a customized web site that suits both an individual's needs, as well as enterprise's needs. Although Joomla! can be used as a blog, WordPress, or other popular blog engines, are usually used for personal blogs or blog style web sites. Here are some examples where Joomla! can be used and is also most suitable for:

- **Corporate intranets, web sites, or portals**: Joomla! has excellent content management functionalities, which can enhance building corporate web site or portals, and help update and manage a site's content. Joomla!'s WYSIWYG editing screen allows even non-technical persons to add, edit, and update web contents at anytime, from anywhere, by just using a web browser.
- **Non-profit and organizational web sites**: Joomla! can be a great tool for a non-profit organization's web site, as it gives freedom to customize the CMS and build it as they need. As Joomla! is open source and free, it also helps the non-profit organizations to minimize investment in building and maintaining web sites.
- **Small business web sites**: Small businesses need web sites to advertise their presence to their customers. However, they usually need to do so with minimum investment in technology adoption. Free and open source Joomla! can help them jumpstart building their web site, without investing in highly priced commercial content management systems, or developing their own CMS.
- **Government, school, college, and charity web sites**: Joomla! can be the best choice for government organizations, schools, colleges, and charity organizations as it is open source, and they have freedom to adopt it to their context. It also saves money for buying CMS.
- **Personal web sites or family homepages**: In addition to company portals or online commerce, Joomla! can also be used as a simple personal blog or home page. Its blogging functionality enables it to be a primary choice for blogging software. Similarly, you can use it as a common web site for your whole family.
- **Community-based portals**: Many community web sites are built on Joomla!. Joomla! has some excellent components, such as Community Builder, for building and managing a community web site. Users can register and express their views in a Joomla! community portal by blogging, posting to forums, exchanging personal messages, instant messaging, and even by building their own homepages.

- **Magazines and newspapers**: Joomla! can be used for building web sites for daily newspapers and magazines. There are some components which help Joomla! turn into a newspaper or magazine site. Its design flexibility allows Joomla! to be used for such sites.
- **Online commerce**: Joomla! can also be used as an online commerce site. There are many components which enable Joomla! to serve as an online shop, and implement other e-commerce functionalities. This book discusses details of implementing e-commerce functionalities in Joomla!. The following screenshot shows an online shop for selling books:

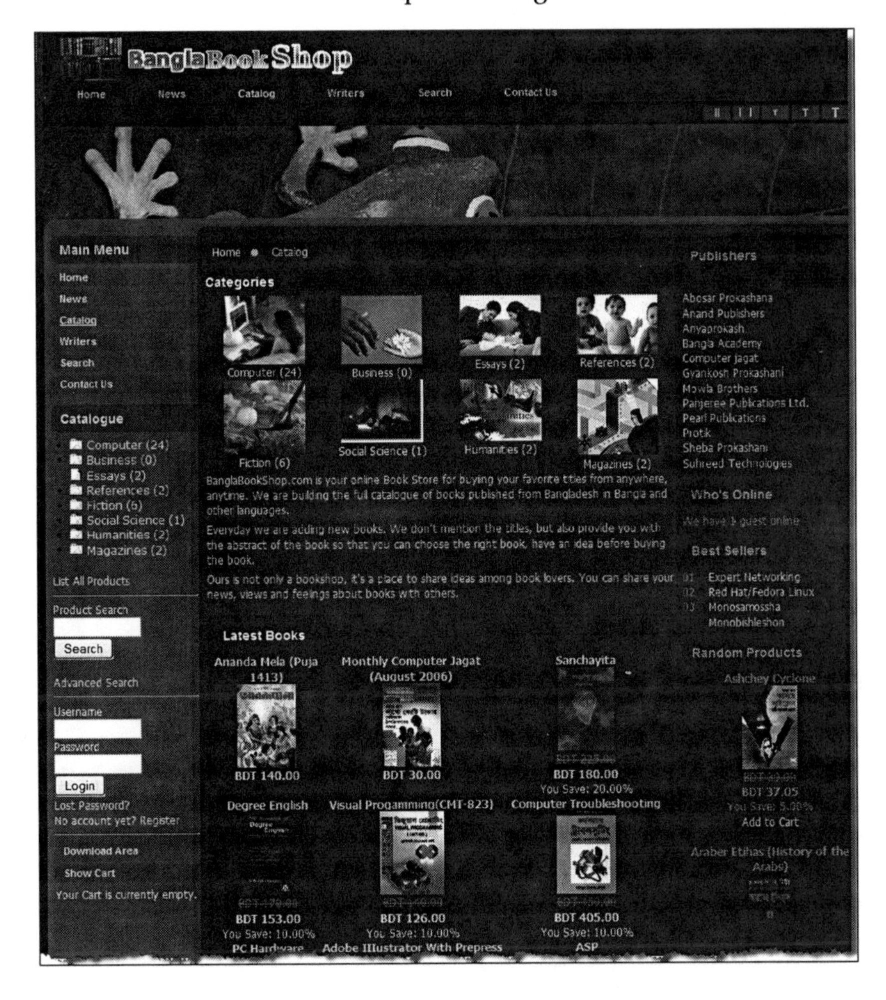

- **Multimedia Gallery**: Joomla! can build stunning photo galleries, multimedia sharing, and podcasting sites. Several Joomla! components allow you to build a photo gallery, implement podcasting, and make your site like the YouTube video sharing site.

In fact, the possibilities for using Joomla! have no limit. You can use it for almost any purpose with some design modification and programming some code. There are already a range of components available for extending Joomla!'s functionalities, which can be used to build:

- Document management systems
- Image and multimedia galleries
- Business directories
- E-commerce and shopping carts
- Forums and chat software
- Calendar and event management software
- Banner advertising, data collection, and reporting tools
- Personal blogging and newsletter system

There are many other possibilities, like integrating some other open source applications to it, and thus, enhances its functionalities.

> You can learn more about extending Joomla! and adding its functionalities by reading the following books published by Packt:
> - *Building Websites with Joomla! 1.5* by Hagen Graf
> - *Learning Joomla! 1.5 Extension Development: Creating Modules, Components, and Plugins with PHP* by Joseph L. LeBlanc
> - *Joomla! Template Design: Create your own professional-quality templates with this fast, friendly guide* by Tessa Blakeley Silver

Joomla! and e-commerce

There are various types of components and modules for Joomla! which can be used for e-commerce. Due to a large number of components available, e-commerce in Joomla! is not only limited to selling products, but it can also adopt other forms of e-commerce activities such as running affiliate shops, charging money for access to premium content, running an auction site, and so on. A brief overview of available components for such e-commerce activities are described in the following sections.

Affiliate carts

Affiliate carts are one form of e-commerce where you show products from other shops or catalogs. Visitors to your shop can browse the products on your shop and buy it from that shop or catalog. You don't need to manage the inventory, fulfill the orders, process the payment, and such things. You get the commissions for each sell you generate through your affiliate store. For example, Amazon has a great affiliate scheme which you may be familiar with.

Joomla! has a number of components for adding affiliate shops to your Joomla!-based web site. The following are some of the widely used affiliate shop components for Joomla!:

- **CJ Catalog Builder**: This is the Commission Junction catalog builder component for Joomla!. This commercially licensed component works natively with Joomla! 1.0.15, and works as 'legacy' in Joomla! 1.5.x. It is a great component for building an affiliate shop by selecting products from the Commission Junction catalog. The products from Commission Junction can be added to your content, or to VirtueMart's categories and sub-categories. This gives you opportunity to customize the layout of how a product is displayed, and also edit the product description.
- **J!Cafe**: J!Cafe is a commercially licensed component which enables you to build an affiliate shop using products from Cafepress(the popular online marketplace). This component natively runs on Joomla! 1.0.x and runs in legacy mode on Joomla! 1.5.x. This component allows customer commenting and bookmarking, and also supports search engine friendly URLs. This is a good choice for Joomla! administrators if you want to sell products from Cafepress.
- **Easy Amazon Associates**: This free component is designed to run on Joomla! 1.5.x. This allows you to include Amazon ads in your content. Once installed and configured, it can generate appropriate codes for your Amazon products.

Paid access to content

Paid access to content is another form of e-commerce. If your Joomla!-based site provides premium content for which you want to charge some fees, the following components can help you charge fees to the content, or simply sell access to content:

- **Account Expiration Control - Membership Manager**: This component allows Joomla! administrators to manage membership for paid content sites. Once the members pay a certain amount of fees, and get membership for a certain period, this component can manage their membership status. The membership is expired if not renewed in due time. This component runs on Joomla! 1.0.x and available for free at no cost.

- **Pay to Download XT**: If you are uploading files to your Joomla! site and want to charge some fees for allowing viewers to download a file, you can use this component. This will allow you to charge an amount through PayPal against each file download. This free component runs on Joomla! 1.5.x (native) and Joomla! 1.0.x (native).
- **DOCman PayPal IPN (Pay Per Download)**: This component allows you to charge a fee for each download from the DOCman document repository. After installing and configuring DOCman, and uploading your files to DOCman, you have to install and configure this component. It will start showing a **Pay with PayPal** button. Once customers pay the amount, they will be redirected to the download URL. This simple and easy to manage component runs on Joomla! 1.5.x (legacy) and Joomla! 1.0.x (native).
- **Subscription Deluxe**: This commercially licensed component allows Joomla! site owners to implement subscription based services for visitors. Subscription may be configured for the entire site, or only part of the site. This component works on Joomla! 1.5.x (legacy) and Joomla! 1.0.x (native).
- **JContentSubscription (Pay and Read Content)**: This commercially licensed component is suitable for implementing subscriptions to news and articles-based sites. When installed and configured, visitors can see the intro text of the news and articles, but they need to pay for viewing the full news or article. With this component, site owners can sell an individual article to individual user. This component runs on Joomla! 1.0.x (native).

Billing and payment systems

There are some billing and invoicing system components for Joomla! which are mostly used for managing subscriptions and recurring billing. The following are two such components (commercially licensed) that can be used with Joomla!:

- **nBill - a complete billing system**: This component can be used for billing recurring payments. It can generate invoices and record all income, expenditures, subscriptions, and orders. It gives users the opportunity to login and view their invoices online. Several payment gateways can be used to pay the invoices. However, this component does not include shopping carts or product catalog. This is good for selling a few products where an order form can be configured manually from the backend. Another drawback of this component is that some of the files are encoded with **ionCube**, which means you need ionCube installed on the server for decoding these files.

- **jAccounts – Quotes and Invoices**: This component is suitable for managing invoices and quotes for service-oriented sites. For example, if you run a Joomla!-based site and provide some consultancy services through that site, you can use it to generate and submit quotes. Upon completion of your work, you can submit invoices to your clients. Clients then pay the invoices online using one of the popular payment gateways, including PayPal, Google Checkout, 2Checkout, and so on.

Auction systems

Auction is another form of e-commerce where sellers advertise their products and customers bid for those products. The highest bidder gets the product. Auctions can also be reverse, where a buyer gives his or her requirements and sellers place their bids. In this case, the lowest bidder wins the bid. You can implement such auction systems in a Joomla! site by using some components. The following are two popular components for auction:

- **Auction Factory**: This is a complete auction system for Joomla!. It can also be used with Joomla!'s Community Builder component. This component supports all types of auctions, including proxy bidding. It has built-in support for multiple languages and SEF. Its user-friendly administrative interface provides easy tracking of auctions and bids. This commercially licensed component runs on Joomla! 1.0.x (native) only.
- **AuctionFun2**: This component enables you to add bidding to content items. Each content item in the Joomla! site can be included in bidding. This component is AJAX integrated and supports multiple types of bidding, including Regular (integrated), CountDown, and eBay style (optional). It supports checkouts through PayPal and Moneris. This can also be used for basic integration with the Community Builder component. The drawback is that it only runs of Joomla! 1.0.x.

Shopping carts

There are very few shopping cart components for Joomla! which can truly be an alternative to VirtueMart. The components which can be considered as near-to-be alternative to VirtueMart are mostly commercially licensed. The following are some of them:

- **JoomShopping Online Shop**: This component allows you to run a shop on a Joomla! web site. Besides general products, it can also sell music and video files. It runs on both Joomla! 1.0.x and 1.5.x. One nice feature of this shopping cart is that, besides text and images you can also add audio and video in product descriptions. It also includes search engine optimization, customized PDF bills, and payment providers. The only downside of this component is that it is in German and all texts do not translate into English.
- **IXXO Cart for Joomla!**: This commercially licensed shopping cart component works with Joomla! 1.5.x (native) and Joomla! 1.0.x. It has some great features for shop owners. It focuses on marketing and selling, and provides a powerful design. This shop can be customized for most of the payment gateways and shipping providers. It has built-in support for search engine friendly (SEF) URLs, multilingual content, customer relationship management, wholesaler management, and easy customization of the look and feel of the store frontend.
- **SimpleCaddy for Joomla! 1.5 with PayPal support**: SimpleCaddy for Joomla! 1.5 is a small component to add shopping cart functionality to a Joomla! web site. It has very few features which helps building a minimalist shop.
- **ECJC Online Shop**: This commercially licensed shopping cart component is derived from osCommerce and has most of the functionalities of osCommerce. It runs on Joomla! 1.5.x (native) and Joomla! 1.0.x (native). Comparing the features with VirtueMart, this can be a substitute if you are willing to pay for it.

What is VirtueMart?

VirtueMart is an open source e-commerce component for Joomla!. It enables Joomla! site administrators to build a product catalog, configure payment and shipping methods, and allows the selling of products online.

Like any other shopping cart (such as osCommerce, Zen Cart, Magento, and so on), VirtueMart allows administrators to configure the shop, configure the selling workflow, configure the payment and shipping options, configure product categories and catalog, and manage customers and orders. However, the difference between VirtueMart and shopping cart applications like osCommerce and Zen Cart, is that

VirtueMart runs as part of Joomla! CMS. It is fully integrated to a Joomla! site, shares the same authentication and authorization mechanism, and also the same look and feel of the Joomla! site. osCommerce and Zen Cart can run independently, but VirtueMart cannot run independently (it runs as component of Joomla!).

Like Joomla!, VirtueMart is also developed using PHP and uses MySQL as a backend database. It also works with Mambo, the predecessor of Joomla!. As VirtueMart uses GNU and GPL licensing, you are free to download it, distribute it, use it, and also to modify it.

VirtueMart is derived from another shopping cart called phpShop. phpShop is a standalone shopping cart based on PHP and MySQL. Initially, the port was for Mambo and was known as Mambo-phpShop. Later, after the initiation of Joomla!, Mambo-phpShop was renamed VirtueMart.

For more information on VirtueMart and getting a copy of it, visit `http://www.virtuemart.net`. You can also have a look at phpShop at `http://www.phpshop.org`.

Features of VirtueMart

VirtueMart is a feature-rich, e-commerce component for Joomla! and Mambo. As it is derived from a standalone shopping cart, it has all of the features needed to run an online shop. The following sections highlight the major features of the VirtueMart shopping cart.

General features

As a component of Joomla! and Mambo, VirtueMart is fully integrated with Joomla! and Mambo and shares the common features of Joomla! and Mambo. It uses the security architecture of Joomla! and also has the capability of using **Secure Sockets Layer (SSL)** encryption, up to 128-bit. This encryption of HTTPS communication makes VirtueMart much safer for the buyers and sellers.

In addition to security features, another good feature of VirtueMart is its flexible tax model. In VirtueMart, sales taxes can be calculated based on a ship-to address, store address, or EU mode. In EU mode, taxes are calculated based on store the owner's address when the customer comes from an EU country.

Customers in VirtueMart are registered users of the Joomla! or Mambo site. Once a customer is registered with Joomla! or Mambo site, that user can maintain their addresses, and also can view their order history and order details.

Whenever a product is sold in VirtueMart shop, an order confirmation email is sent to shopper and the store owner. The administrator of the shop can customize the order confirmation mail and other emails sent to customers.

VirtueMart has excellent localization capability. As part of the Joomla! CMS, you can use multiple languages for the Joomla! site and the VirtueMart shop. Once you install and configure the Joom!Fish component for Joomla!, you can use multiple languages for the VirtueMart store, too. There are several language packs for VirtueMart available on VirtueMart's web site: `http://www.virtuemart.net`. We can download these free of charge, install the language packs, and use them on our VirtueMart shop. However, if we do not find our desired language pack, we can easily translate the language strings using a Language Translator and Joom!Fish component.

As with multiple languages, we can also use multiple currencies for our VirtueMart shop. When multiple currencies are configured, shoppers can view the product price in configured currencies and also buy using those currencies.

Product catalog features

The VirtueMart component can handle thousands of products and categories in its catalog. We can use multiple nested categories to arrange products, and also add products to any category. The entire product catalog is searchable. Shoppers and shop owners both can search the products, categories, and manufactures. We can also filter for discontinued products.

In VirtueMart, the product catalog can be managed through a powerful, web-administration interface. The web interface can use both normal HTML and a JavaScript powered, AJAX-like interface. Like other shopping carts, a VirtueMart product catalog can also be used as a catalog only, where products will only remain for display purposes without displaying prices and **Buy Now** button. For each product, we can set special attributes and mark any product as special or featured.

Product rating is an excellent feature in VirtueMart. This allows customer ratings on products to be moderated or published automatically without moderation. We can also use a **Product is back in Stock** feature to notify subscribed customers. VirtueMart can also display how fast a product can be delivered.

In addition to physical products, VirtueMart can handle virtual and downloadable products. Once you configure and upload the downloadable products, customers can view the details of that product, add it to their cart, pay for it, and get it delivered via download.

Administration features

Administering VirtueMart and catalog configurations is done through its administration panel, which is integrated with the Joomla! and Mambo administration panel. The latest version of VirtueMart has an AJAX integrated interface. The following screenshot shows its AJAX-powered administration panel:

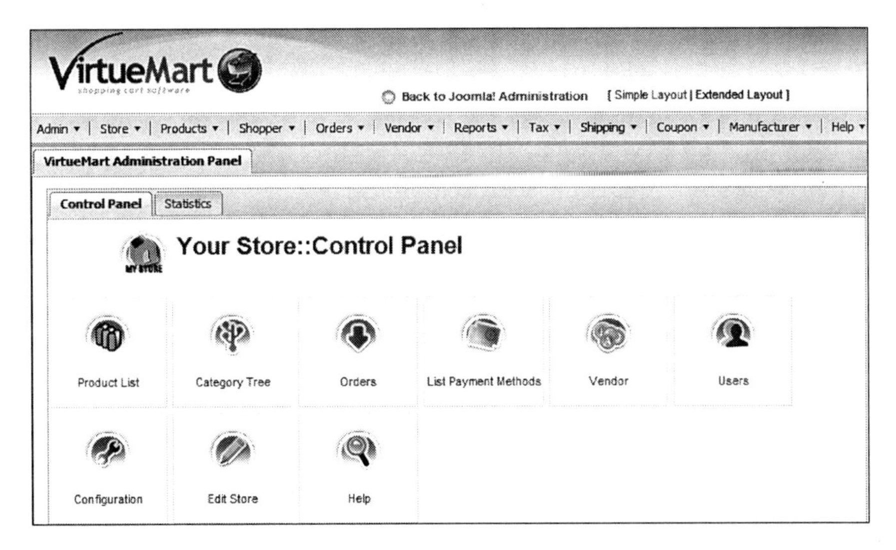

In VirtueMart, we can add multiple images and files for a single product. This gives administrators the opportunity to display multiple product images to demonstrate several product attributes. Similarly, multiple documents may help showing product specifications, technical notes, and so on. The following screenshot shows the product add, edit, and update screen in VirtueMart:

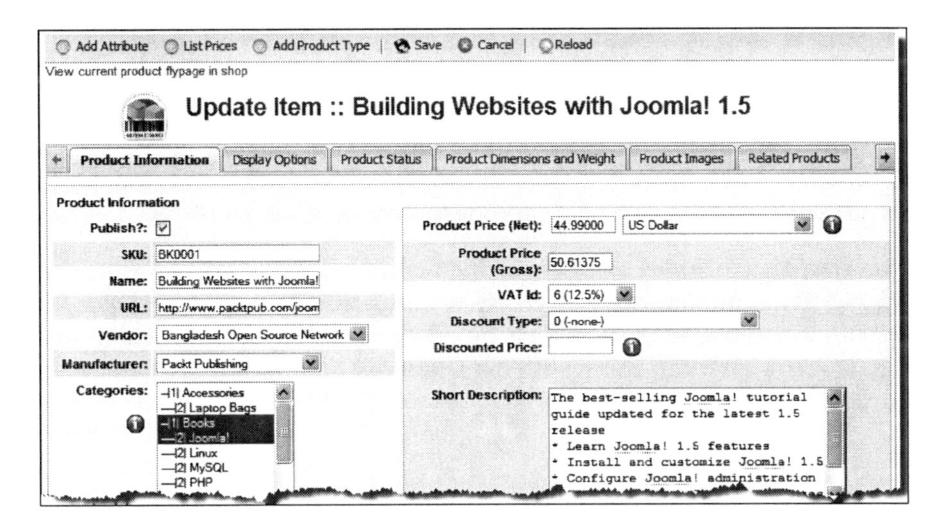

We can add attributes to a product in the VirtueMart catalog. For example, when we are selling a T-shirt, it may have different sizes and colors. Instead of adding multiple products of size and color variations, we may add these as attributes of the product. Once attributes are configured, shoppers can choose appropriate attribute for the product. Some products may be read-only where customers do not have option to select value of that attribute. Product prices can also vary based on the attributes selected.

Another great feature of VirtueMart is adding product type. We can classify our products by product types such as Books, T-shirts, Music Album, Software CD, and so on. For each product type, a set of attributes can be assigned. This makes adding similar products easier.

In VirtueMart, the administrator can create multiple shopper groups, and allow different price levels and payment options for these groups. This is useful for categorizing customers, such as retail customers and bulk purchasers, and assigning special prices for them.

In addition to assigning special prices for different shopper groups, there can be price discounts for certain quantities of an order. Assigning quantity-based pricing helps bulk purchasers. Not only multiple pricing, but the display of prices can be done in different ways. VirtueMart can display prices in different currencies and formats. It may show prices including or excluding taxes. While using multiple currencies for the shop, currencies are converted on the fly using live rates from the **European Central Bank** (**ECB**) or some other banks.

In VirtueMart, we can also view some statistics about new customers, new orders, new products added to the catalog, stock levels, and so on. It helps to get an overview of our selling activity. As the administrators can see the stock level for the products, they can help restock the low-quantity items.

The administrative interface also helps in managing orders. The administrative dashboard displays summarys of new orders, orders pending, and so on. From the **Orders** section, administrators can view more detailed information about orders. They can edit, cancel, or fulfill the orders from this section. While editing or updating any order, an administrator can also notify the customer about the latest status of the order.

The VirtueMart also includes some reporting features. It can display a summary report for old items, and monthly or yearly revenue from the products sold. An administrator can generate these reports by selecting the report type and period of reporting. These reports can show both the summary and individual item statements of products sold and revenue earned.

Payment modules

For any shopping cart, payment modules are essential to process payments online. VirtueMart provides multiple payment processing options with a range of payment modules. It can process credit cards in real time. By default, there are some predefined payment processing gateways such as Authorize.Net, PayPal, 2Checkout, eWay, WorldPay, PayMate, and NoChex. We can also extend our shop to use other payment processing gateways by using the Payment Module API.

Shipping modules

A good shopping cart needs multiple shipping modules. These modules help the shop serve its customers better. VirtueMart has multiple shipping modules to serve a wide range of customers. It gives flexibility in adding shipping carriers and rates for the area the store serves. The administrator can configure which carriers they want to use, and at what rate.

Some shipping modules, such as InterShipper, UPS, USPS, FedEx, and Canada Post, can use live update for shipping rates. This helps shop owners to be aligned with the latest shipping rates of the shipping carrier. Some shipping modules can use a shipping rate API. This shipping module API allows administrators to extend the shipping methods.

Joomla! and other shopping carts

There are many other open source, PHP-based shopping cart software available. If you are running an online shop, you may be using one of those shopping carts. If that is the case, you may be wondering how to use that shopping cart with your newly built Joomla! site. It may even be that you have been running a Joomla!-based web site for long time, and now want to implement a shopping cart. The first choice for implementing such a shopping cart will definitely be the VirtueMart. However, if you think that you must use some other shopping cart, such as Zen Cart, osCommerce, or Magento, then you must think beforehand how you are going to integrate the two. The following sections highlight these issues:

osCommerce

osCommerce is a popular open-source, PHP-based shopping cart. It has a large number of modules by which you can easily extend its functionalities. osCommerce has some unique features, such as gift certificates, which are not available in VirtueMart. If you are using osCommerce for your shop, and also want to add CMS functionalities by adding Joomla!, you can try integrating osCommerce shop to Joomla!. For bridging osCommerce and Joomla!, there is a component called oscBridge, which can be downloaded from `http://tinyurl.com/65149d`.

You can also get an osCommerce-like shopping cart in Joomla! by using **ECJC Online Shop** (see `http://tinyurl.com/2frgx8`) and **E-commerce solution for Mambo and Joomla web sites** (see `http://tinyurl.com/59uopt`) components.

Zen Cart

Zen Cart is another popular open source, PHP, and MySQL-based shopping cart licensed under GPL. It has some advanced features like osCommerce, and provides ease of administration and customization of its look and feel. Zen Cart's powerful features may prelude you to use it with Joomla! to get most powerful CMS and shopping cart hybrid. However, at this point, there is no easy way to integrate Joomla! and Zen Cart. There are some discussions on how to integrate these two powerful open source software. If your shop is not yet running Zen Cart, it is best to build the shop on VirtueMart. If you are running the shop on Zen Cart, you can still migrate your product catalog to Joomla! by using a Joomla! component called the **osCommerce Zen Cart Catalog Import Utility**. This component allows you to migrate products from both an osCommerce and Zen Cart catalog. You can download it from: `http://tinyurl.com/68pwns`.

Magento

Magento (see `http://www.magentocommerce.com`) is the newest open source e-commerce project. It is gaining popularity so rapidly that it is assumed, within a few months, it will surpass the popularity of the osCommerce and Zen Cart shopping cart. Magento's popularity is due to its customizability, usability, and extensibility. It is developer-friendly, as well as designer-friendly. Designers can design their shop frontend as they desire. Similarly, with its extensible code framework, developers can customize it and develop new modules easily. However, up to the writing of this book, there is no easy way to use Magento with Joomla!.

Freeway

Freeway, available at `http://www.openfreeway.org/`, is another open source shopping cart which can be used for building an independent online shop. If you would like to use Freeway with Joomla!, there is a bridge called **Freeway Integration** (see `http://tinyurl.com/5qmpcx`). This component runs on Joomla 1.5.x and integrates the Freeway shopping cart with Joomla! 1.5.x.

Store example used in this book

Throughout the book, we will follow an example which builds a shop based on Joomla! and VirtueMart. For this example, we have chosen a web site—it's of an open source network. Now let us look into its requirements.

Bangladesh Open Source Network (**BdOSN**) is a not-for-profit, voluntary organization for promoting open source philosophy in Bangladesh. Like other open source networks, it mainly focuses on promoting open source philosophy through several activities including monthly talks, seminars, boot camps, and so on. It has established a web site using Joomla! CMS and publishes its advocacy materials, schedule of events, and other articles. Now, as part of its advocacy campaign, it also wants to sell some souvenir items for raising funds for this organization. It will sell T-Shirts, caps, and other items with the Tux logo and open source slogans. It will also sell some virtual products like greeting cards, coupons, and so on, to collect money from its supporters.

Therefore, the web site for BdOSN will have two main sections. It will include content for advocacy, and souvenir items to sell. It will also have some other sections such as a help line, forum, and blog. Joomla! is the best candidate for such a web site as it can fulfill all of these requirements out of the box. Throughout the book, we will see how to add e-commerce functionalities to this site.

Summary

In this chapter, we have discussed what Joomla! is and what its major features are. We have also learned in which cases Joomla! will be a good choice. We then moved on to options available for adding e-commerce functionalities to Joomla!. We have seen that there are a variety of components available for adding e-commerce functionalities to Joomla!. We have introduced some of the popular components for different types of e-commerce functions, such as auction, affiliation, membership and paid access, and so on. We then discussed VirtueMart and its features.

VirtueMart is the most popular shopping cart component for Joomla!. We have learned that it supports most of the features a standalone shopping cart should have. VirtueMart is widely used because of its ease of administration, and rich features. It supports multiple payment and shipping modules, as well as multiple currencies and languages. We have also got some idea about how other shopping carts, such as osCommerce, Zen Cart, and Freeway can be used with Joomla!. Finally, we got a preview of the shop we are going to build in the next chapters.

The introduction is over, and it is now time to move to action. We are going to install Joomla! and start running VirtueMart in the next chapter.

2

Installation and Basic Configuration of Joomla! and VirtueMart

In the previous chapter, we were introduced to Joomla! and VirtueMart. It's now time to start building an online shop with Joomla! and VirtueMart. We assume that you have experienced Joomla! as a CMS. However, it will still be useful if we know the installation procedure of Joomla!. In this chapter, we are going to discuss Joomla! and VirtueMart installation, and the basic configuration of VirtueMart component. On completion of this chapter, you will be able to:

- Describe the prerequisites for Joomla! and VirtueMart installation
- Install Joomla!
- Install and uninstall Joomla! components, plugins, and modules
- Configure a Joomla! site
- Install the VirtueMart component and modules
- Configure basic options for VirtueMart shop

At the end of this chapter, we will have a Joomla! site with VirtueMart shopping cart installed.

Pre-requisites for installation

Before starting with the installation of Joomla! and VirtueMart, we must know about the system requirements and other pre-installation requirements. We must ensure that all minimum system requirements have been met and all preparatory works have been done beforehand. In this section, we are going to discuss the minimum system requirements, pre-installation tasks, and creating a development environment.

System requirements

Joomla! runs on Linux, Apache, MySQL, and PHP or a LAMP environment. It is designed for and tested on LAMP. However, many Joomla! sites successfully run on Windows and IIS with PHP support.

The followings are the minimum system requirements for installation of Joomla! 1.5.x:

- Apache 1.3 or above
- PHP 4.3.x or above
- MySQL 3.23.x or above

Although these are minimum system requirements, you must also ensure that PHP is installed with MySQL, XML, and Zlib functionality enabled. These can be enabled from the `php.ini` configuration file. However, for Joomla! 1.5.x, Apache 2.0.x, MySQL 5.0.x, and PHP 5.x are recommended.

VirtueMart has no separate system requirements. All it needs is a working installation of Joomla! 1.0.x or Joomla! 1.5.x, and Apache and PHP compiled with support for HTTPS (OpenSSL) and CURL. The PHP Safe Mode should also be turned off.

At the client side, most current browser versions work fine. Internet Explorer (5.5+), Firefox, Opera 9+, Safari, and Konqueror work fine with VirtueMart. However, the browser should be configured to accept cookies.

Setting a development environment

Whenever you are developing a web application, it is better to first develop and test it in development environment. Once you are satisfied with the results of your configurations and customizations, you can upload that to a production web server.

For the exercise of this book, we are going to setup a development environment, and try all our codes and examples in this development environment. However, we will also learn how to do it on a live server.

We already know that Joomla! and VirtueMart run on a web environment where Apache, MySQL, and PHP need to be present. We can get all these by installing each application separately, or by installing one of the following packages:

- **WAMP**: This package runs on Windows operating systems. It includes latest versions of Apache, MySQL, and PHP. You can download WAMP server's latest version and its documents from `http://www.wampserver.com`.

- **MAMP**: Similar to WAMP, this package includes Apache, MySQL, and PHP, but this runs on computers with Mac OS. You can get MAMP and its documentation from `http://www.mamp.info`.
- **XAMPP**: This package contains Apache, MySQL, PHP, Perl, and more add-ons like PEAR, phpMyAdmin, and so on. XAMPP is available for multiple platforms including Linux, Windows, and Mac OSX. You can download an appropriate version of XAMPP and its documentation from `http://www.apachefriends.org/en/xampp.html`.

For the exercises in this book, we are going to use WAMP. Setting up a development environment by installing WAMP server is discussed in *Appendix B*.

Getting Joomla!

Joomla! is available for download, free of cost, from its web site `http://www.joomla.org`. You will see a download link to the latest version of Joomla!, both for 1.0.x and 1.5.x series. For this book, we are using Joomla! 1.5.9. However, most of the procedures described in this book will also work fine with the Joomla! 1.0.x series.

To download Joomla!, visit `http://www.joomla.org`. On the right side of the page, you will find a box like this:

Click on the **DOWNLOAD JOOMLA** logo. You will be redirected to the Joomla! download page. Here, you will see the following listing of download files for Joomla! 1.5.x and Joomla! 1.0.x:

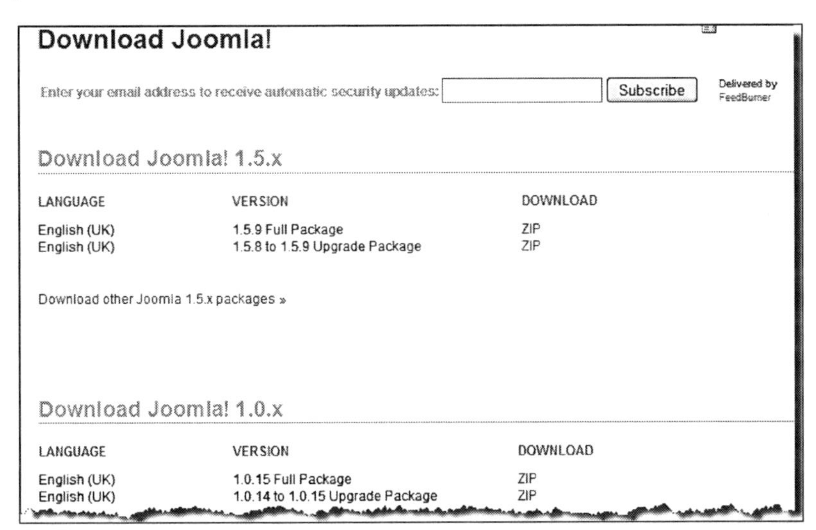

Click on one of the list of packages, for example, **ZIP** beside **1.5.9 Full Package**. The file will start downloading to your computer. Once you finish downloading the file, you can extract the file and see the contents of the folder. These files and folders need to be uploaded to your web server (local or remote).

Getting VirtueMart

Like Joomla!, you can also get VirtueMart from its web site `http://ww.virtuemart.net`. Point your browser to this site and you will get a download link. Before downloading, you must know something about available packages. The following are the VirtueMart package types available for download:

- **Complete Package for Joomla! 1.5**: This package contains the VirtueMart component, modules, and plugins all in one. All of these will work on the Joomla! 1.5.x series. Once you download this package, you must extract the package to get the component, modules, and plugins installation packages separately. The component, modules, and plugins can be installed from Joomla!'s extension installer.
- **Complete Package for Joomla! 1.0.x or Mambo**: If you are running Joomla! 1.0.x, or a Mambo-based site, and want to use VirtueMart in that site, you need to download this package. This package contains installer packages for the component, modules, and plugins.
- **Manual Installation Package for Joomla! 1.5**: This package is good for upgrading an existing VirtueMart installation. If you are using an earlier version of VirtueMart with Joomla! 1.5.x, then download this package and extract the files. You will then need to upload all the files. It will start the upgrade wizard for VirtueMart in Joomla! 1.5.x.
- **Manual installation Package for Joomla! 1.0.x or Mambo**: You need to download this package if you are using Joomla! 1.0.x or Mambo, and want to upgrade from an earlier versions of VirtueMart. This upgrade will happen by uploading the files to Joomla! site, not from the extension installer.
- **Language Pack**: If you want to use more than one language, or another language other than English, you need to download the language pack for VirtueMart.
- **Patch Package (1.1.1->1.1.2) for Joomla! 1.5**: This package is for upgrading from VirtueMart 1.1.1 to VirtueMart 1.1.2 in the Joomla! 1.5.x series. This package needs to be extracted and uploaded to your Joomla! site. It will then start the VirtueMart upgrade wizard.
- **Patch Package (1.1.1->1.1.2) for Joomla! 1.0.x or Mambo**: This is similar to package above, but only works with Joomla! 1.0.x series and Mambo.

- **VirtueMart e-commerce Bundle (with Joomla! 1.5.5)**: This is the Joomla! 1.5.5 package bundled with VirtueMart 1.1.2. If you need to start the e-commerce site from scratch, you may download this package and install Joomla! 1.5.5 from this. Once Joomla! 1.5.5 is installed, you will get VirtueMart 1.1.2 as well. You don't need to install VirtueMart separately.

For our example, we will download **Complete Package for Joomla 1.5**. Once we have downloaded this package and unzipped it on our computer, we will find the following files:

- **VirtueMart_1.1_Installation.pdf**: This is an installation guide for VirtueMart. Read this guide for detail information on the VirtueMart installation.
- **com_virtuemart_1.1.2.j15**: This is main component package which can be installed through the extensions installer. We should first install this package.

We will find the following module files in the `modules` subfolder:

- **mod_virtuemart_1.1.2.j15.zip**: This is the main module for VirtueMart. It will display the products for the VirtueMart catalog. You must install and publish this module to show the products.
- **mod_product_categories_1.1.2.j15.zip**: This module displays the product categories. It is good for displaying product categories in the left or right sidebar, so that it acts like a menu.
- **mod_productscroller_1.1.2.j15.zip**: When installed and published, you will see scrolling products. You can configure how many products will be scrolling and how quickly they will scroll.
- **mod_virtuemart_allinone_1.1.2.j15.zip**: This module alone can display featured products, random products, top ten products, and latest products. These are shown in a separate tab.
- **mod_virtuemart_cart_1.1.2.j15.zip**: This module shows the contents of the cart. This mini cart contains a link to main cart page.
- **mod_virtuemart_currencies_1.1.2.j15.zip**: This module shows currency selector. You only need this module when you are using multiple currencies for your shop.
- **mod_virtuemart_featureprod_1.1.2.j15.zip**: This module only displays featured products. You can configure how many featured products will be displayed in this module.
- **mod_virtuemart_latestprod_1.1.2.j15.zip**: This module displays the latest products added to VirtueMart catalog. You can configure how many latest products will be displayed.

- **mod_virtuemart_login_1.1.2.j15.zip**: This module displays a login module for VirtueMart users. This module ensures that user registration and login work for both Joomla! and VirtueMart.
- **mod_virtuemart_manufacturers_1.1.2.j15.zip**: This module lists the manufacturers. Clicking on a particular manufacturer will show the products of that manufacturer.
- **mod_virtuemart_randomprod_1.1.2.j15.zip**: This module displays randomly selected products. You can configure how many random products will be displayed.
- **mod_virtuemart_search_1.1.2.j15.zip**: This is search module for VirtueMart. When you install and publish this module, visitors will be able to search the VirtueMart product catalog.
- **mod_virtuemart_topten_1.1.2.j15.zip**: This module displays the top-ten selling products. This is similar to the best seller module in other shopping carts.

There are two plugins in `plugins` subfolder:

- **vmproductsnapshots_1.1.2.j15.zip**: This plugin enables the administrator to add a product snapshot in the content items, such as in an article. The snapshot will show a product image, price, and a link to add to the cart.
- **vmxsearch.plugin_1.1.2.j15.zip**: This plugin enables search in the VirtueMart catalog. When this plugin is installed and enabled, Joomla!'s standard search can find the VirtueMart products as well. In that case, you don't need to use VirtueMart's search module.

We now know the package types for VirtueMart and individual component, module, and plugin's functions. We will be looking into these modules in detail later in this book.

Uploading installation files to server

Once you have downloaded and extracted the installation files, you need to upload them to a web server before starting installation. If you are using a local web server for development, copy the files to your web server's webroot. For example, we are using a local WAMP server and its webroot is set to `e:\www`. Therefore, we will create a folder `e:\www\bdosn` and copy the Joomla! installation files to this folder.

If you are using a remote web server, you need to use some FTP client like FileZilla. Connect to the FTP server, and upload the files to appropriate directory.

Creating database for Joomla!

We have learned that we need a MySQL database server to install Joomla! Before proceeding to the actual installation of Joomla!, we need to create a database for Joomla!. We can do this by using a `mysql` command, or through a phpMyAdmin web interface. Let us create one database for our BdOSN site by using a phpMyAdmin interface at `localhost`. For this, point your browser to `http://localhost/phpmyadmin`, and you will get the following screen:

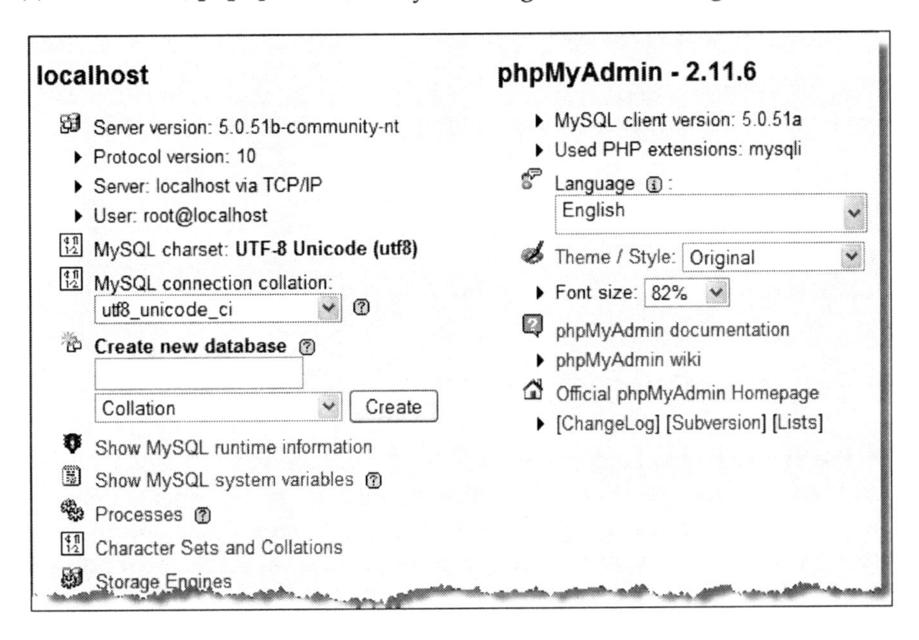

In the **Create new database** field, type the name of database, that is `bdosn`, and select **utf8_general_ci** in the **Collation** drop-down list. Then click on the **Create** button. This will create a database named `bdosn`. However, there will be no tables yet. We don't need to create tables since; these will be created during Joomla! installation. What we need to know at this point is the database name and username for that database. As we are using `localhost`, it will be **root** without any password. However, for a production environment, you need to know the database username and password exactly what is used there.

Brief installation process for Joomla!

Let us start installation of Joomla! now. We are going to install Joomla! on our development environment, that is the localhost. Therefore, follow the steps below:

1. Open your browser and type `http://localhost/bdosn` in the address bar. This will take you to the **Joomla! Installation** wizard. First, you will see the **Choose Language** screen. Select a language for installation steps and click the **Next** button:

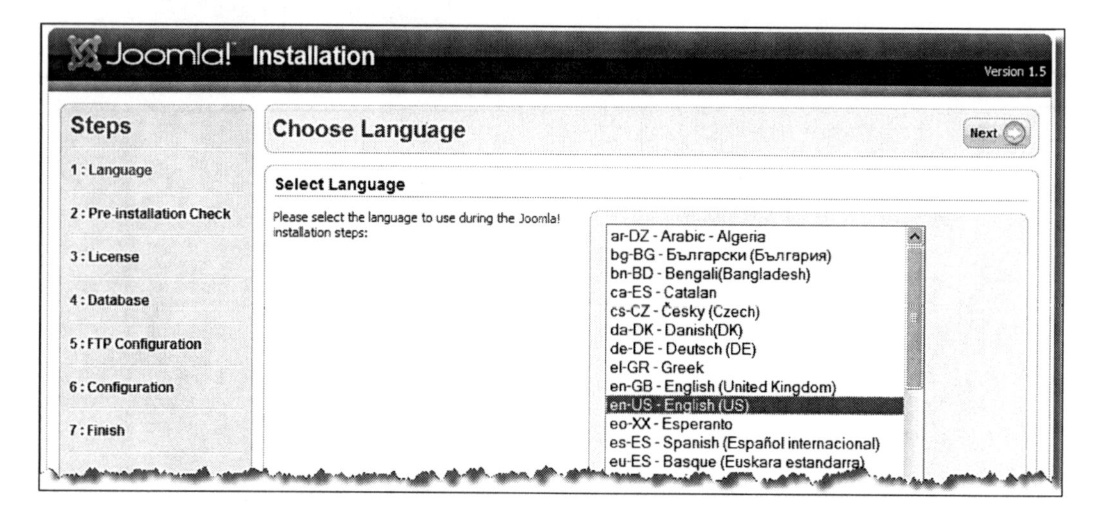

2. A **Pre-installation check** screen will be displayed. This screen has two sections. The first section shows you whether the system meets the requirements for installing the Joomla! version you are installing. The second section shows the recommended settings and actual settings found on the server. Any deviation from the recommended settings will be shown in red. If there is any item in red color in the first section, you cannot install Joomla!. However, items with red color in second section (**Recommended Settings**) will still allow you to install Joomla! successfully. You may change some PHP settings and recheck the setting by clicking the **Check Again** button. To proceed with installation, click the **Next** button:

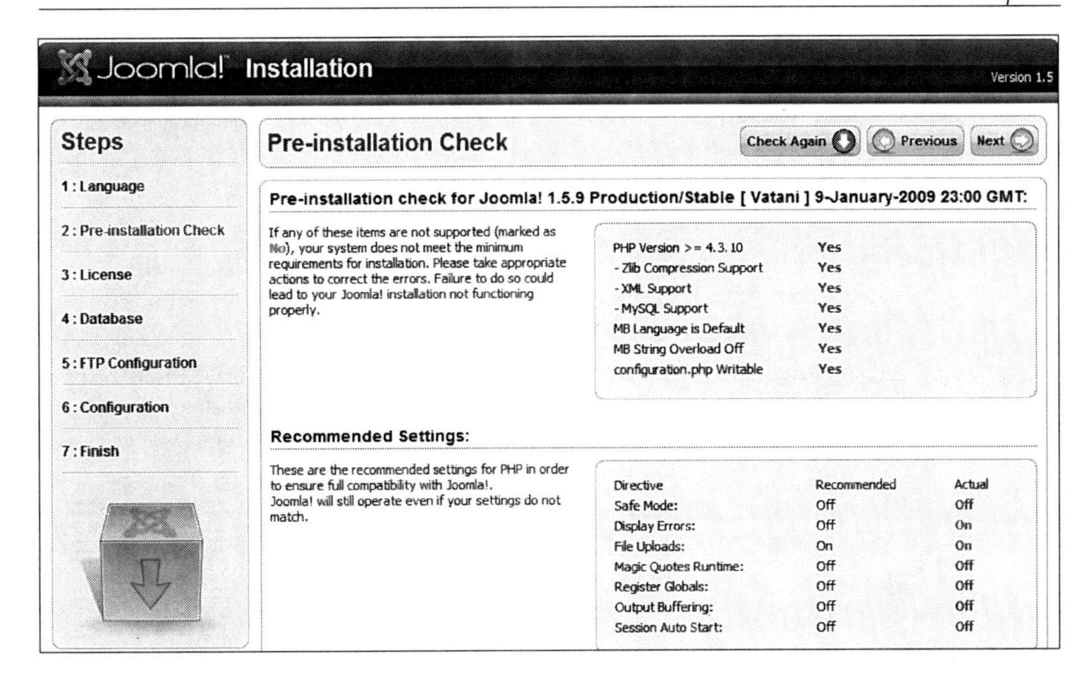

3. Next, the **License** screen will be displayed. This screen displays the **GNU General Public License**. Read the license, if you are not familiar with it. The license describes the terms of use of Joomla!. To proceed with installation, click on the **Next** button. Clicking **Next** means you have accepted the licensing terms:

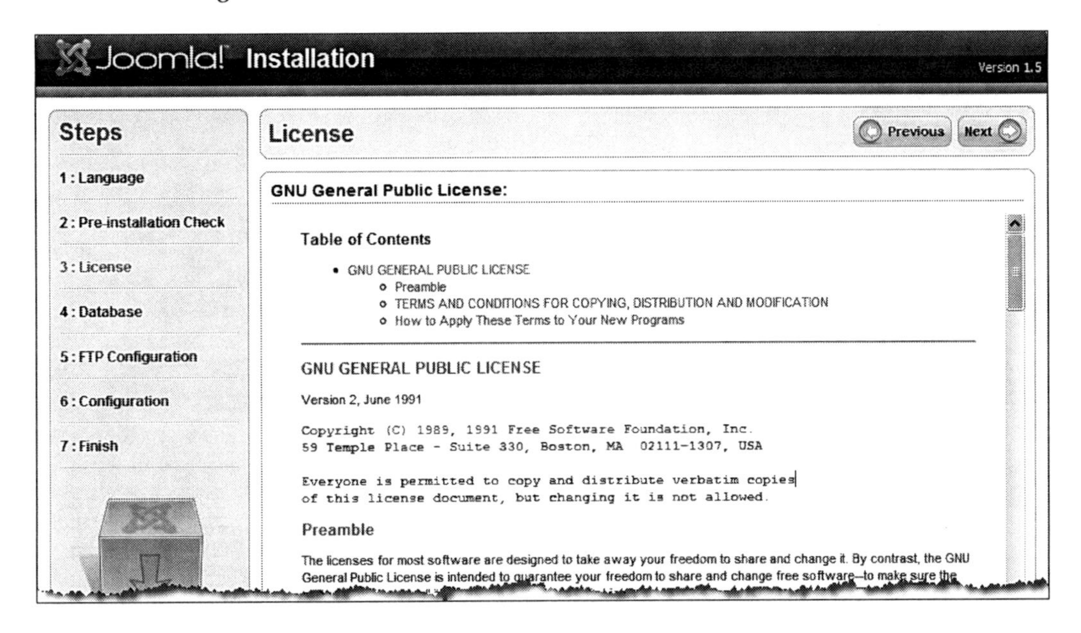

4. The **Database Settings** screen will be displayed next. You need to provide database setting information in this page. It has two sections, the **Basic Settings** and **Advanced Settings**. In the **Basic Settings** section, you must provide the following information:
   - **Database Type**: By default, **mysql** is selected. You can also use **mysqli**. For our database, select **mysql**.
   - **Host Name**: This is the MySQL server's host name. It is usually **localhost**. If you are using a remote server, this name may be different and can be obtained from the host provider.
   - **Username**: This is the username for connecting to the database. The user should have permission to insert, update, and delete a record from the database. For our database, type **root** in this field.
   - **Password**: This is the password for the above username. For our default installation of a WAMP server, root user's password remains blank. Therefore, keep it blank. If you have changed that password, type that password in this field.
   - **Database Name**: Type the name of database to be used for this Joomla! installation. We have created `bdosn` database for this purpose, so type **bdosn** in this field:

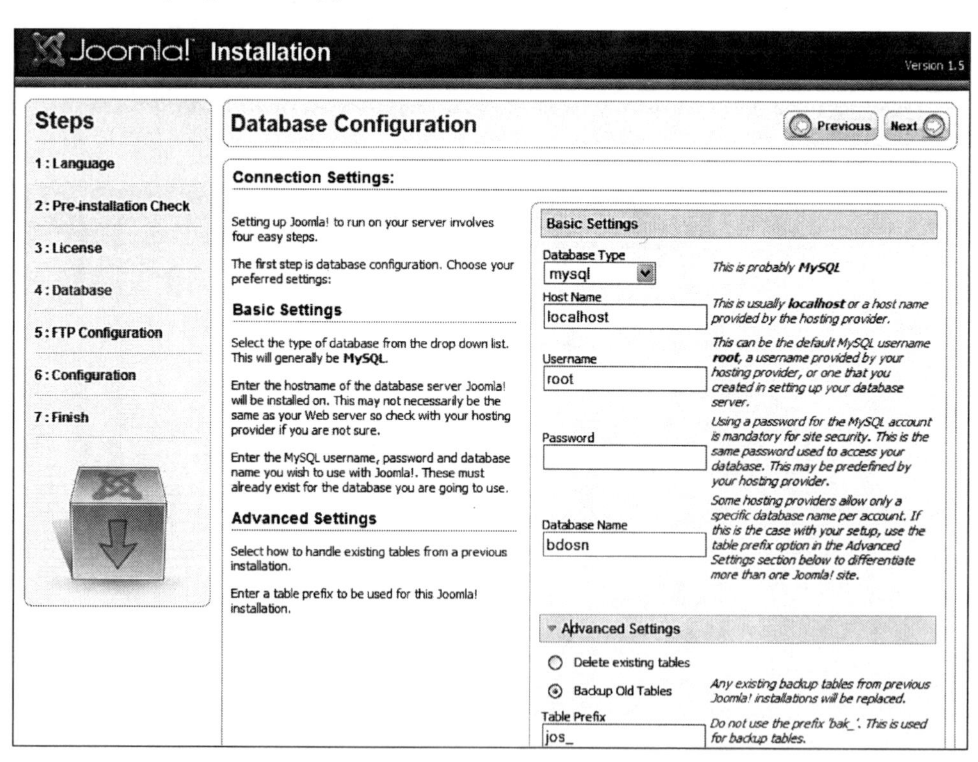

The fields in **Advanced Settings** are not visible by default. Click on the **Advanced Settings** heading, the fields will then be visible. Options in this section are:

- **Delete existing tables**: If you are using an old database and want to delete the existing tables, select this option.
- **Backup old tables**: If you are using an old database and want the backup of the existing tables, select this option.
- **Table Prefix**: Type the prefix you want for Joomla! tables. A prefix is useful when you are sharing the same database for multiple applications. This prefix identifies Joomla! tables. You can type any prefix in this box except **bak_** which is used for backup tables in Joomla!. Default prefix **jos_** is fine with most of the installation, and we will keep it so.

Once all of these settings are configured, click on the **Next** button to proceed with the installation.

5. The **FTP Configuration** screen will now be shown. If you want to use FTP for uploading files to Joomla! your web site, you need to configure the FTP settings in this screen. By default, this is disabled. To enable it, select **Yes**. Then type the **FTP User** name, **FTP Password** for that user, and **FTP Root Path**. In the **Advanced Settings** section, you can type **FTP Host** and **FTP Port**. You can also configure whether **FTP Password** will be saved or not. For our site, keep the defaults (selected **No**) and click on **Next** button:

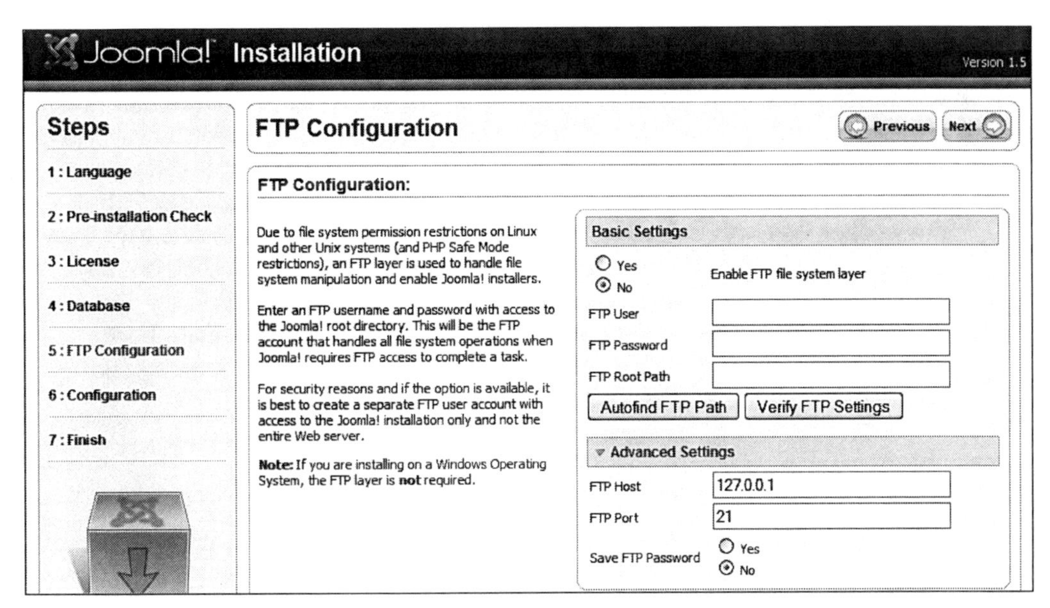

6. Next, the **Main Configuration** screen will be shown. There are three sections including the **Site Name, Confirm the Admin E-mail and Password**, and **Load Sample Data, restore or migrate backed-up content**. In the **Site Name** box, type the name of your site. For example, "Bangladesh Open Source Network". In the next section, type the administrator's email account in **Your E-mail** text field, then type password for the administrator account in the **Admin Password** text field. Then confirm it by retyping the password in the **Confirm Admin Password** text field:

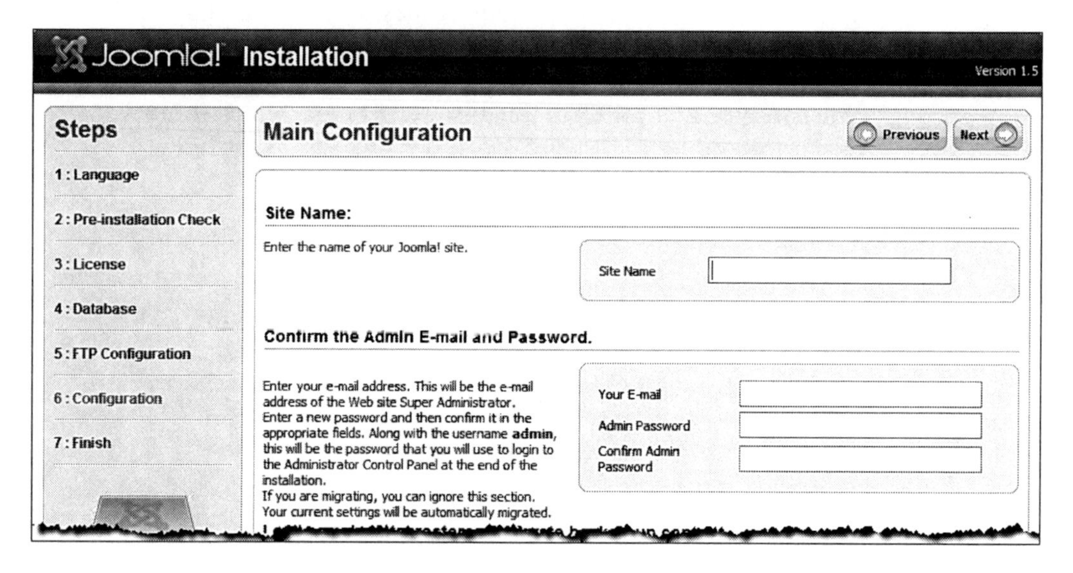

Joomla! comes with some sample data. Installing these sample data will help you understand how Joomla! works. You will get some predefined sections, categories, and articles. The articles, accompanied with Joomla! 1.5, will help you understand how to use it. For installing the default sample data, select **Install Default Sample Data** and click on the **Install Sample Data** button. Remember that only selecting the option to install the default data and then going to next step will not install the sample data. You must click on the **Install Sample Data** button before proceeding to next step. For our site, we are installing sample data, so click on the **Install Sample Data** button. Within a few seconds, a **Sample data installed successfully** message will be displayed in place of the **Install Sample Data** button:

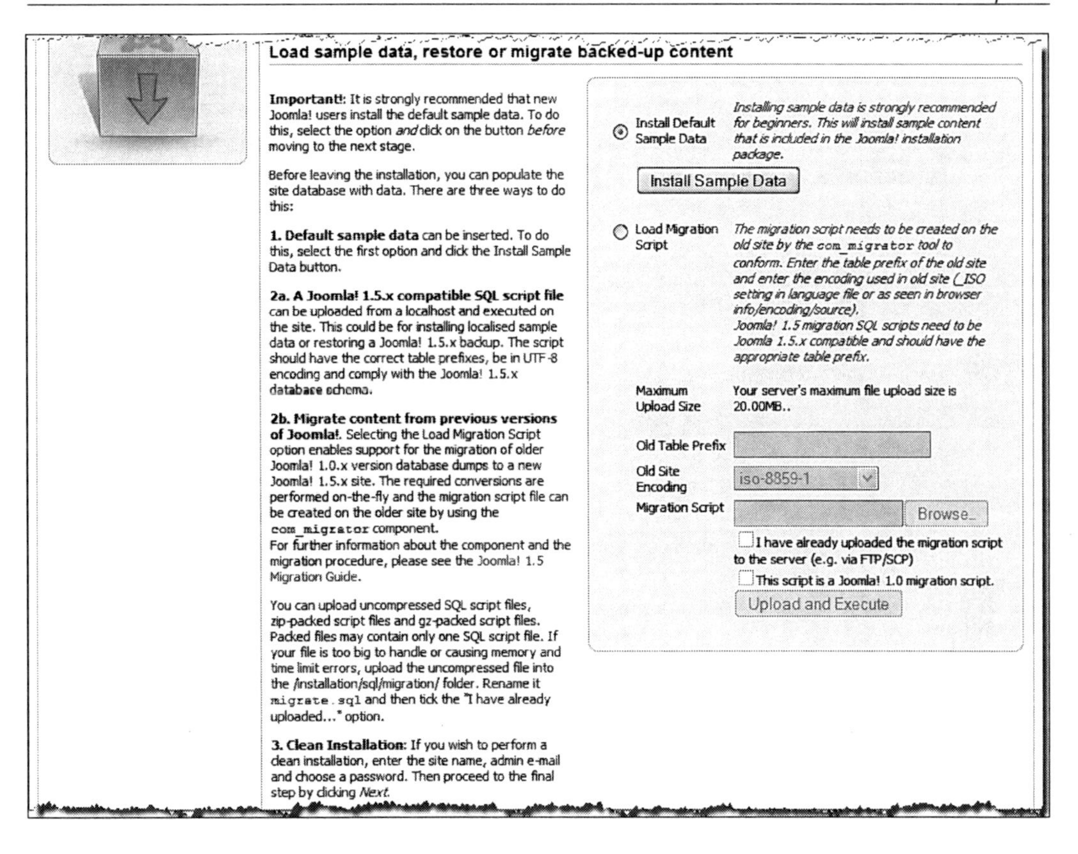

The remaining options in this section are for migrating content from an earlier version of Joomla! to Joomla! 1.5.x. For this to work, you should have the generated migration script in the old Joomla! site using `com_migrator` component. That migration script will be used here. You can browse to the migration script, specify the old table prefix, old site encoding, and click on **Upload and Execute** button. We are not migrating old data, therefore, click onthe **Next** button.

Before trying to upgrade your old Joomla! site, you must backup the site files and database. You'll learn more about the use of the **com_migrator** component and database backup and restoration in Chapter 10, *Maintenance and Troubleshooting*.

7. **Finish** screen will now be displayed. Here, you will see some warning about removing the installation directory. On the top of the right-hand side we will also see the **Site** and **Admin** buttons. By clicking on these, we can go to the web site or administration area. Also notice that the administrative username is admin, and you need it to login to administration panel. Let us click on the **Site** button now:

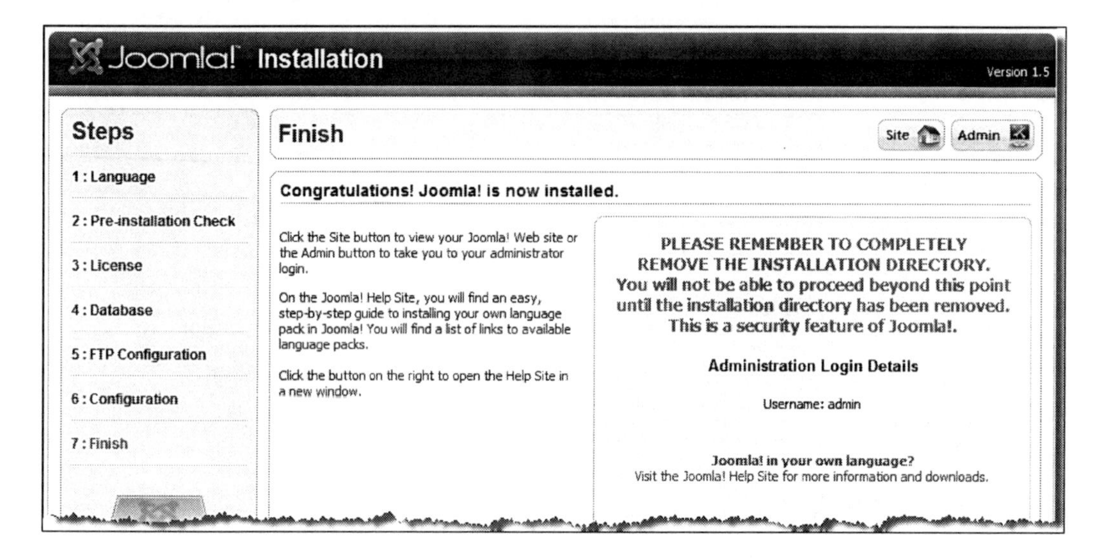

8. We will see a warning message (note the following screenshot). It advises us to remove the Joomla! installation directory named `installation`, which is located under Joomla! installation root. Keeping this directory invokes a security risk, because anyone can point to this directory from his or her browser and start the Joomla! installation again. Let us delete the entire directory `e:\www\bdosn\installation`. Now, point your browser to `http://localhost/bdosn` to look at our newly installed Joomla! site.

We can now see the default installation of Joomla! 1.5.9. As we have installed the sample data, the frontend of the site looks like the following:

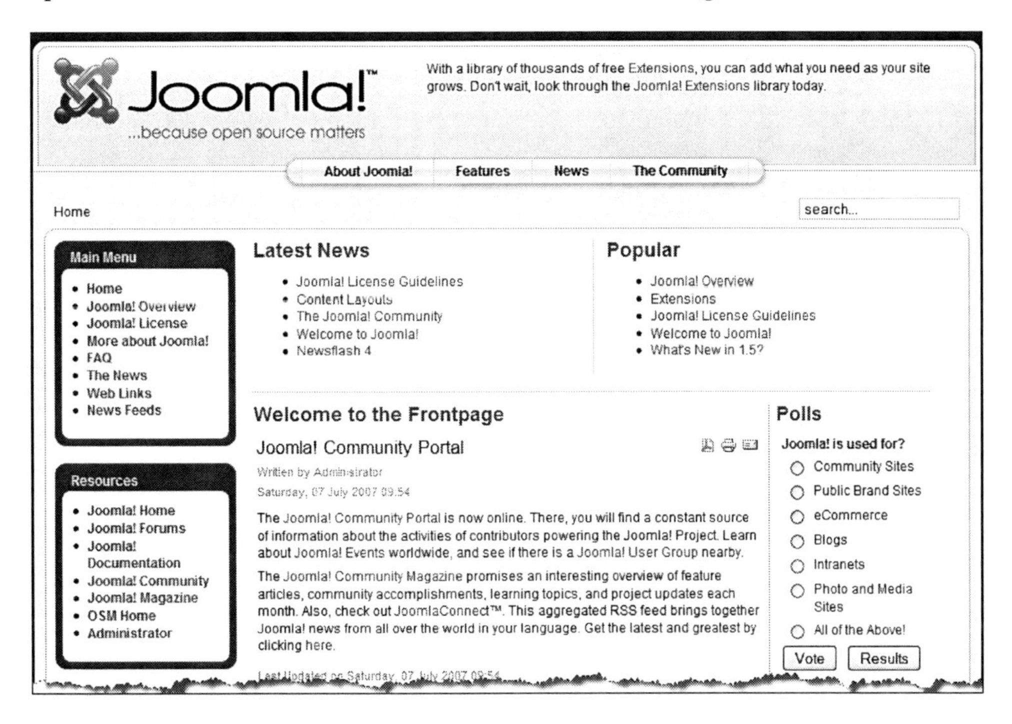

You can now look into the administrative panel as well. Let us type `http://localhost/bdosn/administrator` in our browser's location bar. It will take us to administration section login screen:

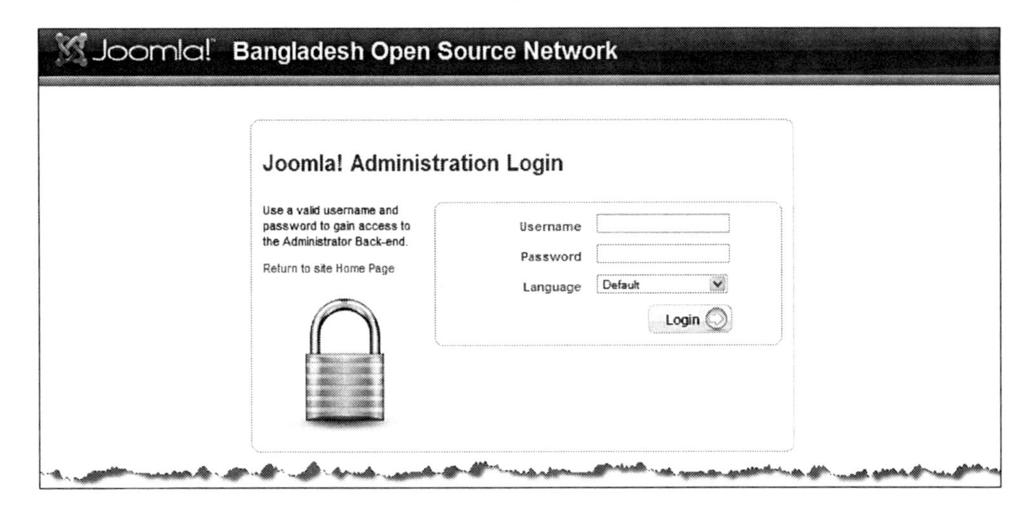

Now, type the administrative username **admin** and password that you assigned during installation. You may select the language too. Then, click the **Login** button. On successful login, you will see the Joomla! administration panel:

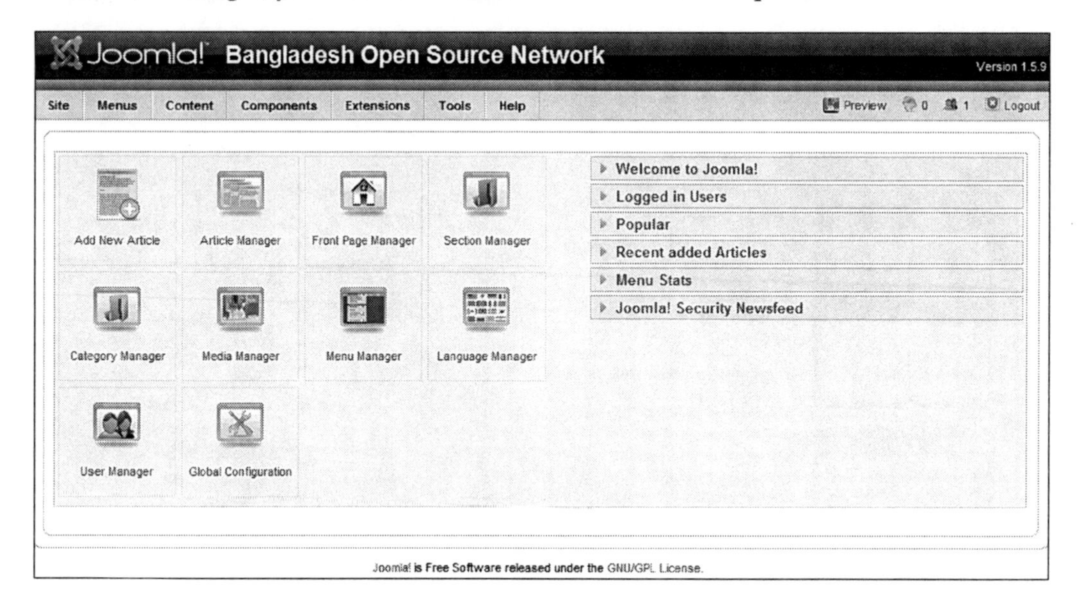

The Joomla! administration panel is the place from where we will configure our Joomla! site and manage its contents.

For a complete discussion onthe Joomla! administration panel and building a generic web site using Joomla!, please read the book *Building Websites with Joomla! 1.5* published by Packt.

Basic configuration of Joomla!

We will now look into the basic configuration of a Joomla! web site so we can start using our site. A detailed discussion on a full configuration of the Joomla! site is beyond the scope of this book. Therefore, we will only be discussing the essential configuration options which we must know for implementing VirtueMart in Joomla!

First of all, you need to configure some global options for your Joomla! site. We can configure these options from the Joomla! administration panel. Go to **Site | Global Configuration**:

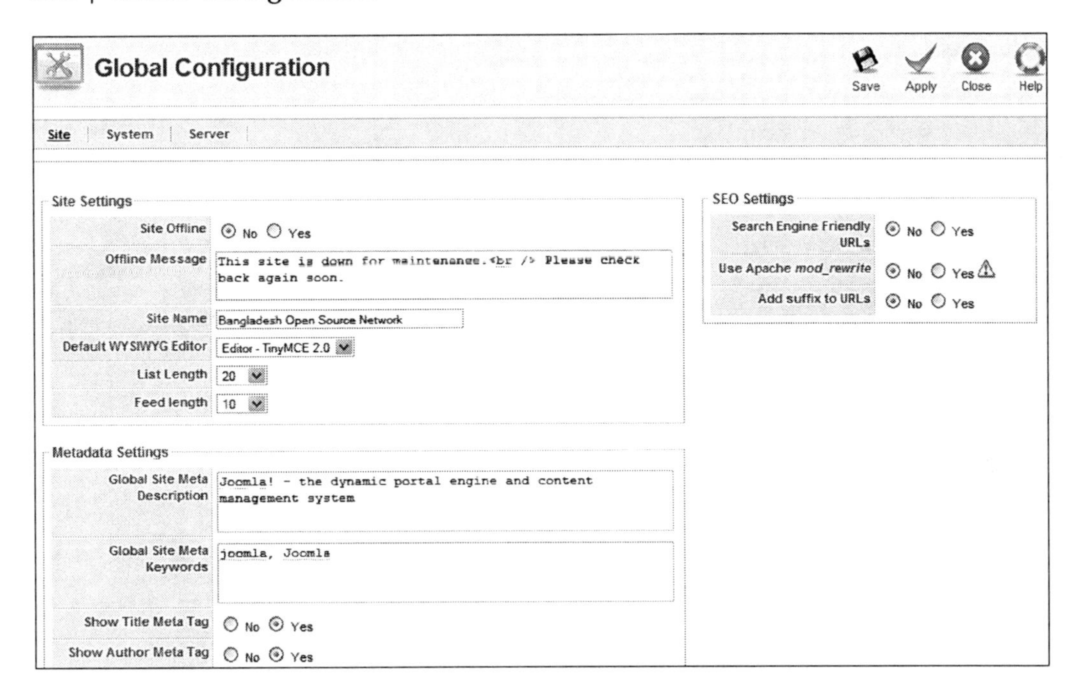

The **Global Configuration** screen's first tab is **Site**, and it has three sections: **Site Settings**, **Metadata Settings**, and **SEO Settings**. The first section, **Site Settings**, gives you the option to make the site offline, and shows a message why it is offline and for how long. You can also set the site's name in the **Site Name** field. You can also select a rich text editor from the **Default WYSIWYG Editor** drop-down list.

In the **Metadata Settings** sections, you can set a meta description for the site and set global site keywords. The description and keywords are helpful for search engine optimization.

In the **SEO Settings** section, you can specify whether **Search Engine Friendly URLs will be used or not. Using SEF may help** your site to be listed in the search engines. For search engine friendly URLs, you may need to enable the Apache `mod_rewrite` module. If you are using Apache and want to enable SEF, select **Yes** in **Use Apache mod_rewrite**.

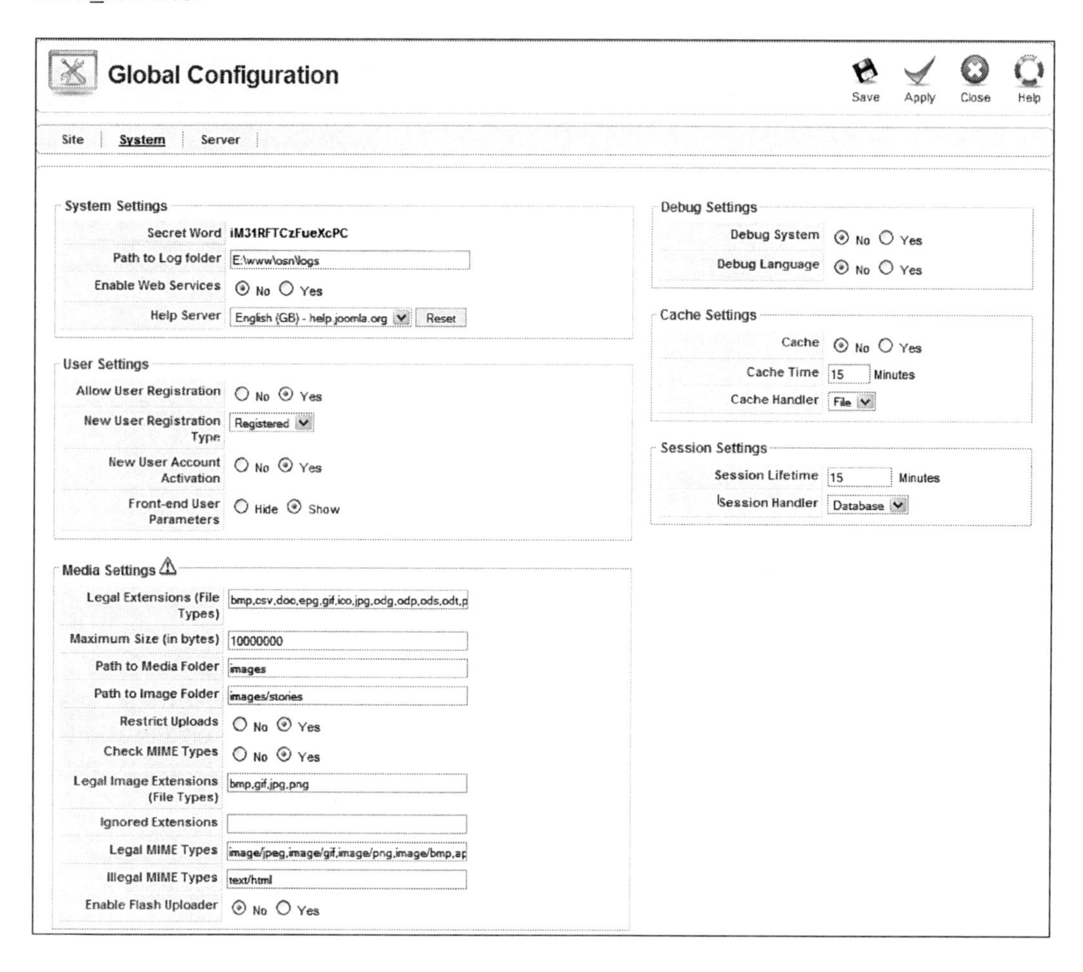

In the **System** tab (seen above), there are six sections. The **System Settings** section allows you to set a path to the log folder, enable web services, and set a help server. For some components, you need to set **Yes** in the **Enable Web Services** field.

In the **User Settings** section, you can configure whether you will allow user registration or not. Check **Yes** in **Allow User Registration**, then select **Registered** in the **New User Registration Type** drop-down list. If you want the user account be verified, select **Yes** in **New User Account Activation**. Enabling this will send an activation link to the users when they have registered.

In the **Media Settings** section, you can set what type of media files can be uploaded to your Joomla! site. Specify the allowed file extensions in the **Legal Extensions (File Types)** field. In the **Maximum Size (in bytes)** field, specify the maximum size of the file to be uploaded. Then, check the default path to the media and images folder. You can disable media uploads by selecting **Yes** in **Restrict Uploads** field. You may also specify what image formats will be allowed on your site. As you will also need to upload images for your products, check the **Legal Image Extensions (File Types)** field and ensure that the necessary file types are present. Here, you will find four image formats: BMP, GIF, JPG, and PNG. You can add more extensions to this field separated by commas. For each image type you add in this field, also add the corresponding MIME types in the **Legal MIME Types** field. If you want to use a flash file uploader, select **Yes** in the **Enable Flash Uploader** field.

In the **Debug Settings** section, you can enable or disable system and language debugging. For a development environment, you may enable these to see the debug messages. But for a production environment, this should be set to **No**.

In the **Cache Settings** section, you may either enable or disable caching, and can also set the cache interval. By default, caching is disabled.

In the **Session Settings** section, you can set the session lifetime and session handler. The default session lifetime is fifteen minutes. If you see that your sessions expire too often, check this setting and set a suitable value in **Session Lifetime** field.

In the **Server** tab, there are five sections, out of which you need to change settings in two sections:

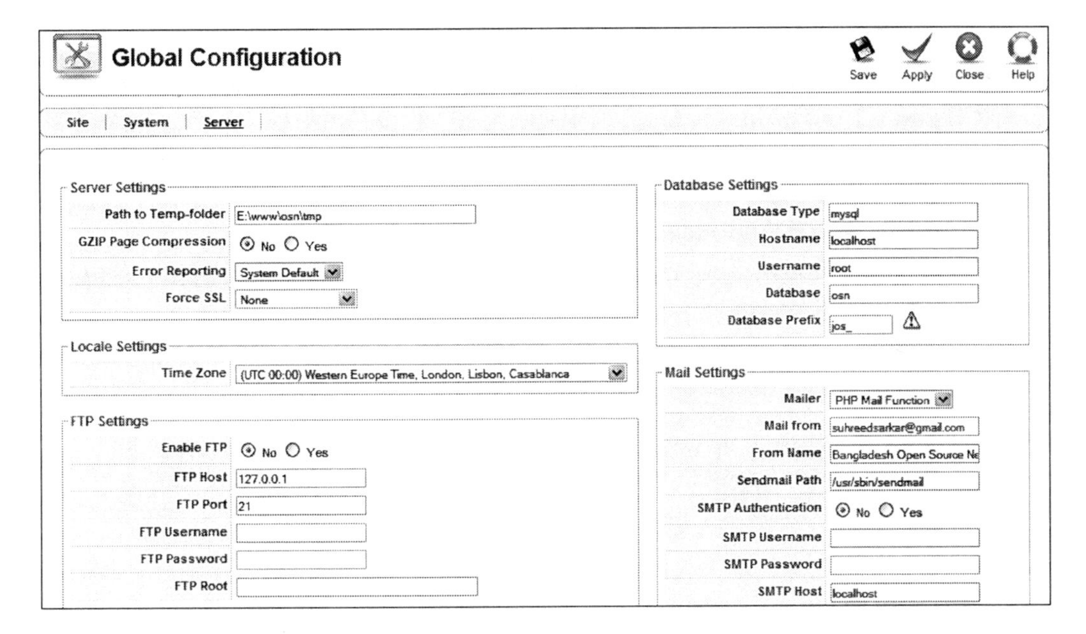

For a faster browsing experience, you may enable GZip compression of web pages. Any browser supporting GZip compression will experience faster browsing speed as pages will be sent to the browser in a compressed form. Select **Yes** in the **GZip Page Compression** field to enable GZip compression. However, for GZip page compression to work, your `php.ini` configuration for the web server should enable the **php_zip** extension.

In the **Locale Settings** section, select the appropriate time zone from the **Time Zone** drop-down list. The **FTP Settings** and **Database Settings** sections show the settings configured during installation. In most cases, you will not need to change these. However, you need to configure the **Mail Settings** section carefully. The following are the configuration options in this section:

- **Mailer**: You can use **PHP mail function**, **Sendmail,** or **SMTP Server** for sending emails from your Joomla! site. This same mailer will be used by other components of Joomla! including VirtueMart.
- **Mail from**: You need to provide an email address from where the mail will be sent. By default, the administrator's email address is used here.
- **From Name**: This will be the name which is shown in the **From** field in an email. By default, the site name is displayed in this field.
- **Sendmail Path**: If you choose **Sendmail** in the **Mailer** field, you will need to specify the sendmail path in this field. The default value is **/usr/sbin/sendmail**, which is appropriate for most Linux servers. You can get this path from your host provider.
- **SMTP Authentication**: If you select **SMTP Server** as a transport method in the **Mailer** field, you will need to configure this and the following fields. If your SMTP server requires authentication, then select **Yes** in this field. If you select **Yes** in this field, you also need to configure the username and password in the next two fields.
- **SMTP Username**: Type the username to be used to login to the SMTP server through which your emails will be sent.
- **SMTP Password**: Type the password for the above username which resides on the SMTP server.
- **SMTP Host**: Type the name of the SMTP server through which your emails will be sent, for example, `smtp.bdosn.org`.

Whenever you change any settings in any field, you must save those changes by clicking on the **Save** or **Apply** button. If you want to go back without making any change, click on the **Close** button. You can get help on that screen by clicking the **Help** button.

Basic administration of Joomla!

We have seen the global configuration of Joomla!. We will now learn about basic administration of Joomla!. This will allow that you to create sections, categories, articles, and menus. We will also see how to change the look and feel of the site by changing templates for a Joomla! site.

Managing contents

In Joomla!, content is managed under sections and categories. One section may contain multiple categories, and one article belongs to one section and one category. For each article, you must assign it to a section and category. Therefore, we will first see how to create sections and categories, and then articles.

Managing sections

For managing sections, go to **Content | Section Manager** from the Joomla! administration panel. The **Section Manager** screen will show list of available sections:

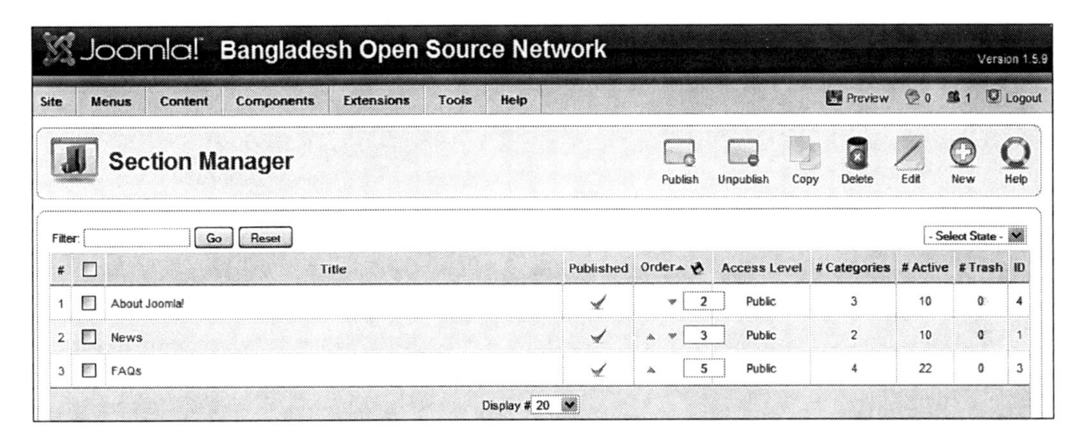

You can manage the sections as follows:

- To unpublish one or more sections, select those sections (check the checkbox left of the section name) and click the **Unpublish** icon in the toolbar.
- To publish one or more unpublished section, select those sections and click the **Publish** icon in the toolbar.
- To delete one or more section, select those sections and click the **Delete** icon in the toolbar.

- To create a new section, click the **New** icon in the toolbar. This will show the following screen:

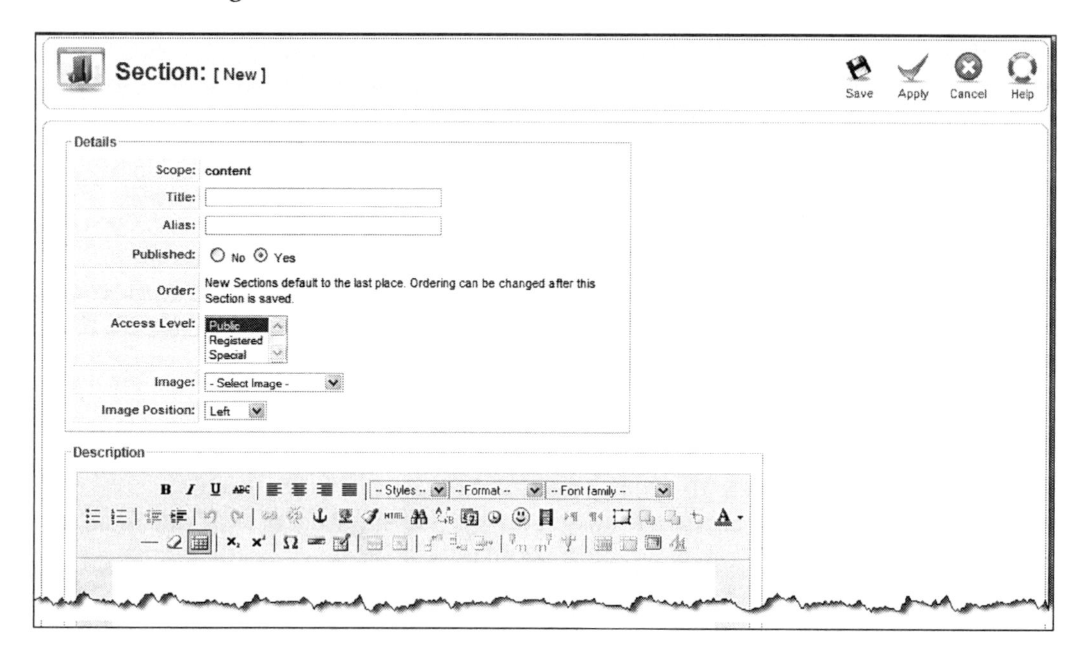

In the **Section: [New]** screen, type the **Title** and **Alias** of the section. The **Title** will be the full name of the section. The **Alias** will be the shortened name of the section, which will be used for generating search engine friendly URLs. Then select **Yes** or **No** in the **Published** field. In the **Access Level** field, you can select which user groups can access this section. **Public** is the default setting. If you want only registered user to access this section's content, select **Registered** in this field. You can select an image for the section in the **Image** drop-down list. An image's position can be set in the **Image Position** field. Then finally, type some description of the section. You can use rich HTML in this description. When all fields are filled, click on the **Save** or **Apply** icon in the toolbar to save the section.

- To edit a section, select the section and click the **Edit** icon in the toolbar. This will show the **Section: [Edit]** screen which is similar to the **Section: [New]** screen. Make changes to any field in this screen and click the **Save** or **Apply** icon in the toolbar.

- To copy a section, select that section and click the **Copy** icon in the toolbar. Remember, copying a section will also copy all categories and articles under that section. If we select the **News** section and click the **Copy** icon, the following screen will be displayed:

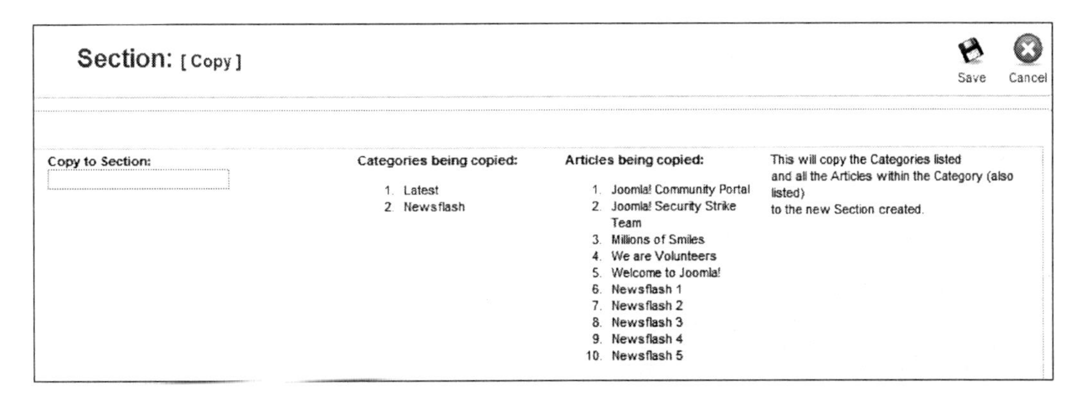

The **Section: [Copy]** screen will list which categories and articles will also be copied. Type the name of the new section (for example, **Tutorials**) in the **Copy to Section** field. Then, click the **Save** icon in the toolbar. You will find the Tutorials section in the **Section Manager** screen:

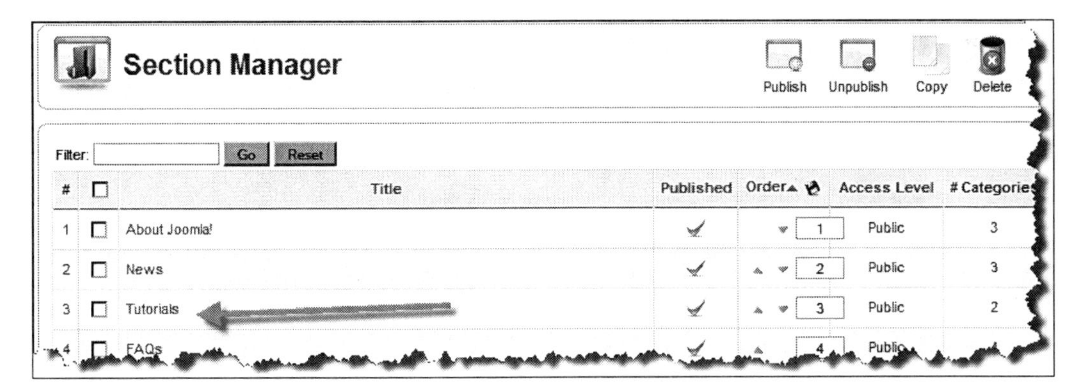

Warning:

You cannot delete a section if it contains child categories. Similarly, you cannot delete a category if it contains articles. Therefore, to delete a section or category, start by deleting the articles, then the category, and finally delete section.

Managing categories

For managing categories from the Joomla! administration panel, go to **Content** | **Category Manager**. The **Category Manager: [Content]** screen will display a list of available categories:

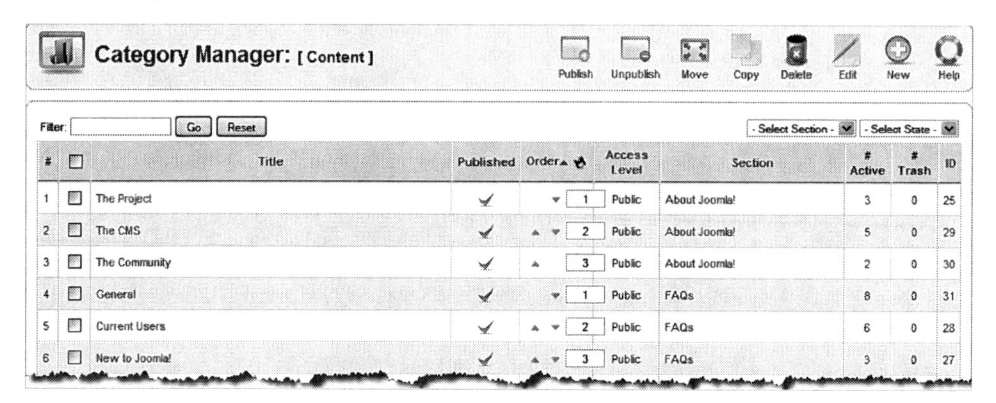

In the **Category Manager: [Content]** screen, you will find two drop-down lists to the right. One is for selecting a section, and another is for selecting a state: published or unpublished. You can filter the list of categories by selecting a section or state from these drop-down lists.

You can publish, unpublish, move, copy, delete, edit existing category, and create new category in the same way as done for sections.

Adding a category is similar to adding a section. The only difference is that when creating a category, we need to assign a parent section.

Managing articles

For managing articles, in the Joomla! administration panel, go to **Content** | **Article Manager**. A list of all articles will be displayed in the **Article Manager** screen:

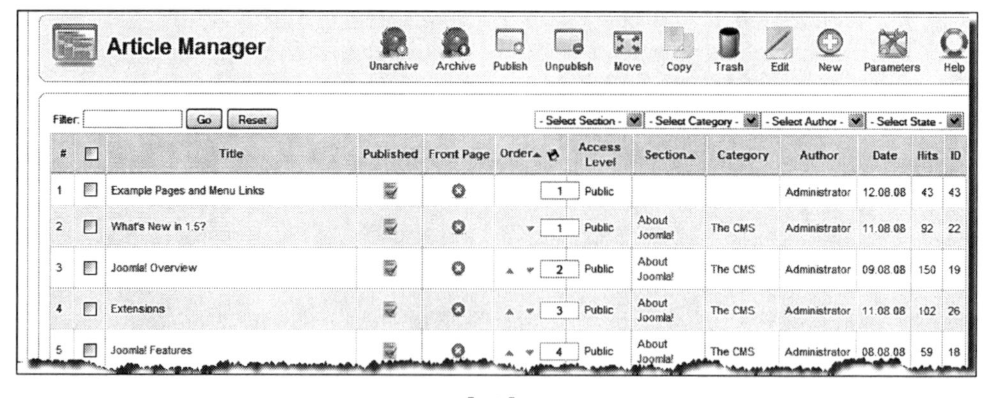

Like the **Section Manager** and **Category Manager**, we will see a set of icons on the toolbar. Through these icons, we can **Unarchive**, **Archive**, **Publish**, **Unpublish**, **Move**, **Copy**, **Trash**, and **Edit** articles. For doing these, we must select the article(s) first, and then click on an appropriate icon in the toolbar. We can also filter the article listing by typing a filter term in the **Filter** text box and clicking the **Go** button. The **Select Section**, **Select Category**, **Select Author**, and **Select State** drop down lists will help us filter the article listing by section, category, author, and by state (either published or unpublished).

We can create a new article by clicking the **New** icon in the toolbar. This will show the **Article: [New]** screen. We can create a new article by completing this form. This form has a rich text edit box. Here, we can enter our article text which will automatically be formatted as HTML:

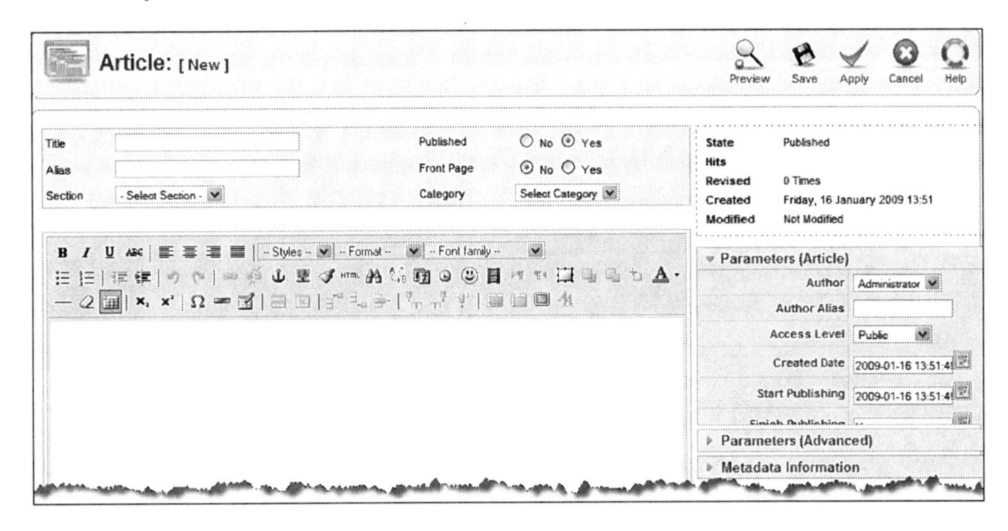

As we see from the screen, creating an article is easy. We need to type the title of the article in the **Title** field, then assign a short name in the **Alias** field, and assign a section from the **Section** drop-down list. In the **Published** field, select **Yes** to publish the article or **No** to not publish it. In the **Front Page** field, select **Yes** to show it on front page or **No** to not show it on the front page. You also can assign a category from **Category** drop-down list. We then need to type the texts of the article in the rich text box. We can apply text and paragraph formatting, insert an image, create a hyperlink, create a bulleted and numbered list, and so on by using the toolbars of this rich text editor.

On the right side, there are some options to configure the article. In **Parameters (Article)**, we can assign the author from the **Author** drop-down list, assign a separate name for the author in the **Author Alias** field, and then select a **Created Date** and **Start Publishing** date.

In **Parameters (Advanced)**, we can configure some advanced options for this particular article. We can globally define these options through the **Parameters** icon in the **Article Manager** screen.

In **Metadata Information**, we can specify a description for the article, assign keywords and author. The information provided in these fields are useful for search engine optimization.

When we have finished adding our content, we can save the article by clicking the **Save** or **Apply** icon in the toolbar. Clicking on the **Save** icon will save the article and bring us to the **Article Manager** screen. Clicking the **Apply** icon will save the article and keep the article editing screen open so we can continue editing the article. We can preview the article by clicking on the **Preview** icon.

In Joomla!, you cannot delete an article directly. For deleting one or more articles, select those using the checkbox to the left of their title, and click the **Trash** icon in the toolbar. The articles are not deleted permanently yet. It's like deleting files in Windows and Linux operating system, where files first go to a recycle bin. In Joomla!, trashed articles can be viewed from **Content | Article Trash**. The **Trash Manager: [Articles]** screen will list all trashed articles. We can restore or permanently delete these articles from here:

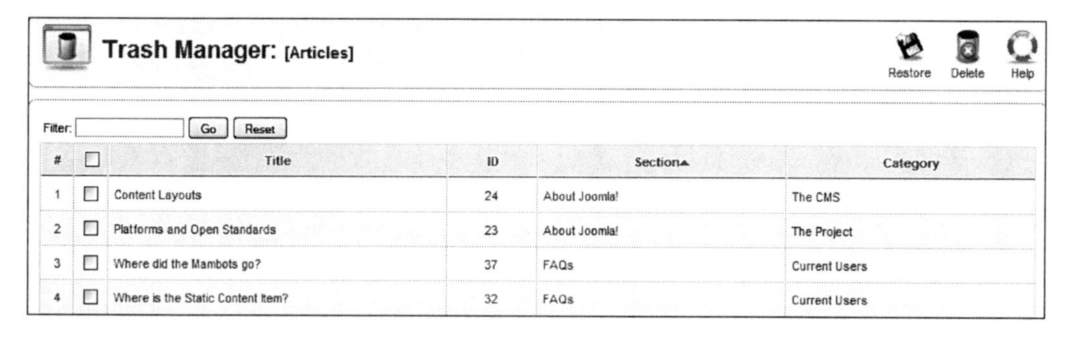

To restore the items, select them and click the **Restore** icon in the toolbar. The **Restore Items** screen will confirm which items will be restored. Click on the **Restore** icon again. Items restored will be in their respective categories with an unpublished status. To permanently delete articles, select the articles and click the **Delete** icon in the toolbar. **Permanently Delete Items** screen will list items to be deleted. Click the **Delete** icon to permanently delete the items. These items will no longer be in the database:

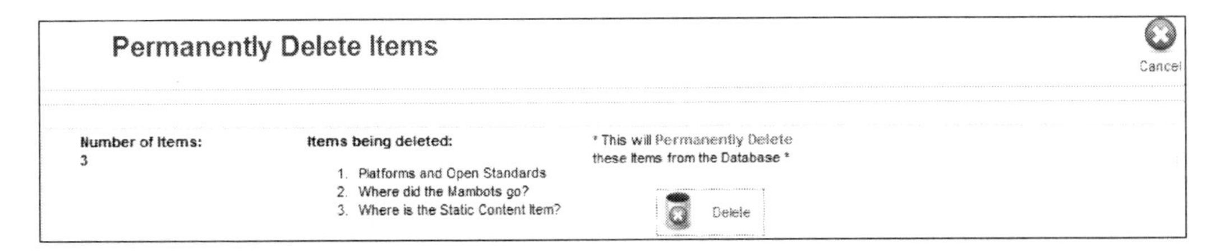

We can promote any published article to front page by selecting **Yes** in the **Front Page** field while creating the article. This can also be done from the **Article Manager** screen. In this screen, find the **Front Page** column. A red cross icon in this column indicates this article will not be shown on front page. To show that article on front page, click on that red cross icon and it will be turned into green tick icon. The article will now be displayed on the front page of your Joomla! site. The order in which the pages will be shown on front page can be managed from the **Content | Front Page Manager** screen:

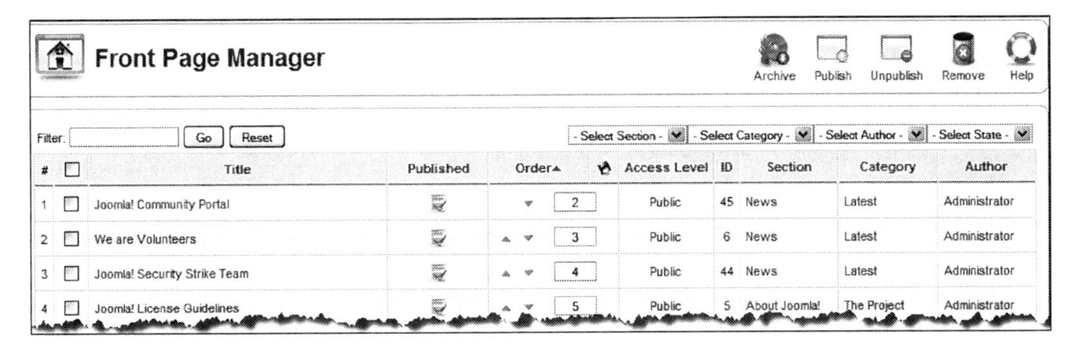

Managing extensions

Extensions are a great feature of Joomla!. We can extend Joomla!'s functionality by installing appropriate extensions. In Joomla! 1.5, there are five types of extensions:

- **Components**: Joomla! components are mini applications which may contain their own database tables, administration settings, and frontend elements. For example, phpShop was an e-commerce shopping cart software. It is now converted to be used with Joomla! and named as VirtueMart. VirtueMart is a component of Joomla! which can be installed, uninstalled, configured, and used under a Joomla! installation.
- **Modules**: Modules are small blocks of code which can be used to show a specific content or information across the site. For example, `mod_latest_news` is a module, which shows the latest content added to a News section of the `com_content` component. Joomla! content may have multiple modules to display its content in different formats.

- **Plugins**: Plug-ins (known as 'Mambots' in 1.0.x versions) are complex codes which works in the background to execute some functions on specific events. For example, **geshi** is a plugin which is used with Joomla! to display the code block in the content in different formats. Whenever content blocks with certain tags (for example, `<code> </code>`) are found, the **geshi** plugin turns that into special format so that codes are more readable to the audience. Similarly, another plugin for SEF transforms the URLs into search engine friendly URLs.
- **Languages**: Languages are a very basic but useful extension through which administrator can add multiple languages to the site and display the site interface in different languages.
- **Templates**: Templates are a visual design of the site. Joomla! uses templates to display its content in different formats. One can represent the site with a different look and feel by changing the template.

All extensions are managed from the **Extensions** menu in the Joomla! administration panel.

We can install or uninstall any extension (component, module, plugin, language, or template) from **Extensions | Install/Uninstall**. This shows **Extension Manager** screen:

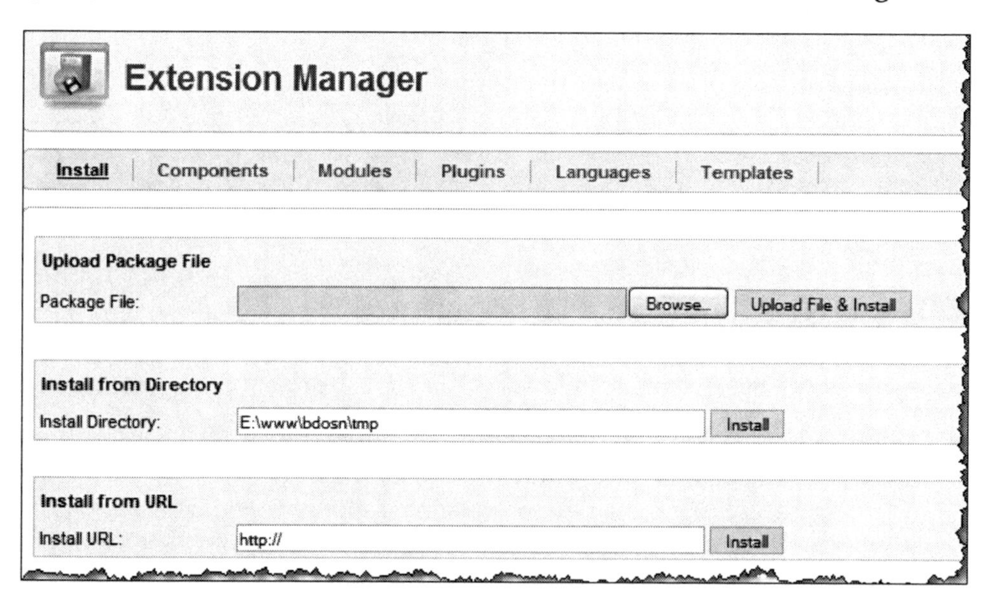

From the **Extension Manager** screen, we see that we can install an extension in Joomla! 1.5 in three ways. This includes uploading the zipped extension package (component, module, plugin, language, or template), using a directory on the web server where the extension files are already present, and starting directly from the web by providing the extension file's URL.

In Joomla! 1.0.x series, you must install or uninstall components, modules, plugins, templates, and languages separately. In Joomla! 1.0.x, this is done from: **Installers | Template - Site**, **Installers | Template - admin**, **Installers | Languages**, **Installers | Component**, **Installers | Modules**, and **Installers | Mambots**. Plug-ins are called Mambots in Joomla! 1.0.x. There is no option for installing any extension directly from the web.

We can see the installed components, modules, plugins, languages, and templates by clicking on the respective link beside the **Install** link. Let us click on the **Components** link. This will show a list of all installed components. We will also see whether the component is enabled or not. We can enable a component by clicking on the disabled red icon, and disable it by clicking on the enable green tick icon in the **Enabled** column. To uninstall a component, select the radio button to left of the component name, and click **Uninstall** icon in toolbar. We cannot uninstall a component which is grayed. Grayed components are core components of Joomla! and required by other components or modules:

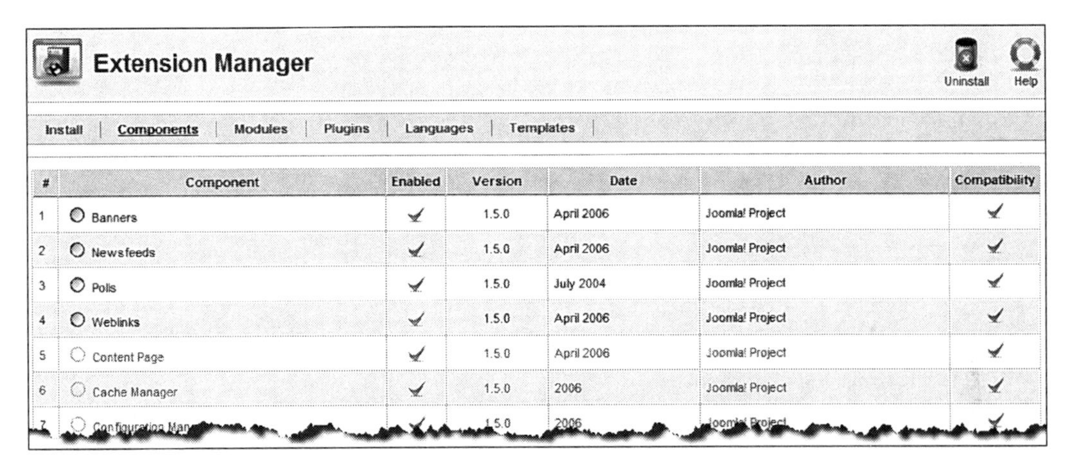

#	Component	Enabled	Version	Date	Author	Compatibility
1	Banners	✓	1.5.0	April 2006	Joomla! Project	✓
2	Newsfeeds	✓	1.5.0	April 2006	Joomla! Project	✓
3	Polls	✓	1.5.0	July 2004	Joomla! Project	✓
4	Weblinks	✓	1.5.0	April 2006	Joomla! Project	✓
5	Content Page	✓	1.5.0	April 2006	Joomla! Project	✓
6	Cache Manager	✓	1.5.0	2006	Joomla! Project	✓

Similarly, we can uninstall modules, plugins, languages, and templates. In each case, some items cannot be uninstalled as those are core or have no alternative. For example, if we have only one site template installed, we cannot uninstall that unless we install another site template.

Installation of VirtueMart

We are now ready to install VirtueMart. Earlier, we discussed that VirtueMart is a component of Joomla!. Therefore, it will be installed as a component. If you have not downloaded the VirtueMart installation package yet, download that now from the URL provided earlier in this chapter. Put the VirtueMart installation package on your desktop and then extract the zip file. You will see the following directory structure:

```
VirtueMart
|    com_virtuemart_1.1.2.j15.zip
|    VirtueMart_1.1_Installation.pdf
|
+---modules
|         mod_productscroller_1.1.2.j15.zip
|         mod_product_categories_1.1.2.j15.zip
|         mod_virtuemart_1.1.2.j15.zip
|         mod_virtuemart_allinone_1.1.2.j15.zip
|         mod_virtuemart_cart_1.1.2.j15.zip
|         mod_virtuemart_currencies_1.1.2.j15.zip
|         mod_virtuemart_featureprod_1.1.2.j15.zip
|         mod_virtuemart_latestprod_1.1.2.j15.zip
|         mod_virtuemart_login_1.1.2.j15.zip
|         mod_virtuemart_manufacturers_1.1.2.j15.zip
|         mod_virtuemart_randomprod_1.1.2.j15.zip
|         mod_virtuemart_search_1.1.2.j15.zip
|         mod_virtuemart_topten_1.1.2.j15.zip
|
\---plugins
          vmproductsnapshots_1.1.2.j15.zip
          vmxsearch.plugin_1.1.2.j15.zip
```

If you see all of the above files, you have downloaded the correct package. If you don't see the above, go to http://www.virtuemart.net and download **Complete Package for Joomla! 1.5**.

When packages are ready, login to the Joomla! administration panel. Once you are in the Joomla! administration panel, go to **Extensions | Install/Uninstall**. In the **Extension Manager** screen, click on the **Browse** button in the **Package File** field. Locate the `com_virtuemart_1.1.2.j15.zip` file on your desktop, select it, and click open. Then click the **Upload File & Install** button. On successful installation of the component, you will see the following screen:

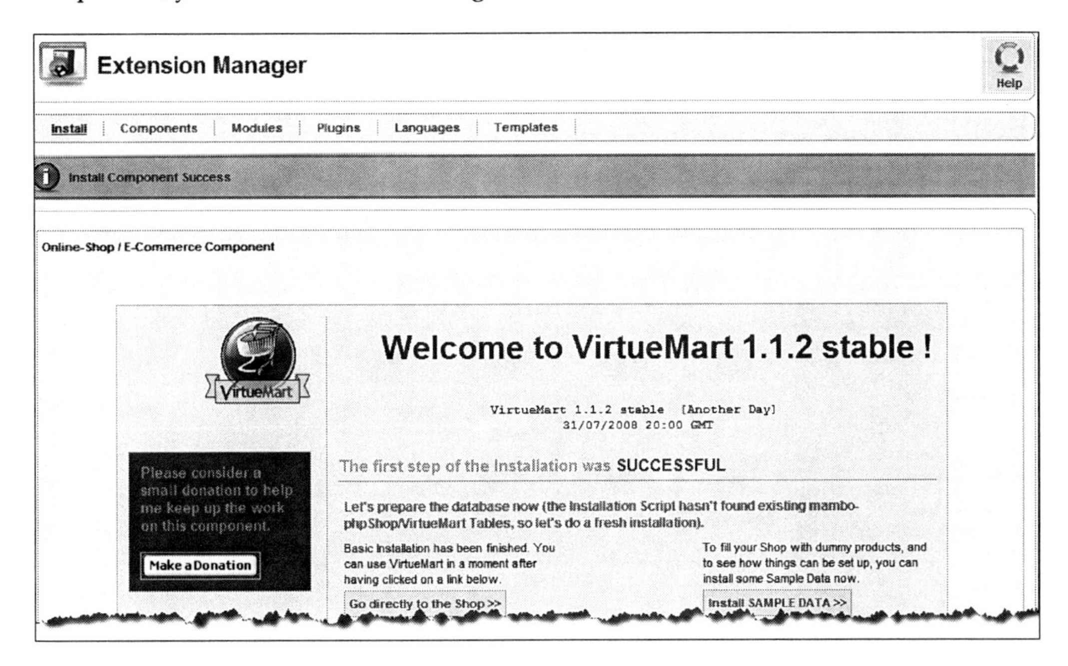

The screen will inform you that VirtueMart has been successfully installed. You can now go to the store by clicking on the **Go directly to the shop>>** button. You can also install sample data for the VirtueMart store by clicking on the **Install SAMPLE DATA>>** button. Installed sample data will be published and browsing that data will help us to understand how VirtueMart works. However, you can delete this data anytime you want to. We will be discussing how to delete the sample data later in this book.

Let us install the sample data by clicking on the **Install SAMPLE DATA** button. A warning message will be displayed asking that the sample data installation not be disturbed. Once the sample data installation is complete, we will get the following screen, the **VirtueMart Administration** panel:

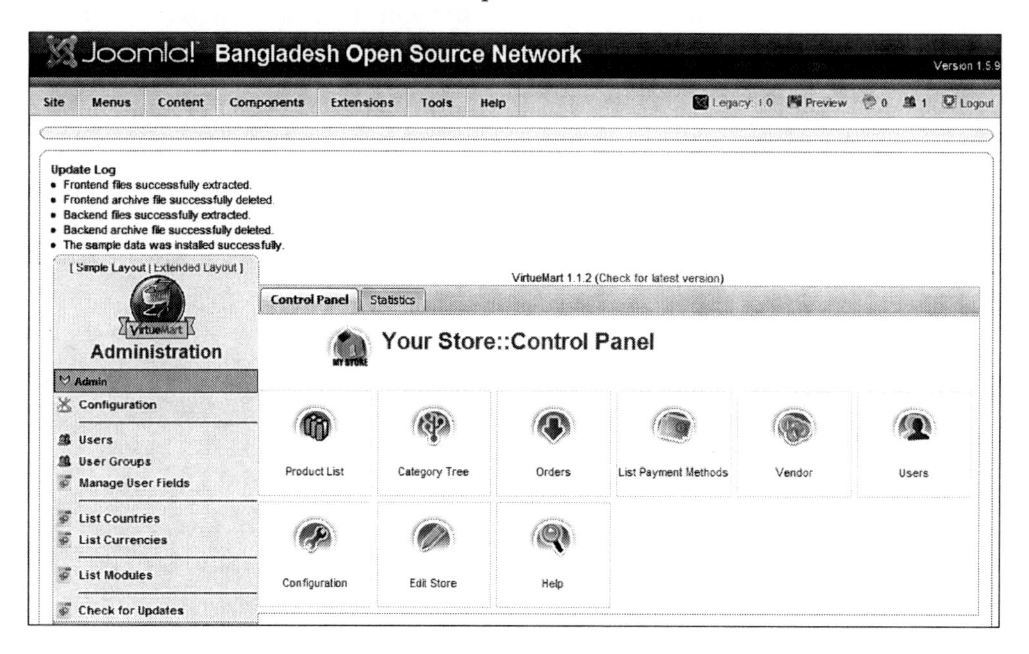

We have just installed the component. However, there are some modules and plugins in the package. Let us install all these modules and plugins in a similar way. Go to **Extensions | Install/Uninstall** and select the files from your desktop. Click open and then click the **Upload & Install** button. Repeat this for all module files (inside `modules` subfolder and starting with `mod_`) and plugins files in `plugins` subfolder. For each successful installation, you will see a message like the following screenshot:

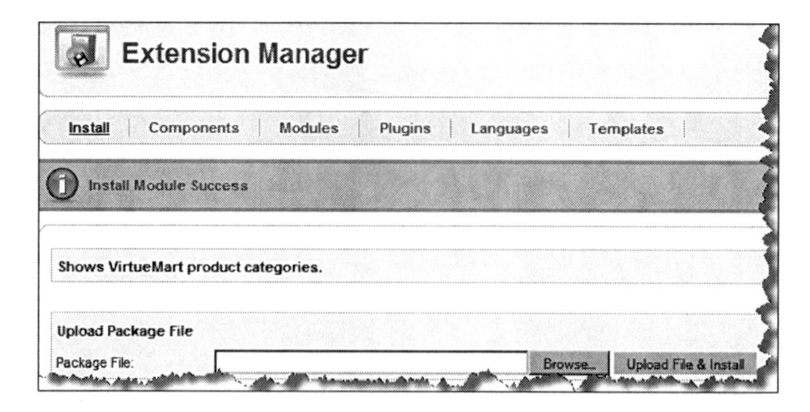

> If you are trying to install VirtueMart packages for Joomla! 1.0.x in Joomla! 1.5.x, you must have Legacy Mode turned on in Joomla! 1.5.x. To enable legacy mode, go to **Extensions | Plugin Manager**. Then select the **System - Legacy** plugin and click the enable icon in the toolbar. By enabling this plugin, you will be able to use extensions designed for Joomla! 1.0.x in Joomla! 1.5.x. An indicator for legacy mode will be displayed on the top, right-hand portion of your administration area.

Basic configuration of VirtueMart

We have completed installing the VirtueMart component, modules, and plugins. It's now time to seen how these work. Before seeing the effect of VirtueMart, we have to configure the store. The full configuration of the VirtueMart store is discussed in the next chapter. In this section, we are going to know how we can see VirtueMart on the frontend.

After installation, the VirtueMart component is enabled by default. You may check it from **Extensions | Install/Uninstall | Components**. Although the VirtueMart component is installed, you cannot see any of it on the frontend. To view your newly installed shopping cart, point your browser to `http://localhost/bdosn/index.php?option=com_virtuemart`. This will show the VirtueMart shop. First, you will see the categories and the featured products. Clicking on any product category (say **Hand Tools**) will display a listing of products in that category:

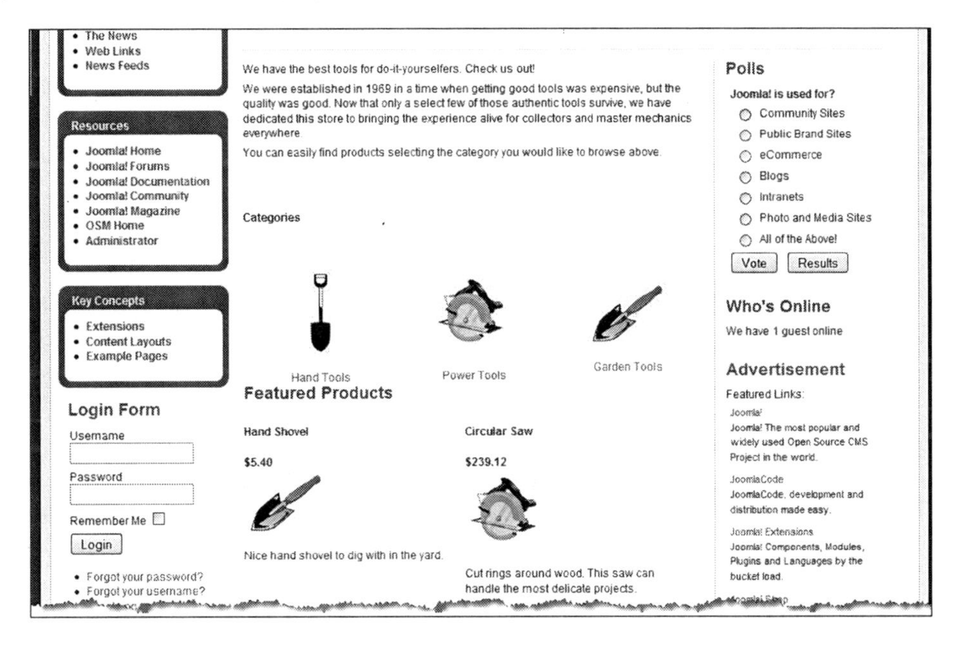

Look in to the VirtueMart store. It is not showing any VirtueMart module, such as **Manufacturers**, **Latest Products**, and so on. We have not published those modules yet. Also note that customers will not visit the shop by typing the direct URL of our shop. We need to provide a menu for our shop on the front page, so that they can visit the shop by clicking on the menu link.

Adding VirtueMart to menu

The best way to show the VirtueMart on the frontend of the Joomla! web site is to publish the VirtueMart modules and adding a link to **Main Menu** and **Top Menu**. We will now see how to add a menu link that leads to VirtueMart.

In Joomla!, menus are created from **Menus | Menu Manager**. In the **Menu Manager** screen, you will find the available menus. You can create a new menu by clicking the **New** icon in the toolbar:

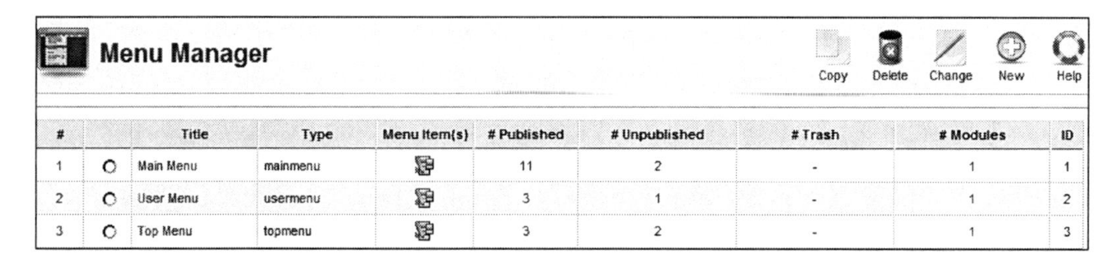

#		Title	Type	Menu Item(s)	# Published	# Unpublished	# Trash	# Modules	ID
1		Main Menu	mainmenu		11	2	-	1	1
2		User Menu	usermenu		3	1	-	1	2
3		Top Menu	topmenu		3	2	-	1	3

You will find at least two menus present in the **Menu Manager**. We will add our shop link to **Main Menu** and **Top Menu**. To view the menu items in the **Main Menu**, click on the icon in the **Menu Item(s)** column. This will show the **Menu Item Manager: [mainmenu]** screen:

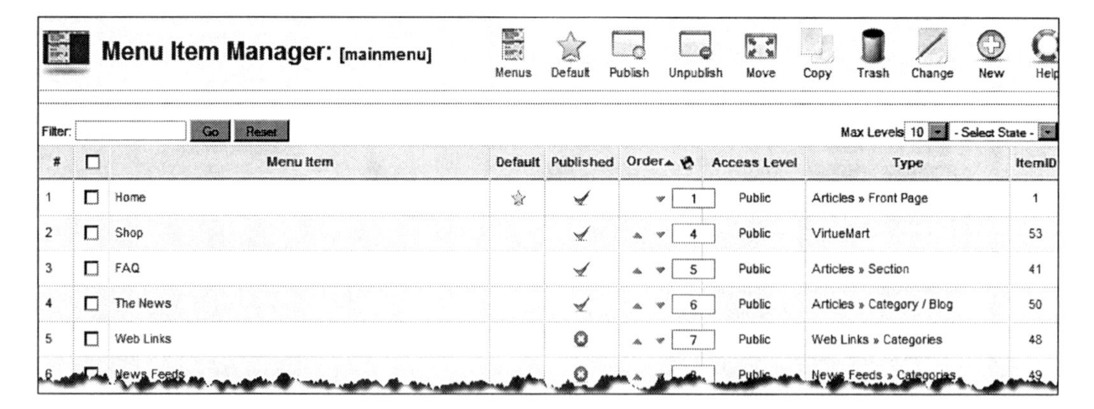

#		Menu Item	Default	Published	Order	Access Level	Type	ItemID
1		Home			1	Public	Articles » Front Page	1
2		Shop			4	Public	VirtueMart	53
3		FAQ			5	Public	Articles » Section	41
4		The News			6	Public	Articles » Category / Blog	50
5		Web Links			7	Public	Web Links » Categories	48
6		News Feeds			8	Public	News Feeds » Categories	49

As we can see from the **Menu Item Manager**, we can publish, unpublish, move, copy, edit, and trash menu items. We can also create new menu items from here. We will now create a menu item for VirtueMart shop.

To create the menu item, click the **New** icon in the toolbar. This will display the **Menu Item: [new]** screen. In this screen we must select a menu item type. There are four types of items: **Internal Link**, **External Link**, **Separator**, and **Alias**:

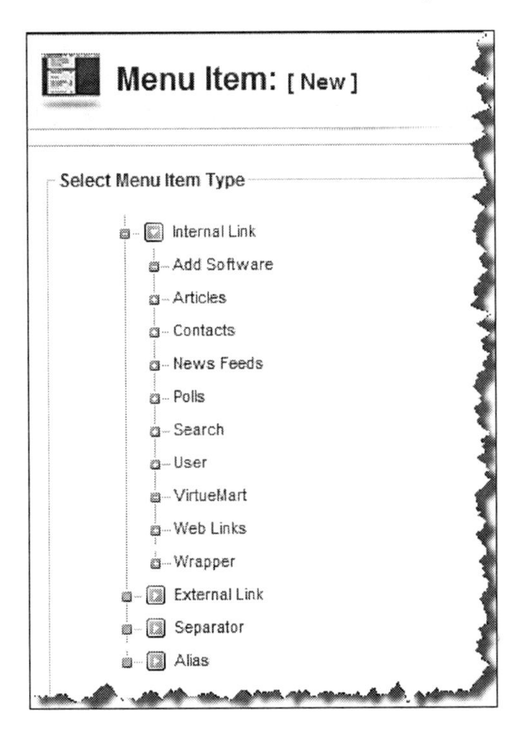

We will create the menu item to link to the VirtueMart component. This will be an internal link to the Joomla! web site. In the **Select Menu Item Type** section, we will see **VirtueMart** under the group **Internal Link**. Therefore, click on **VirtueMart**. This will show the **Menu Item: [new]** screen. We need to provide some information in this screen:

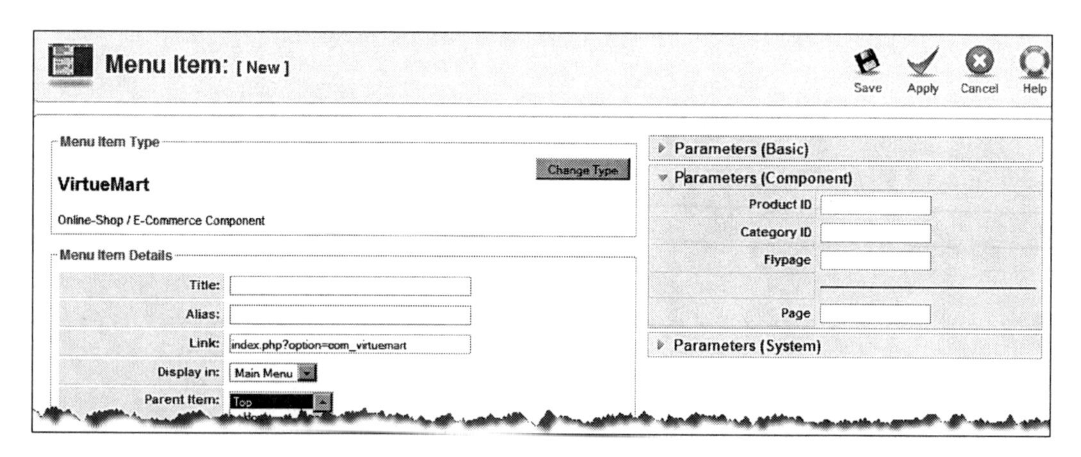

For creating the menu item, most of the default settings are acceptable. We need to type the title of the menu item in the **Title** field, and a short name in **Alias** field. The **Main Menu** will be in the **Display in** drop-down list. As we want to publish the menu item, keep **Yes** selected in the **Published** field. All visitors of our site will be able to visit the shop. Therefore, in the **Access Level** field, keep **Public** selected. In the **On Click, Open in** field, keep the default value. On the right side we see some parameter boxes. In **Parameters (Basic)**, there is nothing to configure. In **Parameters (Component)**, we can configure VirtueMart specific settings. The menu item can be directed to a specific product. If this is the case, we have to specify the product identification number in the **Product ID** field. Similarly, this can be directed to a specific category, whose identification number should be given in the **Category ID** field. We can also specify what will the flypage will be for this menu. We will discuss flypages later in Chapter 6, *Customizing the look and feel*.

When all of these information are provided, click the **Save** or **Apply** icon in the toolbar to save the menu item. We have added the menu item with the title **Shop**. We can now see the **Shop** menu item at the bottom of the menu item list in the **Menu Item Manager: [mainmenu]** screen. To move the menu item up, assign a lower order, say 3, and click the **Save Order** icon beside the **Order** column. The **Shop** menu item will be in third place in the list:

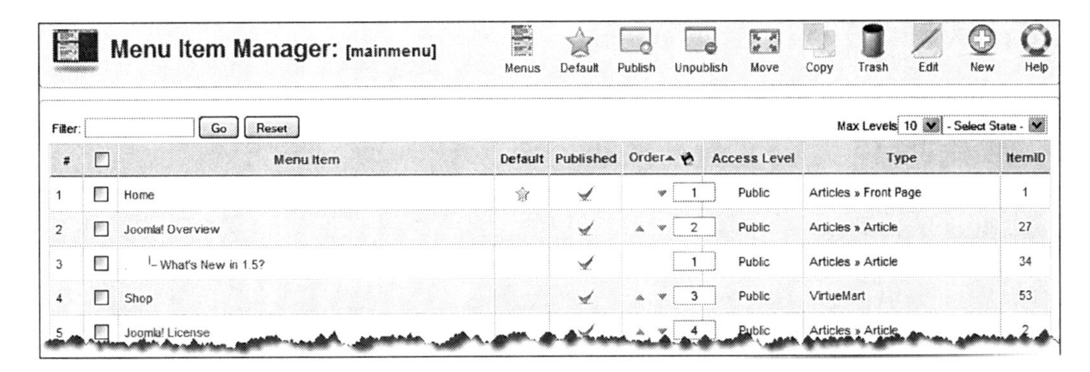

#		Menu Item	Default	Published	Order	Access Level	Type	ItemID
1		Home	☆	✓	1	Public	Articles » Front Page	1
2		Joomla! Overview		✓	2	Public	Articles » Article	27
3		└ What's New in 1.5?		✓	1	Public	Articles » Article	34
4		Shop		✓	3	Public	VirtueMart	53
5		Joomla! License		✓	4	Public	Articles » Article	2

Similarly, we can add the same menu item in the **Top Menu**. We can create a new menu item in the **Top Menu**, or copy the **Shop** menu item we have created just now. To copy the **Shop** menu item, in the **Menu Item Manager: [mainmenu]** screen, select the **Shop** menu item, and click the **Copy** icon in the toolbar. This will display the **Copy Menu Item(s)** screen:

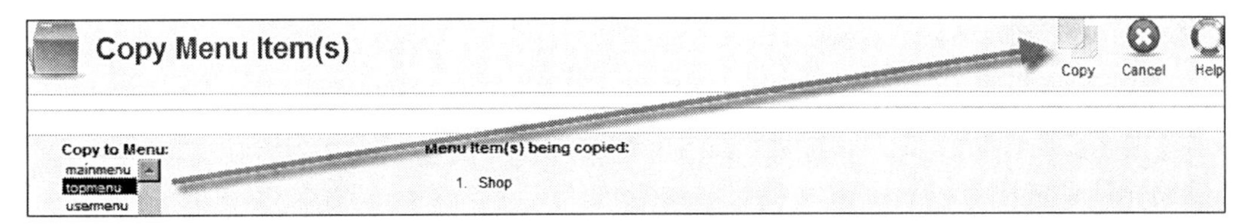

In the **Copy Menu Item(s)** screen, we have must select the menu we want to copy the menu item to. We want to copy it to the **Top Menu**, therefore, select **topmenu** in the **Copy to Menu** list. Then, click the **Copy** icon in the toolbar. It's done. The **Shop** menu item is in the **Top Menu** now. Let us check the web site now. Point your browser to `http://localhost/bdosn/`.

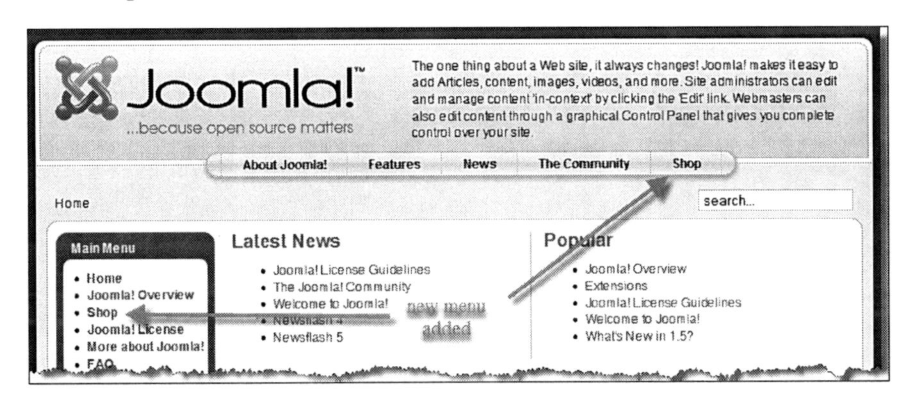

We now see the **Shop** link in both the main menu and top menu (as seen above). Click on these links and see what happens.

Showing the modules

We can publish our VirtueMart modules like any other Joomla! modules. To publish VirtueMart modules, in the Joomla! administration panel, go to **Extensions | Module Manager**. This will show **Module Manager** screen:

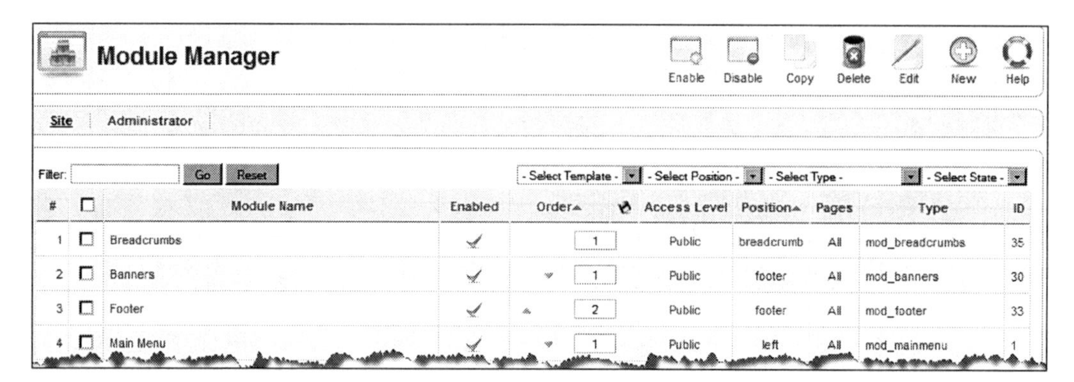

In the **Module Manager** screen, near the bottom of first page and in second page, you will see the list of VirtueMart modules. All VirtueMart module names start with VirtueMart. Let us publish the **VirtueMart Manufacturers** module. We want to show the manufacturer's name in the left column of our site. To do so, click on the **VirtueMart Manufacturers** module, or select the module and click the **Edit** icon in the toolbar. We will see **Module: [Edit]** screen:

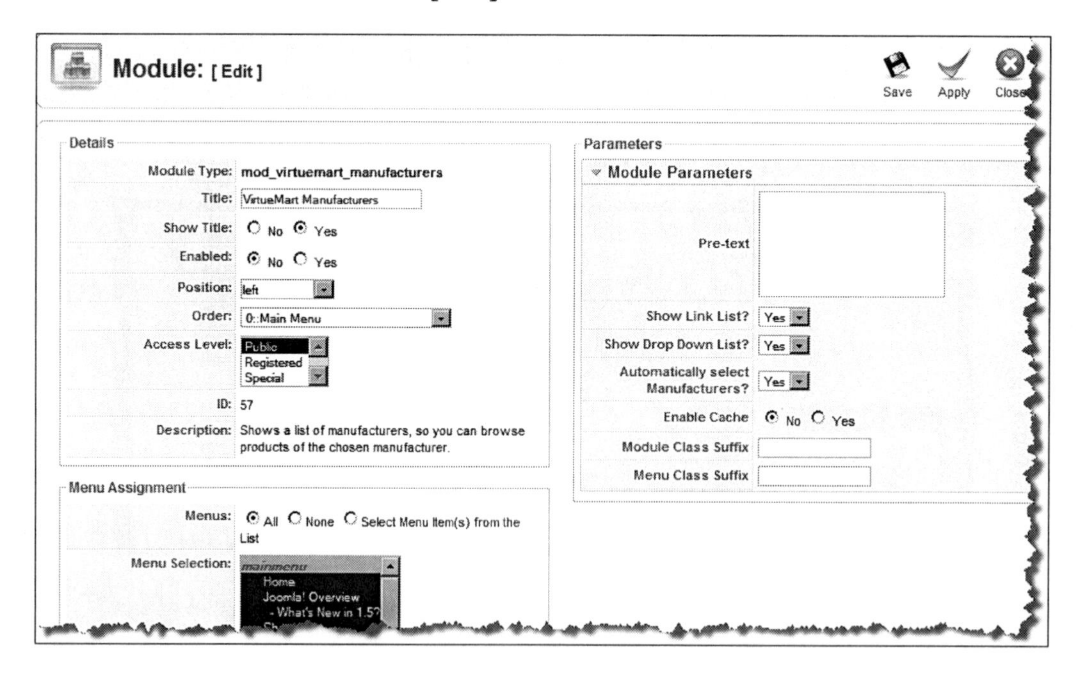

The **Module: [edit]** screen for the **VirtueMart Manufacturers** module has three sections: **Details, Menu Assignment**, and **Parameters**.

In the **Details** section, type a title of the module in the **Title** field. There is a default title of the module. We can type a title as we want. For example, we can type only **Manufacturers** in this **Title** field. Select **No** in the **Show Title** field, if you do not want to show the title of the module. Select **Yes** in the **Enabled** field. Now select the position to display the module from the **Position** drop-down list. We want to show it on the left navigation bar. Therefore, select **Left** in the **Position** drop-down list. In the **Order** drop-down list, select the module after which you want to show the current module. We want to show it just after the **Main Menu** module. Therefore, select the item after **0: Main Menu** from the **Order** drop-down list. The module will be displayed after the item is selected in this box. To display the module to all visitors, select **Public** in the **Access Level** list box.

In the **Menu Assignment** section, we can configure which menus the current module will be displayed. Select **All** to display this module for all menus, and **None** to not display in any menu. We can set it visible for specific menus. For example, we want to show the **VirtueMart Manufacturers** module only when the visitors are in VirtueMart shop and have come via the **Shop** menu. Therefore, check **Select Menu Item(s) from the List**, and in the **Menu Selection** list box, select **Shop** under **mainmenu** and **topmenu**.

In the **Parameters** section, we can set parameters for this specific module. If you want to show some text at the beginning of the module, type that text in the **Pre-text** field. To show the manufacturers list with a hyperlink, select **Yes** in the **Show Link List?** drop-down box. If you want to show the manufacturers list as a drop-down list, select **Yes** in the **Show Drop Down List?** box. We want a plain bulleted list, therefore, select **No** in this field. If you want, select **Yes** in the **Automatically select Manufacturers?** box, then when you are viewing a product's detail, the manufacturer will be highlighted in the list. Caching this module can be enabled by selecting **Yes** in the **Enable Cache** field. Assigning a **Module Class Suffix** and a **Menu Class Suffix** is helpful for adding CSS declarations in style sheets.

When all of these fields are configured, click the **Save** or **Apply** icon in the toolbar to save the module settings. You can also publish the module with default settings by clicking the icon in the **Enabled** column in the **Module Manager** screen.

Now, preview the web site, and go to your shop by clicking the **Shop** link either in the **Main Menu** or in the **Top Menu**. You will see the **Manufacturers** module, just after the **Main Menu**. As we have not added other manufacturers, only **Manufacturer** will be shown in this module:

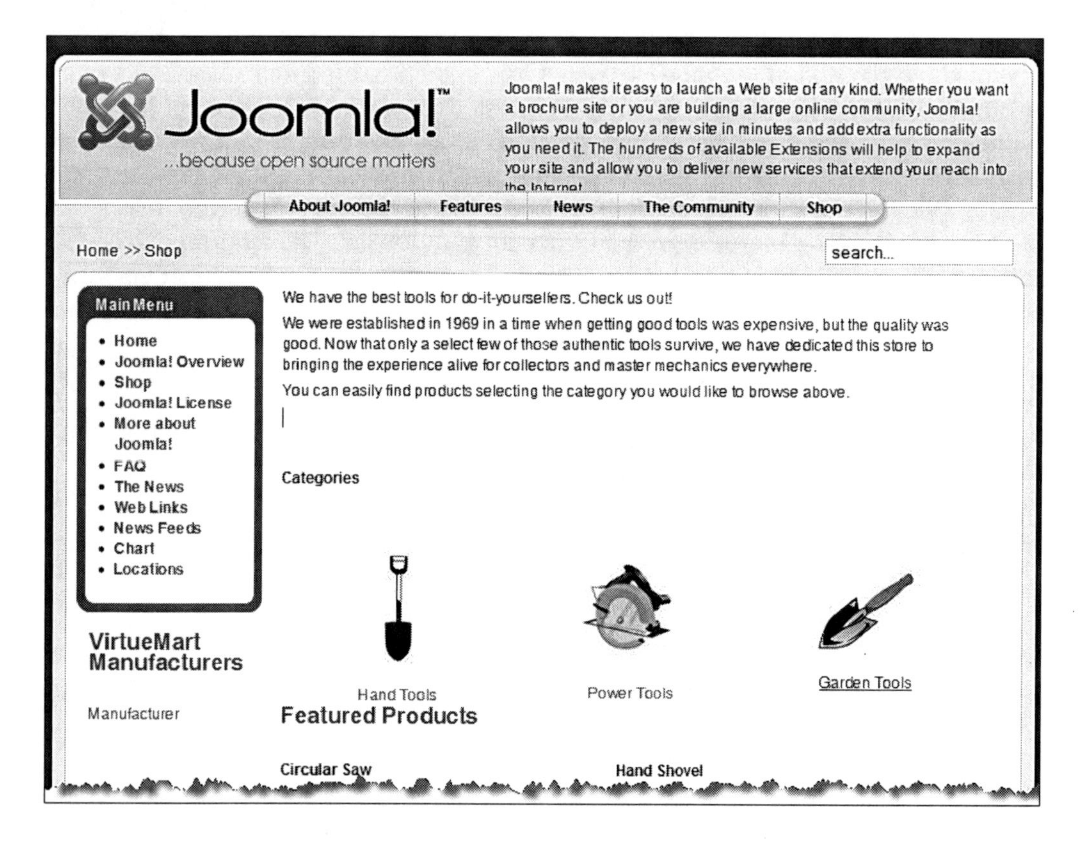

We can publish the other modules in the similar way. However, it is always suggested that you edit the module settings before publishing those modules, instead of publishing with default name and settings.

Summary

In this chapter, we have discussed the prerequisites of installing Joomla! and VirtueMart, the installation process of Joomla!, and basic configuration for Joomla!. We have also seen how to manage sections, categories, and articles. We have learned about managing extensions as well.

We then moved to discuss installing the VirtueMart component, modules, and plugins. Finally, we made menu items for the VirtueMart component, and published one VirtueMart module. We have seen how the VirtueMart shop looks and how the module is displayed in the Joomla! frontend. With this basic knowledge, we are now ready to delve into configuring a VirtueMart store.

In the next chapter, we are going to explore configurations of our VirtueMart store.

3
Configuring the VirtueMart Store

In the previous chapter, we installed Joomla! and VirtueMart and also saw what the VirtueMart shop looks like. Before we operationalize our VirtueMart shop, we need to configure it with appropriate settings. In this chapter we are going to see how to configure a VirtueMart shop. On completion of this chapter, we will be able to:

- Configure the shop
- Create and use appropriate time zones, currencies, and locales
- Install/Uninstall appropriate modules and configure them
- Configure payment methods for our shop
- Configure shipping methods for our shop
- Configure taxes for our shop

VirtueMart administration panel

We can configure the VirtueMart store from the VirtueMart administration panel. To get to the VirtueMart administration panel, select **Components | VirtueMart** in the Joomla! administration panel. This will show the **VirtueMart Administration** panel in the **Simple Layout** mode. VirtueMart's simple layout mode shows the traditional administration panel, with a left sidebar where a list of configuration groups and items are shown. Clicking on one of the items will display the configuration options in the main area.

The following screenshot shows the **VirtueMart Administration** panel in the **Simple Layout**:

On the other hand, the **Extended Layout** is powered by JavaScript and provides elegant looks. It also takes less space to show the configuration options. Click on the **Extended Layout** link to switch to the extended layout mode. We can switch back to simple layout at any time by clicking on the **Simple Layout** link. The following screenshot shows the **VirtueMart Administration** panel in the **Extended Layout**:

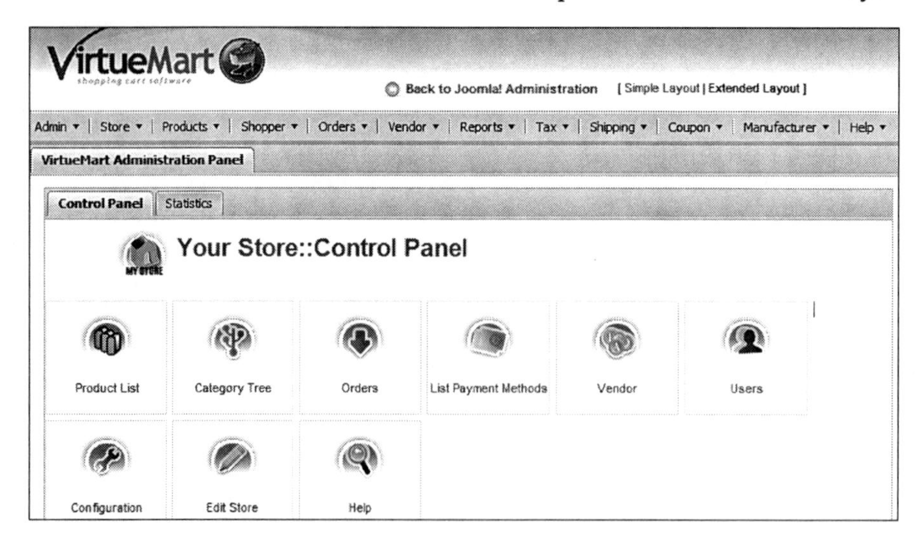

Note that, in the **Extended Layout** view, Joomla! menus are not displayed. It's fully the **VirtueMart Administration** panel. On the top there are two links: one is **Back to Joomla! Administration**, and another is the **Simple Layout**. These are our return paths to the desired interfaces. Throughout the book, we will use the **Extended Layout** mode for explaining VirtueMart configurations.

Store information

Let us first start by configuring our store. Our store should have a name, address, owner, contact number, and so on. For credibility of our store, we must publish where our store is physically located. We should also provide an introduction to our store explaining who we are, what we sell, and so on.

We can configure the store's information from **VirtueMart Administration Panel | Store | Edit Store**. This will show **Store Information** screen:

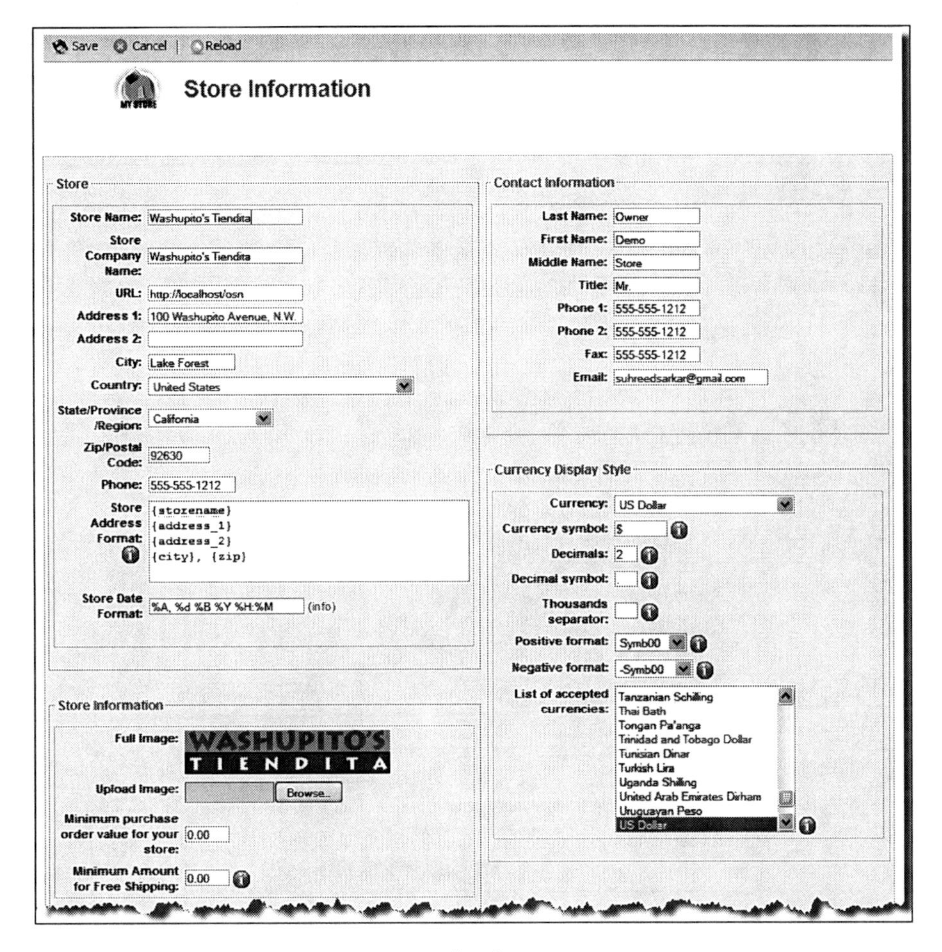

The **Store Information** screen has six sections. The first section, the **Store**, gives us fields for configuring the physical address of our store. We need to type a store name, store's company name, address, city, state, country, and so on. In the **Store Address Format** field, we can define how the store address will be displayed. We can use some placeholders to define this address format. You can see the available placeholders by hovering your mouse pointer on info icon beside the field. In the **Store Date Format** field, we can define the date format to be used for the store. The format should be indicated as per PHPs `strftime` function format. To know more about the supported syntax, click on the (info) link next to this field.

In the **Store Information** section, we can upload an image as the logo of our store. The uploaded image will be displayed in the **Full Image** field. There are other two options to configure in this section. We can define a minimum purchase order value for our shop. To do this, specify a value in the **Minimum purchase order value in your store** field. This is the amount a customer must purchase to successfully checkout from the store. For example, if we set it 50, the customer must purchase products amounting to at least 50 in default currency of the shop. For a certain amount of purchase, we may offer free shipping. Specify this amount in the **Minimum Amount for Free Shipping** field. The amount we specify will be in the default currency of the shop including tax. For example, we specified 50 in this field, and when a customer's purchase, including tax, amounts to 50, that customer will be eligible for free shipping.

In the **Contact Information** section, we provide contact details of the store owner. These details will include the name, title, phone number, fax number, and email.

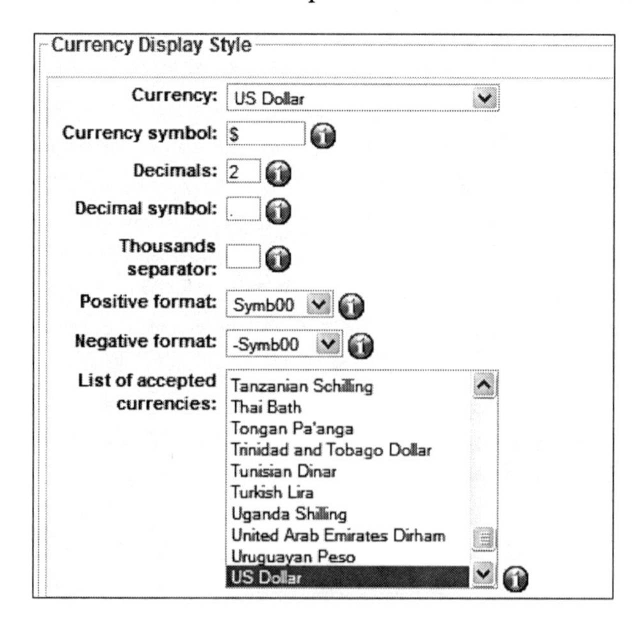

In the **Currency Display Style** (seen in the previous screenshot), we can specify which currency will be shown by default, what symbol will be shown for the currency, and so on. Select the default currency in the **Currency** field. In the **Currency Symbol** field, specify a symbol for the currency. We can use an HTML entity for this. For example, if we select **Bangladeshi Taka** as the default currency, then **BDT** will be the symbol in this field. In the **Decimals** field, we can specify how many digits after the decimal we want to use. It can be zero, and in that case, fractions will be rounded to nearest value. We then specify the **Decimal symbol**, **Thousands separator**, **Positive format**, and **Negative format**. Then come to the **List of Accepted Currencies**. From the list box, select the currencies you want to allow customers to use for checkout. We can select multiple currencies by pressing the *Ctrl* key, and then clicking the currency name. To use a single currency, select only the default currency, which you have already assigned in the **Currency** field.

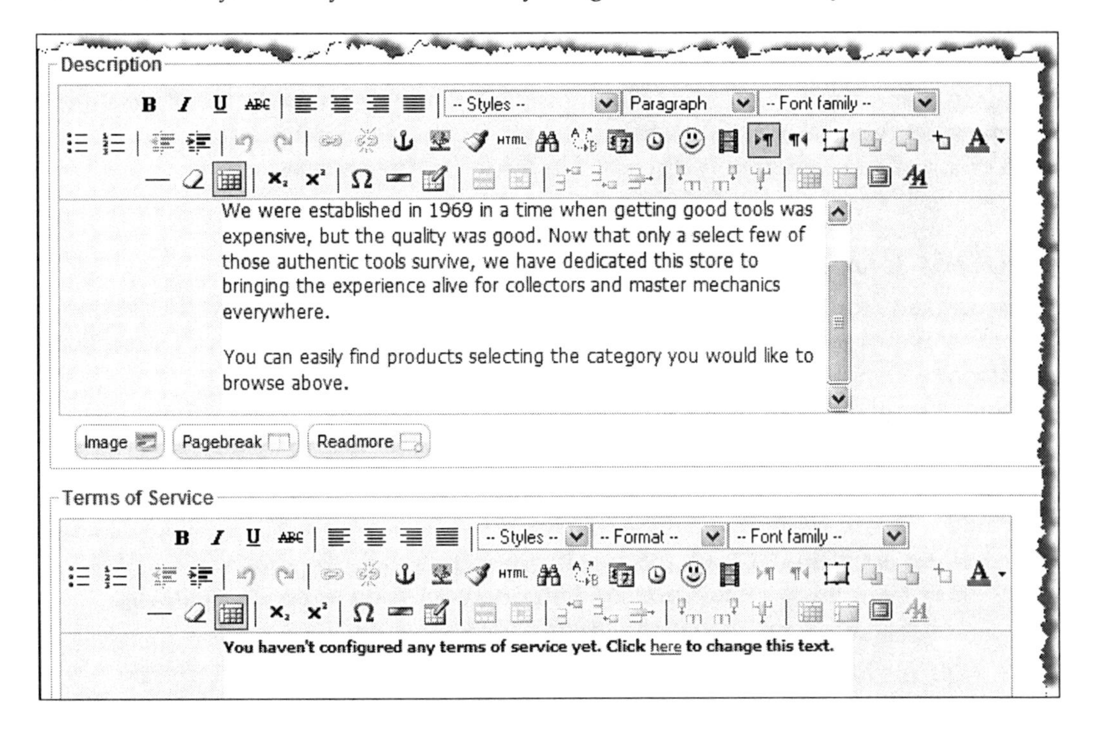

In the **Description** section (seen in the above screenshot), we will find a rich text edit box. Type the store's description in this box. We can use rich HTML formatting which includes images and hyperlinks. Similarly, in the **Terms of Service** section, type the terms of service for our store.

Although anything can be typed in the **Terms of Service** box, in a real shop, this text should be well thought and acceptable by the customers. You may consult your legal advisor to formulate the terms of service for your store. You can download and customize the privacy and terms of service documents available at: `http://tinyurl.com/9677bw`.

When we have configured all the fields in **Store Information** screen, click on the **Save** button on top to save the settings.

Shop configuration

Besides configuring the store information, we also need to configure some options for the entire store before putting it in action. This is done from the **VirtueMart Administration Panel | Admin | Configuration**. This will show the **Configuration** screen, where we will see some tabs and many sections for configuration groups. Each group of configuration is discussed in the following sections.

Global configurations

There are some configuration options in the **Global** tab of the **Configuration** screen. This tab contains seven sections to configure several aspects of our shop. The sections are discussed below.

Shop status configuration

Global section defines a site's status. It has three options to configure:

- **Shop is Offline?**: Check this box if you want to take the shop offline. This may be necessary when you are building your shop or product catalog, or doing some maintenance activities for your shop.
- **Offline Message**: While taking the shop offline, you can show a special message to the customers. Explain why the shop is offline and when it will be back online.
- **Use only as catalog**: For some shops, you may need to only show the products without selling them, which mean you maintain a product catalog only. If you use your shop to only display product catalog, select this checkbox. Once this is checked, customers will not be able to see the **Buy Now** button besides products and will not be able to place orders for the products.

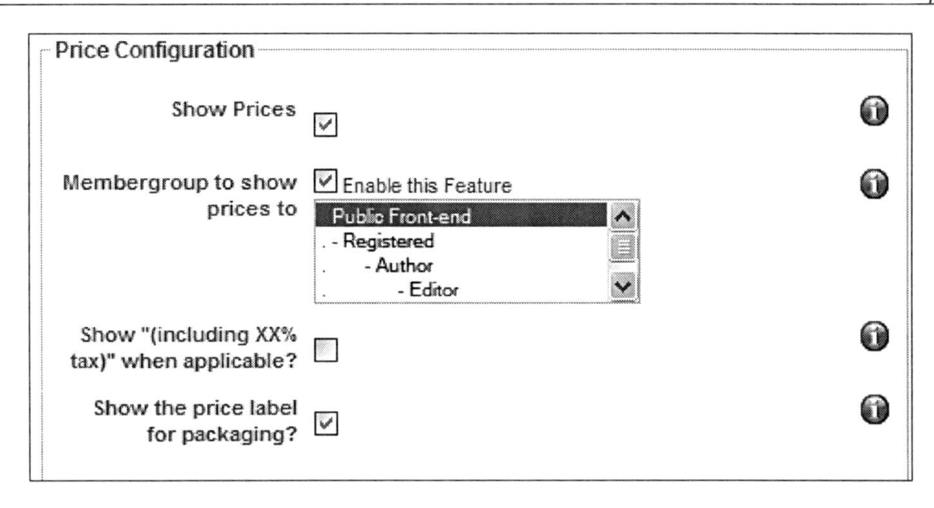

Price configuration

The **Price** section (seen in the screenshot above) of the **Global** tab gives us an opportunity to configure how prices of products will be displayed. The following are the configuration options in this section:

- **Show Prices**: Check this box if you want to show prices. You generally need to show the prices when you are really selling the products. You may turn it off if you are using the shop as catalog only.
- **Membergroup to show prices to**: You may also choose to show the prices only to a particular group of users. By default, all users from the frontend can see the prices. You may restrict it to only **Registered**, **Author**, or **Editor** user. When you are selecting a group, another group with higher permissions automatically gets permission to that. For example, when you choose the **Author** group, members of the **Editor** group also can see the prices. In this case, **Public Front-end** will not be able to see the prices, as it has lower permissions.
- **Show "(including XX% tax)" when applicable?**: For some cases, it is useful to indicate the prices including taxes. If you check this box, percentage of tax included will also be displayed besides the price of the product, for example, $ 44 (including 10 percent tax). However, whether tax is displayed with prices or not, it will be displayed during checkout and on the invoice.
- **Show the price label for packaging?**: If you check this box, the price will be displayed for a package, for example, Price Per Unit (10 pieces). Normally, the price is shown for a single item.

Frontend features

The **Frontend Features** section of the **Global** tab contains some options for configuring review, rating and coupon usage settings:

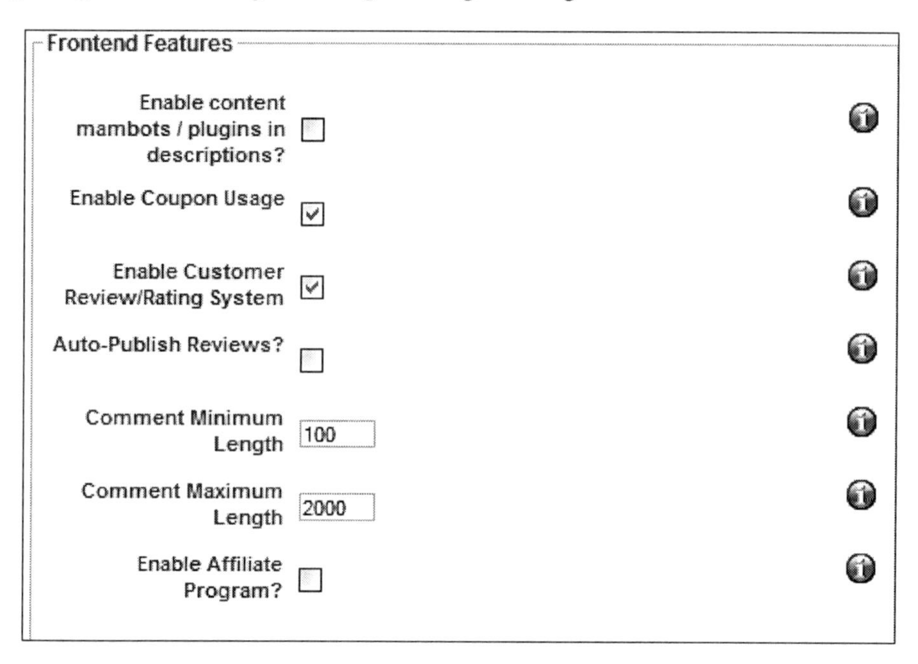

Followings are the options in the **Frontend Features** section:

- **Enable content mambots/plugins in descriptions?**: If you enable this feature, category and product descriptions will be parsed by all published mambots/plugins. Some mambots/plugins may replace some words in the description automatically. Therefore, you may want to keep the descriptions out of mambots/plugins parsing. However, VirtueMart's extended search plugin will work irrespective of the setting of this option
- **Enable Coupon Usage**: Check this box to allow the use of coupons on your shop. When this feature is enabled, customers can get discounts/special prices using coupons sent by you.
- **Enable Customer Review/Rating System**: Check this box to enable product reviews and ratings by the customers. When enabled, customers can share their experiences of using the product, and that often acts as a testimonial, and subsequently contributes to higher sell.

- **Auto-Publish Reviews?**: If you check this box, reviews submitted by the customers will be published automatically. You may often have trouble with review auto-publishing, as some customers may use offensive languages. In that case, you need to uncheck this box, moderate the reviews, and publish them manually.
- **Comment Minimum Length**: Specify the minimum length of the comment. Type number of characters in this box. The minimum length is specified so that comments at least describe something about the product, instead of just writing '+', 'good', or 'thumbs up'. The default value is 100, which is a reasonable minimum length for comments.
- **Comment Maximum Length**: Like the minimum, you may also specify the maximum length in characters for comments. The default value is 2000, and for most of the cases, that should be enough.
- **Enable Affiliate Program?**: Check this box if you want to track affiliate programs. You can enable this if you have installed an affiliate program in the backend.

At present, the affiliate program feature in VirtueMart does not work properly. However, this is going to be fixed soon.

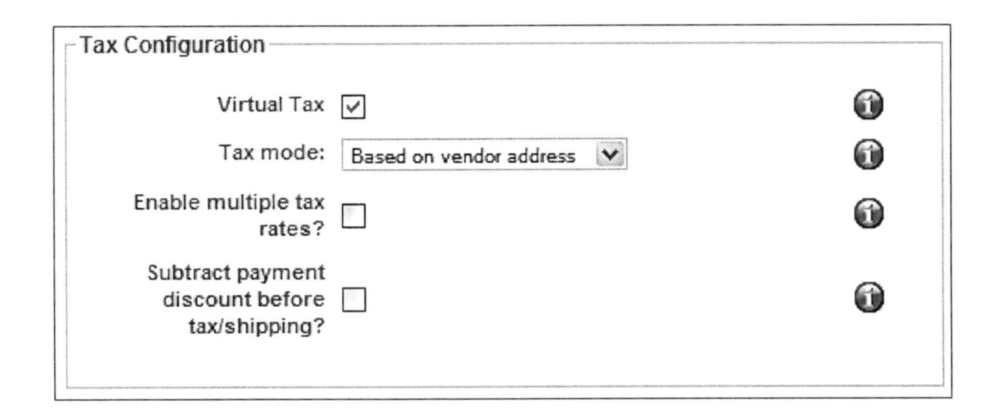

Tax configuration

The **Tax Configuration** section (seen in the previous screenshot) of the **Global** tab allows us to configure how taxes will be applied to the product prices. The options in this section are:

- **Virtual Tax**: Check this box if you want to apply tax to products with zero weight. Generally, downloadable or information products are considered virtual products.
- **Tax Mode**: Taxes can be configured based on the shop owner's origin or the shopper's origin. You can select three options here. If you want to apply tax based on shop owner's location (country) then select the **Based on Vendor Address** option. On the other hand, if you want to apply tax based on the shopper's location (country), then select the **Based on Shipping Address** option. Another option is the **European Union Mode**. When this is selected, per product tax is applied, if the shopper is from any country in the European Union.
- **Enable multiple tax rates?**: You can apply multiple tax rates for different types of products. For example, for books it may be 7 percent, for CD and DVDs it is 10 percent, and for electronic items it is 4 percent. If this is the case, check this box to allow multiple tax rates.
- **Subtract payment discount before tax/shipping?**: Check this box if you want to subtract discounts from the total before applying the tax. If this option is not selected, the tax will be applied on the total and then the discount will be deducted. This discount is for the payment method used. For example, you may give a discount to customers who pay by PayPal.

This section defines how taxes will be applied. However, it is not defining what the tax rates will be. Tax rates are defined separately and will be discussed later in this chapter.

User registration settings

The **User Registration Settings** section in the **Global** tab gives us options to configure how users of VirtueMart will be created, and whether they need to agree to some terms while signing up to our shop:

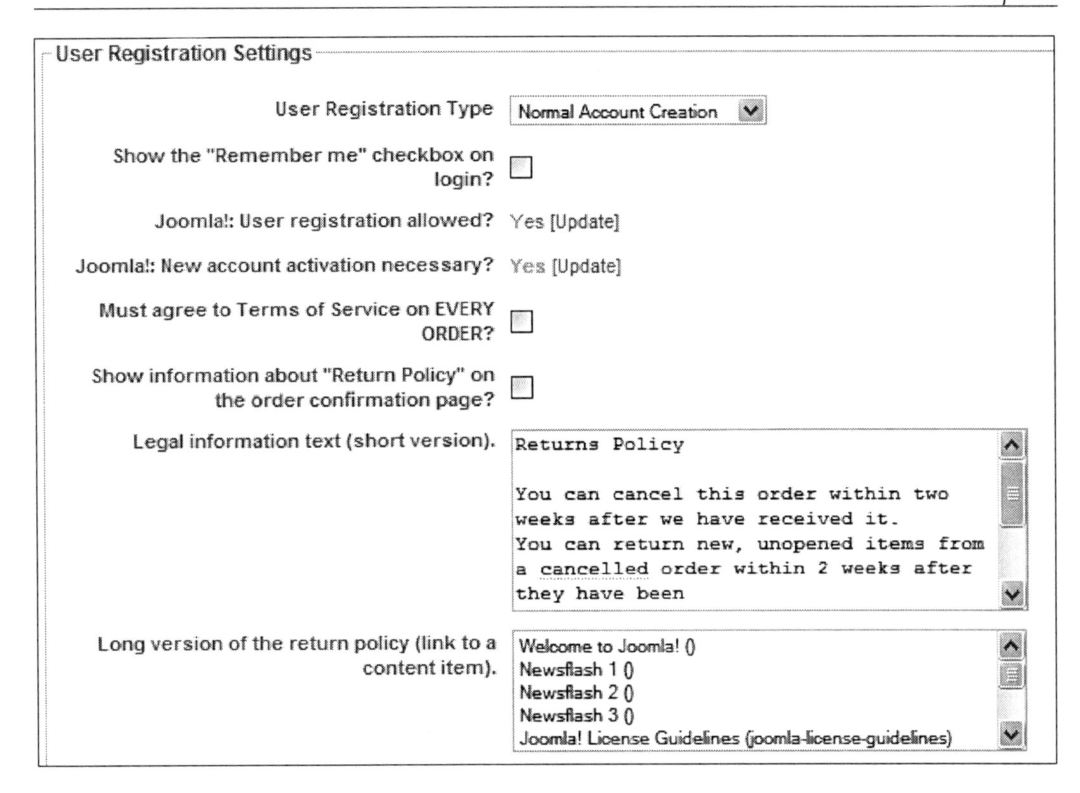

The **User Registration Settings** section gives us the following options to configure:

- **User Registration Type**: This sets how users will register to your shop. There are four options to select. Selecting the **Normal Account Creation** option will allow the shopper to choose a username and password, and provide billing and shipping information. Selecting the **Silent Account Creation** option will ask the user email address and billing address. Based on this email address, it will automatically create a username and password, and mail those to the customer. Thus, the customer does not need to choose a username and password while registering. If you select the **Optional Account Creation** option, the customer will be provided an option to create an account. However, that will not be mandatory. If the customer chooses not to create an account, a hidden account will be created for that customer's login. If you select the **No Account Creation Possible** option, the customer cannot create a persistent account to get back to the shop. In this case, a dummy account is created each time to keep the data of that customer's purchase. The default setting is to create a normal account, which is fine for most of the shops.

- **Show "Remember Me" checkbox on Login?**: The **Remember Me** feature allows a customer to return to the shop without logging in again. When the customer checks the **Remember Me** box, a cookie is set to his or her computer. This is done by default. Although it may seem beneficial for the customer, it has security risks, especially when customers are using public computer. Therefore, it is better to give an option to the customer to control whether they want this cookie to be set or not. Check this box to give this option to your customers.
- **Joomla! User registration allowed?**: This field simply shows whether user registration from Joomla! is allowed. By default, it is enabled and shown here in green color, which means this is an appropriate setting for VirtueMart. However, if you see **No** in red color, click on the **Update** link and set **Yes** in the **Allow User Registration** field.
- **Joomla! New account activation necessary?**: This shows whether new account activation in Joomla! is enabled. This should be disabled. If you see **Yes** in red color, click on the **Update** link and set **No** in the **New User Activation** field.
- **Must agree to Terms of Service on EVERY ORDER?**: If you want to remind customers of the **Terms of Services** every time the customer buys something, select **Yes** in this field. This will show the terms of service to the customers during checkout and they must agree to it for a successful checkout.
- **Show information about "Return Policy" on the order confirmation page?**: A return policy is important for any online shop. Customers must know about the return policy. Select **Yes** to show the return policy on an order confirmation page. Showing this policy is legally binding for some European countries. Therefore, always keep this enabled.
- **Legal information text (short version)**: In this box, you must type the legal information text describing the return policy and the order cancellation policy. This box is for providing a shorter version of the text.
- **Long version of the return policy (link to a content item)**: You can show a long version of the return policy. For doing so, first create an article in Joomla! which contains the return and order cancellation policies. Select that article in this list box.

Core settings

The **Core Settings** section of the **Global** tab gives us some options to configure stock checking, mail format, and so on. Following are the options to configure in this section:

- **Check Stock?**: When this box is checked, every time the customer adds a product to cart, the stock level is checked. The customer can add the maximum available units of products. For example, 10 books are in stock and the customer tries to add 14 books in the cart. If this box is checked, a maximum 10 pieces of that book will be added to the cart.
- **Enable the Cookie Check?**: If you check this box, every time a client visits the shop, it checks whether the client's browser supports a cookie or not. By default, this is enabled. If this is disabled, or the client's browser does not support cookie, session ids are appended to the URL to identify the session.
- **Select a currency converter module**: You can select a currency conversion module in this drop-down list. At present, only one module **convertECB.php** will be displayed. The currency converter module contains logic and currency exchange rate servers' addresses. This is used to convert currency exchange rates automatically.
- **Order-mail format**: Select in which format the order mail will be sent to customers. There are two available options: **HTML Mail** and **Text Mail**. For compatibility with most of the email clients, you may select the **Text Mail** format.
- **DEBUG?**: Check this box to enable debugging. When this is enabled, a debugging page is shown in the bottom of each page. This is very helpful during shop development as you can see error messages, queries, and values of several variables in debug messages. However, this should be set to **No** for a live shop.
- **Limit by IP Address?**: You can enable the debugging output for a specific IP address. Check this to do so.
- **Client IP Address**: When the previous option is checked, enter the IP address of the client's computer, which will be allowed to view the debugging output. Other clients, except one having this IP address, will not see the debug messages. This can be seen in the following screenshot:

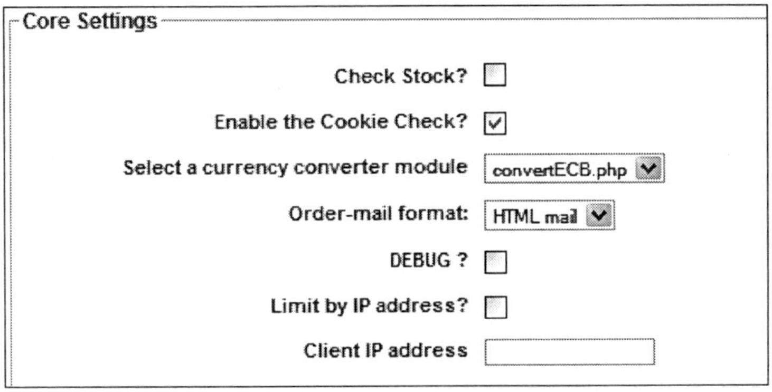

Logfile configuration

The **Logfile Configuration** section of the **Global** tab contains the following options to configure:

- **Enable logging?**: Check this to enable logging in the VirtueMart. Logging will provide useful troubleshooting information.
- **Logfile name**: Type the path and name of the logfile. The path must be accessible and writable by the web server process.
- **Logging level**: Select a logging level. There are eight levels of logging: **Emergency**, **Alert**, **Critical**, **Error**, **Warning**, **Notice**, **Info**, **Debug**, and **Tip**. **Emergency** has the lowest threshold value of 0, whereas **Tip** has the maximum threshold value of 8. When you select a level, logging for the other levels having greater threshold value are not logged. For example, when we select **Warning - 4**, **Emergency**, **Alert**, and **Critical** messages are logged. But **Notice**, **Info**, **Debug**, and **Tip** are not logged.
- **Logfile format**: Specify the log format in this box. The default value is fine for most cases. The variables that can be used in this field are listed below the field. This can be seen in the following screenshot:

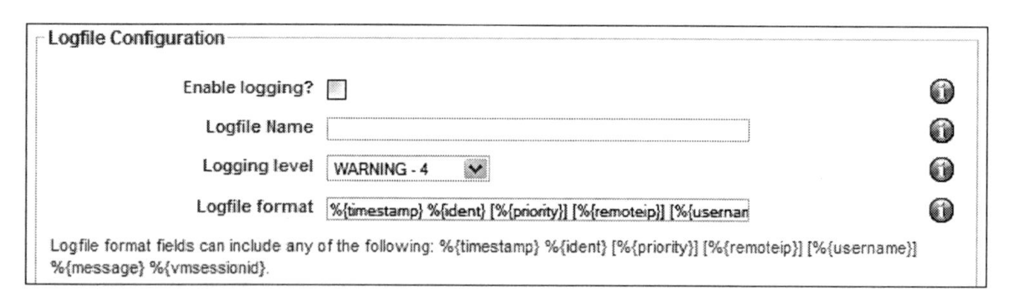

Security settings

The **Security Settings** tab has three sections: **Security Settings**, **more Core Settings,** and **Global Proxy Settings**.

Main security configurations are done from the **Security Settings** section, which has the following options:

- **Site URL**: This is the shop's URL. For example, `http://yourshop.com/`.
- **SECUREURL**: This is the URL for secure server using SSL. For example, `https://yourshop.com/`. Always write the trailing slash.

- **Shop areas which must use https**: Select the modules which must use the secure URL. Whenever customers switch to these modules, their connection is also changed to HTTPS. By default, the **account** and **checkout** modules are selected.
- **Generally prevent https connections?**: When you check this box, customers will be forced to use a normal http connection when not browsing areas identified for using a secure connection.
- **Encryption Function**: Specify which encryption function will be used. Default is **AES_ENCRYPT**, which provides strong security. Another option is **ENCODE**, which is less secure.
- **Encryption Key**: This is the encryption key used for encrypting sensitive data before storing in the database. This key is generated randomly.
- **Store Credit Card Information?**: By default, VirtueMart stores credit card information in the database, although an external payment processor is used. The card information is stored in an encrypted form. Turn this setting off if you do not manually process the credit card information.
- **Allow Frontend-Administration for non-Backend Users?**: Check this box if you want to allow store administration from the frontend. Users in the **Registered** and **Editor** group have no access to store backend, therefore, they can administer the store from the frontend if this is enabled:

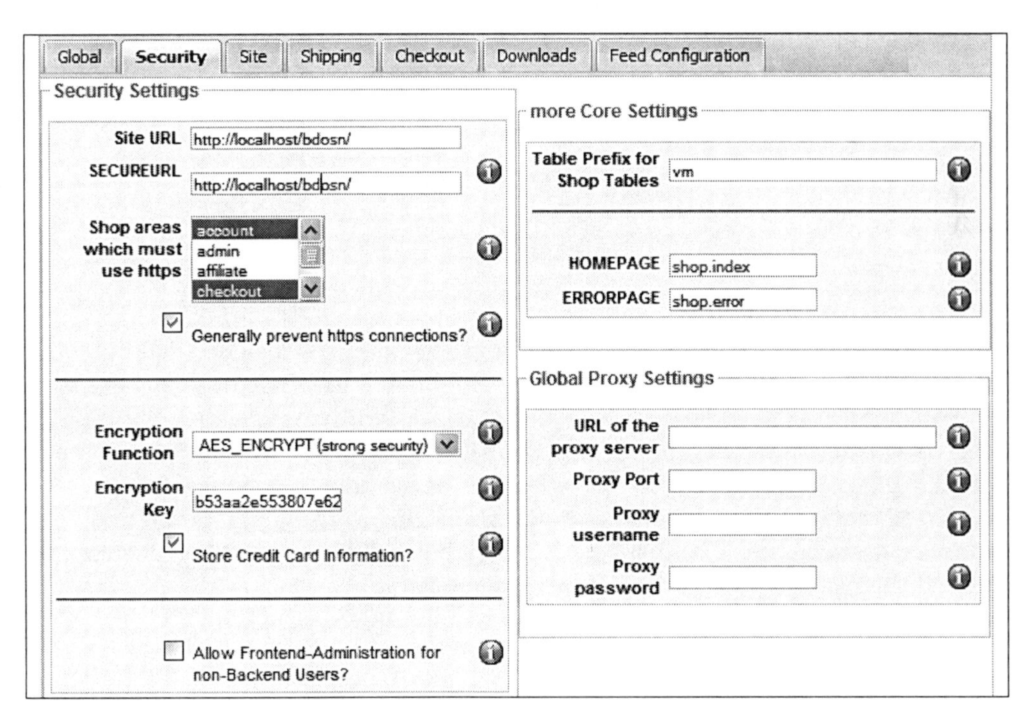

In the **more Core Settings** section, we can set the **Table Prefix for Shop Tables**. The default **vm** is fine, unless you have already changed the table prefix in the database. In the **HOMEPAGE** and **ERRORPAGE**, we can set the default pages to be displayed in the shop's homepage and error page respectively. The default values are fine for most of the cases. However, we can change those if we have designed separate layouts for these pages.

In the **Global Proxy Settings** section, we can set the proxy server's URL, port number, username, and password. These settings are used by the web server for fetching shipping rates from UPS/USPS. For most cases, you do not need to fill these settings.

Checkout configuration

The **Checkout** tab gives options to configure how the checkout steps will be presented to the customer. By selecting the **Enable the Checkout Bar**, we can show a graphical checkout bar while customers are checking out:

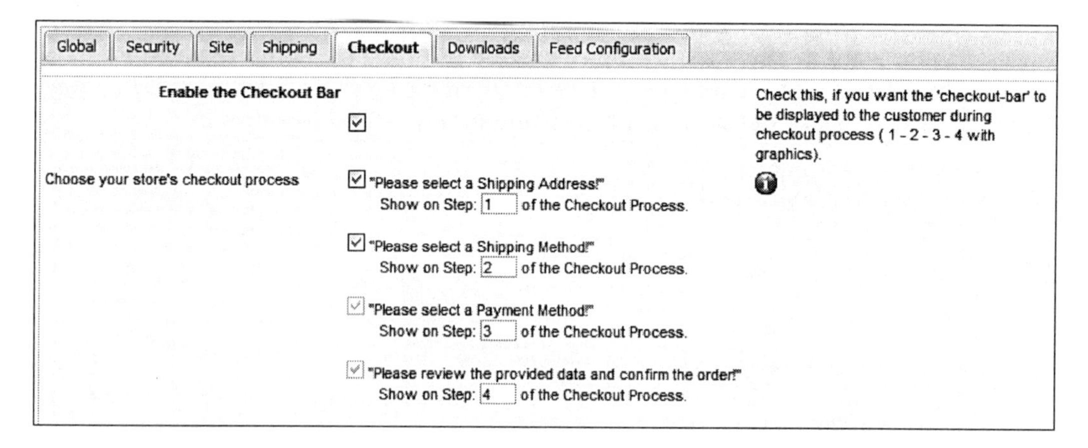

The **Checkout** bar shows customers which step they are in of the checkout process. From this tab, we can set which steps will be shown and in which order. There are four steps in the checkout process: selecting shipping address, selecting shipping method, selecting payment method, and confirming the order after reviewing the selected options. Out of these four steps, we can select only two steps not to be shown in the checkout process. An option for selecting a payment method and confirming the order must be displayed. On enabling the **Checkout** bar, customers will see the steps as shown in the following screenshot:

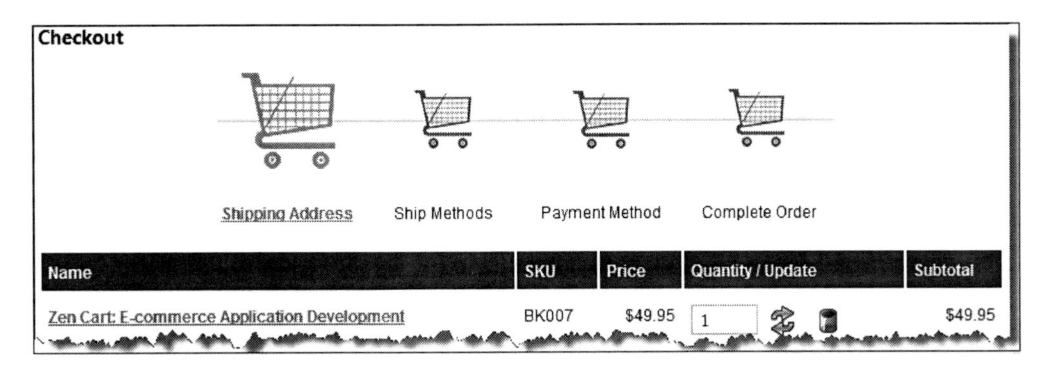

In VirtueMart, we can sell downloadable products. If you plan to sell downloadable products, you will first have to configure options for this in **Downloads** tabs:

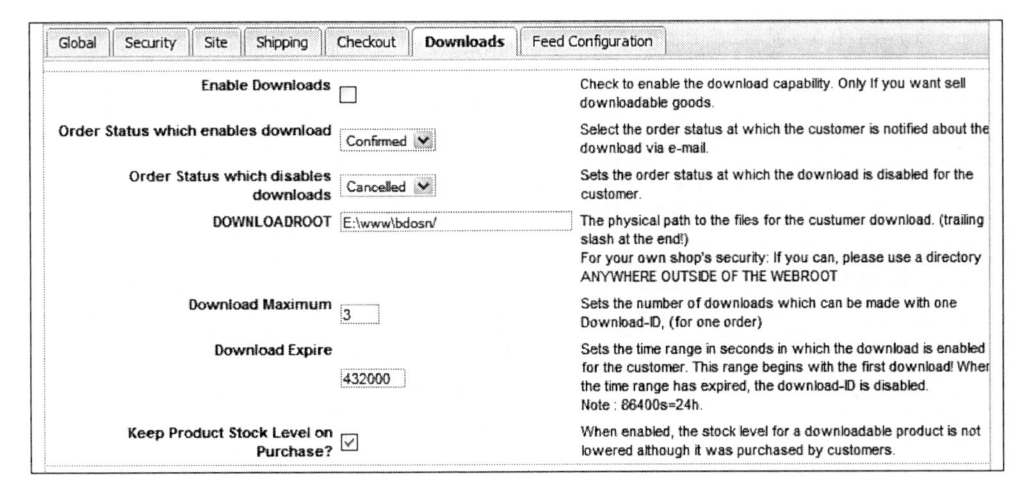

Options in the **Downloads** tab are:

- **Enable Downloads**: This must be checked if you want to sell downloadable products.
- **Order Status which enables download**: After placing the order, the customer will be able to download the product when the order status is updated to settings provided in this field. The default value is **Confirmed**, which means when the order's status is changed to **Confirmed**, the customer can download the product.
- **Order Status which disables downloads**: This is the opposite of the previous settings. Set the order status for which download will be disabled. The default value is **Cancelled**, which means when an order is cancelled, the customer cannot download the product.

- **DOWNLOADROOT**: This is the physical path where the downloadable products are stored. For enhanced security, this path should be outside of the webroot. Specify the path with a trailing slash (/) at the end.
- **Download Maximum**: Specify how many times the products can be downloaded for a single order. The default value is 3, which means the customer can download it three times.
- **Download Expire**: Set an expiration time for the download. After the order is placed, the download should be available for this amount time. This time should be specified in seconds. For example, the default value is 432000, which means twelve hours. After twelve hours, the customer cannot download it anymore. To be practical, set this value in between three days to seven days.
- **Keep Product Stock Level on Purchase?**: When a physical product is sold, the stock level goes down. However, for downloadable products, stock level remains same. Therefore, there is no need to lower the stock level with each download. Select this checkbox to keep the stock level the same after processing the orders. Despite this setting, the number of items sold will be reported in product sold report.

Feed configuration

Product feeds are an excellent feature is VirtueMart. Customers can know about the latest products in the VirtueMart shop through product feeds. From the **Feed Configuration** tab, we can enable and configure how product feeds will be displayed:

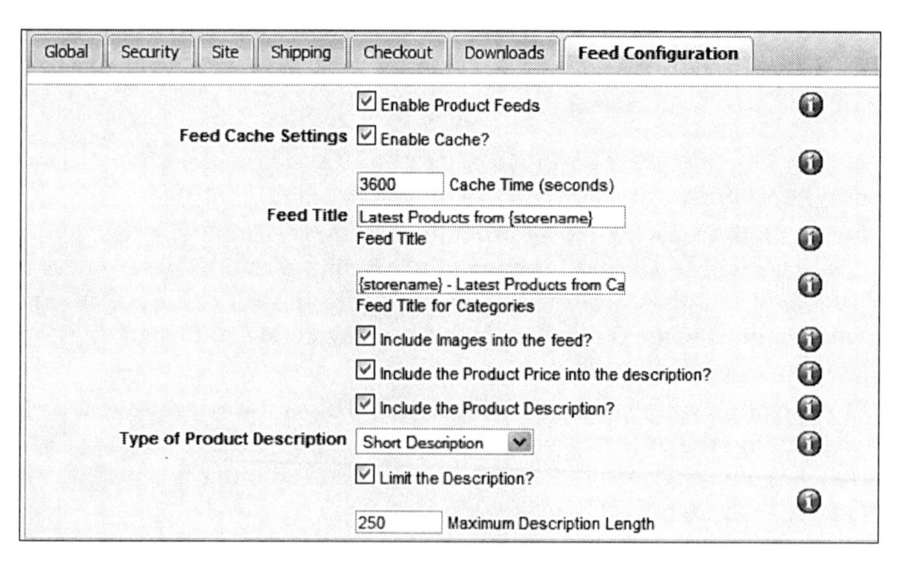

The following are the options to configure in the **Feed Configuration** tab:

- **Enable Product Feeds**: Check this box to enable product feeds. The other settings will have no effect unless this is checked.
- **Feed Cache Settings**: Select **Yes** in the **Enable Cache?** field to enable caching of product feeds. Caching provides faster performance and reduces server load. Also, specify time for caching in the **Cache Time (seconds)** field.
- **Feed Title**: Specify what the title of your product feed will be. the default value is **Latest Products from {storename}**. Note the use of the **{storename}** variable, which will be replaced with store's name.
- **Feed Title for Categories**: Feeds can be used for a specific category. In that case, the title of the feed should contain the category name. The default setting in this field is **{storename} - Latest Products from Category: {catname}**, which includes both the store name and category name.
- **Include Images into the feed?**: Select this to include product images in the feed. Including product images may be useful for the customers.
- **Include the Product Price into the description?**: Select this to include the product's price in the product description provided by the feed.
- **Include the Product Description?:** Check this to include product descriptions in feed items.
- **Type of Product Description**: Specify what type of product description you want to include in the feed. For each product, there is one short description, and a long product description. Select the **Short Description** option to show the summary description. Otherwise, select the **Product Description** option to show the full description of the product. While showing the product's description, you can also limit it by checking the **Limit the Description?** box and typing number of characters in the **Maximum Description Length** field.

We have not discussed the **Site** tab. We will discuss this in Chapter 6, *Customizing the Look and Feel*.

Managing countries

By default, VirtueMart includes 244 countries and we can see the list from **Admin | List Countries**. The **Country List** screen shows a list of all countries available. We can also add, edit, or remove a country definition from this screen:

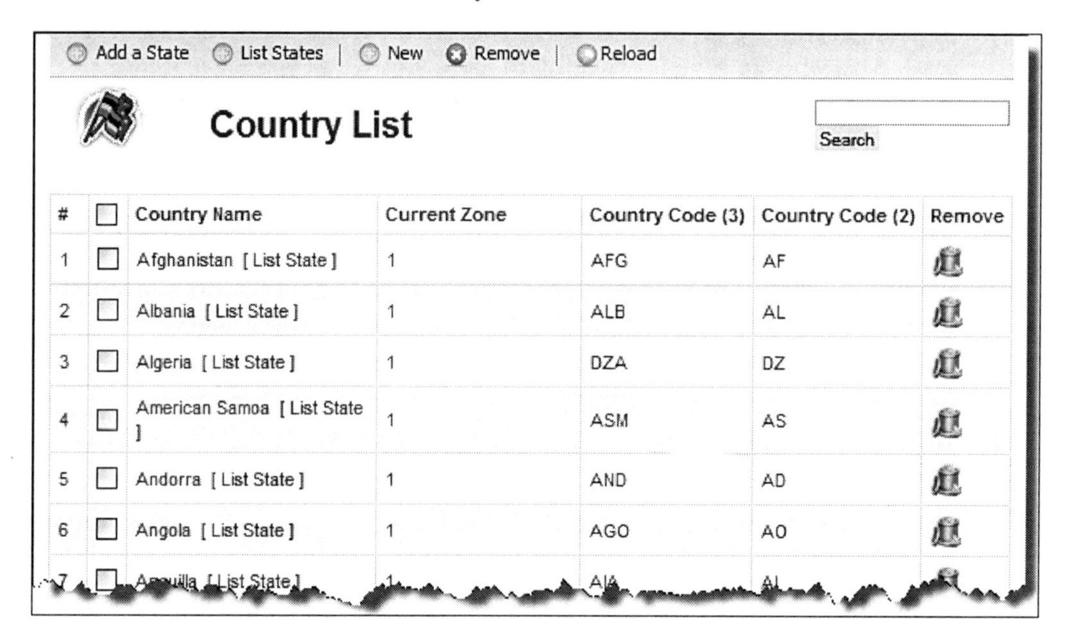

For adding a country, click on the **New** icon in the toolbar. This is will show the **Add Country** screen:

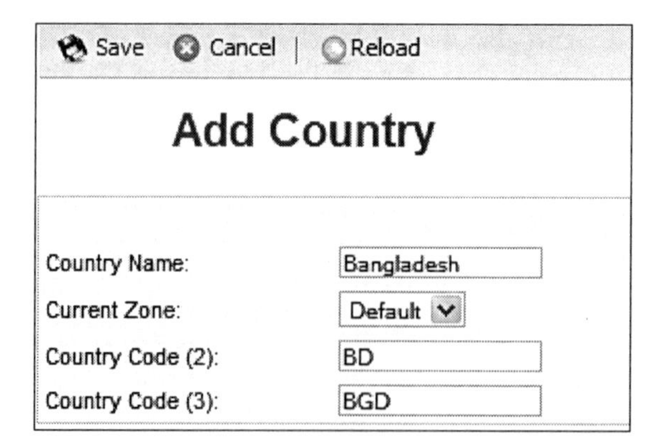

For a country we are adding, we must provide a name, two letters ISO Code in **Country Code (2)** field, and also three letters ISO Code in **Country Code (3)** field. For example, Bangladesh has two ISO country codes: **BD** and **BGD**. These ISO codes are standard based. The zone we select here is "Shipping Zone", which is used in Zone Shipping module.

[Please visit `http://tinyurl.com/2d22r3` for details on country codes.]

For editing the country information, click on the country name in the list. This will show the **Add Country** screen where we can make changes.

Generally, you don't need to remove a country. However, if you wish to do so, click on the trash icon in the **Remove** column in the **Country List** screen. This will ask you whether you really want to remove that country. To remove multiple countries at a time, select the countries from the list and click on the **Remove** icon in the toolbar.

We can add and view a list of states for the countries listed in the **Country List** screen. To view the list of states, select the countries for which you want to see the list of states, and then click on the **List States** icon in the toolbar. For adding States to a country, select the country and click on the **Add a State** icon in the toolbar. This will show the following screen for adding a state:

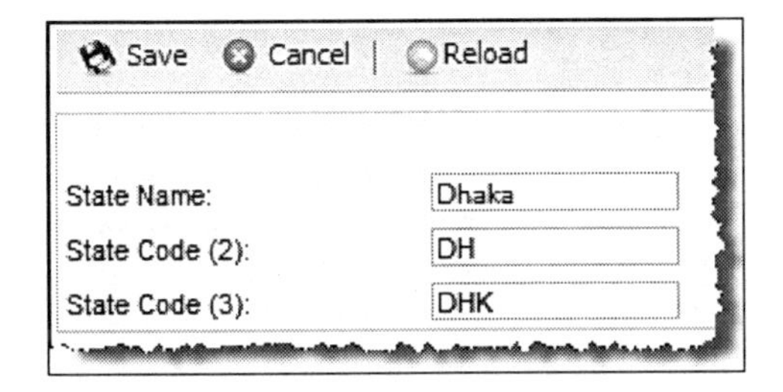

For defining a state, we must provide a **State Name**, two-digit, and three-digit state codes. Once these are given, click on the **Save** icon to save the state.

Managing currencies

Like countries, VirtueMart has defined most of the currencies. You can manage currencies from the **Admin | List Currencies**. This shows the **Currency List** screen:

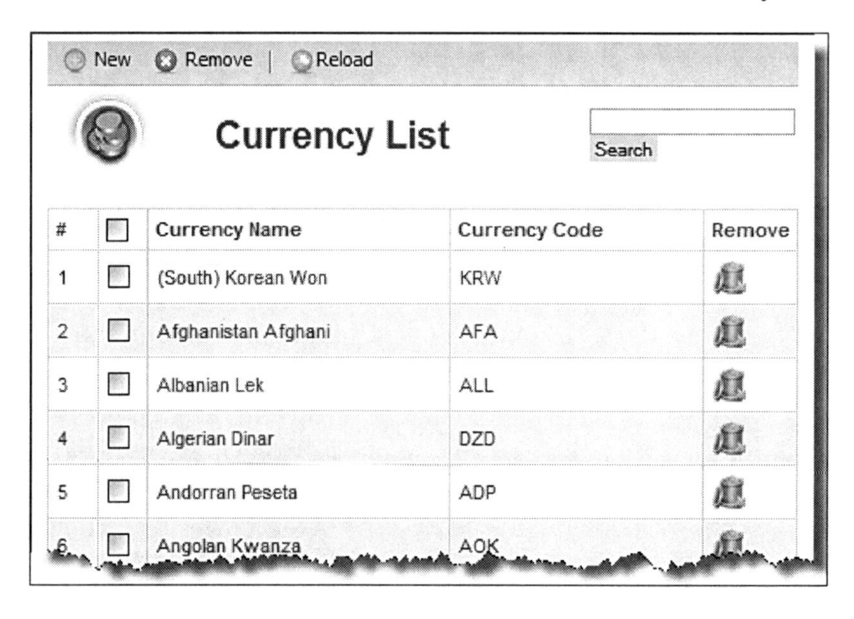

For each currency, there is a full name of the currency and three-letter currency code. This is the ISO currency code. You can remove any currency by clicking on the trash icon in the **Remove** column. To edit the currency, click on the currency name. Similarly, to add a new currency, click on the **New** icon in the toolbar. This will show the **Add Currency** screen, where you have to type the currency name and currency code as seen here:.

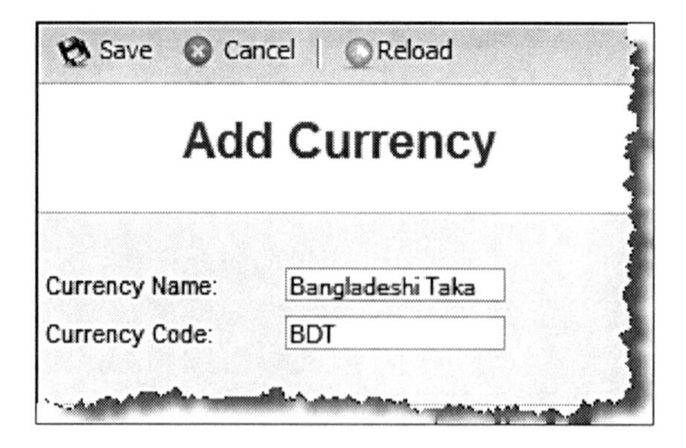

Most currencies are already defined in VirtueMart. However, if you need to define a new currency, and need to know the ISO code for that currency, please visit list of currencies and their codes at `http://tinyurl.com/22zxwj`.

Using shipping modules

Before starting our business, we need to decide how we are going to ship our products to our customers. Once we have decided on shipping methods, we need to configure the appropriate shipping modules in VirtueMart. By default, VirtueMart has several shipping modules available. We can view the list of available shipping modules and enable/disable them for our store from the **Admin | Configuration | Shipping** as seen here:

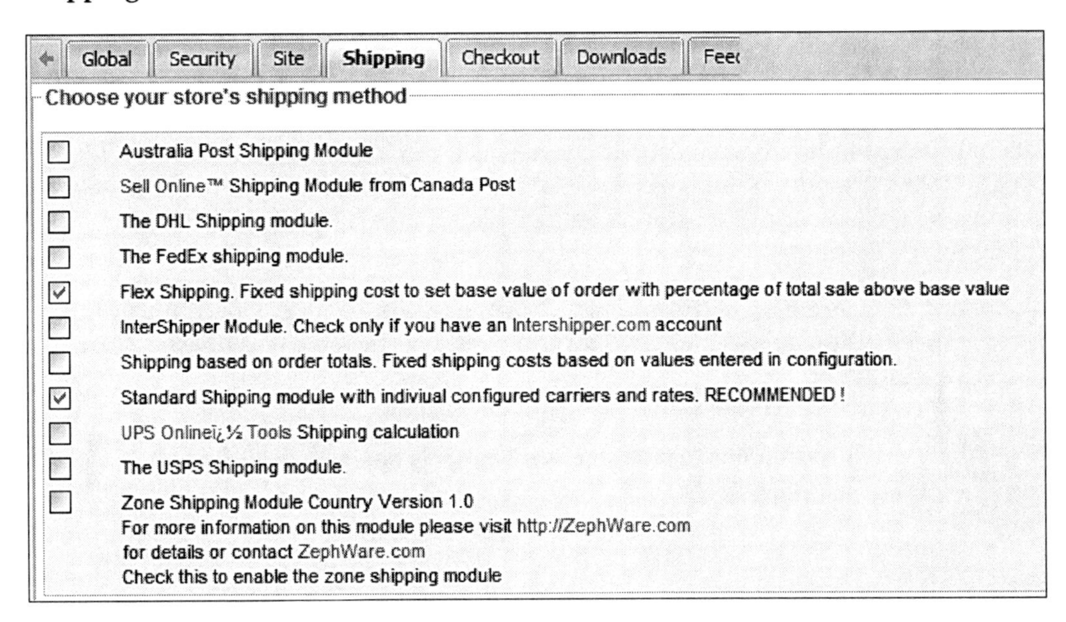

Once we have enabled the shipping modules, we can view the list and configure them from the **Store | Shipping Module List** as seen here:

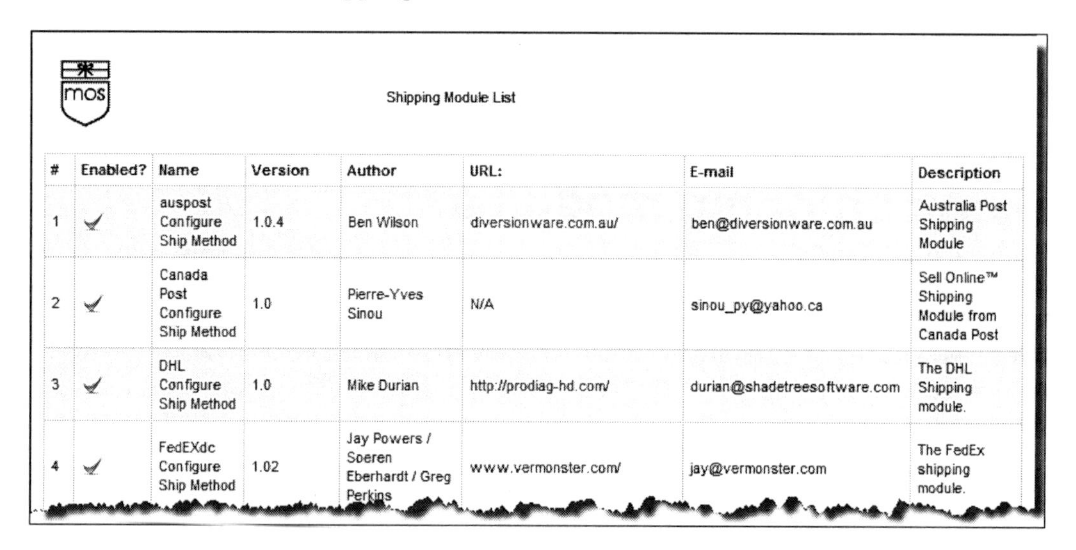

#	Enabled?	Name	Version	Author	URL:	E-mail	Description
1	✓	auspost Configure Ship Method	1.0.4	Ben Wilson	diversionware.com.au/	ben@diversionware.com.au	Australia Post Shipping Module
2	✓	Canada Post Configure Ship Method	1.0	Pierre-Yves Sinou	N/A	sinou_py@yahoo.ca	Sell Online™ Shipping Module from Canada Post
3	✓	DHL Configure Ship Method	1.0	Mike Durian	http://prodiag-hd.com/	durian@shadetreesoftware.com	The DHL Shipping module.
4	✓	FedEXdc Configure Ship Method	1.02	Jay Powers / Soeren Eberhardt / Greg Perkins	www.vermonster.com/	jay@vermonster.com	The FedEx shipping module.

The **Shipping Module List** screen, displays which modules are enabled and which version of those modules are used. An enabled module will show a green tick mark in **Enabled** field. Notice that below the name of each module, there is a link to configure the module.

By default, there are two modules enabled: **Flex shipping** and **Standard Shipping**. We will discuss how to use these two modules, and also enable and use the **Zone Shipping** module.

Configuration options for other shipping modules are discussed in *Appendix A*.

Flex shipping

The flex shipping module provides value based shipping cost calculation. It takes a base shipping cost and adds a percentage of the order's value. Click on the **Configure Ship Method** link below the **Flex** module in the **Shipping Module List** screen. This will show the **Shipping Module Configuration: flex.php** screen:

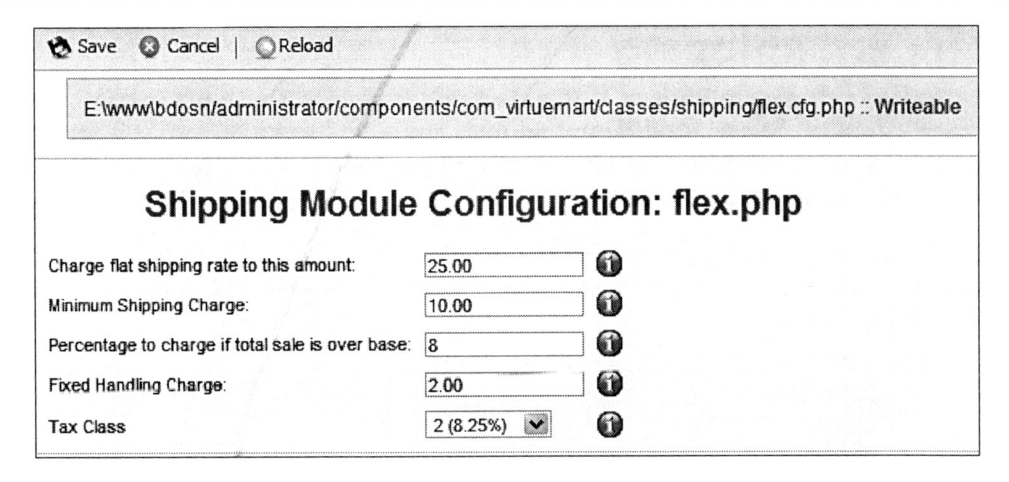

We must configure the following options for the **Flex** module:

- **Charge flat shipping rate to this amount**: Specify the amount for which the flat rate shipping charge will be applied. If the order total is more than this value, then a percentage of that value will be considered a shipping charge. For example, you provide 50 in this field. Therefore, orders of $50 and less will be applied a minimum shipping charge specified in the field below.
- **Minimum Shipping Charge**: This is the minimum shipping charge that will be applied for any amount below the base value set in the previous field. For example, you set 10 as the minimum shipping charge.
- **Percentage to charge if total sale is over base**: This is the percentage to be charged as a shipping cost, if the total sale is above the base value specified earlier. For example, you entered 8 percent here. Earlier, you set base value at 50. If a purchase totals $90, then shipping charge will be $ 7.425. However, if the purchase totals $40, the shipping charge will be the minimum charge, that is, $10.
- **Fixed Handling Charge**: You may charge a handling fee for this shipping method. This amount will be added to the shipping charge calculated by the previous conditions.
- **Tax Class**: Select a tax class for this shipping method. Whenever, a customer chooses this shipping method, that is the tax that will be applied.

When all these are configured, click on the **Save** icon in the toolbar to save the configuration options.

Standard shipping

The standard shipping module of VirtueMart provides great flexibility to configure our own shipping charges for different regions, cities, and so on. In fact, it is our own shipping charge table which we may design and use for our shop's purpose. We don't need to depend on other rates.

For using the **Standard Shipping Module**, we first need to create a shipper. We can see available shippers list by selecting **Shipping | Shipper**. This will show the **Shipper List** screen:

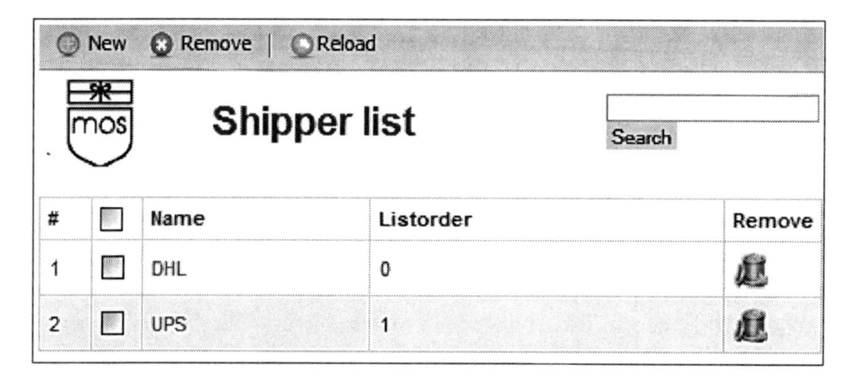

To create a shipper, select **Shipping | Create a Shipper**, or from the **Shipper List** screen, click on the **New** icon. This will show the **Shipper edit/ create** screen (seen below). Type the name of the **Shipper Company** and a list order number, and then click on the **Save** icon to save the shipper.

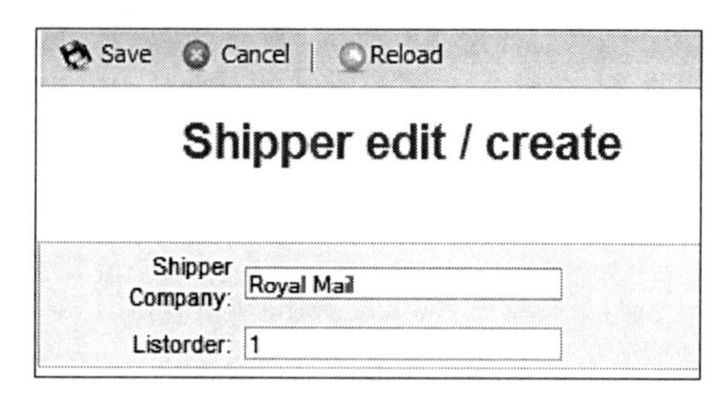

Once shippers are added, we may proceed to configure the standard shipping rates. Click on the **Configure Ship Method** below the **Standard Shipping Module** in the **Shipping Module List** screen. This will show the **Shipping Rates List** screen, listing all the available standard shipping rates. We can also define new shipping rates from this screen:

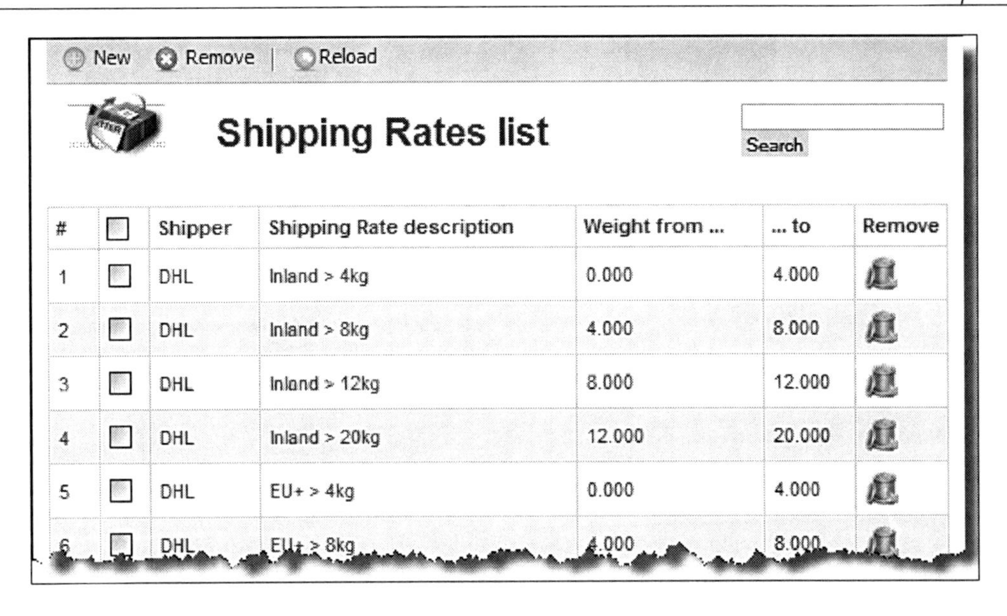

#		Shipper	Shipping Rate description	Weight from ...	... to	Remove
1		DHL	Inland > 4kg	0.000	4.000	
2		DHL	Inland > 8kg	4.000	8.000	
3		DHL	Inland > 12kg	8.000	12.000	
4		DHL	Inland > 20kg	12.000	20.000	
5		DHL	EU+ > 4kg	0.000	4.000	
6		DHL	EU+ > 8kg	4.000	8.000	

To create a new shipping rate, click on the **New** icon in the toolbar in the **Shipping Rates List** screen. This will show the **Create/Edit a Shipping Rate** screen:

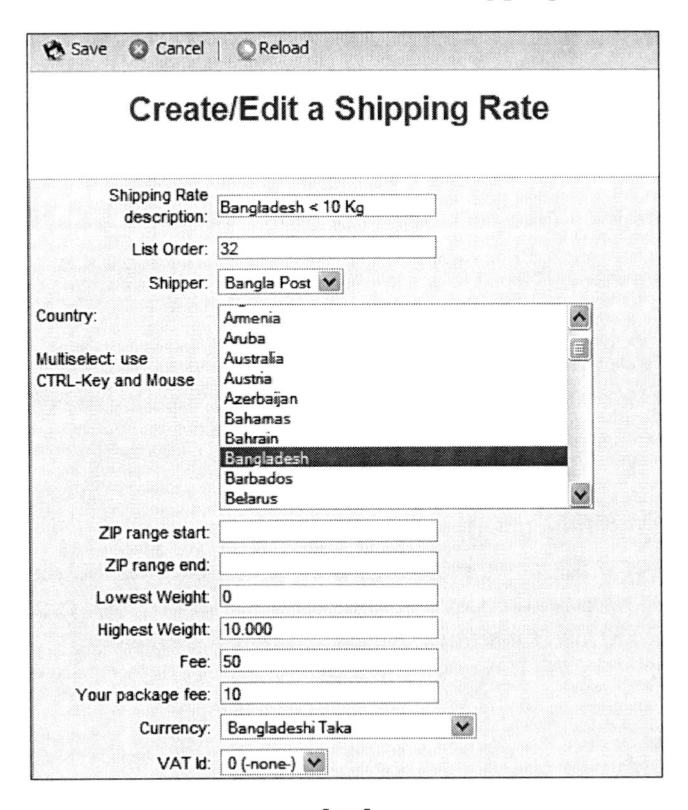

The following information will need to be provided in the **Create/Edit a Shipping Rate** screen:

- **Shipping Rate Description**: Type a description of the shipping rate. For example, if you want to create the shipping rate for inside Bangladesh, then it may be Bangladesh < 10 kg.
- **List Order**: Type a number as list order.
- **Shipper**: Select a shipper from the list. You will find the shippers which you created earlier. For example, select **Bangla Post**, which we created earlier.
- **Country**: Select one or more countries for which the shipping rate will be applicable. As we are configuring the rate for Bangladesh only, we will select Bangladesh from the list.
- **ZIP range start**: Type the ZIP code range start. Starting from this ZIP, the rate will be applicable.
- **ZIP range end**: This is end of ZIP code range.
- **Lowest Weight**: Specify the lowest weight for which this rate will be applicable. Just type the number, not 'Kg'.
- **Highest Weight**: Specify the highest weight for which this rate will be applicable.
- **Fee**: Specify the shipping fee in this field.
- **Your package fee**: Specify the package fee, if any, for this shipping method.
- **Currency**: Select the currency in which the above fees will be charged.
- **VAT Id**: Select a tax class which will be applied for this shipping method.

When all the above information has been entered, click on the **Save** icon to save the shipping rate.

In the **Standard Shipping Module**, we need to define all of the shipping rates for the regions we will be shipping. There are some example rates to help us understand how to create different rates using this module.

Zone shipping

The **Zone Shipping** module provides shipping rates per zone. In this module, we can configure zones and add countries to the zones. We can then configure per item cost for that zone and also maximum shipping cost for the zones.

Once enabled in **Admin | Configuration | Shipping**, we can configure this module from the **Store | Shipping Module List**. Click on the **Configure Ship Method** link below the **Zone Shipping** in the **Shipping Module List** screen. This will show the **Zone List** screen:

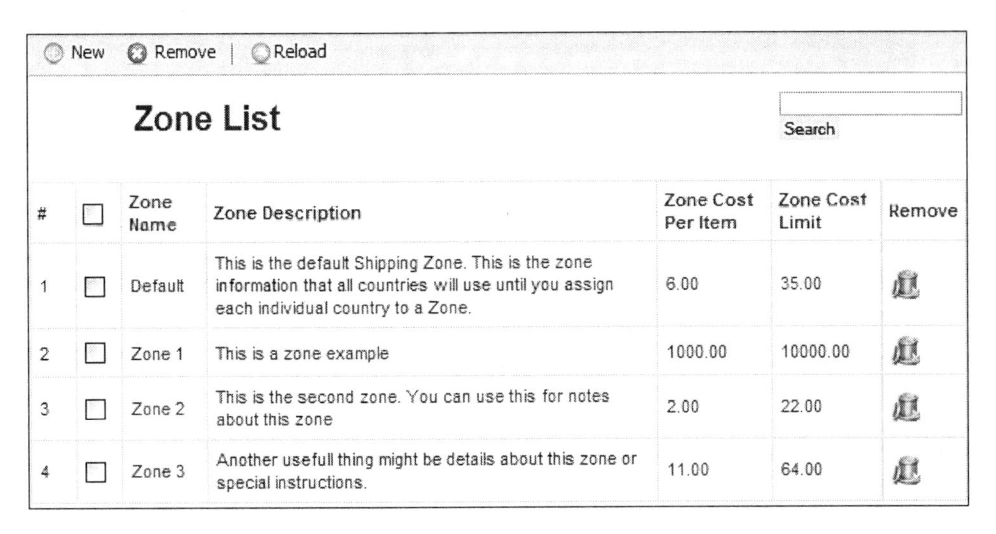

By default, there are four zones defined. The **Default** zone is for all countries which are not included in any other zone. Other zones have rates specified and countries are added to these zones. To create a new zone, click on the **New** icon in the toolbar in the **Zone List** screen. This will show the **Zone Shipping** screen as shown here:

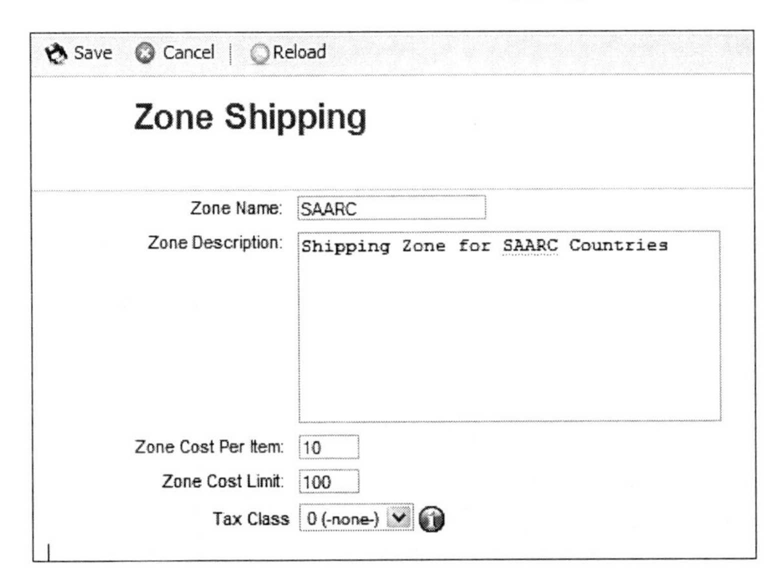

In the **Zone Shipping** screen, provide the following information:

- **Zone Name**: Provide a name for the zone. For example, we want to create a shipping zone for SAARC countries. In that case, the name may be SAARC.
- **Zone Description**: Provide a brief description of the zone.
- **Zone Cost Per Item**: Specify the per item shipping cost for this zone. Collect information on shipping rates for the countries included in the zone and calculate the per item shipping cost. This will cover the actual shipping cost in all countries. For example, 10 for SAARC zone.
- **Zone Cost Limit**: Although we have specified a per item shipping cost, the total shipping cost cannot be unlimited in the **Zone Shipping** module. There should be a maximum threshold. Type that threshold in this box. For example, 100 for SAARC zone.
- **Tax Class**: Like other shipping modules, select a tax class which will be applied to this shipping method.

Once all the information above is provided, click on the **Save** icon in the toolbar to save the zone.

Adding a zone will not apply the shipping cost. We must add the countries to that zone. For example, we have created the **SAARC** shipping zone. Now we need to add the SAARC countries in this zone. To do this, we need to edit the country definitions. Go to **Admin | List Countries**. This will show the **Country List** screen. In the **Country List** screen, click on the first country in SAARC region, that is, **Bangladesh**. This will show the **Add Country** screen. Now select **SAARC** in the **Current Zone** drop-down list and click on the **Save** icon in the toolbar.

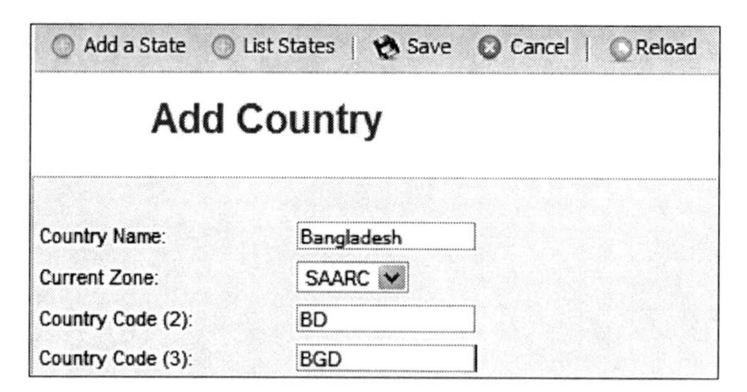

Using the same process, add other countries, that is, India, Pakistan, Sri Lanka, Bhutan, Maldives, and Nepal to the SAARC zone. When this is done, customers from these countries, or products shipped to these countries, will have the shipping rate configured in the **SAARC** zone.

> For many shippers, we need special modules. For example, we have the InterShipper shipping module in VirtueMart. When using this module, customers can select a shipper, and based on that shipper, shipping rates are retrieved from an online web service provided by that shipper. Please read *Appendix A* for configuring other shipping modules bundled with VirtueMart.

Using payment modules

Payment processing is one of the vital activities in an online shop. Payment modules help process payment through a payment processing gateway. There are many payment modules available for popular payment processing gateways. For example, we can use the Authorize.net payment module to receive payment through the Authorize.net gateway.

In VirtueMart, we can configure the Payment Processing Modules from **Store | List Payment Methods**. However, before configuring the payment methods for our shop, it is better to define the types of credit cards we are going to accept in our shop.

Adding credit cards

We can see the available credit card types from the **Store | Credit Card List**. This shows the **Credit Card List** screen:

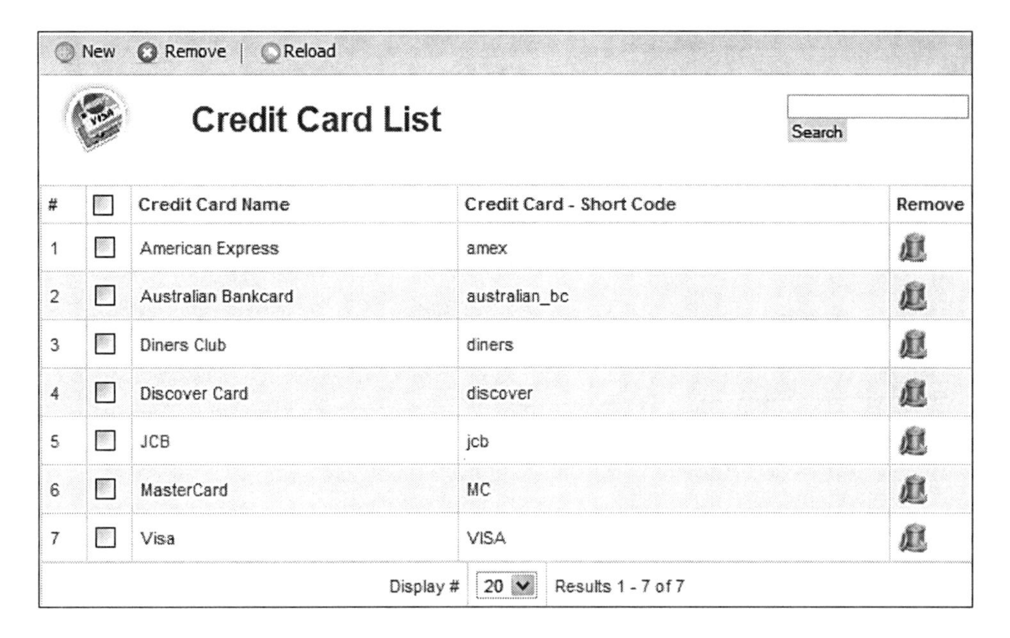

#		Credit Card Name	Credit Card - Short Code	Remove
1		American Express	amex	
2		Australian Bankcard	australian_bc	
3		Diners Club	diners	
4		Discover Card	discover	
5		JCB	jcb	
6		MasterCard	MC	
7		Visa	VISA	

Display # 20 Results 1 - 7 of 7

As we can see, most of the credit card types are listed in this screen. If we do not accept any one of these, we can remove it by clicking on the trash icon in the **Remove** column. We can also add a new card by clicking on the **New** icon in the toolbar. This will show the **Add Credit Card Types** screen. Type the card's name and short code in this form, and click the **Save** icon to add the card:

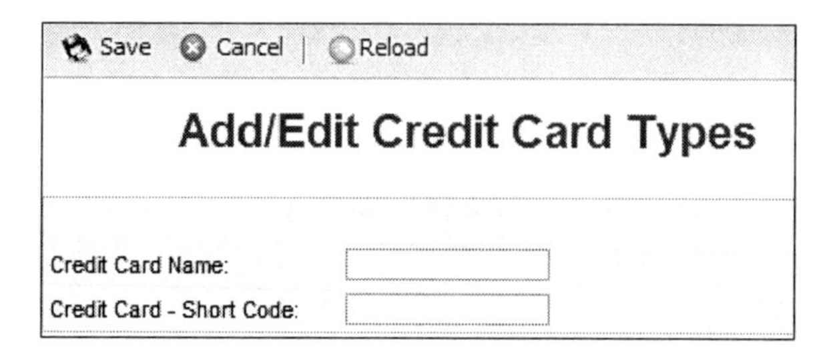

Configuring payment methods

We can see the available payment methods by selecting **Store | List Payment Methods**. This shows the **Payment Method List** screen listing all available payment methods:

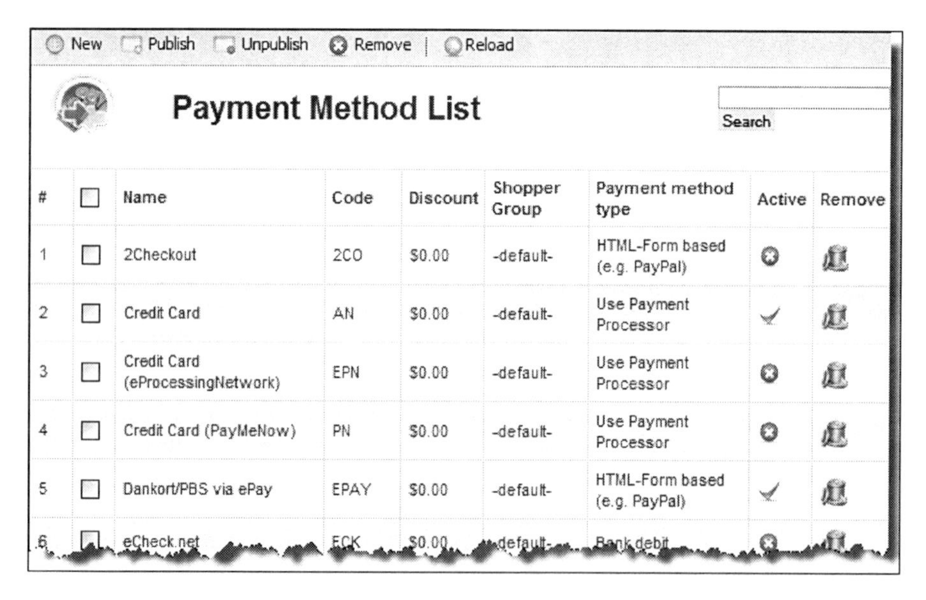

#		Name	Code	Discount	Shopper Group	Payment method type	Active	Remove
1		2Checkout	2CO	$0.00	-default-	HTML-Form based (e.g. PayPal)		
2		Credit Card	AN	$0.00	-default-	Use Payment Processor		
3		Credit Card (eProcessingNetwork)	EPN	$0.00	-default-	Use Payment Processor		
4		Credit Card (PayMeNow)	PN	$0.00	-default-	Use Payment Processor		
5		Dankort/PBS via ePay	EPAY	$0.00	-default-	HTML-Form based (e.g. PayPal)		
6		eCheck.net	ECK	$0.00	-default-	Bank debit		

The list shows the name of the payment method, code, discount for the payment method, shopper group who can use this payment method, payment method type, and whether the method is active or not. Inactive methods have a red circle with an X icon, active methods have green tick icon. We also see the trash icon in the **Remove** column for removing the payment method.

By default, there are sixteen pre-configured payment methods, out of which six are activated. Each payment method has separate configuration options, and covering all payment methods would make this chapter extremely large. Therefore, we will discuss configuration options for some of the payment methods, and also discuss how to add new payment method.

The configuration details for all other payment methods are discussed in *Appendix A*.

PayPal

PayPal is a widely used payment processing gateway. It has several payment processing services, out of which, HTML form-based processing is the simplest to implement in a shopping cart. The PayPal payment method configured in VirtueMart is such an HTML form-based implementation of PayPal's payment processing. To see this module's configuration options, click on **PayPal** in the **Payment Method List** screen. This will show the **Payment Method Form** screen (as seen below), which has two tabs: **Payment Method Form**, and **Configuration**.

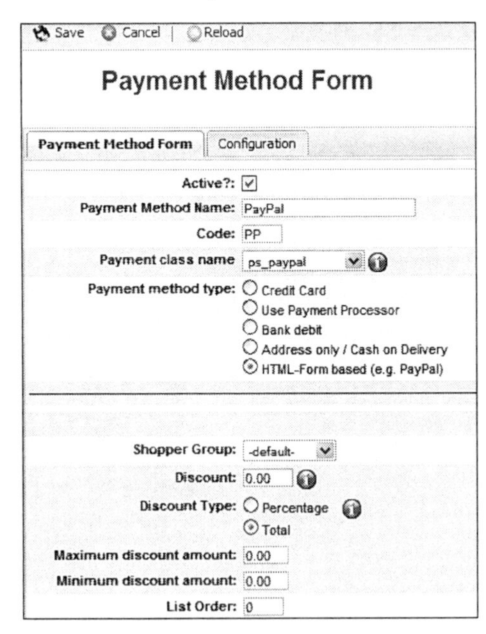

In the **Payment Method Form** tab, we see the definition of the payment method. The fields in this tab are common for all payment methods and needs to be configured when adding the payment method. First, it shows whether the payment method is active or not. Next, there is **Payment Method Name** and **Code**. In the **Payment class name** field, an appropriate class file for the payment processor, in this case **ps_paypal**, is selected. In the **Payment method type**, we see that the **HTML form-based** is selected. For any preconfigured payment module, we do not need to make changes in this tab. However, we may change the **Shopper Group**, **Discount** and other such configurations:

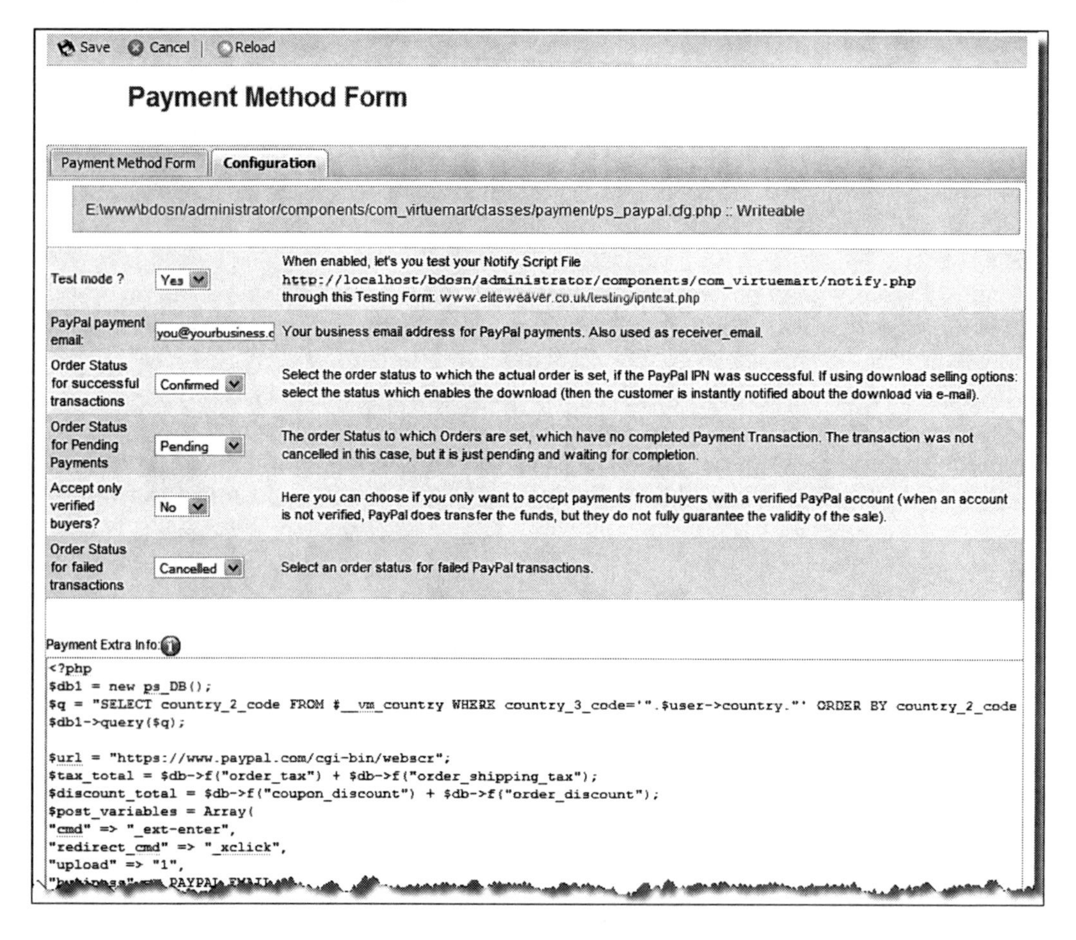

Module-specific configuration options remain in the **Configuration** tab.
For the PayPal module, we will get the following fields to configure in the **Configuration** tab:

- **Test Mode?**: When configuring this module for the first time, you may want to test the configurations. In that case, select **Yes** in this field. This will enable you to test the settings. Once you get the desired results, select **No** to go to production mode. In that case, actual payment processing will take place.
- **PayPal Payment email**: This is the email used for your PayPal business. Type the email address in this field and all payments will be made to this PayPal account.
- **Order Status for successful transactions**: Select the order status which will be set for successful transactions. When **Instant Payment Notification** (**IPN**) is successful, the order status will be set to this status. For downloadable products, this order status should be used for enabling a download so that customers are instantly given the download link when they make the payment. The default setting is **Confirmed**, which is fine for most of the shops.
- **Order Status for Pending Payments**: Set the order status for pending payments. When a payment requested through PayPal is in process or pending, the order status will be set to the status indicated here. The default setting is **Pending**, which is fine for most shops.
- **Accept only verified buyers?**: In PayPal, there are verified and non-verified accounts. When buyers transfer fund from non-verified account, you get the money. However, PayPal does not guarantee the validity of the purchase. Select **Yes** if you want to sell only to verified buyers. Default is **No**, and it is fine for most of the shops.
- **Order Status for failed transactions**: Select an order status for failed transactions. When a transaction fails through PayPal, this status will be set to the order. The default setting is **Cancelled**, and it is appropriate for most of the shops.
- **Payment Extra Info**: This field is for providing extra information to customers during order confirmation. For the PayPal module, the code in this field presents the HTML form through which the customer enters payment information and submits to PayPal.

As we can see from the above field options, we need to provide a PayPal id, generally your email address, and set **No** in **Test Mode** field to make the PayPal module opertional.

Credit card processing through Authorize.Net

Authorize.Net is a popular payment processing gateway. A module for this is already preconfigured in the VirtueMart. However, at first sight, it will be difficult to recognize it from the list. The preconfigured module for Authorize.Net is named as **Credit Card** in **Payment Method List** screen. Click on this to get the configuration options. This will show the **Payment Method Form**. In the **Payment Method Form** tab, we see which payment processing class is used and what payment method type is used:

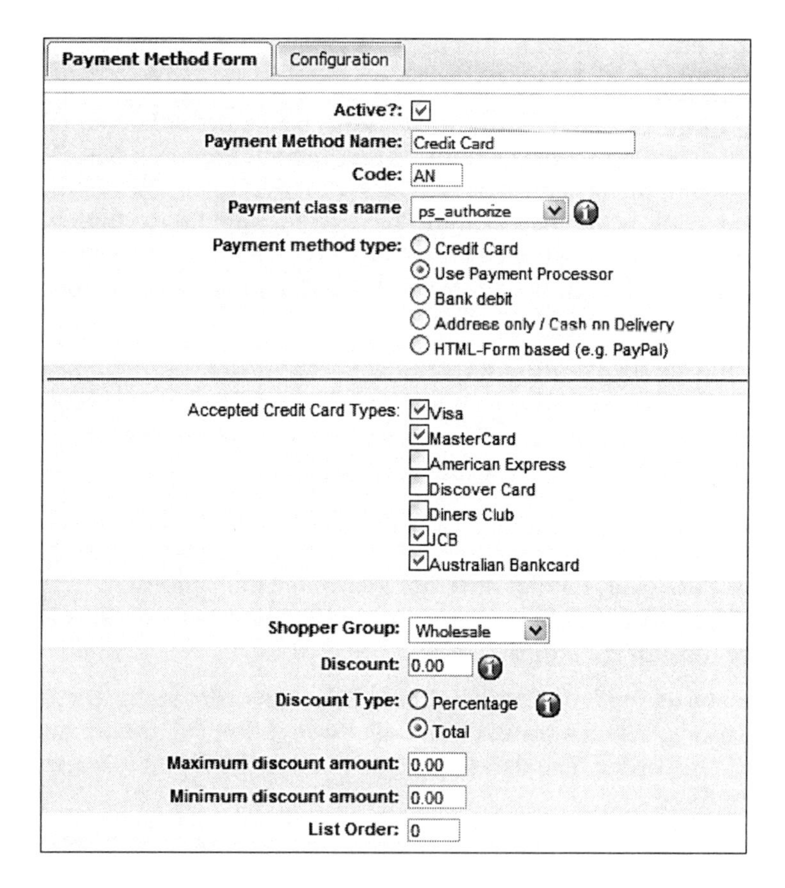

Notice that **ps_authorize** is selected in the **Payment Class Name** field. This class file defines the business logic for using the Authorize.Net gateway. Also note that the **Use Payment Processor** is selected in the **Payment Method Type** field. With this selection, we get the **Accepted Credit Card Types** list. This list identifies which cards can be processed by Authorize.Net. We don't need to change any settings in this tab.

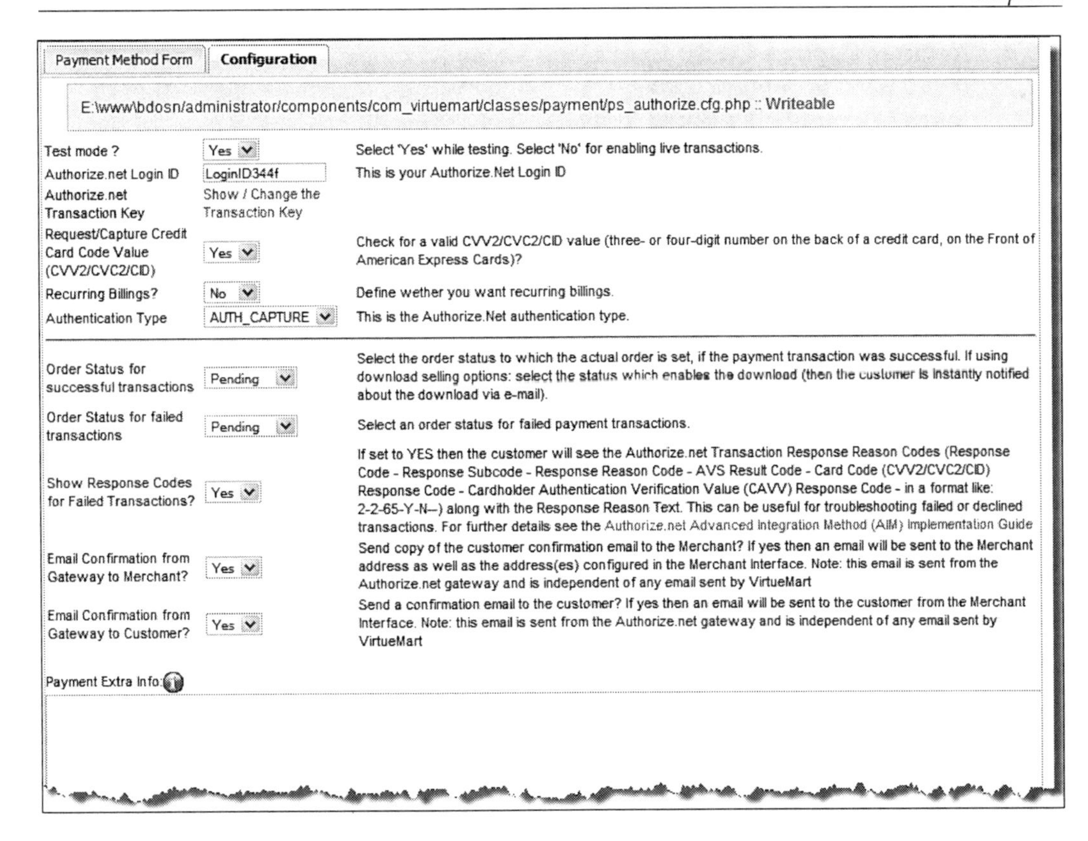

Actual configuration options for the **Authorize.Net** module are in the **Configuration** tab (seen above). We must configure the following options in this tab:

- **Test mode ?**: Select **Yes** to enable test mode. Change it to **No** when you have finished testing the settings.
- **Authorize.net Login ID**: Type the Authorize.Net login ID. You can get this ID by registering at `http://www.authorize.net`.
- **Authorize.net Transaction Key**: When you are registered at Authorize.Net, you get a 16-character alphanumeric transaction key which is randomly generated. This key is used as an additional layer of authentication when submitting transaction requests from your shop. You don't need to enter this transaction key manually. Just click on the **Show/Change the Transaction Key** link. It will ask you for your login password to Authorize.Net. Once you have provided it, VirtueMart connects to the Authorize.Net server and updates the transaction key.

- **Request/Capture Credit Card Code Value (CVV2/CVC2/CID)**: Select **Yes** if you need to capture CVV2/CVC2/CID values, which are three-digit or four-digit numbers printed in the back of the credit cards. For most of the shop, the default value **Yes** will be appropriate.
- **Recurring Billings?**: Select **Yes** if you want recurring billing using Authorize. Net. For most of the shops, this needs to be set **No**.
- **Authentication Type**: Select the authentication type which will be used for Authorize.Net. Options are: **AUTH_CAPTURE** and **AUTH_ONLY**.
    - **AUTH_CAPTURE** uses authorization with auto capture. This transaction process is completely automatic. The transaction is submitted to the processor for authorization and if approved, is placed in your Unsettled Transactions already set to Capture. Usually, settlement occurs within 24 hours.
    - On the other hand, when an **AUTH_ONLY** transaction is submitted to Authorize.Net, the transaction is sent to the processor for authorization. If authorized, the transaction is put in your Unsettled/Pending Capture. When the transaction is captured, funds will be transferred from customer's bank to you. This is appropriate when you want to make the sell but ship the product after some time, and want to get the payment after shipping the product.

  The default value is **AUTH_CAPTURE**, and most of the shops will use this as their default mode of transaction for the Authorize.Net payment gateway.
- **Order Status for successful transactions**: Select the order status which will be set on successful transaction. The default value of **Confirmed** is fine for most shops.
- **Order Status for failed transactions**: Select the order status which will be set on failed transaction. The default value of **Cancelled** is fine for most shops.
- **Show Response Codes for Failed Transactions?**: Select **Yes** to show the response codes for failed transactions to the customers. The response code shows the code, sub-code, reason, card code, and so on. The response codes may be useful for troubleshooting failed or declined transactions.
- **Email Confirmation from Gateway to Merchant?**: Select **Yes** to allow an order confirmation email to be sent from the gateway to the merchant. If this is enabled, you will receive the payment confirmation notification from Authorize.Net. This mail is sent from Authorize.Net, not from VirtueMart.

- **Email Confirmation from Gateway to Customer?**: Select **Yes** to allow a payment confirmation email to be sent from Authorize.Net to the customer. When this is enabled, Authorize.Net will notify the customer about the successful transaction. This mail will be sent from Authorize.Net, not VirtueMart.
- **Payment Extra Info**: This textbox is for displaying some extra information on the order confirmation page. There is no such text in this module.

The **Credit Card** module used in VirtueMart uses Authorize.Net **Advanced Integration Method (AIM)** . We can learn more details about this integration method by reading the Authorize.Net AIM Implementation Guide available at `http://www.authorize.net/support/AIM_guide.pdf`.

Cash on delivery

Cash on delivery is a traditional method of payment where customers pay in cash when the goods are delivered. For some areas, especially areas nearby the shop, this payment method can be used. There is nothing to process through this module. However, we may look into how this module is defined. To do so, click on the **Cash on Delivery** module on the **Payment Module List** screen. This will show the **Payment Method Form** for **Cash on Delivery** module:

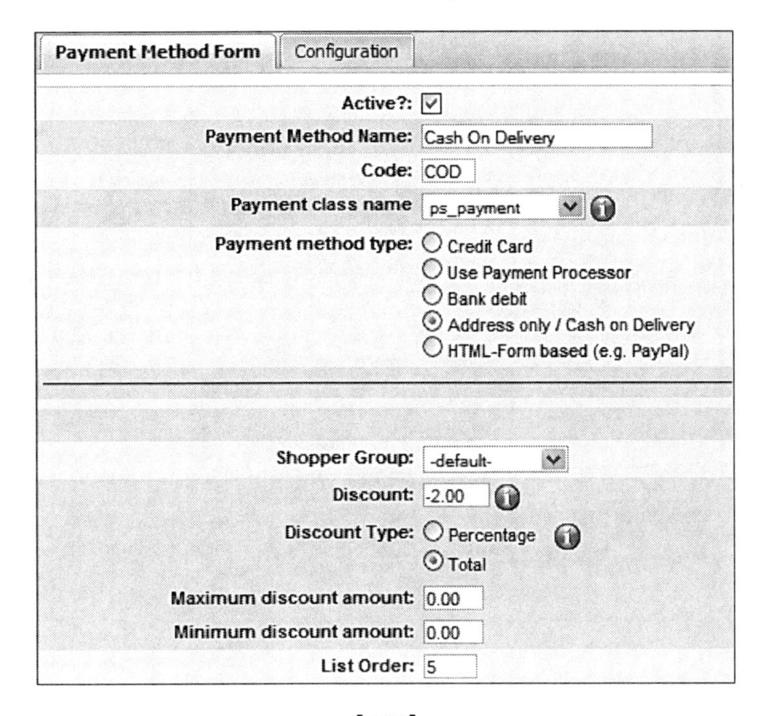

In the **Payment Method Form** tab, we can see how the Cash on Delivery payment method is defined. It is assigned **COD** as the **Code**, and **ps_payment** as the **Payment Class Name.** In fact, the **ps_payment** class is a placeholder, it has no business logic defined for processing payment. Modules like **Cash On Delivery** do not need processing, therefore, the **ps_payment** class is used. This payment method is fully dependent on an address. Therefore, **Address Only / Cash On Delivery** is selected in the **Payment method type** field. Cash on Delivery involves some risks. Therefore a negative discount is specified in the **Discount** field, which means the customer has to pay more when using this payment method.

Adding a payment method

Although there are sixteen preconfigured payment methods in VirtueMart, we can still add another payment method at any time. For example, Money Order may be another payment method used in some regions, which is not preconfigured in VirtueMart. We can add this payment method from the **Store | Add Payment Method**. This will show the **Payment Method Form**. We saw this form earlier, and now it is our turn to use this form and make our payment method Money Order:

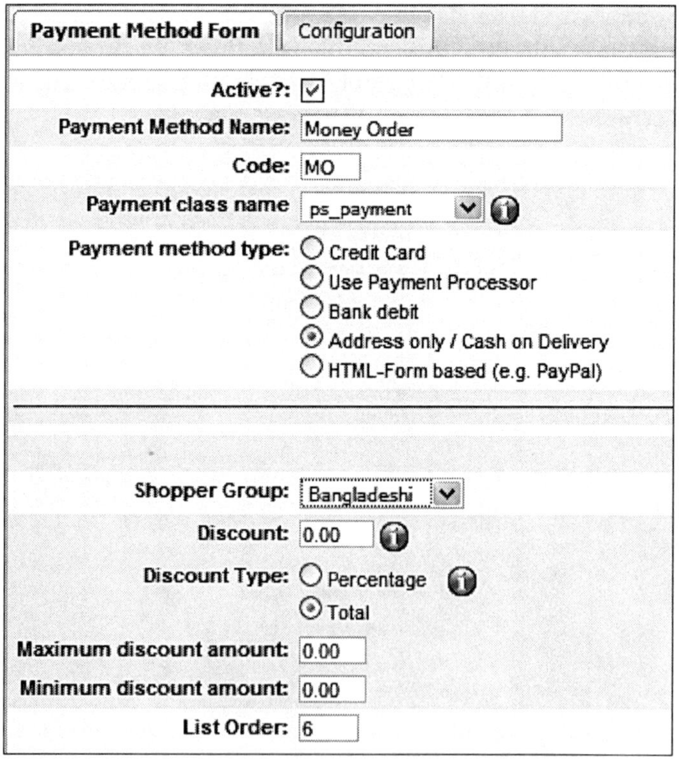

In the **Payment Method Form** tab, we need to define the payment method. The following information must be provided in this form:

- **Active?**: Check this to make this payment method active.
- **Payment Method Name**: Type the name of the payment method. In this case, it is **Money Order**.
- **Code**: Specify a code for the payment method. This will be short name, for Money Order, it will be **MO**.
- **Payment class name**: Select the payment class which will process the payment. The drop-down list will show a range of class names for the different payment processors. The Money Order payment method will not use a payment processor, as it is a manual process. There is a placeholder class named **ps_payment,** which has no business logic defined, and can be used for modules which do not need any processing. Therefore, select the **ps_payment** class in this field.
- **Payment Method Type**: Specify the payment method type you are using. There are five options:
    - **Credit Card**: Select this if you are manual processing the credit card using a terminal.
    - **Use Payment Processor**: Select this type if you are using some external payment processor like Authorize.Net.
    - **Bank Debit**: Select this type if the payment method debits your bank account or needs information on a bank account.
    - **Address Only/Cash On Delivery**: Select this when no processing is done by the module. Manual payment processes should use this type. As Money Orders will need no processing by the module, select this for the **Money Order** payment method.
    - **HTML-form based (e.g. PayPal)**: Select this if the customers are redirected to another web site to provide payment information through a form, for example, in PayPal. Usually, you need to provide some code in the **Configuration** tab's **Payment Extra Info** field to auto-fill the form with customer data retrieved from the VirtueMart database.

- **Shopper Group**: Select a shopper group which can use this payment method. This is a way of limiting use of a payment method to a particular group. For example, we may want only customers living in Bangladesh to be able to use the **Money Order** payment method. In that case, we first have to create a shopper group, **Bangladeshi,** and include all customers from Bangladesh to this shopper group. We then select the **Bangladeshi** group in this field.
- **Discount**: Type the discount amount for this payment method. You may provide a discount to promote your preferred payment method. On the other hand, you may charge a fee for an inconvenient payment method. A fee can be specified as negative. For example, 3.0 will be considered a discount, where customers will be benefitted, but -3.0 will be considered a fee, where customers have to pay extra for using this payment method.
- **Discount Type**: Discounts may be an absolute amount or a percentage. For example, if you specify 4.0 in the **Discount** field and select the **Total** in this field, then whatever the total order amount is, the discount will only be $4.0. However, if you select the **Percentage** in this field, the discount will be 4 percent of the total order amount.
- **Maximum discount amount**: Specify the maximum discount amount for this payment method. This is useful when you have selected **Percentage** in the **Discount Type** field.
- **Minimum discount amount**: Specify the minimum discount amount for this payment method. This is useful for a **Percentage** discount type.
- **List Order**: Specify a value for what order this payment method will be listed in checkout page's payment options. A lower value will place the module in a higher position.

If you want to show some extra text to the customers about this payment method, then type that in the **Payment Extra Info** in the **Configuration** tab. For example, with a **Money Order** payment method you may type, "The order will only be confirmed on receiving the Money Order. Please mention the order ID on your Money Order for faster processing."

When all of the above information is provided, click on the **Save** icon in the toolbar to create the **Money Order** payment method. Once saved, you can see the **Money Order** payment method listed in the **Payment Method List** screen.

Adding tax rates

Store-wide configurations for taxes are defined from **Admin | Configuration | Global**. In the **Tax Configuration** section, we have noticed that we can set how taxes will be applied based on store address, shipping address, or in EU mode. Configuration details for this were discussed earlier in this chapter. However, we have not yet seen how to add tax rates.

Before applying taxes to any product, we need to define the tax rates. We can see the available tax rates from **Tax | List Tax Rates**. This will show the **Tax Rate List** screen:

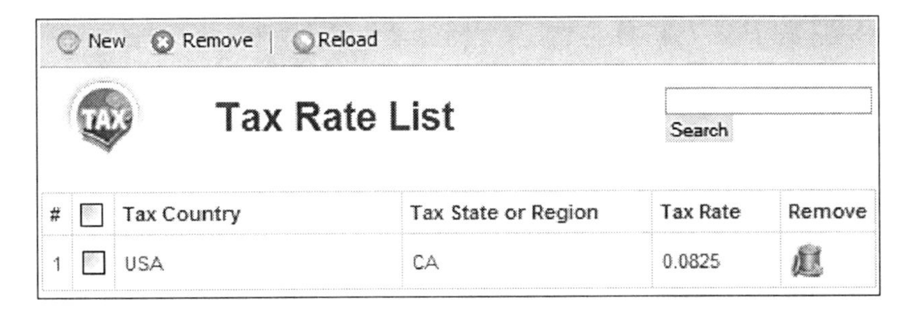

As a sample, there is one tax rate for USA, CA defined. For a real online shop, we need to define our own tax rates. We can define a tax rate by selecting **Tax | Add Tax Rate**, or by clicking on the **New** icon in the toolbar in the **Tax Rate List** screen. In both cases, we will get the **Add Tax Information** screen:

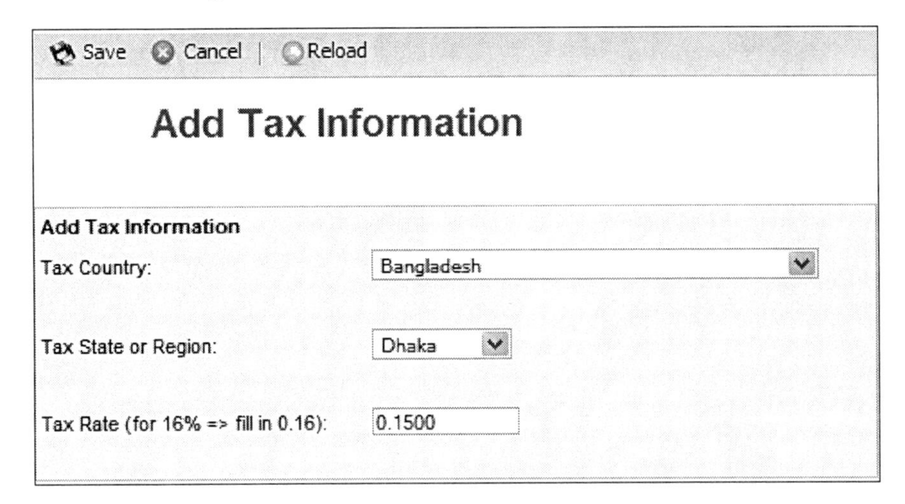

In the **Add tax Information** screen, first select the country for which you want to create the tax rate. The **Tax Country** field has a drop-down list containing all the countries defined in VirtueMart. Once a country is selected, states or region defined for that country will be available in the **Tax State or Region** drop-down list. Select a state or region from this list, if you want to define the rate for a state or region. Otherwise, select none in the **Tax State or Region** list to define the tax rate for an entire country. In the **Tax Rate** field, specify the rate in a decimal format. For example, if the tax rate is 15 percent, type 0.15 in the **Tax Rate** field.

Once all of this information is provided, click on the **Save** icon to save the tax rates. Using the same process, create as many rates as you need.

Remember that creating tax rates will not automatically apply these rates to products. We need to assign the tax rates to every product when we are adding the product. We will know more about this in the next chapter.

Summary

In this chapter, we discussed the configuration options for a VirtueMart store. First, we saw how to update the store information and configure store-wide options. We then moved to adding countries and currencies. As shipping and payment processing are two major concerns for an online shop, we examined available options for these. We also saw how to enable and configure shipping modules, and create shipping rates for standard shipping modules. Then we also saw how to enable and configure default payment methods. We have also created a new payment method for our store. Finally, we saw how to add tax rates for the store.

Based on the knowledge gained in this chapter, we will now proceed to managing a VirtueMart store in the next chapter.

4

Managing product catalog

In the previous chapter, we saw how to configure the VirtueMart store. Once the configurations are set, our next step is to build our product catalog for the store and manage that catalog. In the catalog management functions, there are several tasks including managing manufacturers, vendors, products, product attributes, product types, and bulk import and export of products. In this chapter, we are going to learn about the details of building a product catalog and managing the catalog for a VirtueMart store. On completion of this chapter, you will be able to:

- Manage manufacturers and vendors
- Manage the product categories and products
- Create and use product attributes
- Create and use product types

We are going to add and edit a lot of information for manufacturers, vendors, product categories, and products. Actually, in this chapter, our VirtueMart shop will really take shape with products we want to sell.

Importing and exporting products in bulk helps to build the catalog quickly. However, use of this feature requires some advanced knowledge on managing VirtueMart. Therefore, we will discuss the bulk import/export of products in Chapter 9, *Extending VirtueMart Functionalities*.

Catalogue management

The product catalog for an online shop comprises of the products we sell in the shop. Whatever products we want to sell should be added to this product catalog first. Once products are added to the catalog, customers can browse the products and decide to buy whatever they need. Therefore, managing the catalog is one of the primary tasks of the shop owner.

Products that we add to the catalog need to be organized to help customers easily find the right products. In VirtueMart, customers can sort the products by product categories and manufacturers. Therefore, before adding products to the catalog, we will look into managing manufacturers and product categories.

Managing manufacturers

In VirtueMart, whenever we add a product to the catalog, we also need to assign a manufacturer for that product. In reality, every product has a manufacturer, and for better management of the shop, we should be able to find products by their manufacturer. Therefore, first step will be to identify the manufacturers and enter their information in VirtueMart store. We can also categorize the manufactures as publishers, software developers, and so on.

Adding a manufacturer category

There is a default manufacturer category for use in VirtueMart. We can use that default category for creating a manufacturer. However, when we are selling large number of products from a large number of manufacturers, classifying them into categories will be convenient for managing the manufacturers.

For adding a manufacturer, in the VirtueMart administration panel, click on **Manufacturer | Add Manufacturer Category**. This shows **Manufacturer Category Form**:

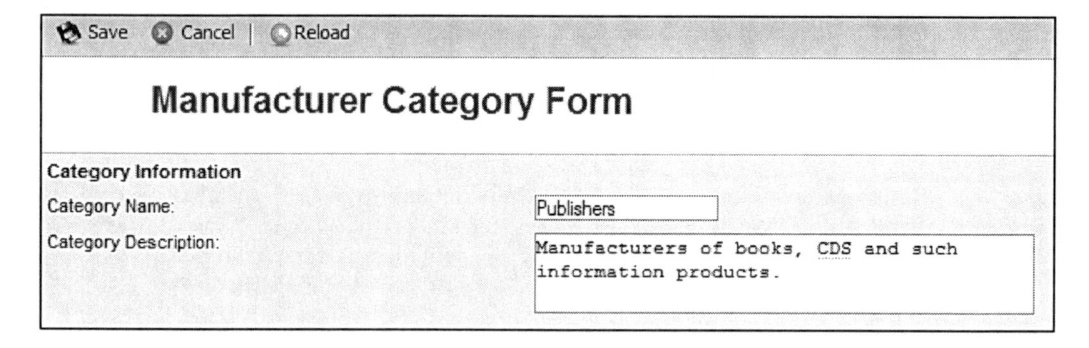

In the **Manufacturer Category Form**, provide information for the **Category Name** and the **Category Description** fields. Once these are provided, click the **Save** icon in the toolbar to save the manufacturer category. In the same process, you can add as many categories as you want.

Adding a manufacturer

For adding a manufacturer, in the VirtueMart administration panel, select **Manufacturer | Add Manufacturer**. This shows **Add Information** screen:

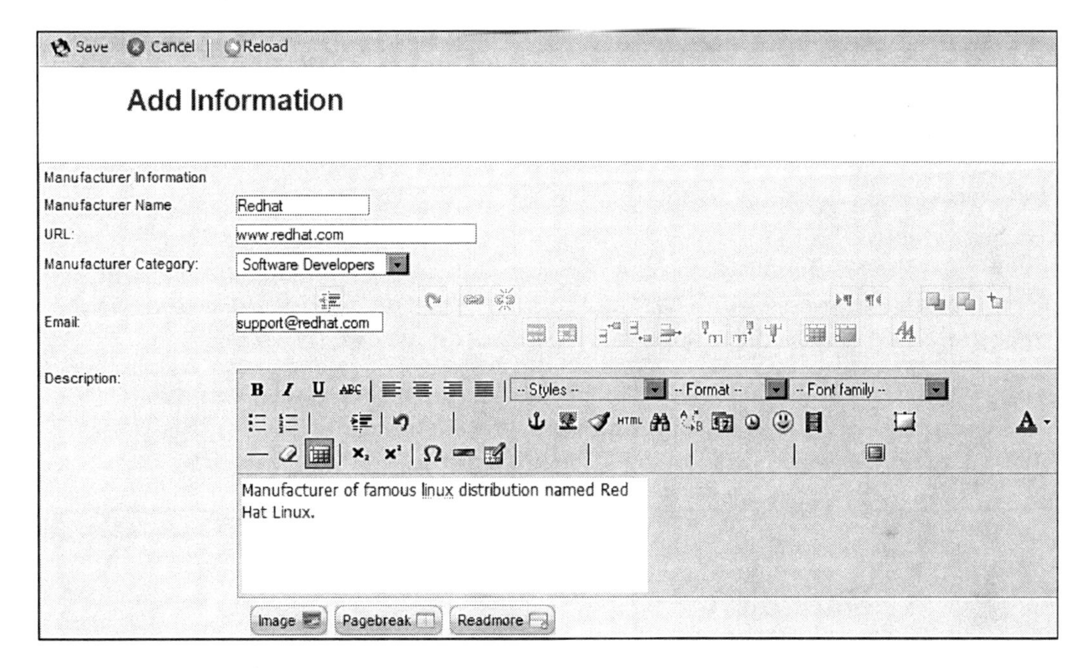

In the **Add Information** screen, type the manufacturer's name, their URL, email address, and a brief description. In the **Manufacturer Category** field, select the category. The drop-down list will show the manufacturer categories you created earlier. Once all the information is provided in this screen, click the **Save** icon in the toolbar to save the manufacturer information.

Listing the manufacturer categories

Once you have added the manufacturer categories, you can view the list of manufacturer categories by selecting **Manufacturer | List Manufacturer Categories**. This shows **Manufacturer Category List** screen:

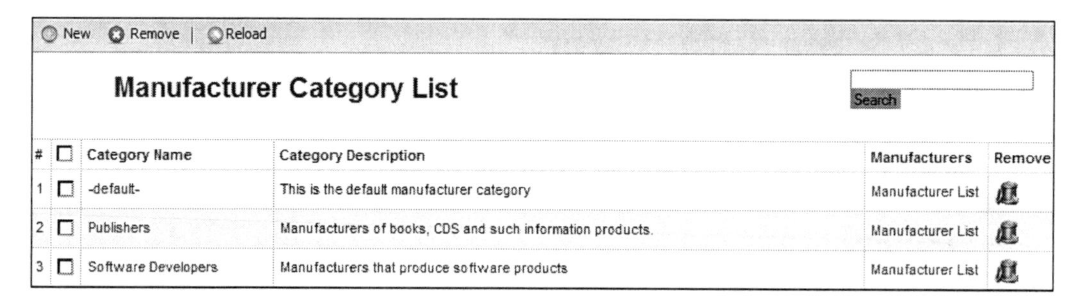

#	☐	Category Name	Category Description	Manufacturers	Remove
1	☐	-default-	This is the default manufacturer category	Manufacturer List	
2	☐	Publishers	Manufacturers of books, CDS and such information products.	Manufacturer List	
3	☐	Software Developers	Manufacturers that produce software products	Manufacturer List	

In the **Manufacturer Category List** screen, you will see all manufacturer categories you have created. From this screen, you can add a new category by clicking the **New** icon in the toolbar. Similarly, you can remove a category by clicking on the trash icon () in **Remove** column, or by selecting the categories and clicking the **Remove** icon in the toolbar. You can edit a category by clicking on the category name.

To view the list of manufacturers, click on the **Manufacturer List** link in the **Manufacturers** column, or select **Manufacturer | List Manufacturers**. This shows **Manufacturer List** screen displaying all manufacturers you have added:

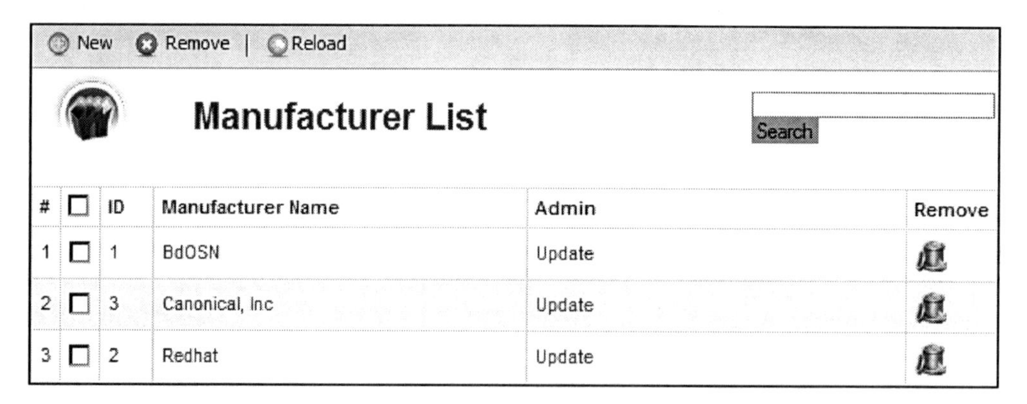

#	☐	ID	Manufacturer Name	Admin	Remove
1	☐	1	BdOSN	Update	
2	☐	3	Canonical, Inc	Update	
3	☐	2	Redhat	Update	

From the **Manufacturer List** screen, you can create a new manufacturer, remove one or more manufacturers, and edit any manufacturer. For editing a manufacturer, click on the manufacturer's name or the **Update** link in **Admin** column. This will bring up the **Add Information** screen again. You can also create a new manufacturer by clicking the **New** icon in the toolbar.

From the **Manufacturer Category List** screen, you may think that clicking on the **Manufacturer List** link against each category will display the manufacturers added to that category only. Ideally, this should be the case. However, until VirtueMart 1.1.2, it shows the list of manufacturers from all the categories. We hope this will be fixed in the upcoming releases of VirtueMart.

Managing vendors

The idea of multiple vendors is something what you can see on `Amazon.com`. Different vendors add their products to sell, when the order is placed, the store notifies the vendor to fulfill the order. The main store usually gets a commission from the vendor for each sell made through the store. However, VirtueMart's vendors feature is still in its infancy and does not yet function properly. You can add multiple vendors in VirtueMart, and assign products to the vendors. However, adding vendors has no effect on selling any product on the VirtueMart store, except when applying different vendor-specific tax rates and shopper groups. At the moment, it also helps to identify products from different vendors. In the following sections, you will see how to add and manage vendors.

Vendor category

Like manufacturers, you can also create vendor categories. For creating vendor categories, go to **Vendor | Add Vendor Category**. This displays **Vendor Category Form**:

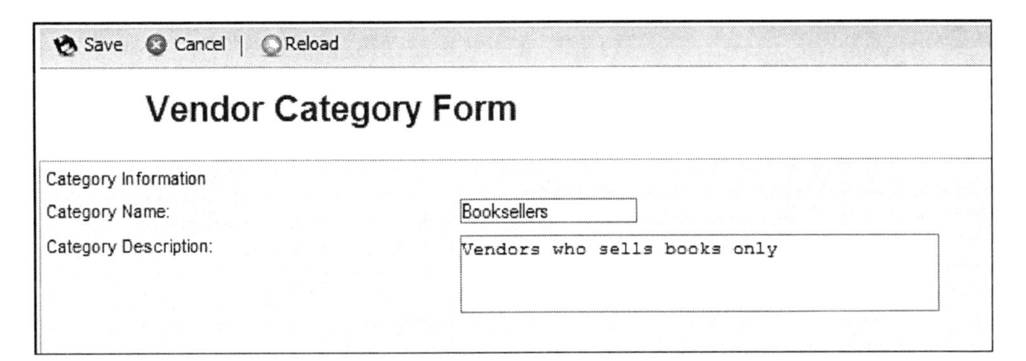

In the **Vendor Category Form**, type the name of the category and its description. Then click the **Save** icon in the toolbar. You can add as many categories as you want.

Before trying to add vendor categories, first plan how you are going to categorize your vendors (for example, based on the product they sell or their location). Have a full category tree on hand and then start creating categories.

Adding vendor

Once you have created the necessary vendor categories, you can proceed to adding vendors. For adding vendors, click on **Vendor | Add Vendor**. This displays the **Add Information** screen:

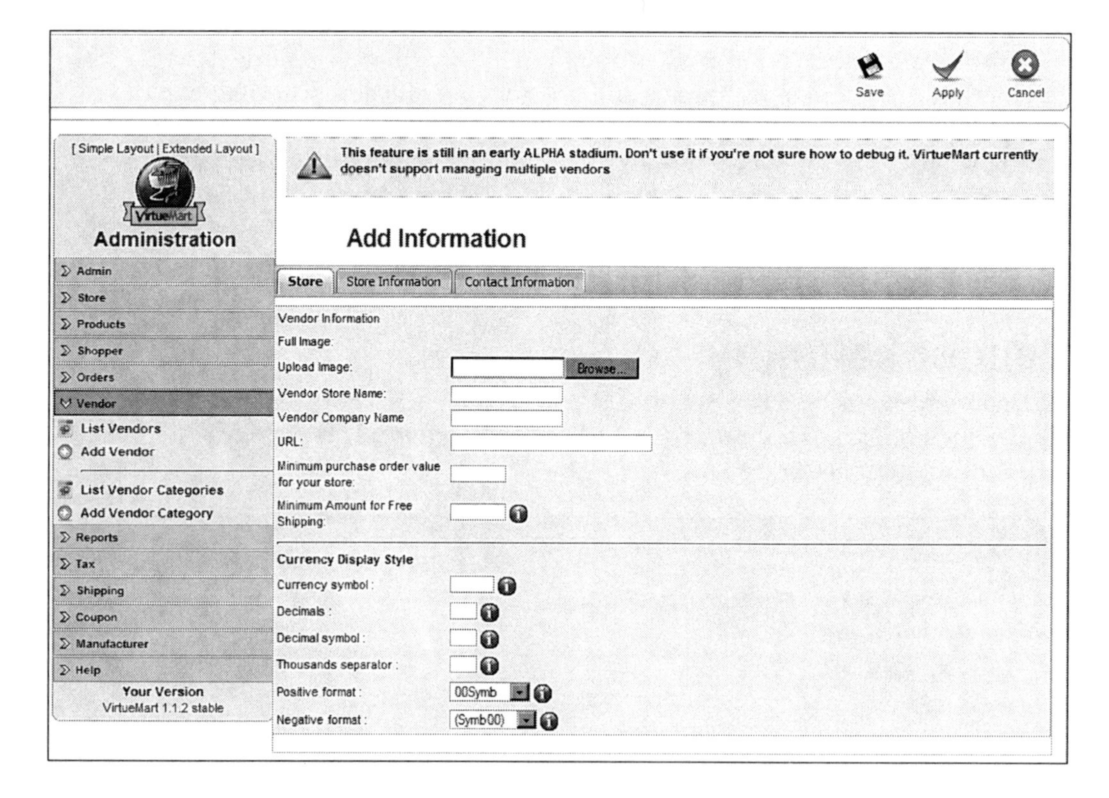

Caution

Note that there is a warning sign at the top of **Add Information** screen. It warns you about using the vendor feature as it is in the 'Alpha' or pre-mature stage. Also note that we have used **Simple Layout** for displaying it. If you try adding a vendor from **Extended Layout**, you will open up an edit screen for existing vendor information, which you already added during the initial configuration of the shop. Up until VirtueMart 1.1.2, a bug has been encountered and which will hopefully be fixed in future releases when it crosses 'Alpha' stage.

The **Add Information** screen shows three tabs: **Store**, **Store Information**, and **Contact Information**.

From the **Store** tab, add the vendor's store name, company name, logo, web site URL, minimum purchase order value, and minimum amount for free shipping. You can also configure the currency symbol, decimal points, decimal symbol, thousand separator, positive format, and negative format.

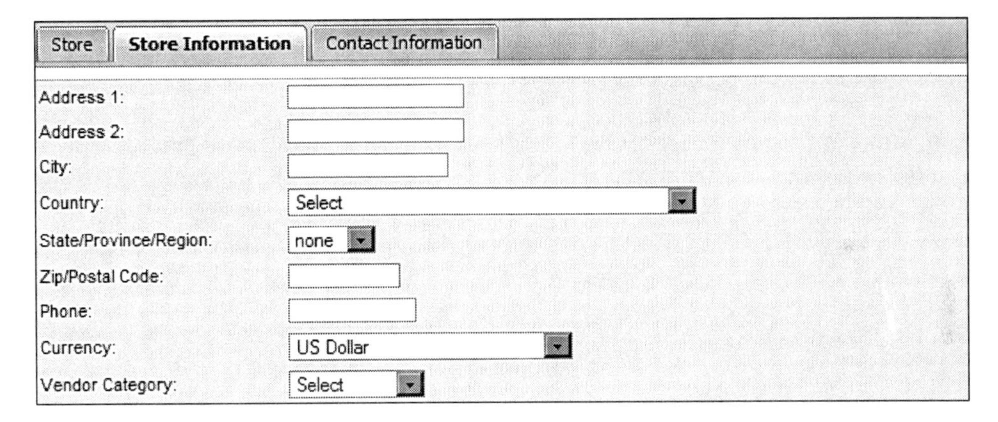

In the **Store Information** tab (seen in the previous screenshot), you can add the address of the store, city, state/province/region, zip/postal code, phone, currency and vendor category. The vendor categories you have created earlier will be available in **Vendor Category** drop-down list.

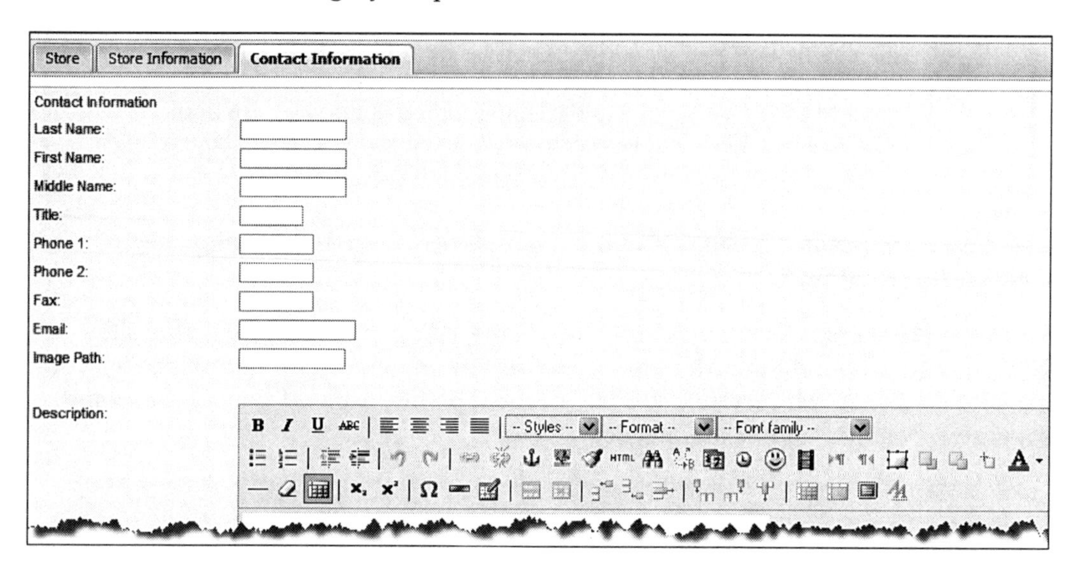

In the **Contact Information** tab (seen in the previous screenshot), you can set the contact details of the vendor, such as name, title, phone, fax, email. You can also add a brief description of the vendor which will be displayed in the vendor details page in the store. Type a brief description in the **Description** rich-text editing box. In the **Terms of Service** rich-text editing box, provide terms of service applicable for that vendor.

Once information in all the three tabs are provided, click the **Save** icon in the toolbar to add the vendor.

Managing vendors and categories

Managing vendor categories is easy. You can manage the vendor categories from **Vendor | List Vendor Categories**. This shows **Vendor Category List** screen:

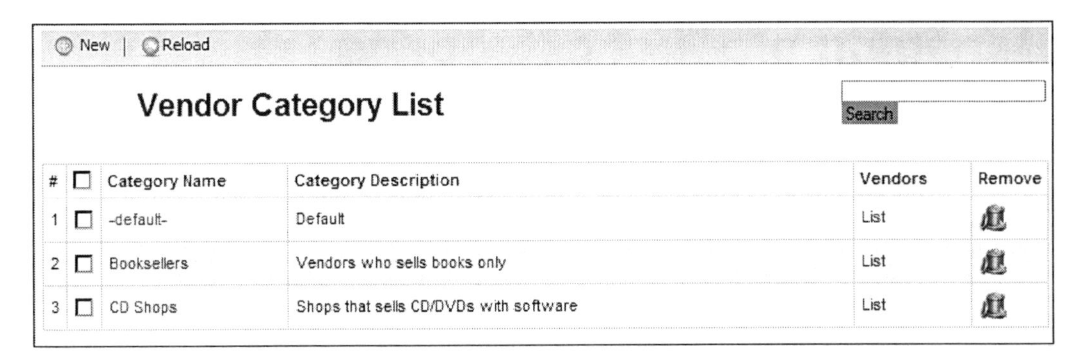

In the **Vendor Category List** screen, you can see all available categories. You can add a new category by clicking on the **New** icon in the toolbar. Similarly, you can delete any category by clicking the trash icon in the **Remove** column. For editing a category, click on the name of the category in the **Category Name** column. Clicking on the **List** link will show the vendors in that category.

You can view the list of vendors from the **Vendor | List Vendors**. This shows the **Vendor List** screen (seen below). Like the **Vendor Category List** screen, you can create a new vendor by clicking on the **New** icon in the toolbar. You can also delete a vendor by clicking on the trash icon in the **Remove** column. For editing a vendor, click on the vendor name link in the **Vendor Name** column.

As the vendor feature is still in a pre-mature stage, some of the links don't behave as intended. For example, clicking the **List** link doesn't show the list of vendors in that category. Instead, it shows all of the vendors. These could be fixed through editing some of the `.php` files specific to this functionality.

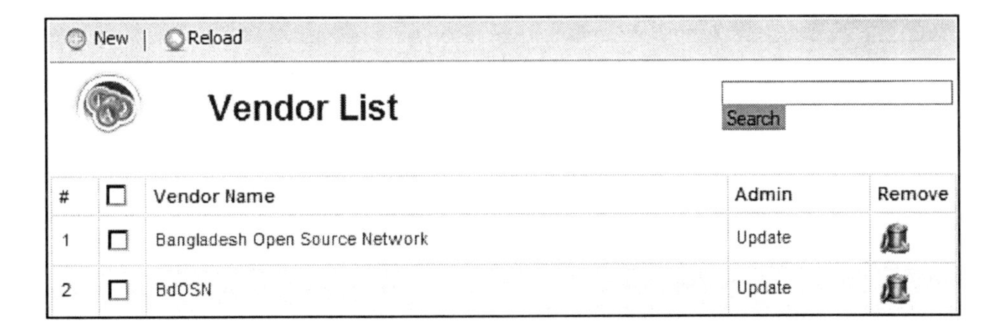

Managing product categories

Products in a shop are categorized for easy searching and for the convenience of the customers. Therefore, when you are planning your shop, also plan how you are going to categorize the products you sell. For our store example, we will divide the products into the following categories: Books, CDs, DVDs, Accessories, Souvenir, and Coupons. Additional sub-categories will be under these categories.

Building a well planned category tree, and adding products to the appropriate categories, is one of the best practices for catalog management. In VirtueMart, you can use multiple product categories which can be nested. Before trying to add product categories, you should also prepare the images to be used for each category.

Adding product categories

You can add product categories from **Products | Add Category**. This shows **Category Information** screen:

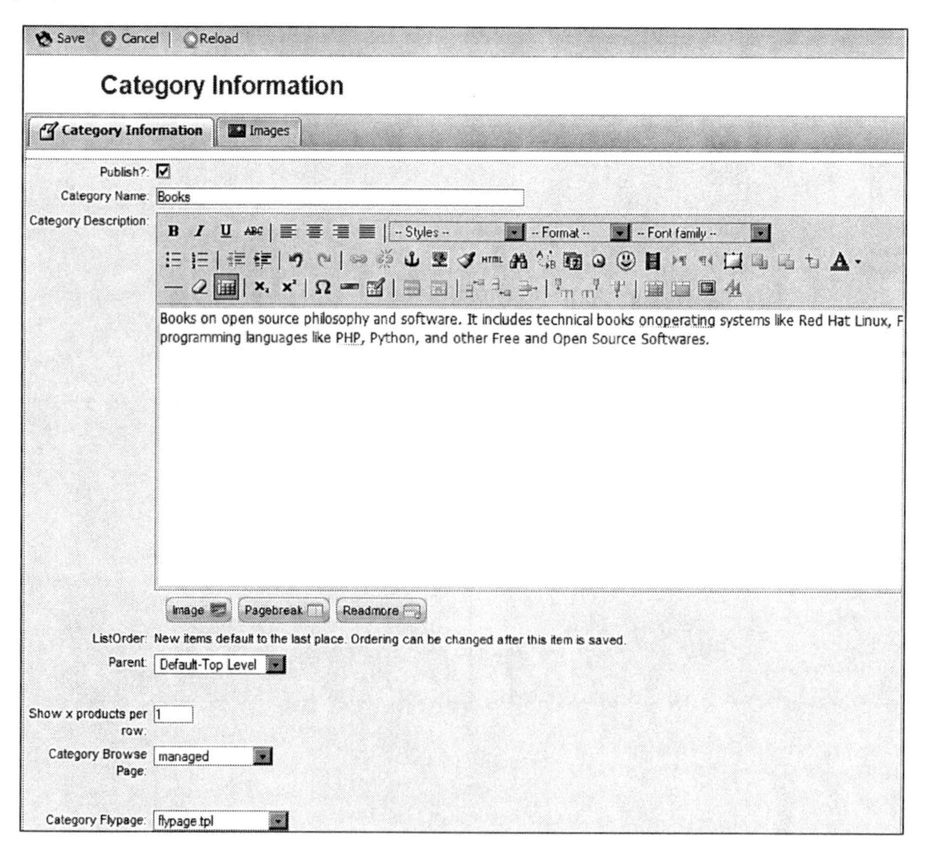

The **Category Information** screen has two tabs: **Category Information** and **Images**. In the **Category Information** tab, configure the following options:

- **Publish**: Check this box if you want to publish the category you are creating. By default, this is checked. Uncheck it if you don't want to instantly publish it.
- **Category Name**: Provide a brief name for your product category in this field. You must type a name for the category.
- **Category Description**: Type a brief description for the category in this rich-text editing field. You can use rich HTML formatting here. The category description should be something that helps customers to understand what's in that category.
- **ListOrder**: You will find this field disabled while creating a new category. When you create a new category, it will be listed at the end. However, when editing the category, you can change the order in which the categories will be listed. A lower number in this field will place that category in upper position.
- **Parent**: This field allows categories to be nested. If you want to make the new category a sub-category of an existing category, select that existing category from this drop-down list.
- **Show x products per row**: Specify, for this category, how many products will be displayed in a row.
- **Category Browse Page**: For each category, you can specify a browse page for showing particular information about the products in that category. You will learn more about a browse page and how to design it in Chapter 6 *Customizing Look and Feel*. For time being, accept the default setting for this field.
- **Category Flypage**: For each category, you can specify a different flypage, which displays product details. For example, for the **Books** category, you may want to show the product details differently. Therefore, you design a flypage for that category and assign that to the **Books** category. You will know more about the design and use of flypages in Chapter 6, *Customizing the Look and Feel*. Until then, accept the default setting for this field.

In the **Images** tab (seen below), you can assign an image for the product category you are creating. You can upload a full image and select the **Auto Create Thumbnail** option to create the thumbnail from the larger image. Otherwise you can upload a thumbnail image separately. You can also specify the URL of the image in **URL** field.

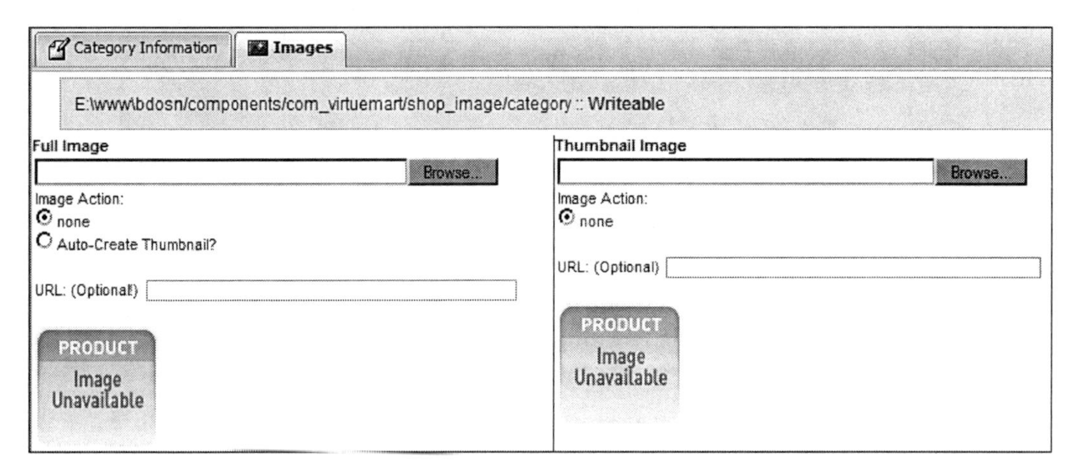

When all of the information is provided in both of the tabs, click the **Save** icon in the toolbar to create the product category. Add as many product categories as you want.

As you remember, we have installed the sample data for VirtueMart which inserted sample product categories and products. As we are now building our own store and do not need those sample products, we can delete those and create our categories and products. Before adding new categories and products, delete all the product categories and products.

Modifying product categories

You can manage product categories from **Products | List Categories**. This shows **Category Tree** screen:

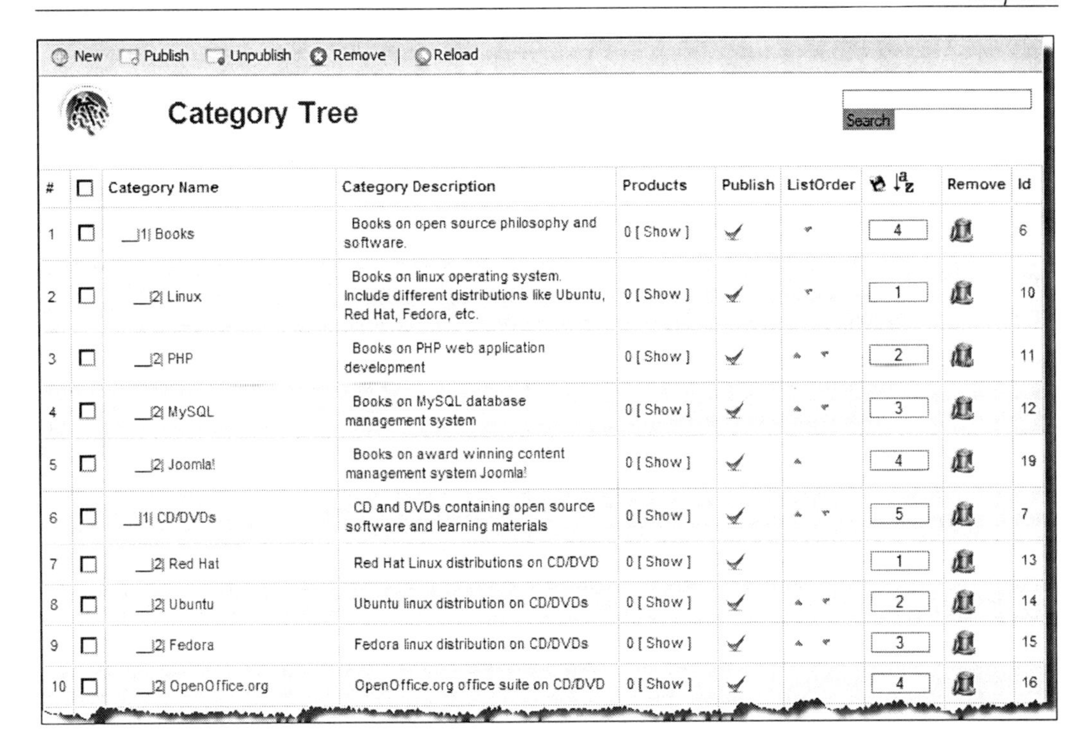

#		Category Name	Category Description	Products	Publish	ListOrder		Remove	Id
1		__|1| Books	Books on open source philosophy and software.	0 [Show]			4		6
2		__|2| Linux	Books on linux operating system. Include different distributions like Ubuntu, Red Hat, Fedora, etc.	0 [Show]			1		10
3		__|2| PHP	Books on PHP web application development	0 [Show]			2		11
4		__|2| MySQL	Books on MySQL database management system	0 [Show]			3		12
5		__|2| Joomla!	Books on award winning content management system Joomla!	0 [Show]			4		19
6		__|1| CD/DVDs	CD and DVDs containing open source software and learning materials	0 [Show]			5		7
7		__|2| Red Hat	Red Hat Linux distributions on CD/DVD	0 [Show]			1		13
8		__|2| Ubuntu	Ubuntu linux distribution on CD/DVDs	0 [Show]			2		14
9		__|2| Fedora	Fedora linux distribution on CD/DVDs	0 [Show]			3		15
10		__|2| OpenOffice.org	OpenOffice.org office suite on CD/DVD	0 [Show]			4		16

In the **Category Tree** screen, you see the list of all product categories you have created. This list also shows category nesting, its description, number of products in each category, whether the category is published or not, and their list order. You can also create a new category from this screen by clicking on the **New** icon in the toolbar. For removing multiple categories, select the categories by checking the checkbox left to the category name and then click on the **Remove** icon in the toolbar. For removing a single category, click on the **trash** icon in the **Remove** column.

Warning:

When you remove a product category, all products under that category will also be deleted from your store. Therefore, be careful about deleting any category. If you really need to delete any category, first move the products in that category to another category. Otherwise, you will lose all the products in that category. In fact, you don't need to delete any category. If you don't want to show any category in the store, you can simply unpublish it.

You can also publish or unpublish any category. For publishing or unpublishing multiple categories, select those categories by checking the checkbox left to the category name, and then click the **Publish** or **Unpublish** icon in the toolbar. For a single category, you can click on the icon in the **Publish** column to publish or unpublish that category. A green tick icon in the **Publish** column means the item is published. A red circle with a white cross inside means the category in unpublished.

> When a category is unpublished (including its sub-categories), the products under the category are also not visible in the store frontend. However, some modules, such as Featured Products, Random Product, and Top Ten Products, may display the products under those unpublished categories.

You can assign the list order for categories by clicking the up or down arrow in the **List Order** column. There is also another way to do this. In the column next to the **ListOrder**, you can assign the order and click on the **Save** icon ( ). Clicking the alphabetically sort icon ( ) will arrange the categories to display in alphabetical order, as shown in the following screenshot:

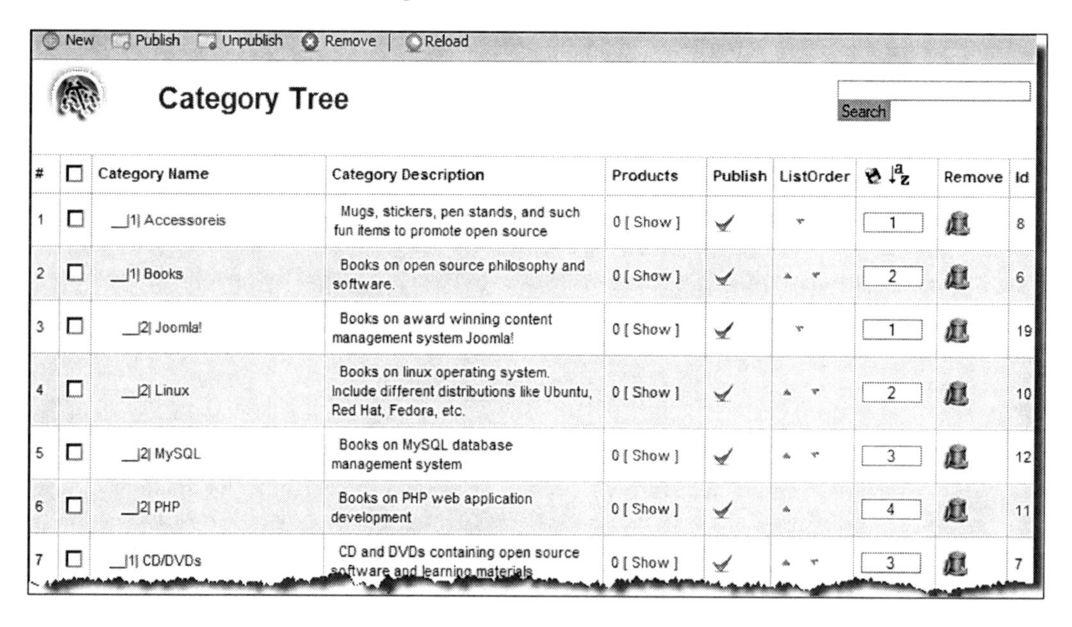

#		Category Name	Category Description	Products	Publish	ListOrder		Remove	Id
1		_|1| Accessoreis	Mugs, stickers, pen stands, and such fun items to promote open source	0 [Show]			1		8
2		_|1| Books	Books on open source philosophy and software.	0 [Show]			2		6
3		_|2| Joomla!	Books on award winning content management system Joomla!	0 [Show]			1		19
4		_|2| Linux	Books on linux operating system. Include different distributions like Ubuntu, Red Hat, Fedora, etc.	0 [Show]			2		10
5		_|2| MySQL	Books on MySQL database management system	0 [Show]			3		12
6		_|2| PHP	Books on PHP web application development	0 [Show]			4		11
7		_|1| CD/DVDs	CD and DVDs containing open source software and learning materials	0 [Show]			3		7

For editing any category, click on the category name. That will open up the same **Category Information** screen, which you have used for adding a category.

We have added several categories with category images. Let us see how it looks in the frontend. Let's browse to `http://localhost/bdson/` (or any other URL where you have installed the VirtueMart shop) and click on **Shop** from main menu. This shows the categories as shown in the screenshot below:

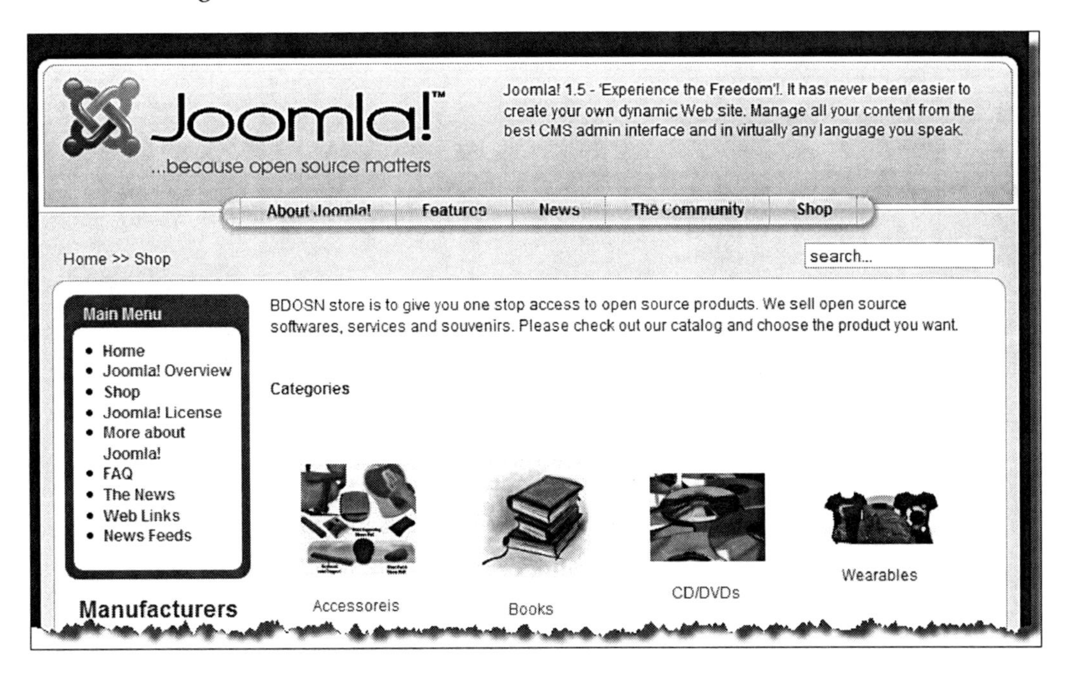

Let us explore more. Click on the **Books** category link and we see the sub-categories as the following screenshot:

Adding a product

After creating the necessary product categories, you can proceed to adding products to your store. You can add products from the **Products | Add Product**. This shows the **New Product** screen:

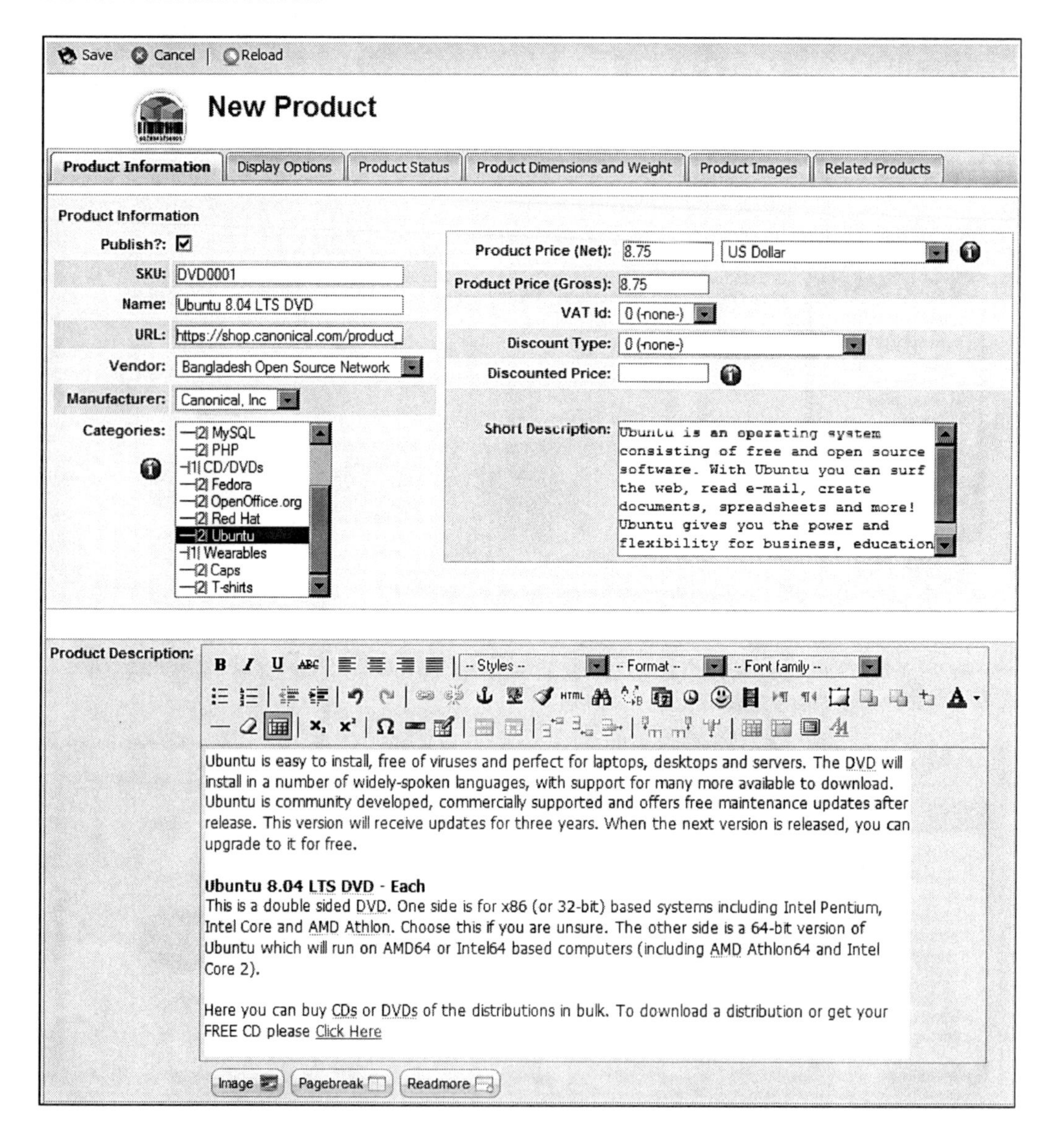

The **New Product** screen has six tabs: **Product Information**, **Display Options**, **Product Status**, **Product Dimensions and Weight**, **Product Images**, and **Related Products**.

In the **Product Information** tab, configure the following options:

- **Publish**: By default, this checkbox is checked. If you don't want to publish the product, uncheck this checkbox. Later, you can publish the product.
- **SKU**: The SKU (Stock Keeping Unit) is a unique number used to keep track of inventory. Usually, for large shops, barcodes are used as SKU. For our VirtueMart shop, we will assign SKU manually. For example, it may be BK0001 for a book, it may be CD0001 for a CD, and so on. However, we have to be careful that all SKUs are unique. Generally, SKUs are not displayed to customers, these are for our administrative purposes.
- **Name**: Type the product's name in this field. The product name should be brief but comprehensive.
- **URL**: If the product has some main page which describes the product in details, you may add that URL in this field.
- **Vendor**: You can select a vendor for this product from this drop-down list. The drop-down list will show the vendors which were added earlier. If you don't see an appropriate vendor, it should be added first in the vendors section using the method described earlier.
- **Manufacturer**: You can select a manufacturer of the product from this drop-down list. The list will show the manufacturers that were added earlier. If you don't see that product's manufacturer in the list, create the manufacturer first using the methods described earlier.
- **Categories**: From the list of product categories, you need to select the appropriate categories for the product. You can select multiple categories by press the *Ctrl* key and clicking on the categories in the list.
- **Product Price (Net)**: Type the net price of the product (price without any tax or discount) and select the appropriate currency from the drop-down list to the right of this field.
- **Product Price (Gross)**: This is the price after adding taxes. However, you do not need to type anything here. The value of this field will be calculated based on your selection in the next field, **VAT Id**.
- **VAT Id**: Select the tax rate applicable for this product. As you remember, we saw, how to create tax rates in Chapter 3, *Configuring the VirtueMart Store*. Tax rates created earlier will be available in this drop-down list.

- **Discount Type**: Select a discount type from this drop-down list. The discount types that were defined earlier will be available in this drop-down list. We will discuss discounts and other promotional tools in detail in Chapter 7, *Promotions and Public Relations*.
- **Discounted Price**: When you select a discount type in the **Discount Type** box just before this field, the discounted price of the product is automatically displayed in this field. However, you can type the discounted price in this field directly. This will override any discount type set earlier and set **Override** in **Discount Type** field.
- **Short Description**: Type a brief description of the product which will be displayed in the product listing page in a category. The short description should be in plain text. HTML cannot be used in this field.
- **Product Description**: Type the full description of the product in this rich-text editing box. The product description should cover all information about a product which customers want to know before buying the product.

Note that this description is shown in product details page. Do not think that the **Short Description** will be shown together with the **Product Description** in the product details page. It shows only product description, not the short description.

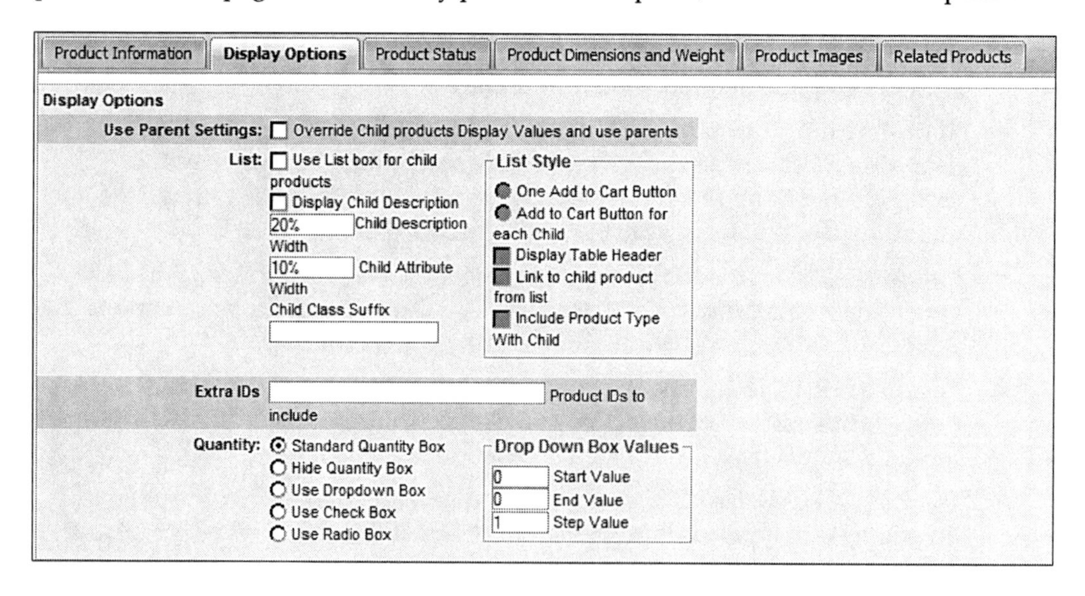

In the **Display Options** tab (seen above), you can configure how the products will be displayed in the shop's frontend. We will discuss these in more detail in Chapter 6, *Customizing the Look and Feel*. For the time being, accept the default settings in this tab.

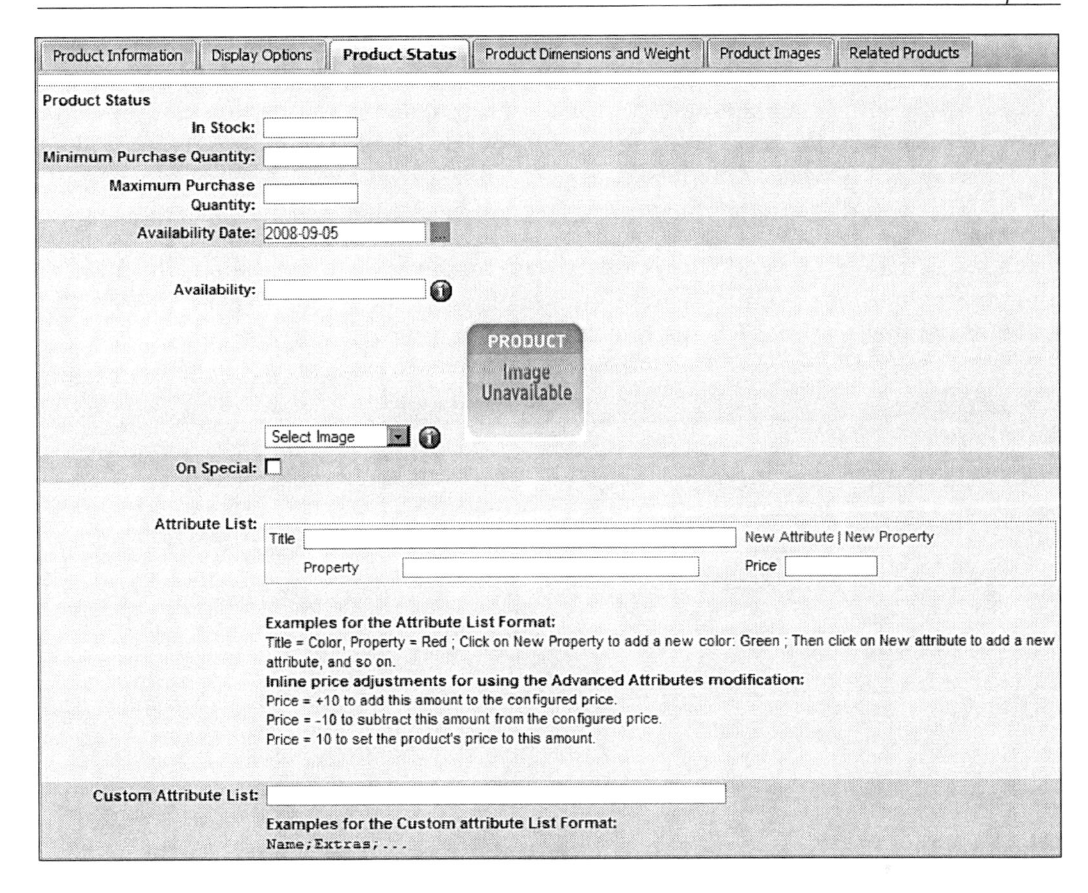

In **Product Status** tab (seen above), configure the following:

- **In Stock**: Type the number of products in stock (for example, 120).
- **Minimum Purchase Quantity**: Specify the minimum purchase quantity for this product in this field. For example, if you type 5 in this field, the customers must order at least five units of the product. It is usually set to 1.
- **Maximum Purchase Quantity**: Like the minimum quantity, specify the maximum number of a product that can be purchased at a time. For example, you may type 10 so that customers can only purchase 10 at a time. This is useful in some cases, especially when you suspect that someone will buy all of the products and try to monopolize.
- **Availability Date**: You can type a date in yyyy-mm-dd (for example, 2008-03-19) format when the product will be available. Alternatively, you can select a date by clicking on the '**...**' icon beside it.

- **Availability**: This field is used to specify the time the product may be delivered to the customers. Type 24h, 48 hours, 2-3 days, 3-5 days, on order, and so on. As an alternative, instead of typing these values, you can select an image from the drop-down list just below this field. Selecting **1-4w.gif** will display 1-4 weeks, **7d.gif** will display 7 days, and so on. This is a very good way to indicate when these products will be available to the customers.

From the **Attribute List** and **Custom Attribute List** fields, we can define attributes and their values for a product. Later in this chapter, we are going to learn how to add attributes to the products. For the time being, keep these fields as they are.

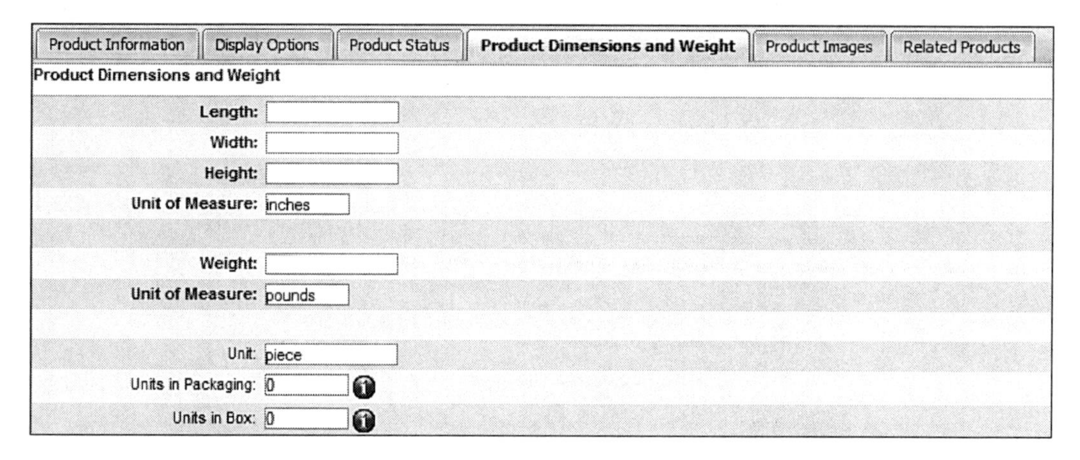

In the **Product Dimensions and Weight** tab (seen above), you can specify the dimensions (length, width, and height) of the product, unit of measurement (inches or millimeter), weight, and unit of measure for weight. For some products, you need to specify how many units of the product will fit in a package. First, specify the unit in the **Unit** field, then specify how many units in a package will fit in the **Units in Packaging** field. You can also specify how many units of the product will fit in the box. This information is essential for calculating packaging and shipping cost.

While product descriptions are important, it is more important to have at least one product image. In VirtueMart, you can add multiple product images. Product images can be added from **Product Images** tab of **New Product** screen:

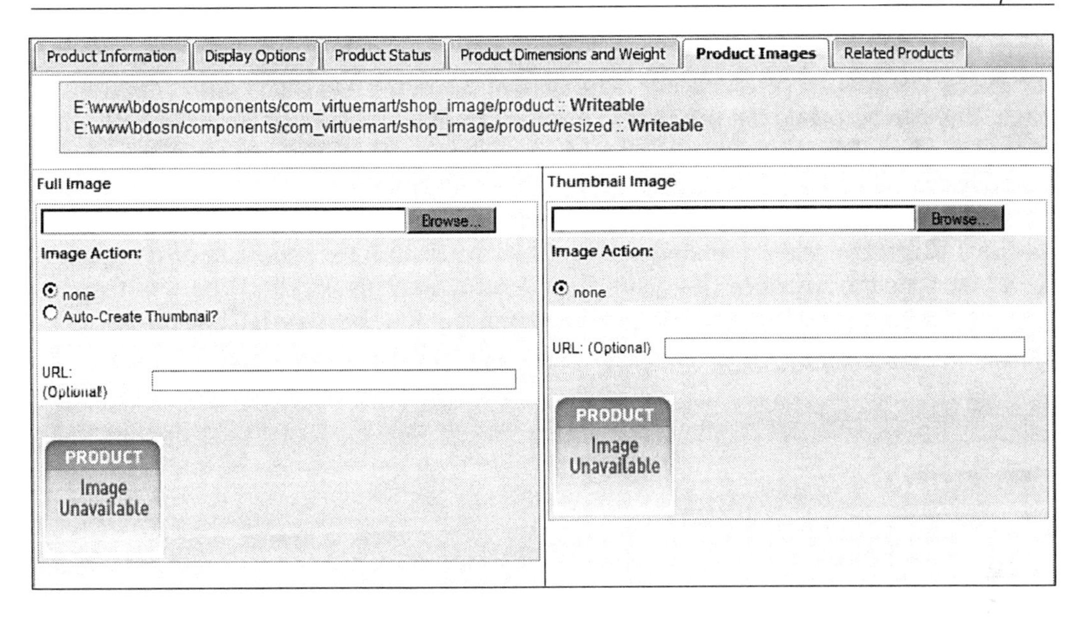

From the **Product Images** tab, you can upload both a full image and a thumbnail image. A thumbnail image is shown by default in the product listing and product detail page. When a special link below the product image is clicked, the full image of the product is shown. Usually, the thumbnail image is smaller in size than the full image. One good thing about VirtueMart cataloging is that it can automatically create thumbnail images from full images.

For adding the image of the product, in the **Full Image** section, click on the **Browse** button and locate the product image you want to add. Then select the **Auto-Create Thumbnail?** radio button to create the thumbnail image from this full image. We can also specify the URL of the image, if it is located on the web. In that case, the image will be loaded from that location.

If you have created thumbnail images separately, you can upload those from **Thumbnail Image** section by clicking the **Browse** button and selecting the thumbnail image from your hard disk. You can also specify the URL of a thumbnail image, if the thumbnail is on the web server.

Thumbnail images are generated using the ratio we mention in the **Admin | Configuration | Site** screen, under the **Layout** section. The default settings for the **Thumbnail Image Width** and the **Thumbnail Image Height** are **90 pixels**. You may adjust the height and width to fit your template.

From the **Related Products** tabs (seen below), you can establish a relationship among products. The related products are displayed at the bottom of the product details page. You can associate the product to another similar product, or an accessory of that product. For example, we are adding a Ubuntu 8.04 LTS Desktop CD. Considering its nature, we can relate these items to a Ubuntu 8.04 LTS Server CD, a Ubuntu 8.04 LTS Desktop DVD, and even with a Ubuntu Organic Circle of Friends Ladies T-Shirt. For adding related products, in the **Search for products or categories here** box, type the keyword (for example, Ubuntu), and press *Enter*. You will then you see the list of product and categories containing that keyword. Click on the products from the list, one by one, and those will be listed in the right side box.

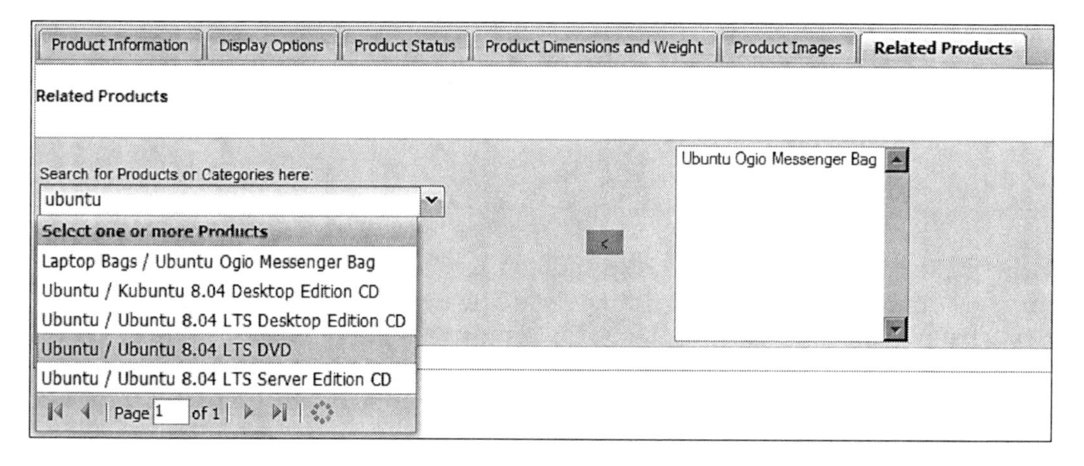

You can add as many products as we want to the **Related Products** box. However, at present, VirtueMart only shows four related products in the product details page. Products with a lower product id (added earlier) will be shown in the related products section, as shown in the below screenshot:

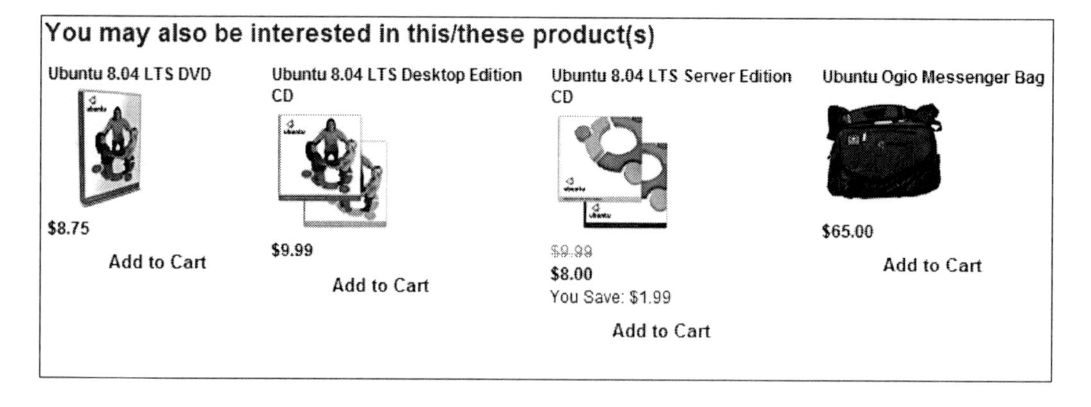

With the addition of related products, most of the required information for the product is complete. You can now save the product by clicking on the **Save** icon in the toolbar.

Using the same process, you can add as many products as you want. In fact, before going to next section, I am adding several products to the catalog. These new products will let us practice the upcoming tasks of managing products.

Managing products

Managing products includes viewing the lists, editing products, deleting products, and publish or unpublish the product if required. All of these can be done from **Products | List Products**. This shows the **Product List** screen:

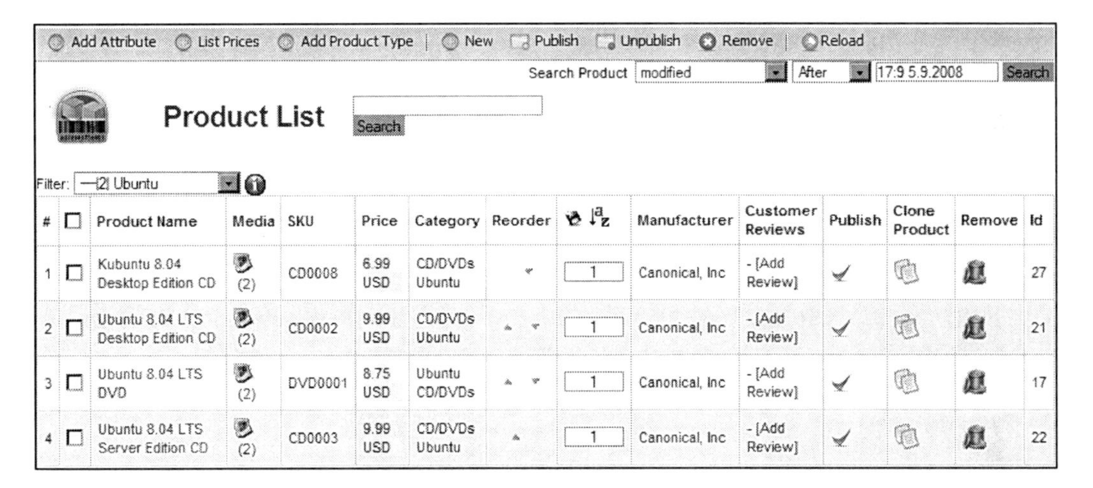

From the **Product List** screen, you can search for a specific product, or products modified or added before or after a certain date. You can also see the list filtered by category. For example, **--[2]Ubuntu** has been selected in the **Filter** drop-down list. This shows products in the **Ubuntu** sub-category.

You can edit any product by clicking on the product name link in the **Product Name** column. This shows a similar screen like the one we have used for adding the new product. In the **Media** column, you can see how many media files have been added to that product. Here, we see the value **2**, because the products use full image and thumbnail image. We can add more images to a product by clicking on the icon in this column. We will learn to do that soon in this chapter.

As you can see, the screen lists **SKU**, **Price**, and the categories the products are associated with. From the **Reorder** column, you can reorder the products by clicking the up or down arrow icon. Alternatively, you can reorder the products by typing the order and clicking on the save icon ( ). For sorting and reordering the products alphabetically, click on the a-z icon ( ).

You can publish or unpublish any product by clicking on the icon in the **Publish** column. You can also remove the product by clicking the trash icon in the **Remove** column. There is another great facility for catalog building, which you can use from this screen. You can create a new product by cloning one product shown in the list. For cloning a product, click on the icon in the **Clone Product**. This will open up the product editing screen. From this screen, you can change the product name, description, price, images and other information as required.

If you look at the toolbar, you will see some buttons for adding attributes, listing prices, and adding product type. We are going to learn about these later in this chapter.

Adding multiple product images

Sometimes, adding multiple product images may help the customers get a clearer idea about the product. For example, a T-shirt's front design and back design may be shown by using two images. You can upload multiple product images from the **FileManager** screen of a particular product. To get that screen, click on the media icon in the **Media** column in the **Product List** screen. This shows the **FileManager** screen listing the media files associated with that product.

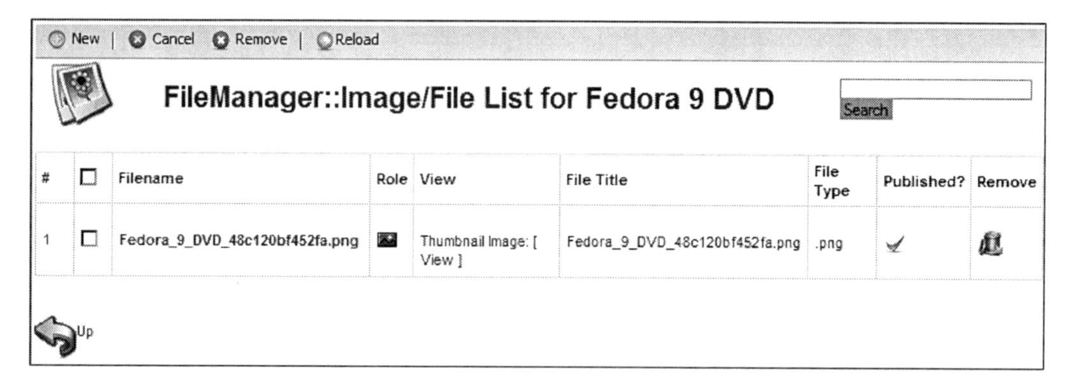

In the **FileManager** screen, you see the list of associated media files. For adding new image to this product, click on the **New** icon in the toolbar. This shows the **Upload a File for** screen. From this screen you can add additional images for the product. As we have selected Fedora 9 DVD as the product (seen in the screenshot above), we want to add a Fedora poster image with it so that customers can use that poster, and be inspired by it.

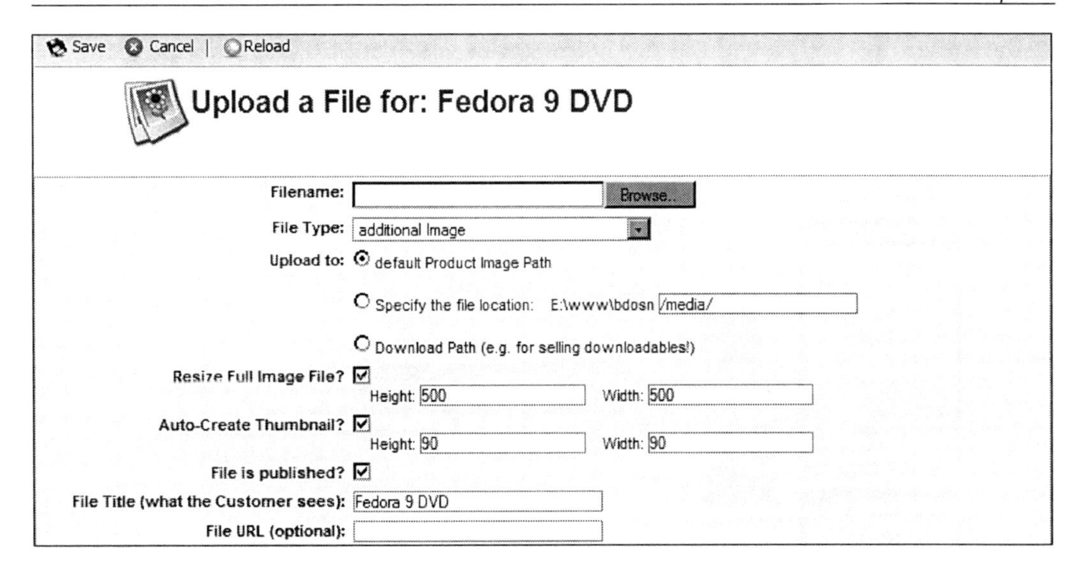

For adding additional images for the product, click on the **Browse** button in the **Filename** field (as seen above). Then, locate and select the file you want to add. In the **File Type** drop-down list, select **additional Image**. In the **Upload to** section, the **default Product Image Path** option is selected. Keep that unchanged. If you want to resize the image you are uploading, check the **Resize Full Image File?** checkbox. You can then specify a **Height** and **Width** to which the image will be resized. For creating a thumbnail automatically, check the **Auto-Create Thumbnail?** checkbox. Again, you can specify a **Height** and **Width** of the thumbnail image. For displaying the file on the product details page, keep the **File is published?** checkbox checked. Click on the **Save** icon in the toolbar to save the file. This will take you back to the **FileManager** screen, where you see another item in the **FileManager** screen:

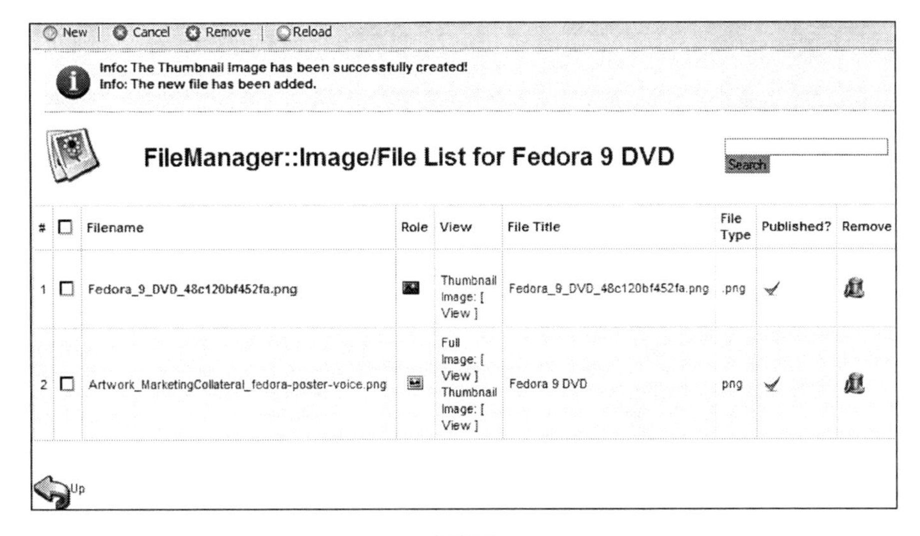

In the same way, you can add as many images as you want to. The additional image just added will be displayed in the product details page, just below the main product image:

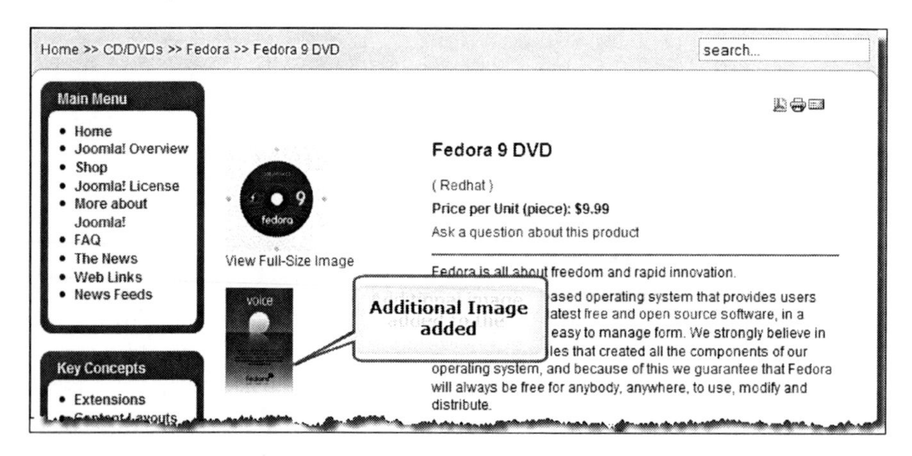

Adding extra files with products

Instead of adding multiple image files for a product, sometimes it is necessary to add some other types of files to provide extra information about the product. For example, with a computer, we may keep detailed technical specifications in a PDF file and add that file to the product. For some software products, adding the installation guide and user manual will also be useful. For example, we are selling an **OpenOffice.org 2 CD**. Therefore, adding an installation guide will be helpful for the customers. However, we need to be aware that these files will be available to the viewers of the product. They can get it without purchasing the product. Such files can be added from the **FileManager** screen. Click on the **New** icon in the toolbar on the **FileManager** screen. That will show the **Upload a File for:** screen:

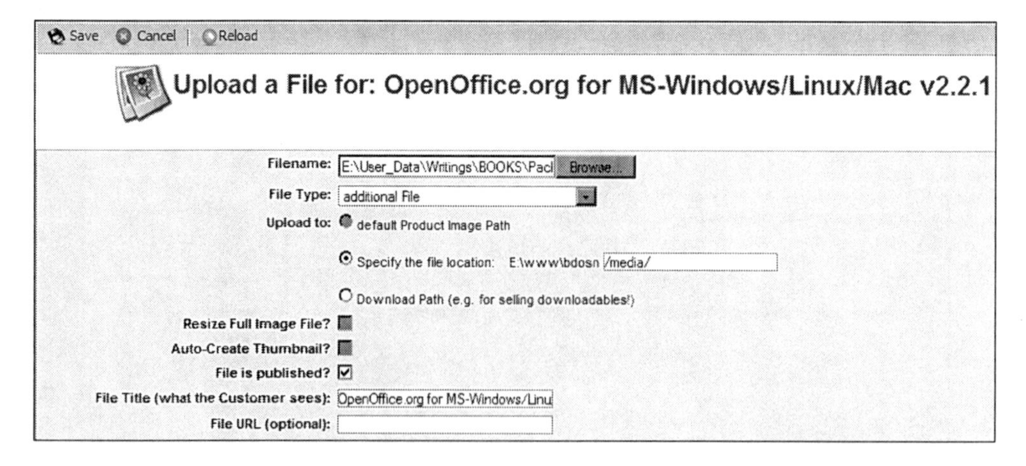

In the **Upload a File for** screen, type the file path, or click on the **Browse** button to locate and select the file. In the **File Type** drop-down list, select **additional File**. Selecting this will change the setting in the **Upload to** field. The **Specify the file location** option will be selected with the default path to media files for Joomla!. You can upload a file with any extension and this upload is not limited to file extensions configured in the Joomla! global configurations for media upload. Note that with changes in the **File Type** field, the other two checkboxes become disabled. Check the **File is Published** checkbox to display the file in the product details page. To end the file adding task, click on the **Save** icon in the toolbar. The file will be added in the product and will be displayed as a link for download at the bottom of product description.

Configuring downloadable products

Some products are virtual or downloadable. For example, when we sell e-books we don't ship them. Instead, the file remains on the server and customers pay for the product and download it. The download link is visible to customers only after paying for the product. If you remember, we discussed configurations for enabling downloadable products in the previous chapter. There, we saw that the downloadable products are enabled from **Admin | Configurations | Download**. From there, you can enable the download, set the order status for which the download link will function, download root (the location where the downloadable files will be stored), and a maximum number of downloads and expiration time. For a quick recap, let us look at the screenshot below:

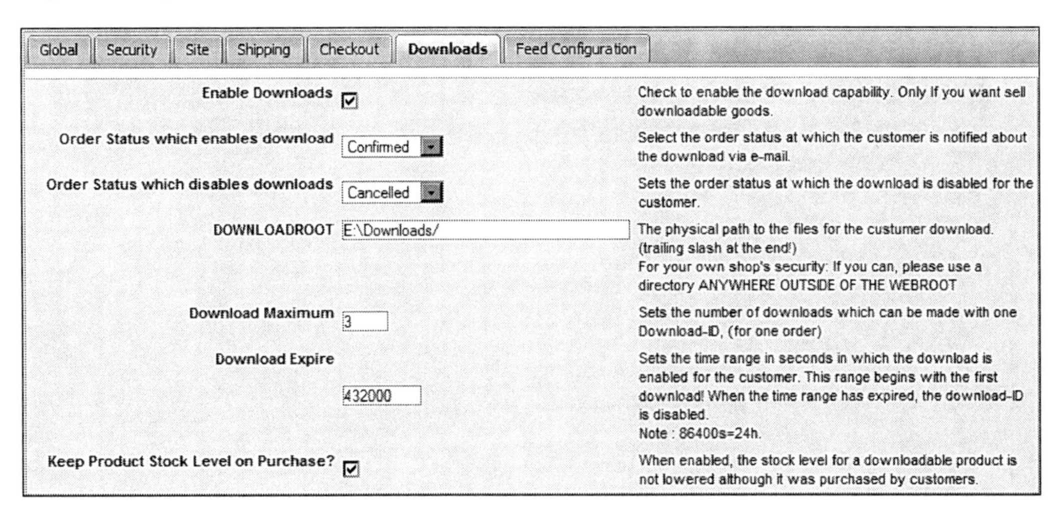

One important thing is that we must specify the download root, and for security, it must be outside the webroot. Our webroot is `e:\www`. Therefore, we will keep the downloadable product files in `e:\downloads/` and type it in the **DOWNLOADROOT** field. Once these are configured and saved, we may proceed to adding downloadable products.

For adding a downloadable product, we first have to add the product with all information, images, and prices as done for normal products. Once we have added the normal product, we can configure it as a downloadable product. For example, we are selling an e-book *Building Website with Joomla! 1.5*. We have added the product information and the cover images. We can now see the product in the **Product List** screen:

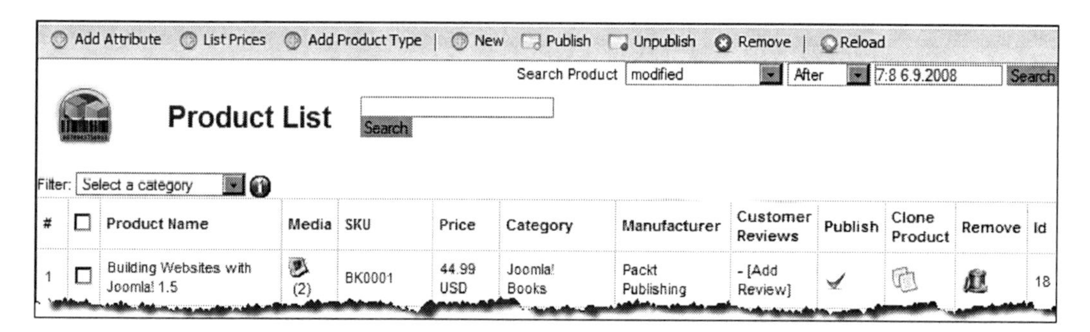

In the previous sections, we learned how to add additional images for a product. We need to use the same screen for configuring this product as a downloadable product. Therefore, click on the media icon () in the **Media** column. This will show the **FileManager** screen. Click the **New** icon in the toolbar of this screen. That opens up the **Upload a File for: Building Websites with Joomla! 1.5** screen. In the **File Type** drop-down list, select the **Downloadable Product File (to be sold)**. This will change the options in the screen as follows:

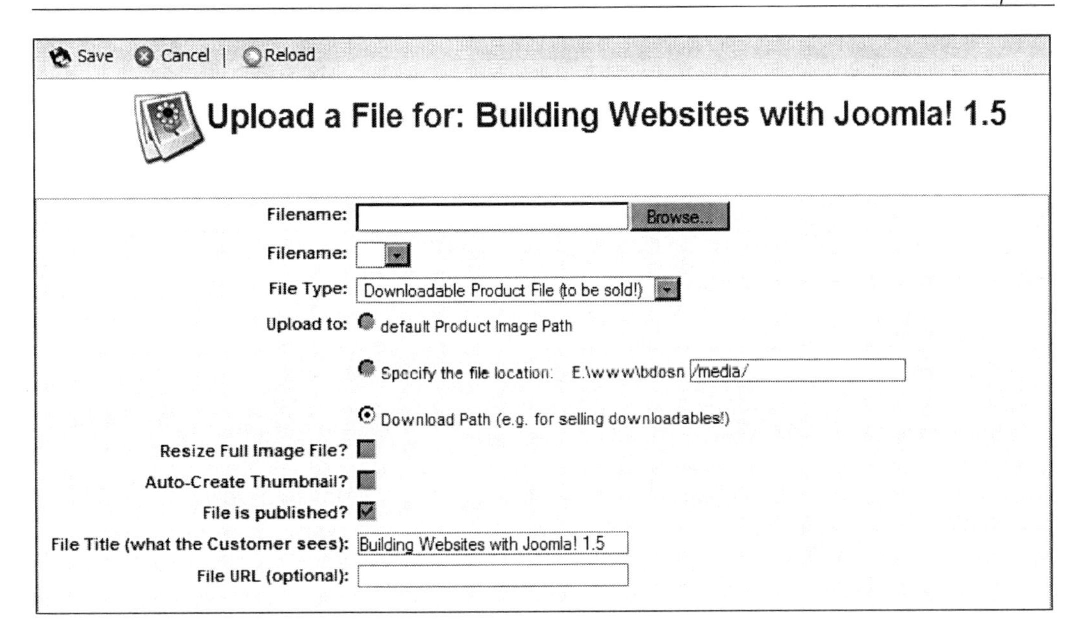

Notice that we have very little to configure in this screen. We will need to upload the file by clicking on the **Browse** button, or selecting the already uploaded file from the list. If you have already uploaded the file(s) in the download directory (`E:\Downloads`, in our case) then files in that directory will be listed in the **Filename** drop-down list. In that case, select the appropriate file name from the list. If the file is yet not uploaded, click on the **Browse** button in the **Filename** field, locate and select the file from your hard disk. Once a filename is given, click on the **Save** icon in the toolbar. The file is now added to the product and you can see it in the **FileManager** screen as follows:

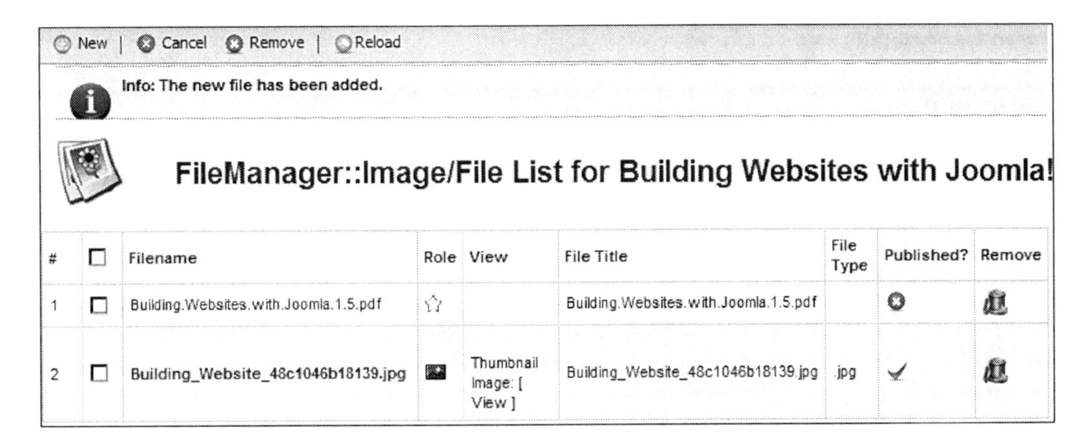

In the list, we see that the file we have just added is not published. To publish this file, click on the red circle in the **Published?** column. The red circle will become a green tick. The product is now downloadable.

From the frontend, whenever a customer purchases the product, the download link will be sent to the customer. Following the download link and code, the customer can download the file within the specified time (three days or seven days, whatever we have configured). The email sent to the customer looks like the following:

```
Hi Suhreed Sarkar,
the file(s) you ordered are ready for your download.
Please enter the following Download-ID(s) in our Downloads Area:
Building.Websites.with.Joomla.1.5.pdf: 856cf6741e167fedba223e9e5d4007
2e
http://localhost/bdosn/index.php?option=com_virtuemart&page=shop.downl
oads&Itemid=53&download_id=856cf6741e167fedba223e9e5d40072e
the maximum number of downloads for each file is: 3
Download until 5 days after the first download
____________________________________________________________
Questions? Problems?
Bangladesh Open Source Network
http://localhost/bdosn/

suhreed@bdosn.org
____________________________________________________________
Download-Info by Bangladesh Open Source Network
```

As you see from the mail, it provided the download ID and download link. An easy way to download the product is to click on the link. The link includes the download ID, so you don't need to type it again. However, if you are logged in to the shop, you can click on the **Download Area** link and then enter this download ID in the following screen:

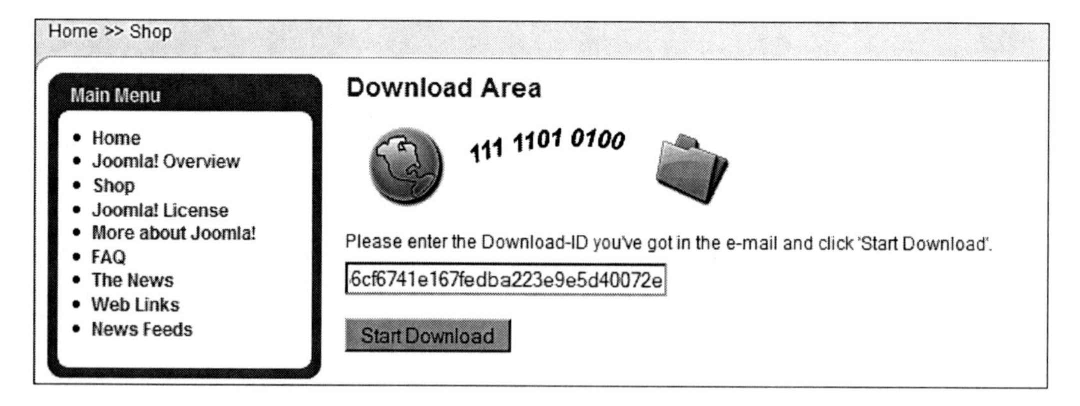

After entering the download ID, click on the **Start Download** button. This will start the download. When prompted to save the file, select a location. The file will be downloaded to your computer. However, note that it does not reveal the physical location of the file. If you look closely, you will get the URL like the following: `http://localhost/bdosn/index.php?download_id=856cf6741e167fedba223e9e5d40072e&func=downloadRequest&option=com_virtuemart&page=shop.downloads.`

This URL gives the customer an opportunity to only download the file three times (as we have set it in the global configuration for the store). With every download, the order status is updated and the store administrators can see how many times that file has been downloaded. To see this, click the **Orders | List Orders**, and then click on the order ID, which has the downloadable product. Clicking the product ID will show the order details. At the bottom, you will notice how many times the product can be downloaded. This also shows the download expiration time. You can also resend the download code to the customer by clicking on the **Resend Download ID** button:

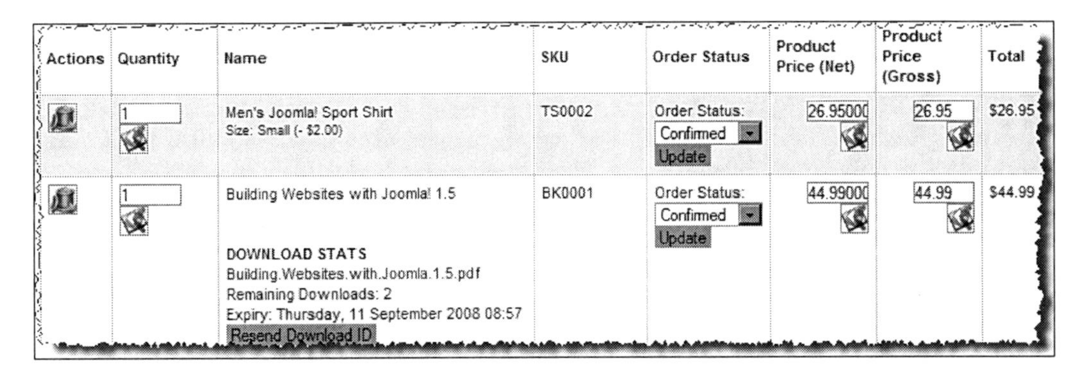

Actions	Quantity	Name	SKU	Order Status	Product Price (Net)	Product Price (Gross)	Total
	1	Men's Joomla! Sport Shirt Size: Small (- $2.00)	TS0002	Order Status: Confirmed Update	26.95000	26.95	$26.95
	1	Building Websites with Joomla! 1.5 DOWNLOAD STATS Building.Websites.with.Joomla.1.5.pdf Remaining Downloads: 2 Expiry: Thursday, 11 September 2008 08:57 Resend Download ID	BK0001	Order Status: Confirmed Update	44.99000	44.99	$44.99

When the customer reaches the maximum number of downloads, or the time has expired, the customer will get an error message while trying to download the file:

The administrator of the shop will notice the case and can also re-enable the download by clicking on the **Re-Enable Download** button in order details page:

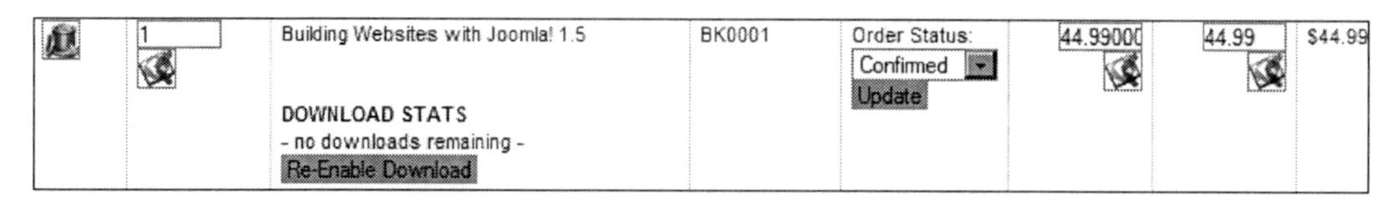

Re-enabling the download will generate a new download code. Therefore, you need to resend the download code again. The customer can download the file three times with the new download code within the new expiration time. This expiration time is set when the customer downloads the file for the first time.

When the shop administrator cancels the order, the download is also disabled as the download ID is removed from the database. The customers can no longer download the file using the download ID they have. However, as a shop administrator, you can change the order's status to confirm again. After changing the order status, you can re-enable the download. In this case, a new download ID is generated. Re-send this new download ID to the customer so that the file can be downloaded again.

While configuring the downloadable product, we can add as many files as we want. The same procedure should be followed for adding another downloadable file to the product. However, as your web server may have a size limit, and the `php.ini` file often restricts to a limit (usually 2MB) for uploading, it is better to upload the larger files directly to the download folder using FTP. When we have uploaded the files to download directory, a list of the files will be available in the **Filename** field of the **Upload a File for** screen.

Using attributes

Attributes are common to most products. When we are selling a T-Shirt, it may have several attributes including size, color, and slogan. Similarly, a book may be hardcover or paperback, and based on the attribute, product's prices may also vary. In VirtueMart, we can add attributes to the products. There are two types of attributes used in VirtueMart: general attributes, and attributes used for stock control. For example, we are selling T-Shirts of four colors: green, yellow, blue, and black. We may configure the color as one attribute and customers can choose the color before placing the order. However, from such simple attribute we cannot say how many green T-shirts are sold, as it only counts T-shirts as general. To solve this issue, VirtueMart introduced the option to create parent-child products based on attribute and value combinations. In this case, there will be four products: green T-shirt, yellow T-shirt, blue T-shirt, and black T-shirt. In the following sections, we are going to learn the details for configuring both types of attributes.

Simple attributes

Adding simple attributes to the product is much easier than configuring the parent-child products based on attribute and value combinations. Let's first try some simple attributes. For example, we are selling the Joomla! Fitted Cap. As you know, caps are of different sizes. Therefore, one attribute of the Joomla! Fitted Cap will be `size`. Another attribute may be the `color` of the cap. Let's try adding these two attributes to the Joomla! Fitted Cap product.

We can add simple attributes to the product when adding the product to the catalog, or later by updating the product information. As we have already added the Joomla! Fitted Cap product in the catalog, we can now update it to add these simple attributes. To obtain this, click on the **Products | List Products**. This shows the **Product List** screen with the list of all products added to the catalog. Find the product named **Joomla! Fitted Cap**, and click on that link in the **Product Name** column. This shows the **Update Item:: Joomla! Fitted Cap** screen. Click on the **Product Status** tab in this screen. This tab has options for adding simple attributes:

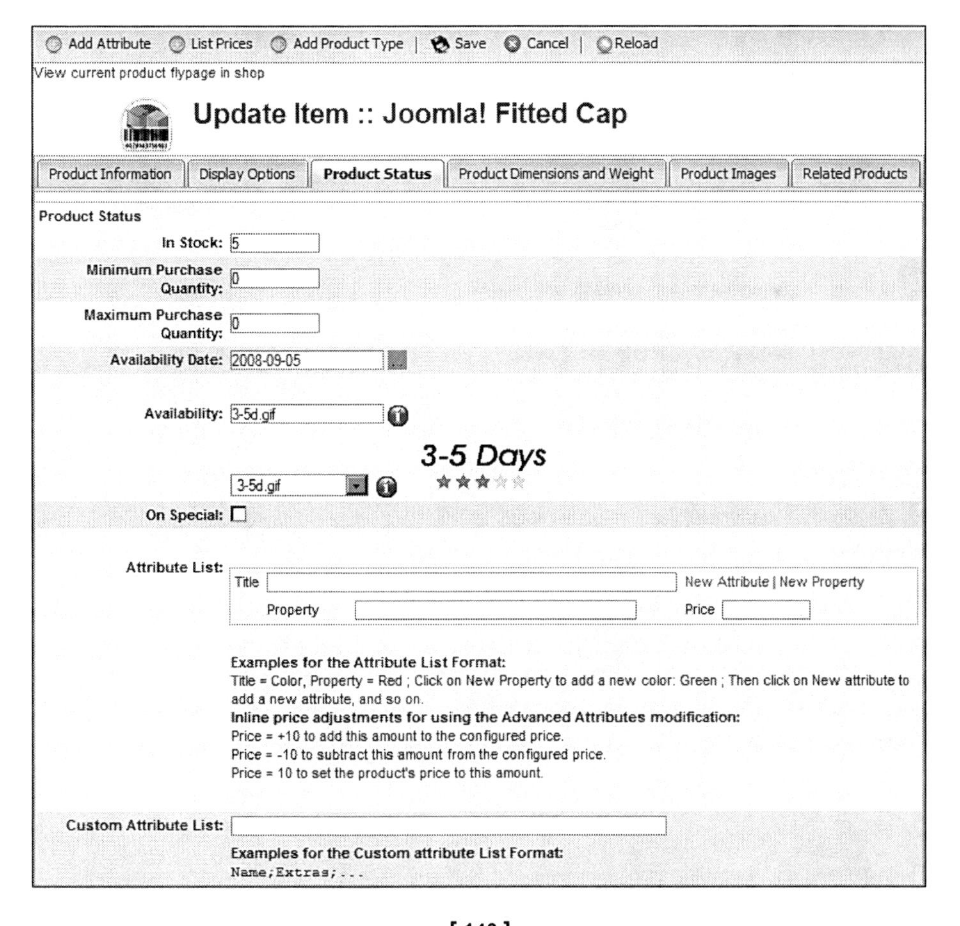

Note that there are two sections: **Attribute List** and **Custom Attribute List**. We will configure the attributes from these two sections. There are instructions on this screen on how to add attributes. In the **Attribute List** section, there are three fields: **Title, Property**, and **Price**. In the **Title** field, type the name of the attribute. Our first attribute for the cap is the **Size**. Therefore, type **Size** in the **Title** field. In the **Property** field, we need to specify the value of the attribute. Type **Large** in the **Property** field. The **Large** sized caps may be more costly than **Medium** size. Therefore, type **+2** in the **Price** field. Similarly, we may add other properties of the attribute **Size**. For adding a new property, click on the **New Property** link. Similarly, click the **New Attribute** link for adding another attribute. After configuring the attribute and properties for those, the screen will look like the following screenshot:

Attribute List:
Title Size — New Attribute | New Property
Property Large — Price +2
Property Medium — Price X
Property Small — Price -2 X

Title Color — New Attribute | Delete Attribute | New Property
Property Black — Price X
Property Blue — Price X
Property Green — Price X
Property Yellow — Price X

Examples for the Attribute List Format:
Title = Color, Property = Red ; Click on New Property to add a new color: Green ; Then click on New attribute to add a new attribute, and so on.
Inline price adjustments for using the Advanced Attributes modification:
Price = +10 to add this amount to the configured price.
Price = -10 to subtract this amount from the configured price.
Price = 10 to set the product's price to this amount.

Custom Attribute List:
Examples for the Custom attribute List Format:
`Name;Extras;...`

From the screenshot above, we see that two attributes and their values have been set. For the variation of size, there is variation in product's price. For example, for the **Large** sized cap, the price will be $2 more than the configured base price. The **Medium** sized cap's price will be equal to the configured base price. However, for the **Small** sized caps, there will be $2 reduction from the configured base price.

For the **Color** attribute, there will be no price variation. We have defined the colors available so that customers can choose their preferred color. However, they don't need to pay extra for their preferred color.

We will now look at the **Custom Attribute** field. This field allows us to add attributes for which the customers must provide a response. For example, for T-shirts and caps, we want to know from the customers, what slogan they want to have printed. In this case, just type **Slogan** in the **Custom Attribute List** field. We can add multiple attribute names by separating them with a semi-colon (;).

When all of the attributes and values are configured, click on the **Save** icon in the toolbar. Attributes are added to the product. We can now see the product details page. We will see the attribute selection box and we must select a value for each attribute before adding that product to the cart:

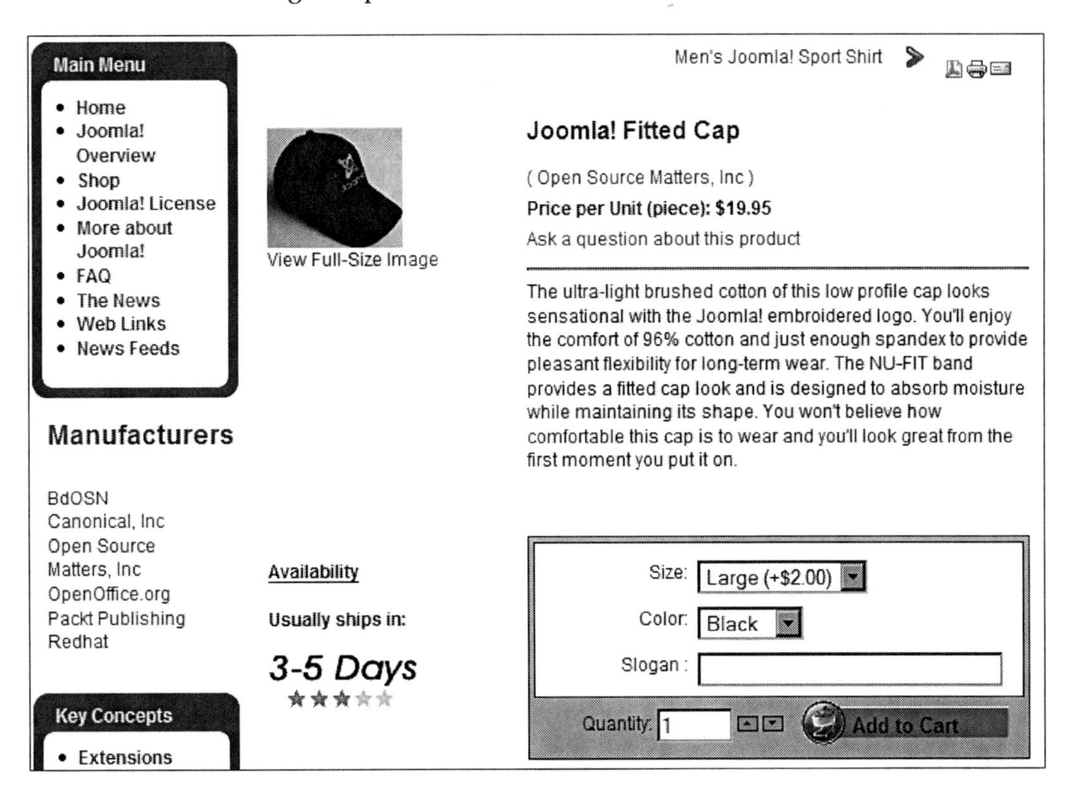

When a customer adds the product to cart, the attributes and their values are also displayed in the cart items. These are always mentioned in the product invoice and order details:

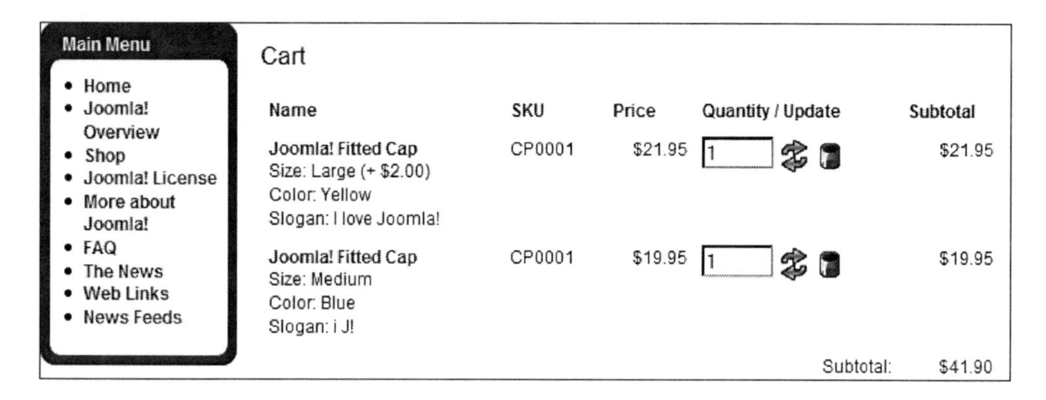

We can now see that due to variations in size, the caps prices are adjusted. However, for changes in color, there is no variation in product prices.

[If you have created any attribute, the customers must choose a value for that attribute. Otherwise, they cannot add the product to the cart. It is applicable for custom attributes as well.]

Parent-child products

We have already added simple attributes to the product and seen that adding simple attributes is very easy. One limitation of using a simple attribute is that it does not allow us to know the stock by attributes. For example, we have configured the Joomla! Fitted Cap with two attributes. We won't know how many green or how many large sized caps have been sold. What we know from the stock information and product order report is that **x** number Joomla! Fitted Caps have been sold. This happened because inventory is maintained by SKU, not by attributes. If we really want to keep track of sales by attributes, we need to create separate products for each attribute variation. When we add a separate product, a separate SKU is used and the inventory is maintained by that SKU. However, creating a separate product for each attribute variation may be a huge task, and customers may be confused. For example, we sell a **Women's Joomla! Black T-shirt**. It has different sizes: small, medium, large, extra large. If we create four products, how will the customers know that it's actually a single product, but of different sizes. To solve this issue, VirtueMart introduced the parent-child products.

In the parent-child relationship, the parent product is the main product added to the catalog. For example, a small size of T-shirt is added as the main product. Then, for variations of the attribute value, child products are added. In the catalog, only the parent product is listed. Customers can see the child products only from the parent product's page.

For our example store, I have added a **Women's Joomla! Black T-shirt**. It is priced for the small size. We can now add the **Size** attribute to this product, and create child products for it, so that inventory of this T-shirts is maintained for different sizes. Let's start adding child products in the following sections.

Adding product attributes

Before creating the child products, we first need to create at least one attribute for the parent product. Therefore, go to the **Products | List Products** screen and select the parent product from the list. In our case we want the **Women's Joomla! Black T-shirt,** then click on the **Add Attribute** button in the toolbar. This shows the **Attribute Form** for the product. In this form, type the name of the attribute in the **Attribute Name** field. Then, type a sort order in the **List Order** field. Click on the **Save** button in the toolbar to save the attribute:

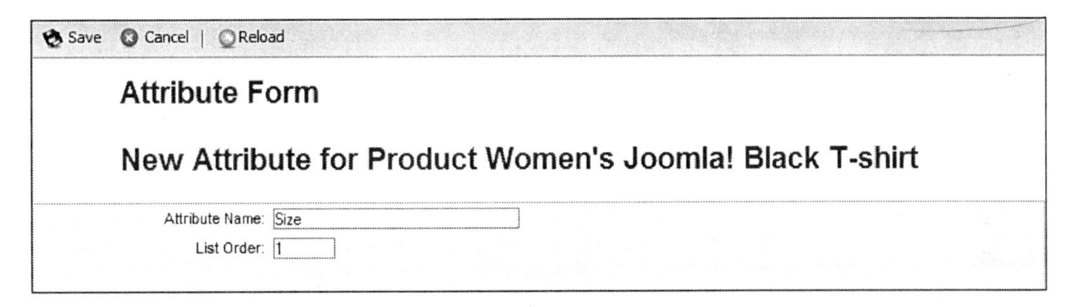

After clicking the **Save** button in the toolbar, the attribute is added and the **Attribute List for - Item: Women's Joomla! Black T-Shirt** screen is displayed. This screen lists all of the attributes added to the product. We can create a new attribute for the same product by clicking on the **New** icon in the toolbar. Attributes can also be removed by clicking on trash icon in the **Remove** column:

When all of the required attributes are added for the product, we may begin adding child products. Note that the attributes listed in this screen will be available when we create child products. Child products will be created for variations of these attributes.

Creating a new item

Child products are known as items in VirtueMart. For adding a child product, we need to create an item. First, go to the **Update** screen of the parent product. From the **Products | List Products** screen, click on the parent product (for example, **Women's Joomla! Black T-Shirt**). This shows the **Update Item :: Women's Joomla! Black T-shirt** screen. This screen is similar to the screen we have used for adding the product:

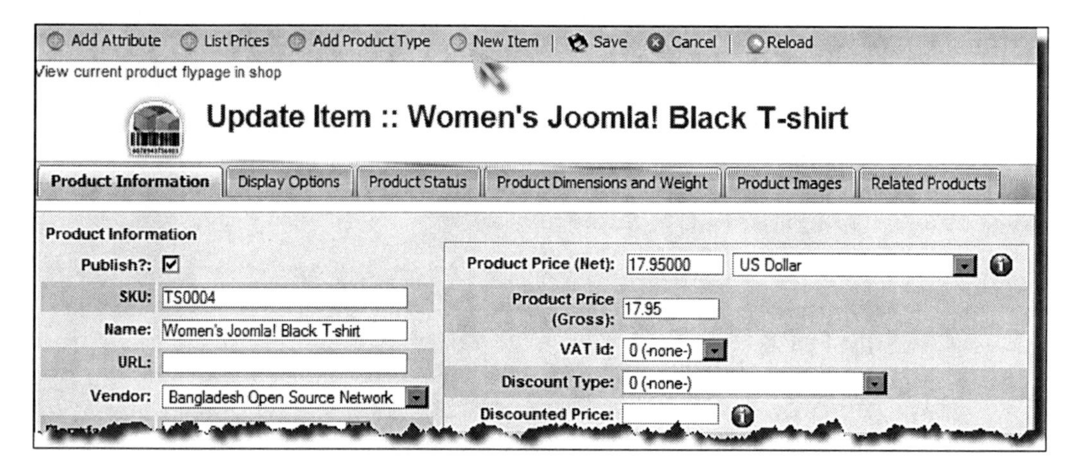

Note that there is a new icon, **New Item,** in the toolbar. This will only be available when some attributes have been added to the product. For adding an item (child product), click on the **New Item** icon in the toolbar. This opens up the **New Item :: Women's Joomla! Black T-shirt** screen, which is similar to the form used for adding new products:

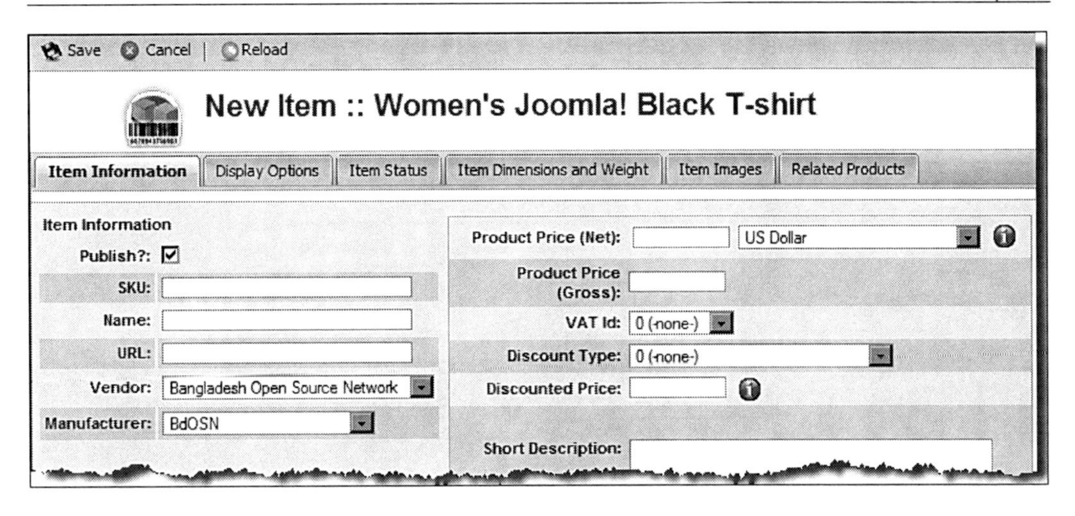

Like adding a new product, fill in the form by providing the appropriate information. If you look at the form carefully, you will notice that all the tabs are named with **Item**, instead of **Product**. Although the tab names have changed, most of the fields in the tabs remain same as **New Product** form. However, we will find a section named **Item Attributes** in the **Item Status** tab. This section shows the attributes we have added to the product. For each item, we need to set a different value in these attributes. As we have added only one attribute, **Size**, to this product, we see the **Size** field in this section. Type a value in this field, say **Large**:

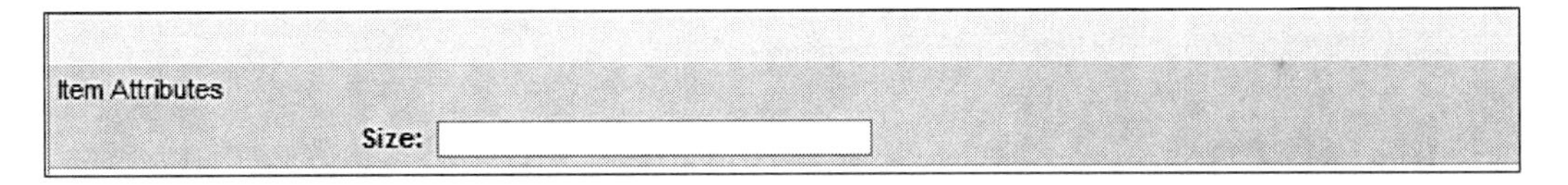

With changes of the attribute, we may price the item differently. Therefore, set the price for the **Large** sized T-shirt in the **Product Price (Net)** field in the **Item Information** tab. We may also add a separate image for the item from the **Item Images** tab. When all of these are configured, click on the **Save** button in the toolbar to save the item information.

We need to add more items for other attribute values (for example, medium, small, and extra large size) in the same process. When we have added an item to a product, in the **Product List** screen, the **[Item Information]** link will be displayed beside the product name. Clicking on this link will show the available items for that product indicating its parent product in **Category** column:

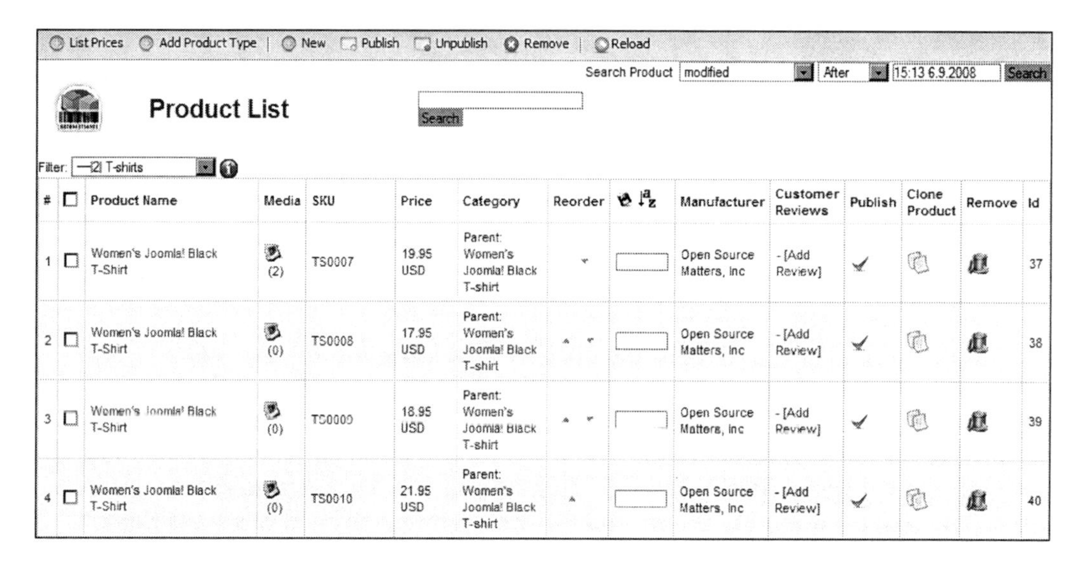

We can add new items from this screen by clicking on the **New** icon in the toolbar. Similarly, we can publish, unpublish, clone, or remove any item from this screen. We can also edit an item by clicking on its name.

Editing items

From the item list, click on the item name which opens the **Update Item** screen. This screen looks similar to the product update screen. We can make any necessary changes in this form and save the changes by clicking on the **Save** icon in the toolbar:

We can also create an item by clicking on the **Add Another Item** button in the toolbar.

Managing product attributes

For managing the product attributes of the product, first change to **Simple Layout** (seen below). Then, go to **Products | List Products**, and click on the product name to open up the product update form. Next, click on the **List Attributes** icon on the left side toolbar. This will open up the **Attribute List for - Item:...** screen. From this screen, you can add a new attribute, edit existing attributes, or remove any attribute. Due to some bug, you don't find the **List Attributes** link in the **Extended Layout**.

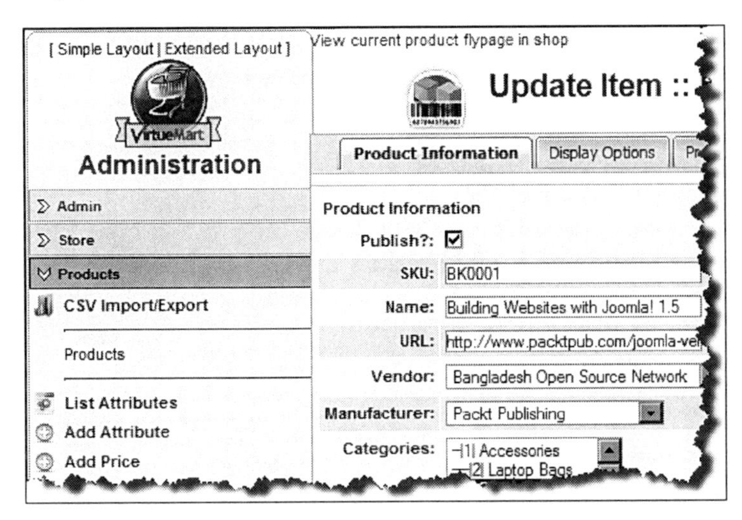

Deleting product attributes is not that easy. As child products are based on the attributes, they cannot exist if you delete the attributes. When you try to delete some attributes, upon which child products are created, you will get an error message saying that you need to delete the child products first, and then attempt deleting the attributes. The same thing happens when we try to delete a parent product without deleting the child products first.

When trying to delete parent-child products, delete the child products first, then attributes, and finally delete the parent products.

Using product types

Product types allow us to present different types of product in the shop in different formats with added information. For example, we are selling books, we need to show some special information, such as author name, edition, ISBN, number of pages, cover type, and so on. A product type of book can collect this custom information in addition to other generic information on that book. Similarly, the product type of software will collect different information (version, OS supported, licensing, download size, and so on) and will be displayed differently.

In VirtueMart, we can use product types with a set of parameters. First, we need to define the product types and define parameters for the product types. Later, we need to add the product types to products. When we add the product type to the product, we get another tab named after that product type, and a set of parameters to configure for that product type. In the following sections, you will learn more about defining and using product types on your VirtueMart shop.

Adding product types

The first step for using a product type is to define the product type. For adding the product type, select **Products | Add Product Type**. This shows the **Product Type Information** screen:

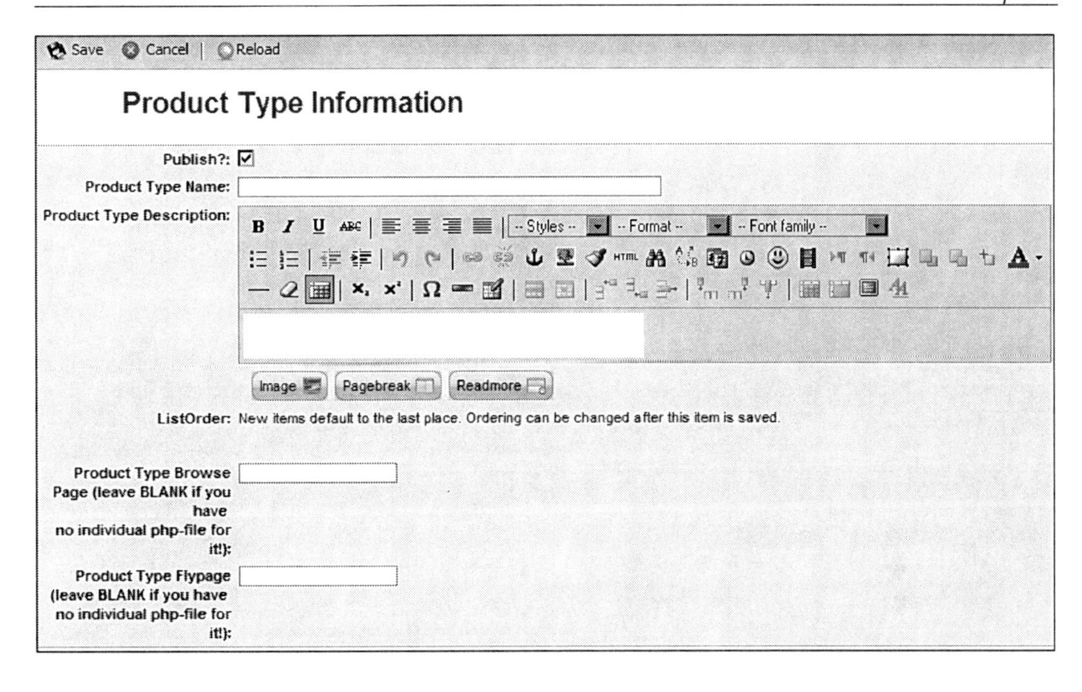

In the **Product Type Information** screen, fill in the following fields:

- **Publish**: By default, this is checked, which means this product type will be available for use. For any reason, if you want to keep it unpublished, uncheck this checkbox.
- **Product Type Name**: Specify the name of the product type. Type **Books** here to create a product type for books.
- **Product Type Description**: Type a brief description of the product type you are creating. For example, when creating a product type for books, explain when this product type will be used.
- **List Order**: When creating a new product type, you cannot specify the list order. Generally, the last number for the list order is taken by default. You can change this **List Order** when editing that product type later.
- **Product Type Browse Page**: You can specify the browse page for this particular product type. For the books product type, you may want to show the browsing page differently. In that case, you need to design the browse page for that product category, and specify the name of that browse page in this field. As you have not designed a browse page at this point, keep this field blank for the time being.

- **Product Type Flypage**: Like browse page, you can specify a flypage (product details page) especially designed for this product type. For the time being, you are not using any special flypage, therefore, keep this field blank.

> You will learn more about designing and using browse pages and flypages in Chapter 6, *Customizing the Look and Feel*. We will be coming back to this configuration for product types after designing some browse pages and flypages.

After filling in the fields of this screen, click the **Save** icon in the toolbar to add the product type. You will see the list of the product types in the **Product Type List** screen:

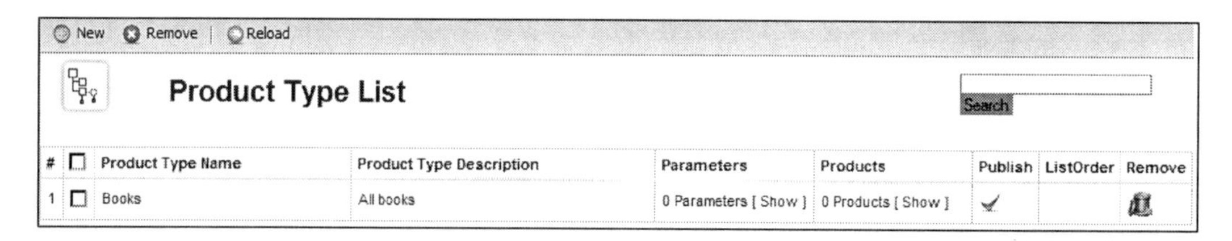

#	☐	Product Type Name	Product Type Description	Parameters	Products	Publish	ListOrder	Remove
1	☐	Books	All books	0 Parameters [Show]	0 Products [Show]	✓		

From the **Product Type List** screen, we can create a new product type, edit an existing product type by clicking on the product type name, see the parameters for the product type, see the list of products included in the product type, and publish or unpublish the product type.

We have added a product type named **Books**. However, it is of no use at this time. To make it usable, you need to add parameters for this product type.

Adding parameters to product types

Why are you adding the product types? We do this to add some extra information to the product. For example, you are creating the **Books** product type for adding some information to the product, which is very much specific for books. For a book, there need to be an authors' name, number of pages, cover type, ISBN, edition, and so on. You have created the product type **Books**, but can you add this information through that product type? Yes, I know you have no clue on this until now. Because, you have not added any field like authors, ISBN, cover type, and so on. VirtueMart allows us to add such fields to a product type by adding parameters to the product type.

For creating parameters for a product type, in the **Product Type List** screen, click on the **[Show]** link in the **Parameters** column. This shows the **Parameters of Product Type: Books[Product Type List]** screen:

As we have not added any parameter to **Books** product type, the screen will not list any. To create new a parameter for the product type **Books**, click on the **New** button in the toolbar. This shows **Parameter Information** screen:

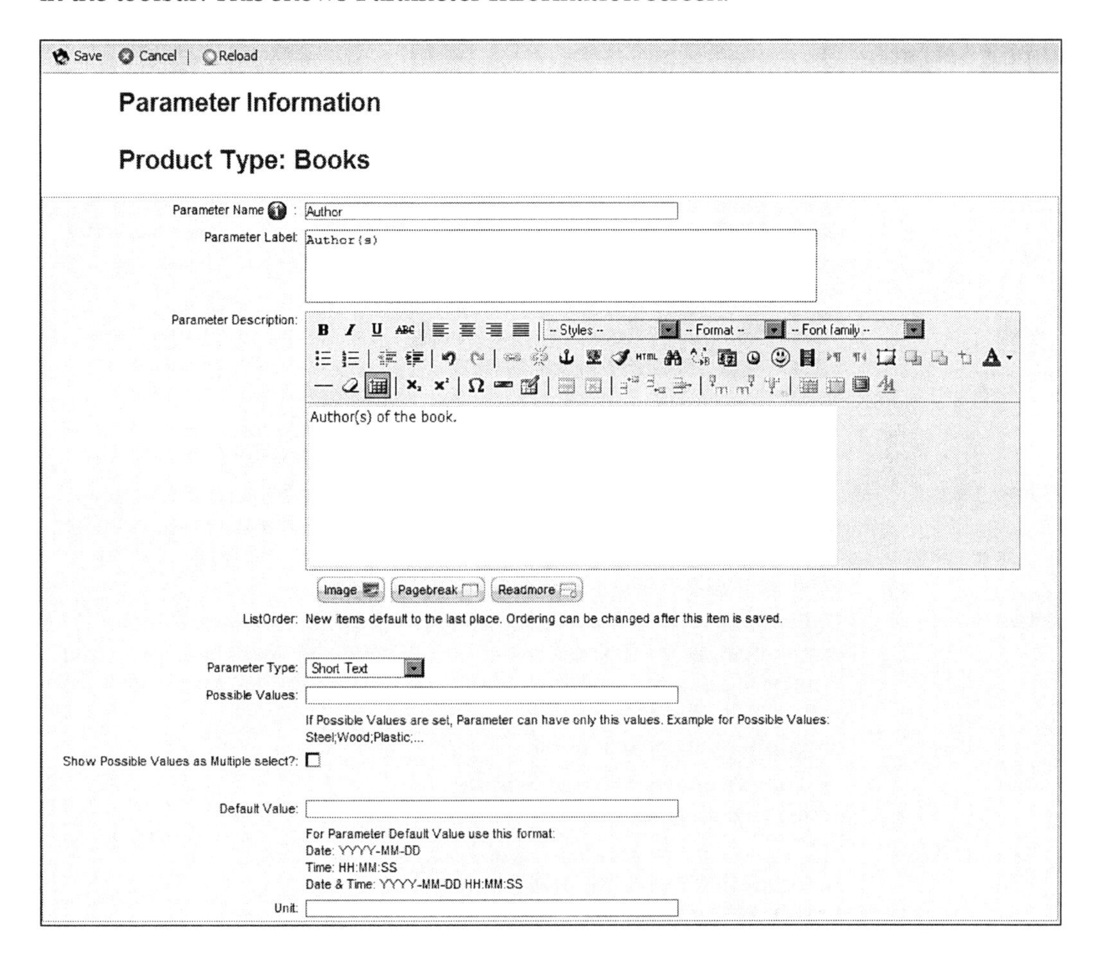

For each book we sell from our store, we want to add author information for it. Therefore, we want to add a parameter named **Author**, where we will be able to provide author's name. Let us first add this **Author** parameter.

In the **Parameter Information** screen, type the name of the parameter, that is **Author**, in the **Parameter Name** field. The parameter name can be a short string and not necessarily descriptive to express its full meaning. However, for displaying the meaningful name of the parameter in the product details page, you can add a label for it in the **Parameter Label** field. Type **Author(s)** in this field. This will be displayed as the field label. In the **Parameter Description** field, type a description of the parameter. This will be displayed as a tooltip in that field on the product details page.

The critical field which you need to select carefully is the **Parameter Type**. The options available in the drop-down list are shown in the table below with their appropriate use:

Option	**Description**	**Example**
Integer	Selecting this allows only integer values to be added, that is, numbers without decimal or fraction. Select this when the parameter value will be a number without a fraction or decimal.	For the books product type, the Pages parameter can be of integer type, as number of pages is always an integer.
Text	Select this option when you need to add something descriptive as parameter.	For the books product type, you may add a parameter named AuthorBio where a short biography of the authors will be published.
Short Text	Select this option for parameters where only short text is needed. This option only allows up to 255 characters to be inserted.	For the books product type, the Author parameter can be of short text type.
Float	Unlike Integer, this allows you to enter decimal values for the parameter. Whatever decimal value you enter, VirtueMart rounds that up to three digits after the decimal point.	For the software product type, this will be appropriate for a Size (MB) parameter.
Char	This option allows a character to be added as the value of that parameter.	
Date and Time	This option allows a date to be entered and time, in YYYY-MM-DD HH:MM:SS format, for a parameter.	

Option	Description	Example
Date	This option allows a date to be entered, in YYYY-MM-DD format, as a value of the parameter.	For the books product type, the publication date parameter may be of this type.
Time	This option allows a time to be entered, in HH:MM:SS format, as a value for the parameter.	
Multiple Values	This option allows single or multiple values for the parameter to be selected from a list of values.	For books, the cover type parameter may be of this type, as it will have only two values: Hard Cover, and Paperback.
Break Line	This type doesn't allow any value to be entered for the parameter. You can use this type of parameter to label a section of parameters.	You may add a parameter labeled 'Other Info' with this type, which will separate some of the parameters under this label.

For the **Author** parameter, you will only enter short texts. Therefore, select **Short Text** in the **Parameter Type** drop-down list.

In the **Possible Values** field, you can add options which can be selected for that parameter when product information is added. For almost all parameter types, you can add the possible values. The possible values for all the parameter types, except **Multiple Values**, will be displayed as a drop-down list, from where you can select only one value. For **Multiple Values** parameter type, this list is shown as a multiple select list box, from where you can select multiple values. To show other types of parameters as multiple select list boxes, check the **Show Possible Values as Multiple select?** checkbox. You can also specify a default value in the **Default Value** field, which will be shown in the parameter field when updating the product information. For **Date** and **Time** types, specify the default value in an appropriate format shown below the field, that is, YYYY-MM-DD HH:MM:SS, YY-MM-DD, and HH:MM:SS.

In the **Unit** field, you can specify the unit of that parameter. For example, when adding the **Size** parameter to the Software product type, you can show text like Size: 10.3 MB by adding MB as unit.

Add the following parameters for the **Books** product type, with the values shown in the table below:

Parameter Name	Parameter Label	Parameter Type	Possible Values
Author	Author(s)	Short Text	-
AuthorBio	Author Bio	Text	-
PubDate	Published on	Date	-
NumPages	Number of pages	Integer	-
ISBN10	ISBN-10	Short Text	-
ISBN13	ISBN-13	Short Text	-
CoverType	Cover Type	Short Text	Hardcover; Paperback

When you have completed adding these parameters to **Books** product type, go to **Products | Product Type List**. On the **Product Type List** screen, click on the **[Show]** link in the **Parameters** column. This will list the parameters as shown in the following screenshot:

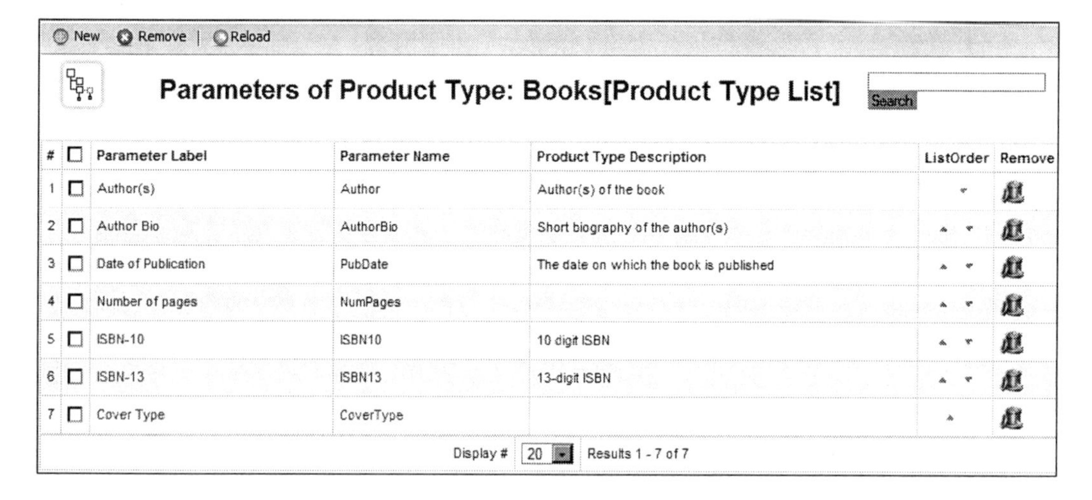

Similarly, you can create product types for other products. For example, our example shop will sell software as well. For software products, we need to provide some special information to customers. Therefore, it will be convenient to create a product type named software with the following parameters:

Parameter Name	Parameter Label	Parameter Type	Possible Values	Remarks
Version	Version	Short Text	-	This cannot be set at integer or float as the version number is usually like 1.2.11.
Size	Size	Float	-	Specify **MB** in the **Unit** field
OS	Supported OS	Multiple Values	Windows XP; Windows Vista; Windows 2000; Linux 2.4.x	
Licensing	Licensing	Short Text	Commercial; GPL; Other Open Source	
Media	Installation Media	Multiple Values	CD; DVD; Download Only	
SystemReq	System Requirements	Break Line	-	This will create section for System Requirements
Processor	Processor	Multiple Values	x86; x64; AMD Athlon; AMD Turion; Intel Pentium; Intel Core; Intel Celeron; Other	
RAM	Memory (minimum)	Integer		Specify **MB** as unit.
HDD	Free Hard Disk Space (minimum)	Integer		Specify **MB** as unit.

After adding the **Software** product type, you can see the list of parameters as we have seen for the **Books** product type. After adding the parameters to product types, we are now ready to configure the products with these product types.

Adding product type to products

Once we have created all of the product types we need, and added appropriate parameters for the product types, we are ready to add those parameters to our products, which are already been added to the catalog. By this time, you will have noticed that in the **Product List** screen, there is **Add Product Type** button:

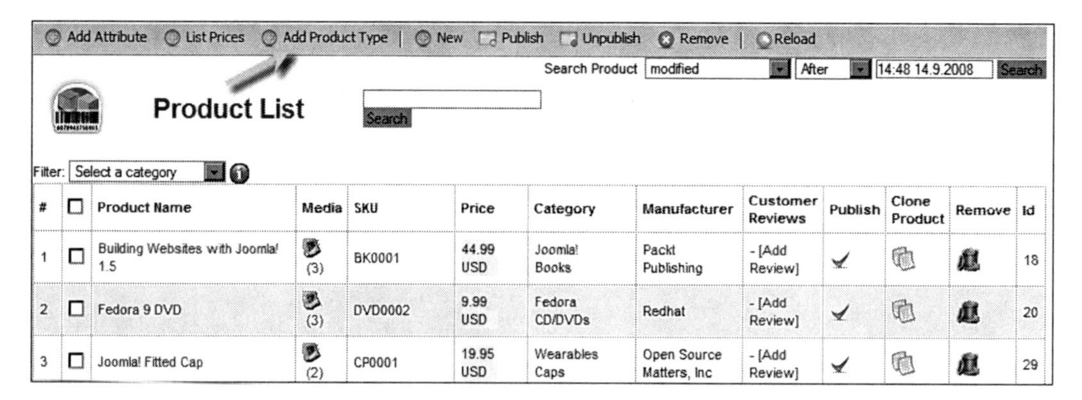

First, you need to select the product and click on the **Add Product Type** button. This will show the **Add Product Type for Product:...** screen (seen below). From the **Product Type** drop-down list, select one product type and click on the **Save** icon in the toolbar. This will add the product type to this product.

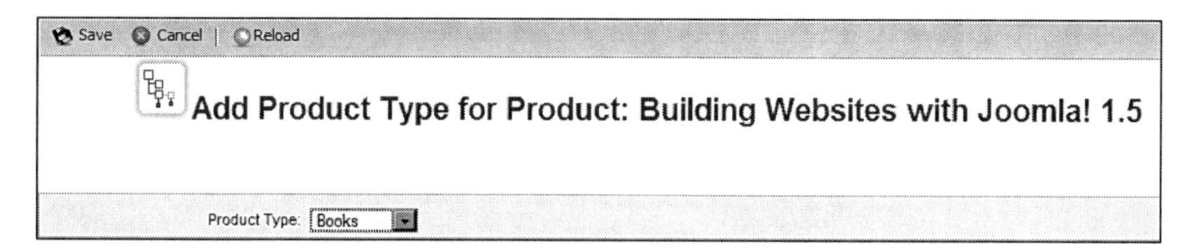

From the **List Products** screen, you may think that you can select multiple products of the same type (for example, all books), and click on the **Add Product Type** button to add that product type to multiple products at a time. In fact, this should be the case. However, for some limitation of VirtueMart, until version 1.1.2, it is not possible to add product type to multiple products at a time. You need to add a product type to individual products, one-by-one. Also, remember that you cannot add a product type while adding the new product.

After adding the product type to the product, we need to provide the information for the product type parameters. Suppose you have added the **Books** product type to a product named **Building Websites with Joomla! 1.5**. Now go to the **Products | List Products**, and click on **Building Websites with Joomla! 1.5**. This will show the **Update Item ::** screen. You will now see a new tab named **Books**. Click on this **Books** tab:

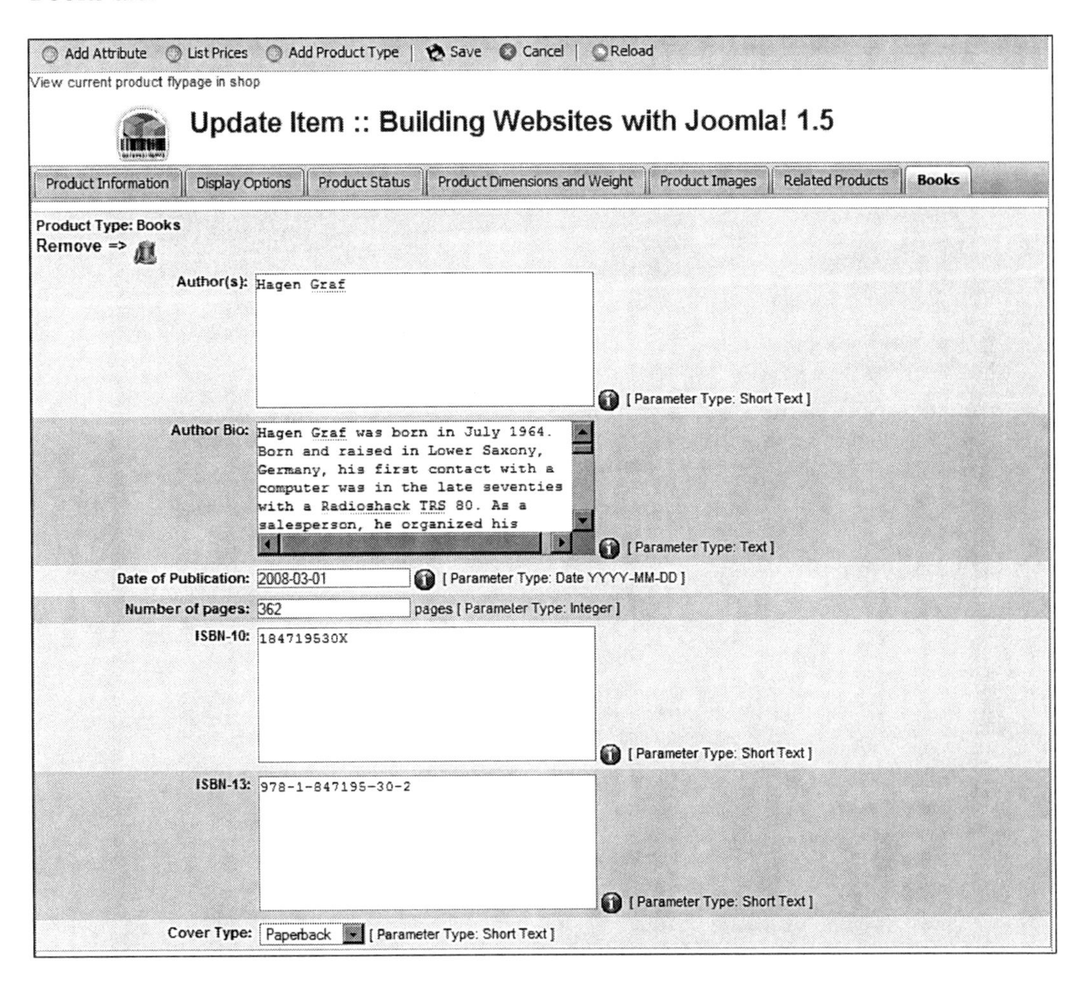

You already know what information needs to be provided in this screen, because you have designed the product type and parameters. The parameters added to the product type **Books** will be available in this screen. Enter the information (as shown in the screenshot above) and click on the **Save** icon in the toolbar.

While adding parameter information, you can get tooltips by hovering your mouse pointer over the info icon (i). In fact, you will see the text entered in the description field when the parameter was created. The same text will also be shown as a tooltip in the frontend. Now, let us have a look at how these parameters appear in the product details page.

From the shop's page, go to the **Books** category and find the book **Building Websites with Joomla! 1.5**. Click on the book name to get the book details. In the book details page, scroll down and you will see a section labeled **Parameters of Category: Books.** This section shows the value of all the parameters, as shown in the following screenshot:

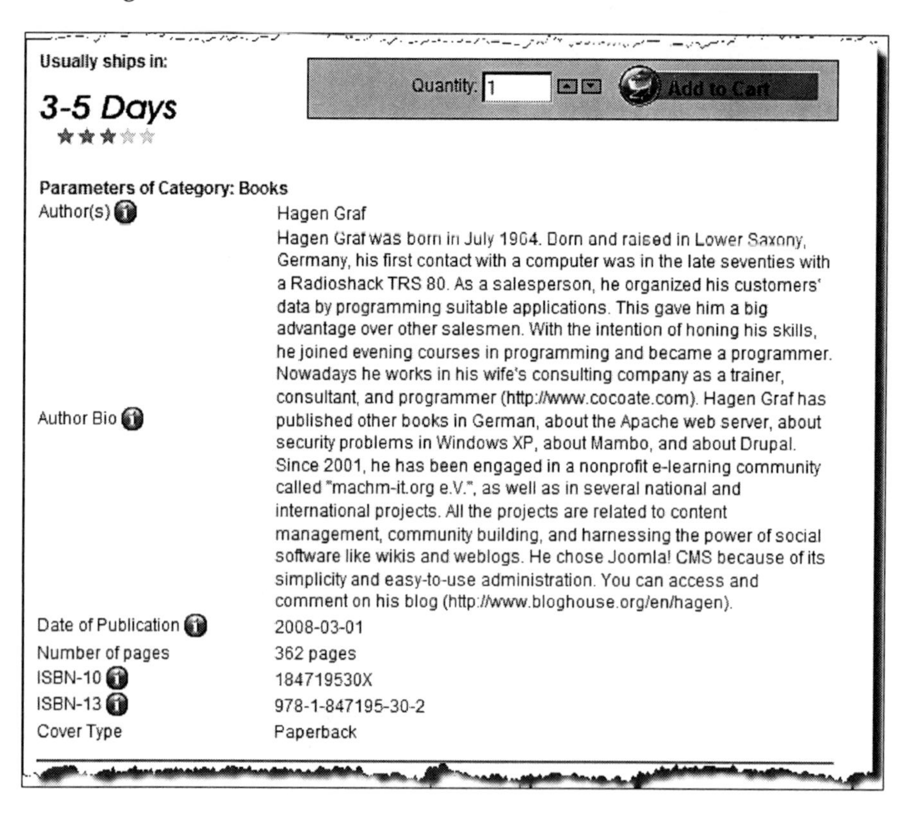

If you are not satisfied with the presentation of this parameter section, wait a little longer. You will learn how to change its display in Chapter 6, *Customizing the Look and Feel*. However, let us add a **Softwares** product type to one software product in our catalog, and see how that looks in the frontend.

When a **Softwares** product type is added to a product, you will see a **Softwares** tab in its **Update Item** screen. The screen will look as the following screenshot:

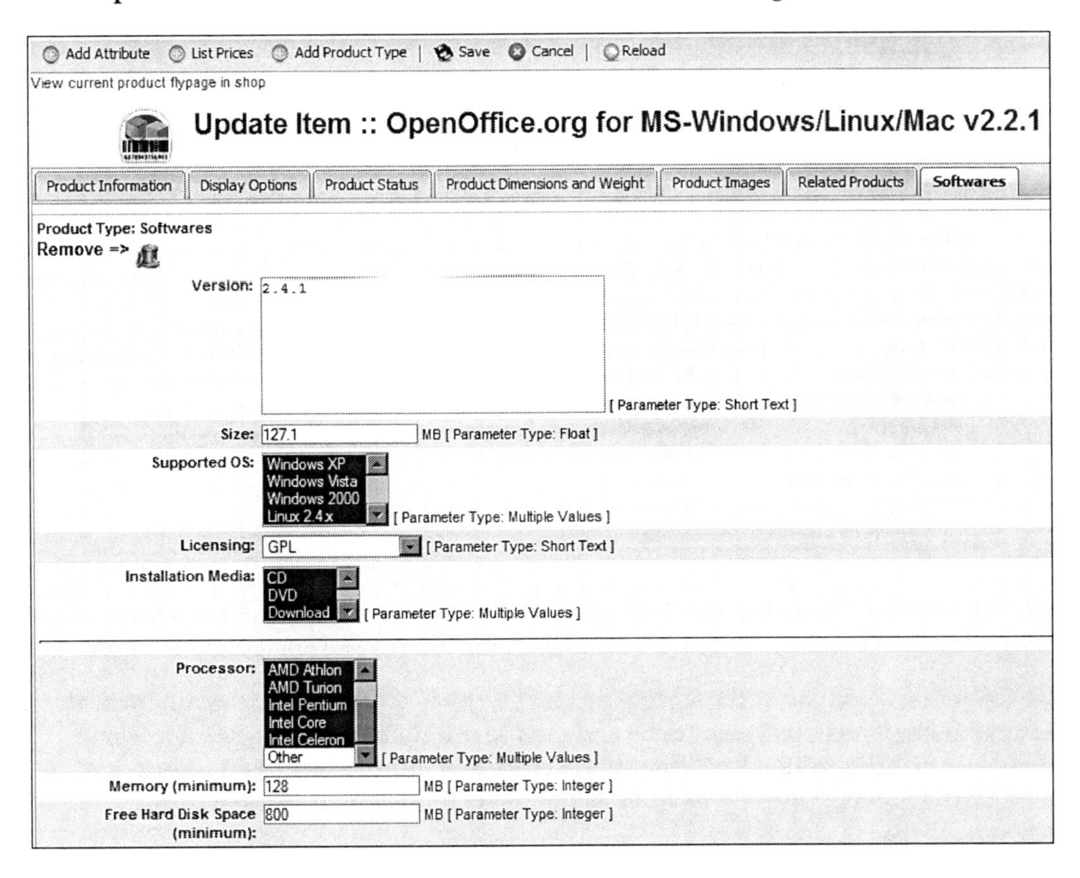

Enter the required information for each parameter, and then save by clicking on the **Save** icon in the toolbar. Once saved, you can view the product details page by clicking on the **View current product flypage in shop** link at the top, or browse from the shop frontend.

In the product details page, scroll down to see the parameters for that software product. These will look like the following screenshot:

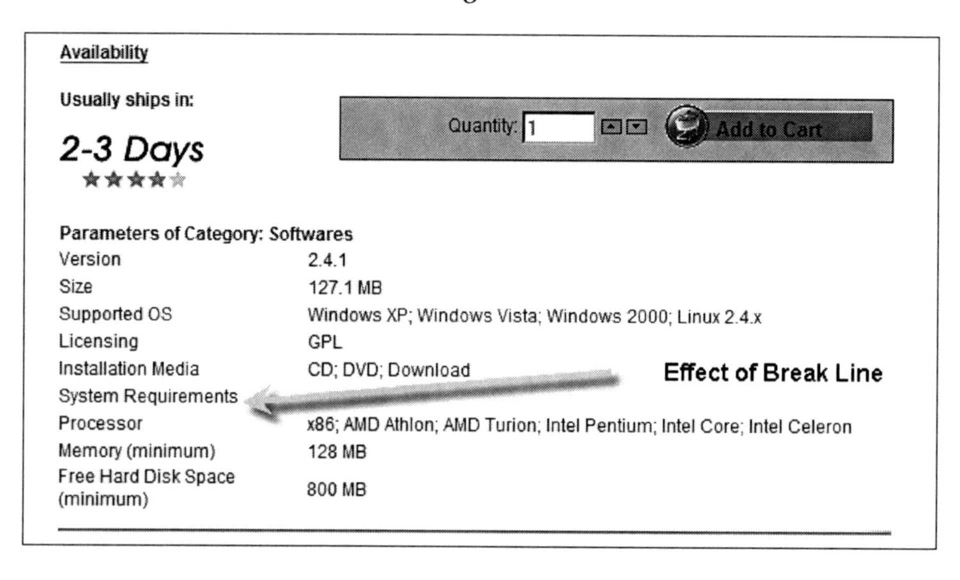

For the software products, note that the **System Requirements** label has separated the parameters below it. This is the effect of using the **Break Line** parameter type.

In VirtueMart, you can add multiple product types to a product. Although for real life products, items don't need to be assigned to multiple product types. However, this gives an opportunity to add multiple groups of information to a product, and overall gives an opportunity to add custom fields for product addition form.

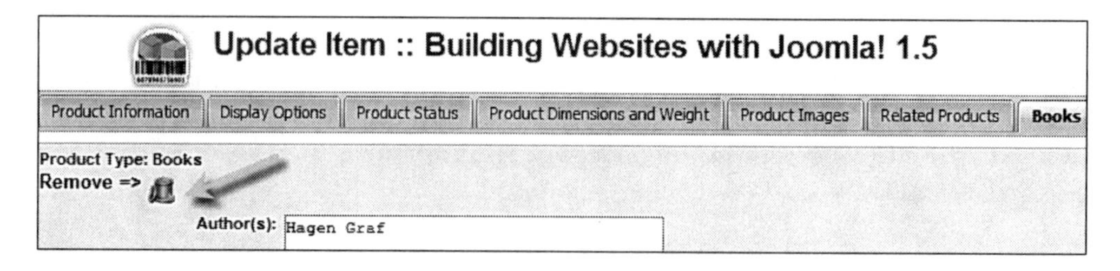

After assigning the product type to the product, you can also remove that product type from the product. If you do so, all information added to that product through the product type parameters will be lost. You can remove the product type from the product by clicking on trash icon (🗑) in the product type info addition screen (seen above).

While adding information to the product type, you can type in the parameter field as you like. However, when you save the entry, only information that is compliant to the field type will be saved. For example, in the **Short Text** type of field, you can type more than 255 characters. When saved, only 255 characters will be saved for that field.

Summary

In this chapter, we have seen how to build a product catalog for our VirtueMart shop. First, we explored adding manufacturers, vendors, and product categories. We then moved to adding products into different categories. We saw how a basic product looks in the shop frontend. Later, we saw more advanced features of product catalog management. We saw how to use product attributes with products. There are two types of product attributes—general attributes and attributes used for controlling inventory. We learned how to add simple attributes, and how to maintain product inventory through the use of advanced attributes and parent-child product relationships. At the end, we examined a more advanced feature of using product types with products. We saw how to create a product type, add parameters to a product type, assign a product type to a product, and update product type information for each product.

Now, after building our product catalog, the shop has taken shape. It is the time for customers to browse the products and buy what they like. Therefore, in the next chapter, our focus will be on managing customers and orders.

5
Managing Customers and Orders

So far, we have seen how to configure a store and build a product catalog. When our product catalog is ready, it is time to test the user registration and order management functionalities. In this chapter, we are going to discuss how to manage customers and orders. On completion of this chapter, you will be able to:

- Configure the user registration settings for VirtueMart
- Manage users for a VirtueMart shop
- Create and manage fields for a customer registration form
- Create and manage user groups
- Create and use order status types
- View order statistics
- View details of an order
- Update an order
- Manage inventory

Note that all VirtueMart customers must be registered with Joomla!. However, not all Joomla! users need to be the VirtueMart customers. Within the first few sections of this chapter, you will have a clear concept about user management in Joomla! and VirtueMart.

Customer management

Customer management in VirtueMart includes registering customers to the VirtueMart shop, assigning them to user groups for appropriate permission levels, managing fields in the registration form, viewing and editing customer information, and managing the user groups. Let's dive in to these activities in the following sections.

Registration/Authentication of customers

Joomla! has a very strong user registration and authentication system. One core component in Joomla! is `com_users`, which manages user registration and authentication in Joomla!. However, VirtueMart needs some extra information for customers. VirtueMart collects this information through its own customer registration process, and stores the information in separate tables in the database. The extra information required by VirtueMart is stored in a table named `jos_vm_user_info`, which is related to the `jos_users` table by the user id field. Usually, when a user registers to the Joomla! site, they also register with VirtueMart. This depends on some global settings. In the following sections, we are going to learn how to enable the user registration and authentication for VirtueMart.

Revisiting registration settings

If you remember, we discussed the global settings for user registration in VirtueMart, in Chapter 3, *Configuring the VirtueMart Shop*. For convenience, we are going to recap the global configuration settings for user registration in the VirtueMart store.

We configure it from VirtueMart's administration panel **Admin | Configuration | Global** screen. There is a section titled **User Registration Settings**, which defines how the user registration will be handled:

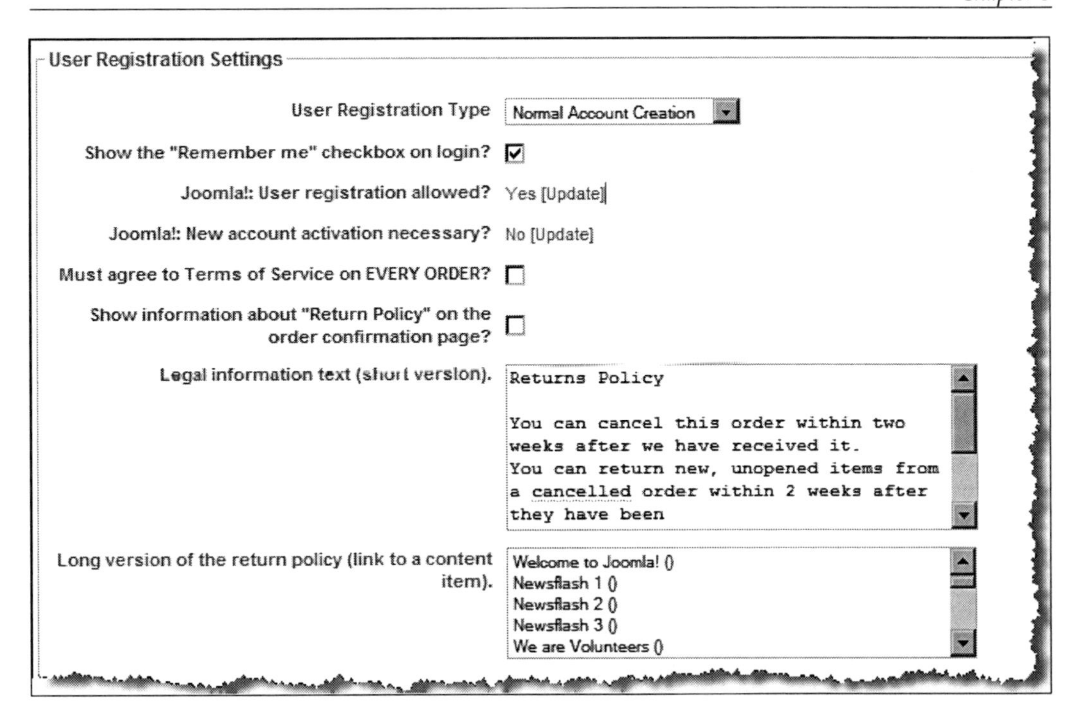

Ensure that your VirtueMart shop has been configured as shown in the screenshot above. The first field to configure is the **User Registration Type**. Selecting **Normal Account Creation** in this field creates both a Joomla! and VirtueMart account during user registration. For our example shop, we will be using this setting.

In Chapter 3, we also warned that Joomla!'s new user activation should be disabled when we are using VirtueMart. That means the **Joomla! New account activation necessary?** field should read **No**.

Enabling VirtueMart login module

There is a default module in Joomla! which is used for user registrations and login. When we are using this default **Login Form** (**mod_login** module), it does not collect information required by VirtueMart, and does not create customers in VirtueMart. By default, when published, the **mod_login** module looks like the following screenshot.

As you see, registered users can log in to Joomla! through this form, recover their forgotten password by clicking on the **Forgot your password?** link, and create a new user account by clicking on the **Create an account** link. When a user clicks on the **Create an account** link, they get the form as shown in the following screenshot:

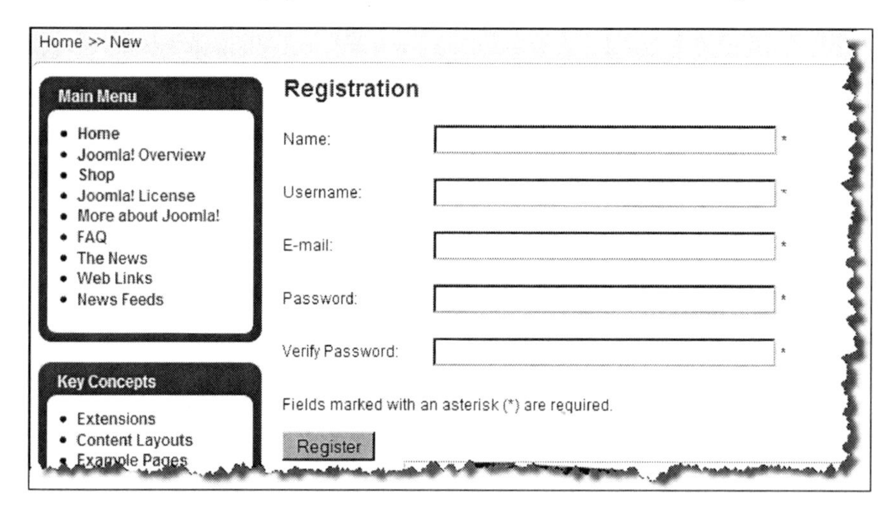

We see that normal registration in Joomla! only requires four pieces of information: **Name**, **Username**, **Email**, and **Password**. It does not collect information needed in VirtueMart, such as billing and shipping address, to be a customer. Therefore, we need to disable the **mod_login** module and enable the **mod_virtuemart_login** module. We have already learned how to enable and disable a module in Joomla!. We have also learned how to install modules. If you followed the instructions from Chapter 2 and installed all of the VirtueMart modules, you will find it from Joomla! control panel by clicking on **Extensions | Module Manager**:

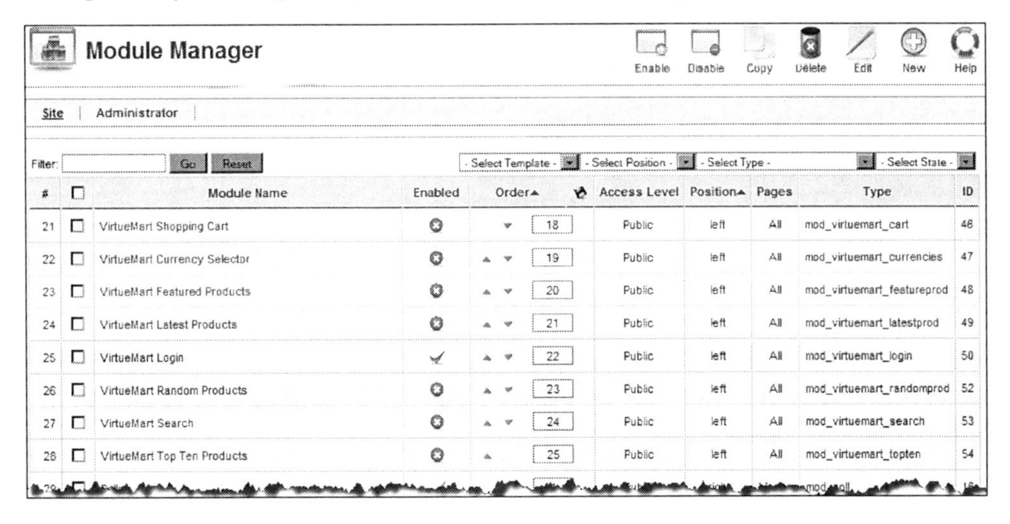

By default, the **mod_virtuemart_login** module's title is **VirtueMart Login**. You may prefer to show this title as **Login** only. In that case, click on the **VirtueMart Login** link in the **Module Name** column. This brings the **Module: [Edit]** screen:

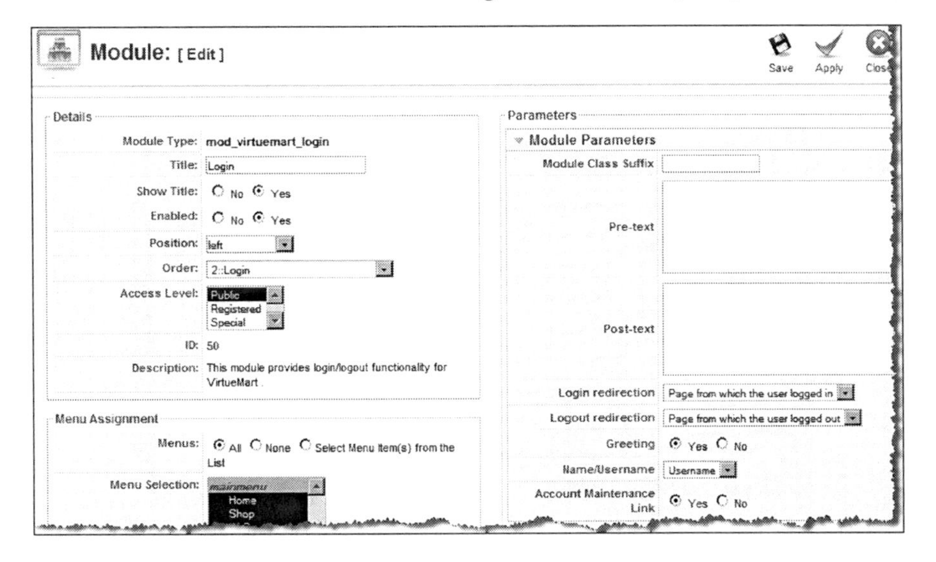

In the **Title** field, type **Login** (or any other text you want to show as the title of this module). Make sure the module is enabled and position is set to left or right. Click on the **Save** icon to save your settings. Now, browse to your site's front-page (for example, `http://localhost/bdosn/`), and you will see the login form as shown in the following screenshot:

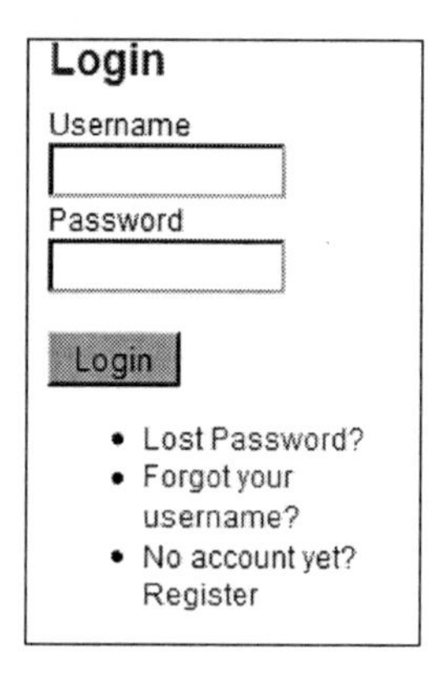

As you can see, this module has the same functionalities as we saw in the **mod_login** module of Joomla!. Let us test the account creation in this module. Click on the **Register** link. It brings the following screen:

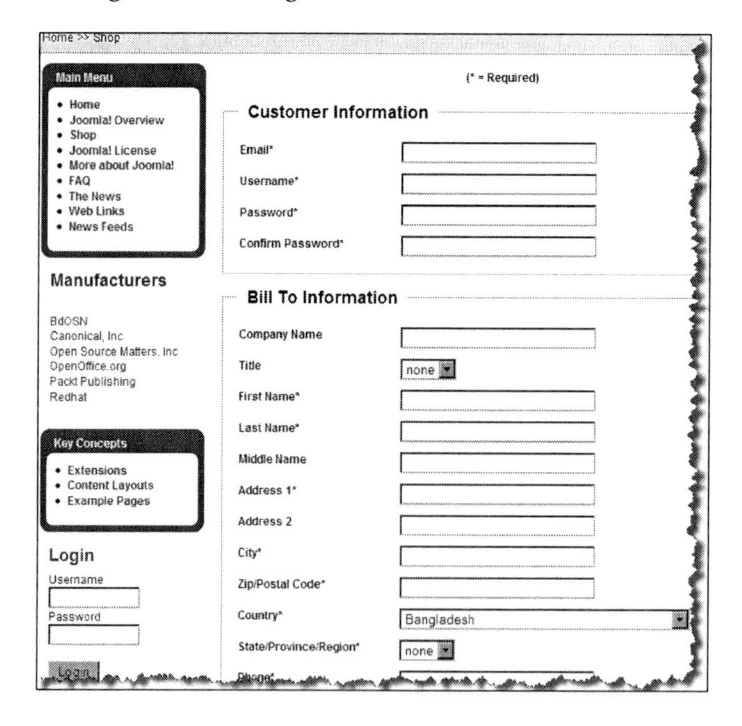

The registration form has three main sections: **Customer Information**, **Bill To Information**, and **Send Registration**. At the end, there is the **Send Registration** button for submitting the form data. In the **Customer Information** section, type your email address, the desired username, and password. Confirm the password by typing it again in the **Confirm password** field. In the **Bill To Information** section, type the address details where bills are to be sent. In the entire form, required fields are marked with an asterisk (*). You must provide information for these required fields.

In the **Send Registration** section, you need to agree to the **Terms of Service**. Click on the **Terms of Service** link to read it. Then, check the **I agree to the Terms of Service** checkbox and click on the **Send Registration** button to submit the form data:

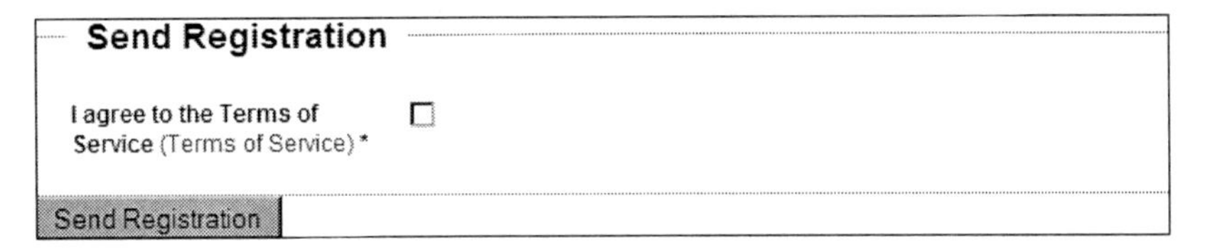

If you have provided all of the required information and submitted a unique email address, the registration will be successful. On successful completion of registration, you get the following screen notification, and will be logged in to the shop automatically:

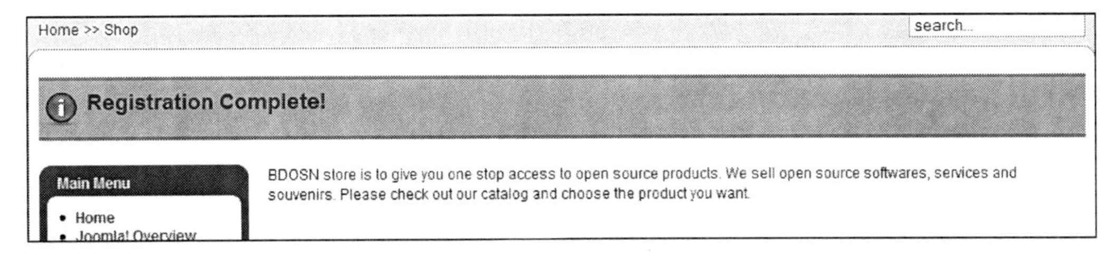

If you scroll down to the **Login** module, you will see that you are logged in and greeted by the store. You also see the **User Menu** in this screen:

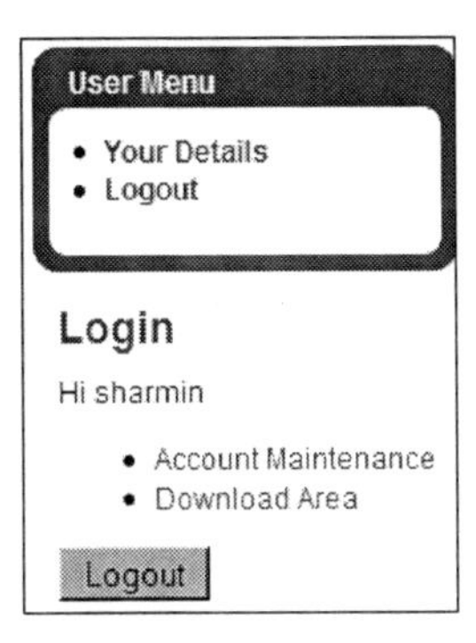

Both the **User Menu** and the **Login** modules contain a **Logout** button. Click on either of these buttons to log out from the Joomla! site. In fact, links in the **User Menu** module are for Joomla! only. Let us try the link **Your Details**. Click on the **Your Details** link, and you will see the information shown in the following screenshot:

As you see in the screenshot above, you can change your full name, email, password, frontend language, and time zone. You cannot view any information regarding billing address, or other information of the customer. In fact, this information is for regular Joomla! users. We can only get full customer information by clicking on the **Account Maintenance** link in the **Login** module. Let us try it. Click on the **Account Maintenance** link, and it shows the following screenshot:

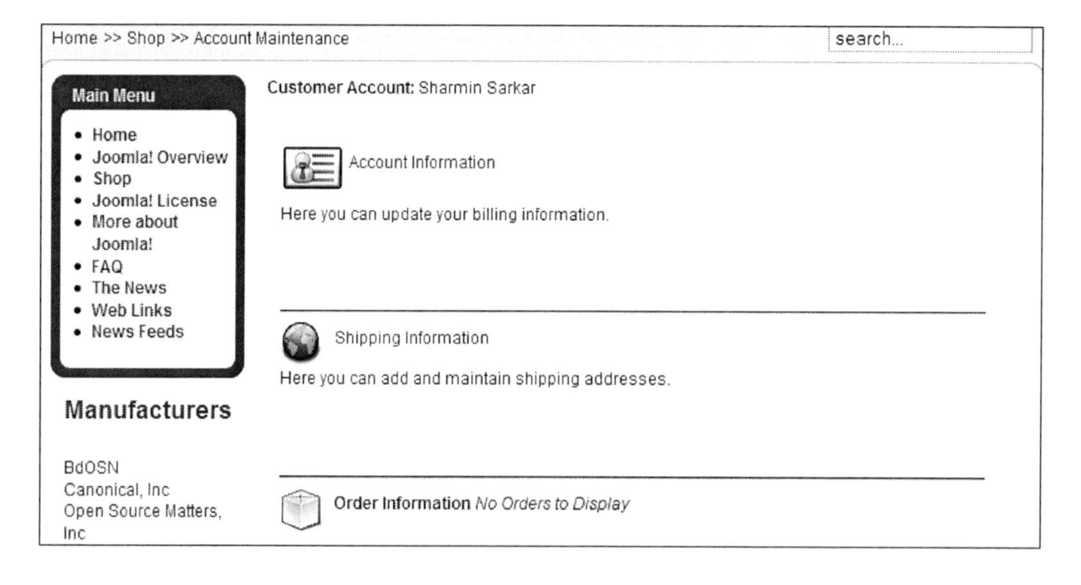

The **Account Maintenance** screen has three sections: **Account Information**, **Shipping Information**, and **Order Information**. Click on the **Account Information** link to see what happens. It shows the following screen:

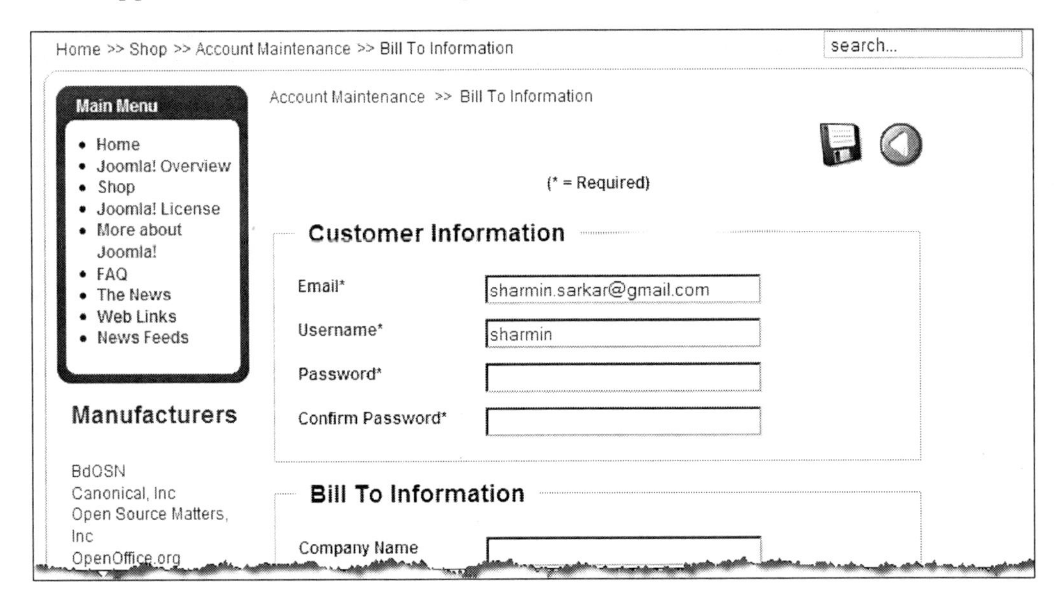

This shows Customer Information and Bill To Information, which have been entered during user registration. The last section on this screen is the **Bank Information**, from where the customer can add bank account information. This section looks like the following screenshot:

Bank Account Info

Account Holder

Account Number

Bank sorting code numb

Bank Name

Bank Account Type — Business Checking

IBAN

Save

As you can see, from the **Bank Account Info** section, the customers can enter their bank account information including the account holder's name, account number, bank's sorting code number, bank's name, account type, and IBAN (International Bank Account Number). Entering this information is important when you are using a Bank Account Debit payment method.

Now, let us go back to the **Account Maintenance** screen and see the other sections. Click on the **Shipping Information** link, and you get the following screen:

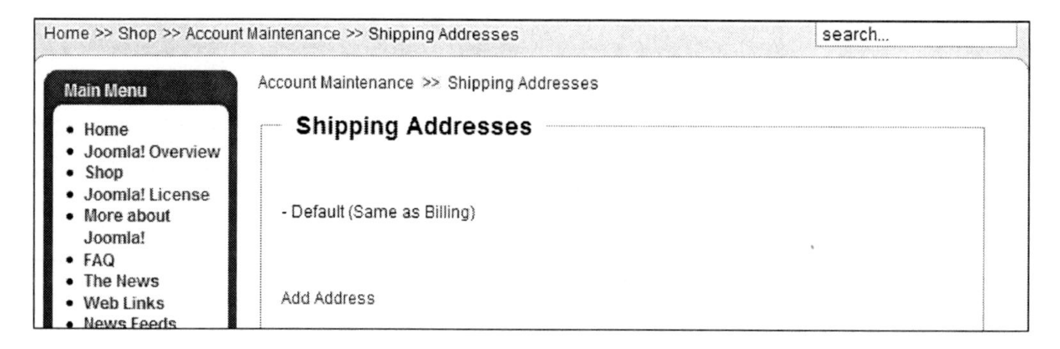

There is one default shipping address, which is the same as the billing address. The customers can create additional shipping addresses. For creating a new shipping address, click on the **Add Address** link. It shows the following screen:

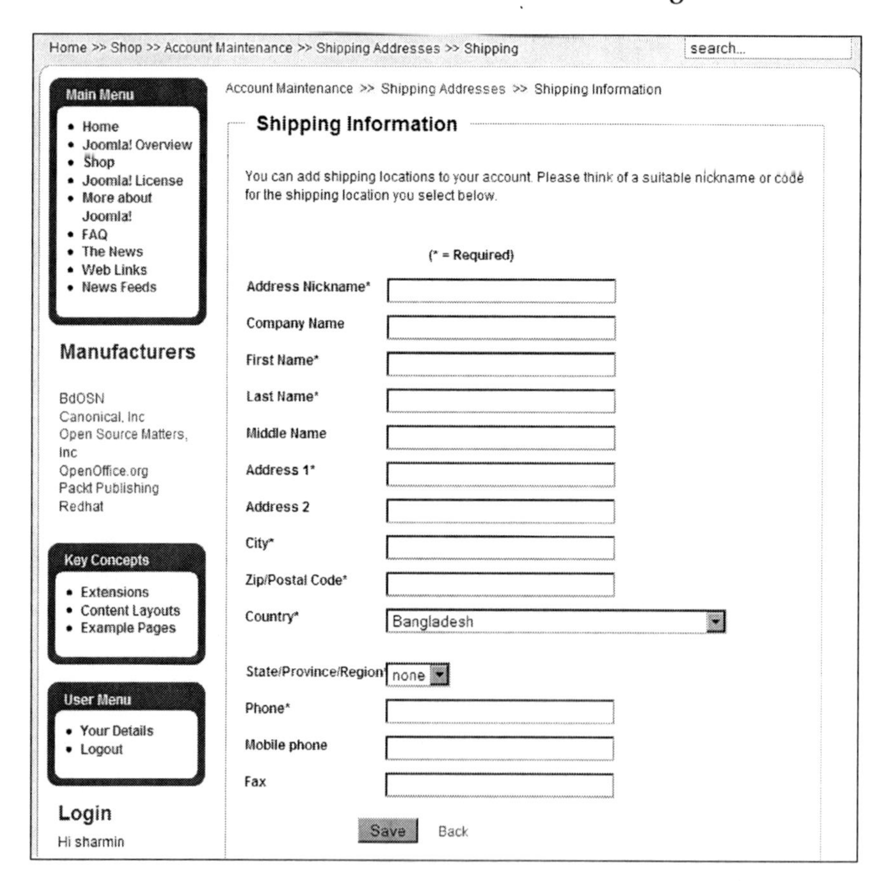

As you see in the above screenshot, customers can add shipping address information. Mandatory fields are marked with an asterisk (*), and must be filled in. The customer also needs to provide a nickname for the address, which will be displayed for selecting the shipping address during checkout. After filling in the form, save it by clicking on the **Save** button.

Now, let us again move to the **Account Maintenance** page. For a new customer, the order information section will not show any orders. When the customer places some orders, this section will look like the following screenshot:

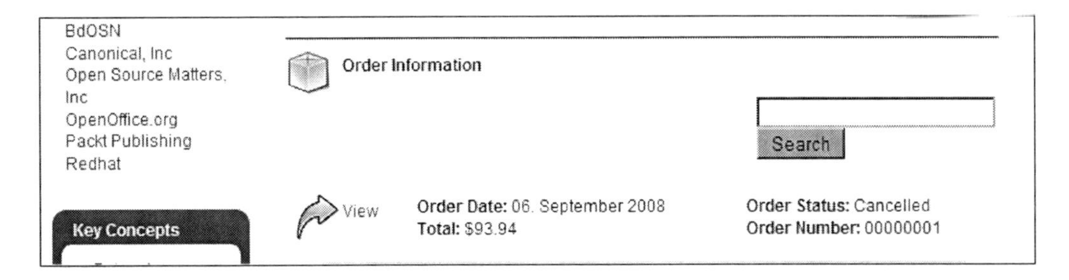

To see the details of a particular order, click on the **View** link. This opens up details of the purchase order. The first part of the purchase order looks like the following screenshot:

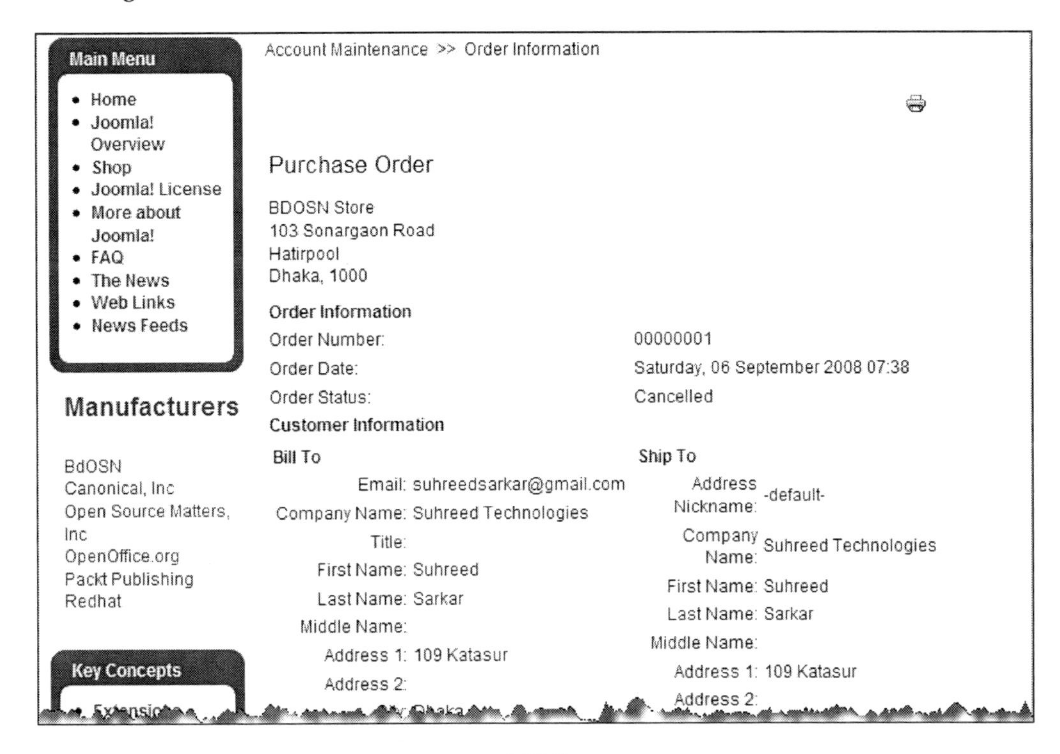

The first part of the **Purchase Order** contains the store's address, order information like order number, order date, and its status. It also contains the customer's information including the **Bill To** and **Ship To** addresses.

The second part of the **Purchase order** contains shipping information, a list of order items, total price, shipping and handling fee, taxes, and payment information. This part looks like the following screenshot:

Login

Hi suhreed

- Account Maintenance
- Download Area

Logout

Shipping Information

Carrier	Shipping Mode	Price
5	BGD	$20.00

Order Items

Qty	Name	SKU	Price	Total
1	Men's Joomla! Sport Shirt Size: Small (- $2.00)	TS0002	$26.95	$26.95
1	Building Websites with Joomla! 1.5	BK0001	$44.99	$44.99

SubTotal :	$71.94
Shipping and Handling Fee :	$20.00
Fee:	+ $2.00
Total:	**$93.94**
Tax Total :	$0.00

Payment Information

Payment Method : Cash On Delivery

Customers can view purchase orders they have placed, but cannot modify those purchase orders.

When you enable the **VirtueMart Login** module, it is wise to disable the **User Menu** module of Joomla!. We have seen that account details provided by the link in the **User Menu** do not show customer information. Therefore, it is recommended that you disable the **User Menu** and the **Login** modules of Joomla! and keep the **VirtueMart Login** module enabled.

Managing fields for user registration form

In the previous section, we saw how customers can register to a VirtueMart shop. To enable registration and login of customers, we have disabled Joomla!'s **Login Form** module, and enabled the **VirtueMart Login** module. When registering through the **Register** link provided by the **VirtueMart Login** module, customers get some extra fields which are used for the shop's purpose such as billing and shipping to addresses. VirtueMart gives us the flexibility to define additional fields for the form, and also decide which fields will be shown in which page—registration, account information, and so on.

For managing the fields in user registration form, go to the VirtueMart administration panel and click on **Admin | Manage User Fields**. This shows the list of user fields currently used:

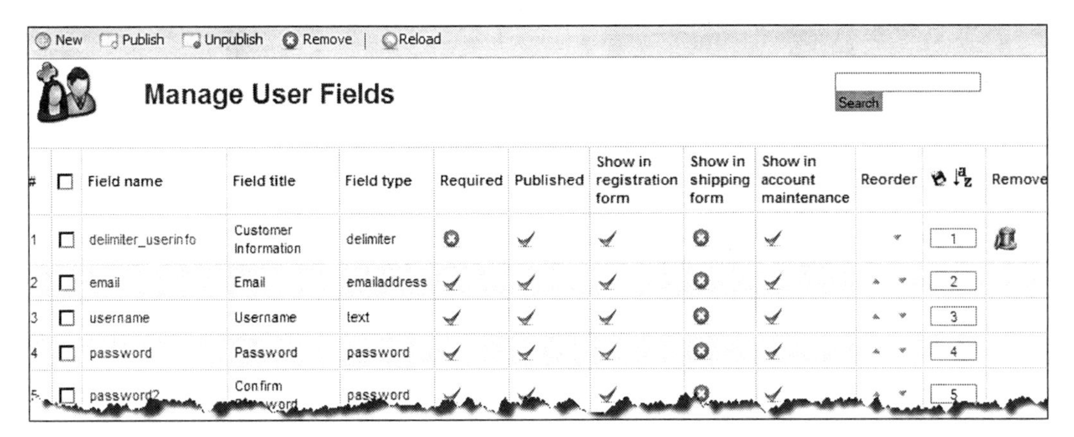

The **Manage User Fields** screen lists the available fields for the registration form. This list indicates what type of fields these are, whether any field is required or not, its published or unpublished status, and in which forms the fields will be displayed. Note the **Show in registration form**, **Show in shipping form**, and **Show in account maintenance** columns. A checkbox in these columns against any field indicates that the field will be available in that form (registration, shipping, or account maintenance). You can also reorder the fields from the **Reorder** column by clicking the up or down arrow icon. Another way to reorder the fields is to type the order number and then saving it by clicking on the **Save** icon ( ). Clicking the **a-z** ( ) icon reorders the fields alphabetically. Also note the trash ( ) icon in the **Remove** column is available only for the fields which are a non-system field, that is, either a delimiter or a custom field.

Adding a new field

As an administrator of the VirtueMart shop, you can add a new field to the customer registration form from the **Manage User Fields** screen. To add a new field, click on the **New** button. This shows the **Add/Edit User Fields** screen:

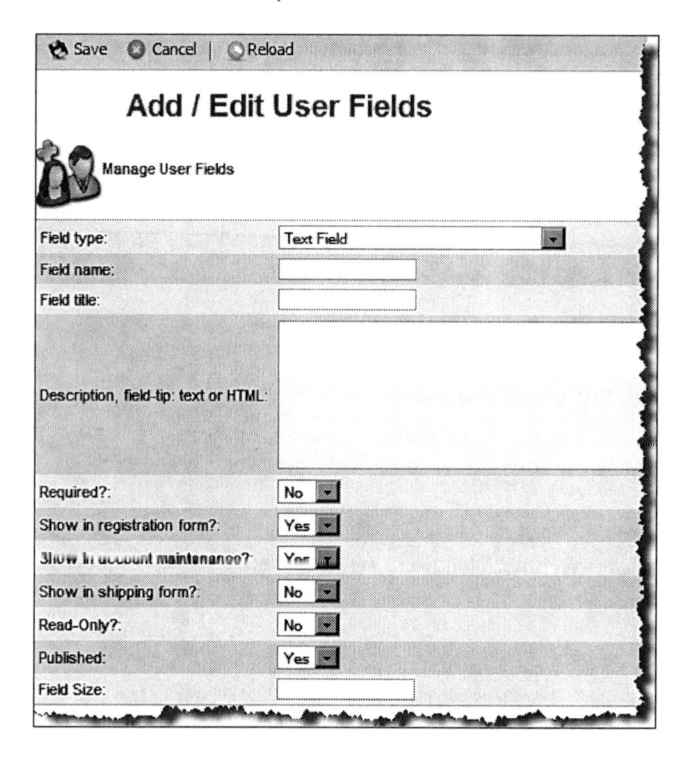

The first field in the **Add/Edit User Fields** screen is **Field type**. You need to specify what type of field you are going to add. Then, provide a name for the field in the **Field name** text box. This name is for internal use only and will not be displayed. Type the label for this field in the **Field title** box, which will be displayed in the form. In the **Description, field-tip** text area, type the description of the field which will be shown as a tooltip in the form. Select **Yes** or **No** in the **Required?** field to indicate whether the user must provide a value for this field or not. As you can see, you can also select in which forms (for example, registration, account maintenance, and shipping) the field will be displayed. When you select **Yes** in the **Read-Only** field, users cannot change the value for that field. In the **Published** field, select **Yes** to publish that. For the **Text Field**, you can specify a **Field Size** which will be the size of the text box.

As you can see from the **Manage User Fields**, most of the fields necessary to collect customer information are available by default. However, sometimes you may need to add some extra fields. Let us see in the following sections how we can create different types of fields.

Text field

This type of field allows up to 255 characters to be added. This is suitable for short text information, such as a username, first name, last name, and so on. Most of the fields available in the VirtueMart user registration form are of this type. For adding such fields, click on the **New** button in the **Manage User Fields** screen. This brings the **Add/Edit User Fields** screen. Select **Text Field** in the **Field type** drop-down list. Then, fill in the other fields as shown in the following screenshot:

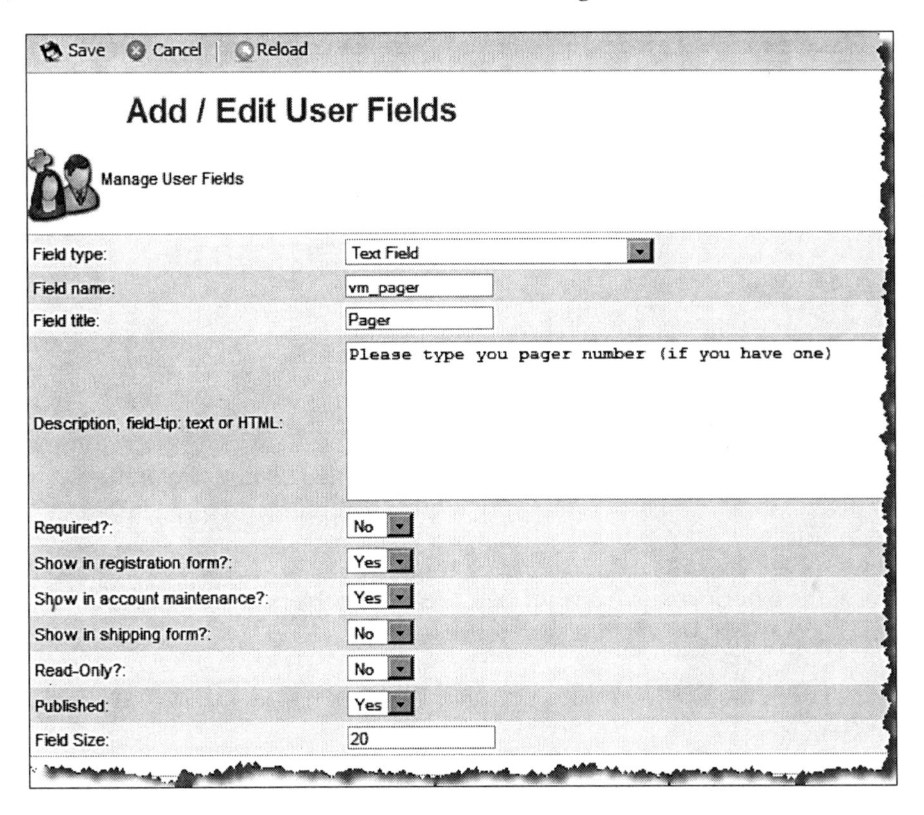

When finished providing all information, click on the **Save** icon, and go back to the **Manage User Fields** screen. Now, reorder the fields and position the field where you want it to show. To see how this field looks, go to store frontend and click on the **Register** link in the **Login** module. That will show the registration form and in that form, you see the field as shown in the following screenshot:

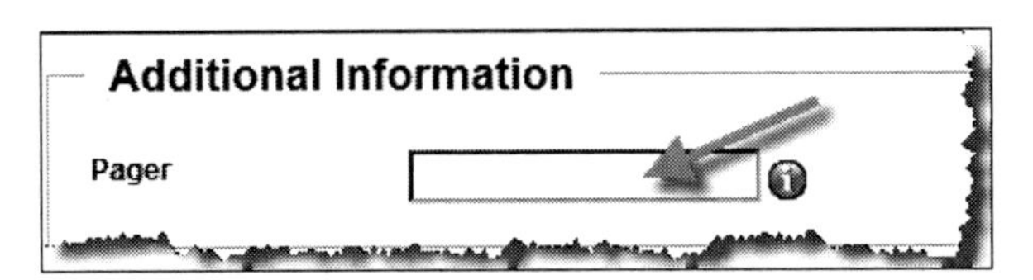

As you can see, the **Pager** field is added to the form. Hover your mouse pointer over the info icon (ⓘ) besides the field. It shows the text you typed in the **Description, field-tip** field during the creation of this field.

Checkbox (Single)

This type of field shows a single checkbox, which can be checked or unchecked by the users. Use this type for fields such as terms of agreement, where users need to agree by checking the checkbox. For creating such fields, follow the same procedure as creating a **Text Field**, but choose the **Checkbox (Single)** in the **Field type** drop-down list. Fields of this type look like the one shown in the following screenshot:

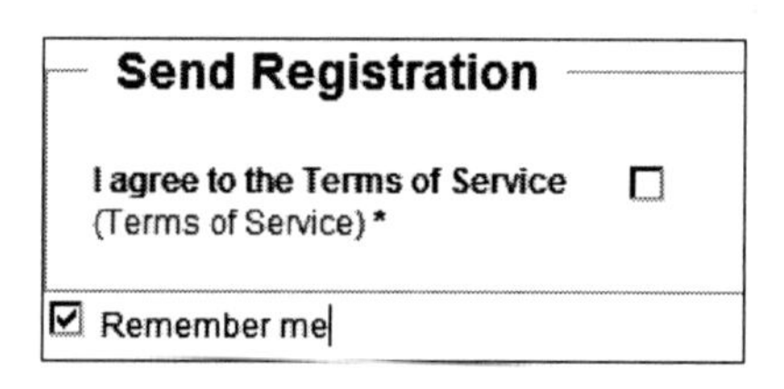

Checkbox (Multiple)

Fields of this type show multiple checkboxes from where users to check multiple options. Use this type for fields where you want to collect some preferences. For example, you may create a field to know the customer's preferences for product categories.

For creating the **Checkbox (Multiple)** field, select this from the **Field type** drop-down list on the **Add/Edit User Fields** screen:

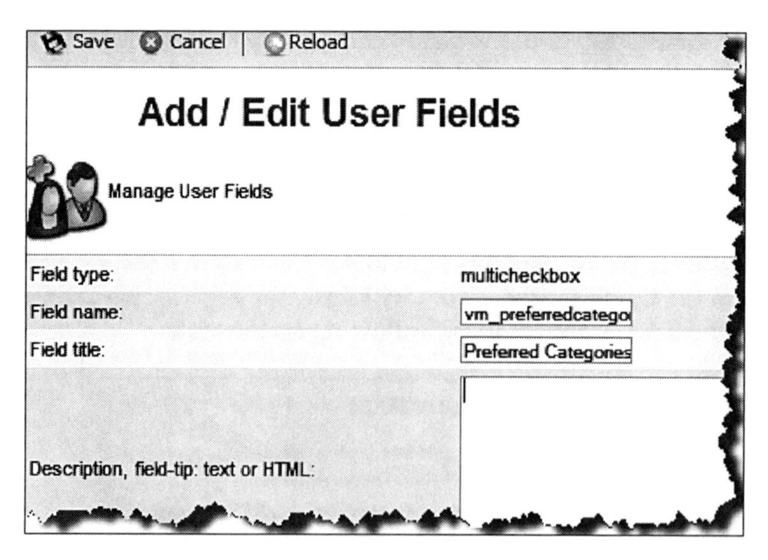

All other fields are same as adding the **Text Field**. However, at the end of the form, you need to define the options and values. Click on the **Add a Value** button to add new option title and values. This will show two columns, where you can type a **Title** and **Value** for the option. Add as many options as you want:

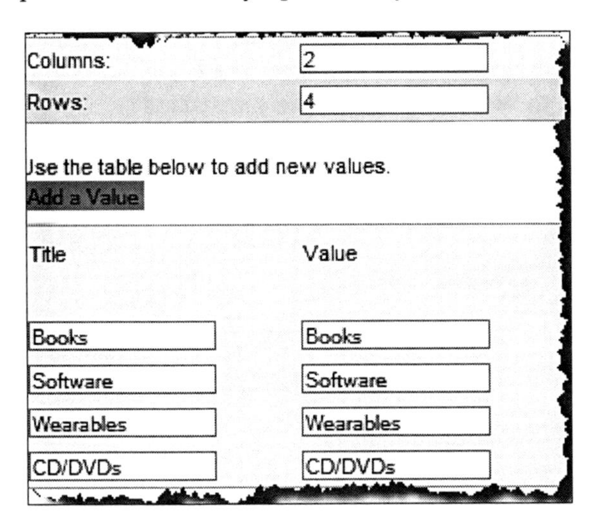

When entering values for all fields is done, click on the **Save** button. Then, go back to the **Manage User Fields** screen, and reorder the field to show it in preferred order. The field you have created will look like the screenshot below:

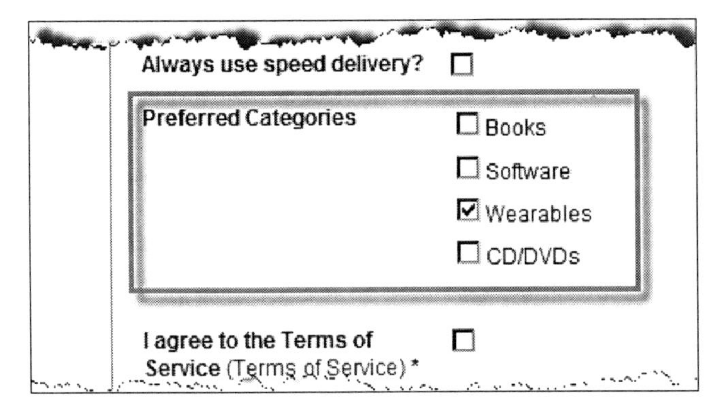

Date

This type is to show a field for entering date with a date picker. In the same way as with the other field types, you can create this type of field by choosing **Date** in the **Field type** drop-down list in the **Add/Edit User Fields** screen. All other information is the same as other types of fields. For example, we want to collect information on a customer's date of birth. In that case, we need to add a field of the **Date** type. Let us configure the field as shown in the following screenshot:

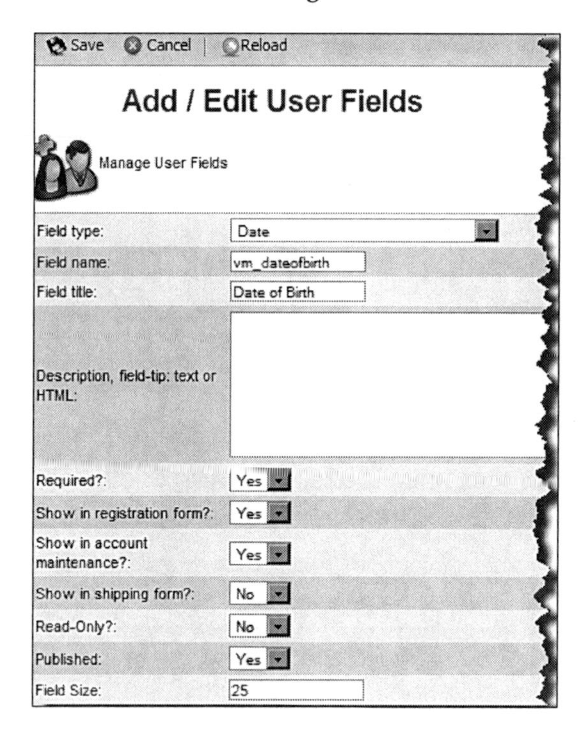

Save the field by clicking on the **Save** icon in the toolbar. Then, go back to the **Manage User Fields** screen and reorder the fields so that our new field shows after the password confirmation field. Now, go to the user registration form to see the result. It will look like following screenshot:

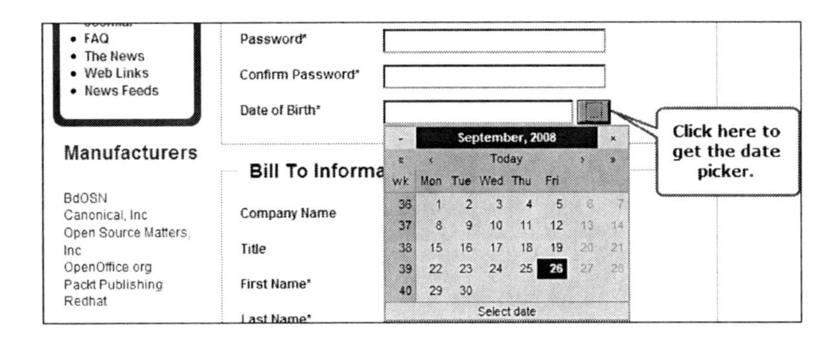

The **Date of Birth** field is marked with an asterisk (*) to indicate that users must enter a value for this field. This happened as we selected **Yes** in the **Required** drop-down list while creating the field.

Age verification (date select fields)

Fields of this type provide a drop-down list for selecting a month, day, and year to indicate a date of birth. While creating a field of this type, the administrator can set a minimum age for registration. Selecting the date from a field of this type, and submitting the form, will automatically calculate the user's age and notify whether he or she is eligible for registration or not. For some sites, registration is restricted to adults only (for example, 18+ years old). Adding a field of this type can help ensure implementing the restriction policy. To enforce such a policy, let us create a field of this type with the configurations shown in the following screenshot:

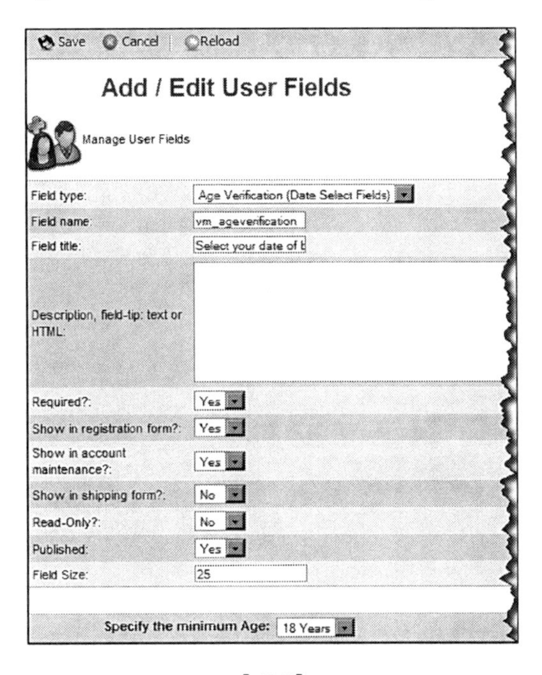

As you can see, we have made this field mandatory by selecting **Yes** in the **Required** drop-down list. The minimum age for registration is set to **18 years** in the **Specify the minimum age** drop-down list. In the registration form, this field will look like the following:

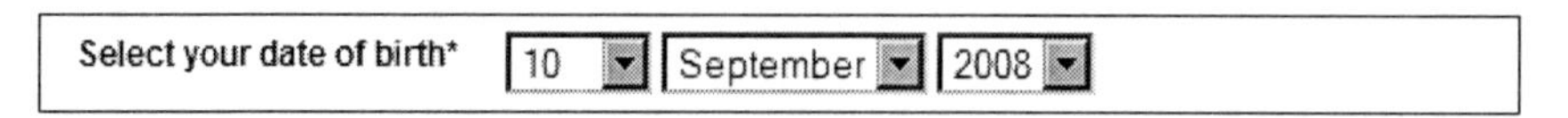

As per the condition of this field, anyone who wants to register must be aged 18 years or above. Let us see how it works. In the registration form, fill in all the required fields and select "10 September 2008" in the **Select your date of birth** field. Then, submit the form for registration. What do you see? It throws a JavaScript error message as shown below:

Click on the **OK** button, and you see the registration form with the information you provided. Scroll down and you find that the **Select your date of birth** field is marked in red color to indicate error in value provided for this field:

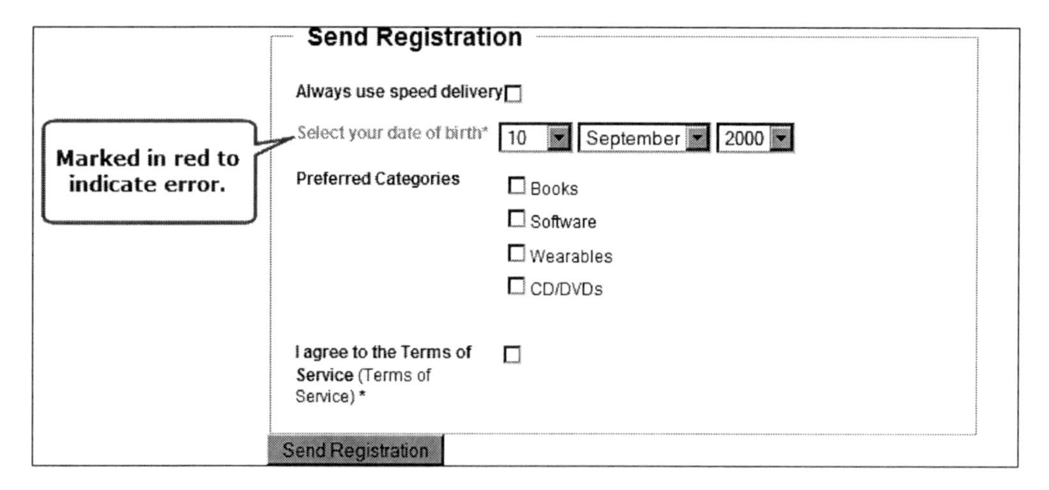

Now, select the birth date as "10 September 1985", and click on the **Send Registration** button. Voila! It works! You are now registered, because the date of birth indicates that your age is more than 18 years.

Drop Down (Single Select)

Fields of this type show a drop-down list with some options to select, from where users can select only one option. For example, you want to collect information on the user's sex (male or female). In that case, you can create a field with the configurations shown in the following screenshot:

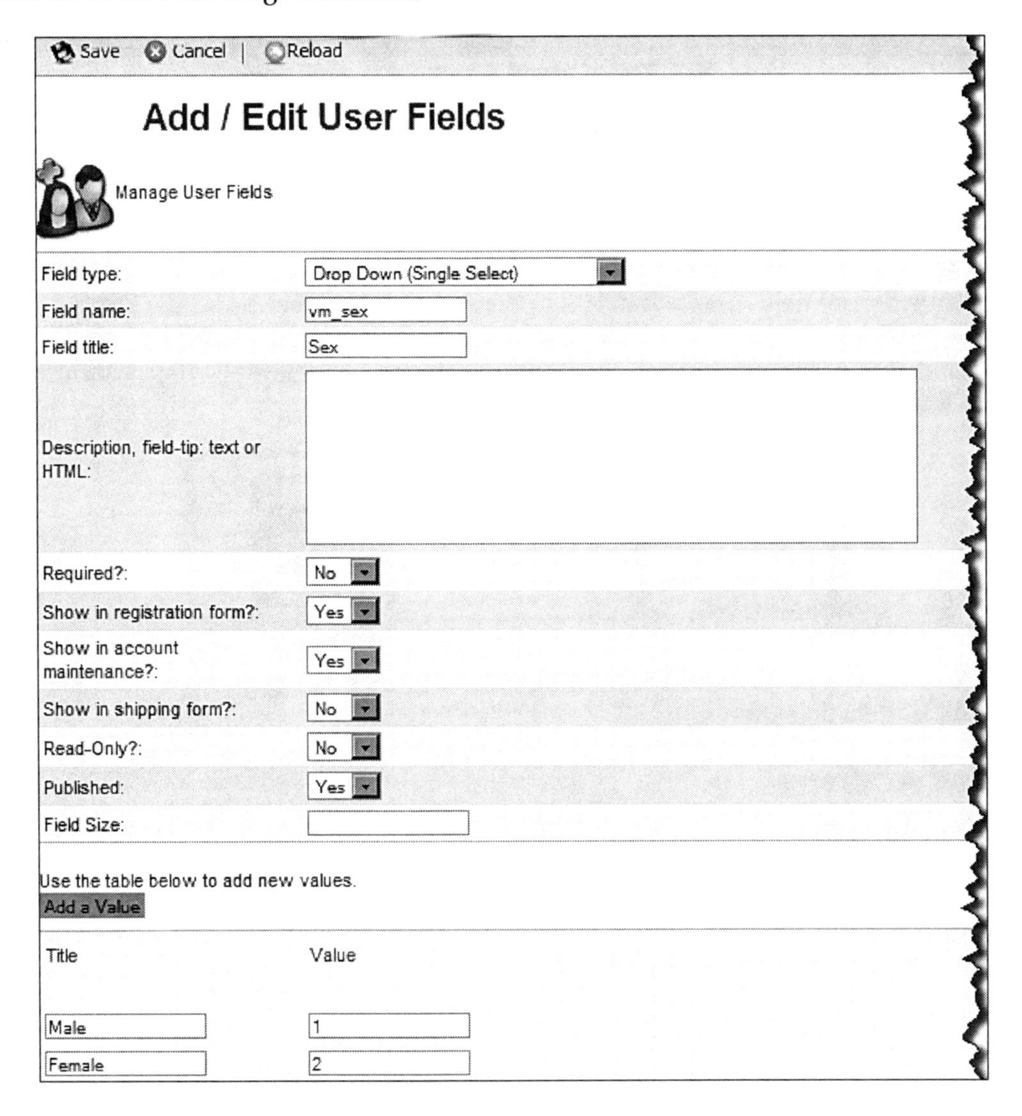

Save the field, and from the **Manage User Fields** screen, reorder the field to show after the **Date of Birth** field. Now, on the frontend, click the **Register** link in the **Login** module. That shows the registration form. In the registration form, the drop-down field we have created will look like the following screenshot:

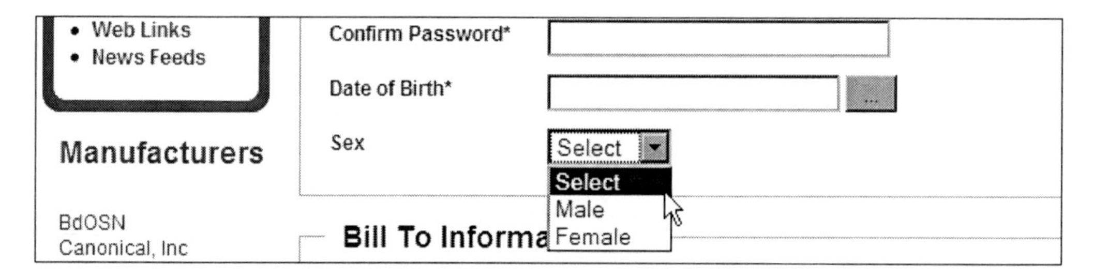

Drop Down (Multiple Select)

Fields of this type show a multiple-select combo box from where users can select multiple options. In the previous example of creating the **Checkbox (Multiple)**, we saw that users can select multiple options. Let us convert that into the **Drop Down (Multiple Select)** field. Create the field in the same process, but select the **Drop Down (Multiple Select)** in the **Field type** drop-down list in the **Add/Edit User Fields** screen. At the bottom, add the same option-value pairs. In the registration form, this field will look like the following:

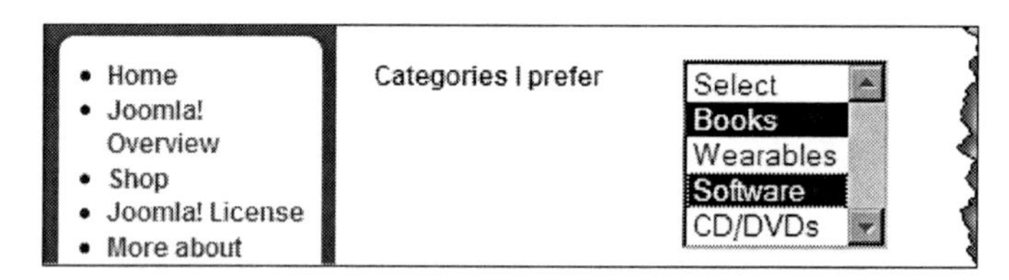

In fields of this type, you can select multiple options by holding down the *Ctrl* key and clicking on the options.

Email Address

Fields of this type are similar to text fields. The difference between the **Text Field** and **Email Address** types is that the latter has built-in validation criteria for ensuring an email address pattern. By default, there is one email address type field in the user registration form. You may want to add another email address field, for collecting an alternative email address, using this type.

EU VAT ID

While doing business with European Union (EU) countries, you need a valid **Value Added Tax (VAT)** ID. Customers who are from EU countries may use their EU VAT ID, if you add a field of this type and collect that information. When you define a field of this type, you can also configure which shopper group the customer will be moved to after successfully validating of his or her VAT ID. For example, we may create a shopper group named EU Wholesale, and add all the customers to this shopper group upon successful validation of their EU VAT ID.

For creating the **EU VAT ID** field, follow the similar steps for other types of fields. In the **Add/Edit User Fields** screen, configure the fields as shown in the following screenshot:

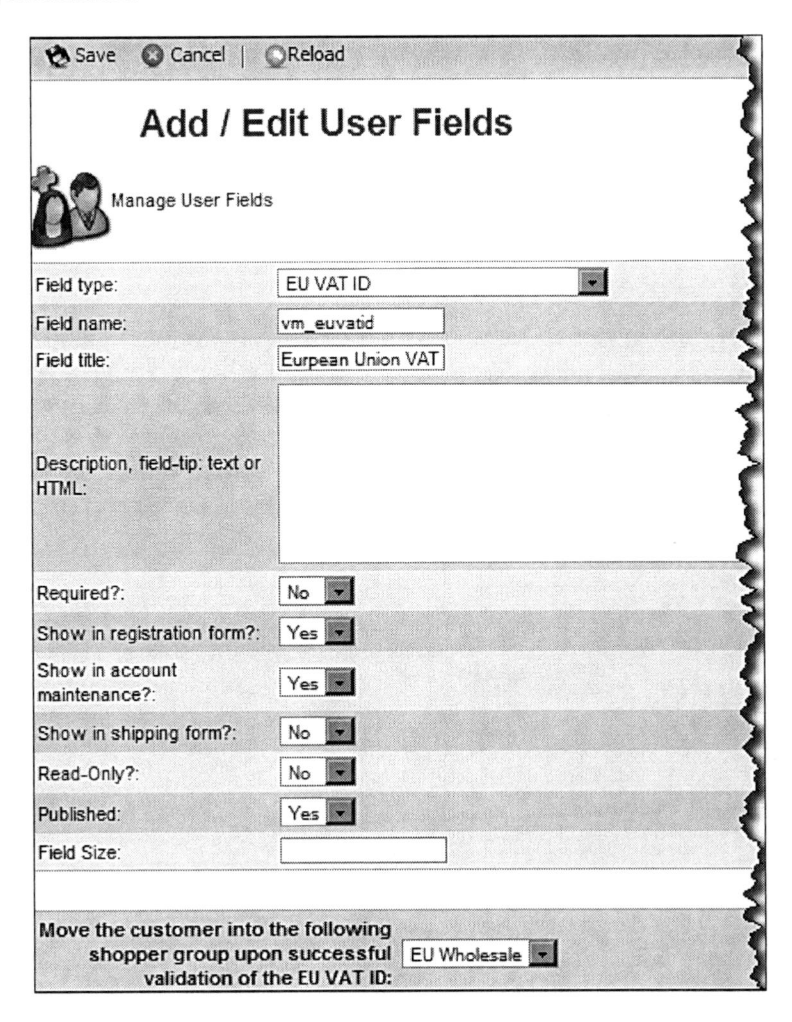

As you can see, we have selected the **EU Wholesale** shopper group where customers will be moved upon successfully validating their EU VAT ID. The field we created now, will be displayed in the user registration and account maintenance form same as text input field:

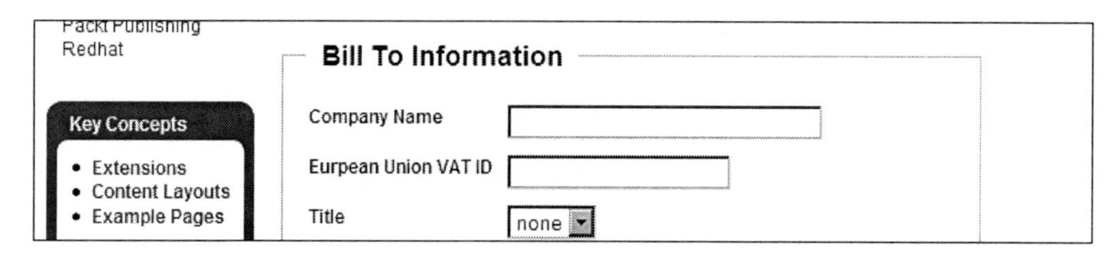

When customers enter their EU VAT ID in the **Eurpoean Union VAT ID** field, and along with other information submits the form for registration, VirtueMart connects to the online database at `http://ec.europa.eu/taxation_customs/vies/api/checkVatPort?wsdl` and verifies the validity of the VAT ID provided by the customer. If it finds the VAT ID invalid, the customer will not be registered, or the VAT ID information will not be saved and an error message will be displayed. This type of field should remain optional, as not all customers will have EU VAT IDs.

Editor text area

Fields of this type are in fact a text area with the rich text editor enabled. Creating such fields may help you collect descriptive information with rich text. For example, we create a text area with the rich text editor where the customers may write something about themselves, with fancy formatting, color, bullets, and links.
For creating a field of this type, just select **Editor Text Area** from the **Field type** drop-down list in the **Add/Edit User Fields** screen. Once created and published, the field will look like the following:

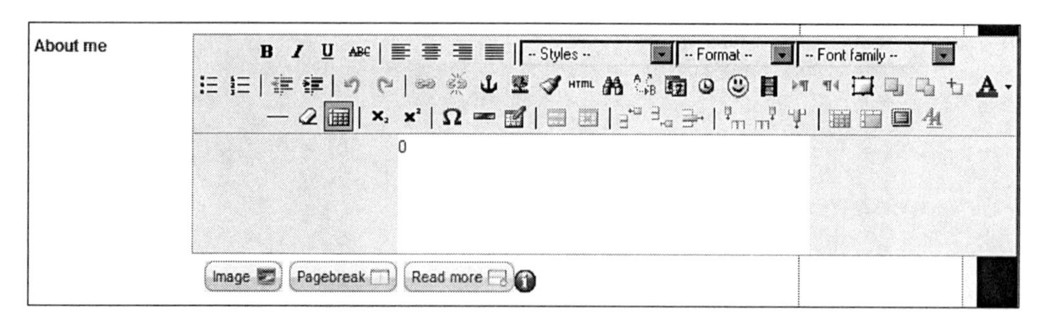

Text area

Fields of this type are a simple text area where customers can enter ample descriptive information. This does not show the rich text editor in the text area. For creating such field, select **Text Area** as the field type and specify other information. At the end of the **Add/Edit User Fields** screen, specify the **Columns** and **Rows** (for example, 40 and 10, respectively). Once saved and published, the field will look like the following screenshot:

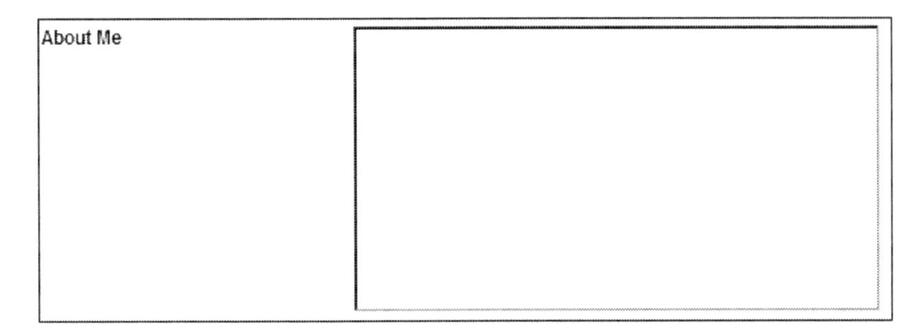

You can make this text area smaller or larger by changing the values in the **Columns** and **Widths** fields in the **Add/Edit User Fields** screen.

Radio button

Fields of this type show radio buttons with options you provide allowing customers to check only one radio button. For example, we can add the **Sex** field using radio buttons. For creating such a field, select **Radio Button** from the **Field type** drop-down list in the **Add/Edit User Fields** screen. Enter other information, and at the end, add the option title and value pairs by clicking on the **Add a value** button. When saved and published, it looks like the following in the registration or account maintenance forms.

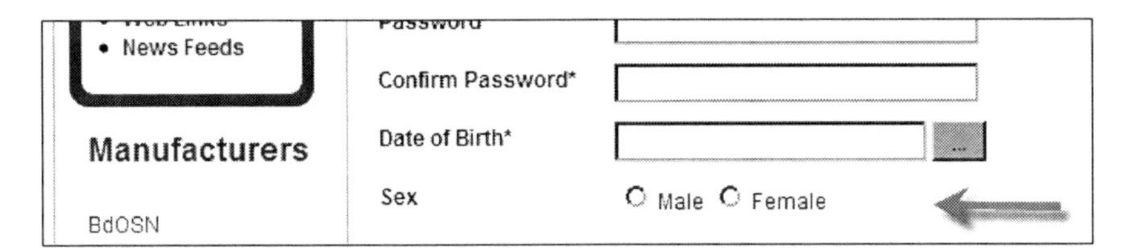

Sometimes, it is better to use a **Radio Button** instead of a **Drop Down (Single Select)**, especially when the options are limited. The benefit of using this is that the user can see all the options without clicking on the field. However, if there are many options (for example country field), then it is better to use a drop-down, otherwise it will be difficult to show all the options as radio buttons.

Web address

Fields of this type allow web addresses to be entered, and validates the input to ensure that these fields are in the URL format. In the **Add/Edit User Fields** screen, select **Web Address** as the field type and at the bottom, select the **URL Only** or the **Hypertext and URL** from the **Field type** drop-down list.

Fieldset delimiter

Fields of this type are used to group several fields and label that group. We have already seen that used. In the registration form, there are three groups of fields: **Customer Information**, **Bill To Information**, and **Send Registration**. You can create such a delimiter by selecting **===Fieldset Delimiter===** from the **Field type** drop-down list in the **Add/Edit User Fields** screen. You just need to provide a name and title for this field type:

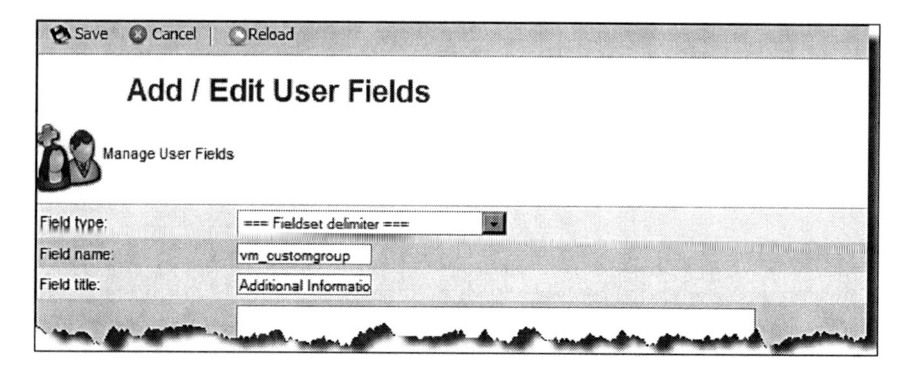

Once you have saved the field, go back to the **Manage User Fields** screen and reorder the field. Fields that are going to be under this group should be placed under the delimiter. As we have created some additional fields, we can group these under this delimiter. Then, the list looks like the following:

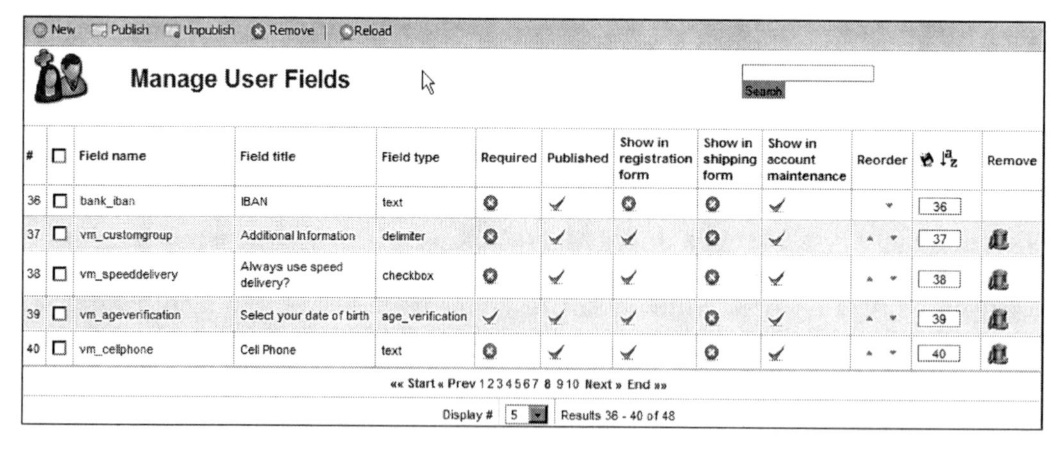

#		Field name	Field title	Field type	Required	Published	Show in registration form	Show in shipping form	Show in account maintenance	Reorder		Remove
36		bank_iban	IBAN	text							36	
37		vm_customgroup	Additional Information	delimiter							37	
38		vm_speeddelivery	Always use speed delivery?	checkbox							38	
39		vm_ageverification	Select your date of birth	age_verification							39	
40		vm_cellphone	Cell Phone	text							40	

«« Start « Prev 1 2 3 4 5 6 7 8 9 10 Next » End »»

Display # 5 Results 36 - 40 of 48

From here, you can see that under our new delimiter **vm_customgroup**, there are three fields. Now, go to the user registration page in the frontend, and you will see the group as shown:

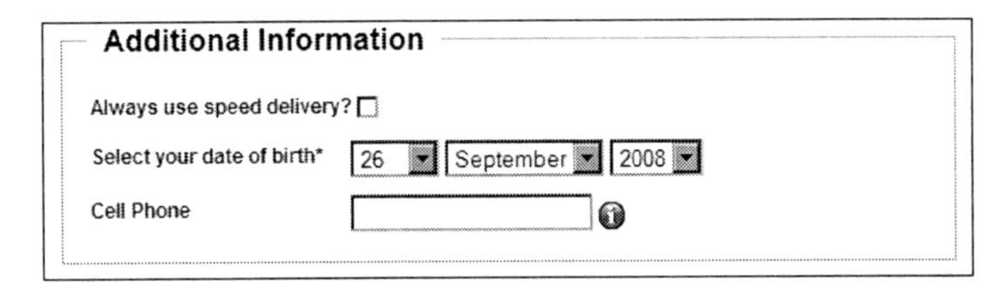

So far, we have discussed all the available field types. If you have installed components like Letterman, YANC, ANJEL, or CCNewletter, another field type for subscribing to newsletters will be available. We will discuss more on implementing newsletters in Chapter 7, *Promotion and Public Relations*.

Editing a field

From the **Manage User Fields** screen, you can edit a field. Just click on the **Field name** in the list and that opens the **Add/Edit User Fields** screen:

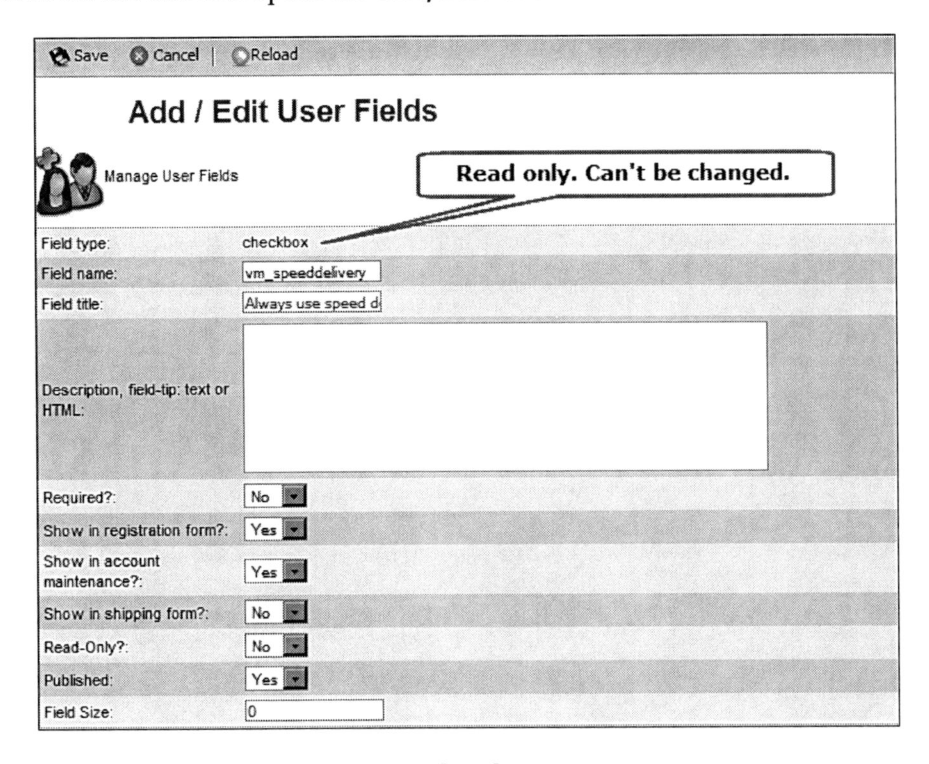

Although you can edit all of the information provided in the screen, you cannot change the field type. For example, a field created as a checkbox cannot be changed into a drop-down list or a text box. However, you may delete the field and create another field of your desired type. In that case, any data collected through the fields will be deleted.

> In creating additional fields, we have typed plain English in the **Field title** text box, which is displayed in the frontend as a label for that particular field. If you look into the built-in or system fields, you see the values in the **Field title** field are something like **PHPSHOP_*****. These language constants are defined in the language files for VirtueMart. These constants are required for localization of VirtueMart. Since we have not yet discussed language files or localization, we just typed English words. We are going to see details of VirtueMart localization and language files in Chapter 8, *Localization of VirtueMart*.

User manager

In Joomla!, there is one **User Manager** component from where you can manage the users of that site. However, for the VirtueMart component, there is another user manager which should be used for the VirtueMart shop. To be clear about the differences of these two user managers, let us look into both.

Joomla! user manager

Let us first try Joomla!'s user manager. Go to the Joomla! control panel and click on the **User Manager** icon or click on **Site | User Manager**. This brings the **User Manager** screen of Joomla!:

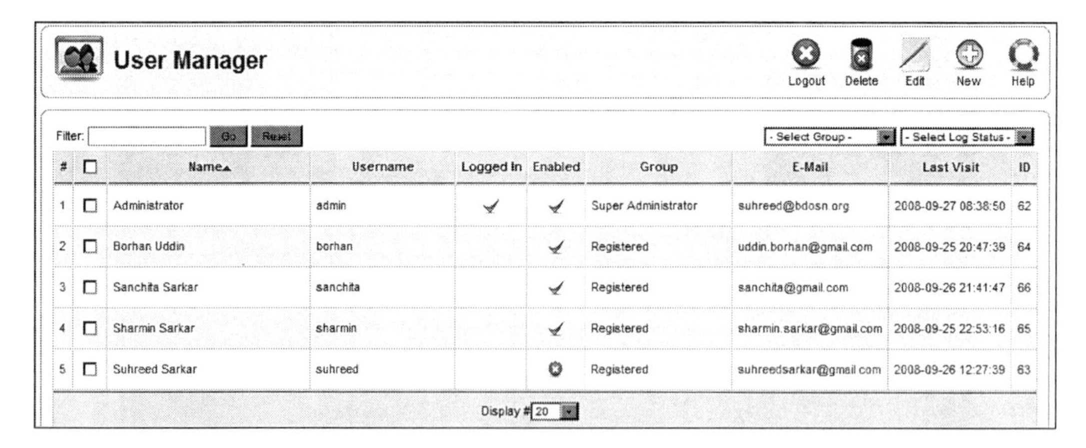

We see that the users registered to the Joomla! site are listed in this screen. This screen shows the username, full name, enabled status, group that the user is assigned to, email of the user, date and time when they last visited, and user ID. From this screen, you may guess that any user can be enabled or disabled by clicking on the icon in the **Enabled** column. Enabled user accounts show a green tick mark in the **Enabled** column.

For viewing the details of any user, click on that user's name in the **Name** column. That brings up the **User: [Edit]** screen:

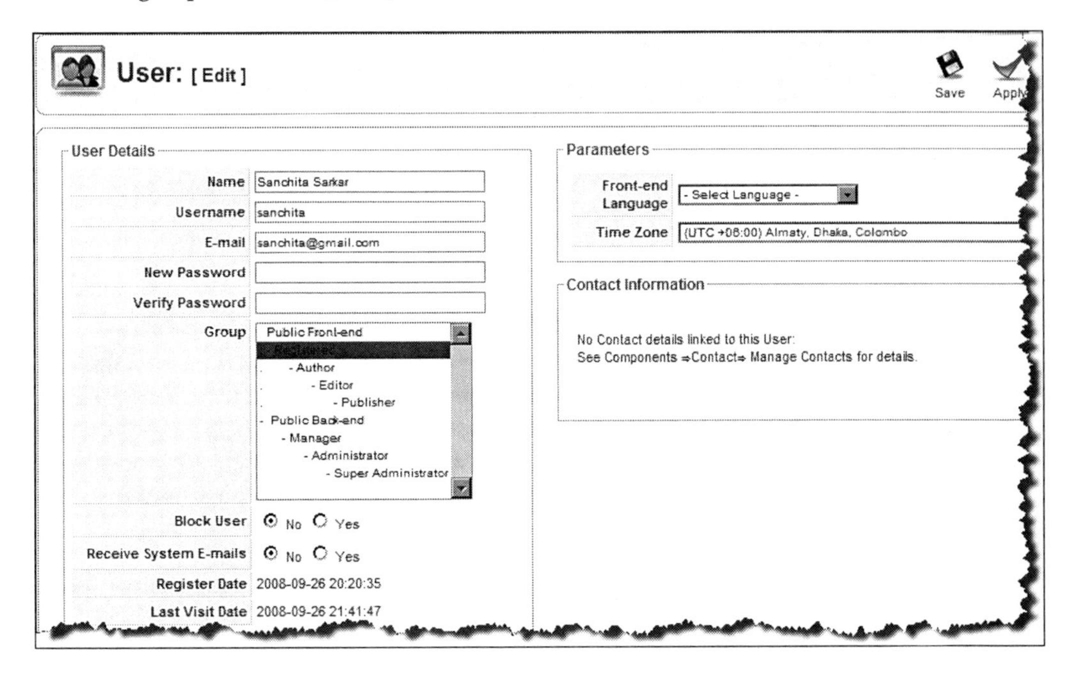

As you see, the **User Details** section shows some important information about the user including **Name**, **Username**, **E-mail**, **Group,** and so on. You can edit and change these settings including the password. In the **Group** selection box, you must select one level. The deepest level gets the highest permission in the system. From this section, you can also block a user and decide whether they will receive system emails or not.

In the **Parameters** section, you can choose the **Front-end Language** and **Time Zone** for that user. If you have created contact items using Joomla!'s **Contacts** component, you may assign one contact to this user in the **Contact Information** section.

VirtueMart user manager

Let us now look into VirtueMart's user manager. From the Joomla! control panel, select **Components | VirtueMart** to reach the **VirtueMart Administration Panel**. To view the list of the user's registered to the VirtueMart store, click on **Admin | Users**. This brings the **User List** screen:

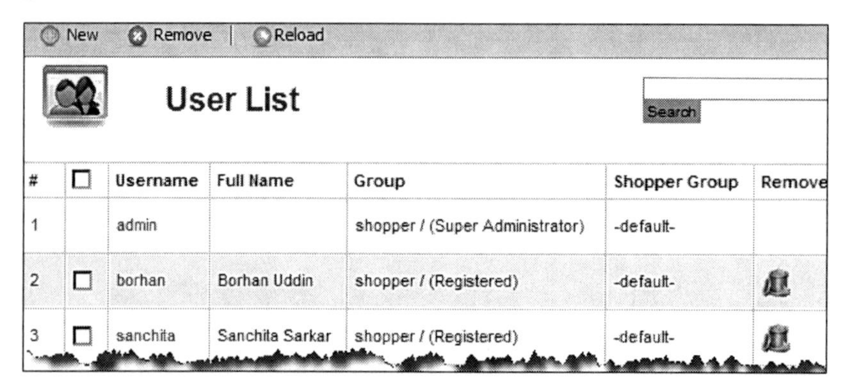

As you can see, the **User List** screen shows the list of users registered to the shop. The screen shows their username, full name, group the user is assigned to, and their shopper group. In the **Group** column, note that there are two groups mentioned. One group is without brackets and another is inside brackets. The group name mentioned inside brackets is Joomla!'s standard user groups, whereas the one without brackets is VirtueMart's user group. We are going to learn about these user groups in the next section.

For viewing the details of a user, click on the user's name in **Username** column. That brings the **Add/Update User Information** screen:

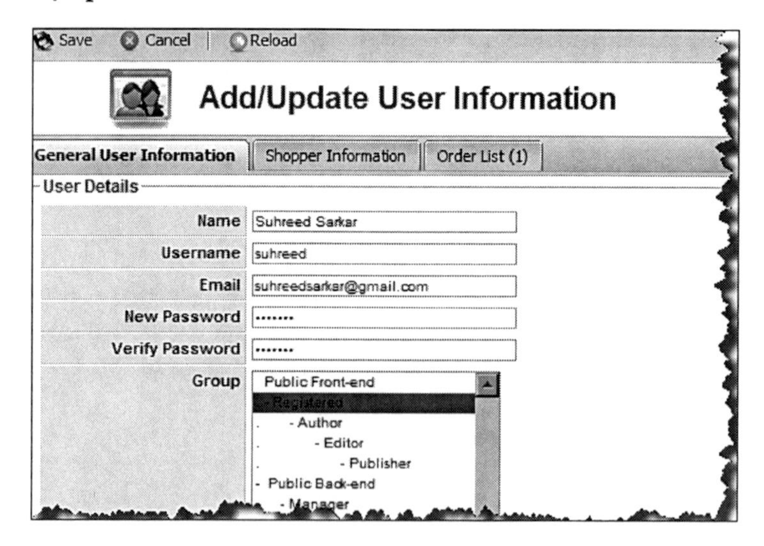

The screen has three tabs: **General User Information**, **Shopper Information**, and **Order List**. The **General User Information** tab contains the same information which was shown in Joomla!'s user manager's **User: [Edit]** screen. The **Shopper Information** tab contains shop related information for the user:

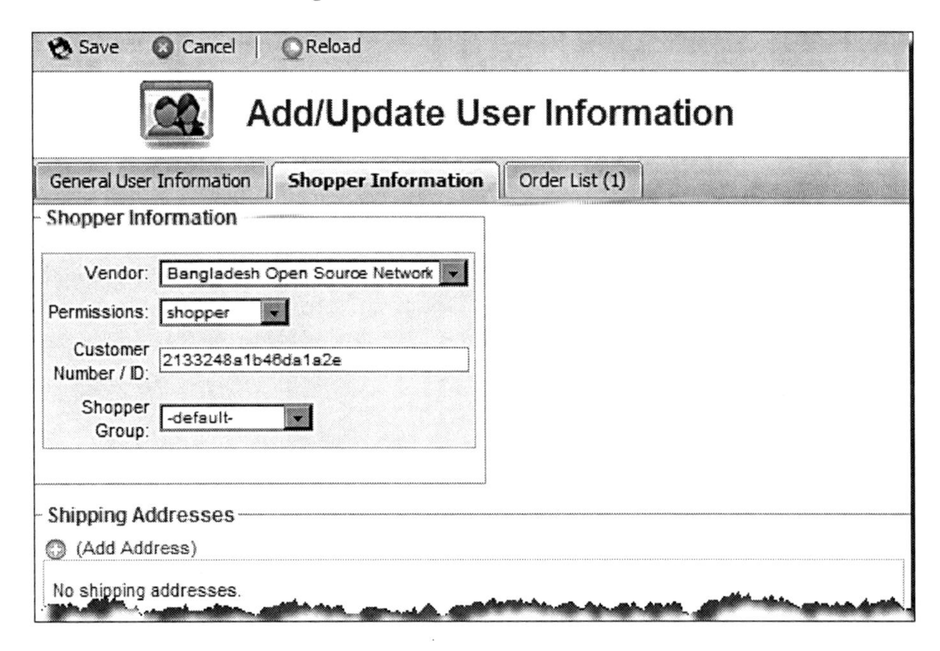

The **Shopper Information** section contains:

- a vendor to which the user is registered
- the user group the user belongs to
- a customer number/ID
- the shopper group

Other sections in this tab are: **Shipping Addresses**, **Bill To Information**, **Bank Account**, and any other section you have added to the user registration or account maintenance form. These sections contain fields which are either available on the registration or account maintenance form. If the user has placed some orders, the **Order List** tab will list the orders placed by that user. If no order has been placed, the **Order List tab** will not be visible.

Which user manager should we use?

As we can see, there is a difference between Joomla!'s user manager and VirtueMart's user manager. VirtueMart's user manager shows some additional information fields, which are necessary for the operation of the shop. Therefore, whenever you are managing users for your shop, use the user manager in the VirtueMart component, not Joomla!'s user manager. Otherwise, all customer information will not be added or updated. This may create some problems in operating the VirtueMart store.

User groups

Do you want to decide who can do what in your shop? There is a very good way for doing that in Joomla! and VirtueMart. Both Joomla! and VirtueMart have some predefined user groups. In both cases, you can create additional groups and assign permission levels to these groups. When users register to your site, you assign them to one of the user groups.

Joomla! user groups

Let us first look into Joomla! user groups. Predefined groups in Joomla! are described below:

User Group	Permissions
Public Frontend	
Registered	Users in this group can login to the Joomla! site and view the contents, sections, categories, and the items which are marked only for registered users. This group has no access to content management.
Author	Users in this group get all the permissions the Registered group has. In addition to that, users in this group can submit articles for publishing, and can edit their own articles.
Editor	Users of this group have all the above permissions, and also can edit articles submitted by other users. However, they cannot publish the contents.
Publisher	Users in this group can login to the system and submit, edit, and publish their own content as well as contents submitted by other users.

User Group	Permissions
Public Backend	
Manager	Users in this group can login to the administration panel and manage content items including articles, sections, categories, links, and so on. They cannot manage users, install modules or components, manage templates and languages, and access global configurations. Users in this group can access some of the components for which the administrator has given permission.
Administrator	In addition to content management, users in this group can add a user to Super Administrator group, edit a user, access the global configuration settings, access the mail function, and manage/install templates and language files.
Super Administrator	Users in this group can access all administration functions. For every site, at least one should be in this group to perform global configurations. You cannot delete a user in this group or move him/her to another group.

As you can see, most of the users registering to your site should be assigned to the **Registered** group. By default, Joomla! assigns all newly registered users to the **Registered** group. You need to add some users to the **Editor** or **Publisher** group if they need to add or publish content to the site. The persons who are managing the shop should be assigned to other **Public Backend** groups such as **Manager**, **Administrator** or **Super Administrator**.

VirtueMart user groups

Let us now look into the user groups in VirtueMart. To see the user groups, go to VirtueMart's administration panel and click on **Admin | User Groups**. This shows the **User Group List** screen:

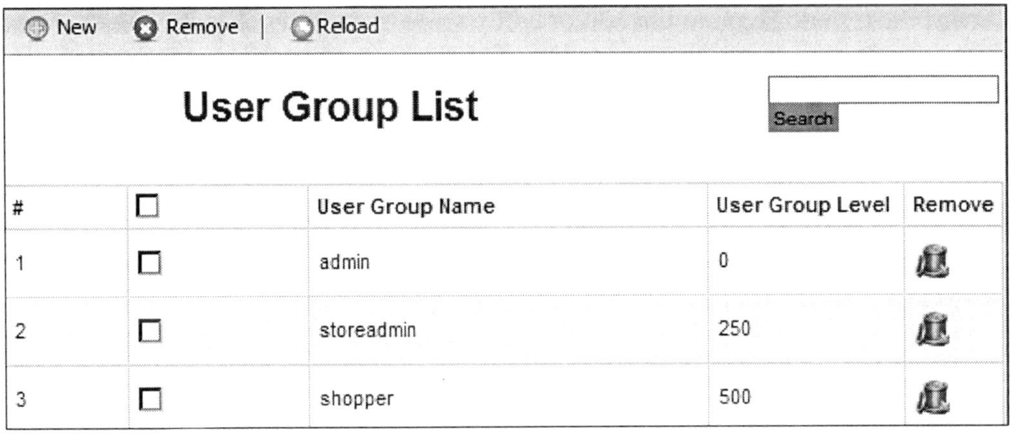

New | Remove | Reload

User Group List

Search

#	☐	User Group Name	User Group Level	Remove
1	☐	admin	0	
2	☐	storeadmin	250	
3	☐	shopper	500	

By default, you will see four user groups: **admin**, **storeadmin**, **shopper**, and **demo**. These groups are used for assigning permissions to users. Also, note the values in the **User Group Level** column. The higher the value in this field, the lower the permissions assumed for the group. The **admin** group has a level value of **0**, which means it has all of the permissions, and of course, more than the next group **storeadmin**. Similarly, **storeadmin** group has more permissions than the **shopper** group. These predefined groups are key groups in VirtueMart, and you cannot modify or delete these groups. These groups have the following permissions:

Group	Permissions
admin	This group has permissions to use all of the modules except **checkout** and **shop**. The admin group does not need these because admin users usually do not shop in their store.
storeadmin	This group has fewer permissions than **admin** group. Users in this group can access all the modules except the **admin**, **vendor**, **shop,** and **checkout** modules. They cannot set the global configurations for the store, but can add and edit payment methods, products, categories, and so on.
shopper	This group has the least permission among the three key groups. By default, users registered to the shop are assigned to this group. Users in this group can fully access the account module, and can use some functions of the **shop**, **coupon**, and **checkout** modules.
demo	This is a demo group created by default so that administrators can test and play with it.

For most of the shops, these four predefined groups will be enough to implement appropriate permissions. However, in some cases you may need to create a new user group and assign separate permissions to that group. For example, you may want to employ some people as store managers who will add products to the catalog and manage the orders. They cannot add or edit payment methods, shipping methods, or other settings, except product and orders. If you add these people to the **storeadmin** group then they get more permissions than required. In such situations, a good solution is to create a new group, add selected user accounts to that group, and assign permissions to that group.

Creating a new user group

For creating a new user group, click on the **New** button in the toolbar on the **User Group List screen**. This brings **Add/Edit a User Group** screen:

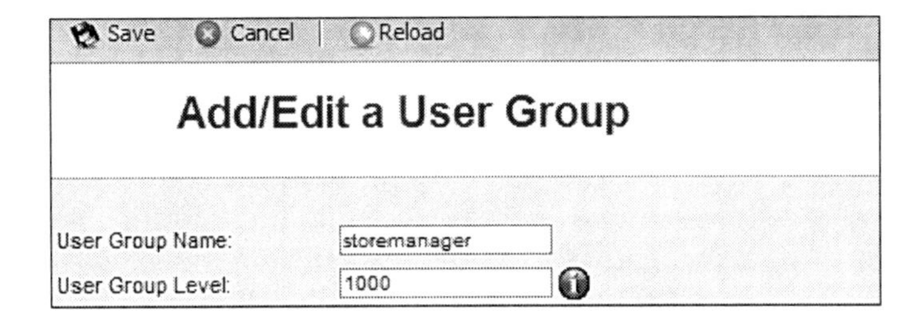

In the **Add/Edit a User Group** screen, enter the group's name and group level. You must type a higher value than existing groups (for example, 1000). Click on the **Save** icon to save the user group. You will now see the newly created user group in the **User Group List** screen.

Are you thinking of how this group will control a user's permissions? Yes, there is still something more to do. Creating a new group and adding users to that group will not assign any permission to users. We have to set the permissions for each group (that we create) and then users in those groups will get those permissions. We are going to learn about viewing and setting group permissions in next section.

Group permissions

Each user group has permissions associated with it. Although there is no simple way to view all of the permissions a user group has, we cans still view the associated permissions for all user groups. To view the permissions associated with the user groups, click on **Admin | List Modules**. This brings the **Module List** screen:

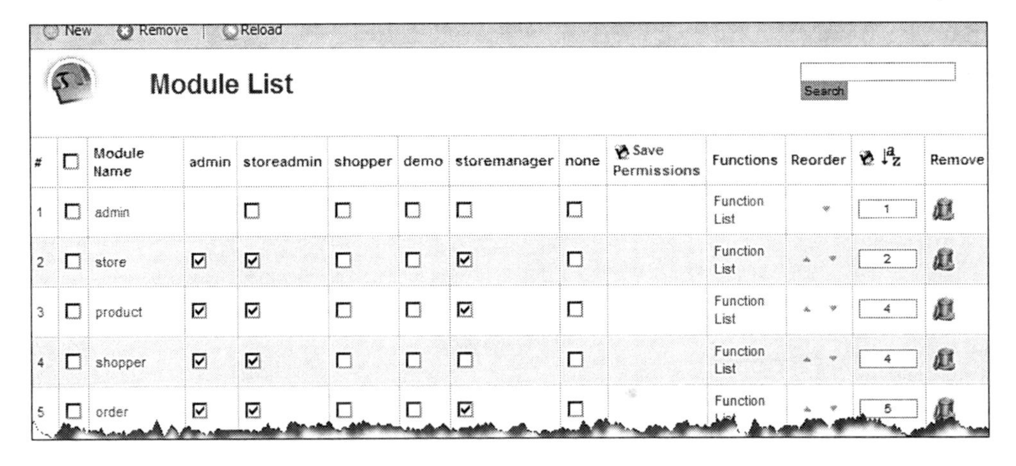

The **Module List** screen shows the modules and the group's permissions to access those modules. As you can see, our newly created **storemanager** user group is also in the list.

Assigning permissions to user groups

We must now assign appropriate permissions to the **storemanager** group. First, select the **store** module. This module allows us to see store-wide configurations and store information. We don't want to allow the **storemanager** group to change the store information. However, we are selecting this store module, because to display the VirtueMart Administration Panel, this module is necessary. Click on the **Function List** link against the **store** module. That shows **Function List: store** screen:

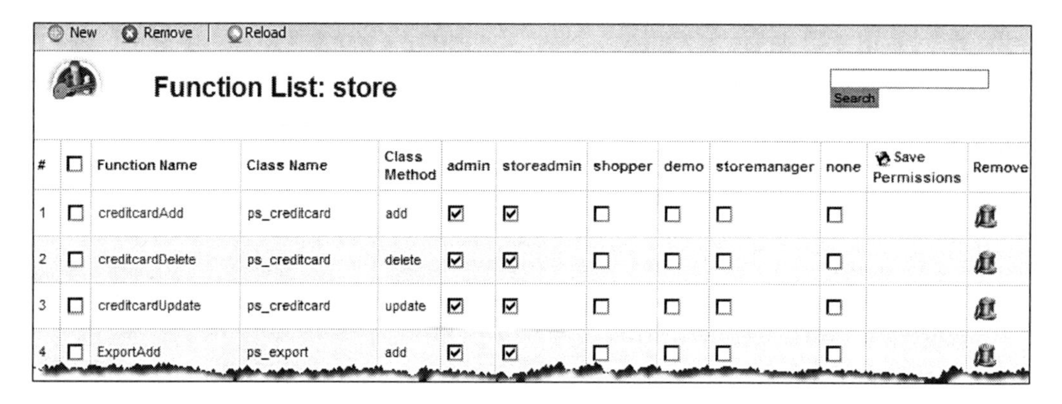

In the **Function List: store** screen, you can see the main functions available in the **store** module. From here, you can select functions that will be available to the **storemanager** group. To know what each functions do, click on the function name to see the **Function Information** screen:

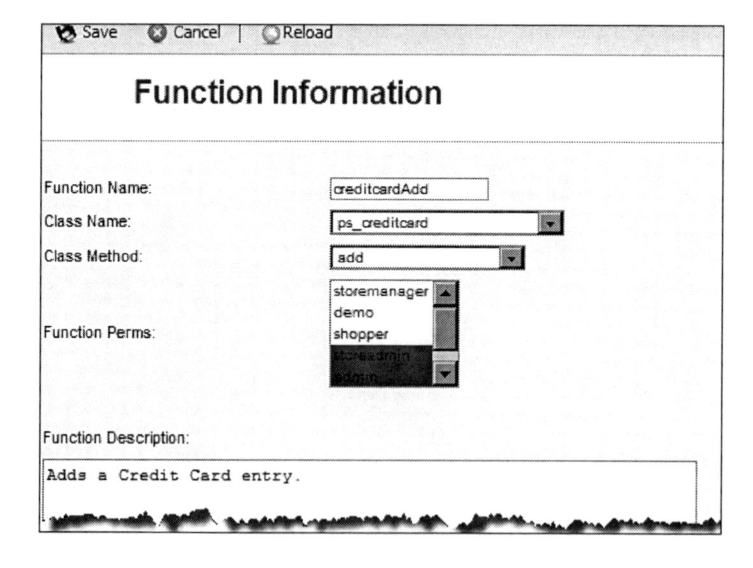

The **Function Information** screen shows the function name, class name, class method, groups which have permission to use that function, and a description of the function. This will help you understand where the function comes from and for what purpose it serves.

Are you pondering the fields in this screen? We are going to explain the fields available in this screen later in this chapter, under the **Adding New Function** section.

As our store managers will not change any settings regarding credit cards, payment and shipping methods, and export modules, in the **Function List: store** screen, we need to uncheck all modules for the **storemanager** group.

For the **storemanager** group, select the **store**, **product**, **order**, **reportbasic**, **account**, and **help** modules. Then, click on the **Save Permissions** link.

After giving access to these modules, we can assign permissions to specific functions under these modules. Click on the **Function List** link against each module and select the functions you want to allow for store managers. For example, we want store managers to add new products, but not to delete products once added to the catalog. To implement this rule, click on the **Function List** link against the **product** module. You get the **Function List: product** screen:

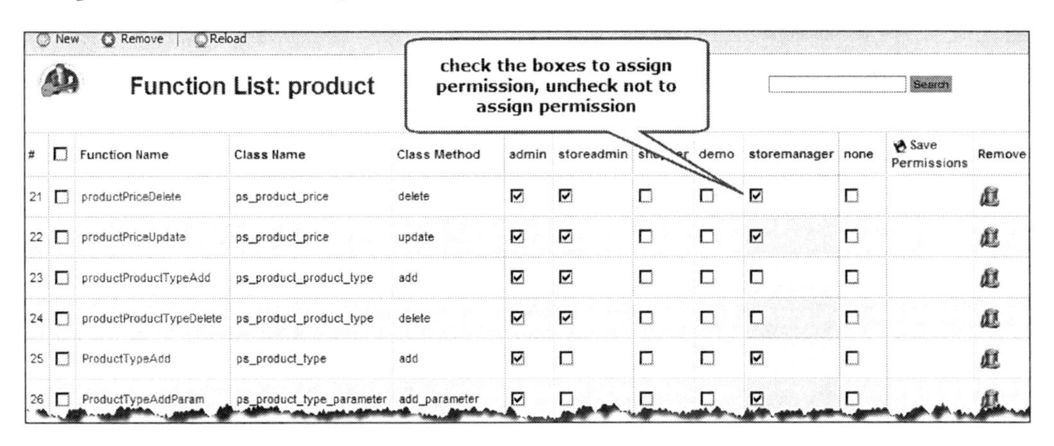

In the **Function List: product** screen, you may select all of the functions for the **storemanager** group except the **productDelete** function. After checking and unchecking the checkboxes under the **storemanager** column for different functions, click on the **Save Permissions** link to save the permissions you have set.

When you see the **none** column checked, that means no restriction is applied for that function or module. Also note that, in both the **Module List** and **Function List** screen, there is a **New** button in the toolbar. You can add a new module or function by clicking on this **New** button.

Adding new module

Why do you need to add a new module while assigning permissions to groups? Generally, the default modules listed in the **Module List** screen are enough for assigning permissions to most of the functions. However, in some cases, you may like to assign permissions to a group of functions, which have not been explicitly assigned, to any group. For example, by default, functions related to managing payment methods are listed under the **store** module. Someone may like to make another module named **payment** and put the related functions under this module. This will help assign permissions to payment functions easily. Therefore, the first step will be to create a module named **payment**.

For creating a module, go to the **Module List** screen by clicking on **Admin | List Modules**. In the **Module List** screen, click on the **New** icon in the toolbar. This opens up the **Module Information** screen:

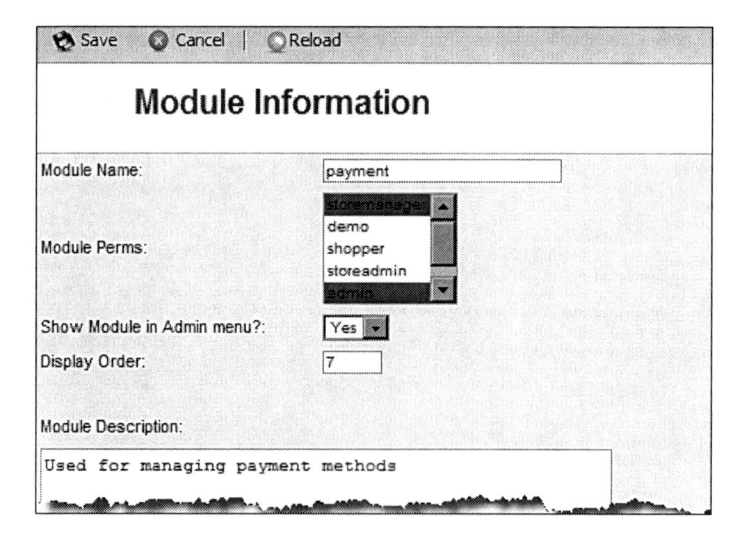

In the **Module Information** screen, we need to provide the name of the module, and some additional information. In the **Module Name** field, type **payment** (or any other name which is not used as a module name already). In the **Module Perms** list, select the groups to which you want to give permissions to access this module. Select **Yes** in the **Show Module in Admin menu?** drop-down list. This will show a section named **Payment** in the admin menu. Assign the display order, say 7, in the **Display Order** field. Finally, give a description what the module does. Click on the **Save** icon to save the module. You can now see this module in the **Module List** screen.

Adding new function

After adding the module, we need to add functions to the module. In the **Module List** screen, go to the **payment** module and click on the **Function List** link. The **Function List: payment** screen will show no function. This is because we have not yet added any function to the **payment** module. For adding a function, click on the **New** icon in the toolbar on the **Function List** screen. This shows the **Function Information** screen:

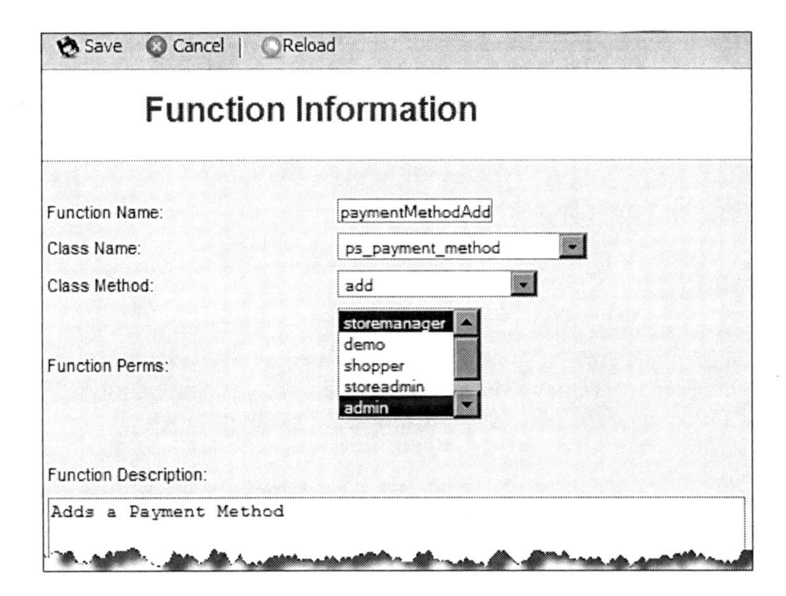

From the **Function Information** screen, you need to configure the following fields:

- **Function Name**: Provide a function name. If you are adding the function for allowing the group to add a payment method, the function name will be **paymentMethodAdd**.

- **Class Name**: From this drop-down list, select an appropriate class file. As we are adding functions for payment methods, select the **ps_payment_method** class file here.
- **Class Method**: When you select a class file in the **Class Name** field, you will see the available functions from that class in this drop-down list.. You will notice that, in the **ps_payment_method** class, there are **add**, **update**, **delete**, **list_method,** and some other functions. The functions named here are usable by user groups. Other functions, such as **validate_add**, **validate_delete**, **validate_update**, and so on, are automatically executed upon use of the **add**, **delete** or **update** functions. For the time being, select the **add** function from the drop-down list.
- **Function Perms**: Select the user groups who will be able to use this function. You can select multiple groups from the list.
- **Function Description**: Provide a description of the function to help administrators understand what this function is for. As the **paymentMethodAdd** function will add a payment method, type **Adds a payment method** in this text area.

When you have entered all this information, click on the **Save** icon in the toolbar. That adds the function to the **payment** module. Similarly, add three more functions named **paymentMethodUpdate**, **paymentMethodDelete**, and **paymentMethodList**. All of these will use the same **ps_payment_method** class and use the **update**, **delete,** and **list_method** class methods respectively.

Warning:

You may get an error message while adding new functions. It happens if another function exists with the same name. As the **paymentMethodAdd**, and other functions we have added now, are part of store module, you will first need to delete those functions in store module.

After adding all the functions, go back to the **Function List: payment** screen, and you will see the function listed there:

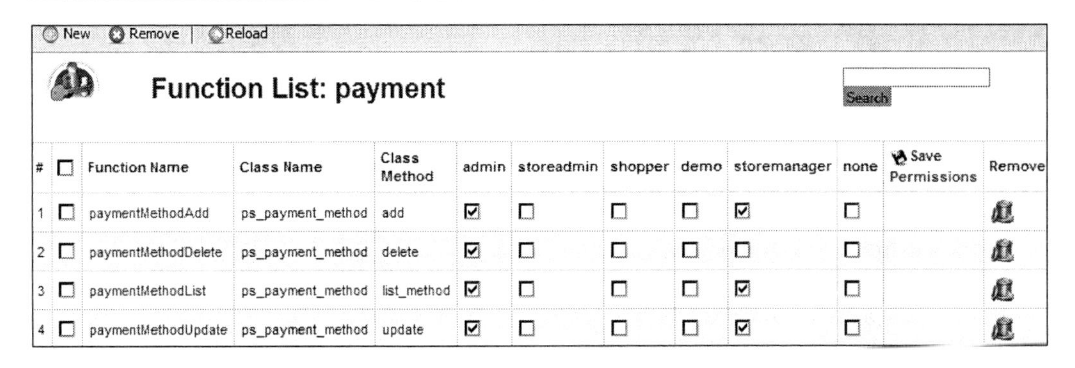

From the **Function List: payment** screen, you can see the permissions assigned to the different user groups. If you want to change some of these permissions, do so, and click on the **Save Permissions** link to save the settings.

In principle, the function name field should take any string that is not the same as other functions. However, you may find it strange when you name the `update()` function as **updatePaymentMethod** instead of **paymentMethodUpdate**. You will get a message saying that the function is not registered:

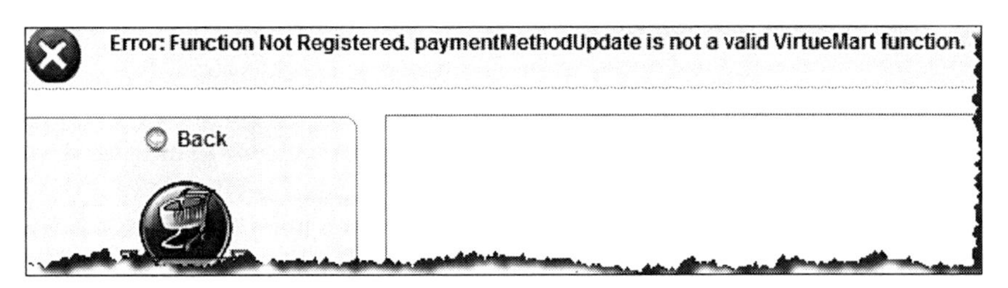

Let us investigate why this happens. Open the file `../administrator/components/com_virtuemart/html/store.payment_method_form.php`. Now, go to line #186. The variable `$funcname` specifies what functions will be used. The line looks like the following:

```
$funcname = !empty($payment_method_id) ? "paymentMethodUpdate" :
"paymentMethodAdd";
```

As you can see, function names are specified in the file. Therefore, whenever you are adding such a function, make sure the function name you provide is the same as mentioned in the `$funcname` variable.

Assigning users to groups

We have already seen how to view a user's information in VirtueMart. For viewing and updating user information, go to **Admin | Users**. Then, click on the username whose details you want to view. That brings up the **Add/Update User Information** screen. Go to the **Shopper Information** tab in this screen:

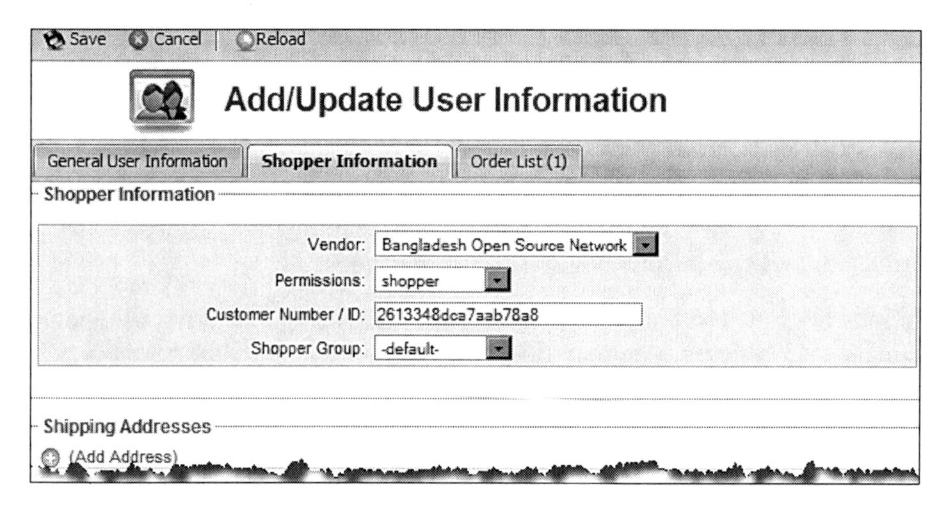

In the **Shopper Information** tab, you can assign appropriate permissions to the user. Select the user group from the **Permissions** drop-down list. For example, we assign the user to the **storemanager** user group, which we created earlier. When the user group is selected from the **Permissions** drop-down list, click on the **Save** icon in the toolbar. Now, the user is a member of the **storemanager** group and will have the permissions that are assigned to the **storemanager** group.

Checking how these work

We will now check how our user groups and permissions work. We have created a user group named **storemanager**, given permissions to manage products and orders to this user group, and finally added a user to this user group. Now, to see the effect, we need to log in as that user, and see whether we can add products and manage orders. Before testing, we need to publish the **mod_virtuemart** module, because a link to administration section is visible in this module when the user has the necessary permissions.

Lets try it first! Go to the shop frontend and log in using that username and password. After logging in, search for the **Admin** link in the VirtueMart module. Is it there? No, you can't see that now:

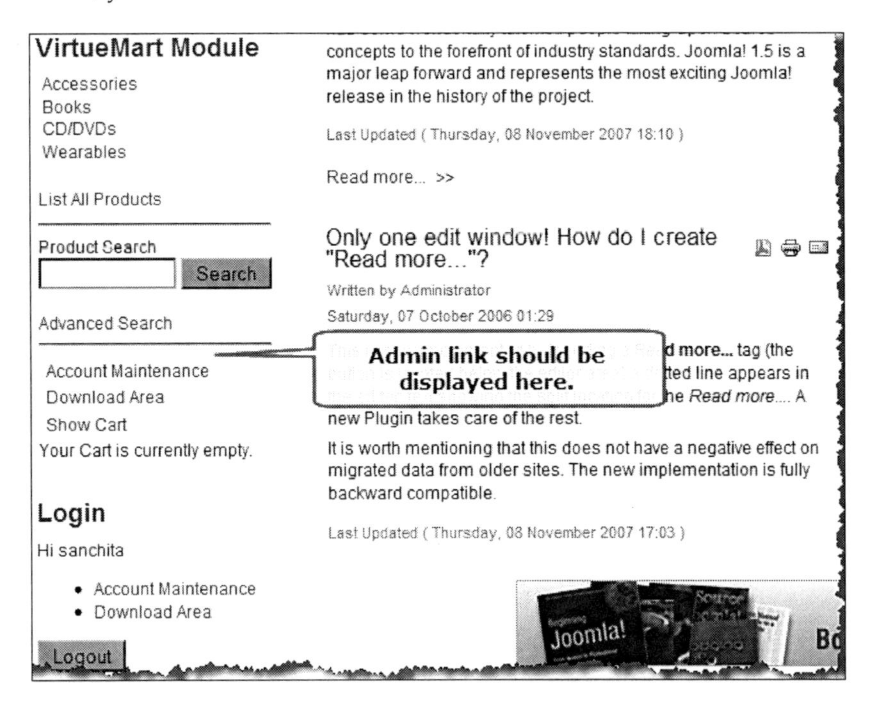

For getting the **Admin** link in the **VirtueMart Module**, and also to get some administrative permission, we have to apply a little hack. We need to edit two files. First, open the file `../components/com_virtuemart/virtuemart.php`. At line #96, you get the following code block:

```
if ( vmIsAdminMode()
      && $perm->check("admin,storeadmin")
      && ((!stristr($my->usertype, "admin") ^
        PSHOP_ALLOW_FRONTENDADMIN_FOR_NOBACKENDERS == '' )
          || stristr($my->usertype, "admin")
          )
      && !stristr($page, "shop.")
   ) {
```

As you will notice, in the second line of the code above, two user groups are mentioned. If we want to give other groups access to the administration panel, we must add that group's name here. So, we change the above code block as follows:

```
if ( vmIsAdminMode()
        && $perm->check("admin,storeadmin,storemanager")
        && ((!stristr($my->usertype, "admin") ^
          PSHOP_ALLOW_FRONTENDADMIN_FOR_NOBACKENDERS == '' )
           || stristr($my->usertype, "admin")
           || stristr($my->usertype, "storemanager")
           )
        && !stristr($page, "shop.")
    ) {
```

The changed lines are highlighted in above code block. We have added the `storemanager` group in second line, and also added another line after || `stristr($my->usertype, "admin")`. With these changes, the user will get the assigned permissions and have access to the administration panel. However, you still will not see the **Admin** link on the VirtueMart Module. For getting that, open `../modules/mod_virtuemart/mod_virtuemart.php` file. In line # 139, you will see the following code block:

```
<?php
}
$perm = new ps_perm;
// Show the Frontend ADMINISTRATION Link
if ($perm->check("admin,storeadmin")
        && ((!stristr($my->usertype, "admin") ^
          PSHOP_ALLOW_FRONTENDADMIN_FOR_NOBACKENDERS == '' )
            || stristr($my->usertype, "admin")
        )
        && $show_adminlink == 'yes'
    ) { ?>
```

In plain language, the above code block says that if the users are of type `admin` or `storeadmin`, then show the admin link. Therefore, to show the admin link to other groups, we need to add that group's name here. Change the above code block as follows:

```
<?php
}
$perm = new ps_perm;
// Show the Frontend ADMINISTRATION Link
if ($perm->check("admin,storeadmin,storemanager")
```

```
    && ((!stristr($my->usertype, "admin") ^
      PSHOP_ALLOW_FRONTENDADMIN_FOR_NOBACKENDERS == '' )
        || stristr($my->usertype, "admin")
        || stristr($my->usertype, "storemanager")
    )
    && $show_adminlink == 'yes'
) { ?>
```

The changed lines are highlighted above. Like the previous code block, we have added the `storemanager` group to the list.

> **Warning:**
>
> While listing the group names, do not use spaces. Using spaces will not show the **Admin** link. For example, `admin,storeadmin,storemanager` will work fine, but `admin, storeadmin, storemanager` will not work. Be careful when applying this hack.

Now, log in again with the same username and password and see what happens. Wow! We got our **Admin** link on the **VirtueMart** module:

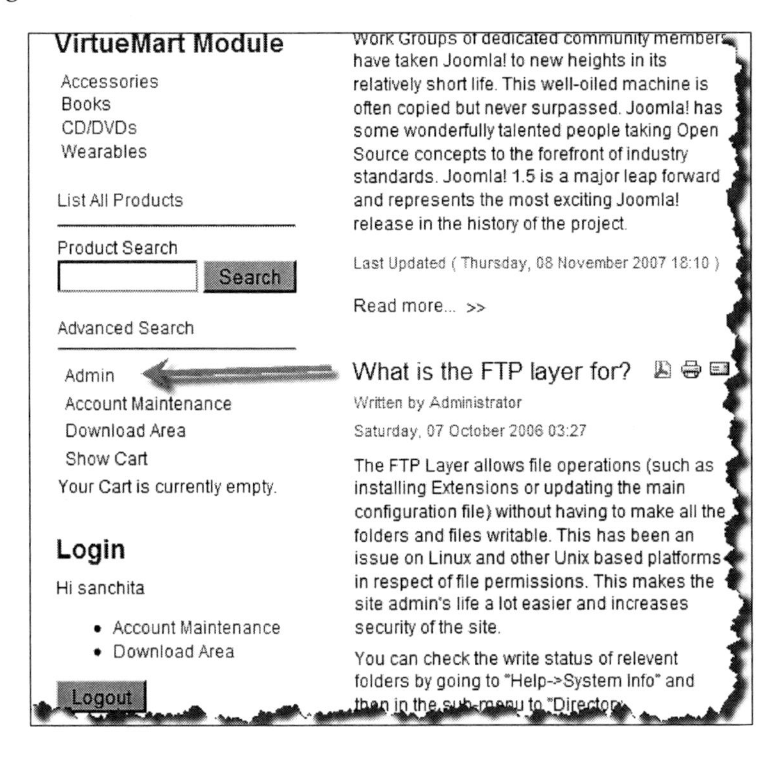

To access the VirtueMart administration panel, and manage products and orders, click on the **Admin** link. You will get the **VirtueMart Administration** panel (in Standard Layout):

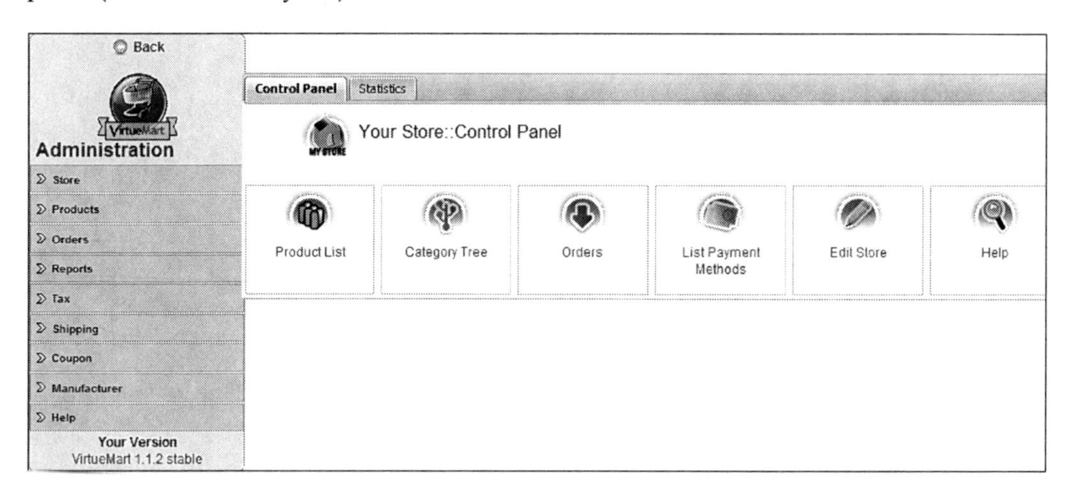

As you can see, there is a **Back** button for going back to frontend. You also get the list of modules in the left sidebar. Clicking on one module will bring out the available functions. I hope you remember that we have assigned permissions to the **storemanager** group to manage products and orders only. They can add new products, but cannot delete any product. Click on the **Products** module, and then on **List Products**. This shows the list of products available in the catalog. Try deleting a product by clicking on the trash icon in the **Remove** column. You get a message like the following:

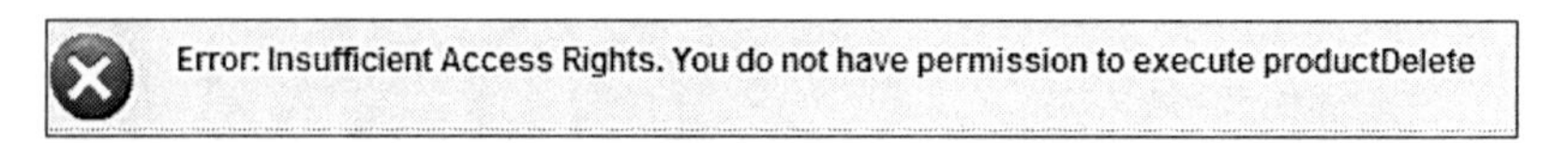

Also, try managing the orders. Click on the **Orders** module and then on **List Orders**. You will see the list of orders placed so far. Try deleting an order from the list by clicking on the trash icon in the **Remove** column. As we have not given permission to the **storemanager** group to delete an order, you will get the following message:

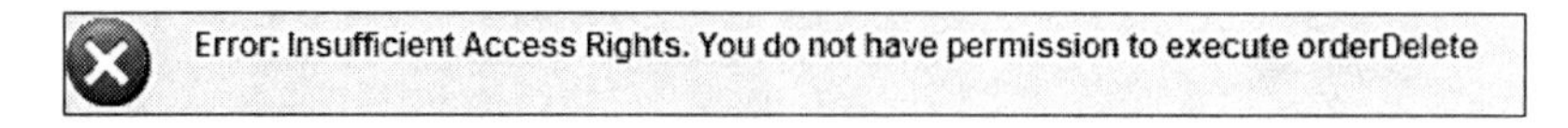

Try to do something else for which the group has no permission, and you will get messages like these. From this, we understand that the permissions we have given to users are in effect. This is one wonderful way for giving access to a frontend user to manage the shop's specific tasks.

What other changes were made? Yes, we created a module named **payment** and added four functions to that module: **paymentMethodAdd**, **payMentMethodUpdate**, **paymentMethodDelete**, and **paymentMethodList**. The **storemanager** group can use all of the methods except the **paymentMethodDelete**. Lets try that.

> But where is the **payment** module in left sidebar? All other modules are there, only our newly created **payment** module is missing. Then how do you try to add, update, and list the payment methods. During creation of the **payment** module, we indicated that this module should be displayed in the administration panel. However, it is not showing there. To showthe module, and other links to that module, we need to edit a file. We will be looking at this issue later, in Chapter 9, *Extending VirtueMart's Functionalities*.

If you click on the **Store** module, you get two payment method related links: **List Payment Methods**, and **Add Payment Method**. As the group **storemanager** has permission to do both, you may try and see what happens. Surely, you will be able to add a payment method, edit a payment method, and to see the list of payment methods. However, you will not be able to delete a payment method, as you have no permission to do so.

Managing orders

Our shop is now ready for customers. They can register to the shop and get some permissions to browse products and place orders. After building the catalog, one of the big tasks of the shop administrator is to manage the orders. Managing an order includes viewing the order, ensuring that payment is made, shipping the product to customers ship to address, and setting the appropriate status of the order. Whenever the status of the order changes, the shop administrator can also notify the customer about its status. When the product is delivered, the status should also be changed. Sometimes, you need to change the status when the customer refunds it for some reason.

Viewing the orders

To view the list of orders placed, click on **Orders | List Orders**. You get the **Order List** screen:

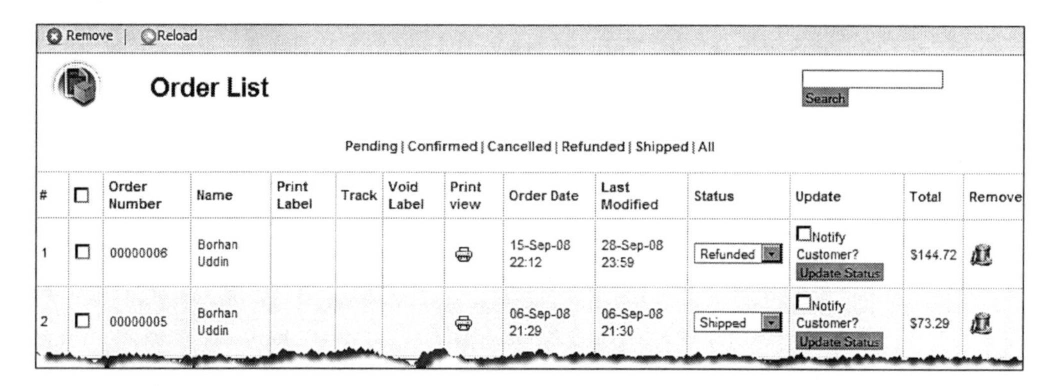

The **Order List** screen shows all of the orders placed so far in that store. It shows the latest order first. As you can see, it shows the order number, name of customer, date of order, date last modified, status of the order, and total price of the order.

As there may be hundreds of orders per day, you need to filter the orders and see which ones need urgent attention. You can filter the orders by their status. For example, clicking on the **Pending** link will show all of the orders which are pending. Viewing the list of pending orders, you may enquire why those are pending. Some may be pending for not making the payment, or you may be waiting for some offline payment. For example, when the **Money Order** payment method is used, the order needs to remain **Pending** until you receive the money order. Once you get the payment, you can change the order status to **Confirmed**.

Viewing an order's details

In the **Order List** screen, you will get an overview of each order. However, sometimes it may be necessary to view the details of an order. For viewing an order's details, in the **Order List** screen, click on the order number link under the **Order Number** column. This shows details of the order:

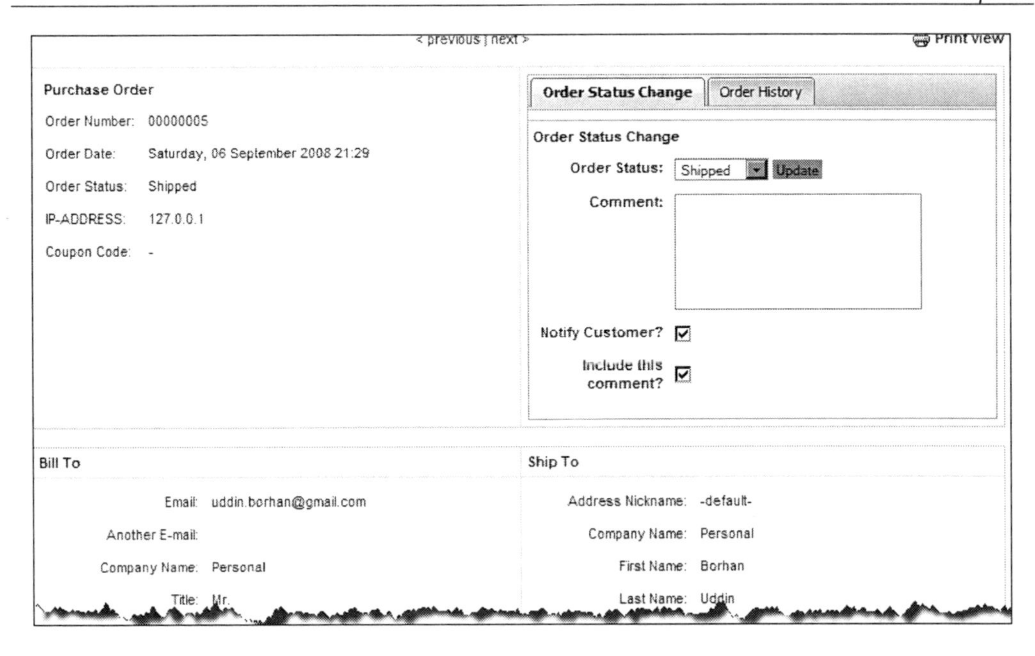

In the **Order Details** page, you will first see the order number, order date, order status, its current status, and IP address from where the order was placed. There is a box section from where you can update the order's status and view the order's history. Then, you get the **Bill To** and **Ship To** addresses. After the **Bill To** and **Ship To** addresses, you get the list of ordered items and their prices. You can also add a new product to this order from this section. This section also shows taxes added, and shipping and handling fees:

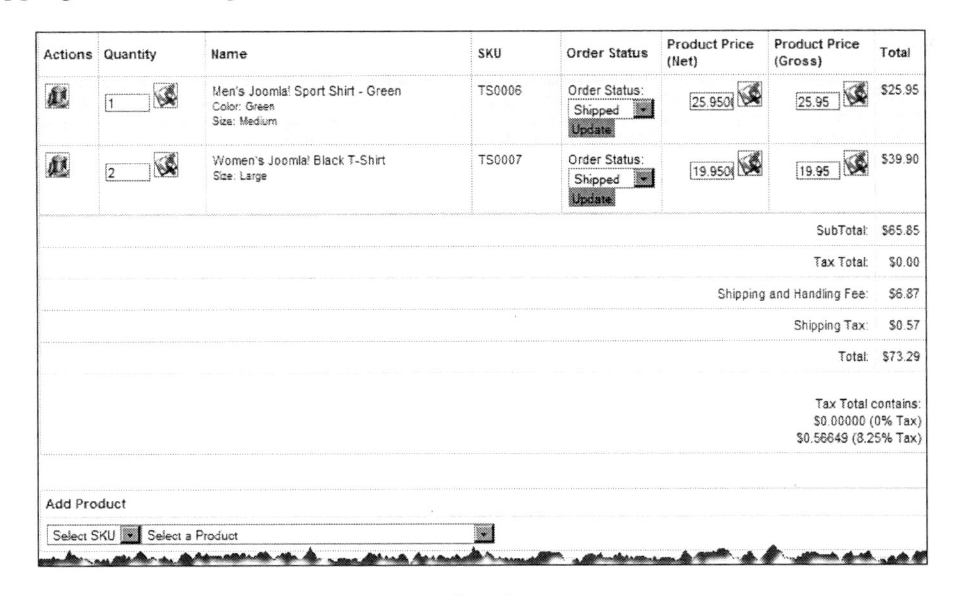

After the product items, you get another section which shows shipping information and payment method used:

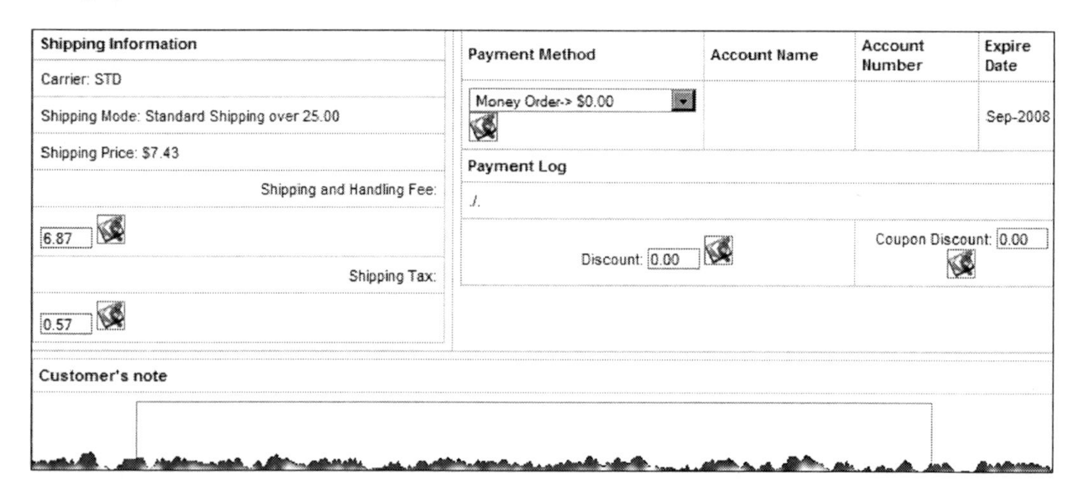

In the **Shipping Information** section, you get the carrier used, shipping mode applied, shipping price, shipping and handling fees, and shipping taxes.

The payment section shows what method was used and when the payment was made. It shows the payment history for this order. It also shows how much of a coupon discount was applied to this order. As an administrator of the shop, you can change the values in the fields where an update icon (update icon) is displayed.

At the bottom, you see the customer's comment. Customers may provide comments while placing the order. These comments may be very much valuable for the shop owner. For example, the customer may want the product to be delivered in a special way. The customer can express that in this comment.

For printing the purchase orders, you may use a printer friendly view. To see the purchase order in a printer friendly view, click on the **Print View** link at top. This formats the purchase order as a plain document, and also shows a printer icon. Click on that printer icon to print the purchase order.

Understanding an order's status

How is the order management workflow maintained? Mainly, this is based on the order status. After receiving an order from the customer, it passes several statuses. An order's life cycle is shown in the following diagram:

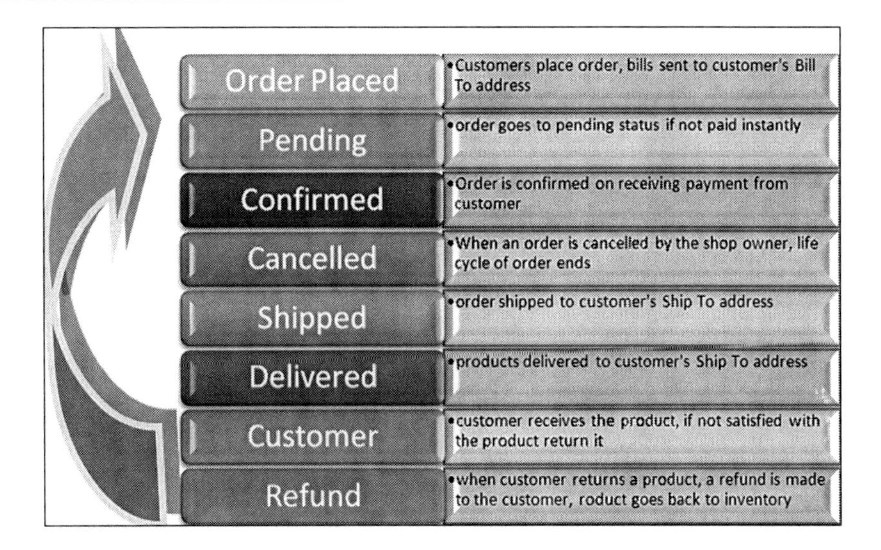

These order status types are defined in advance. At the very outset of starting the shop, the workflow should be clearly defined.

Managing order status types

You can view the existing order status types from **Orders | List Order Status Types**. This shows the **List Order Status Types** screen:

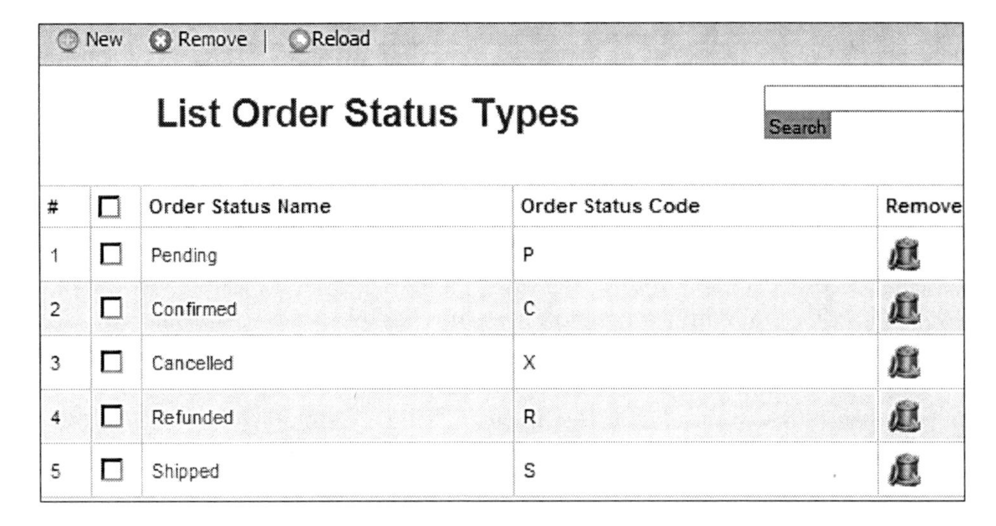

New Remove | Reload

List Order Status Types

Search

#	☐	Order Status Name	Order Status Code	Remove
1	☐	Pending	P	
2	☐	Confirmed	C	
3	☐	Cancelled	X	
4	☐	Refunded	R	
5	☐	Shipped	S	

As you see from the screen on the previous page, there are five status types. We may add another status type of **Delivered**. For adding a new order status type, click on the **New** icon in the toolbar, or on **Orders | Add Order Status Type**. Both brings the **Order Status** screen:

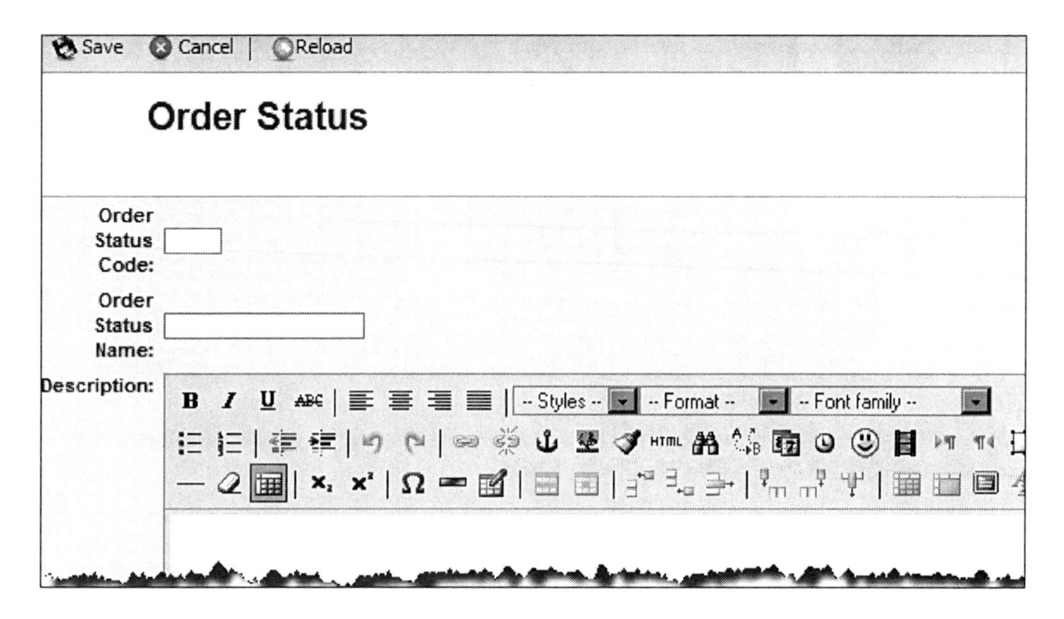

In the **Order Status** screen, first type the **Order Status Code**. For the **Delivered** status, assign **D** as code. Then, type the name of the status type in the **Order Status Name** text box. In the **Description** text area, you may provide a brief description of the order status type. At the end, specify a list order value. Then, click on the **Save** icon in the toolbar. This adds the new **Delivered** order status type. You can create as many order status types as you need.

Changing an order's status

As indicated earlier, while fulfilling the order, the shop owner needs to update the status of the order, and communicate that status change to the customer. You can change an order's status from two places. In the **Order List** screen, you can see the orders and also change status. For changing the status of an order, select an order status type from drop-down list in the **Status** column. Then, click on the **Update Status** button to save the change. If you want to notify the customer about this status change, select the **Notify Customer?** checkbox.

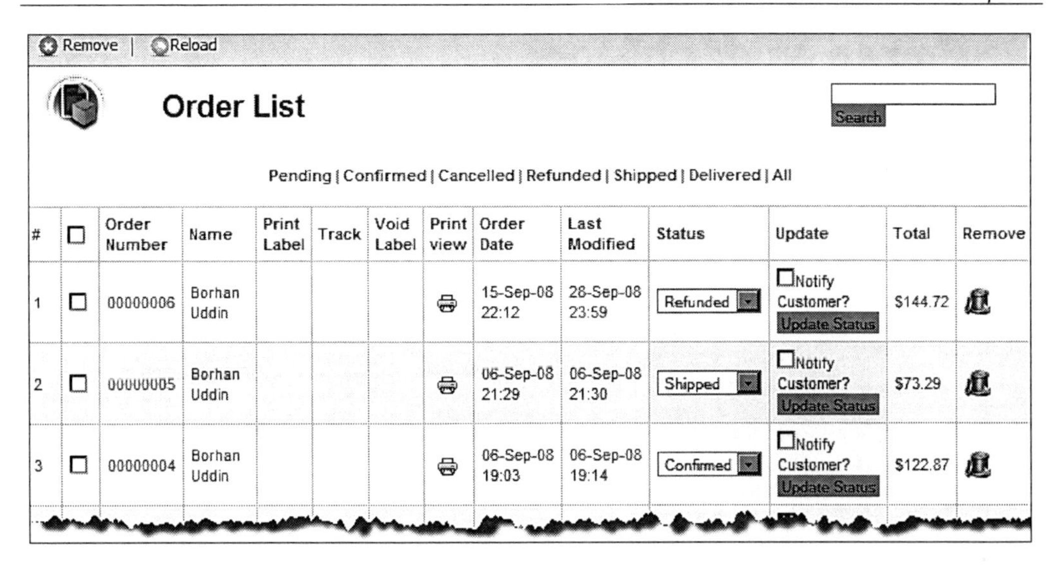

#	☐	Order Number	Name	Print Label	Track	Void Label	Print view	Order Date	Last Modified	Status	Update	Total	Remove
1	☐	00000006	Borhan Uddin					15-Sep-08 22:12	28-Sep-08 23:59	Refunded	☐Notify Customer? Update Status	$144.72	
2	☐	00000005	Borhan Uddin					06-Sep-08 21:29	06-Sep-08 21:30	Shipped	☐Notify Customer? Update Status	$73.29	
3	☐	00000004	Borhan Uddin					06-Sep-08 19:03	06-Sep-08 19:14	Confirmed	☐Notify Customer? Update Status	$122.87	

One disadvantage of updating the order status from the **Order List** screen is that you cannot add a note on changing the status. The other way of updating the order status provides this advantage. For using this, click on the order number link in the **Order List** screen. The order details page will open. On the right side, you will see a box from where you can update the order status. Can you see the **Comment** text area in the following screen?

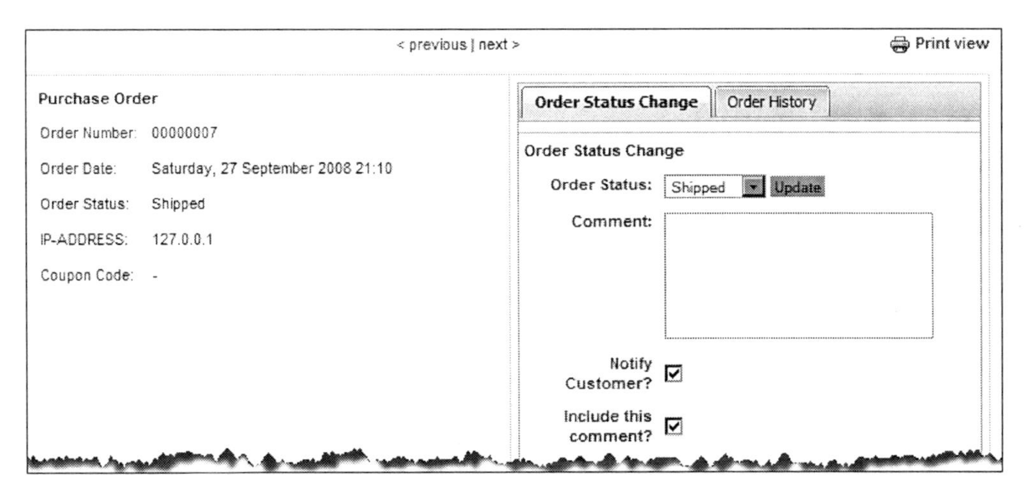

As you can see, from the **Order Status Change** tab, you can change the status, write a comment, notify the customer about the status change, and can also add the comment with that notification.

Viewing an order's history

While viewing an order's details, you can see its history. To see the order history, click on the order number link in the **Order List** screen, and go to order details page. On the right side, you get a box. Click on the **Order History** tab on that box. That shows that order's history:

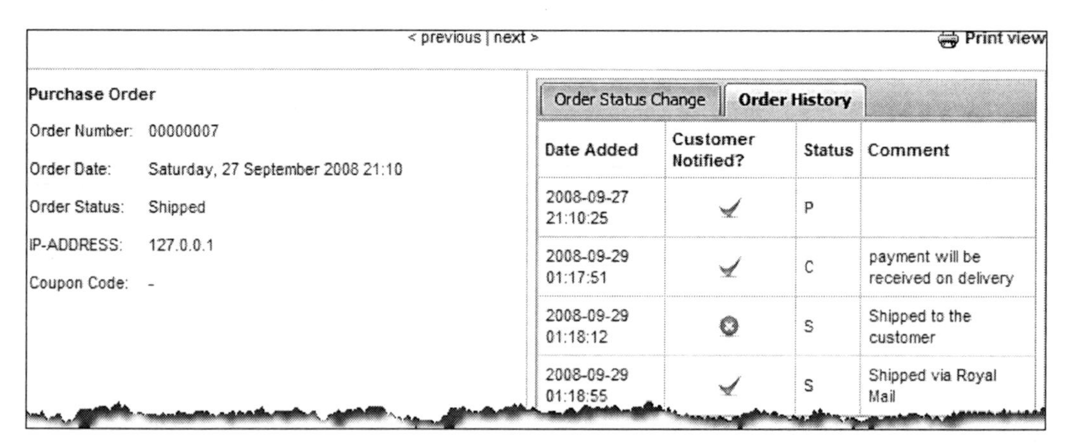

From the **Order History** tab, we know the date and time when the status was changed, whether the customer was notified or not, what status it was changed to (status code only) and the comments we added to the status changes. These are only for viewing, and we cannot change this information.

Order statistics

There are two places from where you can view order statistics. The first is the summary of orders, and another is the detailed report by products, months, weeks, and days.

Let us see the summary of orders statistics first. When you log in to the VirtueMart administration panel, you get a summary of your store's orders in the **Statistics** tab:

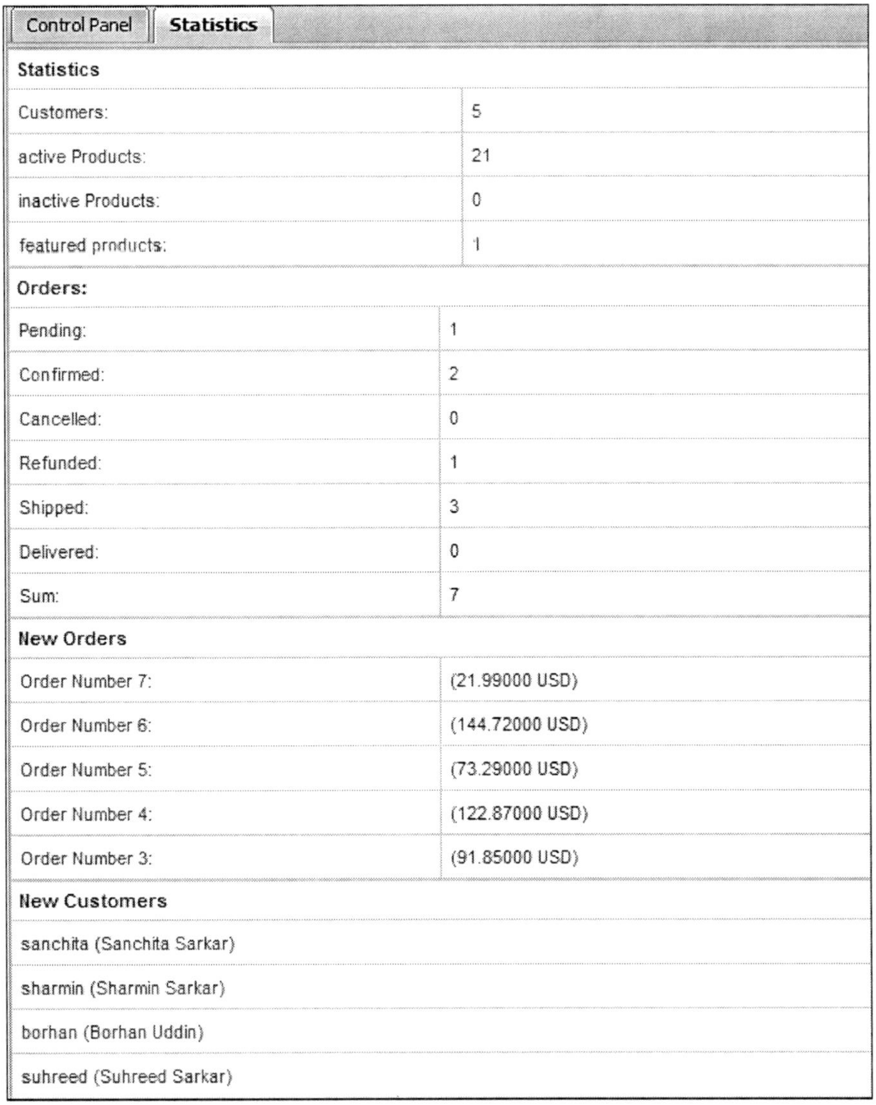

Control Panel | **Statistics**

Statistics	
Customers:	5
active Products:	21
inactive Products:	0
featured products:	1
Orders:	
Pending:	1
Confirmed:	2
Cancelled:	0
Refunded:	1
Shipped:	3
Delivered:	0
Sum:	7
New Orders	
Order Number 7:	(21.99000 USD)
Order Number 6:	(144.72000 USD)
Order Number 5:	(73.29000 USD)
Order Number 4:	(122.87000 USD)
Order Number 3:	(91.85000 USD)
New Customers	
sanchita (Sanchita Sarkar)	
sharmin (Sharmin Sarkar)	
borhan (Borhan Uddin)	
suhreed (Suhreed Sarkar)	

This **Statistics** tab shows the number of customers, the number of active products, inactive products, and featured products. In the **Orders** section, it shows the number of orders by order status type. In the **New Orders** section, we get a listing of new orders and their prices. Similarly, you can see new customers in the **New Customers** section.

Of course, you will not be satisfied with the summary of orders shown in the **Statistics** tab. You want to see more details and analyze which products are selling and on which occasions. For this purpose, you can use the **Report** module in theVirtueMart administration panel. Click on **Reports | Reports**. This shows the **Reports** screen:

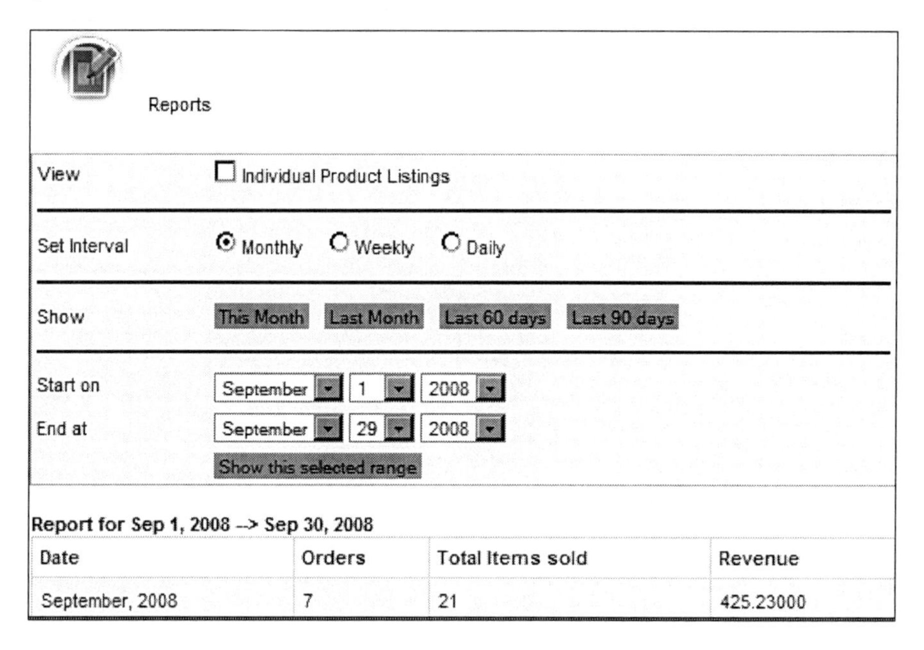

As you can see, from the **Reports** screen, we can view monthly, weekly, or even daily order statistics. We can also select a date range and view the orders placed during that period.

Let us first see how the monthly report looks. For generating such a report, in the **Set Interval** field, select the **Monthly** radio button. Then, click on the **This Month** button to see orders placed in the current month. That displays the sales for that month at the bottom of the screen with a heading like 'Report for Sep 1, 2008 --> Sep 30, 2008' (as shown in the screenshot above). The report shows the period, number of orders, total items sold, and total revenue from these orders.

If you want to know which items have been sold during the current month, check the **Individual Product Listings**, then select **Monthly** in the **Set Interval** field, and finally, click on the **This Month** button. This shows the report as shown in the following screenshot:

Report for Sep 1, 2008 --> Sep 30, 2008

Date	Orders	Total Items sold	Revenue
September, 2008	7	21	425.23000

Product Listing

#	Product Name	Quantity
1	Building Websites with Joomla! 1.5 (BK0001)	2
2	Joomla! Fitted Cap (CP0001)	5
3	Men's Joomla! Sport Shirt (TS0002)	1
4	Kubuntu 8.04 Desktop Edition CD (CD0008)	3
5	Men's Joomla! Sport Shirt - Green (TS0006)	1
6	Women's Joomla! Black T-Shirt (TS0007)	7
7	Fedora 9 DVD (DVD0002)	2

If you set the interval for this report to **Weekly**, uncheck **Individual Product Listings**, and click on the **This Month** button, the report looks like the following screenshot:

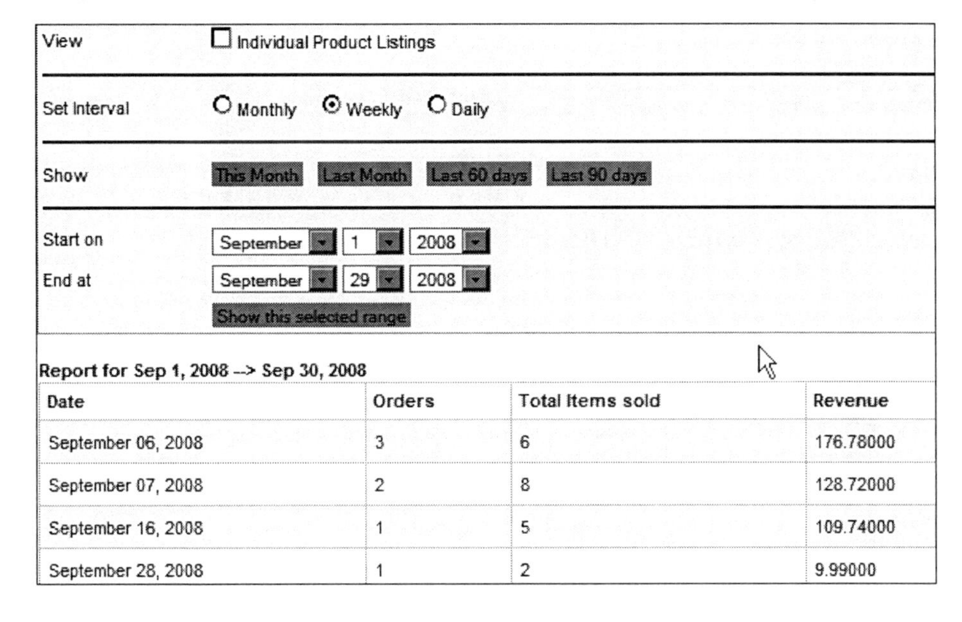

Report for Sep 1, 2008 --> Sep 30, 2008

Date	Orders	Total Items sold	Revenue
September 06, 2008	3	6	176.78000
September 07, 2008	2	8	128.72000
September 16, 2008	1	5	109.74000
September 28, 2008	1	2	9.99000

Similarly, you can see the report for the last month, last sixty days, last ninety days, and selecting the date range, and also by daily interval. These statistics will help you manage your orders and will be of great help for promotion and public relations, which we will discuss in detail in Chapter 7, *Promotion and Public Relations*.

Managing inventory

When orders are placed, and you fulfill the orders, the inventory levels of products tend to reduce. You need to keep an updated inventory of all product items, and proactively restock items that are approaching a low level of stock.

In VirtueMart, you can view the inventory of product items from the **Product Inventory** screen. To reach the **Product Inventory** screen, click on **Products | View Inventory**:

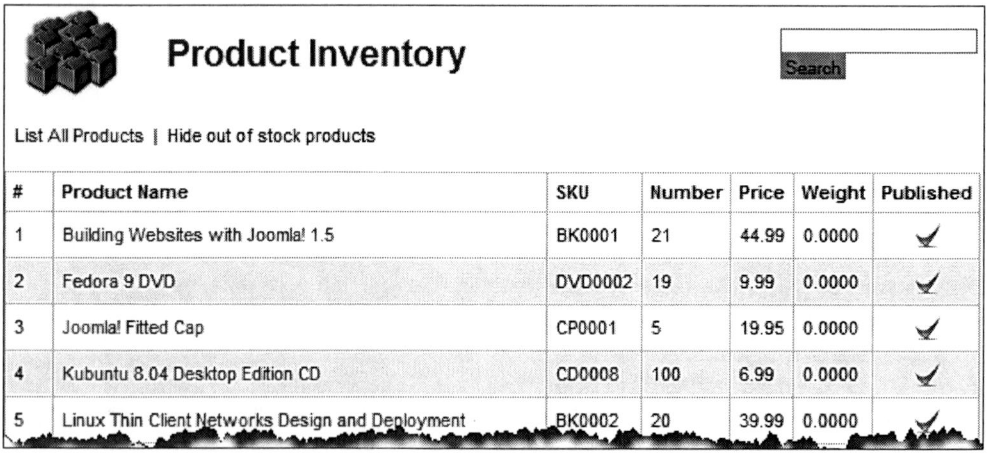

Product Inventory

Search

List All Products | Hide out of stock products

#	Product Name	SKU	Number	Price	Weight	Published
1	Building Websites with Joomla! 1.5	BK0001	21	44.99	0.0000	✓
2	Fedora 9 DVD	DVD0002	19	9.99	0.0000	✓
3	Joomla! Fitted Cap	CP0001	5	19.95	0.0000	✓
4	Kubuntu 8.04 Desktop Edition CD	CD0008	100	6.99	0.0000	✓
5	Linux Thin Client Networks Design and Deployment	BK0002	20	39.99	0.0000	✓

By default, the list hides the products that are out of stock. To view the list of all products, including those that are out of stock, click on the **List All Products** link. This shows the list products with **0** number in stock:

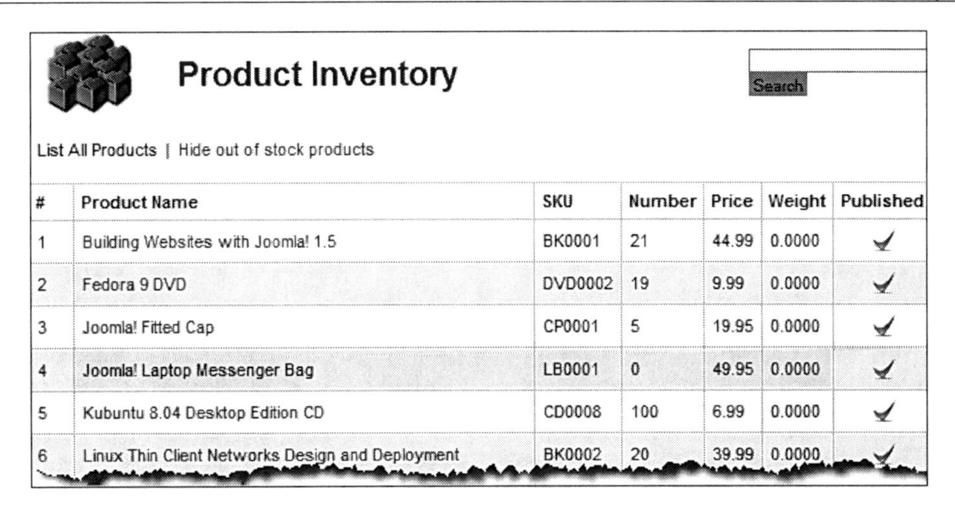
Product Inventory

Search

List All Products | Hide out of stock products

#	Product Name	SKU	Number	Price	Weight	Published
1	Building Websites with Joomla! 1.5	BK0001	21	44.99	0.0000	✓
2	Fedora 9 DVD	DVD0002	19	9.99	0.0000	✓
3	Joomla! Fitted Cap	CP0001	5	19.95	0.0000	✓
4	Joomla! Laptop Messenger Bag	LB0001	0	49.95	0.0000	✓
5	Kubuntu 8.04 Desktop Edition CD	CD0008	100	6.99	0.0000	✓
6	Linux Thin Client Networks Design and Deployment	BK0002	20	39.99	0.0000	✓

As you can see, the item **Joomla! Laptop Messenger Bag** is out of stock, showing **0** in the **Number** field. Suppose you received 10 of that item today, and want to restock it. To do so, click on the product name link. That will open up the **Update Item :: Joomla! Laptop Messenger Bag** screen. On this screen, click on the **Product Status** tab:

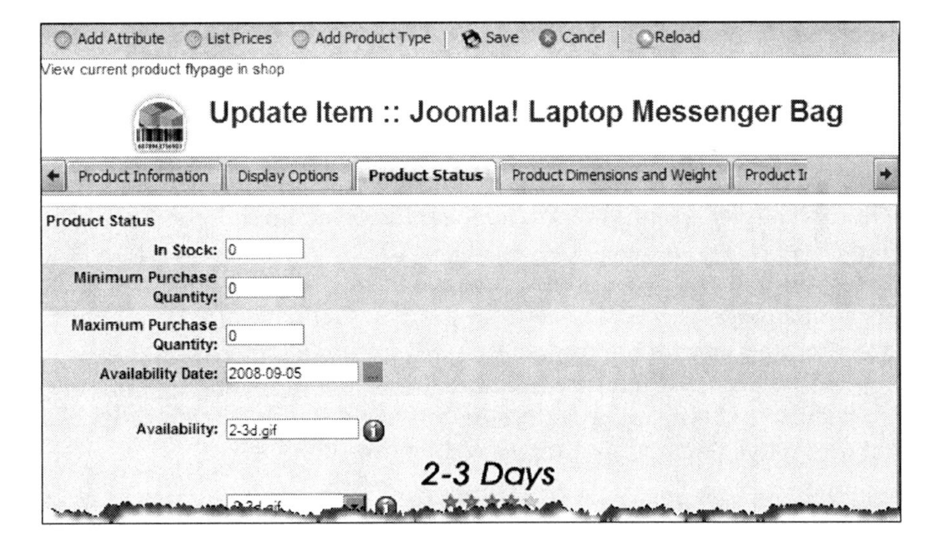

In the **Product Status** tab, the first field is **In Stock**. Type the number of items you have, say 10, in this text box, and click on the **Save** icon in the toolbar. You are done!

Now, go back to **Product Inventory** screen again. You will see that the **Joomla! Laptop Messenger Bag** has 10 in stock:

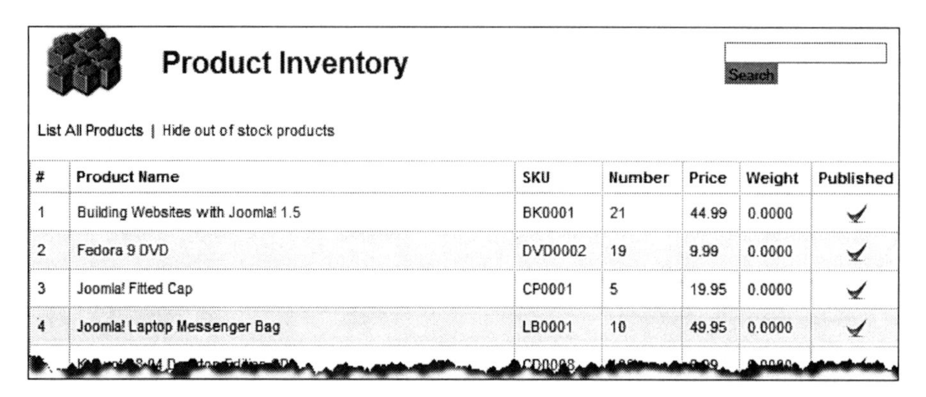

#	Product Name	SKU	Number	Price	Weight	Published
1	Building Websites with Joomla! 1.5	BK0001	21	44.99	0.0000	✓
2	Fedora 9 DVD	DVD0002	19	9.99	0.0000	✓
3	Joomla! Fitted Cap	CP0001	5	19.95	0.0000	✓
4	Joomla! Laptop Messenger Bag	LB0001	10	49.95	0.0000	✓

Using the same process, you can update the stock level of any product item by entering a new value in the **In Stock** field on the **Update Item** screen.

[The limitation of inventory management in VirtueMart is that, like other shopping carts, it does not warn you when a product's stock level reduces to a certain low level. It also does not show the out of stock products at a glance.]

Summary

This has been a long chapter indeed, and I am sure you have learned a lot from this chapter. In this chapter, you have seen how to allow customer registrations to your VirtueMart shop, how to manage the registered users, how to define extra fields for customer registration and account maintenance forms, how to create and manage user groups and assign permissions to user groups. You have also seen how to create permission modules and functions that are used for implementing a permission system for special groups. Finally, you have learned about managing orders, viewing an order's details, updating an order's status, creating and managing order status types, and also managing and updating product inventory.

All the things you have learned in this chapter are very much essential for running a VirtueMart shop, as you must deal with customers, orders, and manage the inventory. So far, we have built the catalog, allowed customers to register, set the order status types, and learned how to manage orders and inventory. Before allowing our shop to go online online, still there is at least one more thing to do. We have to change the look and feel of the store. As you have seen, we are still using Joomla!'s default theme. We must give it a look that we want. Yes, in the next chapter, we are going to learn about customizing the look and feel of our VirtueMart store.

6

Customizing the Look and Feel

I hope you have followed through all of the previous chapters, and built your shop with a product catalog. How does it look? It is using the default Joomla! theme. For branding purpose, and to show your shop differently than others, you need to change the default look and feel. Therefore, it's essential to learn about changing the look and feel of a Joomla! site and VirtueMart shop. In this chapter, you are going to learn about the secrets of customizing the look and feel for both Joomla! and VirtueMart.

On completion of this chapter, you will be able to:

- Install and configure new themes for a Joomla! site
- Customize the Joomla! template to get your desired look and feel
- Explain VirtueMart themes and layouts
- Customize VirtueMart themes and layouts
- Use pretty, or search engine friendly (SEF), URLs for your shop

I assume that you have some basic knowledge on HTML, CSS, and PHP. In this chapter, we are going to deal with some markups. Get ready for tweaking!

Configuring the look and feel of a Joomla! site

The first step in configuring the look and feel of your store is to configure the look and feel of your Joomla! site. As we know, a VirtueMart shop is part of a Joomla! site and gets its overall look and feel from that of the Joomla! site.

Joomla! has a great template system, and there are lots of templates available for Joomla!. To start with your Joomla! site, choose a template first. You may get professionally designed free templates as well as commercial templates for Joomla!. Before choosing a template for your Joomla-VirtueMart shop, search through the web, look at different templates available and decide which one you are going use, and what part of that template you are going to customize.

Installing Joomla! templates

Joomla! templates come in a zipped package. Installing this package is as easy as installing other components or modules. For our example site, we have chosen a free Joomla! template named **Redevo_Aphelion**. You can download it from `http://www.redevolution.com/downloads/download/red-evolution-aphelion-for-joomla!-1.5/`. This template is natively compatible with Joomla! 1.5. A version for Joomla! 1.0.x is also available. The filename for this template is `redevo_aphelion.zip`. Once it has been downloaded, you can proceed to installing the template.

For installing a Joomla! template, follow the steps below:

1. Log in to the Joomla! Administration panel.
2. Click on **Extensions | Install/Uninstall**, which brings the **Extensions Manager** screen:

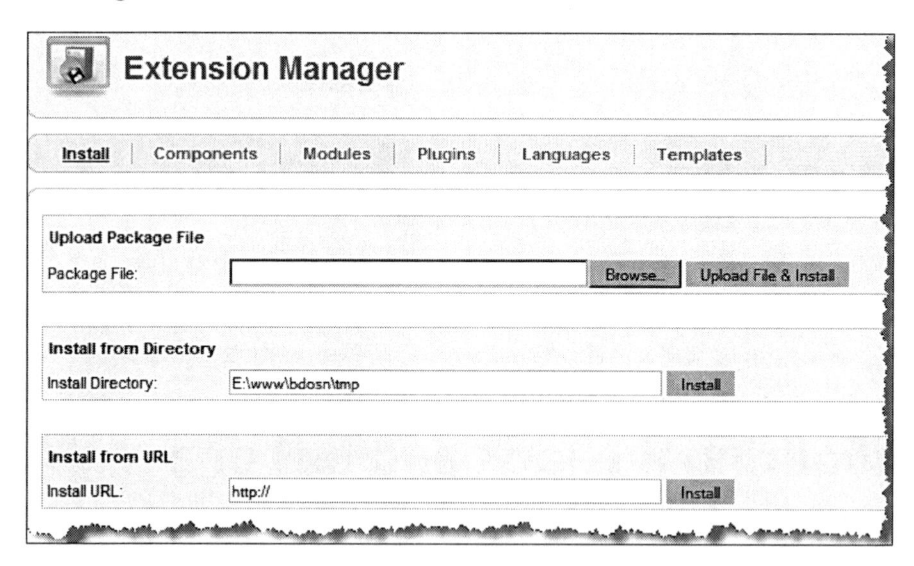

3. In the **Extensions Manager** screen, stay in the **Install** tab, and then click on the **Browse...** button. That shows the open file dialog. Locate the Joomla! template package (in its zipped format), and select it. Finally click on the **Upload File & Install** button. This will upload the file and install the template.

4. On successful installation of the template, a message will be displayed saying that the template has been installed:

5. If you are trying to install the same template that has been already installed, or if the uploaded file is corrupt, you will get an error message on the same screen:

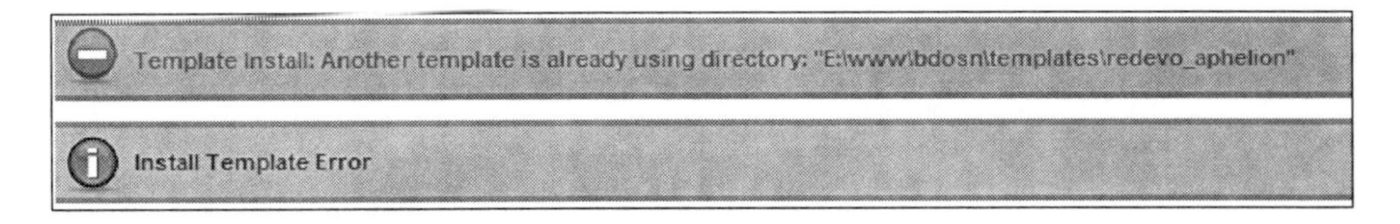

6. After the template has successfully been installed, you can proceed to activate that template for the entire site, or for a part of the site.

You can install as many templates as you like, and apply the templates to the entire site or only a part of the site. We are going to look into that a little later.

Applying a template

Templates are designs for your site. After choosing a template and installing that template, you need to apply that to the entire site or a part of the site. For applying the template you have installed, follow the steps below:

1. From the Joomla! administration panel, click on **Extensions | Template Manager**. This brings the **Template Manager** screen:

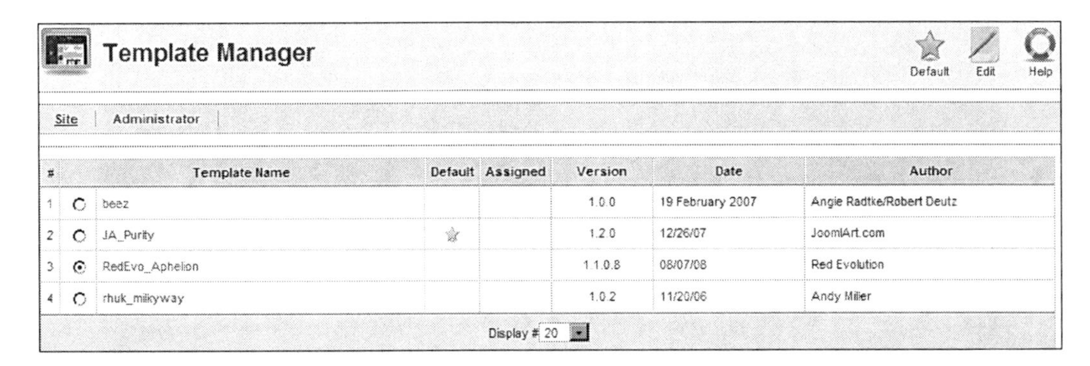

The **Template Manager** screen lists all of the installed templates. You can see which template is assigned as the default template for the site. A default template is marked with a yellow star in the **Default** column. It also shows which templates are assigned to the entire site or part of the site, including the template's date of creation and author name.

2. You can see the name of your installed template in the **Template Manager** screen. If you hover your mouse pointer over the template name, you can see a thumbnail for that template:

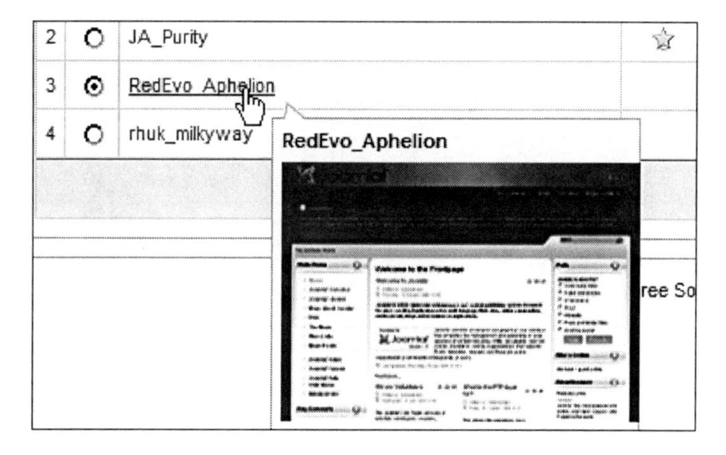

3. For applying the template to the entire site, select the radio button beside the template's name, and click on the **Default** icon in the toolbar. That applies the template to the entire site.
4. To have a look at your site with new template, click on the **Preview** button on the top toolbar. The site will open in a new window. Our example site looks like the following screenshot with the **Redevo_Aphelion** template:

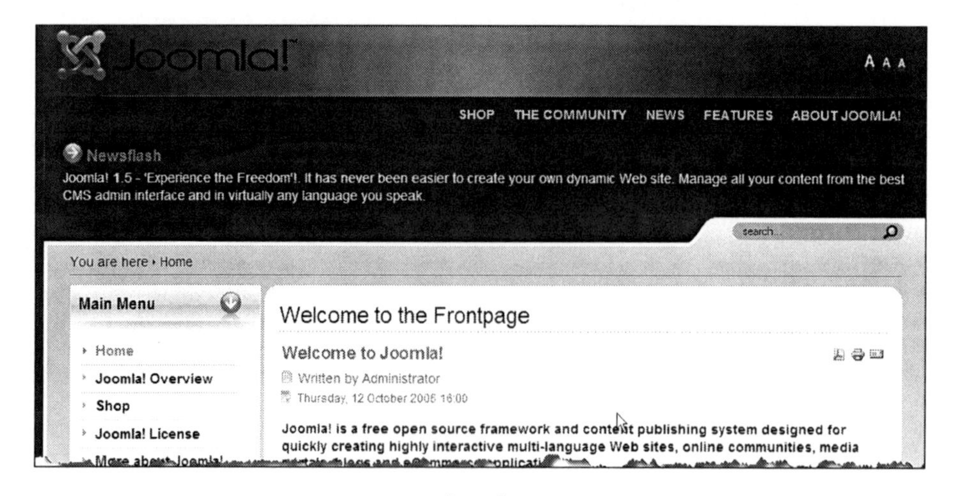

Our site now looks colorful. The top bar is shown in bright colors and then comes the top menu newsflash. This shows the Joomla! logo. We need to customize the template to display the site's logo and slogan.

Customizing a template

Joomla! templates can be customized to get the exact look and feel you want. However, this book's scope is limited to customizations which make the template suitable for your shop. If you are interested to know more about the details of Joomla! template designing and customization, please consult other books on this specific subject (some of which are available from Packt Publishing).

We are now stuck at displaying the logo and site name in the header area. Before trying to display those, let me explain how Joomla! templates work. Joomla! templates contain several placeholders, known as 'positions' in Joomla!, to display the blocks of information. Generally, the header block contains placeholders for the logo and site's name. There is also a placeholder for displaying the top menu.

For viewing the available placeholders, or positions, go to the Joomla! administration panel, click on **Extensions | Template Manager**. Then, click on the template name (for example, **Redevo_Aphelion**). This shows the **Template: [Change]** screen:

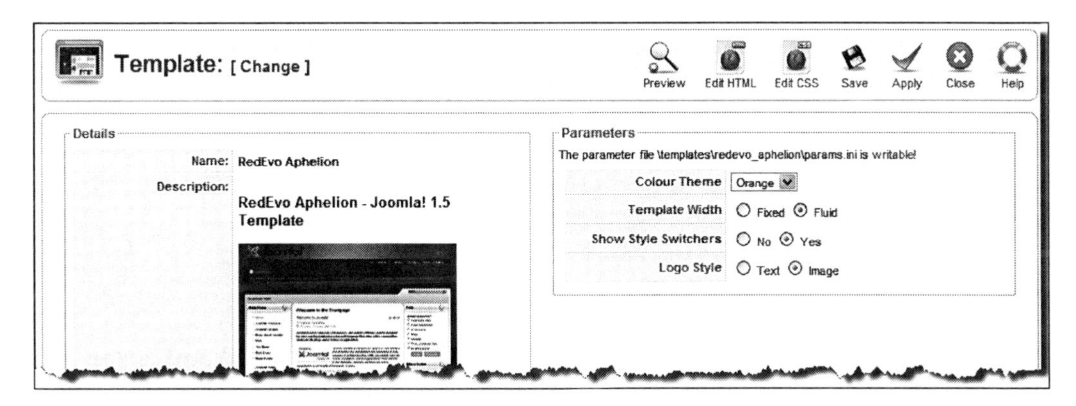

In the **Template: [Change]** screen, we see the template's name, description, and screenshot. From the **Parameters** section, we can configure several parameters to display our template differently. For example, you can select logo a type, its width (fluid or fixed), and logo style. If you select **Image as the Logo Style**, the logo image put inside the `./templates/redevo_aphelion/images` will be displayed. Selecting **Text** as the **Logo Style** will show the site's name only. If you select **Yes in Show Style Switchers** in the frontend, style switcher icons will be displayed from where you can change the font sizes to bigger, normal, or smaller.

The parameters are template specific. Some templates may have other parameters, or no parameter at all.

To view the placeholders, or positions, available in the template, in the **Template: [Change]** screen, click on the **Preview** icon beside the **Edit HTML** icon. This brings a preview of the template as shown in the screenshot below:

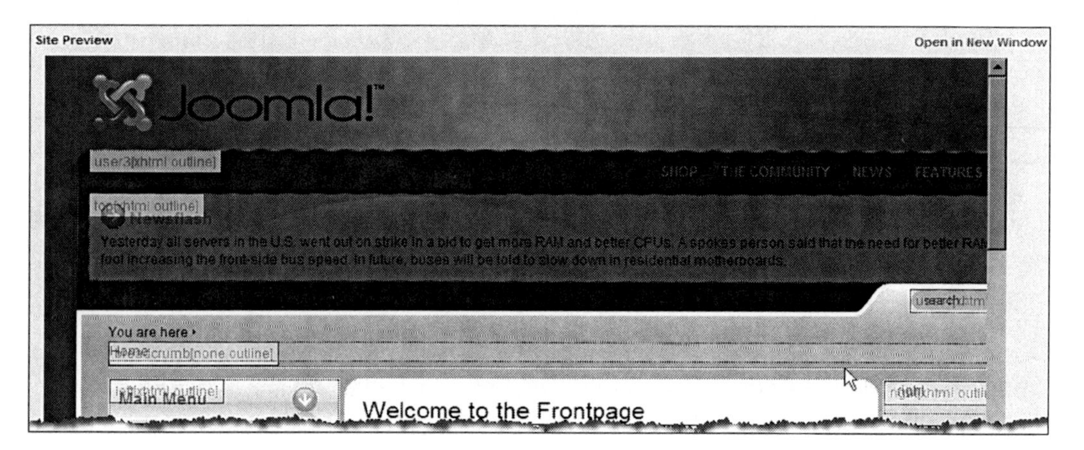

You may click on the **Open in New Window** link to view the preview in a larger screen. Notice that the preview shows the placeholders named **user3**, **top**, **user4**, **breadcrumb**, **left**, **right**, **footer**, **user1**, **user2**, and **syndicate**. We need to place our Joomla! and VirtueMart modules in these placeholders. As we see from the screenshot above, the **Top Menu** is displayed at the **user3** position. Also, note the **top** position, where **Newsflash** is displayed.

Changing a site's logo

So far, the template looks good for our site. The only thing we need to add is our logo. One easy way to do that is to replace `./templates/redevo_aphelion/images/logo_joomla.png` with our own logo image. However, you cannot replace that logo image if your logo is in any other format than `.png`. For example, the logo for our site is named `BdOSN_logo.jpg`. Although you can open the file in an image editing program, such as GIMP, and save the image as `.png`, we want to use the file format and name as it is. For changing the logo, we need to edit the template files. Follow the steps below to change the logo:

1. From the Joomla! administration panel, click on **Extensions | Template Manager**.
2. In the **Template Manager** screen, click on the template name **Redevo_Aphelion**. This brings the **Template: [Change]** screen:

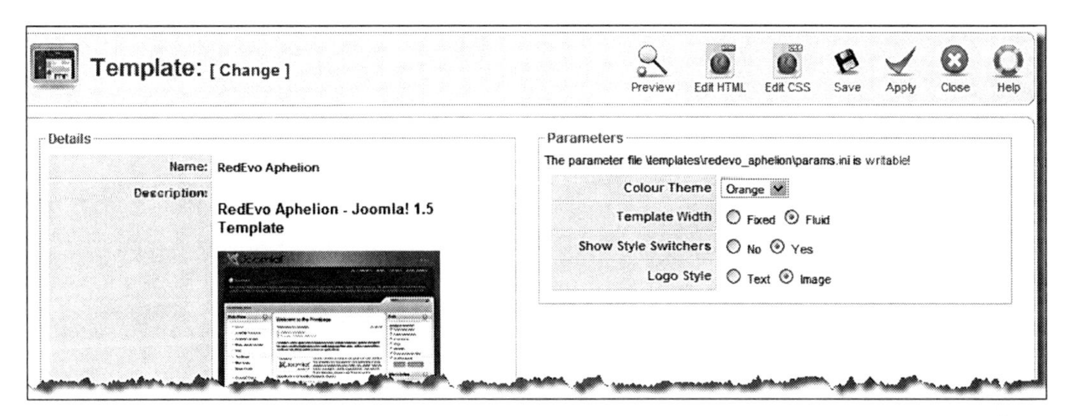

3. In the **Template: [Change]** screen, click on the **Edit CSS** icon in the toolbar. That brings the list of stylesheets available for the template.

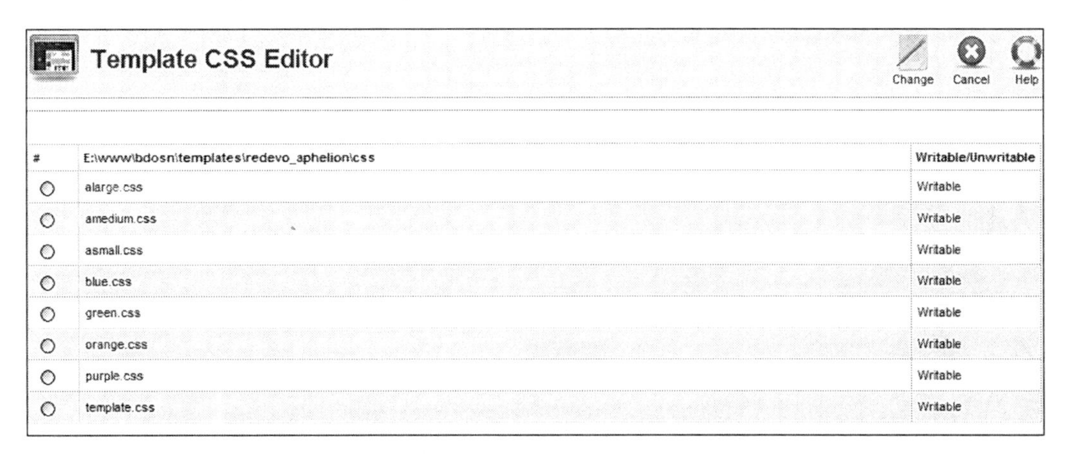

For every style modification to Joomla! templates, you need to edit the `template.css` file. Select `template.css`, and click on the **Change** icon. This opens the CSS file for editing:

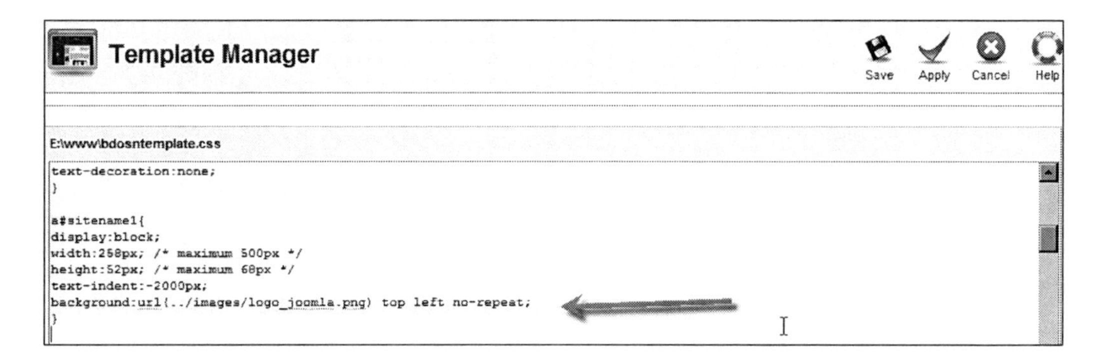

4. Scroll down and find the following section of code:

```
a#sitename1{
display:block;
width:258px; /* maximum 500px */
height:52px; /* maximum 68px */
text-indent:-2000px;
background:url(../images/logo_joomla.png) top left no-repeat;
}
```

5. As you can see, `logo_joomla.png` is used as the background for `sitename1`. To show our logo, we just need to change the `background:url()` declaration. After changing the code block above, it will look like the following:

```
a#sitename1{
display:block;
width:258px; /* maximum 500px */
height:52px; /* maximum 68px */
text-indent:-2000px;
background:url(../images/BdOSN_logo.jpg) top left no-repeat;
}
```

6. Click on the **Save** icon to save the changes.

7. Copy the logo image, `BdOSN_logo.jpg` into the `./templates/redevo_aphelion/images/` directory. Then, preview the site. The site now shows the BDOSN logo:

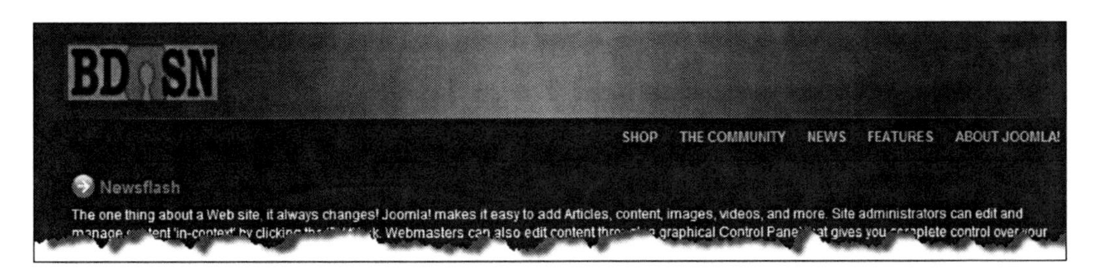

Our template is now almost perfect except for one thing. Scroll down and look at the **Latest News** and **Popular** modules. These are shown after the footer, that is, the copyright notice. We want to show the footer below these blocks. Look at the positions, these modules are positioned at the **user1** and **user2** positions:

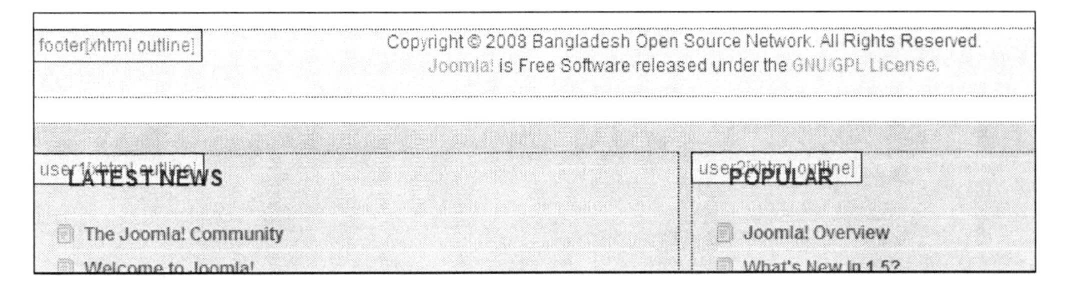

Let us now put the **footer** under the **user1** and **user2** positions. If you are not in the **Template Manager** screen, go there by clicking **Extensions | Template Manager**. Click on the template's name. You get the **Template:[Change]** screen. In this screen, click on the **Edit HTML** icon. This brings up the **Template HTML Editor** screen:

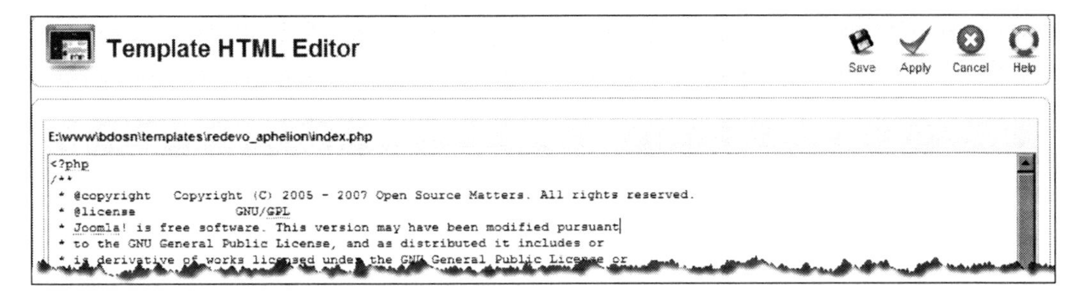

In the **Template HTML Editor** screen, scroll down and find the following code block:

```
<?php if($this->countModules('footer')) : ?>
  <div id="footermodule">
     <jdoc:include type="modules" name="footer" style="xhtml" />
  </div>
<?php endif; ?>
```

Select the code block above, right-click, and select **Cut** from the context menu. Then, scroll down further, and paste the code block above after the following code block:

```
<?php if($this->countModules('user1 or user2')) : ?>
     <div id="bottom"><div class="bottombg">
        <?php if($this->countModules('user1')) : ?>
        <div id="user1">
          <jdoc:include type="modules" name="user1" style="xhtml" />
       </div>
       <?php endif; ?>
       <?php if($this->countModules('user2')) : ?>
       <div id="user2">
          <jdoc:include type="modules" name="user2" style="xhtml" />
       </div>
       <?php endif; ?>
       <div class="clear"></div>
     </div>
</div>
```

After pasting, click on the **Save** icon in the toolbar. Now, preview the site and you will see the footer as shown in the following screenshot:

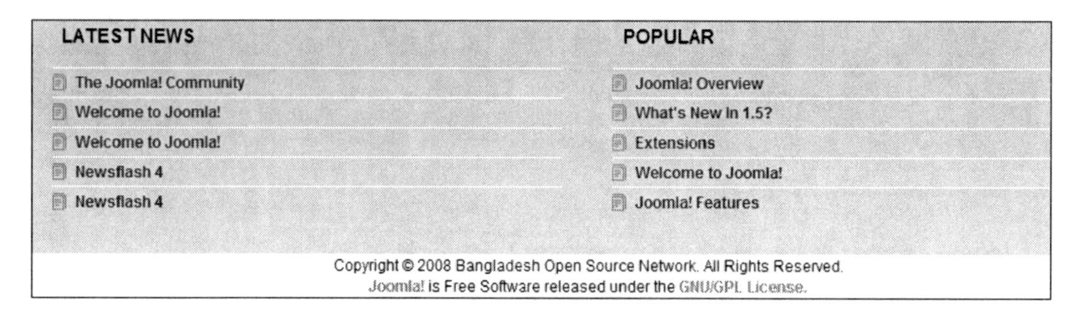

The text in the footer comes from the `./includes/footer.php` file. If you want to change the footer text, open that file. The following code block in this file sets the copyright information and year:

```
<div align="center">
&copy; <?php echo JHTML::_('date',  'now', '%Y' ) . ' ' .
  $mainframe->  getCfg('sitename'); ?>
</div>
```

The highlighted line takes the year from current date and site name from the Joomla! configuration. However, from Joomla! 1.5.x, there is a separate module **mod_footer** to display a footer. Let us look into this file. Open `./modules/mod_footer/mod_footer.php` in your text editor. The code looks like the following:

```
<?php
/**
 .. copyright notice ---
*/
// no direct access
defined('_JEXEC') or die('Restricted access');
global $mainframe;
$date =& JFactory::getDate();
$cur_year = $date->toFormat('%Y');
$csite_name      = $mainframe->getCfg('sitename');
if (JString::strpos(JText :: _('FOOTER_LINE1'), '%date%')) {
   $line1 = ereg_replace('%date%', $cur_year, JText :: _('FOOTER_
LINE1'));
} else {
   $line1 = JText :: _('FOOTER_LINE1');
}
if (JString::strpos($line1, '%sitename%')) {
   $lineone = ereg_replace('%sitename%', $csite_name, $line1);
} else {
   $lineone = $line1;
}
require(JModuleHelper::getLayoutPath('mod_footer'));
```

As you can see from the code block above, it gets the year, site name, and footer line (for example, All Rights Reserved). The constant `FOOTER_LINE1` and `FOOTER_LINE2` are defined in its language file located at `./languages/en_GB.mod_footer.ini`. The constants are defined as follows in this file:

```
FOOTER_LINE1=Copyright &#169; %date% %sitename%. All Rights Reserved.

FOOTER_LINE2=<a href="http://www.joomla.org">Joomla!</a> is Free
Software released under the <a href="http://www.gnu.org/licenses/gpl-
2.0.html">GNU/GPL License.</a>
```

As you can see, the two lines above define what will be shown in footer. Besides variables for the year and site name, it defines some text (All Rights Reserved), and second line of the footer shows the link to the Joomla! site. If you don't want to show this information, or want to show it differently, then you can edit it as you need. For example, we may want to show the first line differently, and not the second line at all. Therefore, the above two lines will look like the following:

```
FOOTER_LINE1=Copyright &#169; %date% %sitename%. Some Rights Reserved.
FOOTER_LINE2=
```

In the first line, we changed a word (you can change or add as many words as you need). For the second `FOOTER_LINE2` constant, we have just kept it blank. After these changes, save the file and preview your site. Now, the footer will look like the following:

Copyright © 2008 Bangladesh Open Source Network. Some Rights Reserved.

Customizing VirtueMart's look and feel

After customizing the look and feel of the main Joomla! site, you can proceed to changing the look and feel of VirtueMart. Generally, the Joomla! template is applied to the VirtueMart shop. However, there is a theming system through which you can change a VirtueMart shop's look and feel. We are going to learn about this theming in VirtueMart.

Look and feel configurations in VirtueMart

You can configure some look and feel parameters from within the VirtueMart control panel. The **Admin | Configuration** screen's **Site** tab gives you the opportunity to set several parameters for the look and feel, and also allows you to apply your desired theme. The **Site** tab of the **Admin | Configuration** screen has two sections: **Display** and **Layout**. The former gives you settings for showing or not showing some elements, whereas the latter sets layout options for product listings, product detail pages, and so on. The following screenshot shows both of the sections:

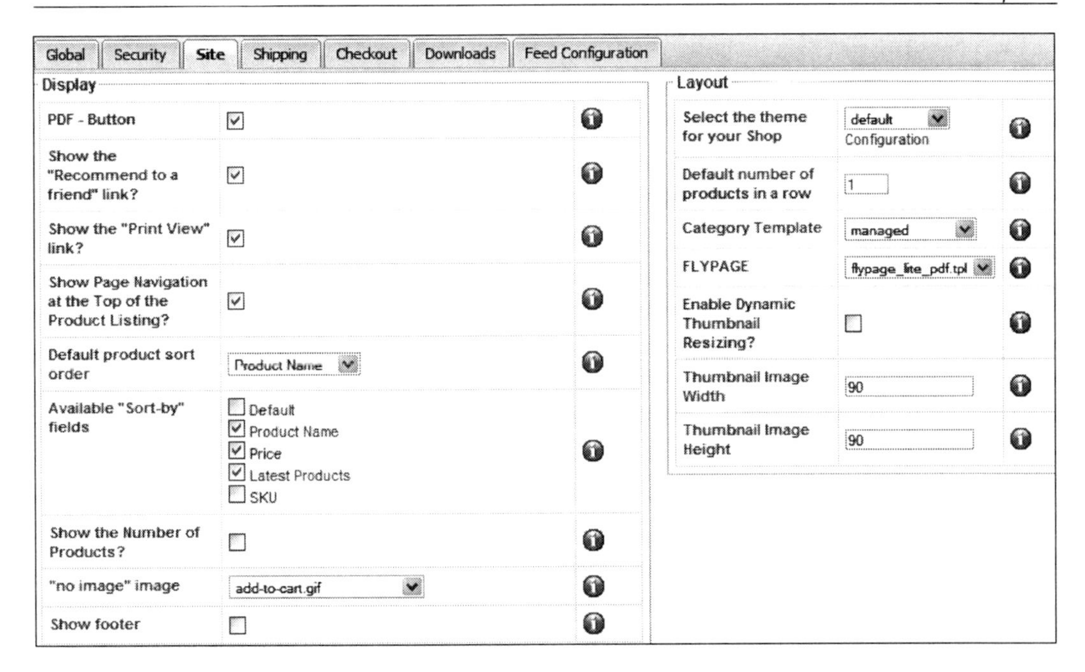

Let us first see the options available in the **Display** section of the **Site** tab:

- **PDF - button**: Check this box if you want to show the PDF button for pages in the shop. Note that this PDF button is independent of Joomla!'s configuration for showing/hiding PDF buttons.
- **Show "Recommend to a Friend" Link?**: Check this box to show the **Recommend to a friend** link on each product page. You should enable this feature so that customers can spread product messages easily. This is also independent of Joomla!'s setting for **Send to a friend** feature.
- **Show the "Print View" link?**: Check this box to easily print the product pages. Checking this shows the **Print View** link on each page and users can see a printer-friendly view of the page and print that page easily.
- **Show Page Navigation at the top of the Product Listing?**: Check this box to display the navigation links on the product listing page.
- **Default product sort order**: Select a default product sort order from this drop-down list. Available options are **Default, Product Name**, **Price**, **SKU**, and **Latest Products**.
- **Available 'Sort-by' fields**: Check the options by which the customers will be able to sort the products.
- **Show the Number of Products?:** Check this if you want to show the number of products besides the categories.

- **"no-image" image**: Select an image to be displayed when the product has no image. A list of images in the drop-down list will be shown from the current theme's images folder, that is, `./components/com_virtuemart /themes/default/images`.
- **Show footer**: Select this check box to show the VirtueMart footer in the shop.

At present, PDF documents generated by VirtueMart do not include product images. Instead, they show some garbage characters in place of product image.

As stated earlier, the **Layout** section gives you the opportunity to define layouts of the product listing, product details page, and so on. Let us now look into the options available in the **Layout** section:

- **Select the theme for your shop**: Select the theme you want to apply to your shop. With the default installation of VirtueMart, only the default theme is available. As you have copied the **vm_orange** theme to theme's folder, the drop-down list should now also show that name. We will come to the details about applying themes later.
- **Default number of products in a row**: Specify the number of products to be displayed in a row. Specifying **1** will be a good choice as that can show product in a decent way. Choosing too many to display in a row may affect the product listing page badly.
- **Category Template**: Specify a browse template for categories. When a user clicks on a category link, products in that category are displayed using this template. Available templates are **managed, browse_1**, **browse_2**, **browse_3**, **browse_4**, **browse_5**, and **browse_lite_pdf**. Use **browse_1** when one product will be displayed in a row. The best way is to select **managed**, this will automatically select an appropriate template based on the configuration of the default number of products to be displayed in a row. We will be looking deeper into these browse pages later and see how to create one.
- **FLYPAGE**: Flypages are for displaying product details. Select a flypage from this list. This will be the default template for displaying product details.
- **Enable Dynamic Thumbnail Resizing**: VirtueMart can dynamically resize images to thumbnails upon being uploaded to the server. Select this option if you want to dynamically resize thumbnails. VirtueMart will resize the thumbnail, using the **gd** extension of PHP, to the height and width specified in the following fields.

- **Thumbnail Image Width**: Specify the width of the resized thumbnail in pixels.
- **Thumbnail Image Height**: Specify the height of the resized thumbnail in pixels.

As we have seen, from the admin panel, we can configure much of VirtueMart store's look and feel. We can further perform additional configurations through themes and customized templates.

Customizing and applying themes

Themes in VirtueMart are different than Joomla! templates. These themes define how VirtueMart pages will look. By default, there only one theme comes bundled with VirtueMart. However, there are some other themes available for download at `https://dev.virtuemart.net/cb/proj/doc.do?doc_id=2079`. Let us download some color themes from this site and put them in the `./components/com_virtuemart/themes/` folder. Each theme should be in its own folder and uniquely named. The default theme is named `default`. If you download `vm_orange.zip`, then unzip the files inside the `./components/com_virtuemart/themes/vm_orange` folder. If you look into the files and subfolder of this theme, you get files and folders like the following:

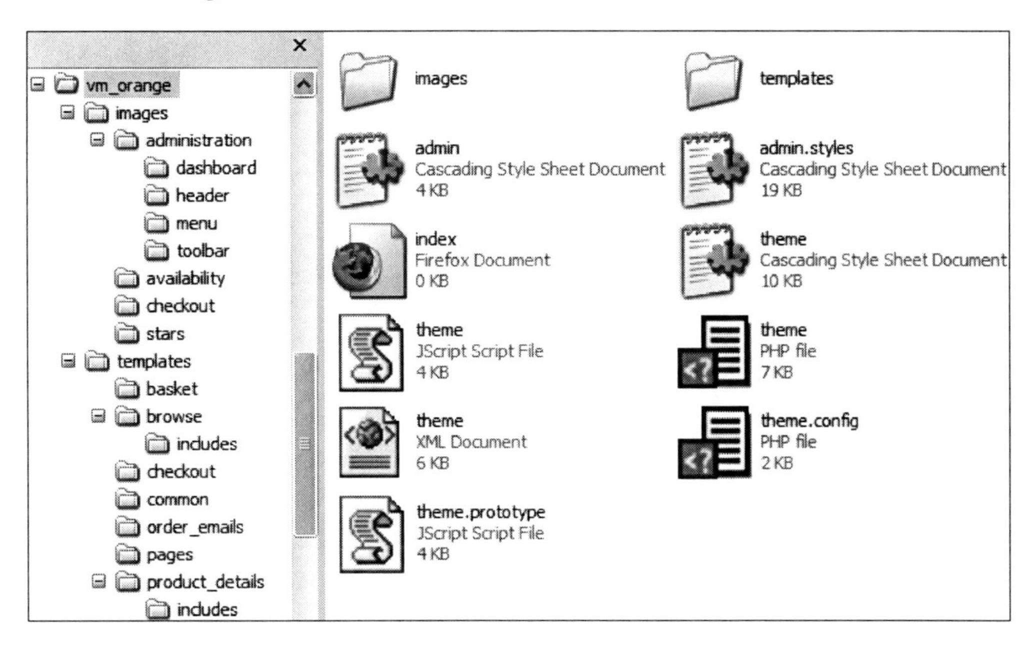

As you can see, the theme directory, `vm_orange`, contains some stylesheets, JavaScripts, a theme configuration file, images and templates for different views. The files available in this theme are described below:

Directory/file	**Role**
`theme.php`	This file acts as the main controller for the theme and includes functions and stylesheets for the theme.
`theme.config.php`	This is the configuration file for the theme. In fact, this file sets the initial configuration of some display and layout variables.
`theme.css`	This is the main stylesheet for the theme. The theme's look and feel are mostly controlled by this stylesheet.
`theme.js`	This is the main script file for the theme. It includes JavaScript functions required by the theme. These functions are mainly for dynamic actions and AJAX requests.
`theme.xml`	This file contains theme-specific configuration parameters and additional information about the theme.
`admin.css`	This is the main stylesheet for the VirtueMart administration panel.
`/images`	This directory contains theme-specific images. For example, the `vm_orange` theme contains orange colored buttons and icons in this folder.
`/templates`	This directory contains templates inside several sub-directories: `basket`, `browse`, `common`, `checkout`, `pages`, `order_emails`, and `product_details`.

Let us now assign the new theme to our VirtueMart store and see the difference it makes. For assigning a new theme, go to the **Admin | Configuration** screen in the VirtueMart administration panel, and click on the **Site** tab. In the **Layout** section, select **vm_orange** from the **Select the theme for your shop** drop-down list. Now, click on the **Save** icon in the toolbar. This will apply the **vm_orange** theme to our shop with the default settings. For customizing the options for **vm_orange** theme, again go to the **Site** tab and click on the **Configuration** link below the drop-down list. That brings up the **Theme Configuration** screen:

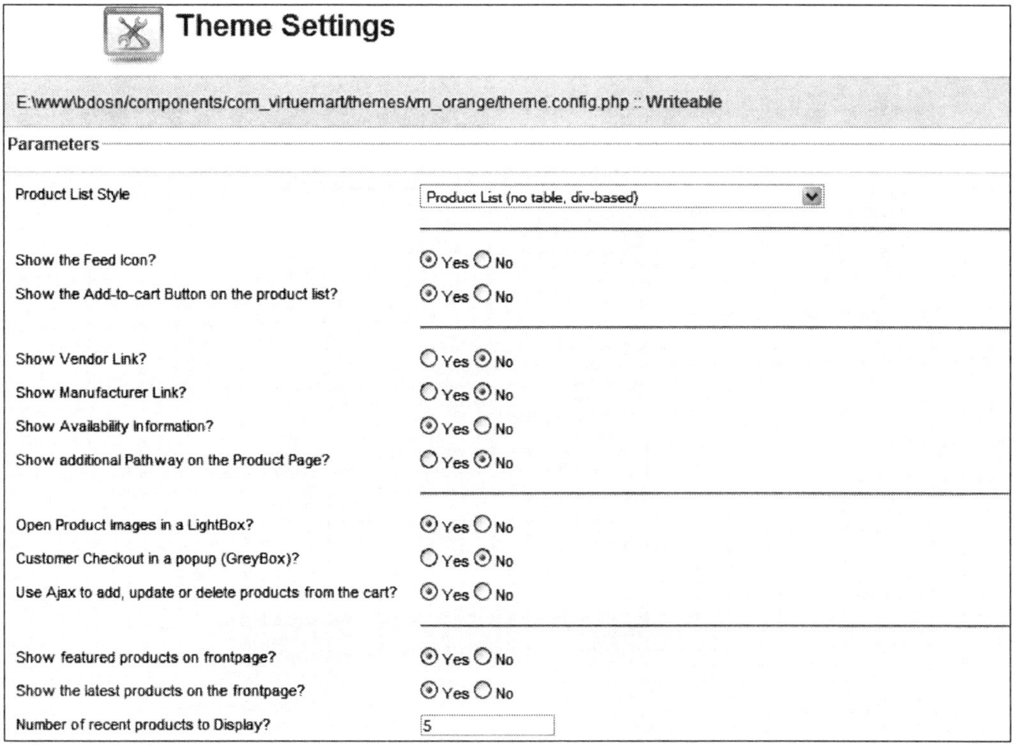

Theme Settings

E:\www\bdosn\components\com_virtuemart\themes\vm_orange\theme.config.php :: **Writeable**

Parameters

Product List Style	Product List (no table, div-based)
Show the Feed Icon?	(•) Yes ( ) No
Show the Add-to-cart Button on the product list?	(•) Yes ( ) No
Show Vendor Link?	( ) Yes (•) No
Show Manufacturer Link?	( ) Yes (•) No
Show Availability Information?	(•) Yes ( ) No
Show additional Pathway on the Product Page?	( ) Yes (•) No
Open Product images in a LightBox?	(•) Yes ( ) No
Customer Checkout in a popup (GreyBox)?	( ) Yes (•) No
Use Ajax to add, update or delete products from the cart?	(•) Yes ( ) No
Show featured products on frontpage?	(•) Yes ( ) No
Show the latest products on the frontpage?	(•) Yes ( ) No
Number of recent products to Display?	5

In the **Theme Configuration** screen, several parameters for the theme are available and we can control the display and layout of our shop item by configuring these parameters. First comes the **Product List Style**, from where you can select how the product list will be displayed by using tables, div, or a flat list using table with one product per row. By default, the **Product List (no table, div-based)** is selected, and for most of the shops, it will be the best choice. Other options are mostly self explanatory. For testing purposes, we will change some of these parameter settings. For example, we select **No** in the **Show Vendor Link**, **Show Manufacturer Link**, and **Show Availability Information** fields. Now, save this configuration by clicking on the **Save** icon in the toolbar, and preview the shop. The product detail page will now show like the following screenshot:

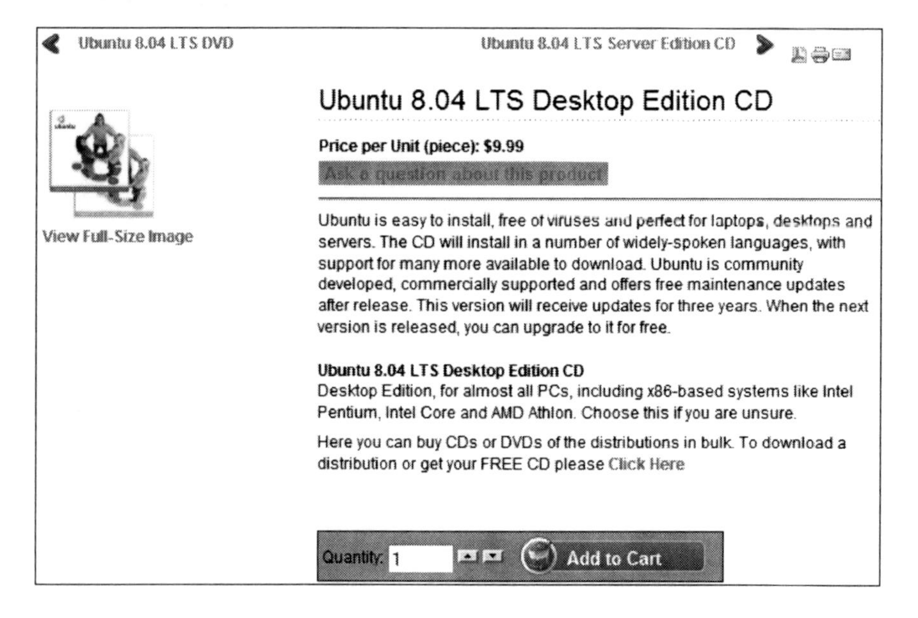

Note that the product detail page no longer shows the vendor link, manufacturer link, and availability information. You can revert to the former settings by choosing **Yes** in for these fields. Then, the above screenshot will look as follows:

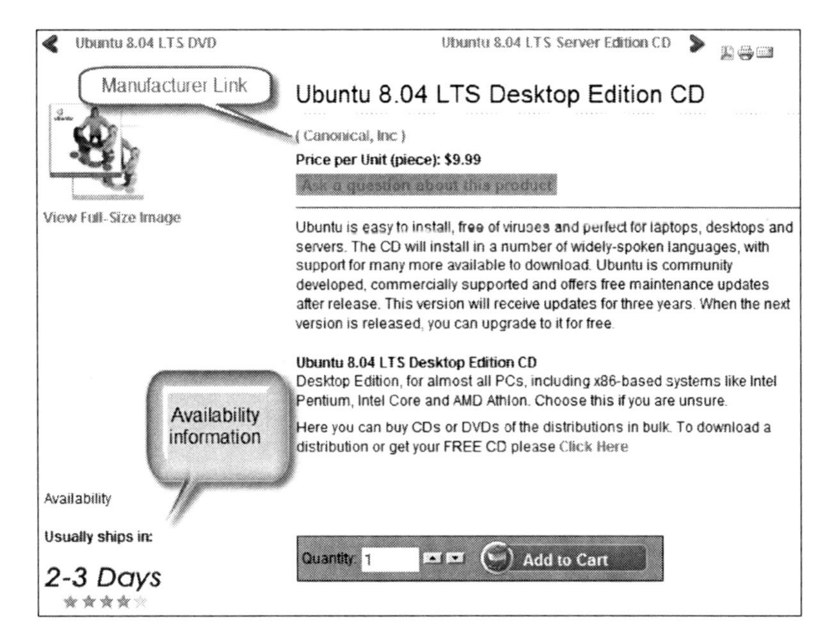

For the shop's front-page, we need to configure the last three parameters. Select **Yes** in the **Show featured products in the front-page** and **Show the latest products in the front-page** fields. Then, type 10 in the **Number of recent products to display** field.

Note that parameters shown in the **Theme Configuration** screen are theme-specific. Parameters to be shown are determined by the `theme.xml` file.

Customizing templates

As we have already seen, VirtueMart uses several templates to display its categories, product listing, and product details. All of these templates are written in plain HTML and PHP. Therefore, you can easily change the templates to suit your needs. In the following sections, we are going to learn about customizing VirtueMart templates.

Shop front-page

Joomla! has a front-page manager from where you can configure which articles will be displayed on the site's front-page. If you want to configure the articles to be shown on the front-page, go to the Joomla! administration panel, and click on the **Front Page Manager** icon. That brings the **Front Page Manager** screen with a list of content items to be displayed in the front-page:

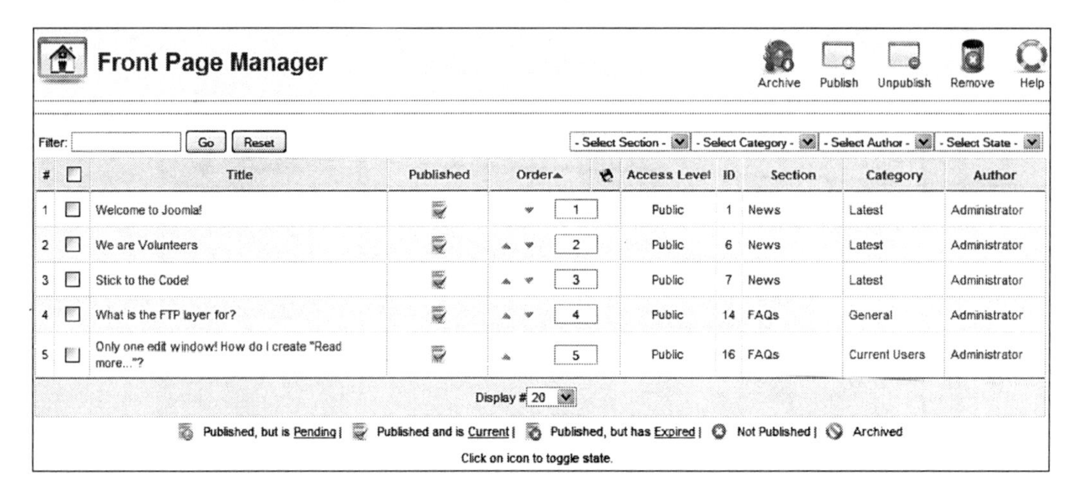

As we can see, from the **Front Page Manager** we can publish, unpublish, reorder, or remove content items. Also note that from this **Front Page Manager**, we cannot assign which products will be displayed on the front page. In fact, VirtueMart has no relation with this **Front Page Manager**. The shop's front-page is defined through a template file in the current theme. If you are using the **vm_orange** theme, then go to the `./components/com_virtuemart/themes/vm_orange/templates/common` folder. The file named `shopIndex.tpl.php` defines the front-page of the shop. Let us examine this file.

Open the `shopIndex.tpl.php` file in your text editor and you will find some code blocks. Let us examine those blocks one-by-one:

```
<?php if( !defined( '_VALID_MOS' ) && !defined( '_JEXEC' ) ) die(
'Direct         Access to '.basename(__FILE__).' is not allowed.' );
?>
```

This is a standard declaration to prevent direct access to the file. In all Joomla! 1.5 files, you'll find this kind of declaration at the very beginning. This is to prevent direct access to the file by typing the URL of the file. Next, you will see something like the following:

```
<?php
defined( 'vmToolTipCalled') or define('vmToolTipCalled', 1);
echo $vendor_store_desc."<br />";
```

The lines above are to check whether the VirtueMart tooltip is enabled. If it is not, it will be enabled. Then, the `echo` statement will print the vendor description. After that, the following lines print the category headings and a list of categories:

```
echo "<br /><h4>".$VM_LANG->_('PHPSHOP_CATEGORIES')."</h4>";
echo $categories; ?>
```

Once the categories are displayed, next comes the code to show the recently viewed products. We have seen that we can configure how many recently viewed products will be displayed. If you don't want to show the recently viewed products, you can simply disable it from the **Theme Settings** screen by typing **0** in the **Number of Recent product to Display** field. If you want to show the recently viewed products list at the bottom, cut the following block of code and paste it at a place where you want to display the list:

```
<div class="vmRecent">
   <?php echo $recent_products; ?>
</div>
```

The following code block is to show the featured products. First, it checks whether the store is configured to show the featured products or not. If it is configured to display featured products, (value is 1) the featured products will be displayed by calling the `$ps_product->featuredProducts()` function. Note that this function takes three parameters: `random (boolean),no_of_products (integer), category_based (boolean)`. You may want to change these parameters, for example, for showing featured products from a specific category. From the frontend of the **Theme Configuration** screen, you can only enable or disable the display of featured products. If you want to change the number of featured products to be displayed, you must specify that number in the highlighted line below:

```
<?php
// Show Featured Products
if( $this->get_cfg( 'showFeatured', 1 )) {
    /* featuredproducts(random, no_of_products,category_based)
     no_of_products 0 = all else numeric amount
       edit featuredproduct.tpl.php to edit layout */
    echo $ps_product->featuredProducts(true,10,false);
}
```

The following code block shows the latest products. First, it checks the configuration for showing the latest products. If it is configured to display, that is, if the value is `1`, the `ps_product::latestProducts()` function is called. It has four parameters. By setting the third parameter to `true`, you can show the latest product in the current month only:

```
// Show Latest Products
if( $this->get_cfg( 'showlatest', 1 )) {

    /* latestproducts(random,
     no_of_products,month_based,category_based)
     no_of_products 0 = all else numeric amount
       edit latestproduct.tpl.php to edit layout */

    ps_product::latestProducts(true,10,false,false);
}
?>
```

As indicated in the code block above, you can edit the layout for displaying the featured and latest products by editing `featuredproduct.tpl.php` and `latestproduct.tpl.php` respectively. We will be looking into these shortly.

As of this writing, there are some bugs in VirtueMart regarding showing the latest products. First, there is no file named `latestproduct.tpl.php`, and in `ps_product.php` file, actions for the `latestProducts()` function are not defined. For these reasons, you don't see the latest products on the front-page, unless you use the VirtueMart Latest Products module.

Let us now look into the `featuredproduct.tpl.php` file. After opening it in your text editor, you can see its structure. First, it checks if the `$featured_products` variable is empty. If it is not empty, only then it will loop through the `$featured_products` array and write other variables, that is, `product_name`, `product_price`, `product_thumb_image`, and so on. The following is a code fragment which displays the information about the featured product:

```
<a title="<?php echo $featured["product_name"] ?>"
  href="<?php $sess->purl(URL."index.php?option=com_virtuemart&amp;
         page=shop.product_details&amp;
         flypage=".$featured["flypage"]."&amp;product_id=".
         $featured["product_id"]) ?>">
<h4><?php echo $featured["product_name"] ?></h4></a>

<?php echo $featured['product_price'] ?><br />

  <?php if ( $featured["product_thumb"] ) { ?>
  <a title="<?php echo $featured["product_name"] ?>"
    href="<?php $sess->purl(URL."index.php?option=com_virtuemart&amp;
```

```
            page=shop.product_details&amp;
            flypage=".$featured["flypage"]."&amp;product_id=".
            $featured["product_id"]) ?>">
<?php echo ps_product::image_tag( $featured["product_thumb"],
  "class=\"browseProductImage\" border=\"0\"
   alt=\"".$featured["product_name"]."\"");?> </a><br /><br/>
<?php
    }?>
 <?php echo $featured['product_s_desc'] ?><br />

 <?php echo $featured['form_addtocart'] ?>
```

As we see from the code snippet above, the featured product template shows the product's name as hyperlink, then it shows the product's price. If the product has a thumbnail image, it shows that thumbnail linking to a full image. After that, it shows the product's short description, and shows a form for adding a product to cart. The variables we get for use on this template are from the `ps_product::featuredProducts()` function.

If you don't want to show any information, you can just delete, or comment out (using `/*` before and `*/` after) the line containing that variable. For example, in the featured product list, we don't wish to show a short description. Therefore, just delete the `<?php echo $featured['product_s_desc'] ?>` line. You may also rearrange the order in which the information is displayed.

Product listing

Product listings for categories are shown through browse pages. Browse pages define the layout for showing a single product in the listing. These pages are located in themes, that is, `./components/com_virtuemart/themes/vm_orange/templates/browse/`. In the default theme, there are several browse files: `browse_1.php`, `browse_2.php`, `browse_3.php`, `browse_4.php`, `browse_5.php`, and `browse_lite_pdf.php`. In the `vm_orange` theme, there is an additional browse file, `browse_color.php`.

Earlier, we saw that we can assign a number of products to be displayed in a row and the browse pages to be used. We have also seen that while setting the number of products in a row, we can select **managed** in the **Category Template** field to choose the appropriate browse page. For example, if the number of products to be displayed in a row is two, then it will use the `browse_2.php` template. Now, we are going to look into the details of these browse page layouts.

Let us first look into `browse_1.php` file. This page provides a layout for displaying one product in a row. It shows the product's name, product's price, short description, product thumbnail image, and customer rating. When this layout is used, a single product is displayed as shown in the following screenshot:

Building Websites with Joomla! 1.5
$44.99
Average customer rating:
Total votes: 1
The best-selling Joomla! tutorial guide updated for the latest 1.5 release * Learn Joomla! 1.5 features * Install and customize Joomla! 1.5 * Configure Joomla! administration * Create your own Joomla! templates * Extend Joomla! with new components, m
Product Details...

In the screenshot above, blocks are highlighted to show where the variables will be displayed. As you can see, first it shows the product's name, then the price thumbnail image, customer rating, and short description. For each product in the catalog, or a specific category, these blocks will be repeated.

Let us now look inside the code of `browse_1.php`. It will look like the following:

```
<div class="browseProductContainer">
     <h3 class="browseProductTitle">
   <a title="<?php echo $product_name ?>"
      href="<?php echo $product_flypage ?>">
   <?php echo $product_name ?></a>
     </h3>
  <div class="browsePriceContainer">
       <?php echo $product_price ?>
  </div>
  <div class="browseProductImageContainer">
    <script type="text/javascript">//<![CDATA[
           document.write('<a href="javascript:void window.open
             (\'<?php echo $product_full_image ?>\', \'win2\',
              \'status=no,toolbar=no,scrollbars=yes,titlebar=no,
                menubar=no,resizable=yes,
                width=<?php echo $full_image_width ?>,
                height=<?php echo $full_image_height
                ?>,directories=no,location=no\');">');
    document.write( '<?php echo ps_product::image_tag
      ($product_thumb_image, 'class="browseProductImage" border="0"
                             title="'.$product_name.'"
                             alt="'.$product_name .'"' ) ?></a>' );
           //]]>
           </script>
   <noscript>
    <a href="<?php echo $product_full_image ?>" target="_blank"
```

```
        title="<?php echo $product_name ?>">
    <?php echo ps_product::image_tag($product_thumb_image,
      'class="browseProductImage" border="0"
      title="'.$product_name.'" alt="'.$product_name .'"' ) ?> </a>
    </noscript>
 </div>
<div class="browseRatingContainer">
   <?php echo $product_rating ?>
</div>
 <div class="browseProductDescription">
     <?php echo $product_s_desc ?> 
     <a href="<?php echo $product_flypage ?>"
        title="<?php echo $product_details ?>"><br />
     <?php echo $product_details ?>...</a>
 </div>
<br />
  <span class="browseAddToCartContainer">
      <?php echo $form_addtocart ?>
  </span>
</div>
```

As we can see from the code above, the variables are printed inside several `<div>`. These `<div>` are positioned using a stylesheet. The variables used here are set by another file: `./administrator/components/com_virtuemart/html/shop.browse.php`. This file provides all of the core functions for browsing products in the VirtueMart catalog.

Let us now look into the `browse_2.php` layout. This provides a layout for displaying two products in a row. When used, the products in a row will be displayed as in the following screenshot:

Building Websites with Joomla! 1.5

The best-selling Joomla! tutorial guide updated for the latest 1.5 release * Learn Joomla! 1.5 features * Install and customize Joomla! 1.5 * Configure Joomla! administration * Create your own Joomla! templates * Extend Joomla! with new components, m
[Product Details...]
$44.99
Average customer rating:
Total votes: 1
Fedora 9 DVD

Fedora is a Linux-based operating system that showcases the latest in free and open source software. Fedora is always free for anyone to use, modify, and distribute.
[Product Details...]
$9.99
Average customer rating:
Total votes: 0

This layout is created using the following code in the `browse_2.php` file:

```
<div style="width:100%;padding: 0px 3px 3px 3px;">
    <h2>
    <a style="font-size:16px; font-weight:bold;"
       href="<?php echo $product_flypage ?>">
           <?php echo $product_name ?>
    </a>
    </h2>
     <div style="float:left;width:32%" >
         <a href="<?php echo $product_flypage ?>">
             <?php echo ps_product::image_tag( $product_thumb_image,
                   'class="browseProductImage" border="0"
                   title="'.$product_name.'" alt="'.$product_name .'"' )
             ?>
         </a>
     </div>
     <div style="float:left;width:60%">
        <?php echo $product_s_desc ?><br />
             <a href="<?php echo $product_flypage ?>">[<?php
              echo$product_details ?>...]
           </a>
     </div>
      <br style="clear:both;" />
      <p><?php echo $product_price ?></p>
      <div style="float:left;width:60%">
        <?php echo $product_rating ?>
      </div>
      <div style="float:left;width:32%">
        <?php echo $form_addtocart ?>
      </div>
   <br style="clear:both;" />
</div>
```

Other browse files also use these types of layout techniques. However, the exception to this is the `browse_lite_pdf.php` file, which is used to generate a simple layout that can easily be converted to PDF. This layout shows the products in a row as the following screenshot:

Building Websites with Joomla! 1.5

$44.99

The best-selling Joomla! tutorial guide updated for the latest 1.5 release * Learn Joomla! 1.5 features * Install and customize Joomla! 1.5 * Configure Joomla! administration * Create your own Joomla! templates * Extend Joomla! with new components, m [Product Details...]

Fedora 9 DVD

$9.99

Fedora is a Linux-based operating system that showcases the latest in free and open source software. Fedora is always free for anyone to use, modify, and distribute. [Product Details...]

The difference between the former layout and this one is that it does not show any customer ratings. The product's name and thumbnail images are also not linked. However, `browse_lite_pdf.php` file's layout is different than the other layout files in terms of its code. It uses a table for layout, whereas other `browse_*.php` files use `<div>` and CSS positioning. The following is the code for the `browse_lite_pdf.php` file:

```
<table width="100%">
  <tr>
   <td>
   <?php echo ps_product::image_tag( $product_thumb_image,
     'class="browseProductImage" border="0" title="'.$product_name.'"
      alt="'.$product_name .'"' ) ?>
   </td>
   <td>
   <h2><?php echo $product_name ?></h2><br>
   <?php echo $product_price ?>
   </td>
  </tr>

  <tr>
   <td colspan="2">
   <?php echo $product_s_desc ?>
   <a href="<?php echo $product_flypage ?>">[<?php echo
     $product_details ?>...]</a>
   </td>
  </tr>

</table>
```

As you can see, the layout is done by using a table. It's simple and convenient for producing PDF files. Look into other layout files and observe the differences with this simple, table-based layout.

Product detail page

Browse pages are for displaying a list of all products in the catalog, or in a category. When you click a product's link on the browse page, the details of the product are displayed. The layout file for displaying a product's details is called flypage.

Like the browse page, you can define store-wide default flypage template, and even specify this for each category. While creating or editing a category, we can specify the **browse** page and **flypage** for that category in the **Category Information** screen.

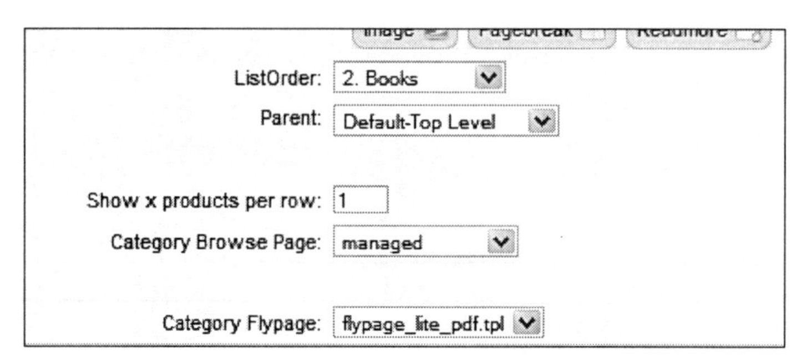

From the category flypage, you can choose one flypage for the category. The flypages available in the theme will be shown in the drop-down list (as seen in the above screenshot).

Flypages for a particular theme resides inside the `templates/product_details` subfolder. For example, the `vm_orange` theme's flypages will be in the `./components/com_virtuemart/themes/vm_orange/templates/product_details/` folder. Let's first try different flypages.

Let us first see how the `flypage.tpl.php` file works. Edit a category, say **Books**, and assign the `flypage.tpl` template to that. Then, from the shop's frontend, click on the book item. The product's detail page will look like what is shown in the following screenshot:

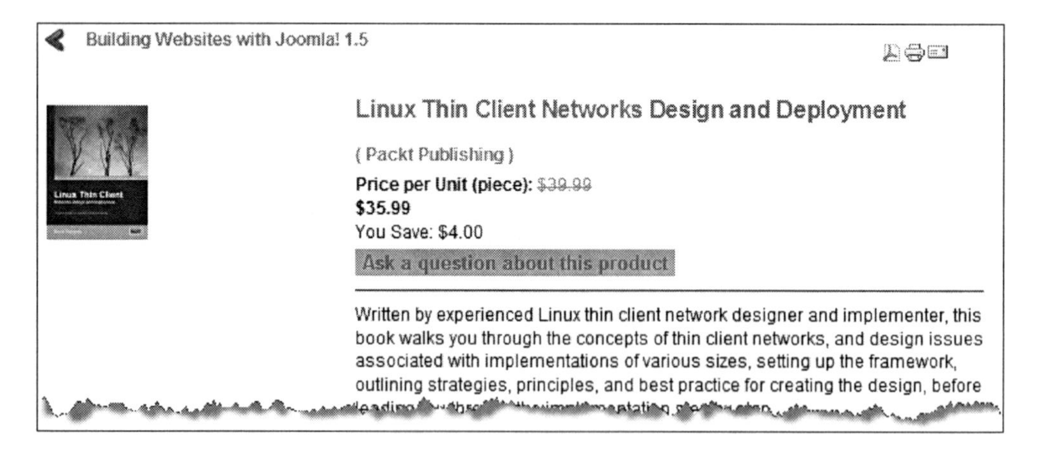

This is the upper portion of the page. As you can see, on the left, a product thumbnail image is shown. Then, on the right, there is a product name, manufacturer's name, price, and description. On the top, we see a navigation link, and buttons (PDF, print, and email). After the product description, product type attributes, availability, and add to cart box are all displayed. If there is a product review, it will be displayed at the bottom, followed by recently viewed products, and more categories.

Let us now try this with `flypage_images.tpl`. This is designed to show the thumbnails of additional images uploaded for the product. Other flypages show link to more images only. With `flypage_images.tpl`, the product detail page will look like what is shown in the following screenshot:

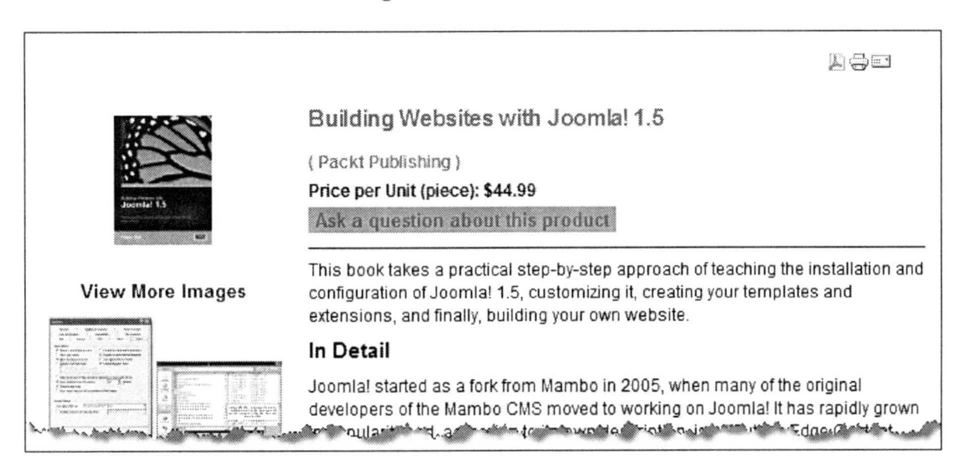

Like the browse page, `flypage_lite_pdf.tpl.php` is also designed to show a simple layout, convenient for converting to PDF. This simply shows the product name, price, thumbnail image, descriptions, product type attributes, and reviews (if any). It doesn't show an add to cart box or availability information. Use this flypage when you are building a catalog only store. The following is the code for this layout:

```
<?php
/* this template must have quirky html, because HTML2PDF doesn't
fully understand CSS and XHTML */
if( !defined( '_VALID_MOS' ) && !defined( '_JEXEC' ) )
  die( 'Direct Access to '.basename(__FILE__).' is not allowed.' ); ?>
<br><br>
<h1><?php echo $product_name ?></h1>
<br><br>
<table width=100%>
<tr><td width=50%><br><?php echo $product_price ?> </td>
<td width=50%><?php echo $product_image ?> </td>
```

```
</tr>
</table>

<?php echo $product_description ?>

<?php echo $product_type ?>
<table width=100%>
<tr><td><?php echo $vendor_link ?></td></tr>
</table>

<table>
<tr><td>
<?php echo $product_reviews ?>
</td></tr>
</table>
```

As we can see, this layout is made of multiple tables. This type of HTML is used so that the HTML2PDF library can convert this to a PDF.

Another available flypage is `garden_ flypage.tpl.php`. This is similar to `flypage.tpl.php`, but shows links to additional product images just after the main product image.

Let us now build a new flypage to show the product details as we want. In the `vm_orange/templates/products_details` folder, create a new file named `flypage_simple.tpl.php`. Type the following code in this file and save it:

```
<?php if( !defined( '_VALID_MOS' ) && !defined( '_JEXEC' ) )
  die( 'Direct Access to '.basename(__FILE__).' is not allowed.' ); ?>

<?php echo $buttons_header // The PDF, Email and Print buttons ?>

<?php
if( $this->get_cfg( 'showPathway' )) {
   echo "<div class=\"pathway\">$navigation_pathway</div>";
} ?>
<br/>

<h1>
   <?php echo $product_name ?>
   <?php echo $edit_link ?>
</h1>

<div style="float:left;margin:5px;">
  <?php echo $product_image ?><br/><br/>
  <?php echo $more_images ?>
```

```
</div>

<?php echo $manufacturer_link ?><br />
<?php echo $product_price ?><br />
<?php echo $product_packaging ?><br />

<hr/>
<div style="float:right;width:35%; border: 1px solid; margin:5px">
    <div style="text-align: center;">
      <?php echo $vendor_link ?><br />
    </div>
   <?php echo $product_availability ?> <br />
   <?php echo $addtocart ?>
 </div>

<?php echo $product_description ?>

<span style="font-style: italic;">
   <?php echo $file_list ?>
</span>

<?php echo $product_type ?>

<hr />
<?php echo $product_reviews ?>
 <?php echo $product_reviewform ?><br />

<?php echo $related_products ?><br />

 <?php echo $navigation_childlist ?>
 <br style="clear:both"/>

 <?php
   if( !empty( $recent_products )) { ?>
   <div class="vmRecent">
      <?php echo $recent_products; ?>
   </div>
<?php
   }
   ?>
```

The code block above is quite straight forward. We have not used any table for the layout. Instead, we used some <div> elements, and positioned those using CSS declarations. The layout above, when applied, will be shown as seen in the following screenshot:

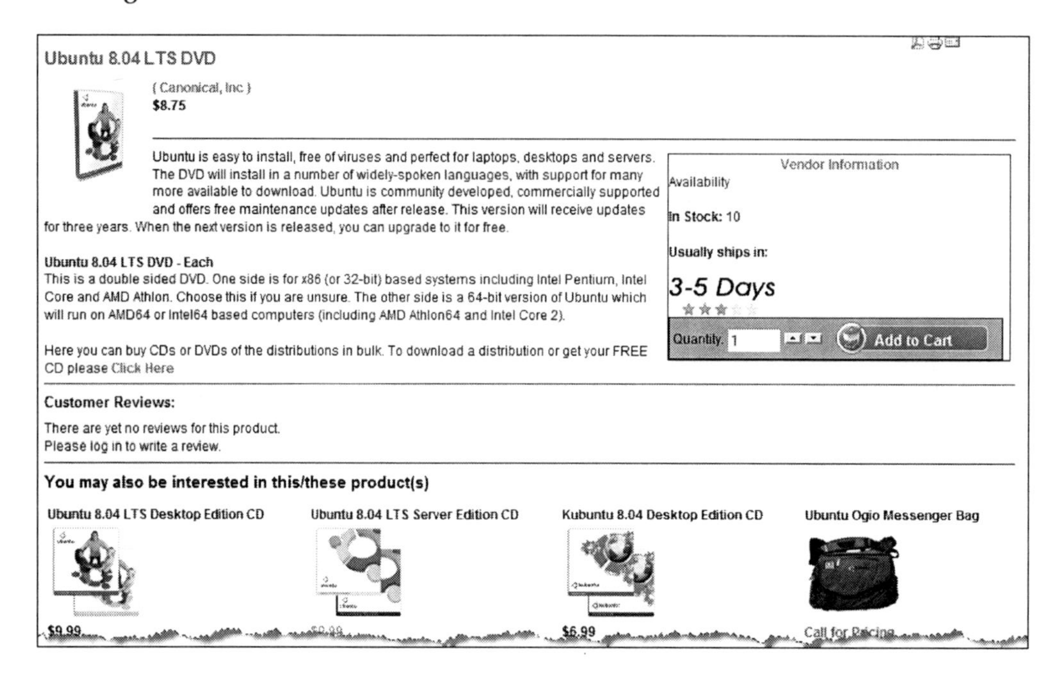

In our new flypage, we first see the product's name, manufacturer's name, and the product prices are displayed. Then, a product thumbnail image is displayed and is left aligned, followed by the vendor link, product availability, and an add to cart box. All of these are kept in a <div> element, and that <div> is floated to the right. This <div> is followed by the product description, product type attributes, customer reviews, related products, more categories, and recently viewed products.

> For a better understanding on how these templates work, look inside the includes subfolder. In this subfolder, you'll see several `.php` files, which are used to display add to cart box.

Basket templates

Templates for showing the items in a basket are located in the `./components/vm_virtuemart/themes/vm_orange/templates/basket/` folder. There are two types of templates: one for B2B (Business to Business) and another for B2C (Business to Customer). Files available in this folder, and their functions, are shown here:

File	Description
basket_b2b.html.php	This template is for showing items in the basket for B2B purchases. Purchases are considered B2B when you set the value **Show Prices Including Tax** to **false**. In this template, first, a list of items with their prices (without tax) is shown. Then, the sub-total is displayed. Discounts, if any, are deducted from the sub-total, shipping fees are added, and then a taxes sub-total is shown and added. Variables used in this template come from the ./administrator/components/com_virtuemart/ html/basket.php file.
basket_b2c.html.php	This template is for showing basket items in the case of a B2C transaction. When you configure your shop to show prices with tax, then that is considered as B2C transaction. This template shows the items with prices (including taxes), an order sub-total, shipping fees, discounts and the order total. It optionally shows the tax amount at the bottom, if you configure your shop to show taxes. It also gets variables from the ../html/basket.php file.
ro_basket_b2b.html.php	This is the read-only version of the B2B basket template. It is shown in the last step of the checkout process. It is read only because customers cannot change the items in this basket layout. Variables used in this template comes from the ../html/ro_basket.php file.
ro_basket_b2c.html.php	This is a read-only version of the B2C basket template. It is shown in the last step of the checkout where customers cannot update the cart's items. It also takes the variables from the ../html/ro_basket.php file.

You may have a look at these files to understand the layout, and if required, can change some lines. In most of the cases, you'll hardly need to do so.

Checkout templates

Checkout templates are for defining the layout of checkout pages. These templates reside in the theme's templates/checkout folder. The template files used for checkout pages are described below:

- checkout_bar.tpl.php: This template defines how the checkout bar will be displayed. The primary logic is to show the step images in the checkout bar and to highlight the current step. You may change the styles used in this layout.
- customer_info.tpl.php: This template shows the layout for customer information which is displayed in the checkout process. This page shows the customer's name, address, email address, and so on.

- `get_final_confirmation.tpl.php`: This template is for showing the final confirmation. It shows the shipping address and shipping method chosen, payment method chosen, checkout note provided by the customer, and legal information provided by the store. Variables used in this template come from the `../html/checkout.confirm.php` file.
- `get_payment_method.tpl.php`: This template is used for getting the payment method from the customer. This page lists the payment methods available for the shop. The customer selects one of the payment methods from the list.
- `get_shipping_address.tpl.php`: This template is for getting the shipping address from the customer, and presenting that address along with the shipping methods available for that shipping address.
- `get_shipping_method.tpl.php`: This template is for prompting customers to select a shipping method, along with the list of shipping methods available.
- `list_payment_methods.tpl.php`: This template is for showing the list of payment methods available. This template is included in the `get_payment_method.tpl.php` file.
- `list_shipping_methods.tpl`: This template is for listing the shipping methods available, and included in the `get_shipping_address.tpl.php` template.
- `list_shipto_addresses.tpl`: This template is for listing the ship to address(es), and is included in the `get_shipping_address.tpl.php` template.
- `login_registration.tpl`: This template provides the registration form for new customers. This also includes the `../html/checkout.login_form.php` file.

The variables used in these templates come from the `checkout.*.php` files in the `./administrator/components/com_virtuemart/html/` folder. You may look at these files to understand how these are linked with the checkout template files.

You rarely need to modify these checkout templates. However, if you want to fine-tune these files to get an exact layout, you may look into their code. The codes are straight—mix HTML, CSS, and PHP. Most of the files contain comments where you can get hints for what to change. For example, in the `list_shipto_addresses.tpl.php`, you may add the display country name, country code (two or three digits), and so on. To do so, open this file in a text editor, and then go to line #65, from which the code looks like the following:

```
echo $db->f("city");
echo ', ';
// for state, can be used: state_name, state_2_code, state_3_code
echo $db->f("state_2_code") . " ";
```

```
echo $db->f("zip") . "<br />\n";
// for country, can be used: country_name, country_2_code,
//country_3_code (not displayed in default template)
echo $VM_LANG->_('PHPSHOP_CHECKOUT_CONF_PHONE').': '. $db->f("phone_
1") . "\n";
echo '<br />'."\n";
```

As we can see in the lines above, we can use some other variables to show a two-digit or three-digit country code and state code. Similarly, you may look at other template files and see the scope of customizing with available variables.

Email templates

VirtueMart sends emails to customers whenever they register with VirtueMart, order an item, or enquire about a product. The registration message is sent from the Joomla! engine, and it maintains the template for user registration and activation mail. VirtueMart uses two templates for order confirmation mail and product enquiries. These templates are located inside the `../themes/theme_name/templates/order_emails/` folder.

First, let's look at the order confirmation template, `confirmation_email.tpl.php`. Like other templates we have seen earlier, this also uses a table for layout. Inside the table cells, some PHP variables are used. This file prints a ship to address, bill to address, the shop's address with vendor logo, product name, quantity, order total, discount total, tax total, payment, and the shipping method chosen and any comments added to the order by the customer.

The enquiry email template, `enquiry_email.tpl.php`, is also table-based and shows the product's name, product thumbnail image, product's description, email subject, question asked by the customer and the customer's contact email.

The variables used in these two template files are coming from the `email_receipt()` function in the `./administrator/com_virtuemart/classes/ps_checkout.php` file.

Other page templates

Templates for other pages in VirtueMart are located in the `./components/com_virtuemart/ themes/theme_name/templates/pages/` folder. This folder contains several page templates including templates for the account's index, billing, orders, billing, shop's cart, info page, checkout, and waiting list pages.

For customizing templates, you should also know about some other files on which the templates depend. These files are located in the `./administrator/components/com_virtuemart/html/` folder. For example, `product.review_form.php` defines what the product review form will look like. Similarly, `shop.index.php` file prepares the variables and sets the template for the shop's front-page. Looking inside the files in this .../`html` folder will help you understand how VirtueMart's look and feel works.

Using search engine friendly URLs

When you are using Joomla! and VirtueMart, the URLs are long and include several parameters. For example, our shop's URL becomes `http://localhost/bdosn/index.php?option =com_virtuemart&Itemid=53`. These types of URLs are generally not indexed by search engines. These URLs are also not human-friendly. Using search engine friendly URLs helps you gain upper ranking in search engines. Therefore, Joomla! included a feature to generate search engine friendly (SEF) URLs. There are also some other components for generating SEF URLs. We will first look into using the built-in mechanism for generating SEF URLs in Joomla!, and then look into other SEF components. Not all SEF components work well with VirtueMart. Therefore, we will look into a component which works with VirtueMart.

Built-in Joomla! SEF

Built-in Joomla! SEF functionality provides basic search engine friendly URLs. Configuring this is easy and straight forward. You can enable Joomla! SEF from Joomla!'s administration panel. Click on **Site | Global Configuration**, and you will get the **Global Configuration** screen. Click on the **Site** tab, if it is not selected already:

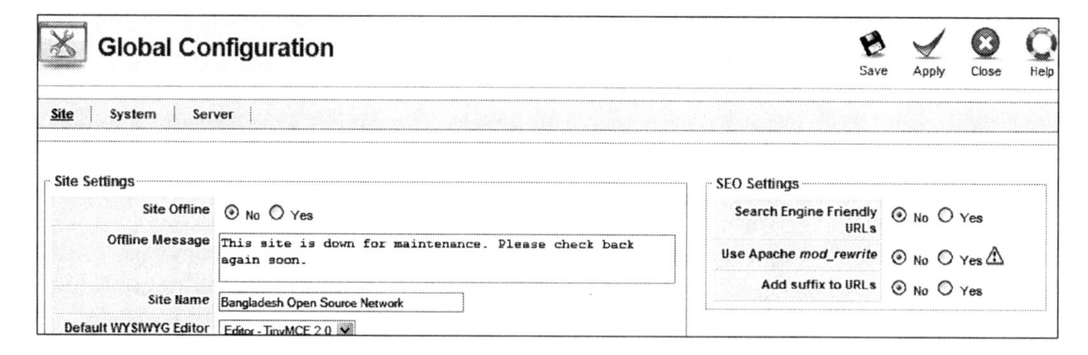

In the **Site** tab, you will see the **SEO Settings** section. To enable SEF, check **Yes** in the **Search Engine Friendly URLs** field. Let us now look into our store's pages. Browse some pages of your site and some products. We will get URLs which look like the following:

- `http://localhost/bdosn/index.php/the-news/1-welcome-to-joomla`: This is Joomla!'s Welcome page whose URL before SEF was `http://localhost/bdosn/index.php?option=com_content&view=article&id=1:welcome-to-joomla&catid=1:latest-news&Itemid=50`.
- `http://localhost/bdosn/index.php/shop`: This is the URL of the shop's frontend whose URL before SEF was `http://localhost/bdosn/index.php? option=com_virtuemart&Itemid=53`.
- `http://localhost/bdosn/index.php/shop?page=shop.browse&category_id=6`: This is one category of the VirtueMart shop. Note that this has not changed much.

From the examples above, and browsing some more products and categories, you will see that SEF works fine up to the shop's frontend, but beyond that (to products and product categories) the long URLs remain the same. We will look into this issue later in this section.

For generating SEF URLs, we may also use Apache's `mod_rewrite`. Check **Yes** in **Use Apache mod_rewrite** field. Make sure that you have enabled the **mod_rewrite** module in Apache, and renamed the `htaccess.txt` file in the Joomla! root directory to `.htaccess`. This will work only for Apache web servers.

The `.htaccess` file defines how URLs will be re-written. You should not touch this file until you know what each line in this file means. If you are an expert in `mod_rewrite`, only then should you think of changing some rules in this file. In most cases, you will not need to change anything in this file. For more information on configuring the `.htaccess` file, you may consult *Joomla! Web Security* by Packt Publishing.

There are many third-party extensions for Joomla! SEF. You can get all of these extensions at `http://extensions.joomla.org/extensions/site-management/sef`. Some of this work fine with Joomla!, but not so fine with VirtueMart. So far, the sh404SEF component works for both Joomla! and Virtuemart. Therefore, in the next section, we are going to learn about implementing SEF URLs in our shop using the sh404SEF component.

SEF with sh404SEF

One excellent SEF extension for Joomla! is sh404SEF. It works with many Joomla! components, including VirtueMart. This component is a hot item and an Editor's Pick at Joomla! extensions directory. You can download it from `http://joomlacode.org/gf/project/sh404sef/frs/`.

Download the sh404SEF package for Joomla! 1.5 or Joomla! 1.0.x. As we are using Joomla! 1.5.x, we have downloaded the Joomla! 1.5.x version from the download site listed above. Once downloaded, install and configure the component as follows:

1. Log in to Joomla! administration panel.
2. Click on **Extensions | Install/Uninstall**. That brings up the **Extensions Manager** screen.
3. From the **Install** tab of the **Extensions Manager** screen, click on the **Browse** button and select **sh404SEF** package, click **Open**, and then click on the **Upload File and Install** on the **Extensions Manager** screen:

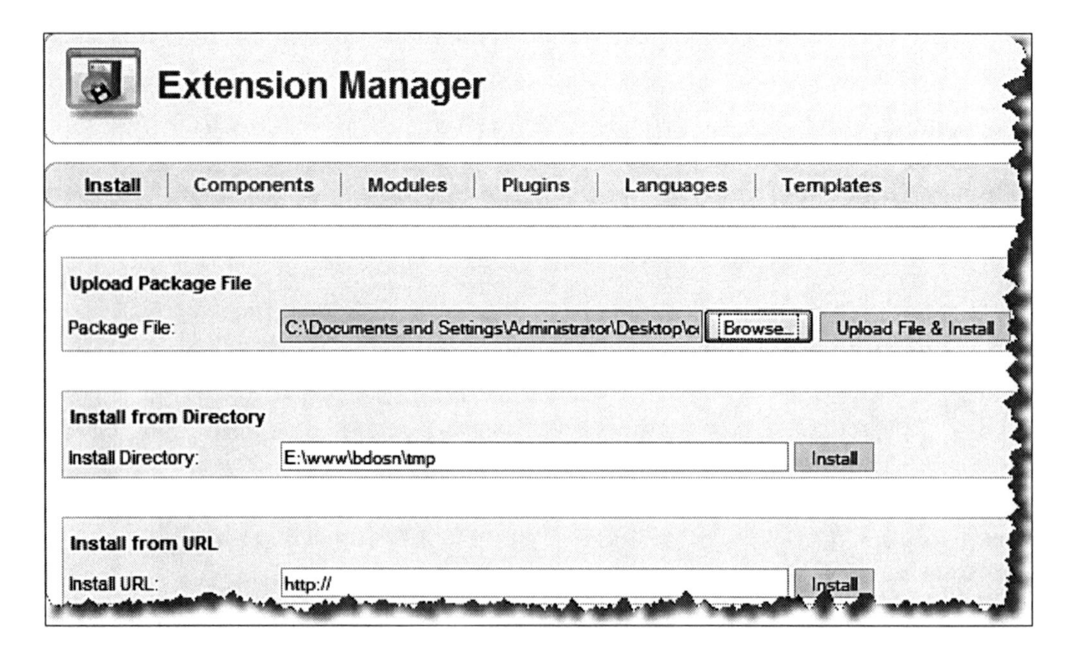

4. Upon installing sh404SEF, you will see the following screen stating that the sh404SEF component is installed successfully. It also provides some instructions. You must read this carefully before proceeding to configuration of sh404SEF component:

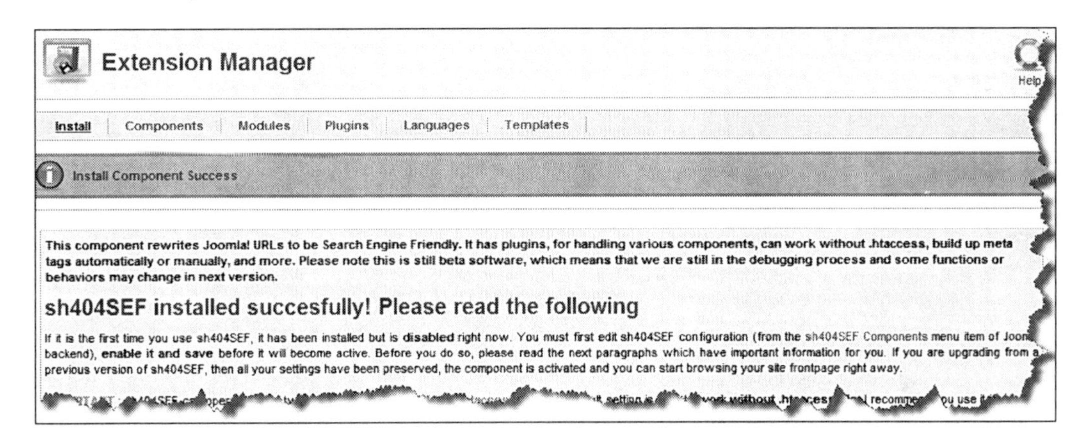

5. Once installed successfully, you'll see the **sh404SEF** link in the **Components** menu. For managing the sh404SEF component, click on **Components | sh404SEF**. This brings the **sh404SEF** control panel:

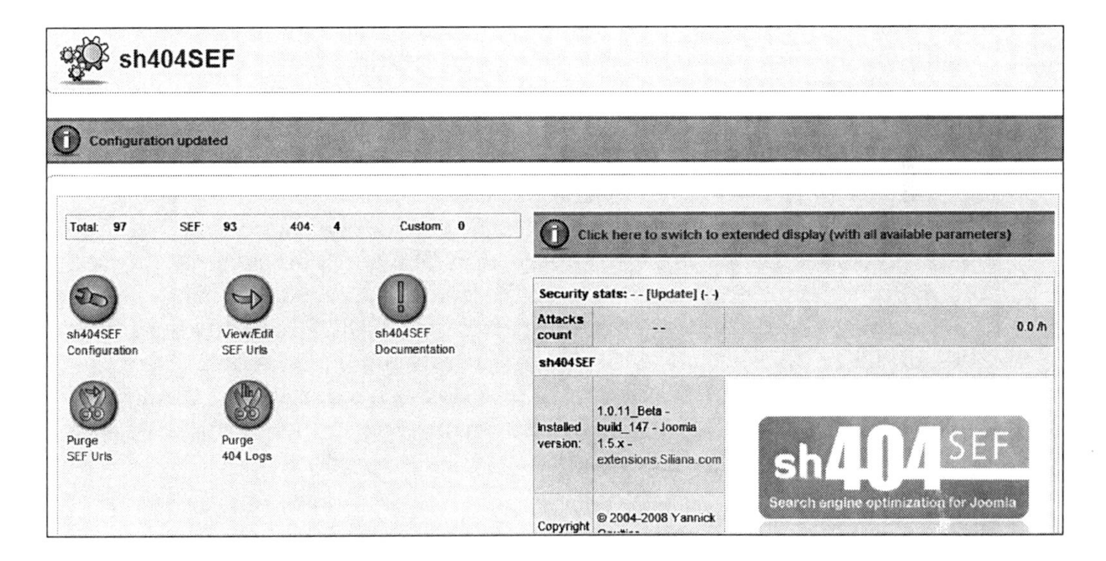

6. For enabling and configuring the sh404SEF component, click on the **sh404SEF Configuration** icon on the **sh404SEF** screen. That brings the **sh404SEF Configuration** screen:

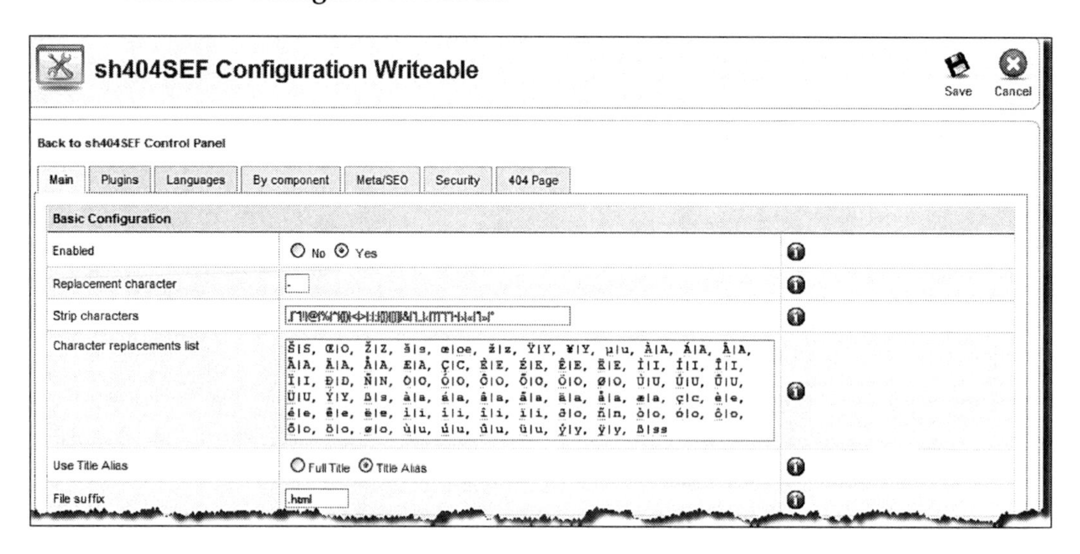

7. One of the advantages of using sh404SEF is that you can use it without `.htaccess`. For many shared servers, you may not have `mod_rewrite` enabled, and site owners with limited technical skills may not be able to configure the `.htaccess` file. Therefore, you may like to use SEF without `.htaccess`. To enable SEF directly, select **Yes** in the **Enabled** field and click on the **Save** icon. However, we can configure something else to get more from the sh404SEF component. In the **Main** tab, you can select which character will be used as a replacement, and which characters should be stripped and replaced. In the **Use Title Alias** field, you can select either **Full Title** or **Title Alias**. Based on your selection, SEF URLs are generated based on either the full title of the article, or the title alias provided during creation of the article. You can also select a file extension in the **File Suffix** field. The default file suffix is `.html`, which means all URLs will end with a `.html` extension. If you select **Yes** in the **Unique ID** field, that will add a unique id (for example, 200811001), to each URL. Finally, you can select the categories for which a unique id will be used.

8. Preview the site and click on the shop items. You will now find URLs like:

    - `http://localhost/bdosn/index.php/Shop.html`
    - `http://localhost/bdosn/index.php/Shop/Books/View-all-products.html`
    - `http://localhost/bdosn/index.php/Shop/Joomla/Building-Websites-with-Joomla-1.5.html.`

    It's very easy to get SEF with sh404SEF.

As you have seen, enabling SEF with the sh404SEF component is very easy. However, you have many options to fine tune how these SEF URLs will be generated and handled by the site. Let us now look into some of the important configuration options for sh404SEF component.

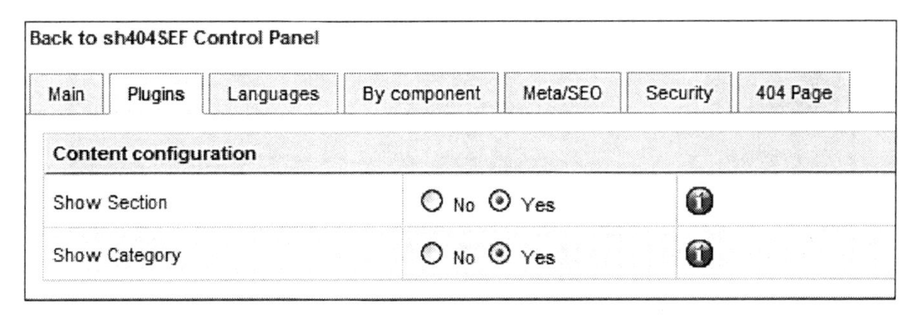

From the **Plugins** tab of **sh404SEF Configuration** screen (seen above), you can configure whether section and category names will be included in SEF URLs or not. This only applies for the content component. However, it is expected that configuration options for the other components will also be available on this screen soon.

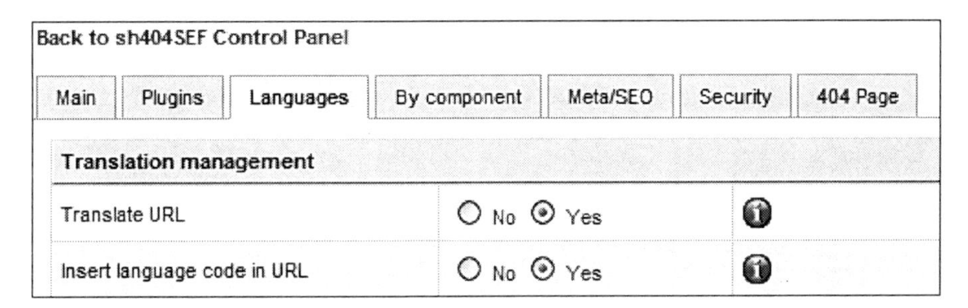

Another advantage of using sh404SEF is that it can generate SEF URLs for multi-lingual web sites as well. From the **Languages** tab of the **sh404SEF Configuration** screen (seen in the previous screenshot), you can specify whether URLs will be translated into a visitor's language or not. Joomla!'s JoomFish component is used for translating contents, and based on the configurations of that component, the SEF may be translated. If you select **No** in the **Translate URL** field, SEF URLs will be displayed in the site's default language. Select **Yes** in the **Insert Language Code in URL** to show the language code in SEF URLs.

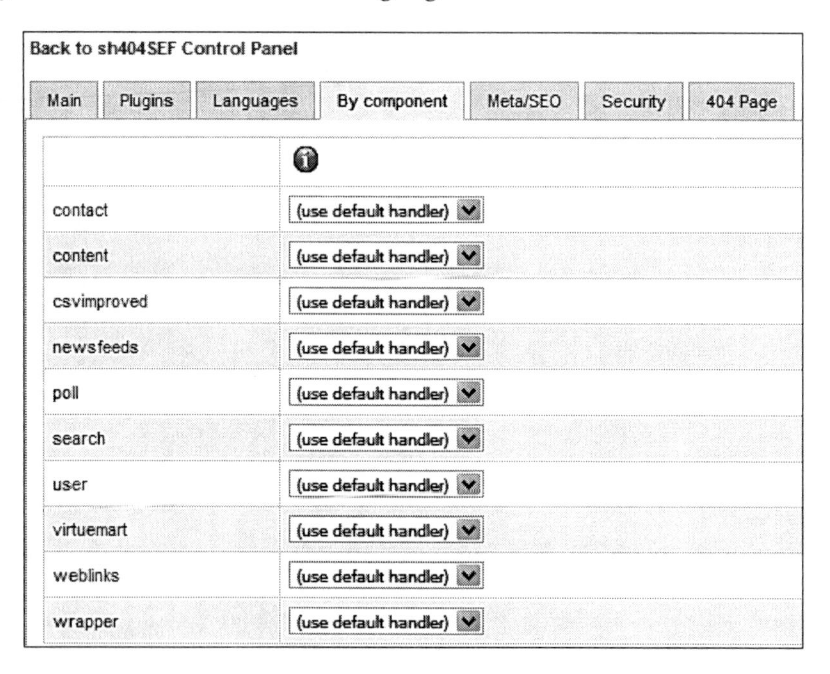

From the **By Component** tab of the **sh404SEF Configuration** screen (seen above), you can configure which components will use SEF URLs. As you can see from the screenshot above, for each component, you can choose the following:

- **Use default handler**: Choosing this will show the default URL. If there is an advanced SEF component available, then a SEF URL will be used.
- **nocache**: SEF URLs generated by the sh404SEF component are stored in your database, so that next time the URL can be served faster from the database. Select this option if you want to disable SEF URLs to be stored in your database. For each request, SEF URL will be generated instantly. For a site with a large number of pages and visitors, selecting this option may result in slow performance.
- **skip**: Select this option if you don't want to use SEF URLs for that component.

The **Meta/SEO** tab of the **sh404SEF Configuration** screen gives you the opportunity to activate meta data management from the sh404SEF component. You don't need to enter the meta information (titles, description, keywords, and so on) of Joomla! contents manually when you have enabled this option:

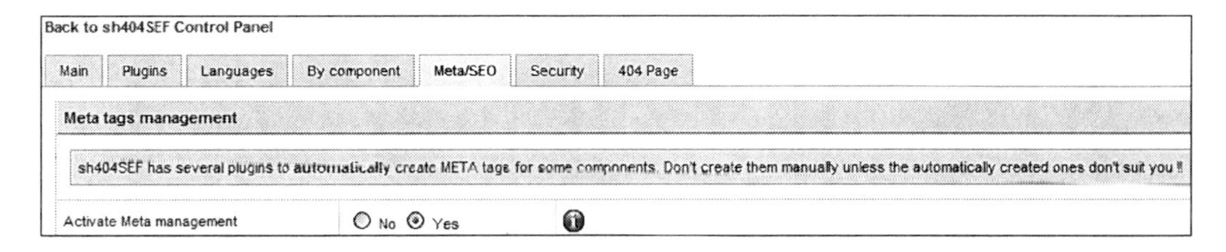

From the **Security** tab of the **sh404SEF Configuration** screen, you can enable security functions. When this is enabled, sh404SEF does some basic checking of URL requests in order to protect your site from some common attacks:

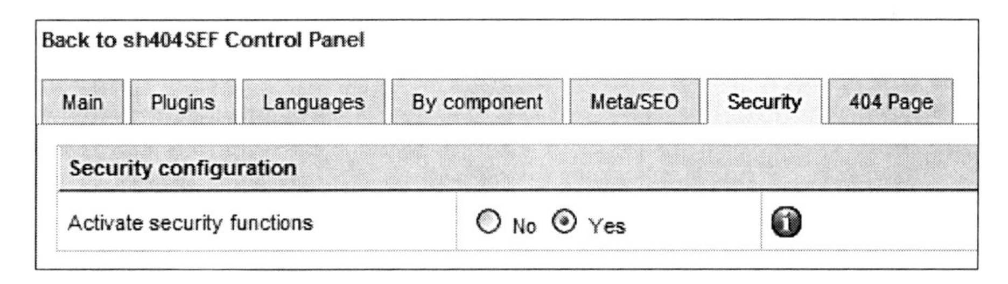

Finally, you can configure a 404 error page from the **404 Page** tab of the **sh404SEF Configuration** screen. The rich text edit box gives you the opportunity to type the message to be shown for a **404 : Not Found** message:

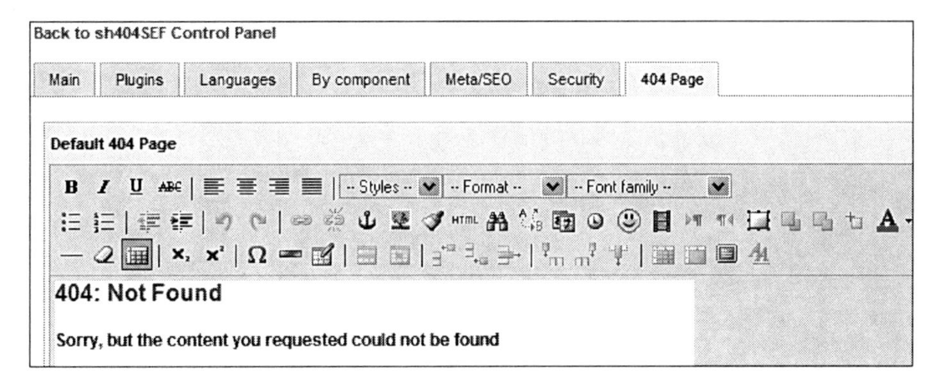

These are the configurations for the sh404SEF component. However, you can manage the SEF URLs, purge the database contents of SEF URLs, and purge 404 logs. All of these can be done from the sh404SEF control panel by clicking on their respective icons. You can view more icons and statistics by clicking on the **Click here to switch to extended display** link in the sh404SEF control panel.

For detailed information and help on sh404SEF, read the documentation that came with the component. Alternatively, you can visit `http://extensions.siliana.com/en/Table/sh404SEF-and-url-rewriting/`.

Summary

In this chapter, you have learned how to configure and customize the look and feel of Joomla! and VirtueMart. First, we saw how to install, apply, and modify Joomla! templates to our site. Then, we moved to VirtueMart's themes and templates. We investigated several theme and template files and found ways to customize them to give VirtueMart a different look and feel. Finally, we saw how to implement SEF URLs for both Joomla!'s main site and our VirtueMart store. First, we tried Joomla!'s built-in SEF functionality. We saw that Joomla!'s built-in SEF feature doesn't generate good looking SEF URLs for VirtueMart products and categories. Therefore, we moved to using a third-party component for SEF. We chose the sh404SEF component as it works fine with both Joomla! and VirtueMart. We have learned about the essential configurations for the sh4004SEF component. With all of these techniques you have learned, it is now time to make the site look like the way you want.

When the look and feel of the site is customized for business, we may proceed to product promotions and public relations. In the next chapter, we will be looking into these aspects.

7
Promotion and Public Relations

Promotion and public relations are the heart of every business. The success of an online business also comes through promotions and public relations. Most online shopping carts consider this aspect and try to provide some tools for promotions and public relations. Like Zen Cart, osCommerce, and Magento, VirtueMart has also has some great tools for product promotions and public relations.

In this chapter, you will learn about the promotion and public relation tools available for your VirtueMart store. On completion of this chapter, you will be able to:

- Use VirtueMart's promotional tools like special and featured products and banner ads
- Use coupons to attract more customers
- Use newsletters and product notifications to keep constant communication with your customers
- Use VirtueMart's product review feature to express customer experiences

In the previous chapters, we have already seen how to build product catalog and change the site's look and feel. When you were building the product catalog, you should have noticed some promotional features. Let us now explore those first, and then move on to public relations through newsletters and product notifications.

Promotions

Promotions are key drivers for attracting new customers to your store. If you have any notion about marketing, then you would continue with new promotions for different categories, mostly based on seasons. For example, during Christmas, you may offer special prices for clothes and gift items. When Christmas is over, New Year's Day will come, and so on. As an online store owner, you have to take these opportunities to promote your products. In VirtueMart, you can put a product in special group, add discounts to products, and send coupons to customers for promoting your products.

Promotional discounts

Discounts can be assigned to an individual product when you are adding a new product, or when editing an existing product. Before that, you can create discounts for different periods of time and apply those later to the products in the catalog.

Creating discounts

In VirtueMart, you can create discounts from **Products | Add Product Discount**. You can also see the available product discounts by clicking on **Products | Product Discount List**. That shows a list of the discounts:

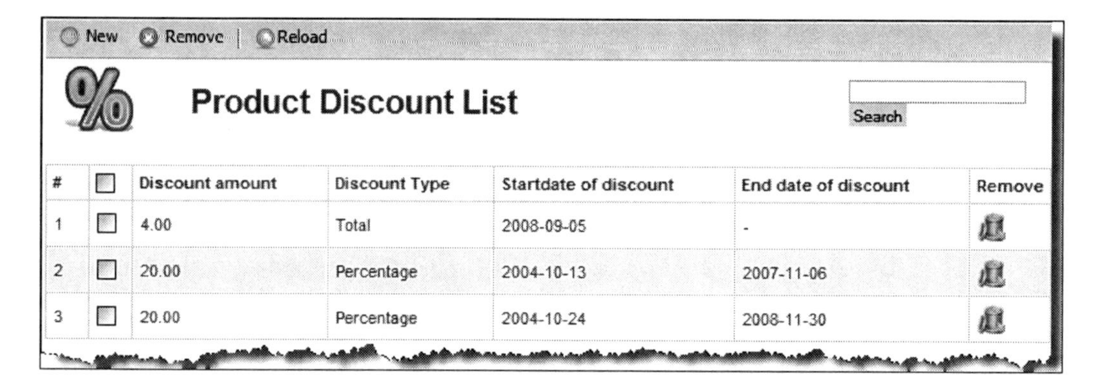

#		Discount amount	Discount Type	Startdate of discount	End date of discount	Remove
1		4.00	Total	2008-09-05	-	
2		20.00	Percentage	2004-10-13	2007-11-06	
3		20.00	Percentage	2004-10-24	2008-11-30	

As you can see, there are two types of discounts: **Total** and **Percentage**. For the type **Total**, the amount specified will be discounted from the product's price, whatever the product's price is. On the other hand, for **Percentage** type of discounts, the specified percentage will be deducted from the product's price. That means, a **Percentage** discount is proportionate to the product's price, whereas the **Total** discount is fixed.

You can create a new product discount by clicking on the **New** button in the **Product Discount List** screen, or on **Products | Add Product Discount** menu. Any of this brings the **Add/Edit Product Discount** screen:

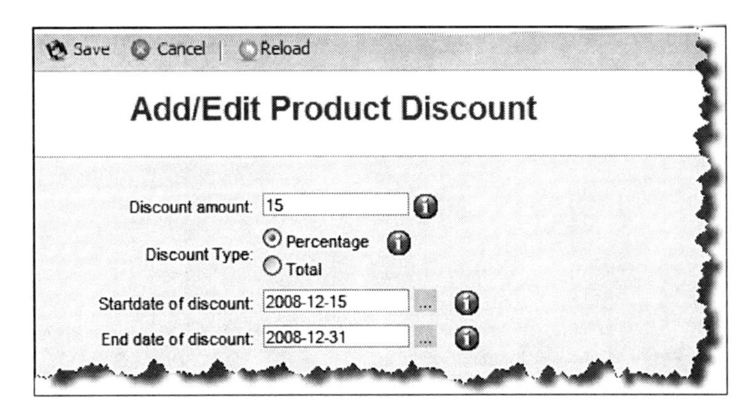

In the **Discount amount** field, type the discount amount you want to offer. Then, select either **Total** or **Percentage** in the **Discount Type** radio box. Optionally, you can specify the start and end date for which the discount will be effective. For example, you decide to offer a fifteen percent discount during the Christmas season. Then type 15 in the **Discount amount** field, select the **Percentage** radio box, type (or select from calendar) 2008-12-15 in the **Start date of discount**, and 2008-12-31 in the **End date of discount** field. Click on the **Save** button to save the discount.

Similarly, you can create as many discounts as you want. Create some discounts for both the **Total** and **Percentage** types, and for different periods. After creating the discounts, you may proceed to next section for adding discount to products.

Adding discounts to products

Once you have created discounts, you can add those to products. In VirtueMart, you can assign the discounts while setting the price for the product. For adding discount to products, follow the steps below:

1. In the VirtueMart control panel, click on **Products | List Products**. This will show the list of products already added to the catalog:

2. If you want to add a new product, click on the **New** button. That will bring up the new product creation screen. As you have already added products to the catalog, you can also add a discount to a product by editing it. Click on the product to which you want to add a discount (for example, the Fedora 9 DVD). That brings **Update Item:: Fedora 9 DVD** screen:

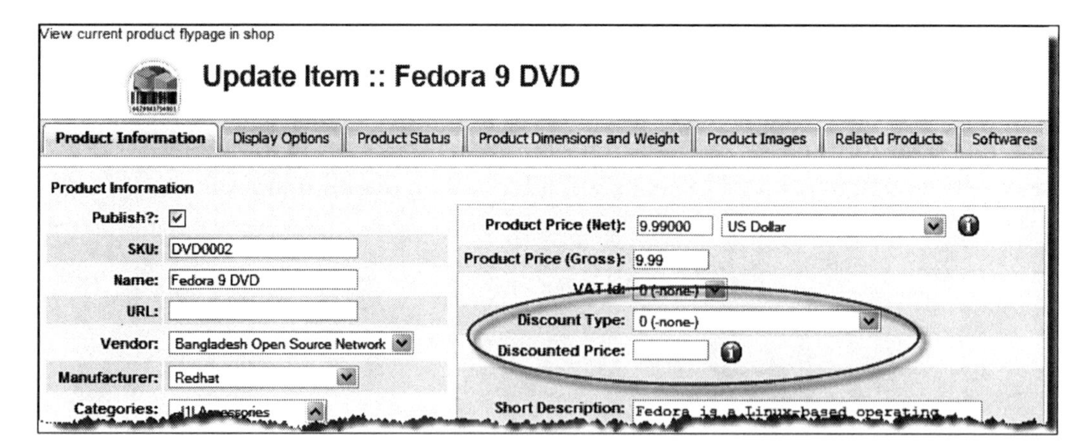

3. In the **Product Information** tab, look into the price information to the right-hand side. There are two fields: **Discount Type** and **Discounted Price**. The discounts created earlier will be available in the **Discount Type** drop-down list. The discounts are shown with the amount and dates for which the discount is effective. Select one of the discounts (for example, **15% (2008-12-15 – 2008-12-31)**), from this list:

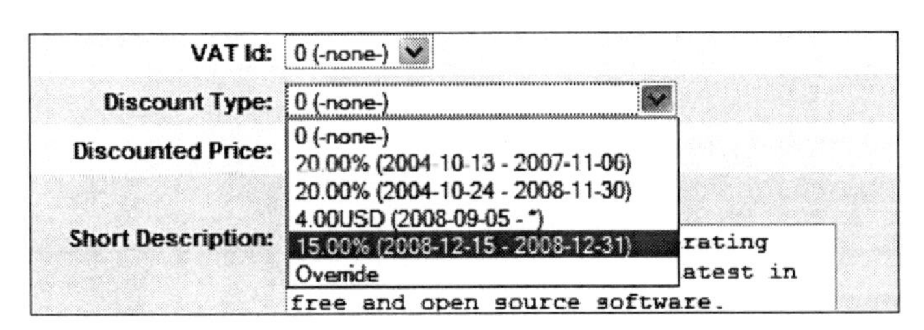

4. On the other hand, if you want to add a new discount, that can be done from this screen as well. Select **Override** from the **Discount Type** drop-down list and type the discounted price in the **Discounted Price** field. That will automatically add the amount of discount in the discount list. Typing any price in this field also selects **Override** in the **Discount Type** field.
5. When you have finished setting either the discount type or discounted price, you can save the product changes by clicking on the **Save** button in the toolbar. That adds the discount to the product.

Let us now see the effect of adding this discount to the Fedora 9 DVD product. Browse to the shop and go to product listing or the Fedora 9 DVD product details page. That will show the original price, discounted price, and the amount the customer saves:

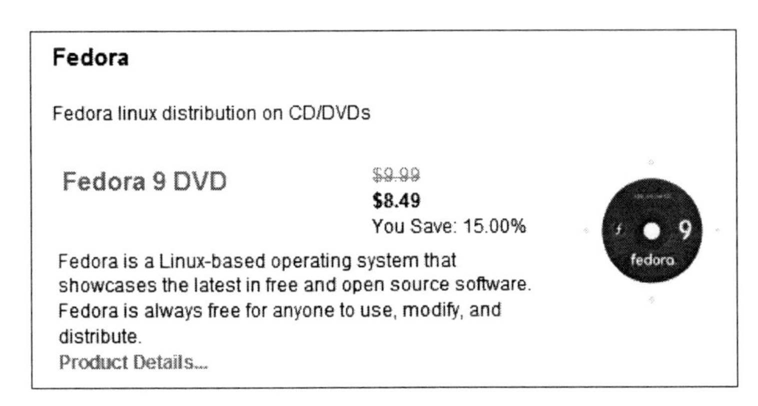

You can add the same discount to as many items as you want. However, at this time, there is no way to apply a discount to multiple items at once.

Special products

Special products may contain both discounted products and featured products. You may mark some products as featured products to have them displayed and highlight those products too.

You can view the special products in VirtueMart by clicking on **Products | Special Products**. That shows the **Featured and Discounted Products** screen:

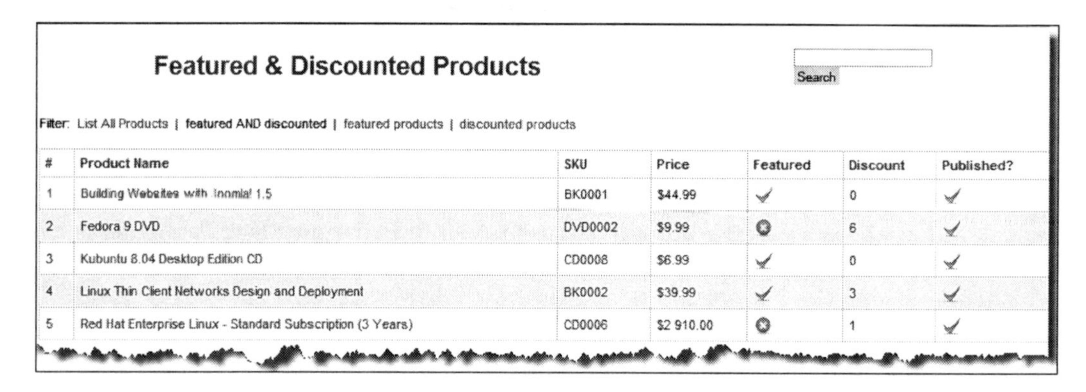
Featured & Discounted Products

Search

Filter: List All Products | featured AND discounted | featured products | discounted products

#	Product Name	SKU	Price	Featured	Discount	Published?
1	Building Websites with Joomla! 1.5	BK0001	$44.99	✓	0	✓
2	Fedora 9 DVD	DVD0002	$9.99	⊗	6	✓
3	Kubuntu 8.04 Desktop Edition CD	CD0008	$6.99	✓	0	✓
4	Linux Thin Client Networks Design and Deployment	BK0002	$39.99	✓	3	✓
5	Red Hat Enterprise Linux - Standard Subscription (3 Years)	CD0006	$2 910.00	⊗	1	✓

As you can see, this screen can displays all products, both featured and discounted products. It is clear that not all featured products need to be discounted, and not all discounted products need to be in a special products group. For displaying a product in the **Featured Products** group, got to the **Product List** screen, and click on the product's name to edit the product information. For example, we want to add the **Ubuntu Ogio Messenger Bag** to the **Featured Products** group. Clicking on the name of this product will show the **Update Item:: Ubuntu Ogio Messenger Bag** screen. Click on the **Product Status** tab on this screen:

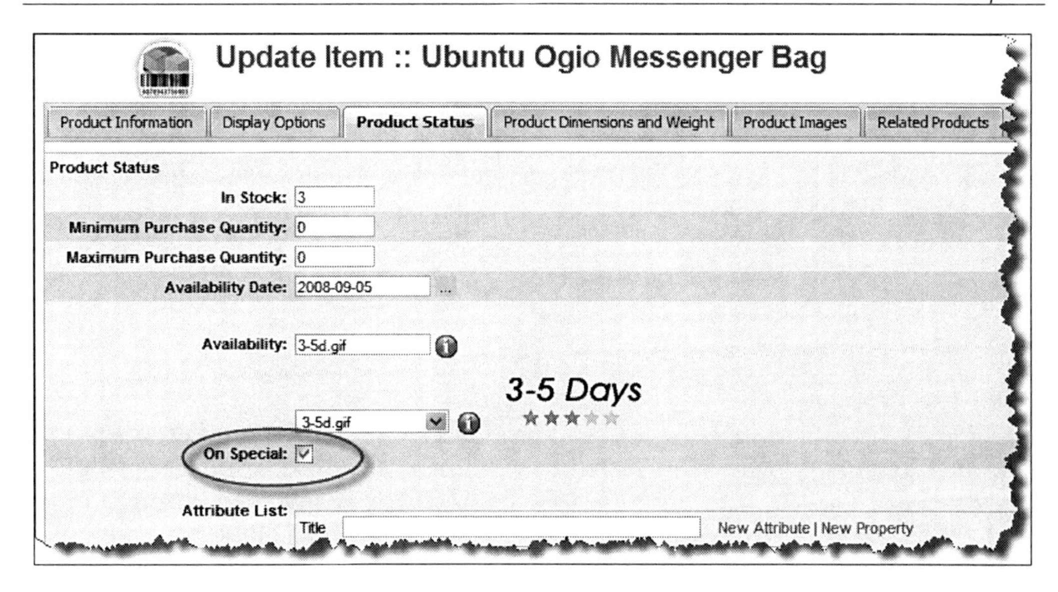

In the **Product Status** tab, you can set the product as special by checking the **On Special** checkbox. You can also set the product's stock, availability, and attributes from this tab, which we discussed earlier in this book.

Products marked as special are displayed in a separate block in the shop's frontend. **Featured Products** are displayed in the shops frontend under the **Categories** list:

If you do not see the **Featured Products** section on the shop's front-page, check the theme settings. As described in Chapter 6, you can change the theme's settings by going to **Admin | Configurations | Site**, and then clicking on the **Configuration** link under **Select a theme for your site** drop-down list. That brings up the **Theme Settings** screen. In this screen, you need to select Yes in the **Show featured products on frontpage?** checkbox.

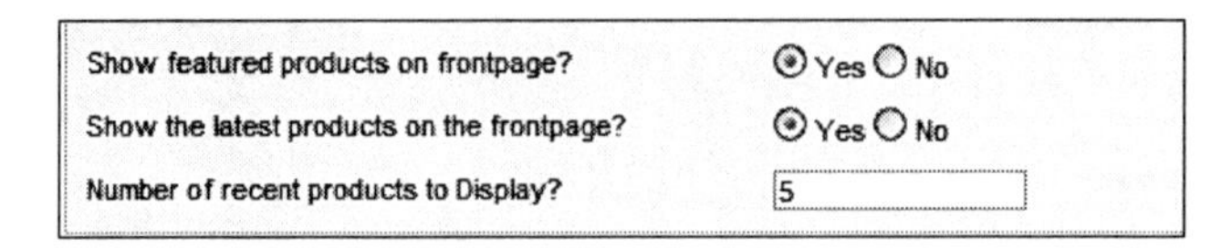

Selecting the option for showing featured products shows the featured products on front page only. When you move to other product categories, or product detail pages, you don't see the featured products. If you wish to display the featured products on other pages of your shop, you need to install and enable the **VirtueMart Featured Products** module.

Like the VirtueMart package, some of the modules are also downloadable from the VirtueMart's site `http://www.virtuemart.net`. The modules are bundled with the `VirtueMart_1.1-complete_package_j15.zip` package which you have downloaded before installing the VirtueMart component. When you unzip the folder, you get the modules in the `./modules` folder. Log in to Joomla!'s administration panel and go to **Extensions | Install/Uninstall**, select the `mod_virtuemart_featureprod_1.1.2.j15.zip` file from `./modules` folder, and click on the **Upload File and Install** button. That will install the **VirtueMart Featured Products** module. Once the module is installed, you can see it listed in the **Module Manager** screen:

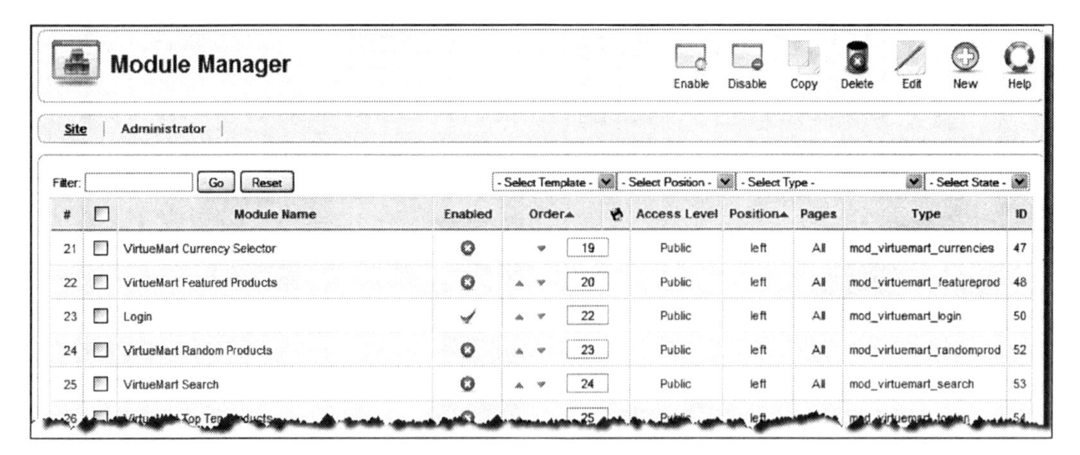

In the **Module Manager** screen, click on the module named **VirtueMart Featured Products**. That brings the **Module: [Edit]** screen, from where we can enable the module and specify its settings:

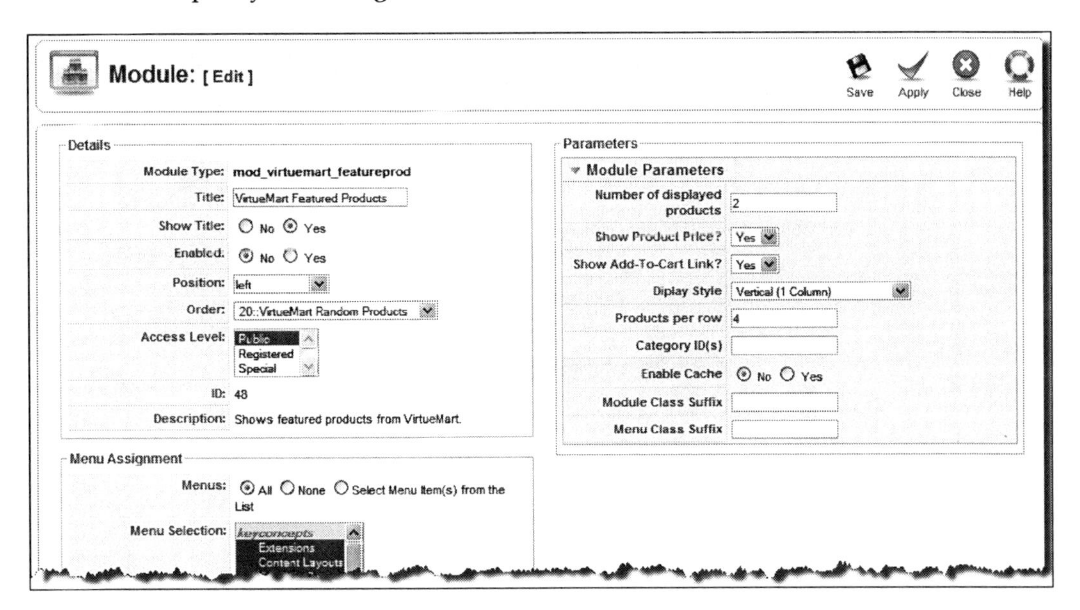

In the **Module: [Edit]** screen, we first need to specify the module title. The default title of the module is **VirtueMart Featured Products**. As you will be displaying the featured products, keeping the title of this module as 'Featured Products' will be fine. Edit the title in the **Title** field. In the **Show Title** field, you can select **No** if you don't want to show the title of the module. The default setting for this field is **Yes**, and you can proceed with this. The **Enabled** field lets you enable or disable the module. To display the module in the shop's frontend, select **Yes** in this field. When you decide to show the module, you can select the position where the module will be displayed.

In the **Position** drop-down list, select a position (for example, **Left**), for displaying the module in left menu bar. In the **Order** drop-down list, you can select the place where the module will be displayed. If you want to display the module after the **Login** module, then select the module listed after the **Login** module in this drop-down list.

In the **Access Level** select box, you can specify which group of users will be able to access this module. The default setting is **Public**, and you should keep this as it is beneficial to show the featured products to all visitors. Selecting **Registered** will only display the module to registered users.

From the **Menu Assignment** section, you can assign the module to all menus or selected menus. If you want to show this module only on some sections of your site, (for example, the **Shop** section), then you may select the menus for which the module will be available. As you want to show the module in shop areas only, you may select the **Shop** menu link in both the **mainmenu** and the **topmenu**:

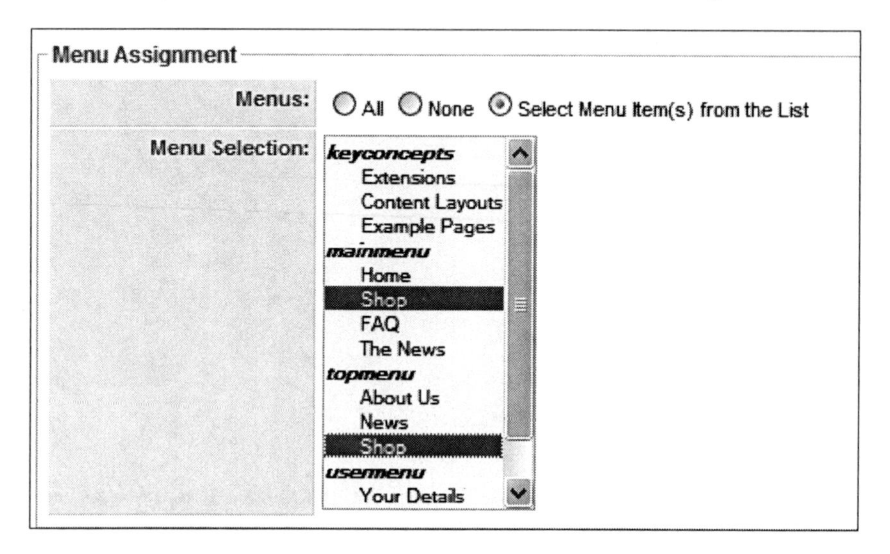

In the **Parameters** section of the **Module: [Edit]** screen, you can specify how many featured products will be displayed, how that will be displayed (vertically or horizontally), if horizontally, then how many in a row. You can also enable or disable having the show product price and add to cart link shown in this module. You may also select one or more specific categories for displaying featured products from. In that case, provide comma-separated list of category IDs in the **Category ID(s)** field. For improved performance, you may enable caching of the module items by selecting **Yes** in the **Enable Cache** field. The **Module Class Suffix** and **Menu Class Suffix** fields can be used to specify suffixes that can be used in the stylesheet for specifying custom styles for this module.

Once all of the settings for the module are configured, click on the **Save** button in the toolbar. That publishes the module in the shop's frontend. Let's preview the shop and you will see the module as the following screenshot:

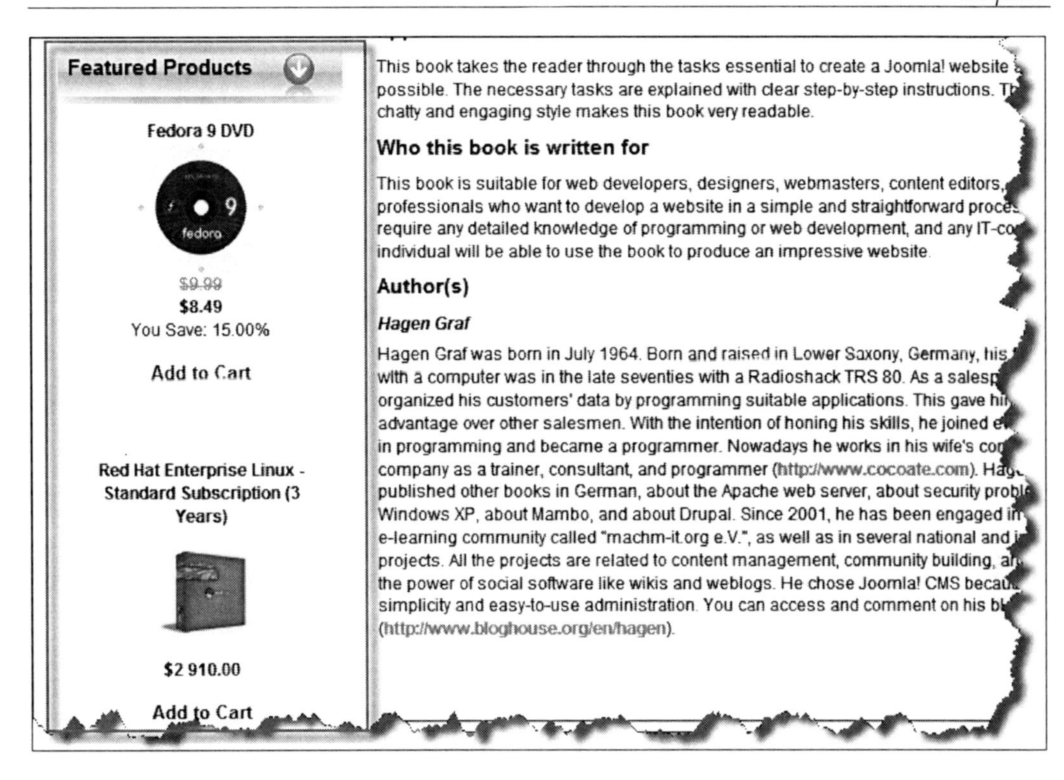

When you are enabling the **VirtueMart Featured Products** module, it is better to disable having featured products shown on the front-page. Change the theme settings to disable, showing the featured products on front-page, and then enable this **VirtueMart Featured Product** module. Otherwise, the customers will see featured products twice: once in the sidebar through the **Featured Products** module, and another in the **Featured Products** section in the front-page under the category list.

Best sellers

Showing best seller items on your shop's frontend can draw the attention of visitors to your site. It becomes conventional for every online shop to show the best seller items. You can also do that in your VirtueMart shop. Installing and enabling the **VirtueMart Top Ten** module will do this for you.

The **VirtueMart Top Ten** module comes along with VirtueMart's complete package. If you have not installed the module yet, then install it through **Extensions | Install/ Uninstall**. Then, click on the module name in the **Module Manager** screen. Like the **VirtueMart Featured Products** module, you will get the **Module: [Edit]** screen, with some different fields to configure:

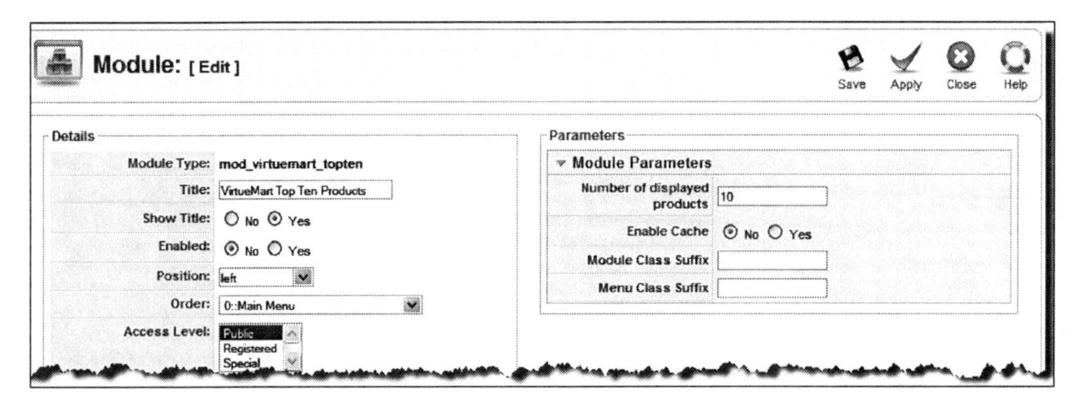

In the **Module: [Edit]** screen, you can edit the title of the module, enable the module, select position, and access level. You can also assign the module to specific menus. All of these are same as shown in the **VirtueMart Featured Products** module. The difference is in the **Parameters** section. In the **Parameters** section, you can specify the number of top products to be displayed. If you type **5** in the **Number of displayed products** field, the title of the module may be 'Top 5 Products'. You can also enable or disable cache, and specify the module class suffix and the menu class suffix. Once these are configured, click on the **Save** button in the toolbar and preview the site. The **Top Ten Products** module will look like the following screenshot:

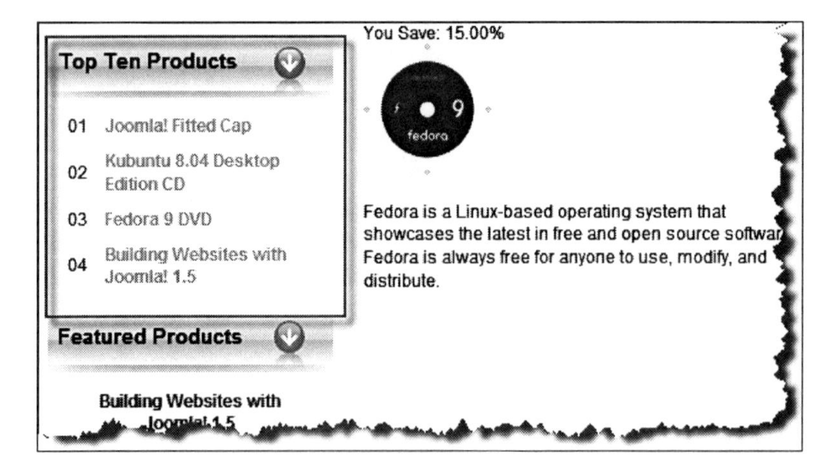

In the screenshot above, you can only see four products in the **Top Ten Products** module. This happened because only four products have been sold so far. When ten products have been sold, ten products will be listed in this module. Showing five products or less in the **Top Ten Module** may be embarrassing. Therefore, it is a good idea to enable this module when you have sold enough products, at least ten.

Latest products

People often check stores for new products. Therefore, displaying a list of the latest products is one promotional tool to attract customers to your store. Like the other shopping carts, VirtueMart can also display the latest products in the catalog. These latest products are displayed based on dates. The products are then added to the catalog.

For showing the latest products in your VirtueMart shop, you can use the **VirtueMart Latest Products** module, which is bundled with the VirtueMart complete package download. If you have not installed the module yet, upload and install it from the **Extensions | Install/Uninstall** screen. Then, click on this module name in the **Module Manager** screen. That also shows the **Module: [Edit]** screen, along with some common settings you can also set module specific parameters:

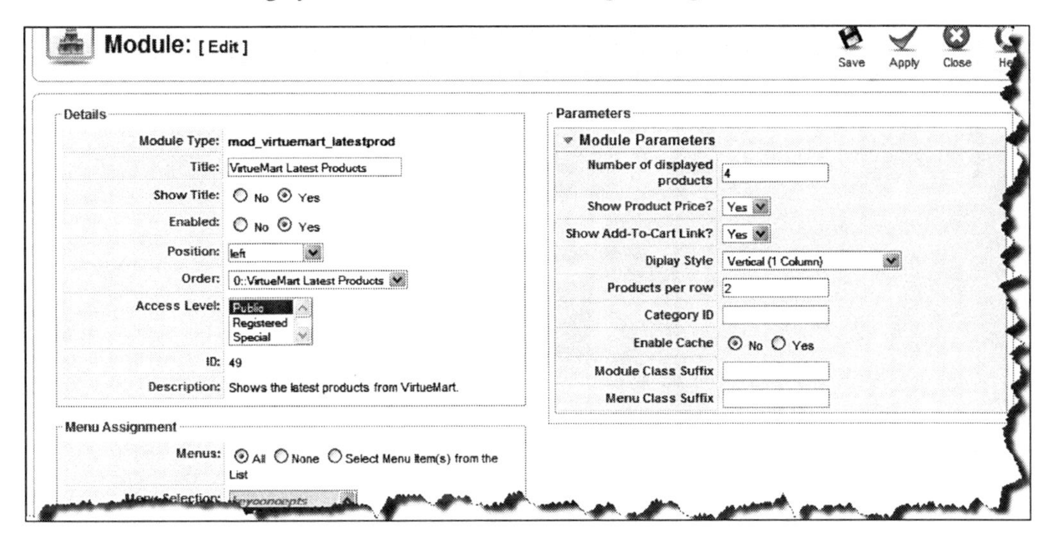

Like the other modules, say from the **Details** section of **Module: [Edit]** screen, you can edit the title of the module, enable the module, select a position, order, and access level for the module. In the **Menu Assignment** section, you can specify the menu items for which the module will be displayed.

The module specific settings are found in the **Parameters** section. You can specify the number of latest products to be displayed, display style (horizontal or vertical), products per row (in case of horizontal display), and so on. You can enable or disable having the product price and add to cart link displayed. The latest products from specific categories can be displayed by providing comma-separated list of the category IDs in the **Category ID(s)** field:

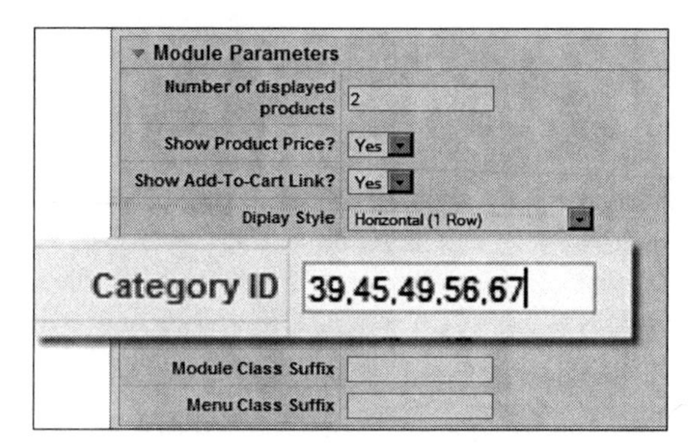

Once all these are set, you can save the module and preview the site to see how the module looks. The module will display the list of latest products added to the catalog:

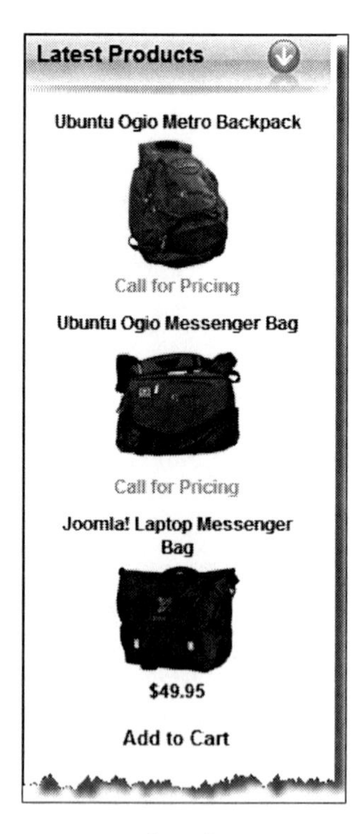

As you can see, the **Latest Products** display the products which have been added most recently to the catalog. The first two items shown here are marked with **Call for Pricing**, therefore, no **Add to Cart** link is shown for these products. However, the third item has a price and shows the **Add to Cart** link.

Random products

While the featured products, latest products, and bestsellers can draw the attention of customers to those products, many other products remain behind the visitor's sight until they dig down into the product categories and search for the product. Showing some products randomly from the catalog surely helps to draw a visitor's attention to some products. In the VirtueMart store, you can display random products by using the **VirtueMart Random Products** module, which is bundled with the VirtueMart complete installation package. If you have not installed this module yet, then upload and install it from the **Extensions | Install/Uninstall** screen. Then, click on the module's name in the **Module Manager** window. That shows the **Module: [Edit]** screen for the **VirtueMart Random Products** module:

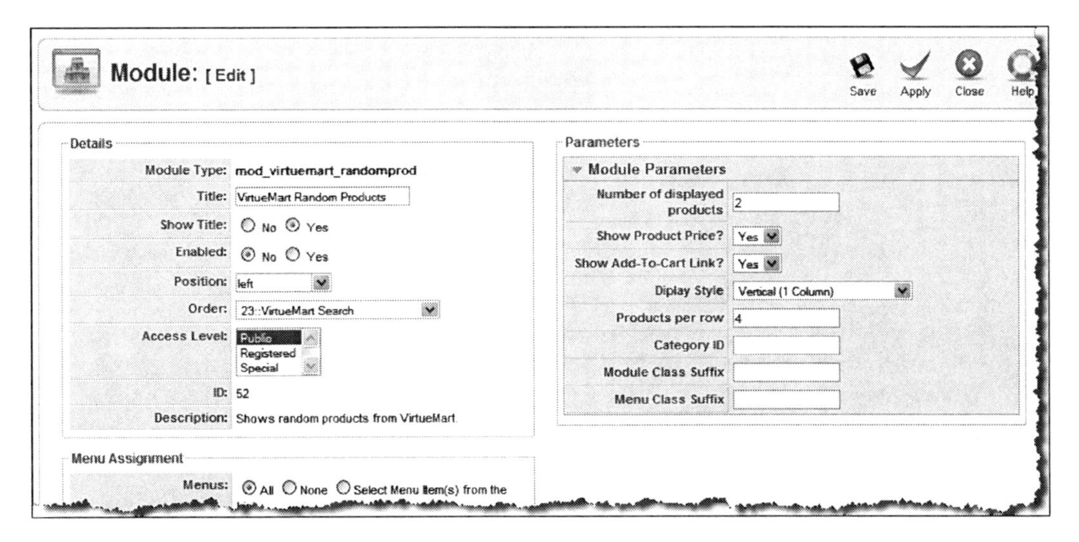

The settings for the **VirtueMart Random Products** module are similar to other modules discussed earlier. Change the title, enable the module, select a position and order. Then, save the changes by clicking on the **Save** button in the toolbar.

You can preview the site to see how the **Random Products** module looks like. It will show different items every time you refresh the page. It will look like the following screenshot:

As you can see, the **Random Products** module will select the specified number of products randomly from your catalog, and display those in the shop's frontend. You may display this module horizontally by selecting **Horizontal** in the **Display style** drop-down list, and placing the module in the **bottom** position. We can put all of the other VirtueMart modules in this bottom position. For example, we want to show the **Latest Products** and the **Featured Products** in horizontal style. Therefore, we select **bottom** as the position, and **Horizontal** as the display style. Then, specify the number of product to display as 4. This shows our modules as in the following screenshot:

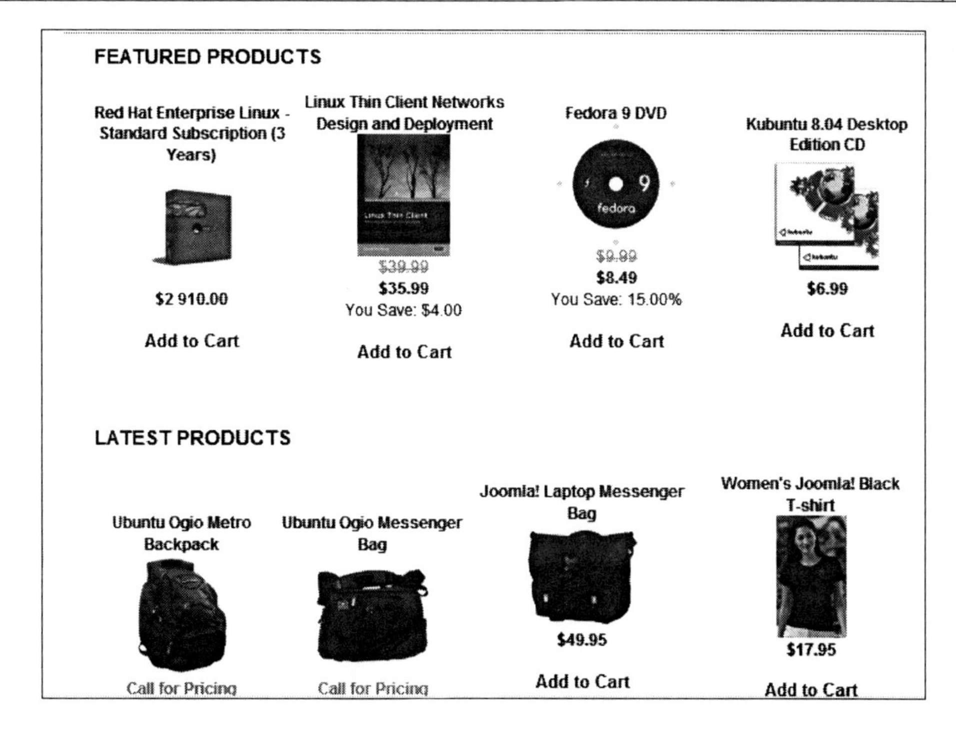

Similarly, you can display the **Random Products** module in this horizontal style. Displaying these products in a horizontal style is often useful as you can display more products than that in the **Vertical** style. While displaying in the horizontal style, you may also select **Table (x rows and Y columns)** as a display style. For example, for the **Random Products** module, we can configure the module as shown in the following screenshot:

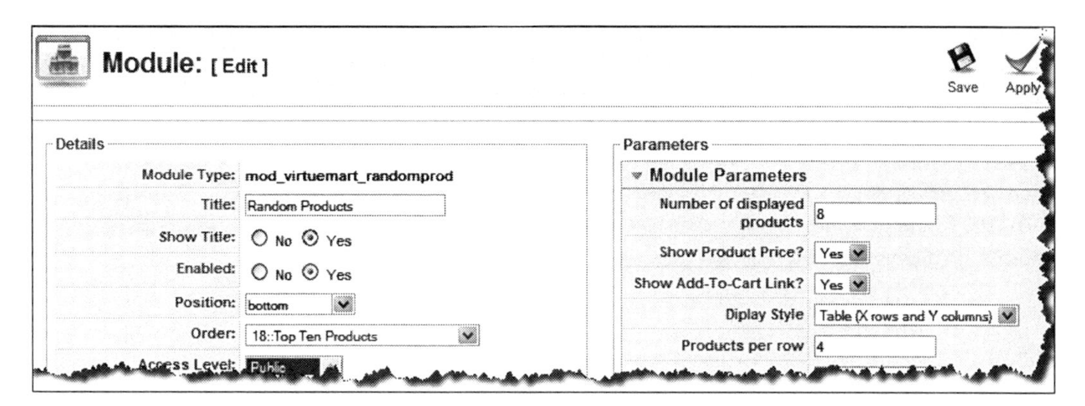

As you can see, the position is set to bottom, the number of products to be displayed is 8, the display style is **Table (x rows and y columns)**, and the products per row is 4. Therefore, we expect that there will be two rows containing four products each. Actually, it happens, and the **Random Products** module now looks like the following screenshot:

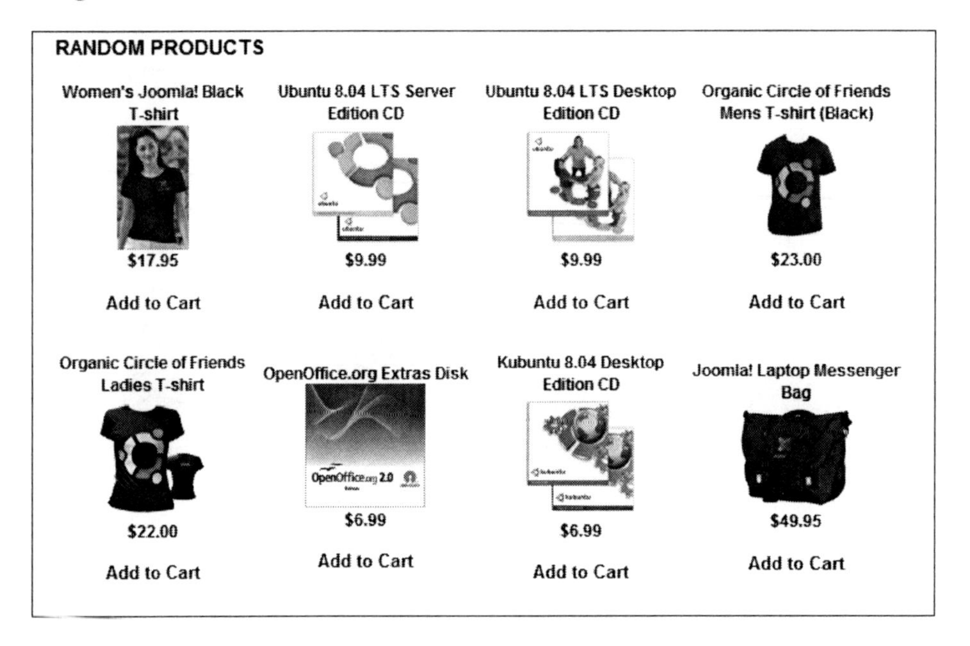

As you can see, it is important to select the number of products to be displayed considering the number of products per row. If you choose the number of products per row as 4, then it is better to select the number of products to be displayed as 8, 12, or 16 (multipliers of 4). Otherwise, some extra rows will be there containing only one or two products.

If you choose to show too many products in one row, the maximum number of product images will be shown based on the available space, others will remain hidden. For example, we choose to display 16 products, all in one row, and that results in a display like the following screenshot:

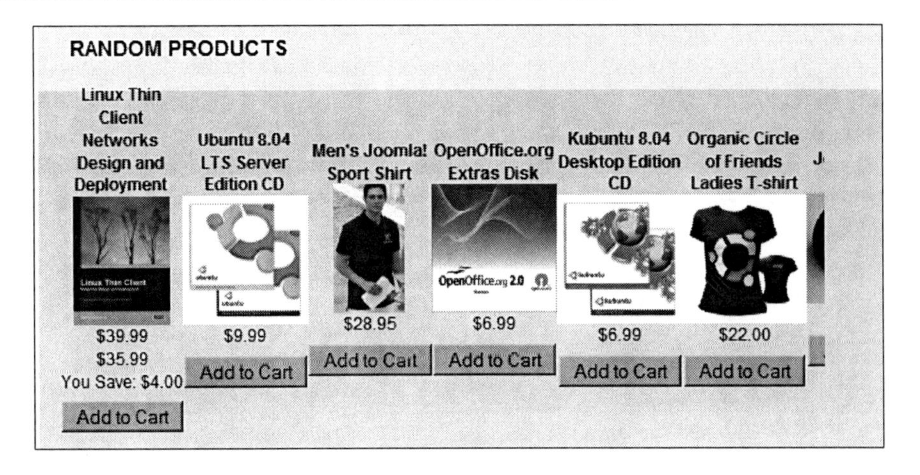

All-in-one

You can display all of modules above (latest products, featured products, top ten products, and random products) using the **VirtueMart All-in-One** module. Although this module shows all these products, there are still some bugs and you may not like it. It comes bundled with the VirtueMart Complete package. If you have not installed it yet, then upload and install this module from the **Extensions | Install/Uninstall** screen. Once installed, configure it by clicking on the module name **VirtueMart All-in-One** in the **Module Manager** screen. Like other modules, you'll see **Module: [Edit]** screen:

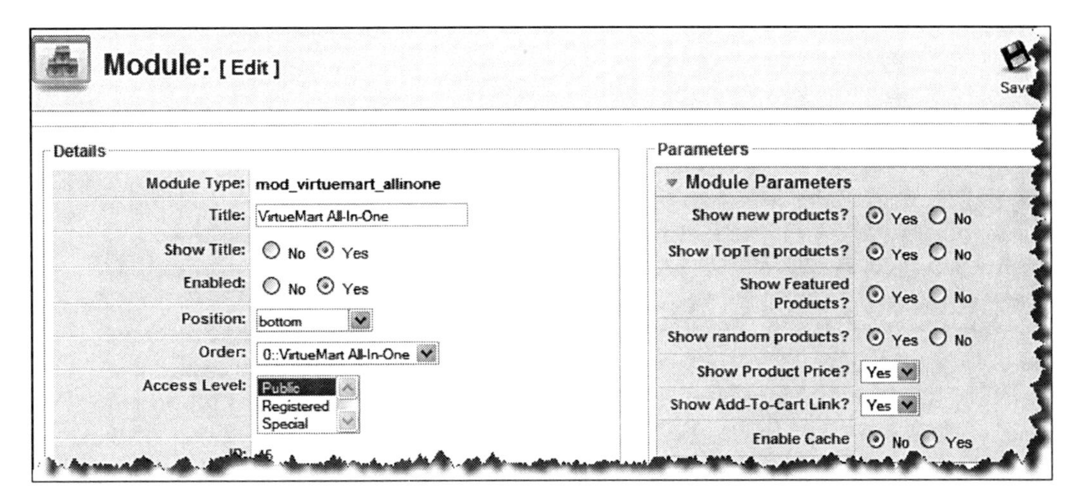

Configuring the **VirtueMart All-in-One** module is similar to other modules. In the **Details** section, you can change the module title, enable or disable the module, select the position and order for displaying on the frontend, and set an access level. In the **Parameters** section, you can select which products (new, top ten, featured, and random) are to be displayed in this module. By default, all of these are enabled for the module. When enabled, the module in the frontend will look like the following screenshot:

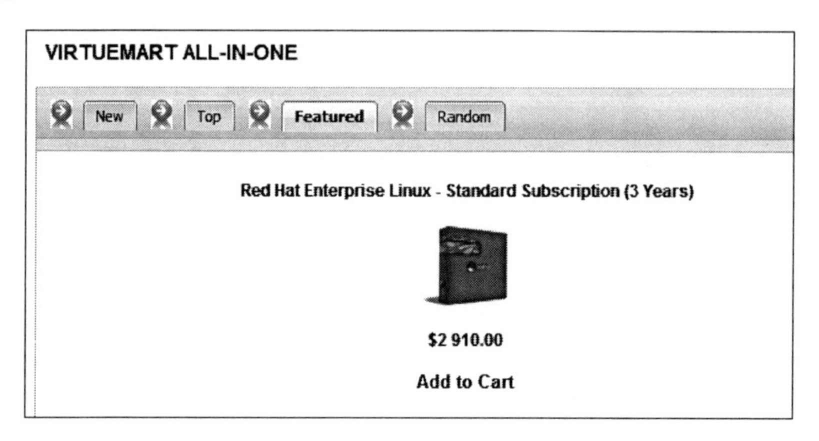

As you can see, the **All-in-One** module uses tabs to display **New**, **Top**, **Featured** and **Random** products. Visitors cannot see all of the products at one time. Another disadvantage of this module is that it shows the products listed vertically, and you cannot change this layout from the module's configurations. For changing the layout, you need to edit the module file `./modules/mod_virtuemart_allinone/mod_virtuemart_allinone.php`.

Scrolling products

Displaying something fancy on the shop's front page attracts visitor's attention easily. Besides showing the featured products, top ten products, and random products, you may also show products scrolling in the sidebar. The products are chosen randomly from the entire catalog or from a specified category or categories. VirtueMart's complete package comes with the **VirtueMart Scrolling Products** module. If you have not installed it yet, then install it and open it for configuring from the **Module Manager** screen. The **Module: [Edit]** screen for this module also displays common settings for the **Details** and **Menu Assignment** sections. In fact, you only need to configure the options in the **Parameters** section:

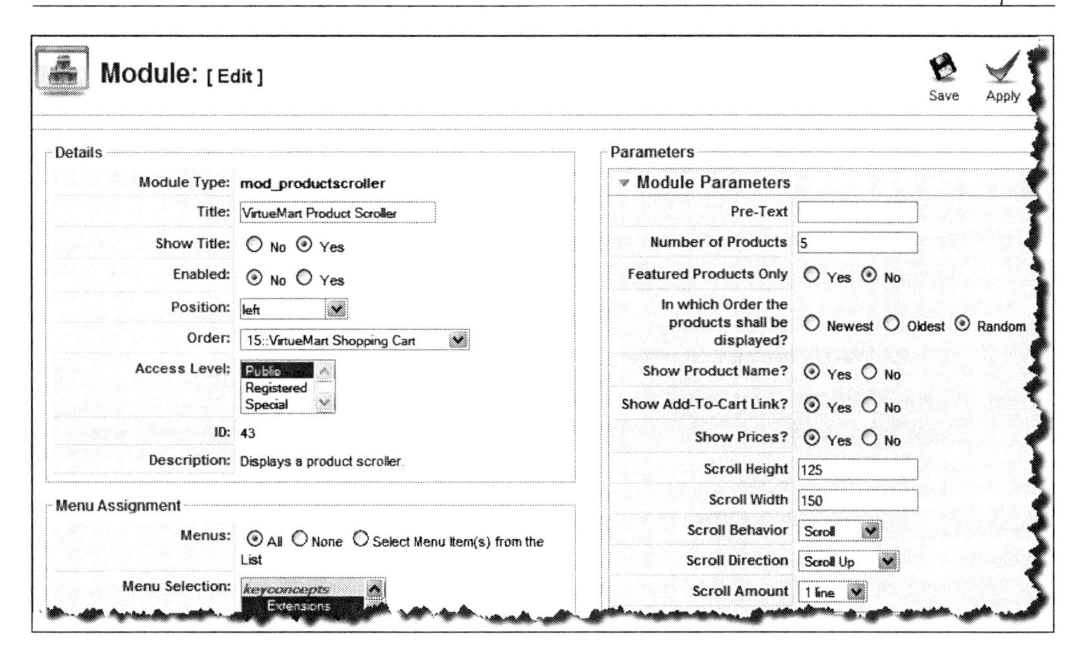

The options available in the **Parameters** section of this module are:

- **Pre-Text**: You can type some text in this field to display at the beginning of the module.
- **Number of Products**: Specify the number of products to be displayed in this scrolling products module. The default value is 5. You can also change it to 10 or 20.
- **Featured Products Only**: Selecting **Yes** in this field will only display the featured products in this module. The default value is **No**.
- **In which order the products should be displayed**?: You can choose one of the three options: **Newest**, **Oldest**, and **Random**. The default value is **Random**, however, if you want to show the products by newest to oldest or oldest to newest, then select **Newest** or **Oldest** respectively.
- **Show Product Name?**: Select **Yes** to display the product's name in the scrolling module. You may select **No** to only show pictures of products.
- **Show Add-to-Cart Link?**: Select **No** if you don't want to show the Add-to-Cart link with the products displayed in this module. The default value is **Yes**.
- **Show Prices?**: Select **No** if you don't want to show the product's prices in this module. The default value is **Yes**.
- **Scroll Height**: Specify the scroll height in pixels for this field.
- **Scroll width**: You can specify scroll width in pixels for this field.

- **Scroll Behavior**: Specify how the scroll will behave. You have three options to choose from: **Scroll, Slide**, and **Alternate**. Try changing these options and see what happens in the module.
- **Scroll Direction**: Select a direction of scrolling from this drop-down list. The options are **Scroll Up, Scroll Down, Scroll Left**, and **Scroll Right**.
- **Scroll Amount**: Select how much scrolling will happen at a time. The default setting is **1** line, you can select 1 to 5 lines as scroll amount.
- **Scroll delay**: Specify the scroll delay. The higher the value in this field, the slower the scrolling will be.
- **Scroll Align**: Select what the alignment of scrolling products will be. You have four options to choose from: **Left Align, Right Align, Center Align**, and **Justify**.

Moreover, there are other fields to configure, such as space character, line character, scrolling text align, and so on. For most cases, the default values will work fine. You can know more about the fields by hovering your mouse pointer over the field names.

For the scrolling products module, the parameters will depend mostly on where you want to show the module. If you choose a **Left** or **Right** position, then the scrolling direction should be configured to scroll up or down. When you are placing the module to top, bottom, or another horizontal position, then the scrolling direction should be set to either **Scroll Left** or **Scroll Right**.

When configured for scrolling up and placed in the **Left** or **Right** position, the **VirtueMart Product Scroller** module will look like the following screenshot:

When the same module is placed in a bottom, top, or any other horizontal position, and the **Scroll Direction** is set to **Scroll Right**, the products in the module scrolls from left to right, as shown in the following screenshot:

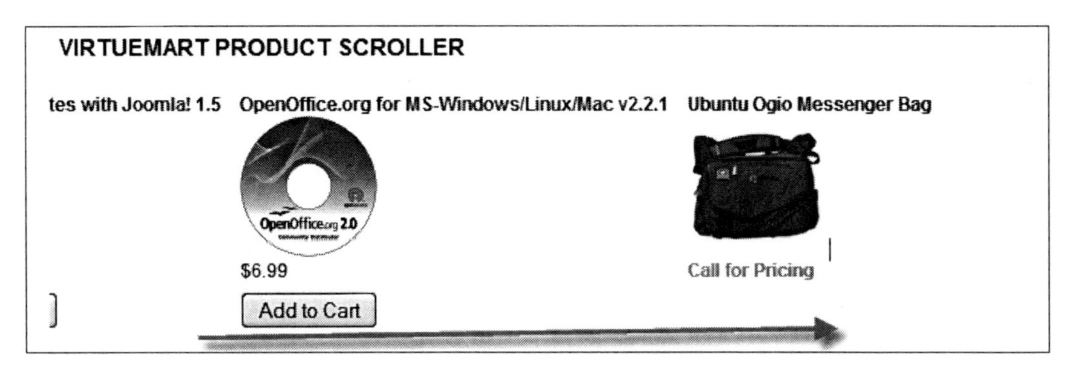

Creative use of the **VirtueMart Product Scroller** module may attract enough customers to your store. You may try to add some flavor to your store by using this module.

Cross-selling and up-selling

Cross-selling and up-selling are common to both online stores, and brick-and-mortar stores. In cross-selling, the salesman sells the accessories or services relevant to the product. For example, when a customer buys a computer, the salesman may try to sell a three-year extended warranty or a wireless mouse with that computer. On the other hand, up-selling is something where salesman suggests a better product. For example, when you are going to buy a laptop, the salesman may try to sell a special brand with higher price or a higher profit margin. Both cross-selling and up-selling are supported in most of the shopping carts. Unfortunately, VirtueMart has not yet implemented the cross-selling or up-selling features in a true sense. However, cross-selling can be implemented with the related products feature of VirtueMart.

You can configure related products when you are adding products to the catalog. You can also add related products afterwards by editing the product's information. For adding related products to a product (for example, to Ubuntu), click on that product's name in the **Products | Product List** screen. That will display the **Update Item :: Ubuntu 8.04 LTS Desktop Edition CD** screen. Here, in this screen, click on the **Related Products** tab:

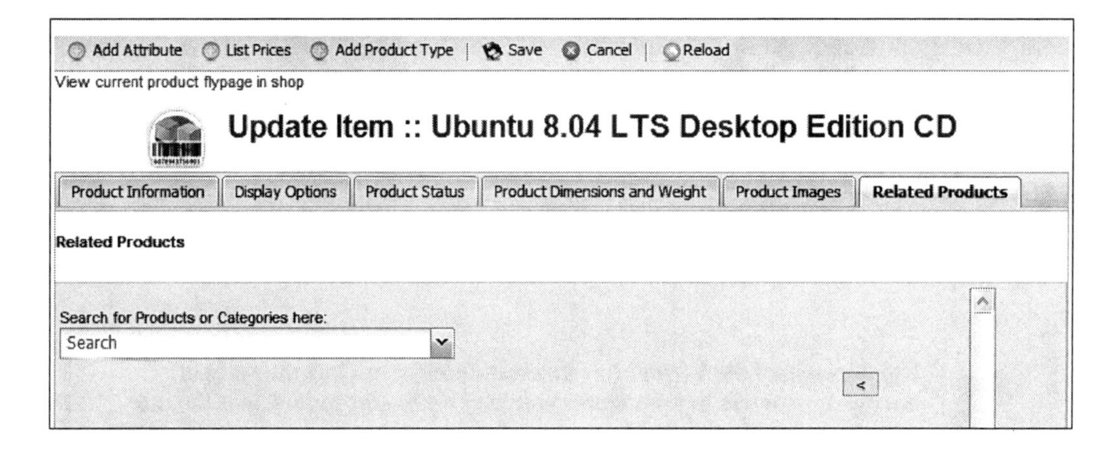

For adding related products, type the name of the product related to current product. For example, for Ubuntu CD, we may add Ubuntu DVD and Kubuntu CD as related products. In the **Search for Products or Categories here** field, start typing the name and that will automatically display a list of available products with that name.

The autocomplete drop-down list shows the category and product name. When you see the autocomplete list **Select one or more Products**, click on the products you want to add as related products. For example, click on the **Ubuntu / Ubuntu 8.04 LTS DVD** and the **Ubuntu / Kubuntu 8.04 Desktop Edition CD** from the list. That will add these products to related products list on the right:

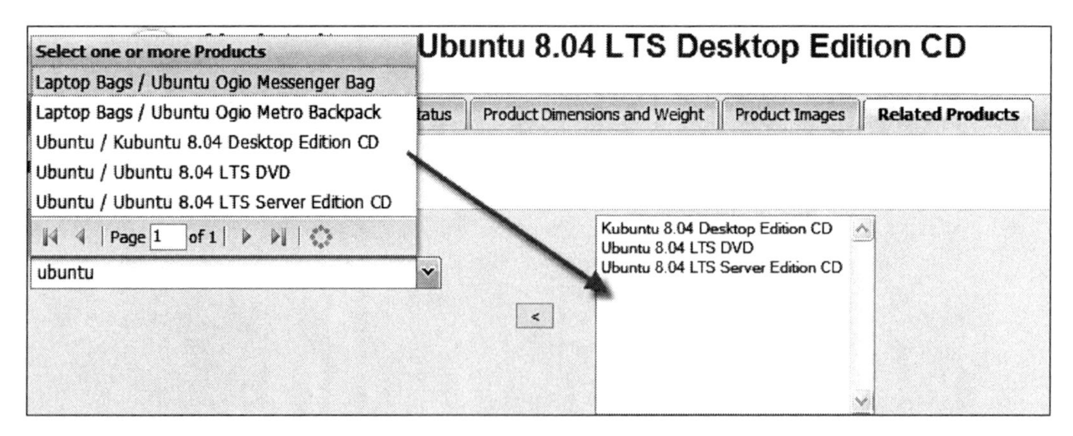

Once you have selected the related products for the product you are updating, click on the **Save** button in the toolbar to update the product information. Similarly, you can add related products to other products. When you see the product's details page, these related products will be listed with a title **You may also be interested in this/these product(s)**:

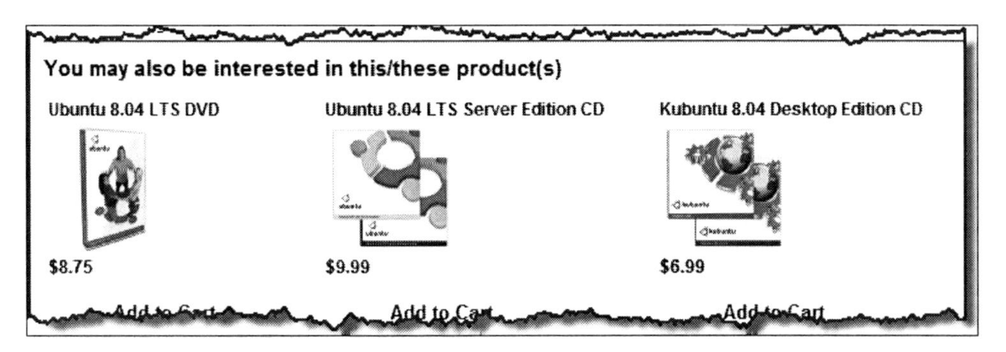

As you can see, through this **Related Products** feature, you can both cross-sell and up-sell products based on what you select as related products. While adding related products to one product, it does not automatically add the reverse relationship. For example, when we add Product B to Product A as a related product, it does not imply that Product A will be listed as a related product, when you see details of Product B.

You may be interested to add related products to multiple products at the same time. Unfortunately, at this time, VirtueMart does not allow adding related products to multiple items at the same time. You need to add related products to individual items.

Use of discount coupons

Discount coupons can be an effective tools for promoting your products and attracting customers to your store. You may offer a discount coupon to each new customer, or all customers who have placed order for a certain amount.

For creating discount coupons, go to **Coupon | New Coupon**. That shows the **New Coupon** screen:

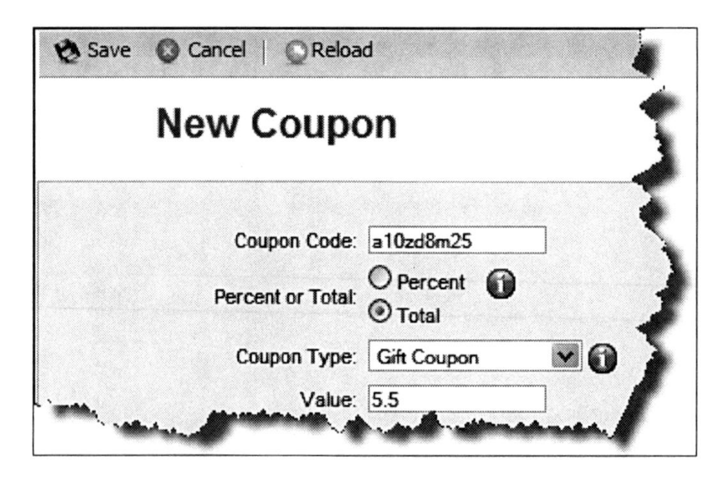

In the **New Coupon** screen, you must define the coupon. First, provide a unique coupon code in the **Coupon Code** field. Customers will need to type this code to redeem the coupon. After providing a coupon code, select the type of discount: percent or total. For sign-up coupons, a fixed discount amount will be fine. It is good to give a percent discount for regular or priority customers though. Select the **Percent** or **Total** radio button in the **Percent or Total** field. Then, select the coupon type. There are two types of coupons: **Gift Coupon** and **Permanent Coupon**.

A gift coupon is for one time use. Once it is redeemed by the customer, it can not be used again. On the other hand, permanent coupons remain forever, and customers can use that discount again and again. For example, for each new sign-up to your store, you offer a fixed amount of discount, say $5.50. As this discount is limited to only $5.50 and can be used with one or two transactions, the coupon type should be set to **Gift Coupon**. If you, for example, want to honor your special customer, say those who have purchased goods of more than $1,000 from you, you may offer a percent discount for all future purchases. Suppose you want to offer a discount of 5.5% for all future purchases. In this case, you should select **Percent** in the **Percent** or **Total** field, and **Permanent Coupon** in the **Coupon Type** drop-down list. You can save the coupon by clicking on the **Save** icon in the toolbar.

Once coupons are added, you can see the list of the coupons by clicking on **Coupon | List Coupons**. That shows the **Coupon List** screen:

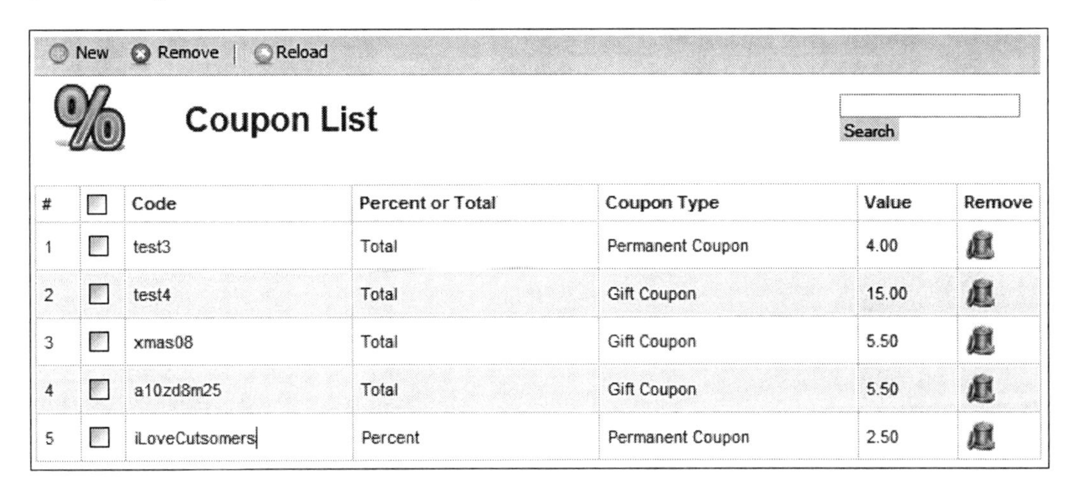

New
Remove
Reload
Coupon List
Search
| Code | Percent or Total | Coupon Type | Value | Remove
1 | test3 | Total | Permanent Coupon | 4.00
2 | test4 | Total | Gift Coupon | 15.00
3 | xmas08 | Total | Gift Coupon | 5.50
4 | a10zd8m25 | Total | Gift Coupon | 5.50
5 | iLoveCutsomers | Percent | Permanent Coupon | 2.50

You may notice that there are some default coupons, test1, test2, test3, and test4. You should remove these coupons first, so that nobody can use these codes on your store. For removing the coupons, select the coupons by checking the checkbox besides the code and click on the **Remove** icon in the toolbar.

As seen in the screenshot above, newly added coupons are also displayed. Once the coupons are created, you need to send the coupon codes to the customers through an email. At this moment, there is no way to automatically send the codes to the customers. You may use Joomla!'s mass-mail feature, or send the sign-up coupons with the welcome message that is sent after registration.

Caution

The coupon feature in VirtueMart is still immature compared to that of other shopping carts, such as Zen Cart, osCommerce, and Magento. It cannot be emailed automatically, cannot generate unique coupon codes automatically, and cannot be specified for a time period or to specific category of products. This also cannot be used as a Gift Certificate, as used in Zen Cart.

Customer reviews

Customer reviews are a great way to increase sales. It has been observed that products with positive customer reviews sell higher than those with no or negative customer review. Like other shopping cart systems, VirtueMart has also implemented a customer review feature. Using this feature, registered customers can add a review to any product. The customer reviews can be published automatically upon submission or be moderated and published by an administrator. When the review is published, it will be displayed in the product's detail page below the product description.

Enabling review

You need to enable the customer review and rating system from VirtueMart's administration panel. You can configure the review system from **Admin | Configuration**. The **Global** tab in the **Configuration** screen shows the review and commenting system options in the **Frontend Features** section:

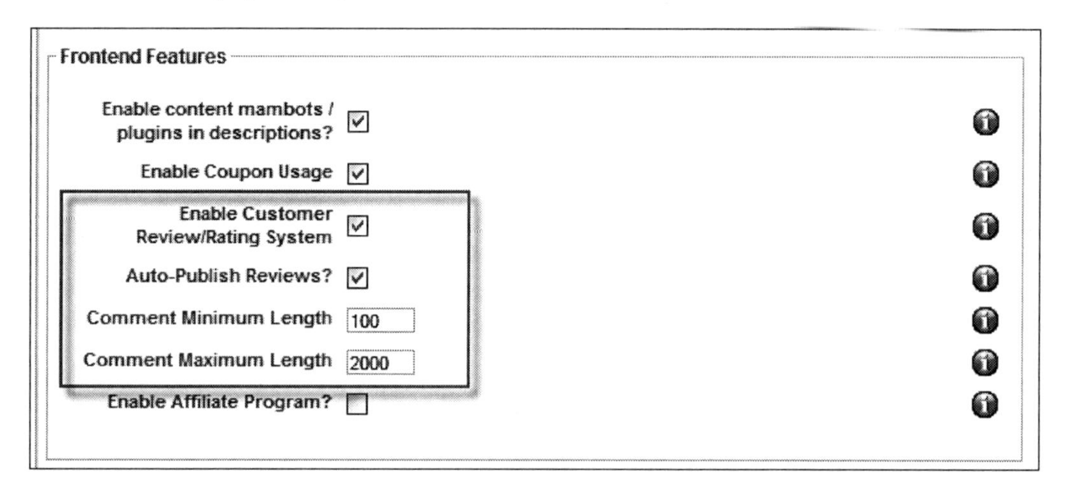

To enable customer reviews and comments, check the **Enable Customer Review/ Rating System** checkbox. As mentioned earlier, customer reviews can be published automatically without moderation. To allow customer reviews to be published without moderation, check the **Auto-Publish Reviews** checkbox. Uncheck it if you want to moderate the customer reviews. While enabling customer reviews, you may also set the minimum and maximum comment length. A minimum length is required so that customers can't only say 'good' or 'bad', but must say something more to qualify their ratings. Some customers may also tend to write an essay while reviewing a product. To stop such customers, set the maximum length of comments.

Remember that lengths specified are in characters, and spaces are also counted as characters. Set the minimum and maximum length while considering this fact.

Submitting reviews

When you have enabled customer reviews and ratings of products, customers can see the existing reviews on the product's details page, below the product description. If the product has no review, it will indicate that and inform the customer that to review the product, the customer needs to log in first.

When customers are logged in to your Joomla! and VirtueMart site, they can rate any product and provide their comments about the product. In that case, the customer sees the rating and review form below the product description:

Customer Reviews:

There are yet no reviews for this product.
Be the first to write a review...

Write a review for this product!

First: Rate the product. Please select a rating between 0 (poorest) and 5 stars (best).

Now please write a (short) review....(min. 100, max. 2000 characters)

Submit Review

Characters written: 0

Logged in customers can rate products by clicking on the star icons and write the comment about the product in the text area. Instructions for the text area show the minimum and maximum characters, the customers can write for the comment. The **Characters Written** box, at the bottom-right corner, shows the number of characters typed by the customer. This reminds the customer about the minimum and maximum characters allowed. Once the customer has rated the product, on five-star scale from the poorest to the best, and have written a comment, they can submit the review by clicking on the **Submit Review** button.

If **Auto-Publish Reviews** is enabled in the VirtueMart configuration, the reviews will be visible to customers within a few seconds. However, if **Auto-Publish Reviews** is disabled, customers will not see reviews until an administrator moderate and publish that review.

> It is good to enable **Auto-Publish Review**. That gives a positive impression to customers, and they become happy seeing their reviews published automatically. When they see you are moderating their reviews, they may tend to think that you do not trust them. However, for getting rid of spam, you need to restrict commenting to only registered users and be vigilant for such activities, and deal with spammers based on the case.

Moderating reviews

As an administrator, you can see the reviews submitted for different products on your VirtueMart store. In the **Product List** screen, you see the reviews for each product under the **Customer Reviews** column:

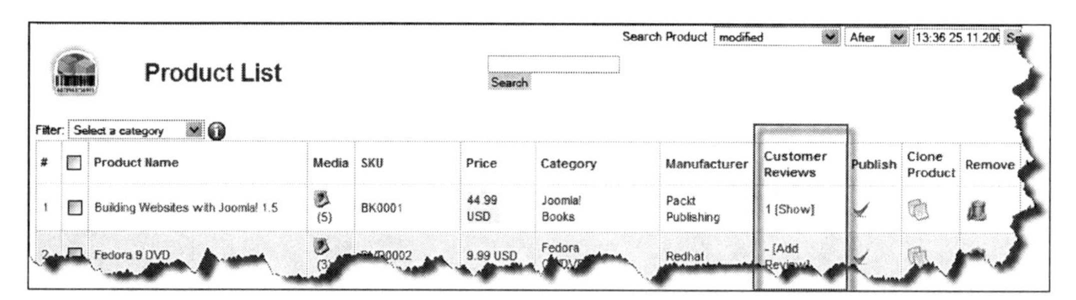

To see the reviews, click on the **[Show]** link under the **Customer Reviews** column. If the product has no reviews, you will see the **[Add Review]** link. You can add a review by clicking on this link.

On clicking the **[Show]** link, you get the **Customer Reviews** screen (seen below). You can also reach this screen from **Products | Customer Reviews**.

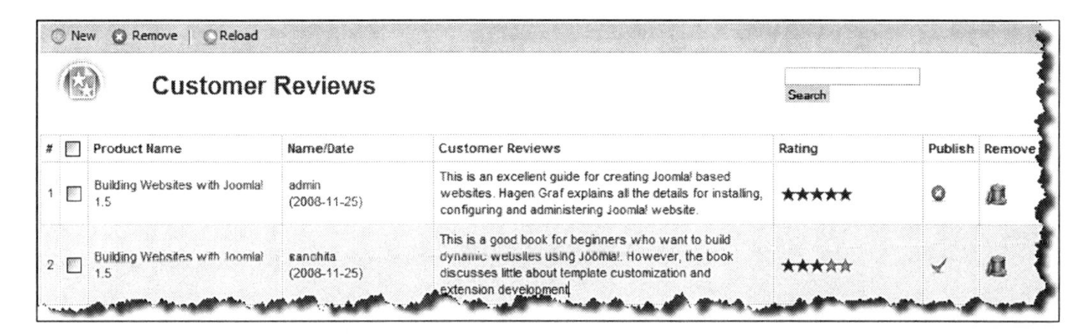

The **Customer Reviews** screen lists the reviews submitted by customers. You can publish or unpublish a customer review from the **Customer Reviews** screen, by clicking on the icon in the **Publish** column. A green tick icon in this column indicates the review has a published status, whereas a red circle with white cross indicates an unpublished status. For deleting a review, click on trash icon in the **Remove** column.

For viewing and editing a review, click on the link in the **Name/Date** column. That brings the **Add/Edit a Review** screen as shown:

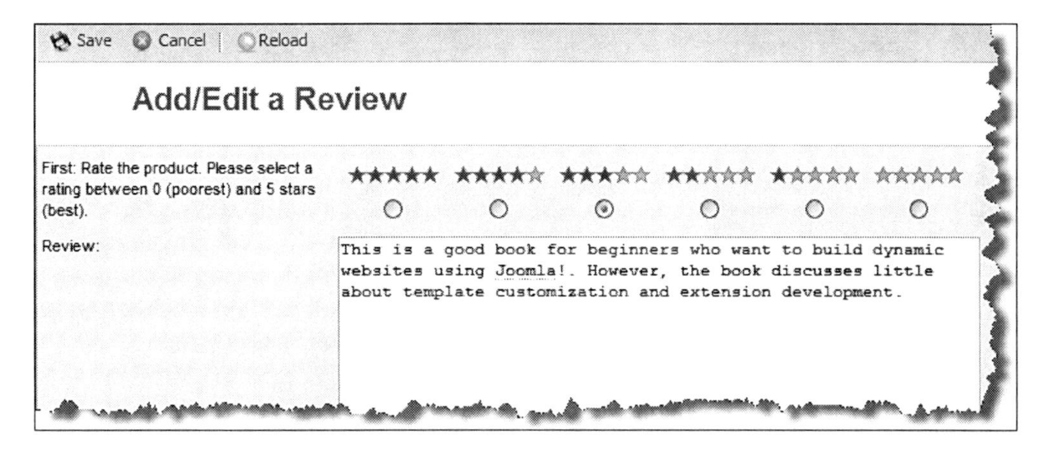

You may edit the review in this screen, if there is something which does not match with your site's policy. The example for this could be when a customer advertises their own product or attacks the manufacturer. Once editing is complete, save the review by clicking on the **Save** button.

When customers submit their reviews and if they are published, either automatically or manually by the administrator, the customer reviews will be displayed under the product description in product's detail page:

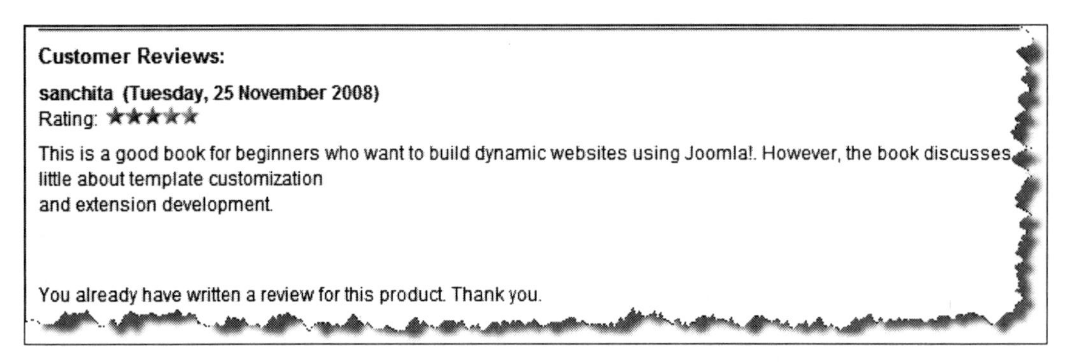

As you can see from the screenshot above, when a customer has already submitted a review for a product, he or she cannot write another review for the same product.

Newsletters and product notification

Newsletters are very effective means of communicating with and updating customers. Through regular newsletters, you can update your customers about new products, special offers, and upcoming products. By default, VirtueMart has no built-in feature for sending newsletters. However, there are several newsletter components for Joomla!, which can be used for a VirtueMart-based store.

You can find the newsletter components, modules, and plugins at `http://extensions.joomla.org`. The **Communication | Newsletter** sections lists the newsletter extensions for Joomla!. There are some very good newsletter extensions, and some of them work fine with VirtueMart. While trying to choose a suitable extension for using with VirtueMart, we should look into how it integrates with VirtueMart. First, it should provide an option to the customers, during registration and afterwards, for opting into a newsletter subscription. Another feature should be inserting Joomla! content into the newsletter so we can send the site updates through the newsletter.

The following table shows the comparative features of the major newsletter components:

Extension Name	Registration for VirtueMart customers enabled?	Inserting Joomla! content into a newsletter?	Remark
Acajoom News	Yes	Yes	Best for using with VirtueMart
ccNewsletter	Yes	No	
Letterman	Yes	Yes	v.2.1.4_RC1 has some problems with language translation
Communicator	No	Yes	
Vemod News mailer	No	Yes	This will be a good choice for automatic product updates

As seen in the above table, we may opt to use Acajoom and Letterman for sending newsletters. However, Vemod News Mailer provides the unique feature of sending updates on Joomla! site content. We can use this extension for product update notifications. Therefore, in the following sections, we are going to see how to install, configure, and use the Acajoom Newsletter, and Vemod News Mailer extensions with VirtueMart.

Using Acajoom Newsletter

Acajoom is an excellent newsletter extension for Joomla!. This is a Joomla! 1.5 native component, and it also has a version for Joomla! 1.x. You can download it from `http://www.acajoom.com/content/blogcategory/13/71/`. Once downloaded from the installation package, install it from the **Extensions | Install/Uninstall** screen.

Configuring Acajoom

For configuring Acajoom, click on **Components | Acajoom | Configuration**. That shows the **Configuration** screen. It has fours tabs: **Mails**, **Subscribers**, **Log & Status**, and **Miscellaneous**.

From the **Mail** tab, you can set the mailing options for this Acajoom news component. First, you need to select a mailer method. It may be an **SMTP server**, **PHP mail function**, and **Sendmail**. If the **SMTP server** method is selected, then you need the SMTP server name and authentication information. For **Sendmail**, you need to specify the path of the sendmail program.

In the **Mailing Settings** and **Sending Settings** section, you can set options for mail bouncing and sending:

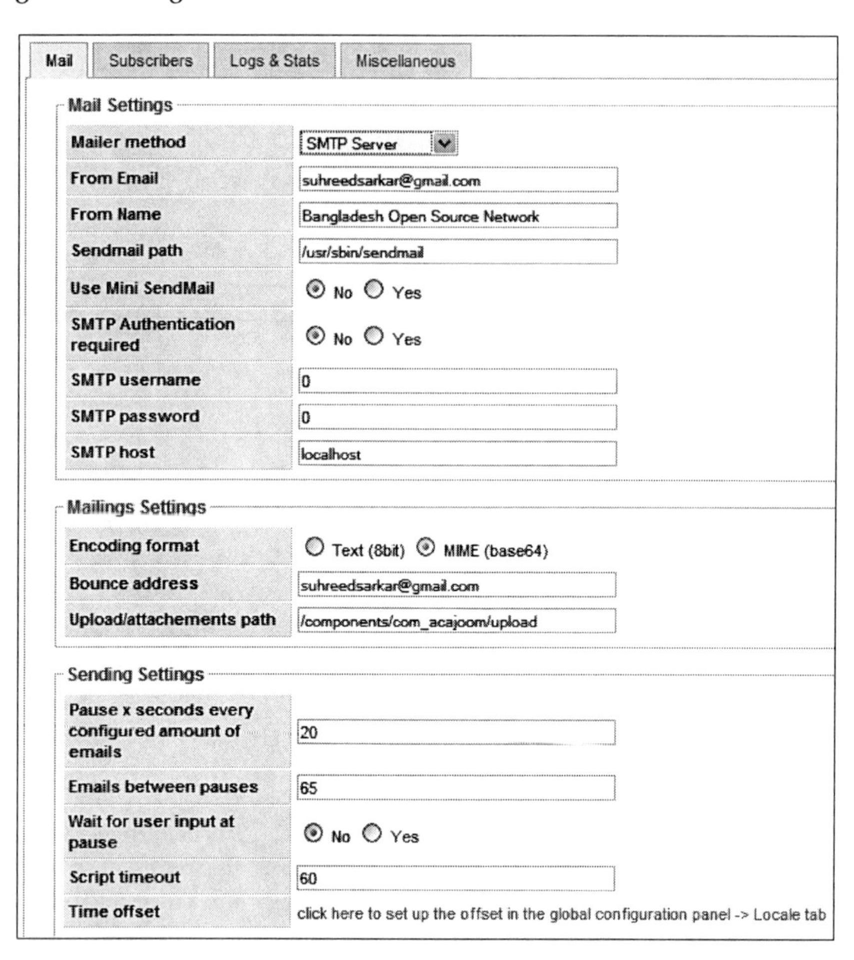

In the **Subscribers** tab, you can specify whether unregistered users can subscribe to the mailing list or not, whether subscriptions need confirmation, and whether to show the mailing list archive button on the frontend:

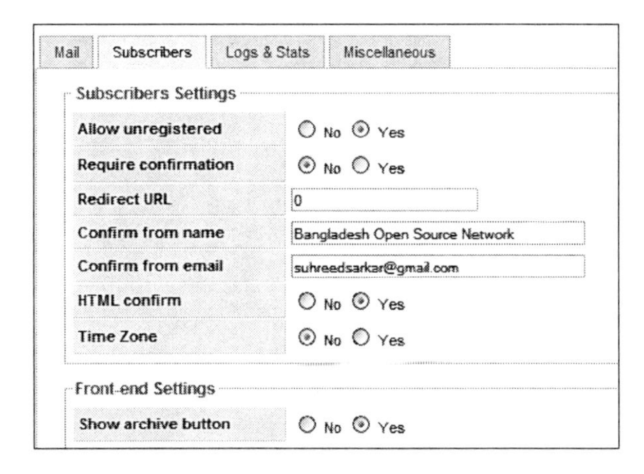

In the **Log & Stats** tab, you can set options for logging and displaying statistics about reading the mailing lists. You need to specify a log format and location, and also you can clear the log.

In the **Miscellaneous** tab, you can specify some other options which will be helpful for newsletter management and readers. Some of the options in this tab are: show guide, show tips, show lists in frontend, SEF in mailings, and show author's name.

Creating a list

One of the nice features of Acajoom is that it can guide you through using Wizard steps. For example, when you first click on **Components | Acajoom | Lists**, it shows the first step for creating a list, as seen in the following screenshot:

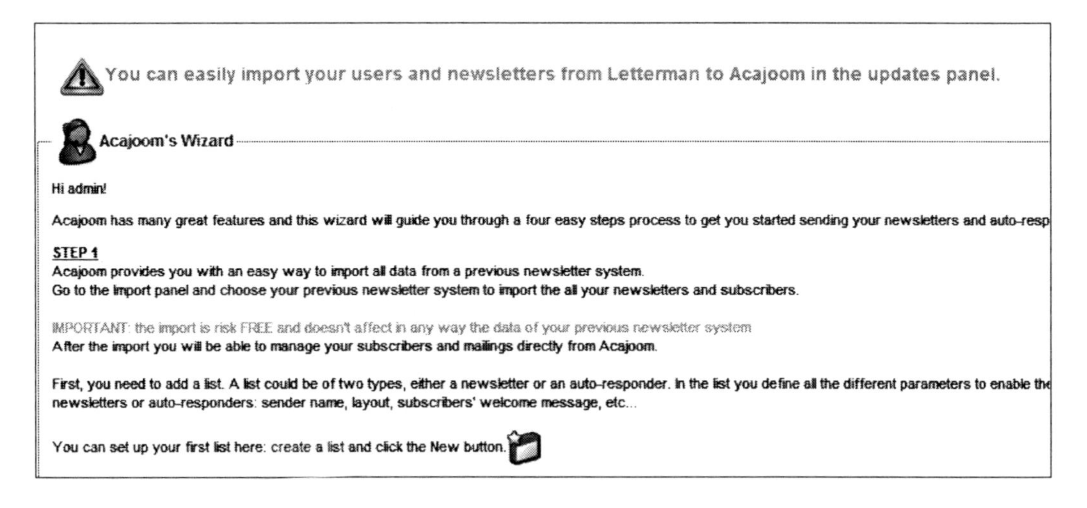

Click on the **create a list** link on Step 1 of the Wizard, or click on the **New** button in the toolbar. That opens up the **New List** screen:

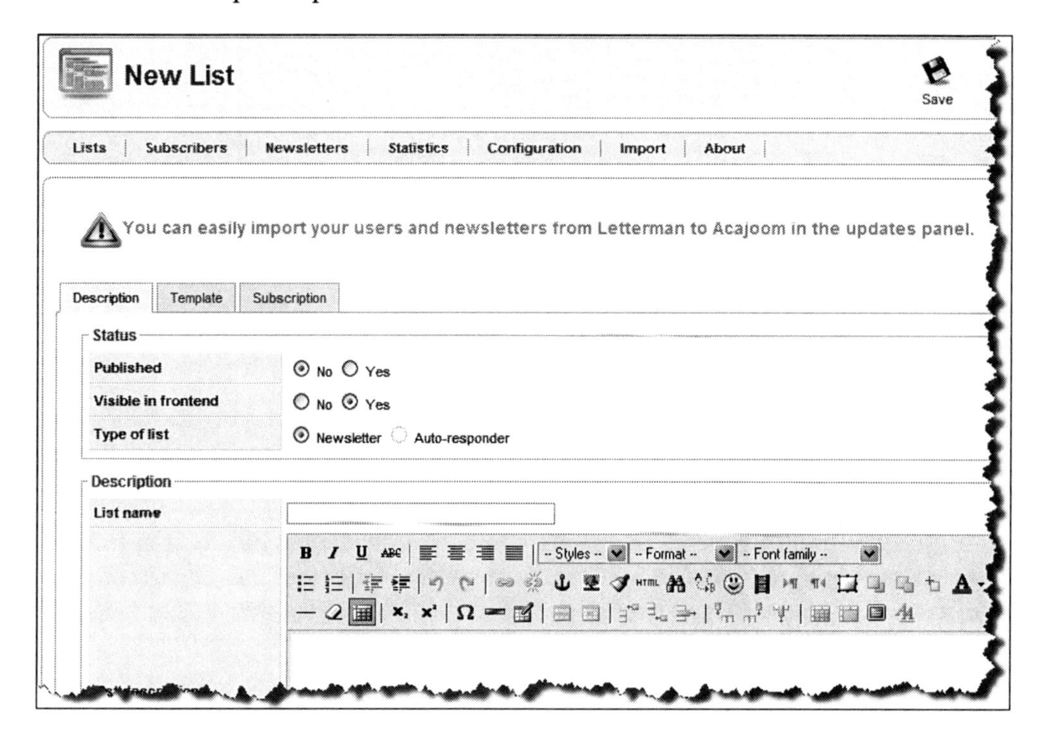

In the **Description** tab, you need to provide a name for the list, say **Monthly Product Updates**, in the **List name** field. Before that, select **Yes** in the **Published** field to publish the list. If you check **Yes** in the **Visible in frontend** field, the list items will be visible on Joomla!'s frontend. In the **Type of List** field, you can either choose **Newsletter** or **Auto-responder** option. First, you need to add a newsletter, and then auto responder, if needed.

In the **List Description** field, provide a description for the list so customers know what the list is for. In the bottom of the list description, you can specify the sender name, sender email address, bounce address, and ID of the creator of the list.

In the **Template** tab, you can specify the layout for the newsletter. The rich text editor allows you to draw the layout. You need to use the **[SUBSCRIPTIONS]** placeholder in the template. An explanation for using this placeholder is given in this screen. Select **Yes** in the **HTML mailing** radio box if you want to send the newsletter in HTML format.

From the **Subscriptions** tab, you can specify how the users will be subscribed to the list. You can select **New**, **All Users**, or **No** in the **Auto Subscribe Users** drop-down list. In the **Unsubscribe Settings** section, select **Yes** in the **Send Unsubscribe Message** field and type the unsubscribe message in the **Unsubscribe email** field:

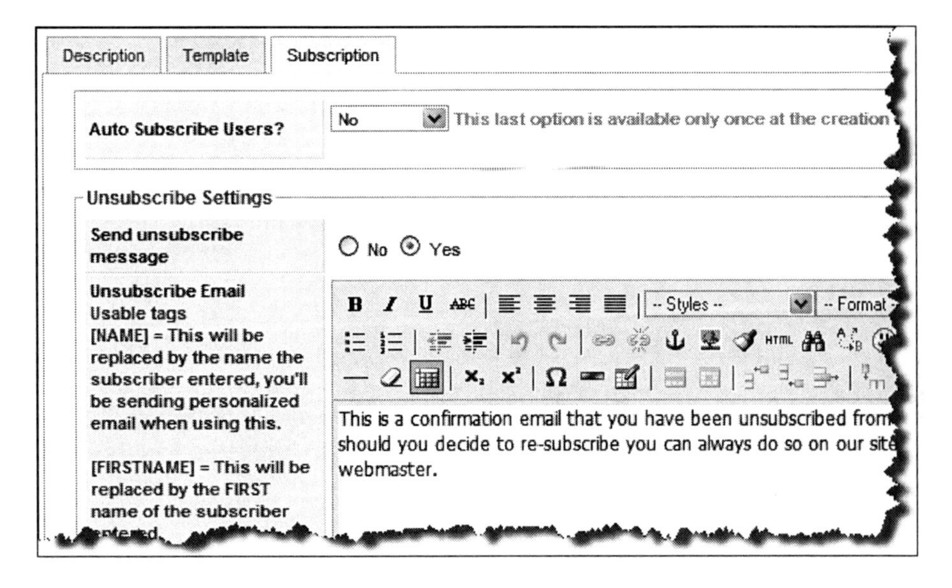

Once all of these settings are configured for the list, click on the **Save** icon in the toolbar to save the list. The list will now be displayed in the **Lists** screen:

You can see the subscribers by clicking on the **View subscribers** link in the **Subscribers** column. As we have selected **All Users** in the **Auto Subscribe Users** field, all existing users of VirtueMart will be displayed as subscribers to this newly created list:

As you can see, the **Subscribers** screen shows the user's name, their email address, sign-up date, and registered and confirmed status. It also indicates whether the user opted for an HTML mailings or not.

In Acajoom and ANJEL, lists and newsletters are different things. Lists may be compared to a magazine, and newsletters are issues of the magazine. By creating a list, you can define the magazine type, layout, and subscription rules. You then need to publish issues of the magazine, that is, newsletters. Newsletters (issues of the magazine) will be mailed to the subscribers to the list. While using these two newsletter extensions, please remember the meaning of these two terms.

Creating newsletters

Once you have created a list, you can create and send newsletters (or issues of that magazine) to the subscribers. For creating newsletters, go to **Components | Acajoom | Newsletters**. Then, in the **Newsletters** screen, select a list, for example, **Monthly Product Update**, from the **Select a list** drop-down list:

Now, click on the **New** button in the toolbar to create a newsletter for the list you have selected, that is **Monthly Product Update**. That shows the **Edit a Newsletter** screen:

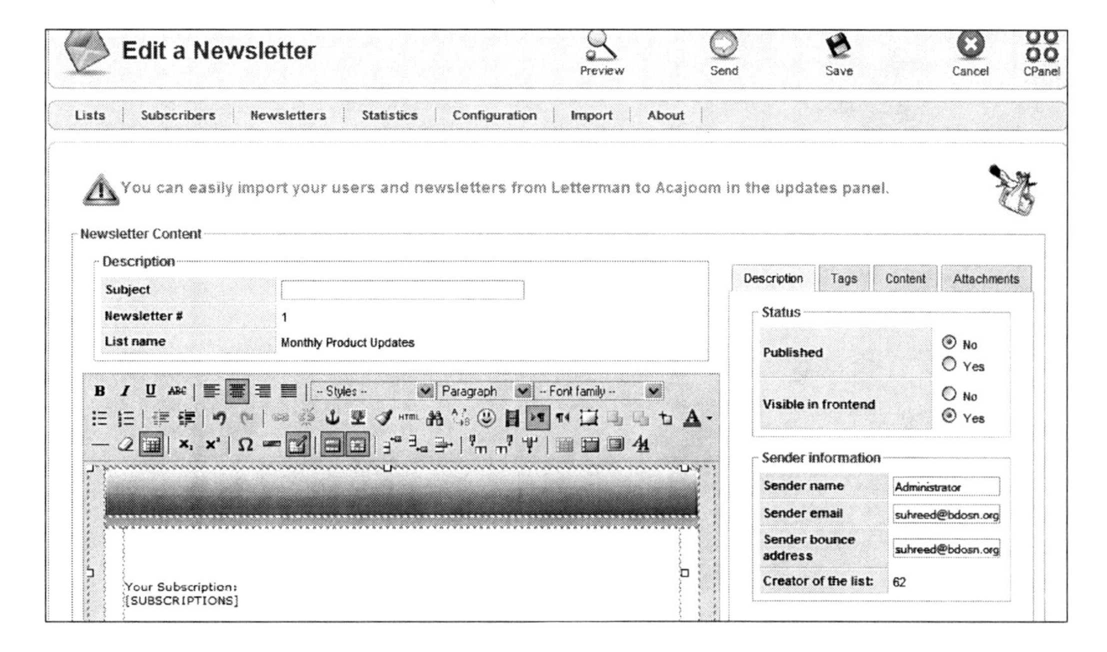

In the **Edit a Newsletter** screen, you must provide a subject for the newsletter, For example, you may type **Christmas Offers 2008** in the **Subject** field. Then, follow the rich text editor showing the template you have designed for the list. Here, you can add your message to the subscribers, and insert Joomla! content.

On the right of the rich text editor, we see four tabs: **Description**, **Tags**, **Content**, and **Attachments**. In the **Description** tab, you can set its status, published or not, visible in the front page or not, and sender information. The **Tags** tab shows available tags (for example, **[NAME]**, **[FIRSTNAME]**), which you can use in the message as variables.

The **Content** tab shows a list of available Joomla! articles which you can add to your newsletter. When you select an article from the list, a tag is shown in the **Content tag** field. You need to copy this tag and paste it in the message to send the article with the newsletter. You can show a full article, only the introduction, or only the title of the article in the newsletter. When you select **Full Article**, **Intro only**, or **Title only**, the content tag also changes. The content tag consists of the article ID and display mode, that is, **0** for **Full Article**, **1** for **Intro only**, and **2** for **Title only**. For example, `{contentitem:6|0}` will show the article with ID 6 as a full article; the `{contentitem:6|1}` tag will display the same article, but with only the introduction.

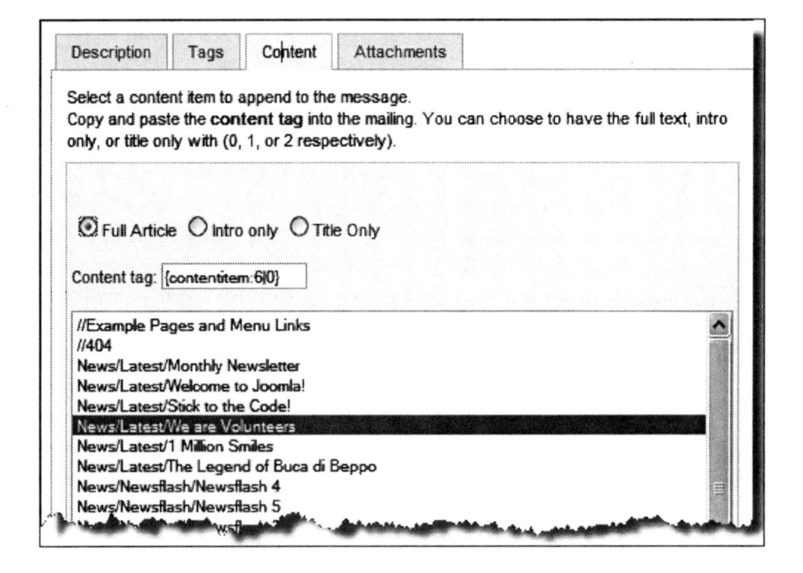

As you can see from the **Content** tab above, you can only add the Joomla! articles to the newsletter, not VirtueMart product items. But our main purpose for sending this newsletter is to update customers about new products available on our store. Therefore, we have to think differently about sending this information through the newsletter.

A good solution for sending product information through a newsletter is to create an article with that product information, publish that article, and then copy the contents for the article to the Acajoom newsletter editor. This doesn't require any hack to the newsletter system. Let us see how we can create an article in Joomla! with VirtueMart's product information.

Creating an article with product information

As you have already endeavored to build a VirtueMart store with Joomla!, we assume that you already know how to create articles, categories, and sections. By default, we have **News** section. Under this section you may create another category titled **Product Updates**. All of our product update articles will belong to this **Product Updates** category.

You can create a new article from the **Content | Article Manager | New** screen. However, our challenge is to add VirtueMart product information into this article. In fact, there is a plugin for inserting VirtueMart product information into Joomla! content. Let's move to **Extensions | Plugin Manager**. The **Plugin Manager** screen lists all of the installed plugins for Joomla!. Find the plugin named **VirtueMart Product Snapshot**, and click on its name. That brings **Plugin: [Edit]** screen:

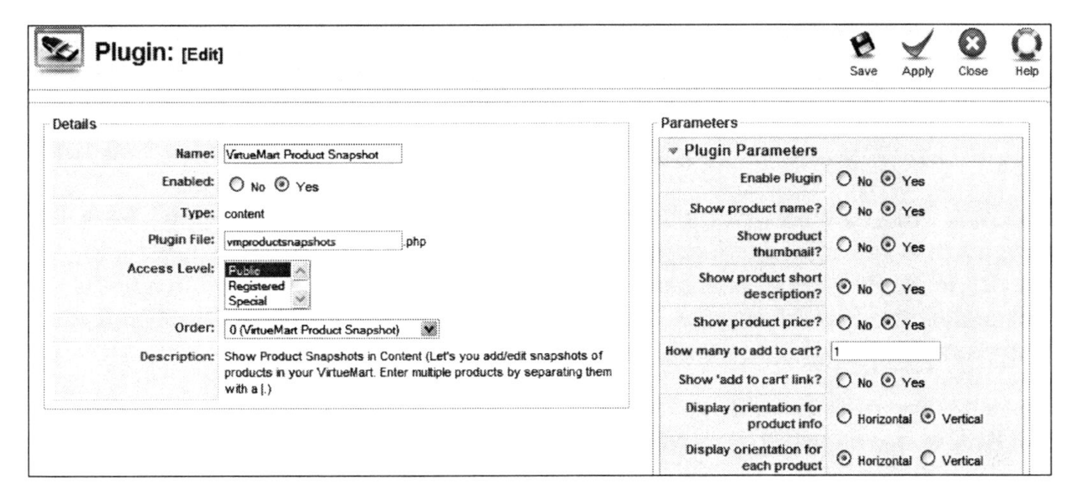

From the **Details** section of the **Plugin: [Edit]** screen, you can enable the plugin, set an access level, and order. Plug-in-specific parameters are displayed in the **Parameters** section. From the plugin parameters section, you can enable the plugin, enable or disable showing the product's name, thumbnail, short description, price, add to cart link, and the amount of products to be added to the cart when the link is clicked. You can also set **Display orientation for product info**, and **Display orientation for each product**. For both of these settings, you can select horizontal or vertical. Select the values as shown in the screenshot above, and click on the **Save** icon in the toolbar.

Let us now try to add an article. Go to **Content | Article Manager**, and click on the **New** icon. That shows the **Article: [New]** screen:

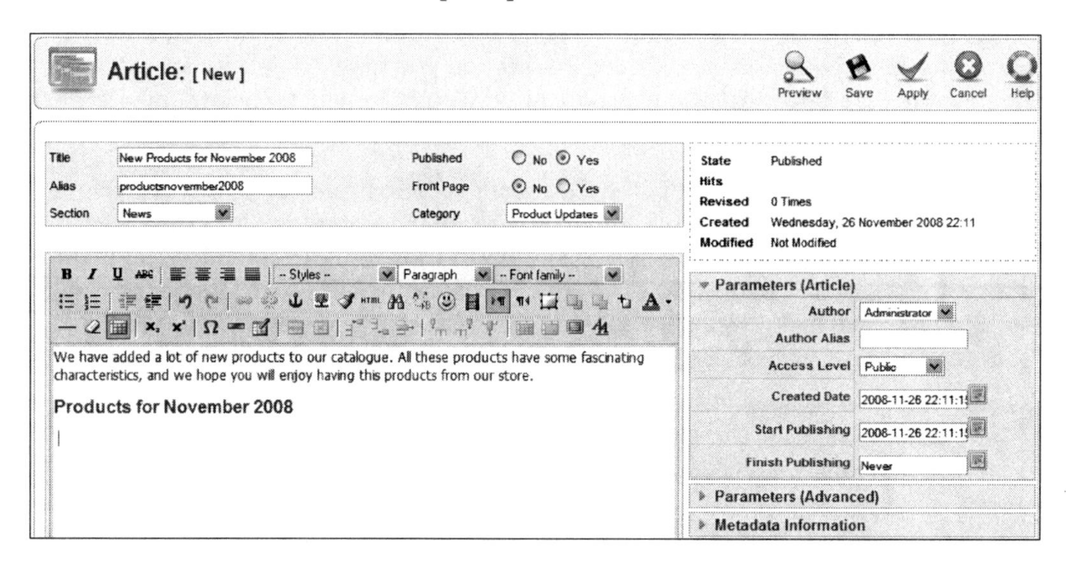

You may proceed with writing the article as shown in the screenshot above. First, assign a title, title alias, section, published and front page status, and category. In the rich text editor, type the introduction for the article. Now, you need to add the VirtueMart product information. We have already enabled the VirtueMart Product Snapshot plugin, but how do we use that?

There are few rules for adding VirtueMart product snapshots to Joomla! contents. We have to use the markup as follows:

```
{product_snapshot:id=XX, showname=y|n, showimage=y|n, showprice=y|n,
 showdesc=y|n, showaddtocart=y|n, displayeach=h, displaylist=v,
 width=90%, border=0, style=color:black;, align=left}
```

As you remember, we have configured a default value for the `product_snapshot` plugin, and therefore, we don't need to provide all of the options shown above. For example, we want to add a snapshot of product ID `21`, and we can do this by simply using this tag:

```
{product_snapshot:id=21}
```

This will display the product snapshot with the default settings. For adding multiple product snapshots, we can separate the IDs by a pipe (|). For example, we add the following tags in the article, save, and publish the article:

```
{product_snapshot:id=18|20|29|33|41}
```

When saved and published, the article will look like the following screenshot:

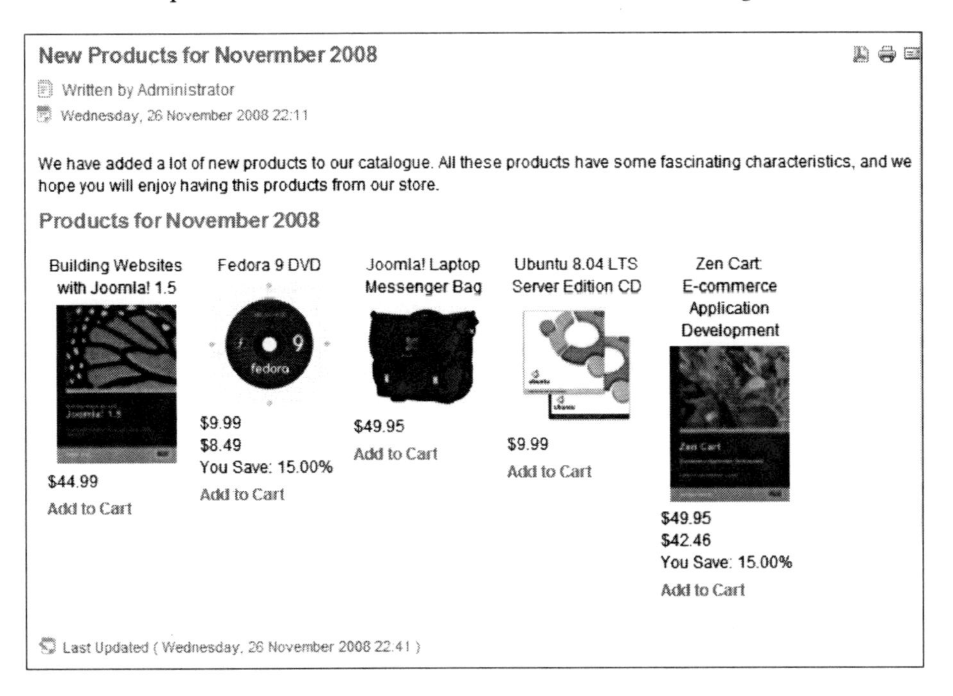

As you can see, the product snapshots for the IDs we have specified are now displayed in the article. If you select **Yes** in the **Show product short description** field during configuring the **VirtueMart Product Snapshot** plugin, the page will look like the following screenshot:

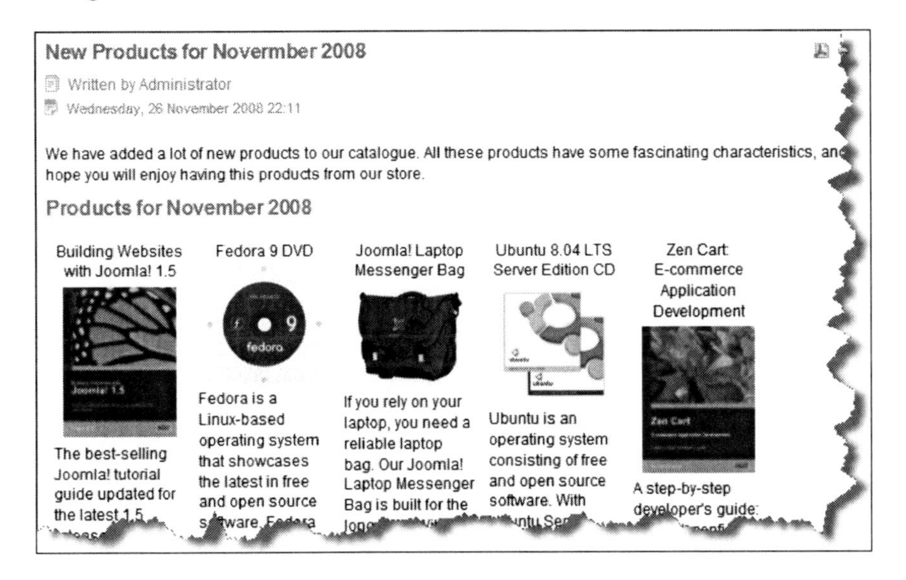

Our article is now ready to be inserted into our newsletter. However, if you select this article and insert the content tag in the newsletter, the product item will not be shown. Instead, you will see the codes like `{product_snapshot: id=18|20|29|33|41}` in the newsletter article sent to the subscriber. To avoid this, publish that article, copy the contents of the article, and insert that in the newsletter editor.

Sending newsletters

When you have created a newsletter and it has been saved, the newsletter will be listed in the **Newsletters** screen. You can send the newsletter to subscribers by selecting the newsletter, and clicking on the **Send** button in the toolbar:

Selecting the newsletter from the list and clicking on the **Send** button will start sending emails to the subscribers using your configured mailing system.

Adding fields in the Registration Form

So far, we have seen how to configure Acajoom, create list and a newsletter, and send the newsletters to the subscriber with VirtueMart products snapshot. As you are using VirtueMart, and for a production environment, users are registered through VirtueMart's Login module, the registration form should provide an option for users to opt-in for such mailing lists. If you are using YaNC, Letterman, or ccNewsletter, then you can easily add an opt-in field.

For adding the subscription field, go to VirtueMart's administration panel, and click on **Admin | Manager User Fields**. Click on the **New** icon to add a field. That will show the **Add/Edit User Field** screen:

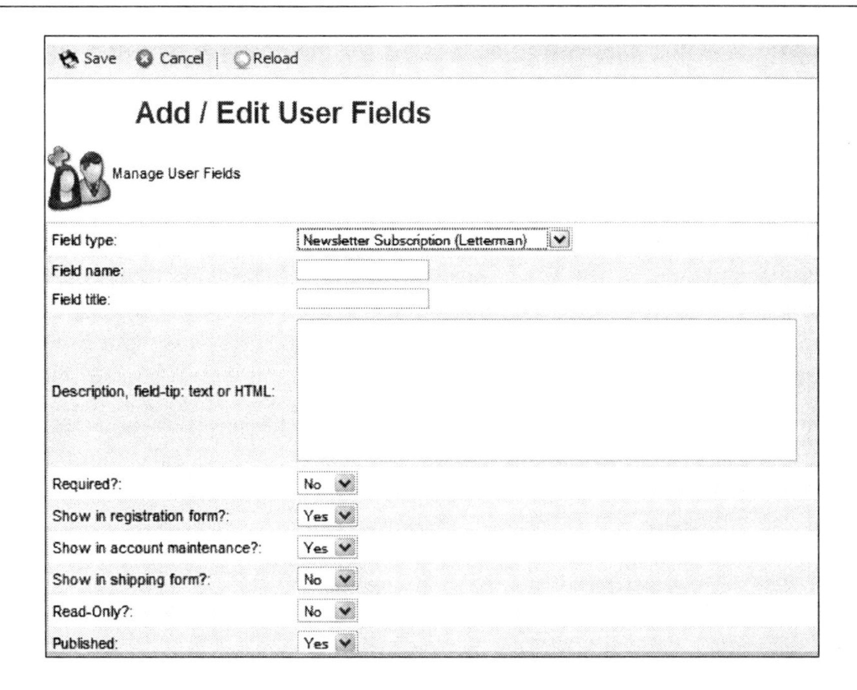

In the **Field Type** drop-down list, select **Newsletter Subscription (Letterman)**, the same field for other newsletters such as ccNewsletter, ANJEL, YaNC. Configure the remaining fields to show this field on the registration form and the account maintenance form.

For Acajoom, there is still no such solution for adding a subscription field in the registration or account maintenance form. However, we can use the Acajoom Subscriber module for subscribing to newsletters. Go to **Extensions | Module Manager** and you will see the **Acajoom Subscriber Module**. Click on the module name to edit the configuration for this module. In the **Parameters** section, you can configure whether to show the introduction text, list names, an HTML subscription option, name field, and so on. Once the module is published, it will look like the following screenshot:

As you can see, all of the lists you have created for the site will be listed in this module, and the visitors can select the lists, provide their name and email address, and then click on the **Subscribe** button to subscribe to the lists selected. They can also choose whether they would like to receive the newsletters in an HTML format or not.

When a user has subscribed to some lists, the module shows a button to change the newsletter subscriptions. When the **Change** button is clicked, an Acajoom page is displayed and the customer sees the **My Subscriptions** icon. Clicking on this icon will bring the **Your Subscription** screen, from where the customer can manage their subscriptions:

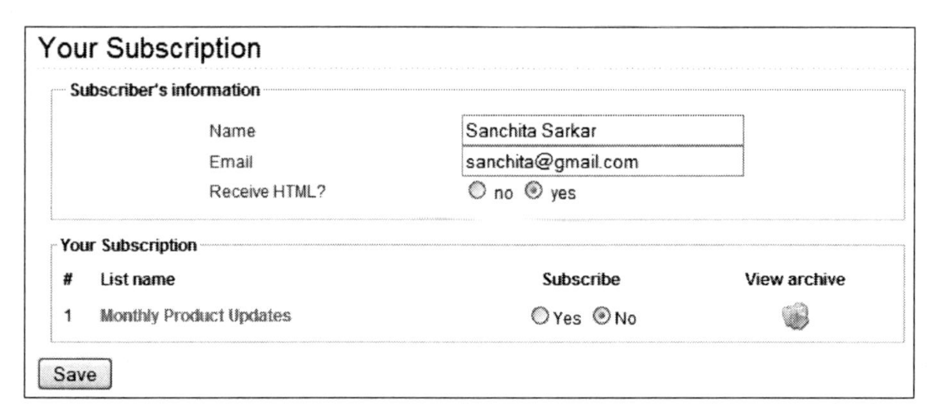

Using the other newsletter components, such as ANJEL, Letterman, YaNC, and so on, is similar to Acajoom. You may try all these and choose one to use with your site.

Using the Vemod News Mailer

The Vemod New Mailer is not a newsletter component like Acajoom. In Acajoom, you can create lists, newsletters, and then send those to subscribers. On the other hand, the Vemod News Mailer provides you great facility for sending news updates to the subscribers. The users of this site can subscribe to one or more sections and categories, and the administrator can specify a time for compilation of available news available. Any news added to these sections and categories will be complied, optionally with an editorial introduction, on the configured time (monthly, weekly, daily, and so on), and will be automatically sent to the subscribers.

For VirtueMart product updates, we can use this extension creatively. We install it and configure the **Product Updates** category to be compiled monthly, and then the users automatically get the product updates.

For using this extension, download it from `http://tinyurl.com/denvxj` and then install it. Then, click on **Components | Vemod News Mailer | Configuration**. That shows the **Vemod News Mailer Configuration** screen:

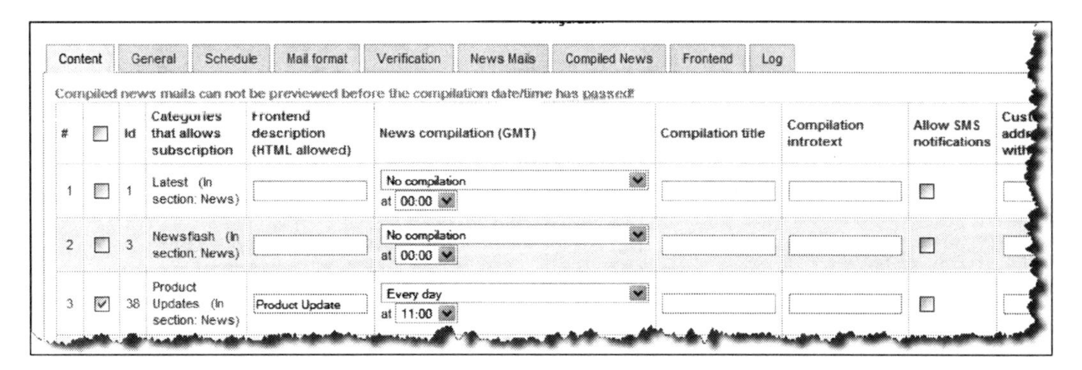

In the **Content** tab (seen above), select the categories and sections which will be sent as an update. Give the compilation a title (**Compilation Title**), introductory text for the compilation, news compilation interval (monthly, weekly, everyday, and so on), and time (in GMT) of compilation. You can also check the **Allow SMS notifications** checkbox, if you want to send updates to mobile devices through an SMS gateway. In the last column, you can add special subscribers to the list by typing their email address.

At the bottom of the **Content** tab, you can set the mailer to compile all news updates and send that as a single newsletter:

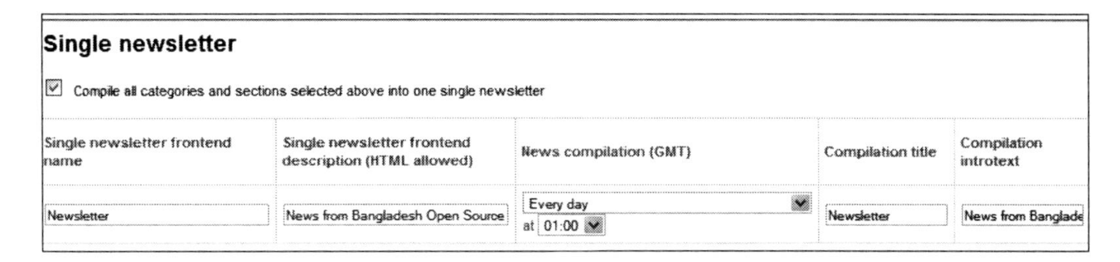

From the **General** tab, you can specify what type of content will be included in the updates, whether guest subscribers are allowed or not, and so on:

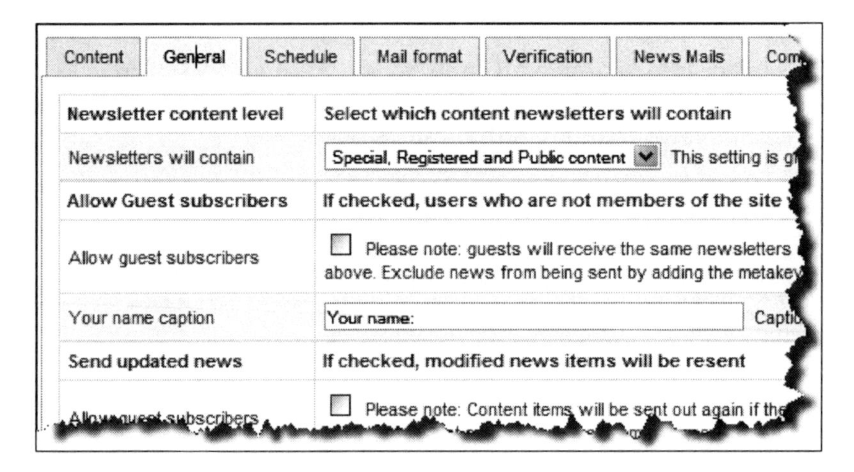

In the **Schedule** tab, you can enable a scheduled scan for updated news, news scan interval in hours, automatically adding newly registered users to subscribers list, automatically re-send failed mailings, and throttling to prevent performance degradation due to bulk mailing:

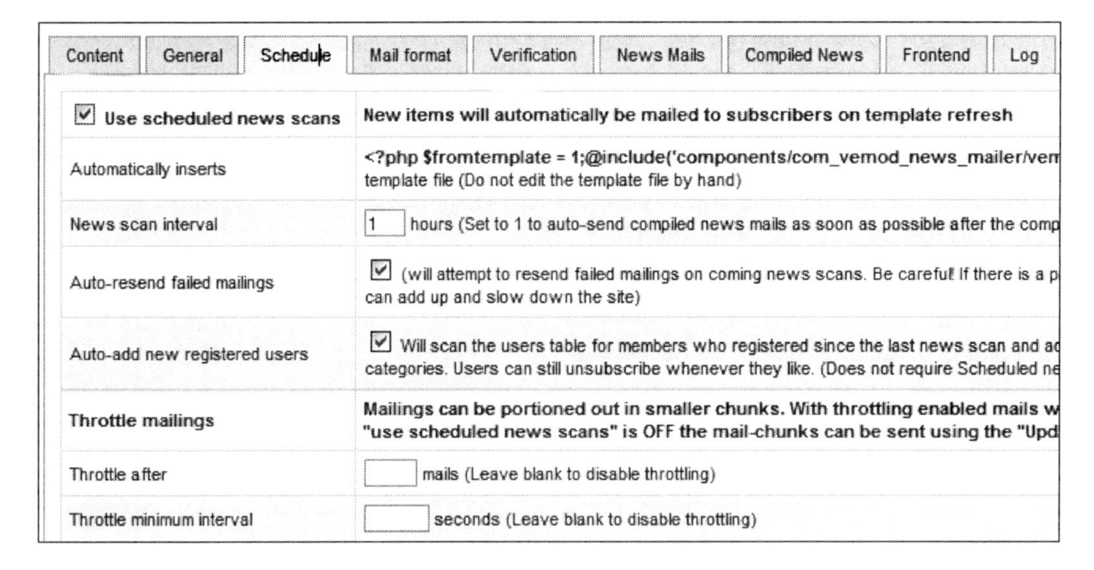

In the **Mail Format** tab, you can set the default mail format (for example, **HTML**, **Plain Text,** or **User Decides**), name of the SMS carrier for sending SMS updates, from address, frontend text, and SMS text.

In the **Verification** tab, you can configure the user verification settings as **No verification**, **For guests**, or **For everybody**. Then, specify the verification email's subject, format, and message (either HTML and Plain text).

In the **News Mails** tab, you can set whether the body of the news updates will be truncated or not. If truncated, how many words will be displayed, and what will be the text of the **Read More...** link:

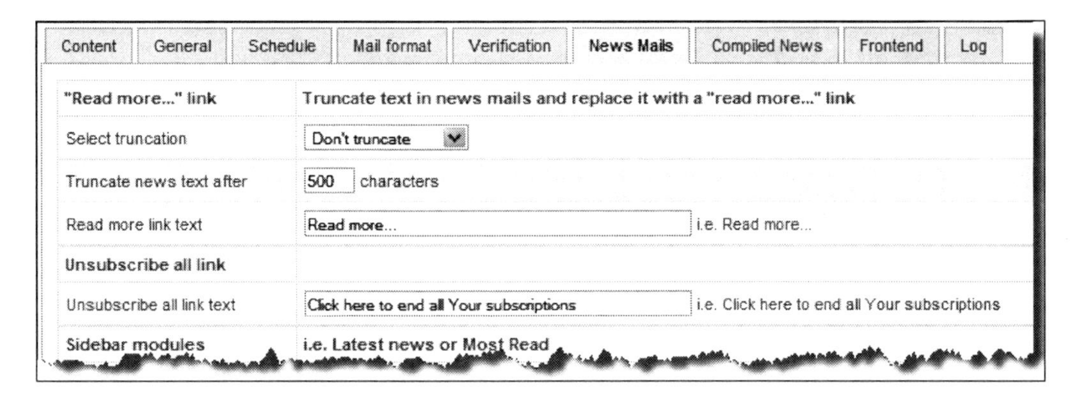

The other tabs also provide some configuration options, and you should explore those too. Help text for every field is provided inline for any administrator with minimum knowledge of Joomla! administration.

Once the categories are selected and configurations are saved, the Joomla! administrator has nothing to do. The news will automatically be compiled and sent to the subscribers. This is a great way to notify visitors about site updates.

The Vemod News Mailer only provides news updates. You cannot use it for sending custom newsletters, as you can do in Acajoom or Letterman. However, if you create a category named Newsletters, configure Vemod News Mailer to send updates of this category, and post your newsletters to this category, then your posted newsletters will automatically be sent to subscribers.

Summary

This chapter has introduced many features of VirtueMart and Joomla!, which you can use for promoting your products and maintaining public relations. Promotions and public relations are important for succeeding in an online business. Therefore, like other shopping carts, VirtueMart has also provided many tools for product promotions and public relations. Through the use of these features, you have learned how to promote your products introducing discounts, special offers, featured products, discount coupons, and so on. You have also learned how to maintain communication with the customers and visitors of your site by using newsletters and mailing extensions. You have learned fair details about the Acajoom News and Vemod New Mailer extension. Both can be used for sending regular newsletters and product updates to both registered and unregistered users of your site.

With this updated knowledge on product promotion and public relations, you may like to further enhance your store's features. Localization of your store is such an advance feature which we are going to discuss in the next chapter.

8
Localization of VirtueMart

So far, we have seen how our Joomla! site and VirtueMart shop can serve our customers. We have used the same language, locales, and settings for all customers. What do you think about adding some flavor to our shop, such as using multiple currencies, multiple languages, locales and so on? Yes, that will surely add some value to our shop, and we are going to learn about the techniques for doing so. On completion of this chapter, you will be able to:

- Understand the need for and importance of localization
- Use different regions and region-specific taxes
- Use multiple currencies for the shop
- Install new languages for the Joomla site and VirtueMart shop
- Translate the language of the site as you require

We assume that you have followed the previous chapters and have already learned how to install and configure the Joomla! extensions (modules, components, and plugins). These skills will be necessary for performing most of the tasks in this chapter.

Why localization?

What is localization? If you are not sure about its definition, just type 'define: localization' in a Google search box and you will get lots of definitions. In short, localization (often called l10n) is the configuration that allows a program to be adaptable to local national-language features. Localization includes the translation of menus and messages into the native spoken language, as well as changes in the user interface to accommodate different alphabets and cultures. It also includes using appropriate locales (date and time format) for that country or region. For example, for customers in France, an online store's frontend language may be changed to French. Only changing the language will not be enough for localization.

For successful localization, appropriate locales (which include currency, date formats, time-zone, and so on) for France, will also be used. So, a localization attempt for France will automatically translate the web site's interface, show the prices in Euros (with a symbol €) and dates will be shown in a dd/mm/yyyy format.

Localization plays an important role upon attracting customers, especially for niche markets. When a store is localized, customers from niche markets are easily attracted to that store. Because they think that it is their 'own' store. Localization also helps understand the content of the store better. As with our example store, customers speaking Bangla will be more comfortable reading the product descriptions in Bangla. Therefore, it will be a good strategy to translate the site's interface into Bangla, and change other settings.

Localizing regions and taxes

Try to recall the discussions in Chapter 3, *Configuring the VirtueMart Store*. In that chapter, we introduced the configuration options for a VirtueMart store. There, we saw that most of the countries in the world have already been added to VirtueMart by default.

Countries

You can see the list of countries by selecting **Admin | List Countries** from VirtueMart's administration panel:

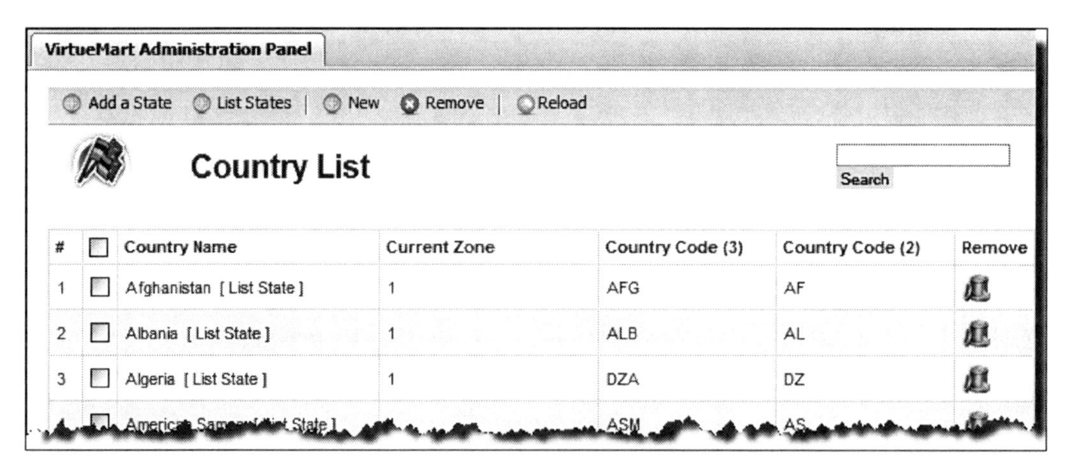

There are 244 countries listed. You can also add a new country by clicking on the **New** button in the toolbar. For creating a new country, you must provide a name, and ISO 2-letter and 3-letter country codes. You can see the list of ISO-2 country codes at `http://www.iso.org/iso/english_country_names_and_code_elements`.

Adding state or region

As most of the countries are already included, we only need to add the regions. If you select a country, and click on the **List State** link or the **List States** button in the toolbar, you will get the list of states in that country. For example, when you select the **United Kingdom**, and click on the **List State** link, you get a list of the states in the UK, as shown in the following screenshot:

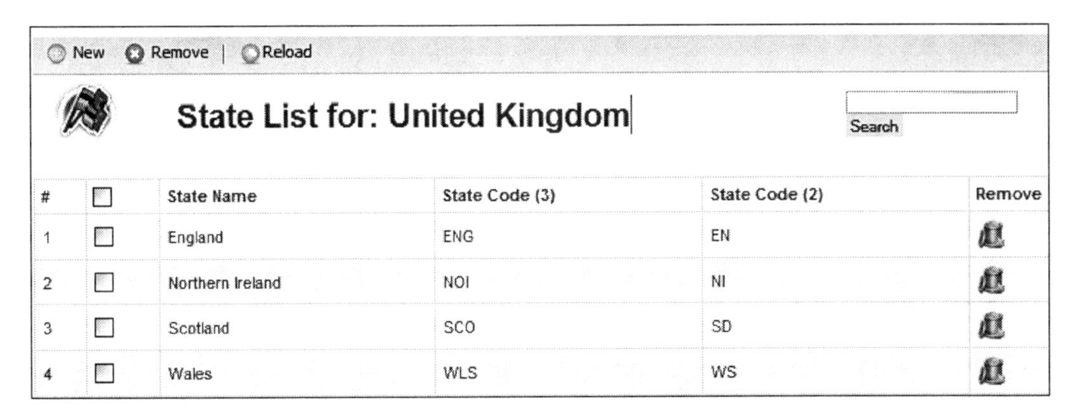

#		State Name	State Code (3)	State Code (2)	Remove
1		England	ENG	EN	
2		Northern Ireland	NOI	NI	
3		Scotland	SCO	SD	
4		Wales	WLS	WS	

As you can see from the **State List for: United Kingdom** screen above, you can edit or remove any of the states listed for that country, and add a new state by clicking on the **New** button in the toolbar. Alternatively, you can select a country (for example, Bangladesh) from the **Country List** screen, and then click on the **Add a State** button in the toolbar. That shows a form like the following screenshot, where you need to provide a name of the state, and 2-letter and 3-letter code for the state:

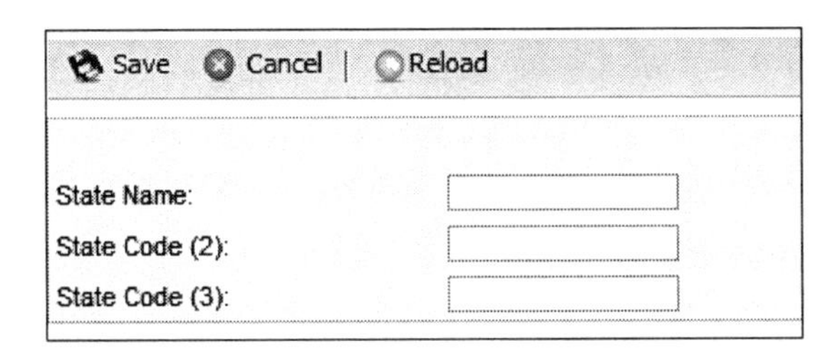

As for Bangladesh, there is no state. However, we have six divisions and sixty four districts, we may add either type as a state. Let us add all six divisions through this form, one by one. Then, the **State List for: Bangladesh** screen looks like the following screenshot:

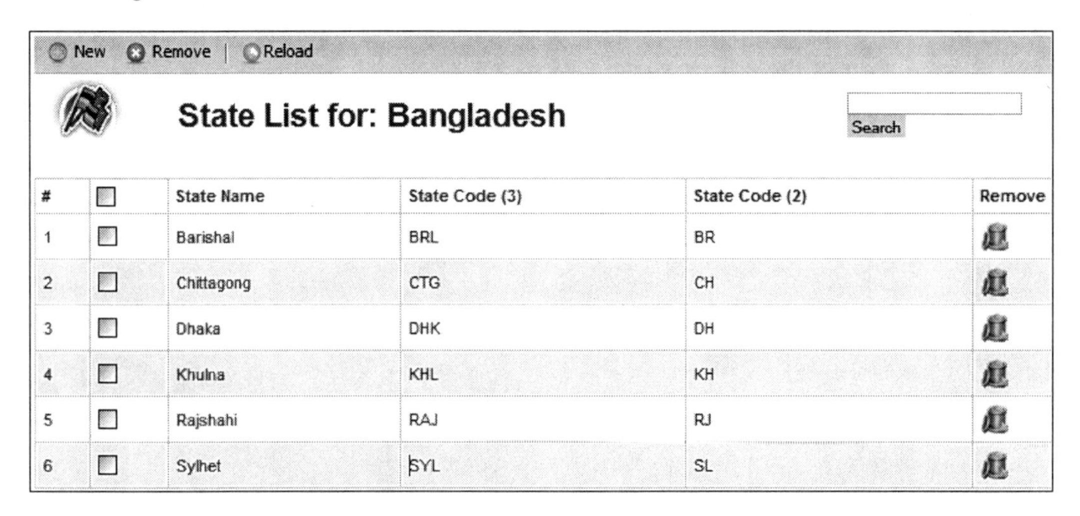
New Remove | Reload

State List for: Bangladesh

Search

#		State Name	State Code (3)	State Code (2)	Remove
1		Barishal	BRL	BR	
2		Chittagong	CTG	CH	
3		Dhaka	DHK	DH	
4		Khulna	KHL	KH	
5		Rajshahi	RAJ	RJ	
6		Sylhet	SYL	SL	

Once these divisions are added, we may configure tax variations by divisions, and can also configure shipping costs by division.

Configuring taxes by region

As indicated earlier, tax rates can be configured by state or region. You can see the list of tax rates by clicking on **Taxes | List Tax Rates** in VirtueMart's administration panel. This shows the **Tax Rate List** screen:

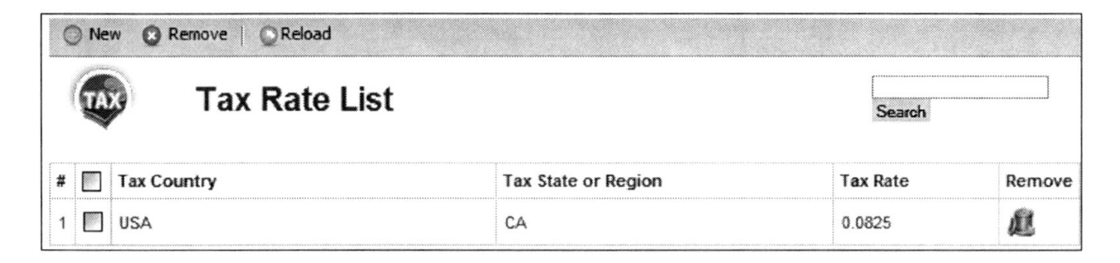
New Remove | Reload

Tax Rate List

Search

#		Tax Country	Tax State or Region	Tax Rate	Remove
1		USA	CA	0.0825	

As you can see, by default, there is only one tax rate defined, and that is for the state of CA in the USA. You can add new tax rates at any time. For adding a new tax rate, click on the **New** button in the toolbar. This shows the **Add Tax Information** screen:

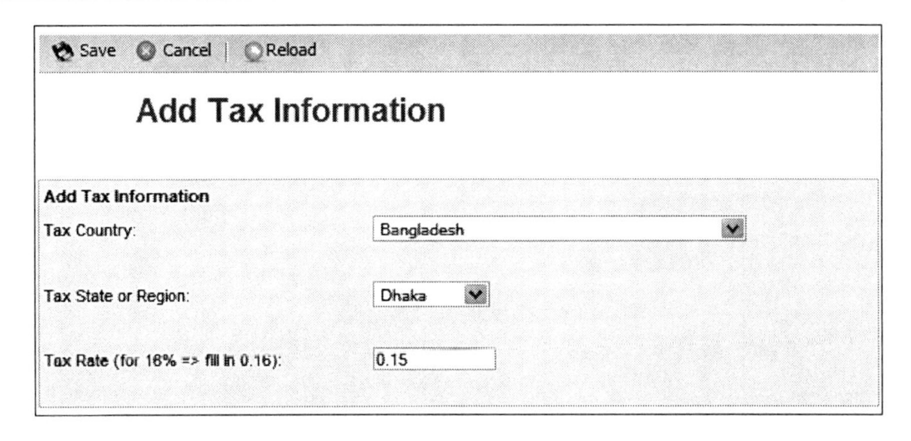

In the **Add Tax Information** screen, select the country from the **Tax Country** drop-down list. The states in the selected tax country will be available in the **Tax State or Region** drop-down screen, select one from this list. Lastly, in the **Tax Rate** text box, type the tax rate as a decimal. For example, for **Dhaka** division the tax rate will be 15%. Therefore, we select Bangladesh in the **Tax Country** list, Dhaka in the **Tax State or Region** list, and type 0.15 in the **Tax Rate** textbox. Finally, you can click on the **Save** button to add this tax rate.

Similarly, we may add tax rates for other regions, and then the **Tax Rate List** screen will look like the following:

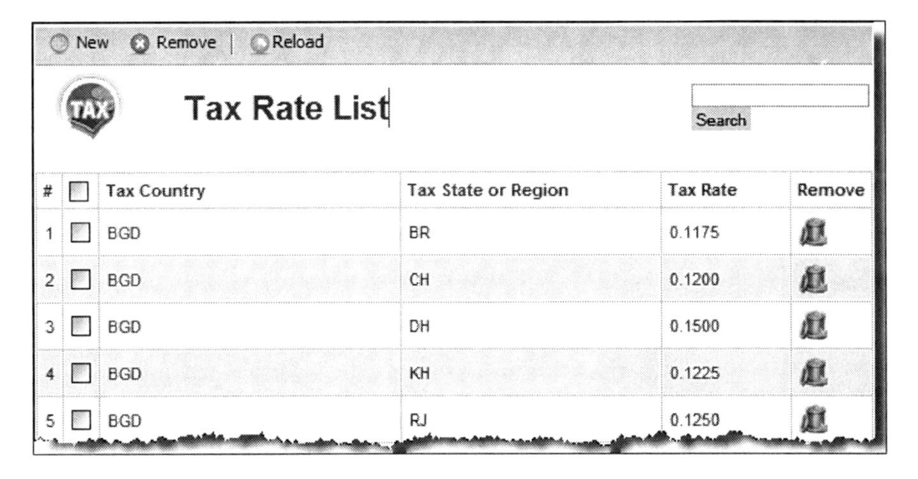

#		Tax Country	Tax State or Region	Tax Rate	Remove
1		BGD	BR	0.1175	
2		BGD	CH	0.1200	
3		BGD	DH	0.1500	
4		BGD	KH	0.1225	
5		BGD	RJ	0.1250	

Yes, now you have added tax rates for each state or region. How are these tax rates used? That depends on how you configure your store for calculating taxes. This is done from the **Admin | Configuration** menu. That brings the **Configuration** screen, and in the **Global** tab of this screen, you find a section **Tax Configuration**:

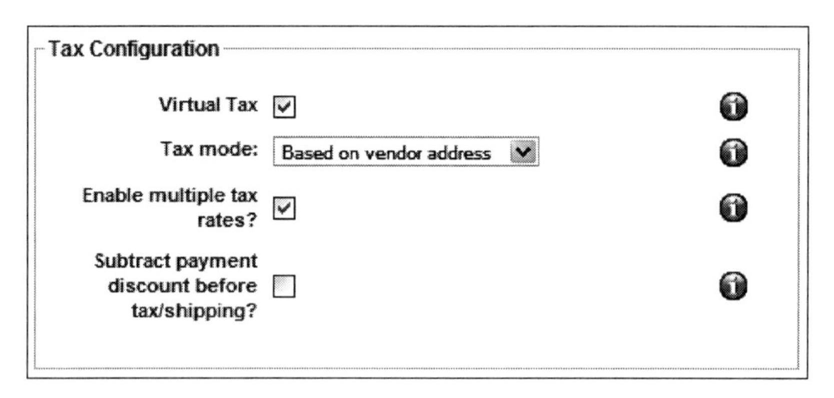

The options in this screen are mostly discussed in Chapter 3, and our concern is for the tax mode. How the taxes to the products will be added depends on the tax mode we set here. There are three tax modes:

- **Based on Vendor Address**: Selecting this will apply taxes based on the vendor's address. For example, the vendor is located in Bangladesh and in the Dhaka division. We have configured 15% tax for the Dhaka division. Therefore, all products of this vendor will be taxed at 15%, irrespective of the address we ship to.
- **Based on Shipping Address**: Selecting this will apply taxes based on the address where we ship to. For example, our store is located in Dhaka, but we are shipping a product to Chittagong, then the tax for that product will be based on the rate we have defined for Chittagong, that is, 12%. Another product shipped to Rajshahi will be taxed at 12.50%.
- **European Union Mode**: When this is selected, a per product tax is applied if the shopper is from any country in the European Union.

As we have seen now, when the tax mode is set to **Based on Vendor Address**, we don't need to configure tax rates for all countries and regions. We only need to configure the tax rate for the state or region where the vendors are. However, when we set tax mode as **Based on Shipping Address**, we need to configure tax rates for all our destinations, where we will be shipping the products.

Using multiple currencies

You can use multiple currencies on your VirtueMart store. You have already seen how to add multiple currencies to your store and set the default currency. In Chapter 3, *Configuring the VirtueMart Store*, you saw how to look for the available currencies, add a new currency, and manage the currencies.

For a brief recap, you can go to **Admin | List Currencies**. That will show all available currencies. By clicking on the **New** button on this screen, you can add a new currency. However, all of the currencies displayed here are not used for the store's transactions. You need to configure the default currency for the store, and other allowed currencies.

For setting default currency and allowed currencies, go to **Store | Edit Store**. It displays the **Store Information** screen, where you find a section named **Currency Display Style**:

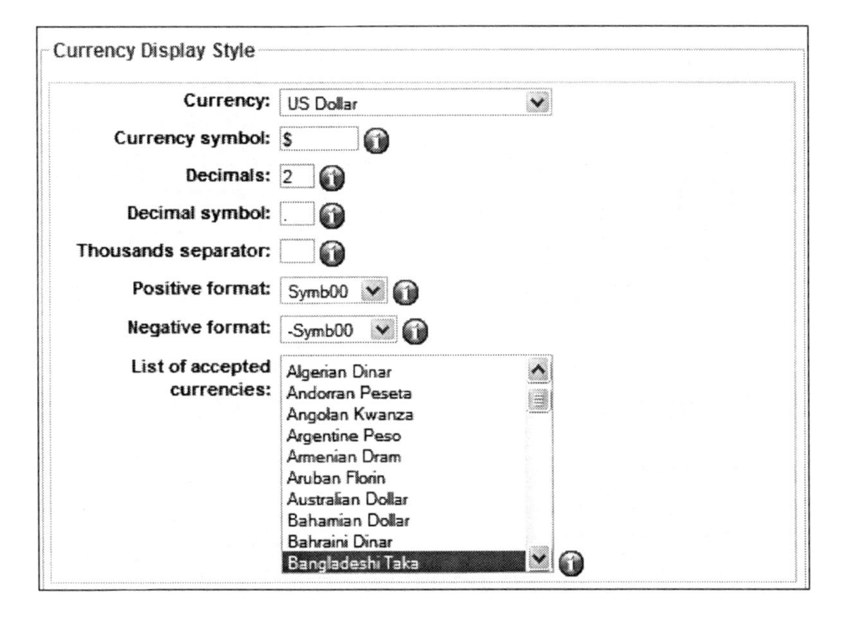

In the **Currency Display Style** section, select the default currency for the store from the **Currency** drop-down list. Then, provide the currency symbol, decimals, thousand separators, and positive and negative format. For enabling multiple currencies for the store, select the currencies from the **List of accepted currencies** list box.

When you add products to the catalog, you specify the prices in the default currency. Then, that will get changed into the desired currency as per the current exchange rate. However, we need to first give the customers an opportunity to see the prices according to their preferred currency. A module bundled with the VirtueMart installation package, `mod_virtuemart_currencies`, allows customers to select a currency from the list.

For enabling this module, go to **Extensions | Module Manager** from Joomla!'s administration panel. Then, click on the **VirtueMart Currency Selector** module in the **Module Manager** screen. The following screenshot shows the **Module: [Edit]** screen:

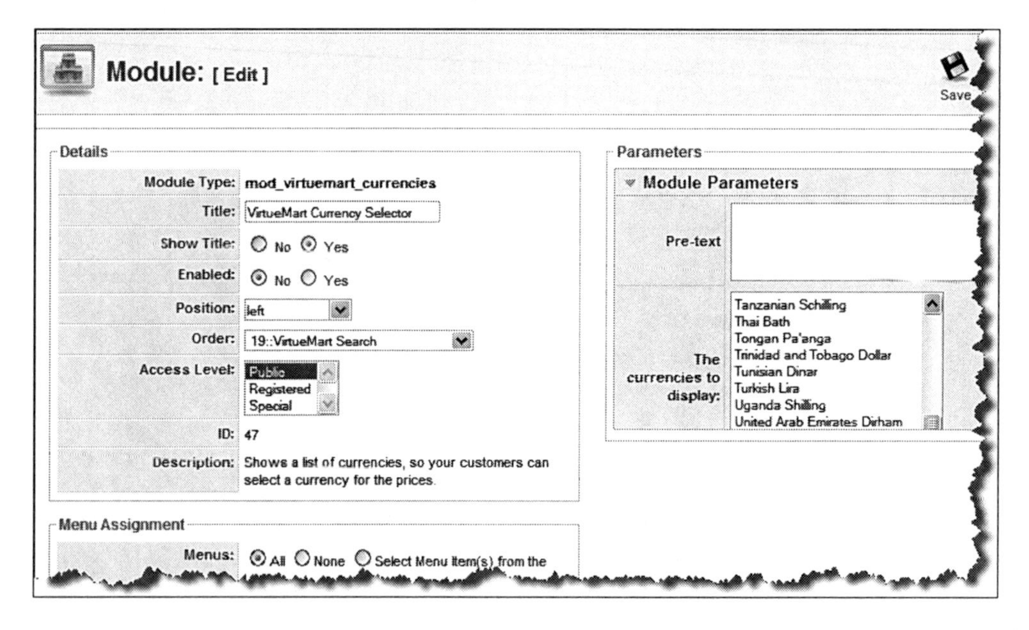

As seen in the other modules, you need to give this module a title (change the default title), enable it, select a position and order for it, and then select an access level for the module. You can also assign this module to all menus or selective modules. The module specific settings can be configured from the **Parameters** section:

- **Pre-text**: Type some introductory text, such as '**Please select your preferred currency from the list:**', in this text box.
- **The currencies to display**: From this list box, select the currencies you want to display in the currency selector drop-down list. Don't forget to select the currencies which you have selected as accepted currencies in the **Currency Display Style** section of the **Store Information** screen. For example, if you have set US Dollar, British Pound, Euro, and Bangladeshi Taka as accepted currencies, then select all these from this list box. Otherwise, the currencies will not be displayed properly.

Once the module is published, it will look like the following screenshot:

Now, select a currency from the list, say **Euro**, and click on the **Change Currency** button. This will display the product prices in Euros, as shown in the following screenshot:

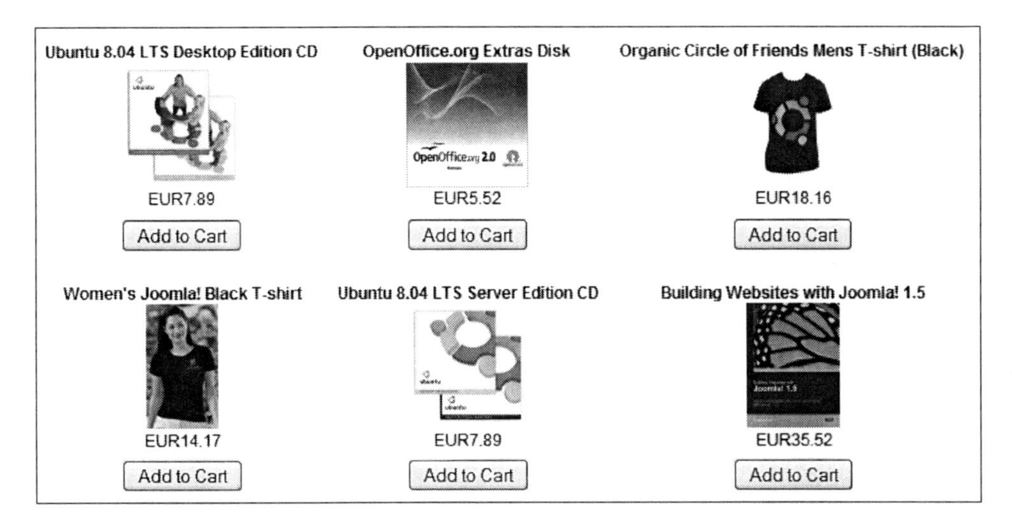

However, when you select **Bangladeshi Taka** from this list and click on the **Change Currency** button, the prices remain the same as the Euro. Before we investigate the reason behind this, let us first understand how this currency conversion is happening.

First of all, for enabling currency conversion, you need to use a currency conversion module. By default, the `convertECB.php` module comes with VirtueMart, which you can find at the `./administrator/components/com_virtuemart/classes/currency/` directory. You can enable this module in the **Admin | Configuration | Global** screen, from the **Core** section. This will work if your web server has enabled the **cURL** PHP extension or the **allow_url_fopen** setting is enabled.

Enabling `allow_url_fopen` may be a security risk for your site. When this is enabled, some extra measure for security is needed. You can refer to the book, *Joomla! Web Security*, published by Packt, for more information on measures for such security threats.

When the customer selects a currency from the list and clicks on the **Change Currency** button, the `convertECB.php` file connects to ECB (European Central Bank) for collecting the daily exchange rates in XML format, stores that XML file in the `./media` folder, parses that XML file, converts the currency, and displays that in the frontend.

One limitation of using this ECB service is that, the conversions rates are defined relative to Euros and only contain popular currencies. For example, exchange rates for Bangladeshi Taka, and some other, is not available in this XML web service.

After selecting `convertECB.php` as the currency converter module with **cURL** and the **allow_url_fopen** setting enabled, if you find that the conversion is not working, check the `convertECB.php` file. Go to line 29, which reads:

```
var $document_address =
  'http://www.ecb.int/stats/eurofxref/eurofxref-daily.xml';
```

Change this to the following:

```
var $document_address =
  'http://www.ecb.europa.eu/stats/eurofxref/eurofxref-daily.xml';
```

Now, try the conversion, and it will work.

Caution:

If the conversion rate for a currency, such as Bangladeshi Taka, is not provided by the ECB, and the customer selects that from the drop-down list, the product prices will not be converted to that currency. Instead, it will show the prices in Euros, but display the symbol of the currency selected.

Using multiple languages

One of the reasons I like Joomla! is that I can make the web site in multiple languages. You'll also like it for its multilingual features. For the Joomla! frontend, translations and language packs are available for the major languages. If you don't find the language pack of your choice, you can also easily translate the interface, with some very basic skills in typing.

Adding a new language to a Joomla! site

Before going to use a language for VirtueMart or any other component, we should know about using multiple languages in the Joomla! site we built. By default, there is only English (United Kingdom) is installed for Joomla!. You can add more language packs from your Joomla! web site and install those for your web site. Language related extensions for Joomla! are available at `http://extensions.joomla.org/extensions/languages`, and language packs at `http://extensions.joomla.org/extensions/languages/translations-for-joomla`. For our example web site, we will install and configure the Bangla language for the site. The Bangla Language pack for Joomla! 1.0.x is available for download at `http://tinyurl.com/j1-1-x-bangla`. As a native language pack for Joomla! 1.5.x is not available for Bangla, we will try to use some other language pack, say Spanish. The Spanish language pack for Joomla! 1.5.x is available at `http://joomlacode.org/gf/project/spanishlanguage/frs/`. Once the package is downloaded, we can proceed to install it.

Like other extensions, language packs are also installed from **Extensions | Install/Uninstall**. When installed, the language will be listed in the **Extensions | Language Manager** screen:

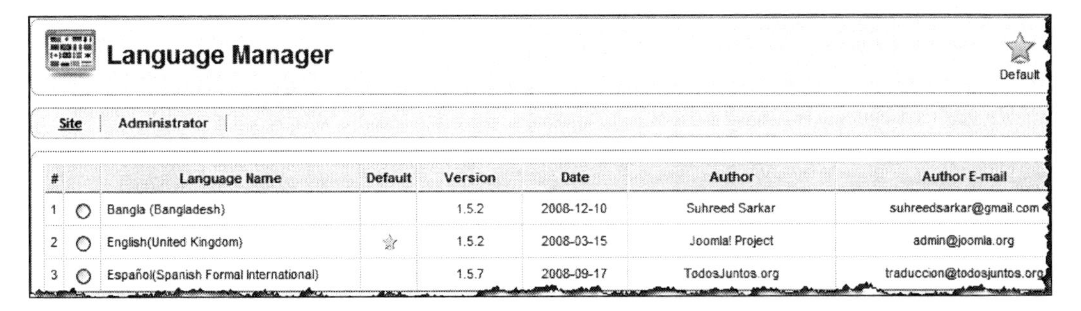

You can set any of the listed languages as the default language for the site. For example, you select **Espanol (Spanish Formal International)** and clicking on the default icon in the toolbar will set Spanish as the default language for the site. If you browse the site after setting Spanish as the default language, some texts in the frontend will be displayed in Spanish:

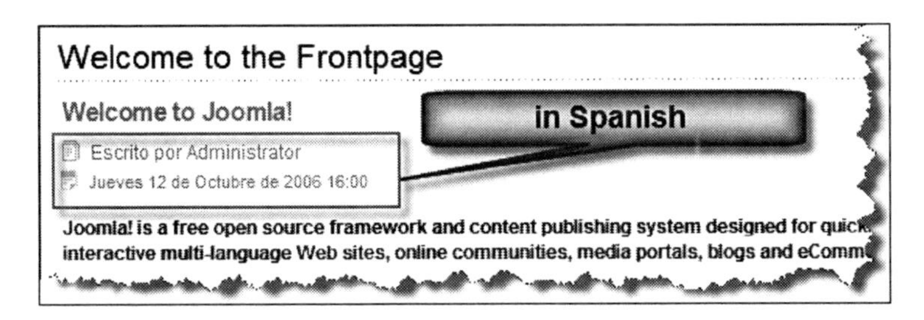

> Remember that installing a language pack shows the frontend (and backend) texts in the specified language. This does not show the content of your site in a different language. For enabling multiple languages for the content, we need to add some other extensions. We will look into such components soon.

Although setting a language as default is easy, we need to give our visitors the option to choose their preferred language. There is no such built-in mechanism. We can implement such a feature using some third-party extensions.

Translating the site language

Although there are some language packs readily available, you may need to translate Joomla! into your desired language. For major languages, language packs are available, however, not for Joomla! 1.5.x. Joomla! 1.0.x and Joomla! 1.5.x language files have many differences. Recognizing that, we should translate Joomla! 1.5.x language files, if Joomla! 1.5.x native translations are not available.

Manual translation

You can translate the Joomla! frontend and backend language files manually by editing them through a text editor. Language files for the frontend are available at the `./language` directory. For each installed language, you will find a sub-directory (for example, *en-GB* for British English, *es-ES* for Spanish language, and so on).

One easy way to create a new language is to copy the default language folder, that is *en-GB*, and rename it into desired language name, that is *bn-BD* for Bengali (Bangladesh). After renaming the folder into *bn-BD*, we may look into the file names. All file names start with *en-GB*, and therefore we should change these to *bn-BD*.

The first file you should edit is `bn-BD.xml` (previous name `en-GB.xml`). This file defines the language. When you open the file for editing for the first time, it looks like the following:

```
<?xml version="1.0" encoding="utf-8"?>
<!-- $Id -->
<metafile version="1.5"  client="site" >
   <name>English(United Kingdom)</name>
   <tag>en-GB</tag>
   <version>1.5.2</version>
   <creationDate>2008-03-15</creationDate>
   <author>Joomla! Project</author>
   <authorEmail>admin@joomla.org</authorEmail>
```

```
    <authorUrl>www.joomla.org</authorUrl>
    <copyright>Copyright (C) 2005 - 2008 Open Source Matters.
      All rights reserved.</copyright>
    <license>http://www.gnu.org/licenses/gpl-2.0.html GNU/GPL</license>
    <description></description>
    <metadata>
      <name>English (United Kingdom)</name>
      <tag>en-GB</tag>
      <rtl>0</rtl>
      <locale>en_GB.utf8, en_GB.UTF-8, en_GB, eng_GB, en,
               english, english-uk, uk, gbr, britain, england, great
                 britain, uk,united kingdom, united-kingdom</locale>
      <winCodePage>iso-8859-1</winCodePage>
      <backwardLang>english</backwardLang>
      <pdfFontName>freesans</pdfFontName>
    </metadata>
    <params />
</metafile>
```

If you have some idea about the structure of XML, the meaning of the above file will be obvious to you. For the Bengali (Bangladesh) language, we will change this file as follows:

```
<?xml version="1.0" encoding="utf-8"?>
<metafile version="1.5" client="site" >
    <tag>bn-BD</tag>
    <name>Bengali  (Bangladesh)</name>
    <description>Bengali language (Bangladeshi) for Joomla!
      1.5.x</description>
    <version>1.5.2</version>
    <creationDate>2008-12-10</creationDate>
    <author>Suhreed Sarkar</author>
    <authorUrl>www.suhreedsarkar.com</authorUrl>
    <authorEmail>suhreedsarkar@gmail.com</authorEmail>
    <copyright>Copyright (C) 2005 - 2008 Open Source Matters.
      All rights reserved.</copyright>
    <license>http://www.gnu.org/licenses/gpl-2.0.html GNU/GPL</license>
    <metadata>
      <name>Bengali  (Bangladesh)</name>
      <tag>bn-BD</tag>
      <rtl>0</rtl>
     <locale>bn-BD.utf8, bn_BD.UTF-8, bn_BD, ben_BD, bn, bengail,
             bengali-bd, bd, bgd, bangladesh</locale>
      <winCodePage>UTF-8</winCodePage>
      <backwardLang>bengali</backwardLang>
```

```
        <pdfFontName>freesans</pdfFontName>
    </metadata>
    <params></params>
</metafile>
```

Changes made in this file are straightforward. We have changed the language name, creation date, author name, author email, and metadata. In the second line, we have mentioned the version of Joomla!. `client = 'site'` means this translation pack is for a Joomla! site, for the administration section, we can specify `client= 'admin'`.

After changing the `bn-BD.xml` file, we may proceed to change other language files. You will notice that for each Joomla! core component, and the components you have installed, there is one language file. For example, `bn-BD.com_contact.ini` is for the Contacts component, `bn-BD.com_search.ini` is for the search component, and so on. There is another file named `bn-BD.ini`, which contains language strings for Joomla!'s core. We may start translating from this file.

Open the `bn-BD.ini` file in your text editor which supports typing in Unicode and saving as a UTF-8 encoded text file. When opened, you will find about 321 lines. The first few lines are as follows:

```
# $Id: bn-BD.ini 10498 2008-12-08 14:10:24 ian ~0 $
# author Suhreed Sarkar
# copyright (C) 2005 - 2008 Open Source Matters. All rights reserved.
# license http://www.gnu.org/licenses/gpl-2.0.html GNU/GPL, see
LICENSE.php

# Note : All ini files need to be saved as UTF-8
```

As you can see, the lines above lines are commented out, and contain author, copyright and licensing information for this language translation. The next section defines how the date will be displayed:

```
DATE_FORMAT_LC=%A, %d %B %Y
DATE_FORMAT_LC1=%A, %d %B %Y
DATE_FORMAT_LC2=%A, %d %B %Y %H:%M
DATE_FORMAT_LC3=%d %B %Y
DATE_FORMAT_LC4=%d.%m.%y
DATE_FORMAT_JS1=y-m-d
%Y-%M-%D=%Y-%M-%D
%A, %B %E=%A, %B %e
```

The above lines are self explanatory. We will define the date formats to be displayed. For Bengali, we don't need to change the date format. The name of the months come next:

```
# Months

JANUARY_SHORT=Jan
JANUARY=January
FEBRUARY_SHORT=Feb
FEBRUARY=February
...
DECEMBER_SHORT=Dec
DECEMBER=December
```

As you see, there are two names for the months: short and full. You need to translate these into your language. For Bengali, the above lines will be translated as:

```
# Months

JANUARY_SHORT= জানু
JANUARY= জানুয়ারি
FEBRUARY_SHORT= ফেব্রু
FEBRUARY= ফেব্রুয়ারি
...
DECEMBER_SHORT= ডিসে:
DECEMBER= ডিসেম্বর
```

Similarly, we have both the short and the full names for the days of week. We can translate those as follows:

```
#Days of the Week
SAT= শনি
SATURDAY= শনিবার
SUN= রবি
SUNDAY= রবিবার
MON= সোম
MONDAY= সোমবার
TUE= মঙ্গল
TUESDAY= মঙ্গলবার
WED= বুধ
WEDNESDAY= বুধবার
THU= বৃহ:
THURSDAY= বৃহস্পতিবার
FRI= শুক্র
FRIDAY= শুক্রবার
```

There are other sections containing some other strings to be translated. For example, Other calendar, Time Zones, Mailer codes, and so on. When all these strings have been translated, save the changes. While saving, make sure that the file is saved with UTF-8 encoding, not the default ANSII encoding or any other encoding.

Similarly, we need to translate other files. For example, we can open the `bd-BD.com_banners.ini` file and change the strings as follows:

```
BNR_CLIENT_NAME= ক্লায়েন্টের জন্য একটি নাম অবশ্যই নির্বাচন করতে হবে।
BNR_CONTACT= ক্লায়েন্টের জন্য যোগাযোগের ঠিকানা অবশ্যই নির্বাচন করতে হবে।
BNR_VALID_EMAIL= ক্লায়েন্টের জন্য অবশ্যই একটি ই-মেইল নির্বাচন করতে হবে।
BNR_CLIENT= অবশ্যই একটি ক্লায়েন্ট সিলেক্ট করতে হবে।
BNR_NAME= ব্যানারের জন্য অবশ্যই একটি নাম দিতে হবে।
BNR_IMAGE= ব্যানারের জন্য অবশ্যই একটি চিত্র দিতে হবে।
BNR_URL= ব্যানারের জন্য URL কিংবা Custom Banner code দিতে হবে।
```

In this way, we can translate all of the language files, and save those with UTF-8 encoding. Once all of the language files are translated, we need to compress the files (for example `.zip, .tar, .gz` archive), including the `.xml` file, to make the installation package. This installation package can be used for installing the language for your Joomla! site.

Caution:

While saving the language file after editing, make sure that the file is saved as Unicode text using UTF-8 encoding. Also, ensure that the file extension remains `.ini`, not `.txt`. Otherwise, the language translation will not work.

For all operating systems, you will find at least one Unicode text editor. The following are some editors which you can use for editing such files:

- For Windows: PSPad (freely available from `http://www.pspad.com/en/`), SuperEdi (freely available from `http://www.wolosoft.com/en/superedi/`);
- For MacOS: jEdit (freely available at `http://www.jedit.org/`)
- For Linux: gEdit and many other available for free.

Translation through the translator component

Translating the languages manually is easy. However, it is possible to make it easier. With this in mind, the **Translations Manager** component has been developed, which can be downloaded from `http://joomlacode.org/gf/project/joomla_1_5_tr1/frs/`. This component allows you to edit the XML file for a language and translate the language strings for each component through the Joomla! 1.5.x user interface, without using any text editor. This eliminates the necessity of knowing the details of the construct of the language files. Not only that, it also helps build the language translation package from the same interface.

Once downloaded and installed from **Extensions | Install/Uninstall** screen, you can access this component by clicking **Components | Translation Manager**. That shows the **Translation Manager** screen listing the available languages:

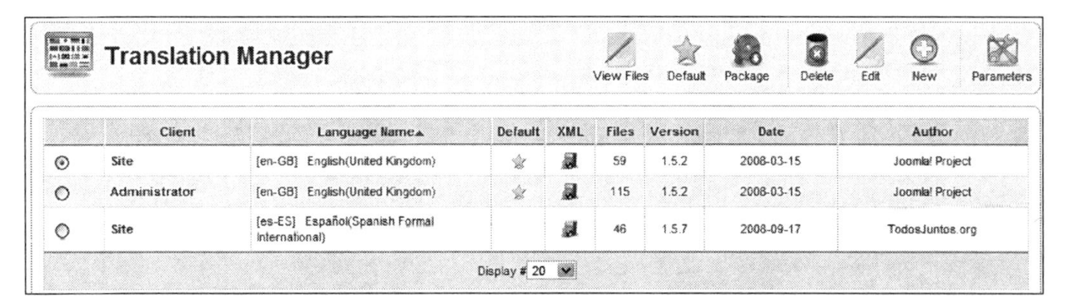

Creating new translation

For creating a new language, click on the **New** icon in the toolbar. That shows the **Create New Language** screen:

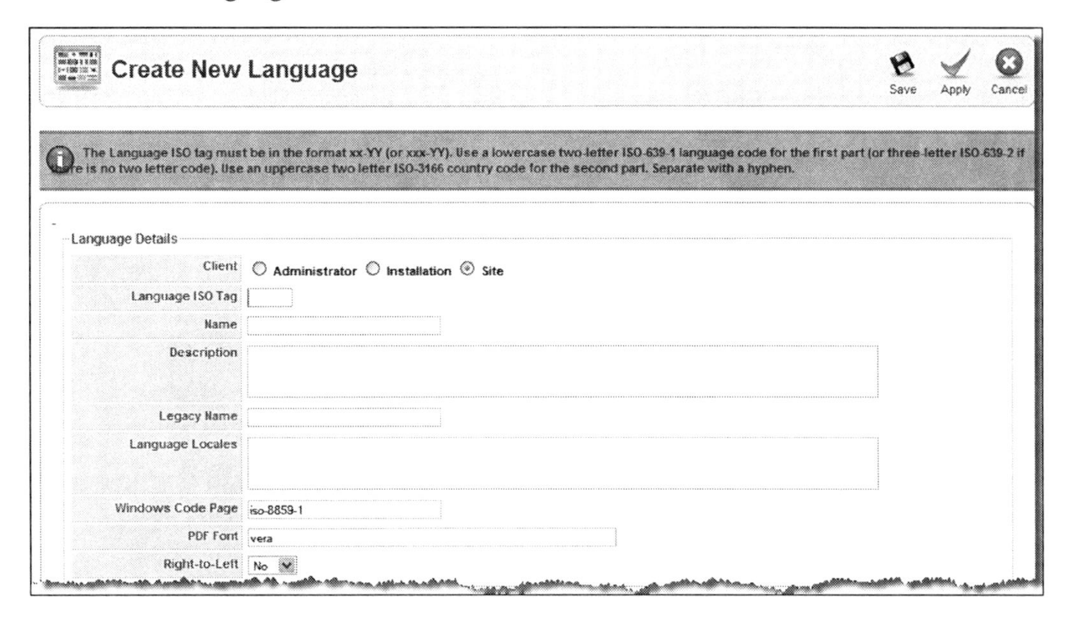

The **Create New Language** screen has two sections: **Language Details** and **Author Details**. In the **Language Details** section, we need to define the language. First, select a type in the **Client** radio box: **Administrator, Installation,** or **Site**. As we will first be creating the Bengali language for the site (Joomla! frontend), we choose **Site**. If you want to create translations for the administration panel or installation screens, then choose **Administrator** or **Installation** respectively.

After choosing the translation client, we need to provide the ISO code for the language. The ISO code will be something like xx-XX (for example, *bn-BD* for Bengali (Bangladesh), *bn-IN* for Bengali (India), *en-US* for English (United States), and so on). As we are creating the translation for Bengali (Bangladesh), we type **bn-BD** in the **Language ISO Tag** field, and **Bengali (Bangladesh)** in the **Name** field. Optionally, we can provide a description of this language in the **Description** text box.

In the **Legacy Name** field, type the traditional name of the language (for example, **bengali** for **bn-BD**). Similarly, we need to provide locales for this language in the **Language Locales** text box. By default, you will see **iso-8859-1** in the Windows **Codepage** field. For languages, such as Bengali, using Unicode, this should be UTF-8. In the **PDF font**, you may keep the default value, or choose another subset of fonts which will be used for generating PDF from the contents. If the language reads right-to-left (for example, Arabic), then select **Yes** in **Right-To-Left** drop-down box. For the Bengali language, it will be **No**.

Let's now look into the **Author Details** section, where we need to provide information about the language translator:

Author Details

Author	Suhreed Sarkar
Author Email	suhreedsarkar@gmail.com
Author Website	http://www.suhreedsarkar.com
Version	1.5.0
Creation Date	2008-12-10
Copyright	Suhreed Sarkar
License	http://www.gnu.org/copyleft/gpl.html GNU/GPL

As you can see, most of the fields in the **Author Details** section are self explanatory. We need to provide the author's name, author's email, author's web site, version of Joomla! for which the translation is being created, translation creation date, copyright, and license.

Once both of the sections are filled in, click on the **Save** icon in the toolbar to create the language translation. You will be taken to the **Translation Manager** screen, where you see the newly created language:

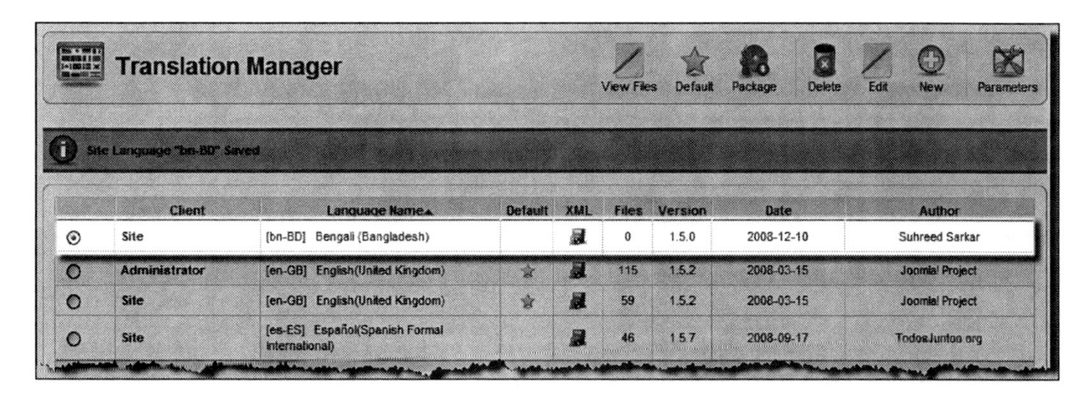

Translating the language files

It is now your turn to edit the language strings for each component. If you want to edit the XML file, click on the icon in the **XML** column. For viewing the files for a language, select the language from the list, and click on the **View Files** icon in the toolbar. As we have created the **[bn-BD] Bengali (Bangladesh)** language, we select it and click on the **View Files** icon. That shows the **Language Files** screen:

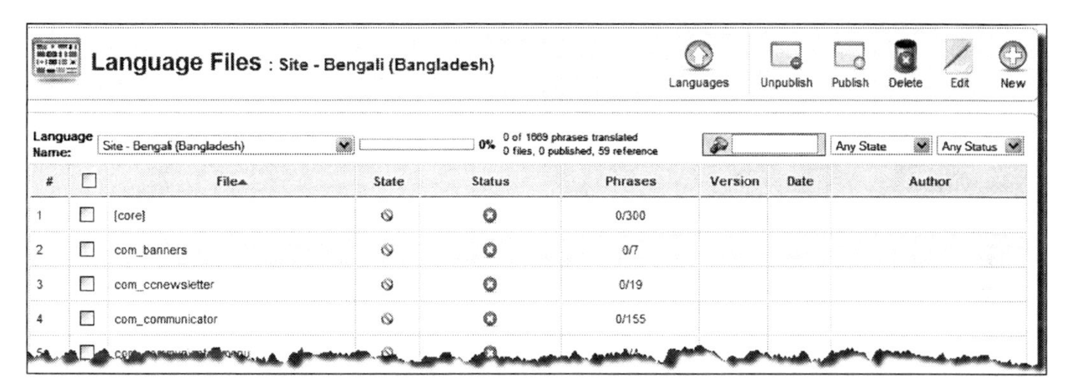

As you can see, the **Language Files** screen lists the language files, their status, number of phrases in that file with translated strings, version, date, and author name. In the screenshot above, we don't see the author or date. These files have been created from the reference language for translation. Now, we need to translate these files into Bengali.

You may start translating from any file. In the manual editing process, we have looked into the core language files. The same phrases will be available if you now click on the **[core]** link in the **File** column. As you can see, this file contains 300 phrases to be translated.

Editing the translation INI file

For starting our translation, let us consider a small language file, such as **com_banners**, which contains seven phrases for translation. Click on the **com_banners** link under the **File** column. That opens the **Edit Translation INI File** screen:

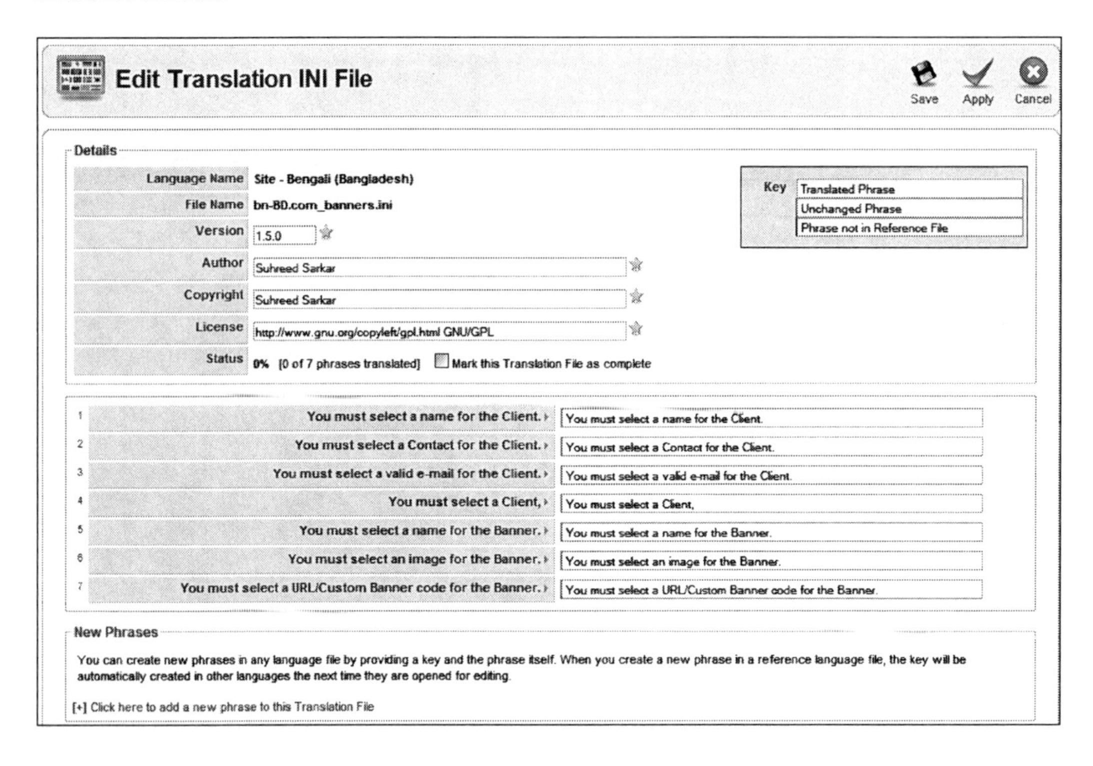

First, let us have a look at the **Edit Translation INI File** screen. In the first section, we get the language name, language file name (`bn-BD.com_banners.ini`), version, author, copyright, and license. These values are taken from the information we provided when creating this language translation project. It then shows the status of translation including the percent and number of phrases completed. There is a checkbox, **Mark this Translation File as complete,** which can be checked when you have finished translating all phrases. On the **Key** section, legends are provided for phrases: unchanged phrases are indicated by red bar, translated phrases without any bar, and phrase not in the language file by green bar.

In the main section, we see the phrases available for a translation. In the left, the original phrases are shown, and just to its right, a text box with the same phrase is displayed. Whatever translation we do, we need to type that in these text boxes. When we translate these phrases, this section will look like the following screenshot:

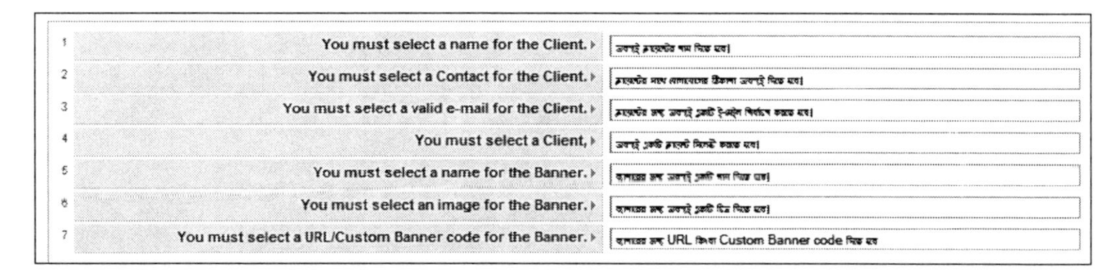

After this translation, click on the **Save** icon in the toolbar, and that will bring you to the **Language Files** screen:

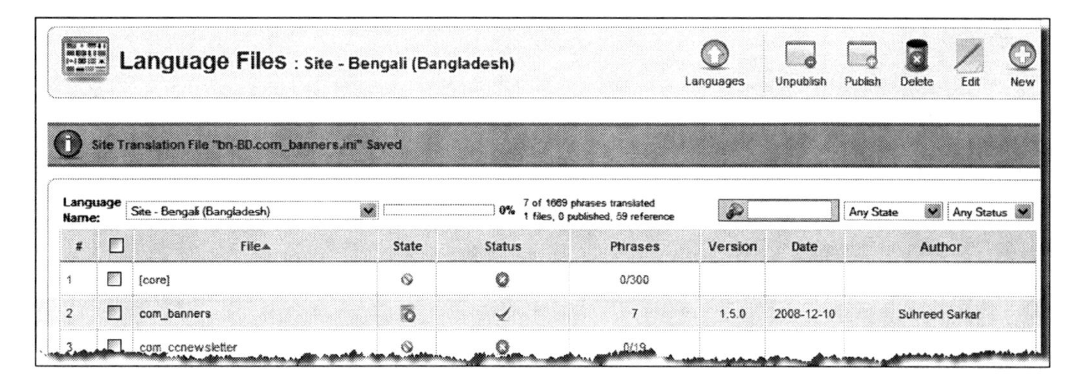

Now, you can see that the **com_banners** file has been translated, and no phrase is remains to be translated. You can also see the date of translation, author name and other information.

Using the translation

When we have completed translating of all of the language files through the **Translation Manager**, we can use those translations instantly without installing. For using the translated languages, we first need to publish the translated language files. You can publish the translated language files by clicking on the icon in the **State** column. A green tick mark in the **State** column indicates that the language file has been published. You can publish multiple language files by selecting them, and then clicking on the **Publish** icon in the toolbar:

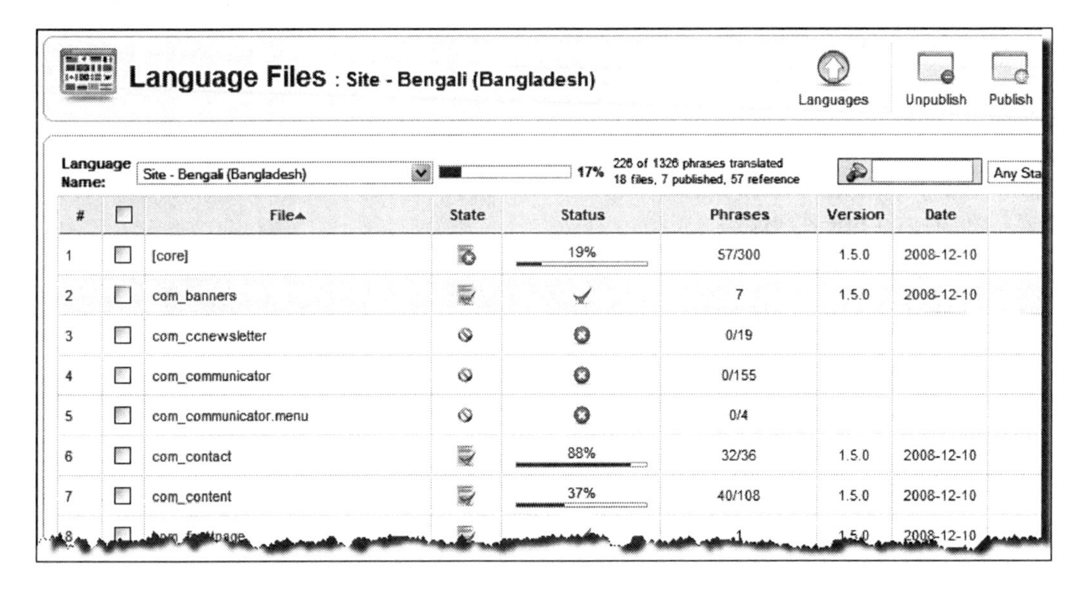

Remember that you cannot publish a file if no phrase in that file has been translated. You can translate only those files from where all or some phrases have been translated.

After publishing the translated files, you need to set the language as default. You can do this from the **Translation Manager** screen. Select the language, that is **[bn-BD] Bengali (Bangladesh)**, and click on the **Default** icon in the toolbar:

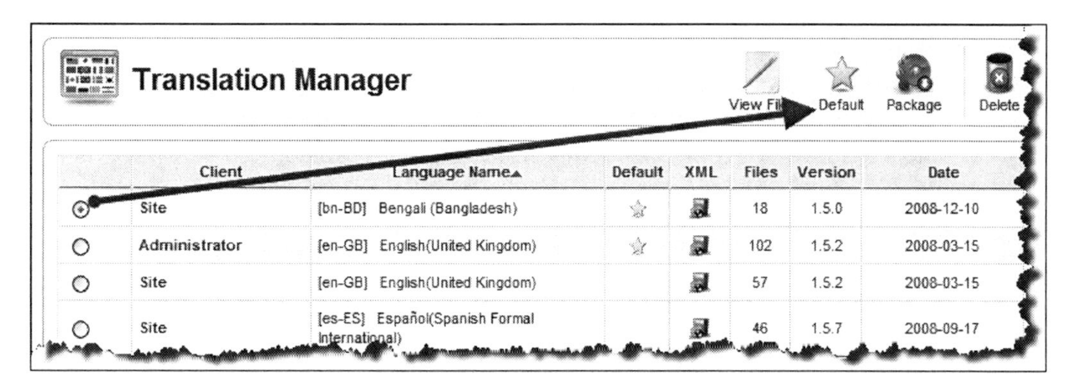

Once the language is set as default, we can try the it on the frontend. As you can see in the screenshot on the previous page, 88% of the **com_contact** file has been translated. Let us see this component in the frontend by clicking on the **Contact Us** menu (if it is not there, create one linking to **com_contact** component). The **Contact** page will be displayed in Bengali and will show the phrases we have translated:

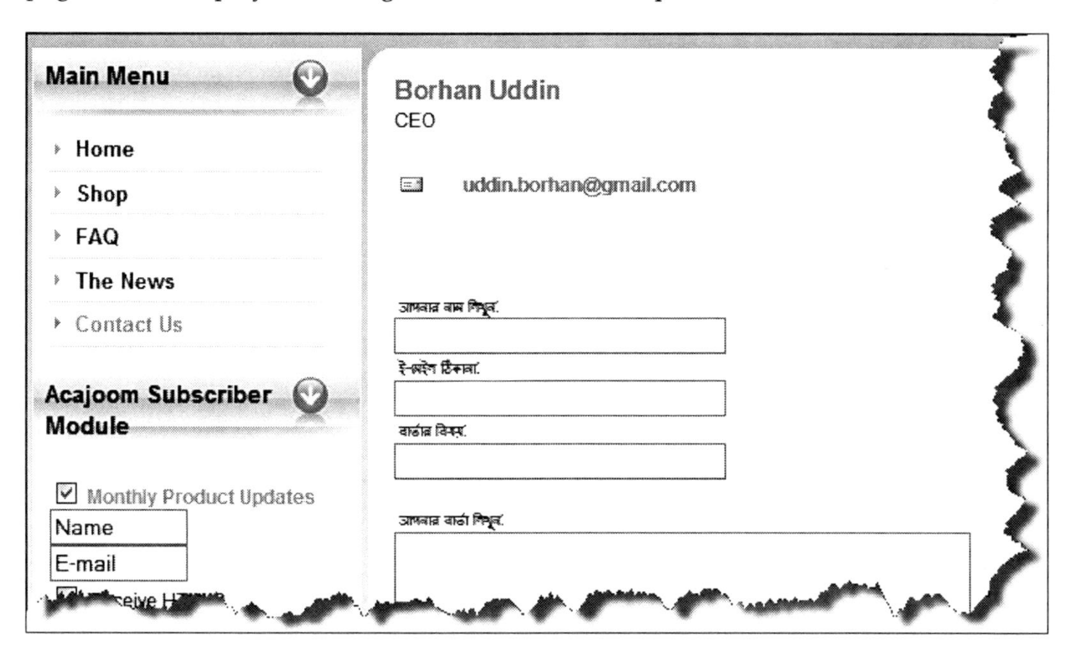

We are now sure that our translation works. Therefore, we can proceed with translating the files, complete the translation of all files, and then publish them for use on our site.

Packaging the translation

When all of the language files have been translated, we can use that translation for our site. However, it will be good if you can distribute your translation to others as well. That's the true spirit of open source; sharing with others, and stopping reinventing the wheel. You can easily make the installation package from these translated files and distribute that package.

For packaging the files, go to the **Translation Manager** screen, select the language you want to package, and then click on the **Package** icon in the toolbar. This will create the package and notify the location where it has been created:

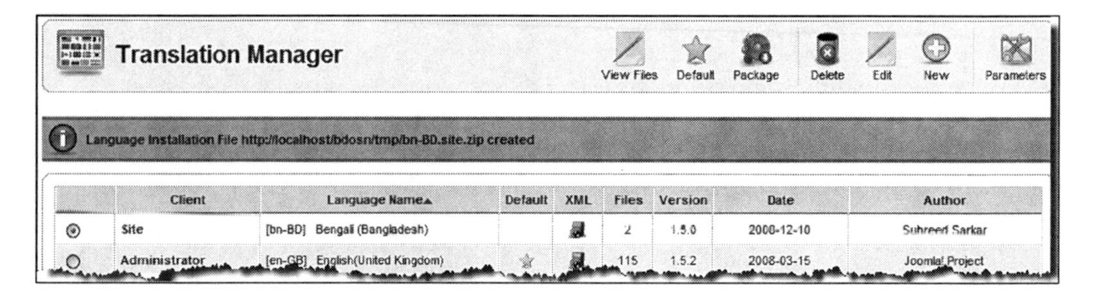

By default, the language package file is generated in the `./tmp` directory. Copy the file from that location and share it with others through the Internet. The best place to add it is into the Joomla! extensions directory.

Showing multilingual content

For showing the multilingual contents in a Joomla! web site we need to use some extensions. To me, the best extension for this purpose is Joom!Fish. You can download it from `http://www.joomfish.net/en/downloads`. Download it and install it from the **Extensions | Install/Uninstall** screen. Once installed, go to **Components | JoomFish**. This shows the Joom!Fish control panel:

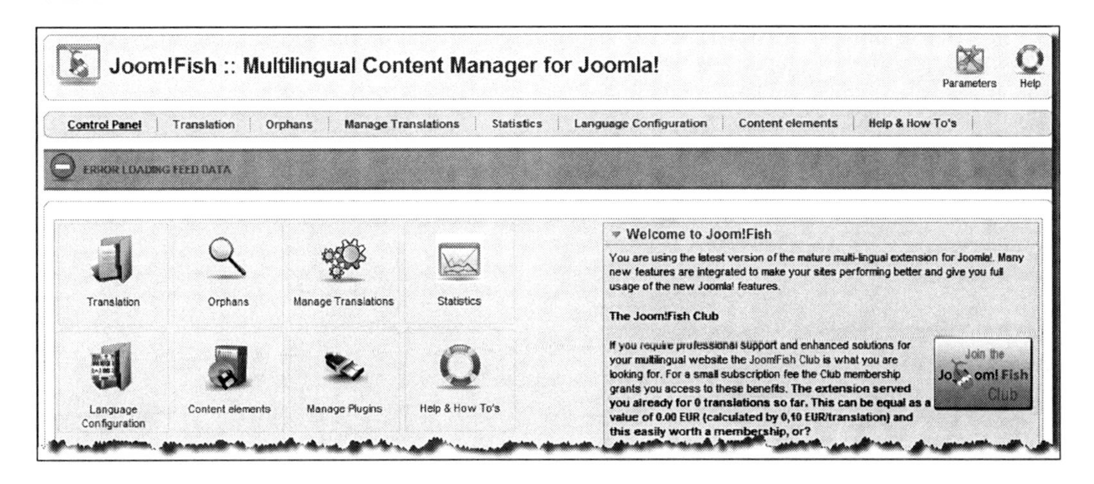

In the Joom!Fish control panel, you can see the links to other parts—**Translation**, **Orphans**, **Manage Translations**, **Language Configuration**, and so on. On the right, you get a brief introduction to the Joom!Fish component. Before you start using Joom!Fish, you may also like to view the documentation by clicking on the **Help & How To's** icon in the control panel.

A detailed discussion on Joom!Fish is out of the scope of this book. The main features and usage of Joom!Fish will be discussed, which are necessary for localizing the Joomla! and VirtueMart store.

Caution:

At present (version 2.0), there are some problems with Joom!Fish and SEF, especially when using the sh404 component for SEF. As we have chosen to use sh404 for SEF, we need to find a solution for this. If you see that Joom!Fish is not working with your installation, for the time being, disable sh404 for your site. We will discuss the solution for making sh404 compatible with Joom!Fish in Chapter 10, *Maintenance and Troubleshooting*.

To start using Joom!Fish, click on the **Language Configuration** link. This section will list the available languages for the site:

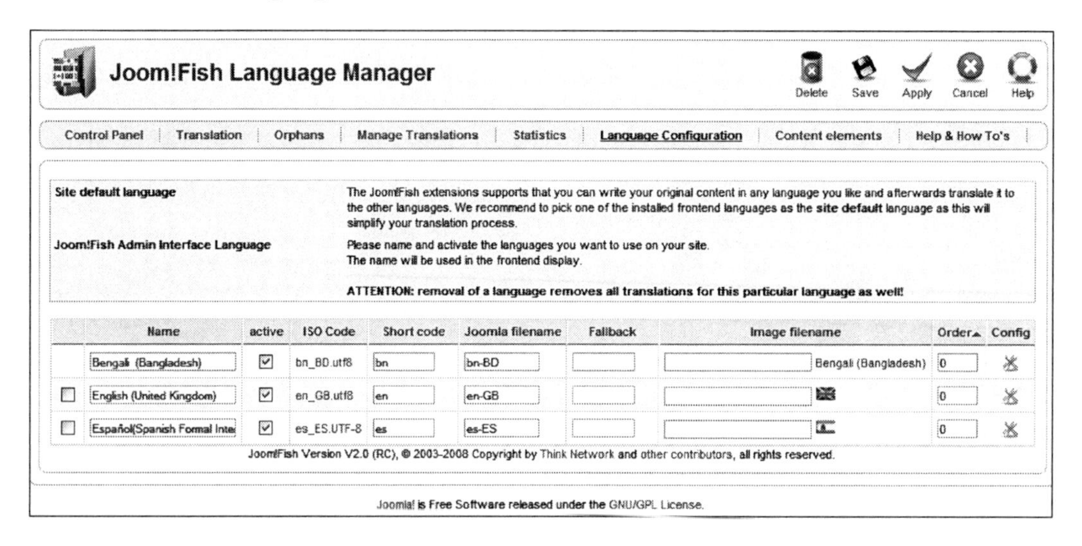

In the **Joom!Fish Language Manager** screen, check the languages which you want to make available for the site users. Check the boxes under the **active** column. For a language, you may also specify the flag image to be displayed. Flag images are located in the `./components/com_joomfish/images/` flags directory. You can copy the flag image in `.gif` format (for example, `bn.gif` for Bengali language), in this folder, and type the file name in the **Image filename** column. Once you have activated the languages, and saved the settings, you can proceed to translating the Joomla! contents including the module names, menus, and articles.

For translating the contents, click on the **Translation** link. That shows the **Translate** screen:

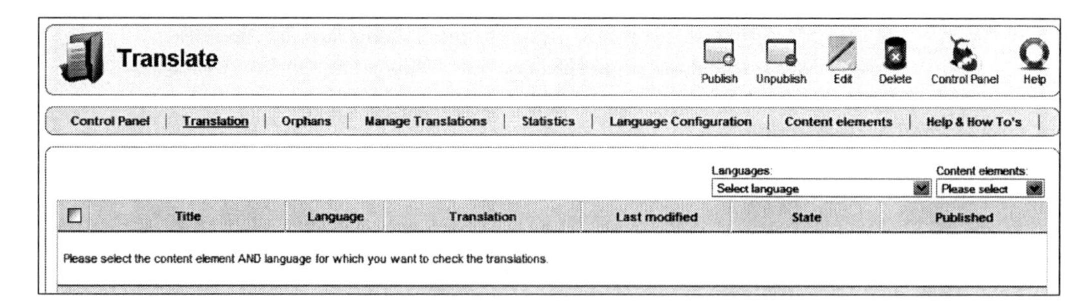

Initially, you see nothing listed in the **Translate** screen. In the **Languages** drop-down list, you will see the list of available languages. Select the language to which you want to translate the content. We want to translate the contents to the **Bengali (Bangladesh)** language. Therefore, we select **Bengali (Bangladesh)** in this drop-down list.

In the **Content Elements** drop-down list, you will see the list of contents which can be translated (for example, Banners, User, Modules, Menus, and so on). We need to select one content element from this list. Let us start with translating the menus. Select **Menus** in the **Content Elements** drop-down list. Now, the translatable elements will be available in the screen:

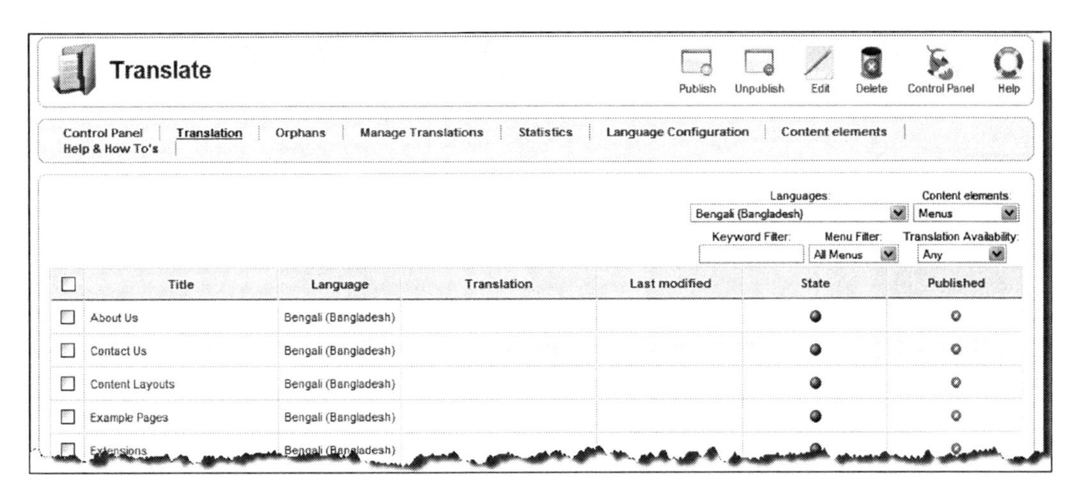

As you see the elements for translation, click on any element, say **About Us**, to translate it. Clicking on the element will display the **Translate** screen, where we can write the translation:

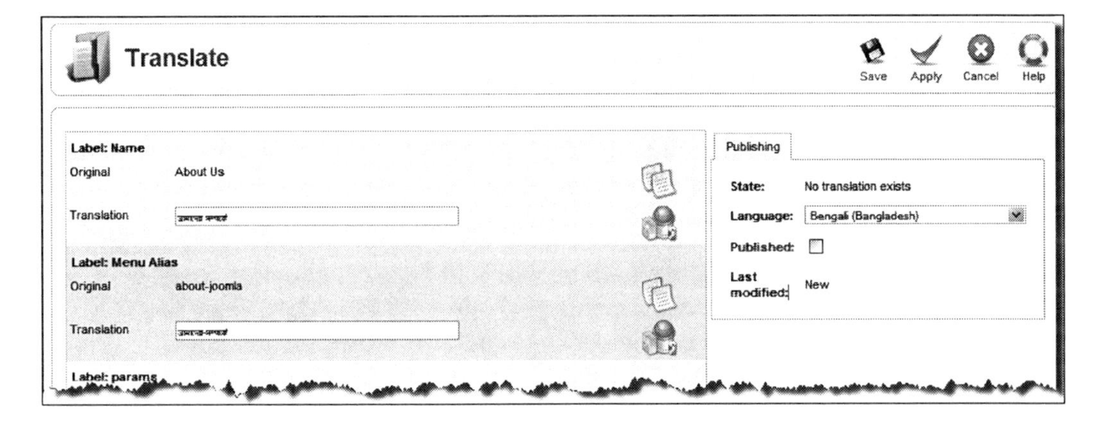

As you can see, this screen provides space for typing the translation in the desired language. Type the translated phrase in the **Translation** text box. You may need to translate multiple phrases depending upon the element you are translating. Once the translation is complete, check the **Publish** checkbox and click on the **Save** icon in the toolbar.

Using the same process, you can translate other elements as well. When the elements are translated, the elements are listed with the translation information:

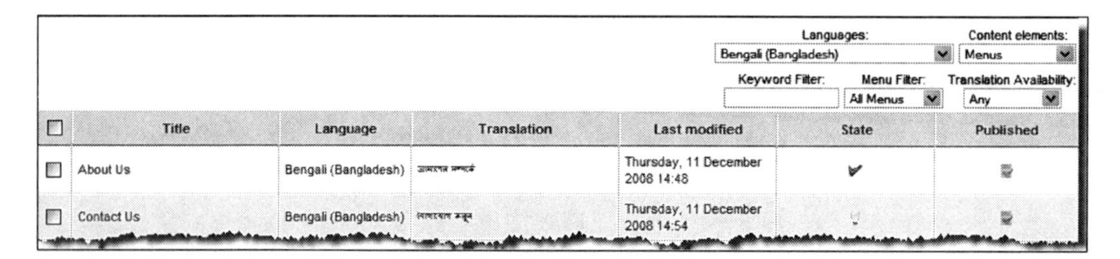

A green tick in the **State** column indicates that all the phrases have been translated, whereas a yellow bulb indicates an incomplete translation.

Let us see how our translation looks. If we look at the frontend, we see that the menus have been shown in Bengali:

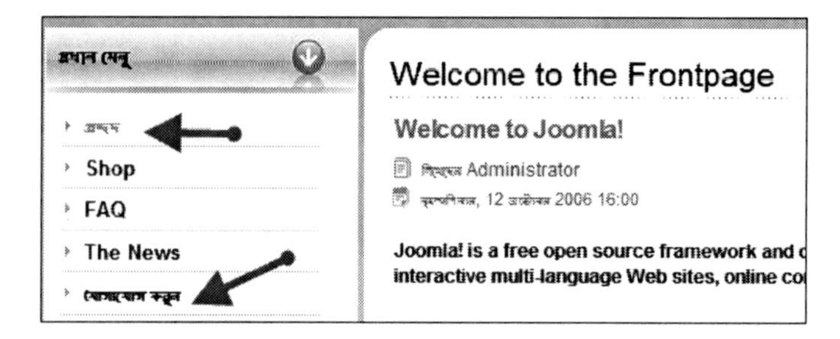

So far, we have seen how to translate Joomla! elements. Joom!Fish allows us to translate phrases through content elements for different components and modules. By default, Joom!Fish contains content elements for the core components of Joomla!. However, we can add content elements for other components, like VirtueMart, Community Builder, and so on.

The content elements for VirtueMart are available at `http://tinyurl.com/jf-vm-ce`. Download the content elements package for VirtueMart. Once the package is downloaded, unzip it. The package contains multiple XML files.

For installing the content elements, copy the XML files to the `./administrator/components/com_joomfish/contentelement` directory. Alternatively, you can go to **Joom!Fish | Content Elements**, click on the **Install** icon in the toolbar, and upload the XML files one by one. The installed content elements will be visible in the **Content Elements** screen:

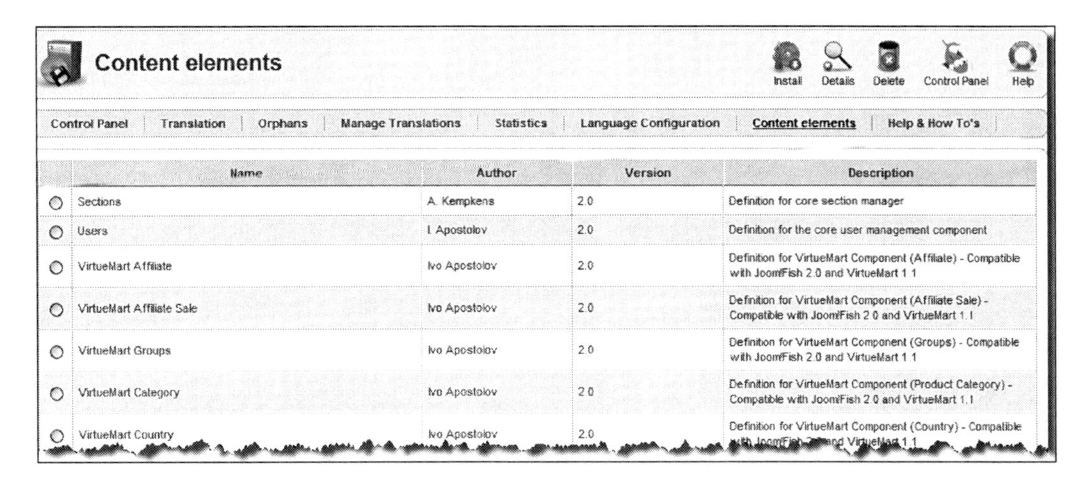

Once you have installed the content elements for VirtueMart, you can add translations for VirtueMart categories, products, countries, groups, and so on. Click on the **Translation** link again to see the **Translate** screen. In the **Languages** drop-down list, select **Bengali (Bangladesh)**, and in the **Content Elements** drop-down list, select **VirtueMart Category**. Now, you see the list of VirtueMart categories to be translated:

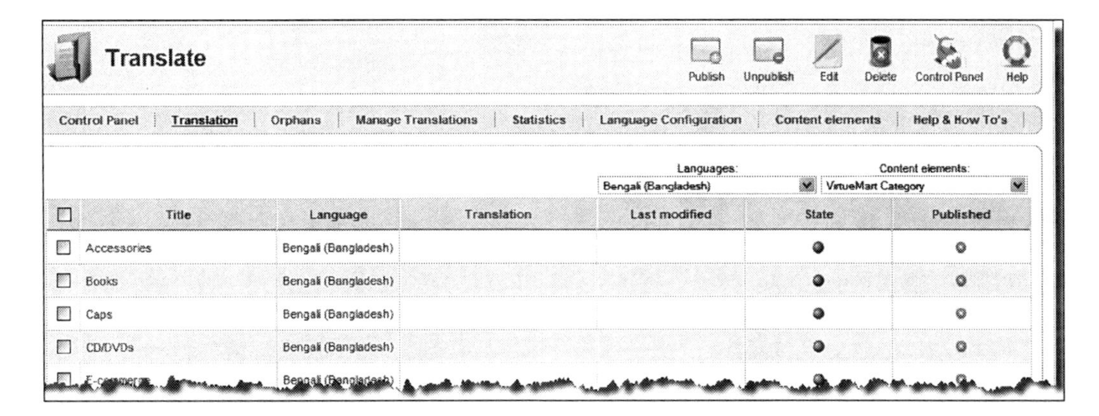

Click on one category title, say **Books**, and you will see the **Translate** screen where you can enter the translation of this category's title and brief description:

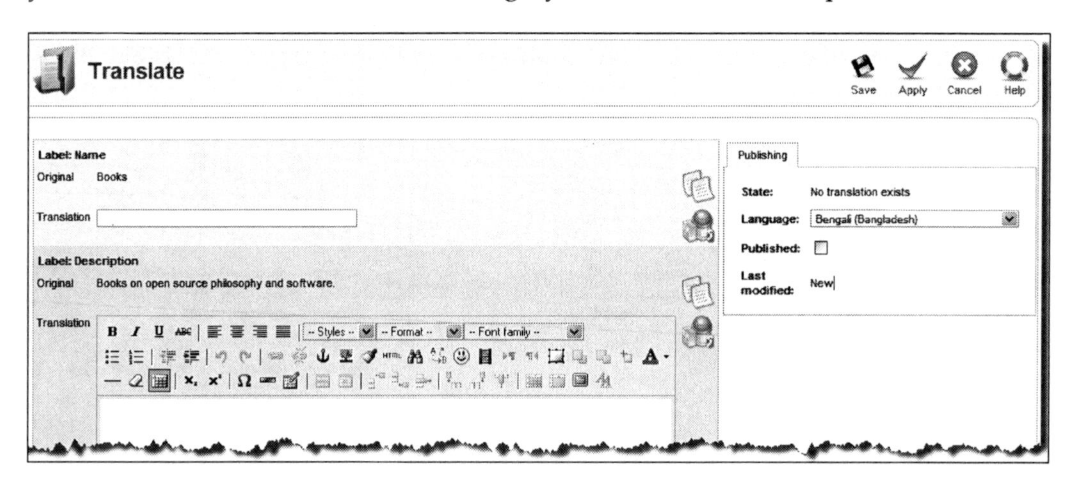

Once the translations are provided, you can publish that translation and save it by clicking on the **Save** icon in the toolbar. Similarly, you can translate the product name, descriptions, and other information. Once you have translated all of the categories and products in VirtueMart, you can see your shop in that translated language:

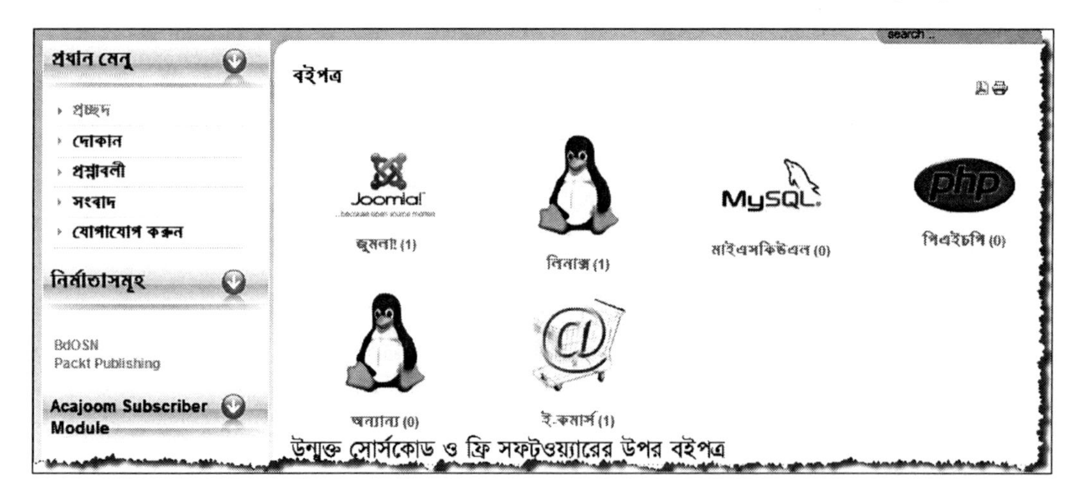

Remember, Joom!Fish translates the contents, not the interface languages. For example, for VirtueMart, it translates the product information, but not the VirtueMart user interface texts. For translating the VirtueMart user interface, we need to translate VirtueMart language files.

Translating VirtueMart language files

Like Joomla!, VirtueMart has its user interface phrases defined in language files. These language files are located in sub-directories under the ./administrator/components/ com_virtuemart/languages directory. However, these language files largely differ from language files of Joomla! 1.5.x. These are .php files, with some old style declarations for language phrases.

In the languages directory of VirtueMart, there are several sub-directories, such as account, admin, affiliate, common, order, product, and so on. In each of these directories, you will find one language file, named english.php. We can take this file as your basis for translation.

For translating a language file, open it in a Unicode compliant text editor, and save it with a separate name (for example, bengali.php). Also, make sure that it is saved with UTF-8 encoding, not in ANSII encoding. Once saved as separate file in the same directory, we can proceed with translating it.

The english.php file in the account folder looks like the following:

```
<?php
if( !defined( '_VALID_MOS' ) && !defined( '_JEXEC' ) ) die( 'Direct
Access to '.basename(__FILE__).' is not allowed.' );
/**
*
* @version $Id: english.php 1071 2007-12-03 08:42:28Z thepisu $
* @package VirtueMart
* @subpackage languages
* @copyright Copyright (C) 2004-2007 soeren - All rights reserved.
* @translator soeren
* @license http://www.gnu.org/copyleft/gpl.html GNU/GPL,
* see LICENSE.php
* VirtueMart is free software. This version may have been
* modified pursuant
* to the GNU General Public License, and as distributed it includes or
* is derivative of works licensed under the GNU General Public
* License or other free or open source software licenses.
* See /administrator/components/com_virtuemart/COPYRIGHT.php for
* copyright notices and details.
*
* http://virtuemart.net
*/
global $VM_LANG;
$langvars = array (
   'CHARSET' => 'ISO-8859-1',
```

```
    'PHPSHOP_ACC_CUSTOMER_ACCOUNT' => 'Customer Account:',
    'PHPSHOP_ACC_UPD_BILL' => 'Here you can update your billing
     information.',
    'PHPSHOP_ACC_UPD_SHIP' => 'Here you can add and maintain shipping
     addresses.',
    'PHPSHOP_ACC_ACCOUNT_INFO' => 'Account Information',
    'PHPSHOP_ACC_SHIP_INFO' => 'Shipping Information',
    'PHPSHOP_DOWNLOADS_CLICK' => 'Click on Product Name to Download
     File(s).',
    'PHPSHOP_DOWNLOADS_EXPIRED' => 'You have already downloaded the
     file(s) the maximum number of times, or the download period has
     expired.'
); $VM_LANG->initModule( 'account', $langvars );
?>
```

As we can see, it starts with a `<?php` tag, followed by a declaration to prevent direct access to this file. Then, the next block is about the file's version, creation date, author and translator, and copyright information. The actual definition of language phases starts with `$langvars = array( … )`. We need to translate what's inside this array. After translating to Bengali, the above block will look like the following:

```
$langvars = array (
 'CHARSET' => 'UTF-8',
 'PHPSHOP_ACC_CUSTOMER_ACCOUNT' => 'ক্রেতার একাউন্ট: ',
 'PHPSHOP_ACC_UPD_BILL' => 'এখানে আপনার বিলিং তথ্য হালনাগাদ করতে পারেন।',
 'PHPSHOP_ACC_UPD_SHIP' => 'এখানে আপনি নূতন শিপিং এড্রেস (যে ঠিকানায় মাল পাঠানো হবে)
   যোগ এবং পুরনো শিপিং ঠিকানা আপডেট করতে পারেন।',
 'PHPSHOP_ACC_ACCOUNT_INFO' => 'একাউন্ট তথ্য',
 'PHPSHOP_ACC_SHIP_INFO' => 'শিপিং তথ্য',
 'PHPSHOP_DOWNLOADS_CLICK' => 'ফাইল(সমূহ) ডাউনলোড করার জন্য পণ্যের নামে ক্লিক
   করুন।',
 'PHPSHOP_DOWNLOADS_EXPIRED' => 'আপনি এরই মধ্যে সর্বোচ্চসংখ্যকবার এই ফাইলটি ডাউনলোড
   করেছেন, কিংবা ডাউনলোডের জন্য নির্ধারিত সময়সীমা পার হয়ে গেছে।'
);
```

For all other files, you need to translate the phrases in this way. As you need to edit the files manually, be careful about typos and don't forget to use the appropriate encoding, that is `UTF-8` for most of the languages.

I apologize to the readers for using Bangla in the example above, which may not be meaningful to most of the readers of this book. But this is my mother tongue, and besides English, I know no other international language which can be used as an example. The main thrust is that you replace the words inside quotation marks with your own translation.

Once all of these language files have been translated, your VirtueMart store is ready to operate in multi-lingual mode. As you enable Joom!Fish, the **Language Selection** module is displayed with flag icons for the languages. Visitors can change the languages by clicking on the flag icons they like. After some translation of both the Joomla! and VirtueMart user interface, and VirtueMart product information, the site will look like the following:

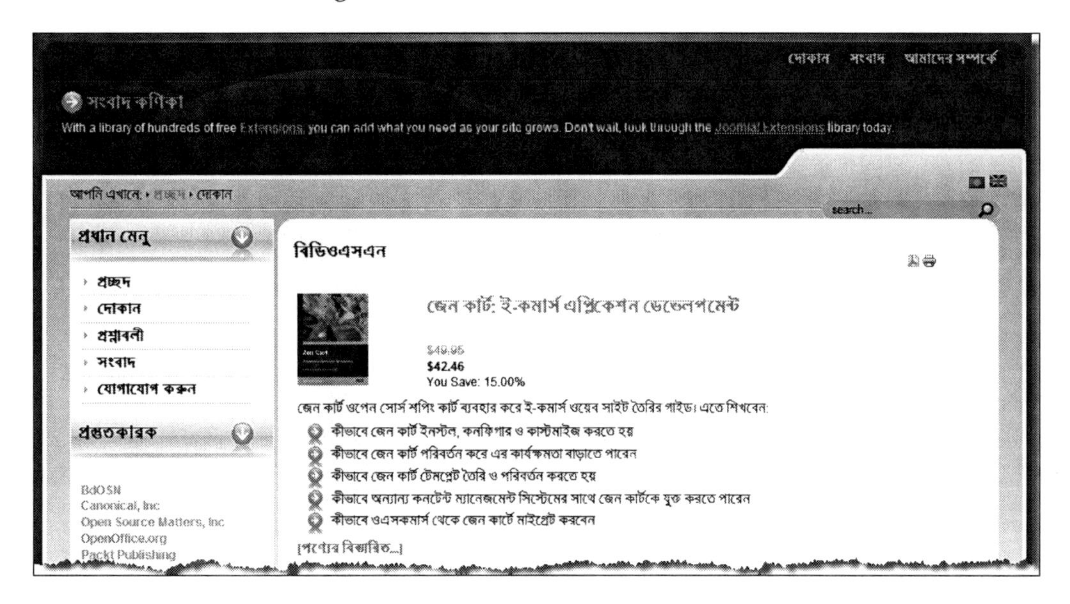

As you can see, almost everything in the Joomla! site and VirtueMart shop can be translated into your desired languages using the combination of methods described in this chapter:

- manual editing of Joomla! language files
- translating the Joomla! user interface using the **Translation Manager** component
- translating Joomla! and VirtueMart contents using Joom!Fish component
- manually translating the VirtueMart user interface language files.

Summary

This chapter has shown you how to localize your Joomla!-VirtueMart shop. First, it showed you how to use region specific tax rates. We then saw how to use multiple currencies on your site. We have also seen how to update the currency conversion rates live from the Internet, and automatically display the product prices in the currency chosen by the customers. Then, we discussed how to make your Joomla! and VirtueMart site multi-lingual. It has shown you how to translate the Joomla! user interface, manage translations, use multi-lingual contents using the Joom!Fish component, and translate the VirtueMart language files.

With these advance skills of localization, we will do something more with VirtueMart in the next chapter.

9
Extending VirtueMart's Functionalities

You have already learned to setup a VirtueMart store, haven't you? Maybe what you have learned so far will be more than enough for most of the stores. However, still there is still a need to further enhance the store with some more functionality. There are some third-party extensions to extend VirtueMart's functionalities, and you may also need to tweak some extensions to suite your need. This chapter shows you how to do this.

On completion of this chapter, you will be able to:

- Use appropriate extensions to import and export products in bulk to your VirtueMart shop catalog
- Use product tag clouds on your shop, which will display the most frequently used tags generated from product name and descriptions
- Use testimonials for the shop
- Use commenting to improve product reviews on your shop
- Use wholesaling, so that orders received through your VirtueMart store can be fulfilled by listed wholesalers
- Provide an opportunity to use social networks and bookmarking sites to spread news about your site and products
- Update the information of multiple products using AJAX
- Spice up your shop to look great by using a new visual cart module, display slideshows with product images, and by include modules in the content items

This chapter mainly focuses on the use of some relevant third-party extensions that add some desired functionalities to your store.

We have not discussed developing a new extension ourselves, as that is beyond the scope of this book. To learn about developing Joomla! (and VirtueMart) extensions, please read the well written book *Learning Joomla! 1.5 Extension Development*, written by Joseph Le Blanc, and published by Packt Publishing.

Bulk product imports and exports

You have now learned how to add products to the VirtueMart catalog one by one. However, it may be convenient to add products in bulk. Most of the shopping cart applications provide some kind of features for bulk importing and exporting of products to the catalog. In VirtueMart, there is also such a feature, which becomes available through installing a third-party extension named CSVImproved. You can get more information and download CSVImproved from the site `http://www.csvimproved.com`. At the time of writing this book, the latest stable version available is 0.9. However, the next release will be CSVImproved 1.5, which will natively work with Joomla! 1.5, and only be available commercially. This section is based on the stable version of CSVImproved 0.8.

Once installed, you can open the CSVImproved control panel by clicking **Components | CSVImproved**:

As you can see, the CSVImproved control panel contains six links. It is better to look at the **Help** area first to know how this component works.

For its use on your store, you may be interested to first define the templates for importing and exporting. Click on the **Templates** icon and you will get the list of available templates for importing and exporting. Also, you can get the options for creating new templates and viewing available fields in the existing templates:

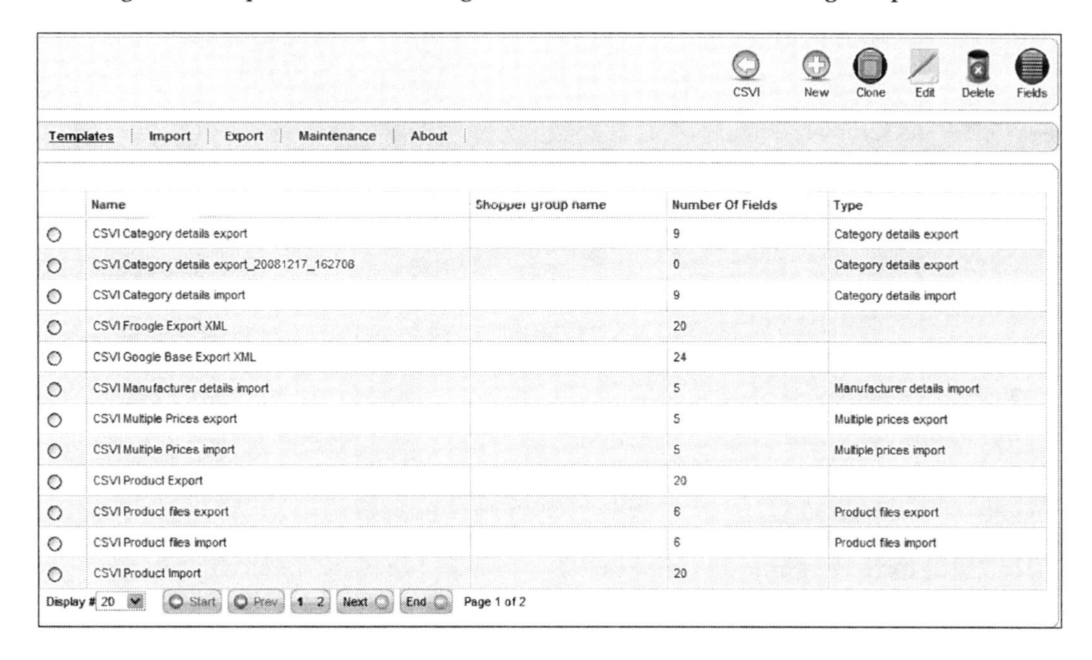

Templates in CSVImproved are a nice way to save your export and import settings that can be used later. The templates contain some general settings and fields for which the data will be imported or exported. By default, there are import and export templates defined for category details, Google base, Froogle, manufacturer details, multiple prices, product details, and so on.

Creating new import and export template

As you can see from the list of templates already defined in CSVImproved, we don't have a template for importing or exporting product types. In our example store, we have defined at least two product types, added parameters to these product types, and added the product types to products. While importing and exporting product information, we also need to import and export product type information.

For such an import or export activity, we can create a new template by clicking on the **New** button on the toolbar. This is shown in the following screenshot:

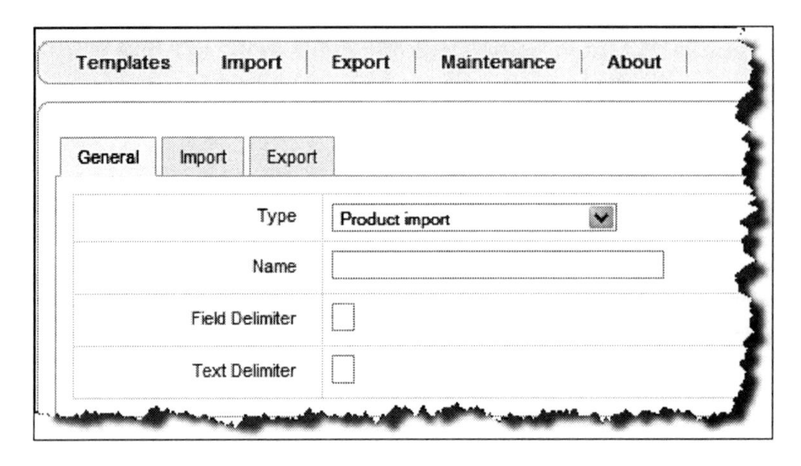

In the **General** tab, you need to select the type of import or export from the **Type** drop-down list. At first, we are going to create a template for a product type export. We will need to select a type of product export in the **Type** drop-down list. Then, provide a name of the template, say **Product Type Export (CSV)** in the **Name** field. In the **Field Delimiter** and the **Text Delimiter** fields, you need to set a character which will be used as a field separator and text separator. In this case, we will put **^** as the **Field Delimiter** and ~ as the **Text Delimiter**.

In the **Import** tab, you can specify how the contents of the CSV file will be imported. As we are creating the export template first, skip the **Import** tab and go to **Export** tab:

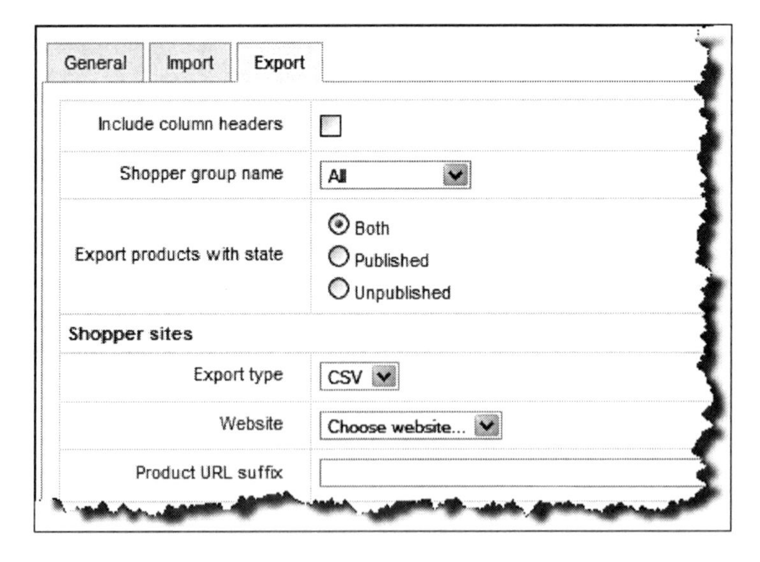

In the **Export** tab, you can check the **Include column headers** checkbox to add column headers in the CSV file. Then, choose a shopper group from the **Shopper group name**. Selecting a specific shopper group will only export the product available for that group. The default setting is **All**, which means all products will be exported. In the **Export products with state** field, you can specify whether to export only published or unpublished products, or you can export all products by selecting **Both** in this field.

You can also specify the export format in the **Export type** drop-down list. You can either select **XML** or **CSV**. The default setting is **CSV** and it works fine with Joomla! 1.1.x and Joomla! 1.5.x.

Although the option for importing or exporting an XML file is available in CSVImproved, up until now, you may experience some problems with exporting and importing the product information in XML format. It is safer to use other formats, like CSV, instead of using an XML format.

On selecting the values above, you can save the template by clicking on the **Save** icon in the toolbar. You can now see the template name in the template list. However, still the template is not ready for use. We need to add the fields to this template.

For adding fields to the template, select the template and click on the **Fields** icon in the toolbar. That lists the available fields for product types, except the unpublished fields. Select all of the fields and click on the **Publish** icon in the toolbar. Then, order the fields by typing a number in the **Field Ordering** column and click on the **Save** icon in the toolbar. Now, the fields will be renumbered and the screen will look like the following screenshot:

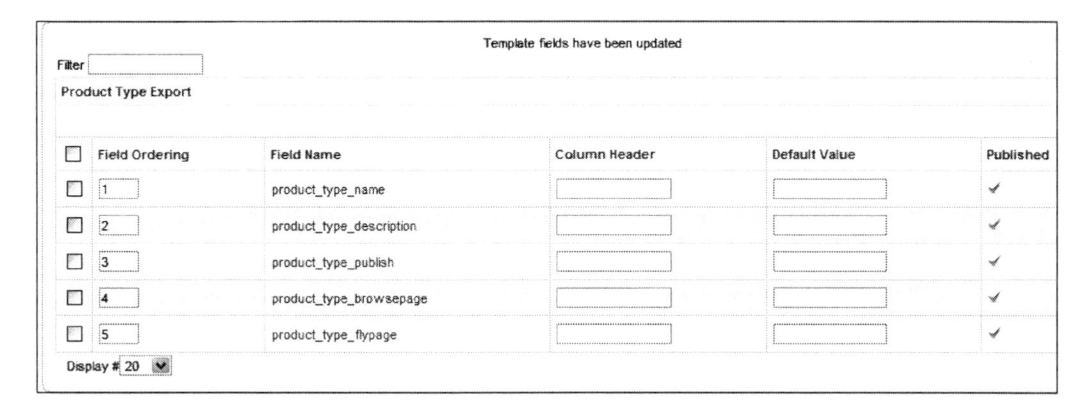

Once you have published the fields and they have been reordered, the template is ready for use. Save the settings for the template.

Before using our newly created template, let us design another template for importing product types. Follow the same procedure outline above, but now select **Product Type Import** in the **Type** drop-down list in the **General** tab and configure the options in the **Import** tab instead of the **Export** tab:

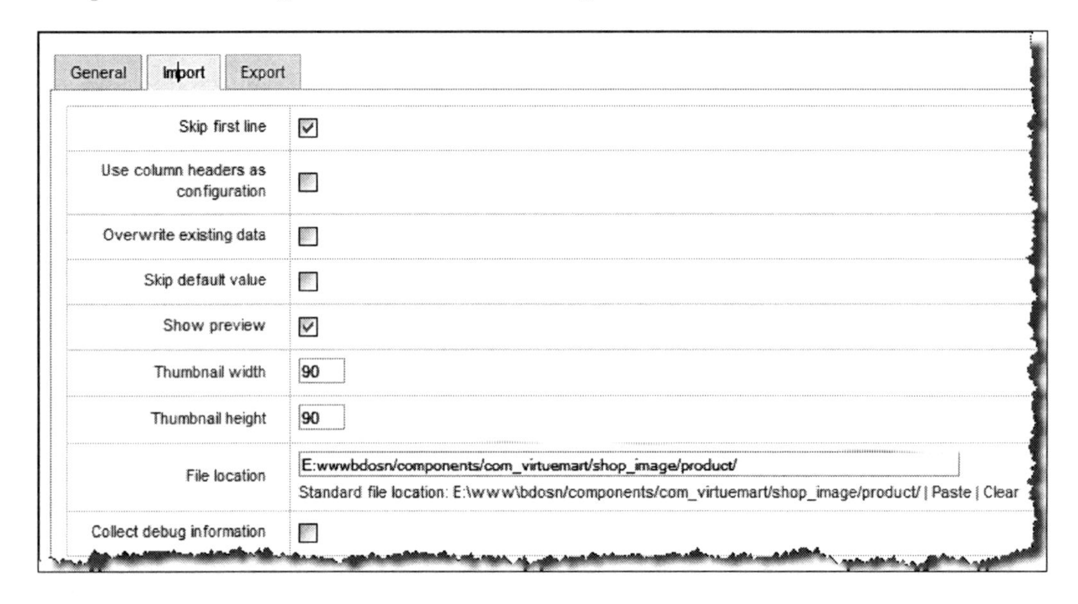

The fields in the **Import** tab are self-explanatory. You can configure it to skip the first line, overwrite existing data, skip default value, show preview before importing, and so forth. Clicking on the **Save** icon will save the template settings.

For this import template, again, you need to specify the fields available for the template. Select the template and click on the **Fields** icon in the toolbar. You will also see a list of available fields. Select all of the fields and click on the **Publish** icon to publish these fields. After publishing, set the order of the fields and save the template.

If the order of fields for the export and import templates are different, you may face a problem in importing the product types from the exported CSV file. Therefore, always maintain the same order of fields.

Using import and export templates

We have just created two new templates. One template is for product exports, another is for importing the product types. Let us now try how these templates work.

From Joomla!'s administration panel, go to **Components | CSVImproved | Export**. You get the **Export** screen:

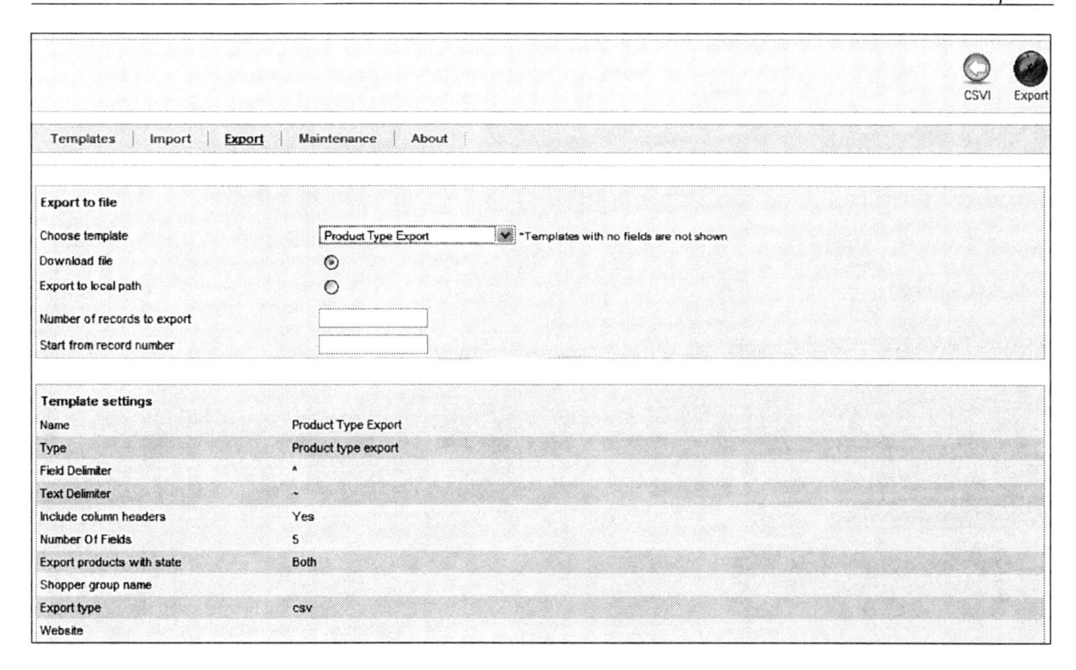

In the **Export to file** section, you first need to select a template from the **Choose template** drop-down list. You will only see the templates with fields published. You can see the **Product Type Export** template, as we have added fields to this template and published the fields. Select this template. You can either download the file or save to a local path on the server. By default, the **Download file** is selected. Then, you can specify the number of records to be exported and from which record number it will start exporting. If you have many product types, it will be better to set a limit for how many records export at a time.

In the **Template settings** section, you see the settings of the template you have selected. As you can see, these were the settings we have set for the **Product Type Export** template.

After selecting the options, click on the **Export** icon in the toolbar. That will export the product types and your web browser will prompt you to save the CSV file. Save the file on your local disk. The file name of the generated CSV file will be something like `CSVI_Export_Product Type Export_19-12-2008_06.25.csv`. If you look into this file, you see the content as following:

```
1  ~product_type_name~^~product_type_description~^~product_type_publish~^~product_type_browsepage~^~product_type_flypage~
2  ~Books~^~All books~^~Y~^~~^~~
3  ~Softwares~^~All Softwares~^~Y~^~~^~~
```

As you can see, the first line contains the field names as column headers. The second and third line contains the actual data of product types. As we have created only two product types, we see only two lines containing data about these product types.

Let us now try importing the items in this CSV file. From the Joomla!'s administration panel, go to **Components | CSVImproved | Import**:

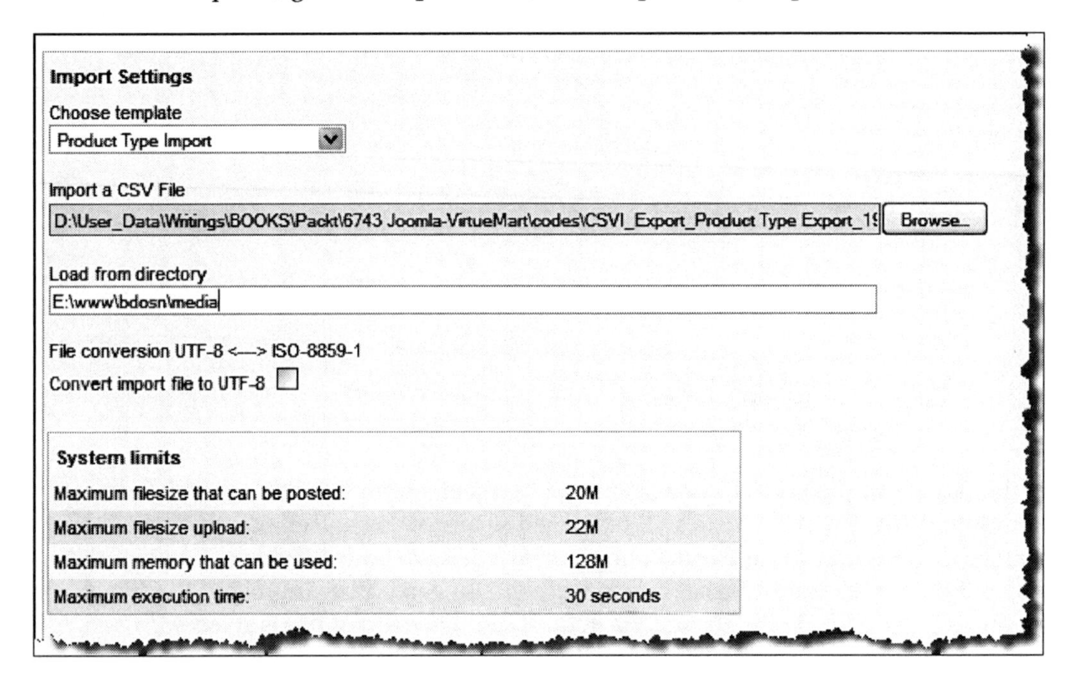

Like exporting, we get the **Import Settings** section, from where first we need to select a template. From the **Choose template** drop-down list, select the **Product Type Import** template. In the **Import a CSV File** field, click on the **Browse** button to select the CSV file you exported earlier. If you want to convert a file into UTF-8 encoding, you may check the **Convert import file to UTF-8** checkbox.

The **System limits** section shows the file size limit that can be uploaded and the amount of memory that can be used for running the script. These limits are set through the `php.ini` file, and you only see the read-only values here so that you don't try to import from files which crosses these limits. Like export, this screen also shows the **Template settings** section listing the settings in the template.

For starting the import, click on the **Import** icon in the toolbar. As we have set previewing of the template, the next screen shows the available records in the CSV file:

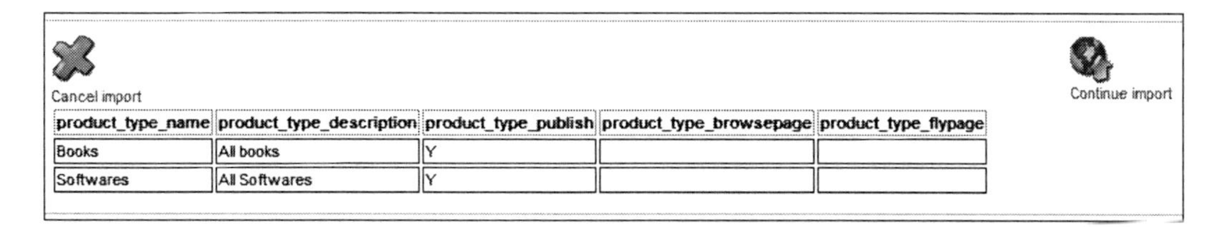

If the information presented in the screen is correct, click on the **Continue import** button. You may also edit the boxes if you like, and then import the modified content. When importing, based on the contents, you will see updated or inserted information in the results screen:

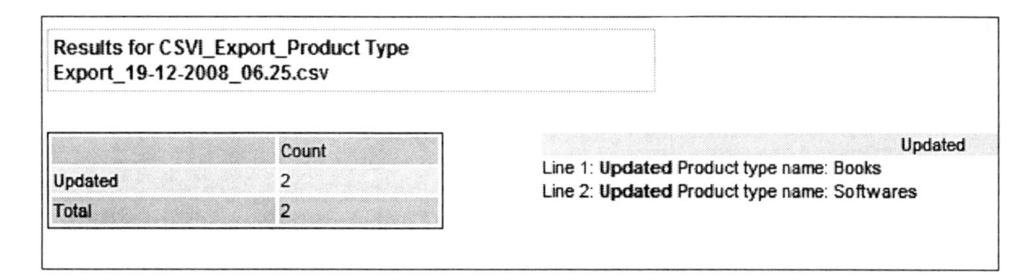

You can use other templates to export and import information, including categories, products, product prices, product type parameters, and so on.

Using CSVImproved for catalog building

Although the main purpose of CSVImproved is to facilitate exporting and importing of catalog items in bulk, it can also be used as an offline catalog builder. Once you have defined templates, and tried those, the blank CSV files can be used for entering product information offline. You can then import those CSV files to product your catalog. Generally, you don't need to import categories, product types, and such things once you have defined those for your store. However, product items need to be imported to your catalog most frequently. You may provide the product template to the vendors and they can enter the product information and send those CSV files to you. Then you, as the shop administrator, can import the product information to the catalog.

> **Warning:**
>
> While using CSVImproved, be careful with the **Maintenance** tab. If you select **Empty database**, and click on the **Continue** button, the product database will be emptied without any warning! That means you get a shop without any products. Before trying this, always backup the database first. We will learn about backing up Joomla! and VirtueMart databases in the next chapters

Using product tag clouds

Tagging, and showing the tag clouds, is a so called Web 2.0 feature, which you can use for your VirtueMart shop. This third-party module simply takes the keywords from the product name, short description and product's description, and builds the tag cloud on the fly. You can specify which words are not to be included in the tag cloud. This free module is available at `http://www.joomlafreak.be/virtuemart/index.php/virtuemart-cloud`. Download this module and install it as other Joomla! modules from **Extensions | Install/Uninstall**.

For configuring and publishing this module, go to **Extensions | Module Manager**, and click on the **VirtueMart Clouds** module link. That shows the configuration options for the module. The **Details** and **Menu Assignment** sections are as usual as with other modules:

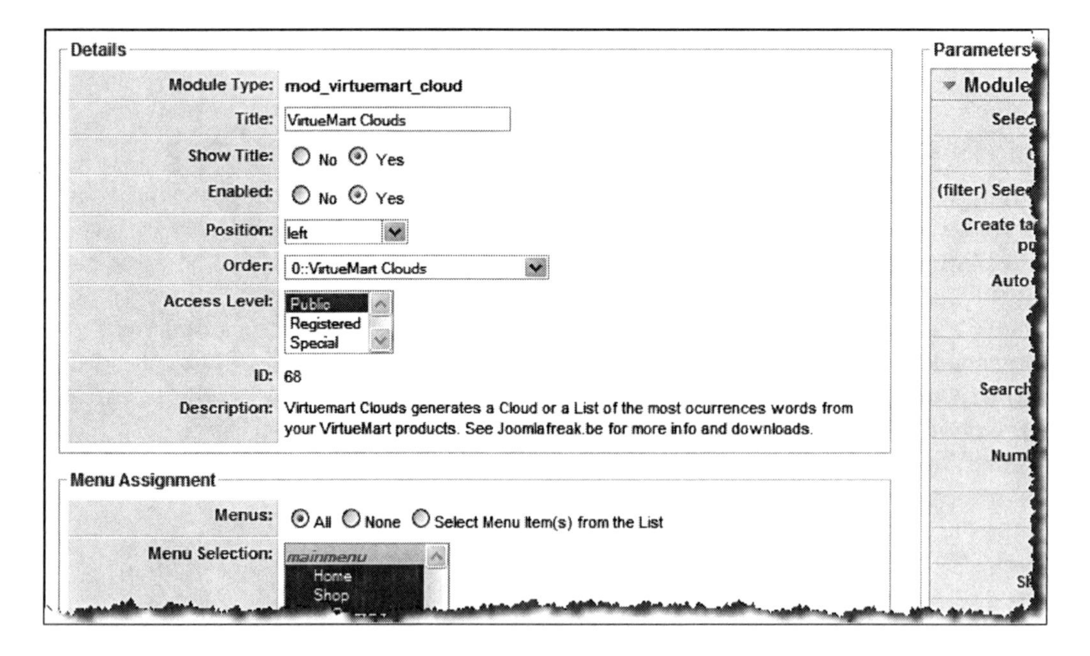

The module-specific configurations are available in the **Module Parameters** section:

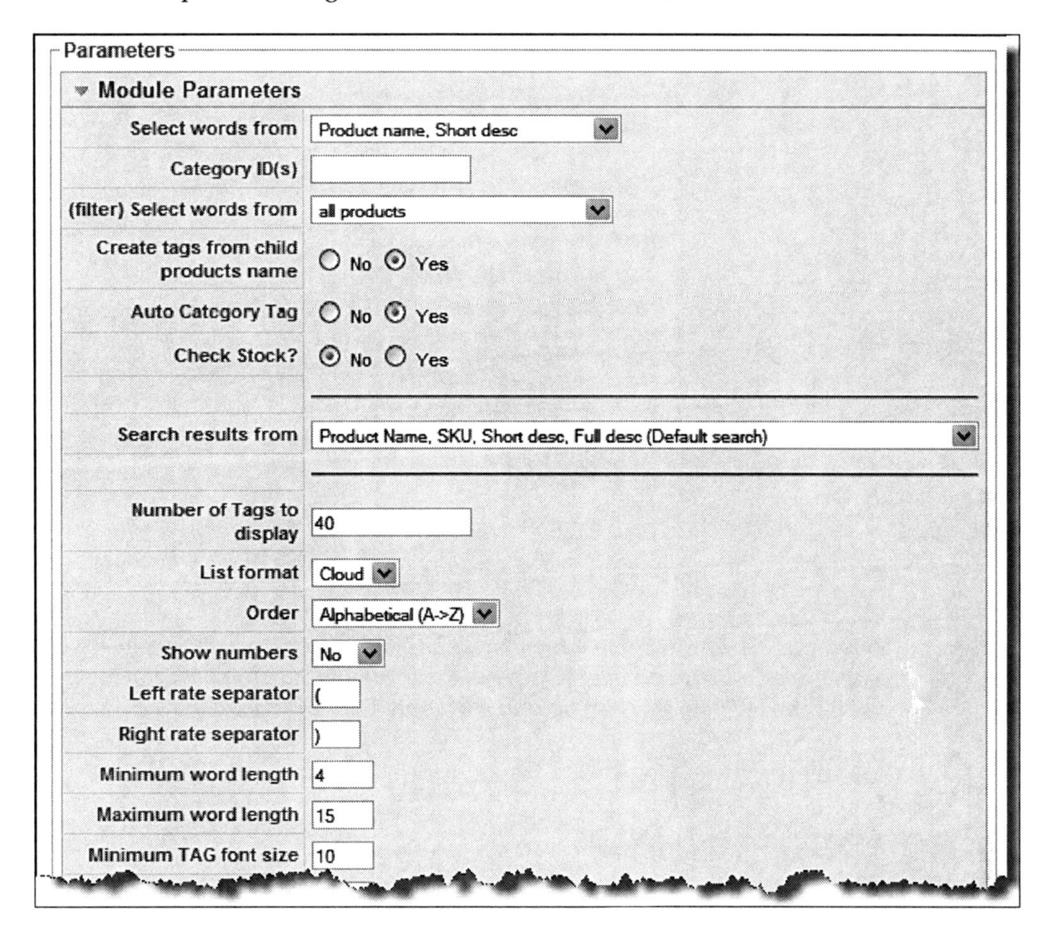

From the **Module Parameters** section, you need to specify where the tags will be built from, whether all or selective categories will be included, how many tags will be displayed, how to order the tags, how the tags will be displayed a (minimum and maximum font size), list format, and so on.

When the tag cloud module is configured and published, it displays the tag cloud generated from the product names and descriptions. A typical product tag cloud will look like the following screenshot:

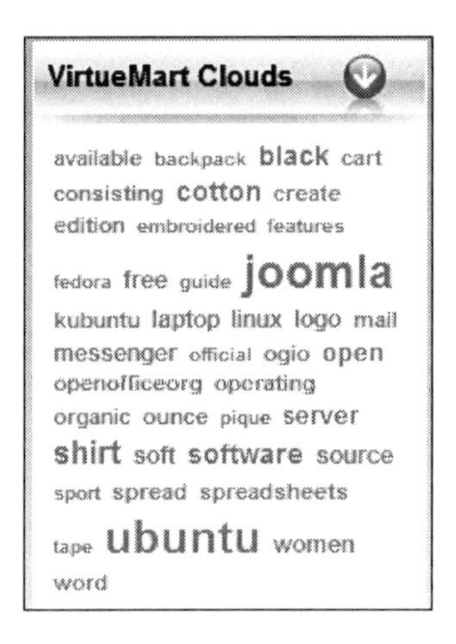

You may find that some unwanted words are in the tag cloud. You can stop these words from being displayed as a tag by typing these words in the **Black List/Stop words** field in the **Module Parameters** section.

Using testimonials

Testimonials can attract your customers to buy some products. Having some testimonials about your web shop, or the after sale service, will make your life easier. That helps build trust on your shop and induces the visitors to buy products from your shop. In one sense, testimonials are different from product reviews. Product reviews are directly related to specific product. However, testimonials may be something about the customer's experience shopping on your site, getting required support after the sale, and about the excellent services you provide.

For a Joomla! site and VirtueMart shop, you can use an extension called JD Testimonial for VirtueMart for collecting and publishing testimonials from the customers. This great module gives several configuration options which will suite the needs of different types of shop owners. This extension is available from `http://www.joomingdales.com/Downloads.html`.

Once downloaded and installed, you can configure it from **Components | JD Testimonial | Settings**. In the **Edit Settings** screen, you find three tabs: **General settings**, **Reminder settings**, and **Mail settings**:

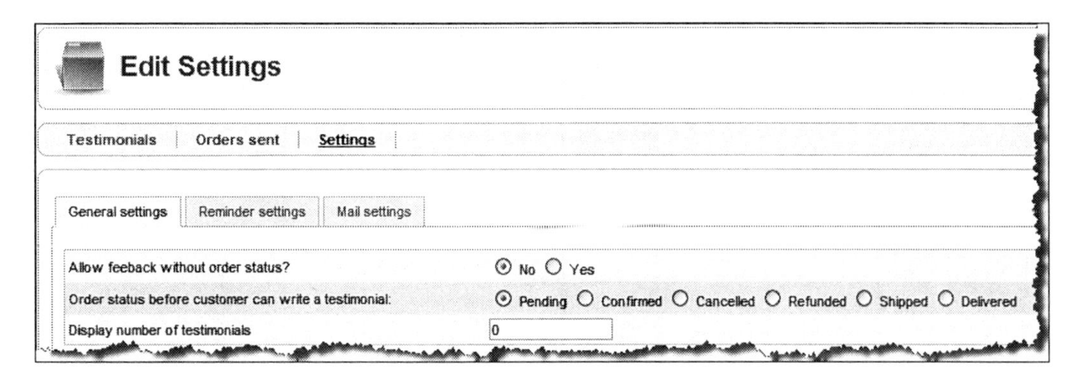

In the **General settings** tab, you can allow feedback based on order status, and also select the order status for customers to provide feedback. It is better to collect such feedback only after the product is delivered. You can also specify the number of testimonials to be displayed at a time.

In the **Reminder settings** tab, you can configure after how many days the customer will be reminded to provide feedback. You can also set a threshold after which the reminder will not be sent again.

In the **Mail settings** tab, you can specify the subject line and the from address of your email sent to customers for feedback.

Once you have configured the component, you can configure the **JD Testimonial** module from the **Extensions | Module Manager**. The configuration screen for this module looks like the following screenshot:

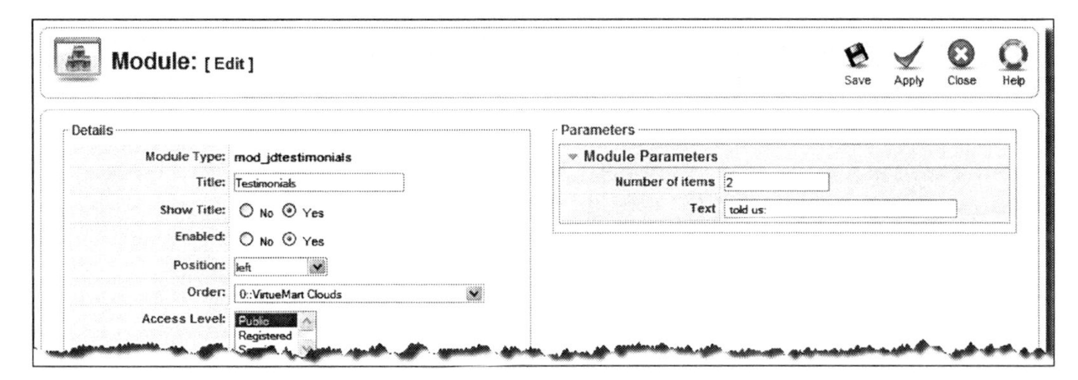

As you can see, in the module parameters section you can configure two options: the number of items to be displayed, and text to be added after the name of the customer. The published module with testimonials will look like the following screenshot:

You can see the list of testimonials from **Components | JD Testimonial | Testimonials**, and edit, publish, or unpublish any testimonial submitted by a customer.

Improving product reviews by commenting

In VirtueMart, customers can review products and submit testimonials. Wouldn't it be great if they could comment on any product or article on your site? There are several third-party extensions for commenting. However, the **JComments** extension is a good choice as it works fine with VirtueMart and Joomla!. The JComments components and module can be downloaded freely from `http://www.joomlatune.com/jcomments-downloads.html`.

Once the component and module are downloaded and installed, we can proceed to configure the JComments component first. Go to **Components | JComments | Settings**. That shows the **Settings** screen with six tabs:

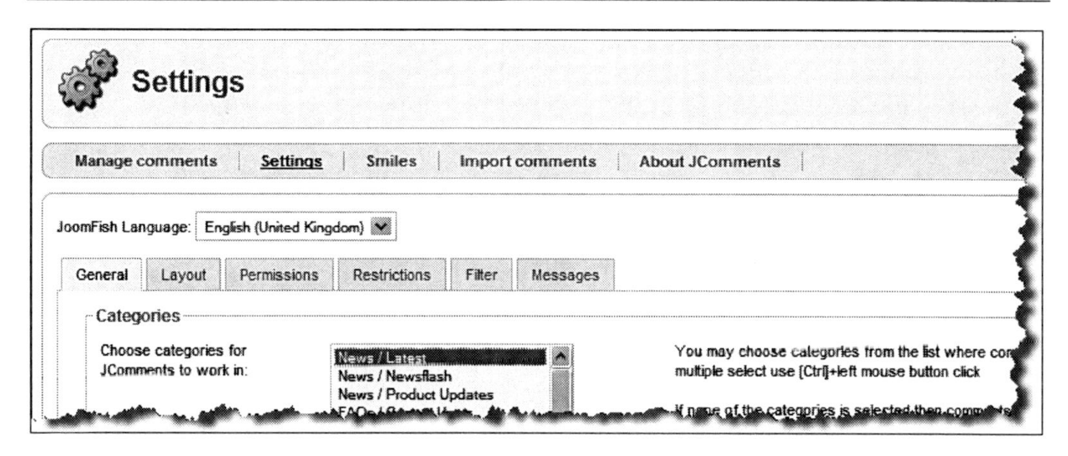

The configuration options available through the six tabs are self explanatory. From the **General** tab, you can select which categories JComments will be used with. By default, it only shows content sections and categories. You can also enable notifications, an RSS feed, and plugins for this component from this tab.

From the **Layout** tab, you can choose a comment template, show smiley's, enable showing votes, choose author name display (username or full name), display order, number of comments per page, maximum number of pages, position of page numbers, and the required fields in comment form.

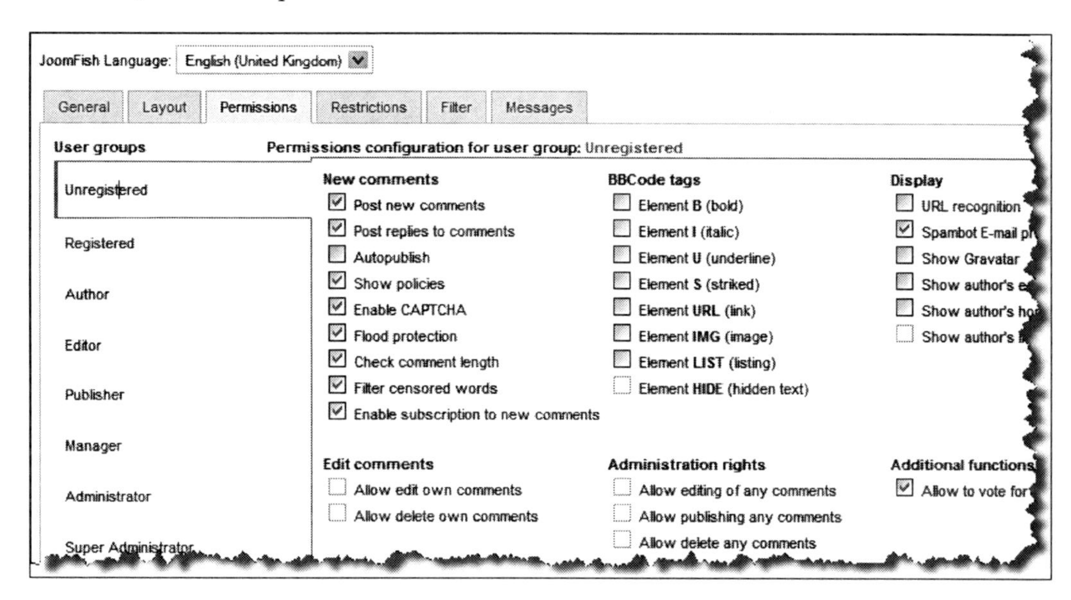

In the **Permissions** tab (seen in the previous screenshot), you can set the permissions for different group of users to perform several tasks related to commenting. For most of the sites, the default configurations will be fine. However, you can fine tune the permissions to secure your site.

In the **Restrictions** tab, you can specify the minimum and maximum values for several fields, such as user name, comment length, interval between posts, and so on. You can also enable name checking of registered users.

From the **Filter** tab, you can specify the inappropriate words which need to be censored from the comments. The **Messages** tab allows you to specify a commenting policy and messages to user not allowed to comment and posts for which commenting is closed.

After configuring the JComments component, you can proceed to configure the JComment module. Go to **Extensions | Module Manager** and click on the **JComments Latest** module. Give an appropriate title for the module, publish it, and select a position where this module will be displayed. Module specific configuration options are displayed in the **Module Parameters** section:

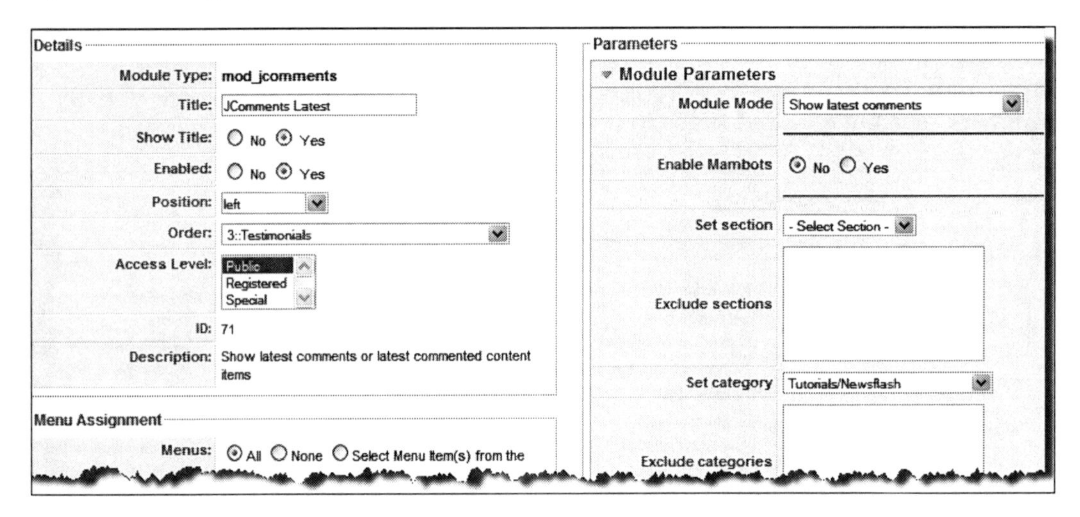

From the module parameters section, you can configure the module mode, enable mambots, set the section, exclude specific sections, set categories, specify categories to exclude, source components, such as **com_content, com_virtuemart**, and some other display options. As you intend JComments to be integrated with VirtueMart in the **Source** field, type **com_content, com_virtuemart**. This will enable commenting both in the content items and the VirtueMart product items.

After configuring the JComments component, we should try it. Go to your site's home page and see the content items. You will see the **Add new comment** link after each article. Click on this **Add new comment** link and it will show the comment editor as seen in the following screenshot:

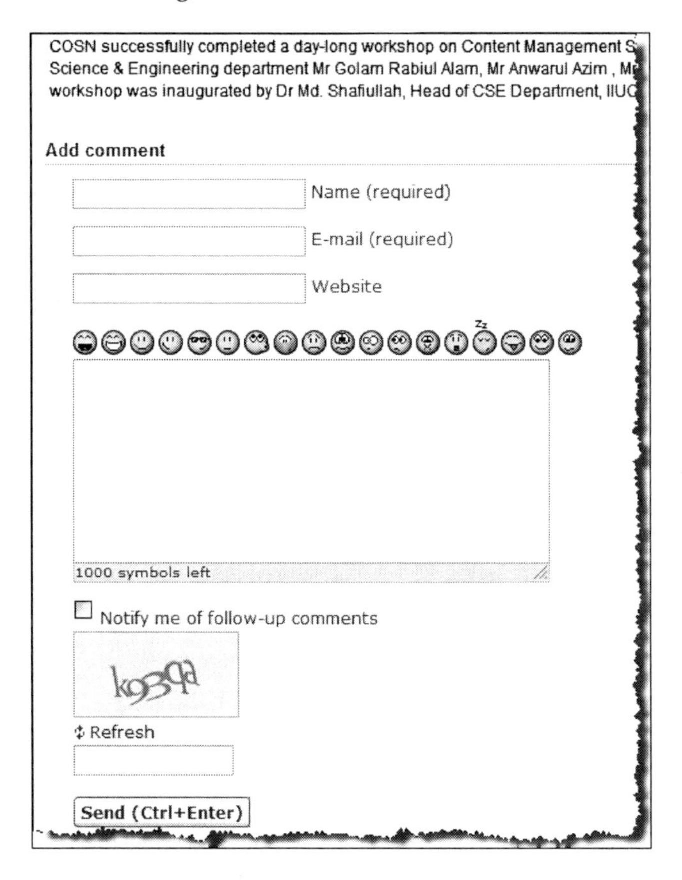

A visitor can fill in the form above and submit the comment. Based on the settings of the JComments component, the comment may be published instantly or stored for moderation. The article with the comment added will look like the following screenshot:

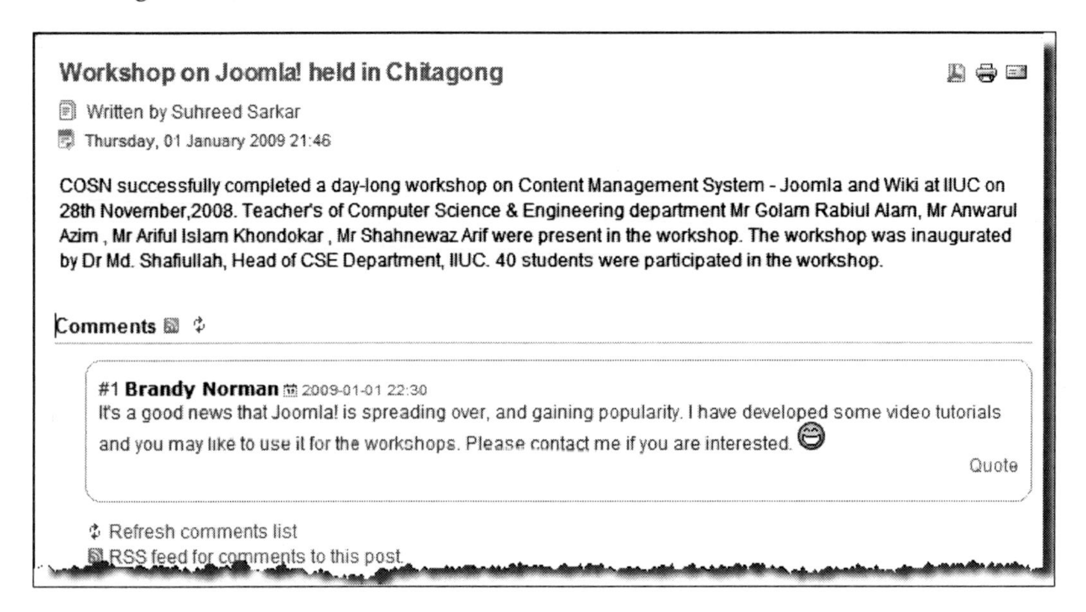

If you try to comment on a VirtueMart product, you still will not be able to do so. This is because of the template used in the VirtueMart. However, you can use the same commenting with some modifications to two files. For allowing commenting to VirtueMart items, follow the steps below:

1. In your favorite text editor, open `./administrator/components/com_virtuemart/html/shop.product_details.php`.
2. Find the following lines (around line number # 347):

```
/*** Show all reviews available ***/
$product_reviews = ps_reviews::product_reviews( $product_id );
/*** Show a form for writing a review ***/
if( $auth['user_id'] > 0 ) {
   $product_reviewform = ps_reviews::reviewform( $product_id );
   }
```

3. Comment out the code block above and add the following code block in that place:

```
$comments = $mosConfig_absolute_path . '/components/com_jcomments/
jcomments.php';
  if (file_exists($comments)) {
    require_once($comments);
```

```
        $product_reviews = JComments::showComments($product_id,
             'com_virtuemart', $product_name);
        $product_reviewform = "";
      }
```

4. Save the changes to the file. Now, open the `./administrator/components/com_virtuemart/html/shop.browse.php` file in your text editor.
5. Find the following code block (around line #398):

```
if (PSHOP_ALLOW_REVIEWS == '1' && @$_REQUEST['output'] != "pdf") {
   // Average customer rating: xxxxx
   // Total votes: x
$product_rating = ps_reviews::allvotes
  ( $db_browse-> f("product_id") );
      }
      else {
         $product_rating = "";
   }
```

6. Comment out the code block above and save the file.
7. Go to **Components | VirtueMart | Configuration** and check **Enable Customer Review/Rating System**. If you have enabled it earlier, keep it checked.

Once the modifications above have been made, try to browse some products and see the product details. Now, you see the comment form instead of the review form:

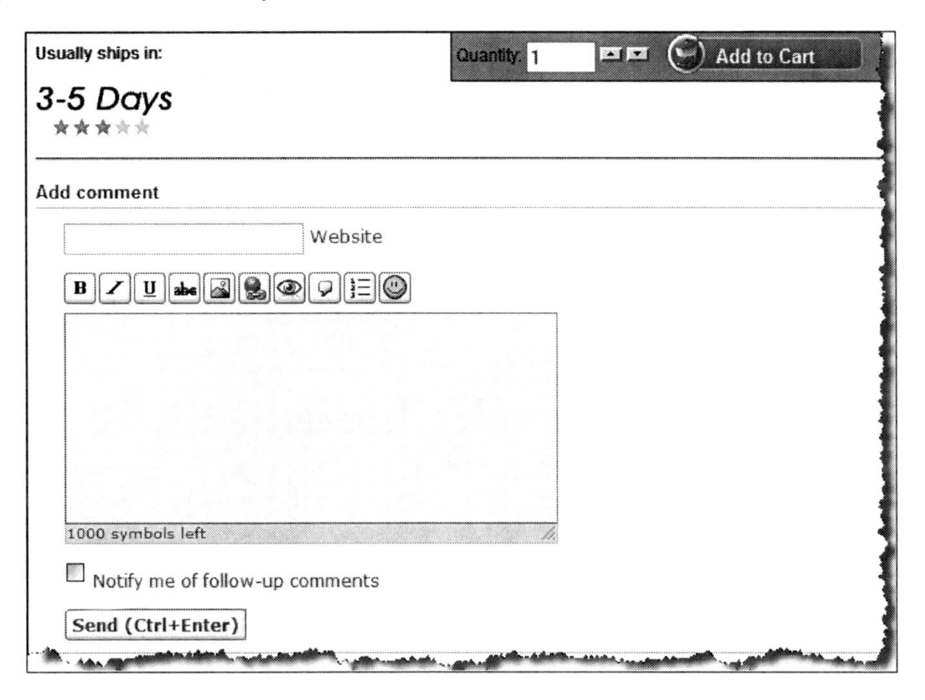

The comment form above looks different than the other form we saw earlier. This is because we are now viewing this logged in as a user, and for logged in users, we don't need to type user name, email address, and use CAPTCHA for a security check. Also, note that the editor is a rich text editor where you can use an image, hyper link, formatting, and so on in your comment. The comments added to the product will be displayed at the bottom of each product:

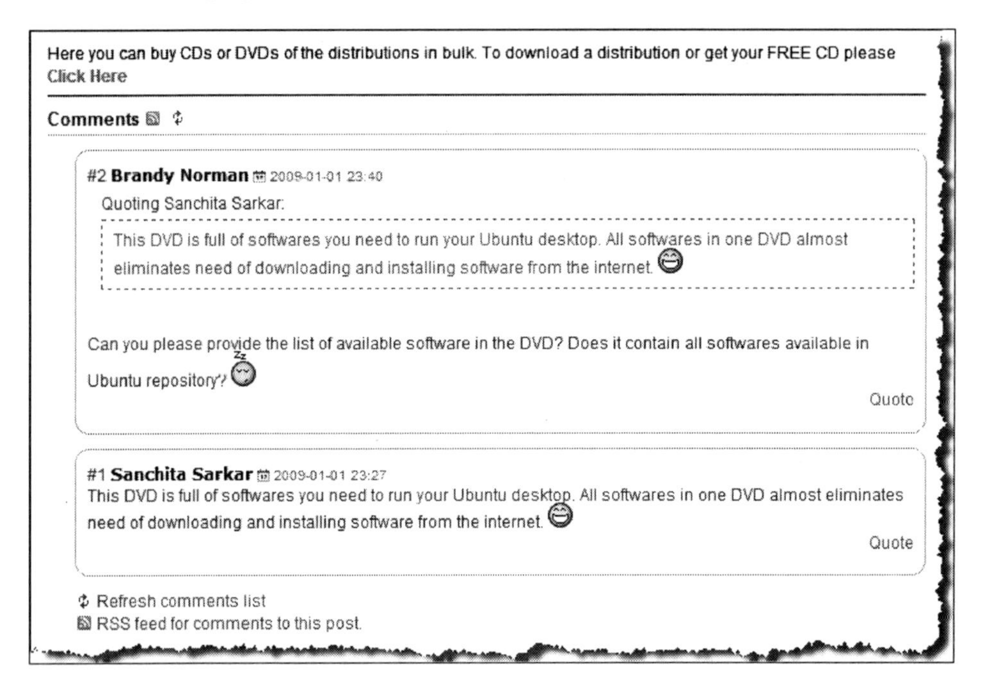

JComments supports multiple languages and works fine with Joom!Fish. When using Joom!Fish, you need to configure JComments for each language available. The administrator can view all of the comments and moderate those from **Components | JComments | Manage Comments**.

Wholesaling from a VirtueMart store

Do you remember the vendor feature in VirtueMart? While discussing the vendor feature, we mentioned that it is a pre-mature feature in the sense that as a shop owner, you cannot tell the vendors to supply the products to the customers. The solution to this is to use a third-party extension wholesaler system for VirtueMart available at `http://www.jmds.eu/wholesaler-system/view-category.html`.

The wholesaler system for VirtueMart replaces some files in the `./administrator/components/vm_virtuemart` directory. Therefore, it is strongly advised that you backup this directory before installing this extension. First, install the **com_wholesaler** component from **Extensions | Install/Uninstall**. Then, unzip the `administrator.zip` file and copy the folder to replace the `./administrator` directory. Once installed, you can see **Wholesalers** in the **Components** menu. Go to **Components | Wholesalers**. That shows the **Wholesalers** screen:

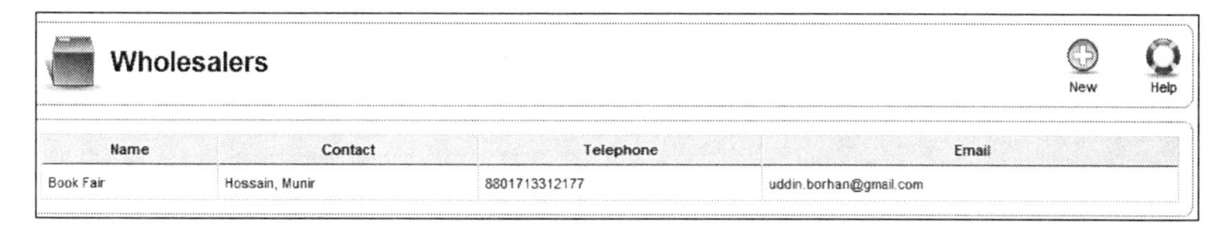

The **Wholesalers** screen lists the available wholesalers. For adding a new wholesaler, click on the **New** icon in the toolbar. That brings a form for adding new wholesaler:

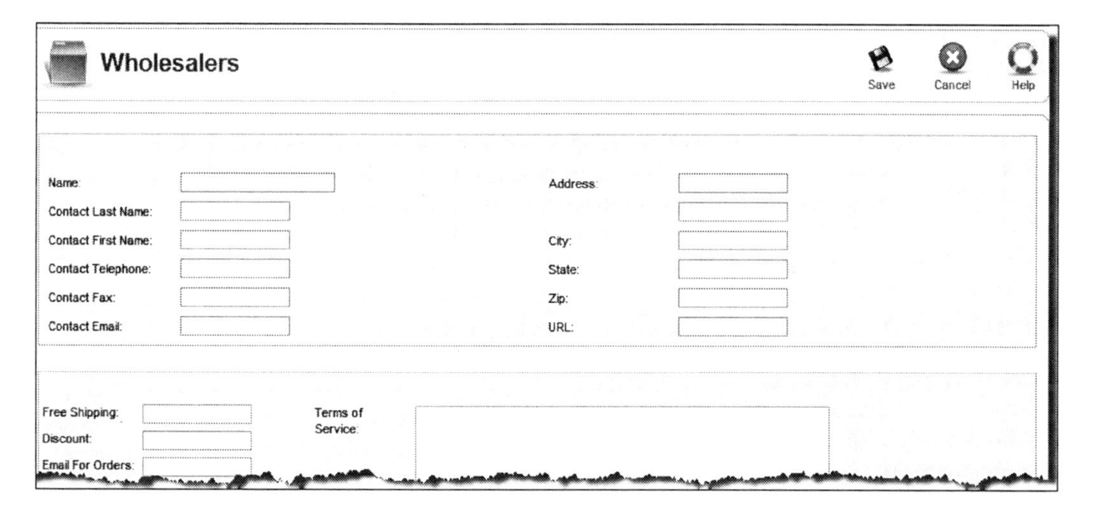

While adding a wholesaler, you need to provide the name of the wholesaler, contact person, telephone and fax number, contact email address, and street address. In addition to this, you can also add whether free shipping will be used or not, what discount the wholesaler will get, and an email address where the orders will be sent. In the **Terms of Service** tex box, you can add the terms of service agreed between you and the wholesaler. When all this information is provided, click on the **Save** icon in the toolbar to save the wholesaler information.

Once you have added the wholesaler, you can edit the products. You will find a new **Wholesaler Details** tab in the **Update Item** screen:

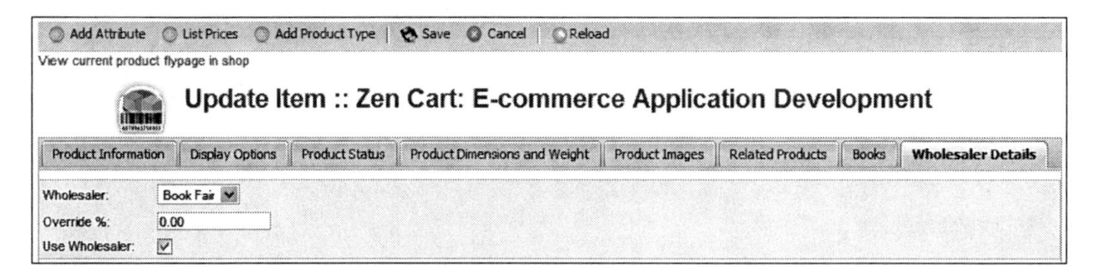

In the **Wholesaler Details** tab, you need to select the wholesaler for that item. You can specify the percentage of discount as well. Check the **Use Wholesaler** checkbox to use this feature.

When a product is configured to use a wholesaler, the wholesaler will be notified through an email after an order is placed and the order status is changed to confirmed. Receiving this notification email, the wholesaler can ship the product to the billing to address.

You can use a number of variables which can be used in product order templates, product browse template, and other places. The variables are briefly listed in a manual bundled with the package.

Using social networking and bookmarking sites

Social networking is becoming a part of our life. Tech savvy people are hooked using one or more social networking sites like Facebook, MySpace and so on. These sites also help spread links of interesting web sites and pages. It would be great if you could give visitors an option to share your shop's link with these social networking sites. A third-party free Joomla! module named JShare for Joomla! 1.5 can help you spread your product information to these social networking sites. You can download the JShare module from `http://joomify.com/mod_jshare.zip`, and install it from **Extensions | Install/Uninstall**.

Once installed, you can configure and publish the JShare module. Go to **Extensions | Module Manager** and click on **JShare Social Bookmarking Module for Joomla 1.5**. From the **Module Parameters** section, you can enable about one hundred social networking and bookmarking sites. The enabled module will look like the following screenshot:

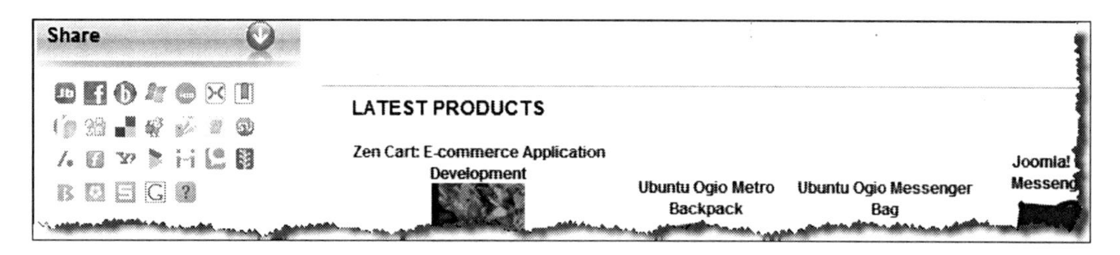

Visitors can share the page with these social networking and bookmarking sites by clicking on the icon of that site displayed in this module.

Using AJAX updates for products

You know what AJAX is. It is changing the web, especially, in new types of design and user interactivity. And you may also think about updating multiple product items at once. In the earlier chapters, we have seen that, as an administrator, you cannot update multiple products at a time unless you export those in a CSV format, update them offline, and again import them to the shop.

A module named the VirtueMart AJAX Updater, available at `http://neonascent.com/`, gives you an opportunity to update multiple VirtueMart products at a time, and uses AJAX to do it. This means fewer page refresh for updating the product information. This module is available both for Joomla 1.0.x and 1.5.x. You need to download different files for these two versions of Joomla!.

Once the module is downloaded and installed, you need to apply a little hack to the VirtueMart template. To apply this hack, follow the steps below:

1. Open the browse template found in the `./components/com_virtuemart/themes/default/templates/browse/` directory.
2. In each browse template (for example, `browse_1.php`), add the following code block at the end:

```
<div class="AJAX" pid="<?php echo $product_sku ?>">
<div class="AJAX_field" field="product_name" title="Name"
content="<?php echo $product_name; ?>"></div>
<div class="AJAX_field" field="product_s_desc" title="order"
content="<?php echo $product_s_desc; ?>"></div>
<div class="AJAX_field" field="product_desc" title="Description"
content=" "></div>
<div class="AJAX_field" field="product_price" title="Price"
content=" "></div>
<div href="<?php echo $product_flypage; ?>"    class="AJAX_detail_
link"></div>
</div>
```

3. Save the browse template file.
4. From **Extensions | Module Manager**, click on **VirtueMart AJAX Updater**.
5. In the **Module: [edit]** screen, select **No** in the **Show title** box, select **Yes** in the **Enabled** field, and select **Special** in the **Access Level** field. Read the instructions in the **Description** field and configure it accordingly:

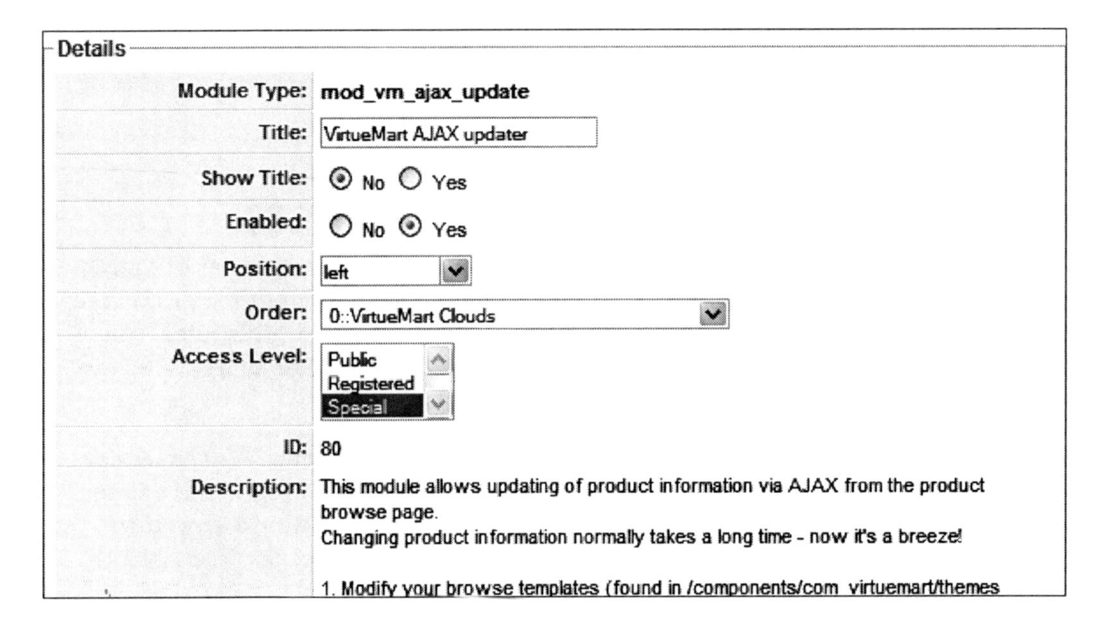

6. Click on the **Save** icon to save the settings.

When the modifications above have been made and the module is enabled, you can login to the shop's frontend using the administrator account. Then, click on a product category from the shop menu and the products in that category will be listed. In the list you will find the fields for updating:

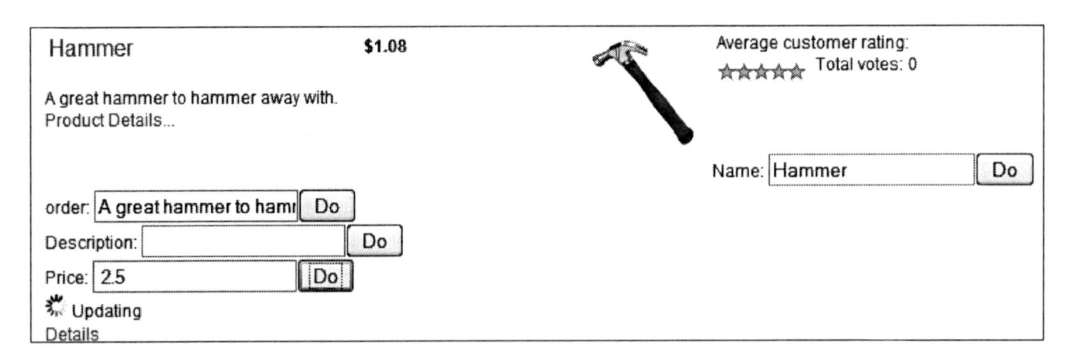

The **Description** and **Price** fields are not filled by default. However, you can type the new value for these fields and click on the **Do** button to update the information. The updating will be done using an AJAX call, without refreshing the page.

For more information on configuring and troubleshooting this module, please visit `http://tinyurl.com/vm-ajax-update`.

Adding some spice to the shop

By default, the modules in VirtueMart are not too spicy. They just work. However, you may like to add some spice and make your shop more attractive. The following sections show you how to use some extensions for this purpose.

Spicy cart

The VirtueMart module shows the number of items and the total price as cart contents. Instead of this, you may like to show the cart contents with images and the total price. You can do this by installing the S5 Column Cart available at `http://www.shape5.com`. Once downloaded, installed, and enabled, the cart items will be displayed as shown in the following screenshot:

Slideshow with product images

We have also seen that there is a VirtueMart module for showing random and scrolling products. You can spice it up by adding another third-party module named **VM Piclens Module**, available at `http://design-joomla.eu/joomla-news/cooliris-formerly-piclens-module-for-virtuemart.html`. This module displays slideshows using VirtueMart product images. When the items in the module are clicked, it displays a slideshow with product image and the details of the product:

PicLens works fine if you also install the PicLens plugins, available at the same site, and enable those. When the PicLens plugin is installed, the slideshow effect can also be used in the content items.

Including modules in content items

So far, we have seen so many modules and these modules provide a lot of information. You may also wish to use this information in the content items of your site. You can do this by using a nice plugin available at `http://www.nonumber.nl/modulesincontent`. The **Modules in Content** plugin allows you to include one or more Joomla! (and VirtueMart) modules in the content items (for example, in news items or articles).

Download the package and install it from **Extensions | Install/Uninstall**. Once installed, go to **Extensions | Plugin Manager**. You will now see the list of the plugins installed on your site. Find and click on the **System - Modules in Content** plugin. That brings the plugin configuration page. In the plugin configuration page, select **Yes** in the **Enabled** field. The plugin specific settings are in the **Plugin Parameters** section:

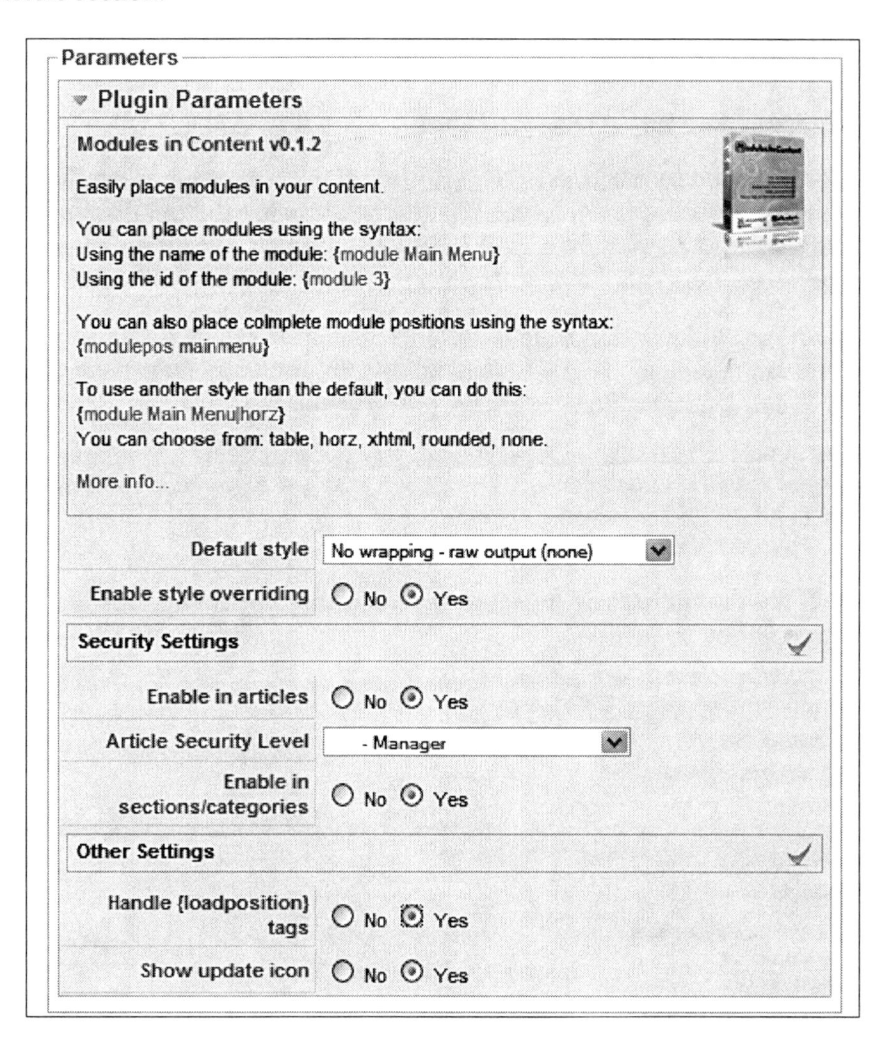

As you can see, the parameter section explains how to use this plugin. It has two forms of syntax: `{module Module Name or id}` or `{modulepos module position name}`. For example, we want to show the **Latest Products** module in an article. In that case, we can simply type `{module Latest Products}` in that article. It will include the products displayed in the **Latest Products** module.

The plugin can display the output in five formats, and you can select your preferred format from the **Default style** drop-down list. The options available in this drop-down list are:

- No Wrapping—raw output (none)
- Wrapped by table—Column (table)
- Wrapped by table—Horizontal (horz)
- Wrapped by Divs (xhtml)
- Wrapped by Multiple Divs (rounded)

Let us select **Wrapped by Multiple Divs (rounded)** from the drop-down list. The word in brackets indicates that you can use this while using the plugin syntax. For example, you want to display the Latest Products module's output as a vertical column. Therefore, the syntax will be `{module Latest Products|table}`.

In the security and other settings section, choose the appropriate options and click on the **Save** icon in the toolbar. That will activate the plugin, and you can start using the plugin. For example, we publish an article with the following text:

```
We have added a lot of new products to our catalog. All these products
have some fascinating characteristics, and we hope you will enjoy
having this products from our store.
{module Latest Products}
```

As the article above will include the latest products module, it will look like the following screenshot:

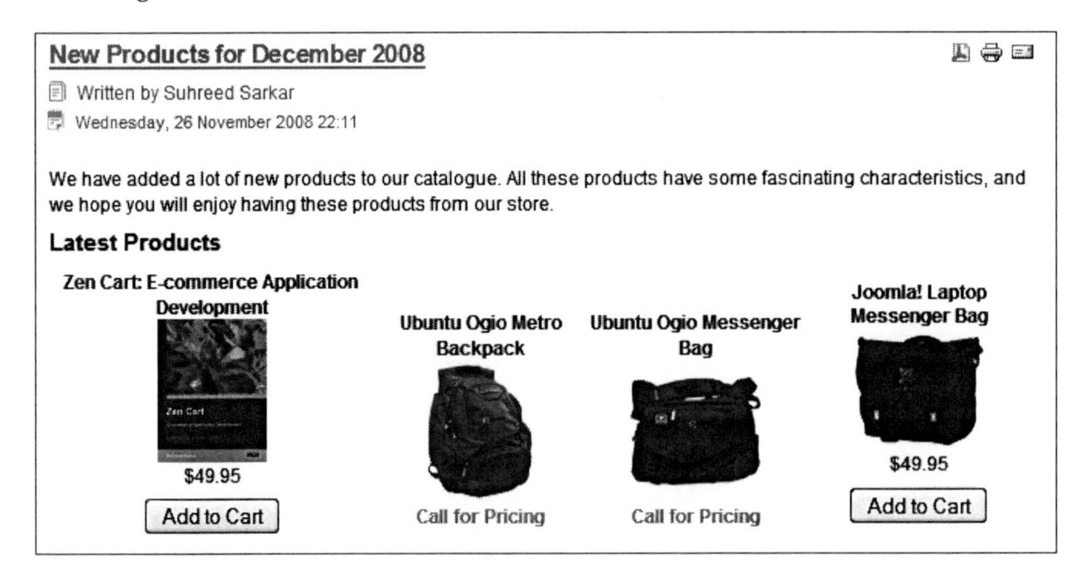

As you see, this plugin can perform a very useful function on your site. You can make one content item and include the modules wherever needed. Therefore, the modules will be displayed in the way you want to display those.

> The structure of VirtueMart modules are the same as that of Joomla! modules. However, as VirtueMart modules are ported from a phpShop script, these modules are not perfectly compliant with the Joomla! modules. For example, the VirtueMart modules use a separate database connection class than Joomla!'s default database connection and management class. The specific programming pattern for VirtueMart is discussed in the *VirtueMart Developer Manual*, which can be downloaded from `http://www.virtuemart.net`.

Summary

In this chapter, we have explored how to extend VirtueMart's functionalities using third-party extensions like modules, plugins, and components. First, you have learned about using CSVImproved for exporting and importing VirtueMart's catalog items. This excellent component can help building the catalog offline, and merge the product information provided by different vendors.

You have also seen how to use other modules to display a product tag cloud, use testimonials, use commenting on products, use a wholesale component so that orders can be fulfilled by wholesalers, and using the JShare module to share your news and product information through social networking and bookmarking sites. You have also learned about using the AJAX Product Update module for updating the information of multiple products using AJAX.

Later in the chapter, we saw how we can make our site more attractive by using some other extensions. We have seen how to use the S5 Column cart and PicLens slideshow module. Finally, we have learned about a magical plugin which can include any module in a content item.

We are in the final stages of building our VirtueMart shop, and in the next chapter, we will be learning about some important things, *Maintenance and Troubleshooting of VirtueMart Store*.

10
Maintenance and Troubleshooting

After building any web application, you need to maintain and troubleshoot it regularly. The Joomla! and VirtueMart store built so far is not an exception. For smooth running of the shop, you need to regularly carry out several maintenance tasks, and also troubleshoot them, if a problem arises. In this chapter, we are going to learn about the necessary maintenance tasks for a Joomla! and VirtueMart online store, and common problems with their solutions. On completion of this chapter, you will be able to:

- Move the shop to your server after building it on your local computer
- Back up and restore files and databases for a Joomla! and VirtueMart store
- Audit security of your site and take necessary measures to harden security
- Identify and troubleshoot common problems
- Find out solutions from online forums

We assume that you have already built the Joomla! and VirtueMart store following the instructions given in the previous chapters. In this final chapter, we are going to transfer that local site to an online web server and learn about maintenance and troubleshooting that online site.

Uploading the local site to web server

From the very beginning of the book, we started building our Joomla! and VirtueMart web site on our local web server. So far, we have built it on a WAMP server or on a LAMP server. It is now time to host this site on an online web server, so that visitors from around the world can access this site and buy our products. We can do this in two ways: transferring the files manually by FTP, recreating the database, and reconfiguring the `configuration.php` file, or by a more automated way using JoomlaPack.

Transferring local site by FTP

When there is no other way, you can start transferring the local site to the online web server and attempt to reconfigure it manually. In this process, we need to transfer the files to the web server using FTP, export the database into a `.sql` file and recreate it on the web server, and finally reconfigure the Joomla! settings.

Step1: Transferring site files

As you are developing the Joomla! and VirtueMart web site, it is expected that you have a plan to host it online, and have already rented or arranged for an online web server which fulfills the requirements for both Joomla! and VirtueMart.

When you have a hosting account, you generally get FTP access to upload your files to the site. Use any FTP program, such as FileZilla FTP client, and upload the files on the application root on your computer. For example, we have created the local site at `E:\www\bdosn\` folder. Therefore, we need to upload all of the files in this folder to our web root on the web server (for example, `/home/username/public_html/` directory on a Linux server).

For downloading the FTP client and learn about using FTP clients to upload files, please consult this web site `http://filezilla-project.org/`.

Step 2: Dumping and recreating a database

As you know, the Joomla! and VirtueMart contents are stored in a database, you need to recreate the same database on the online web server. For doing this, follow the steps below:

1. Open your browser and point it to `http://localhost/phpmyadmin`. This shows the **phpMyAdmin** screen.
2. From the **phpMyAdmin** screen, click on the **bdosn** database, and then on the **Export** tab. This brings the **Export** configuration screen:

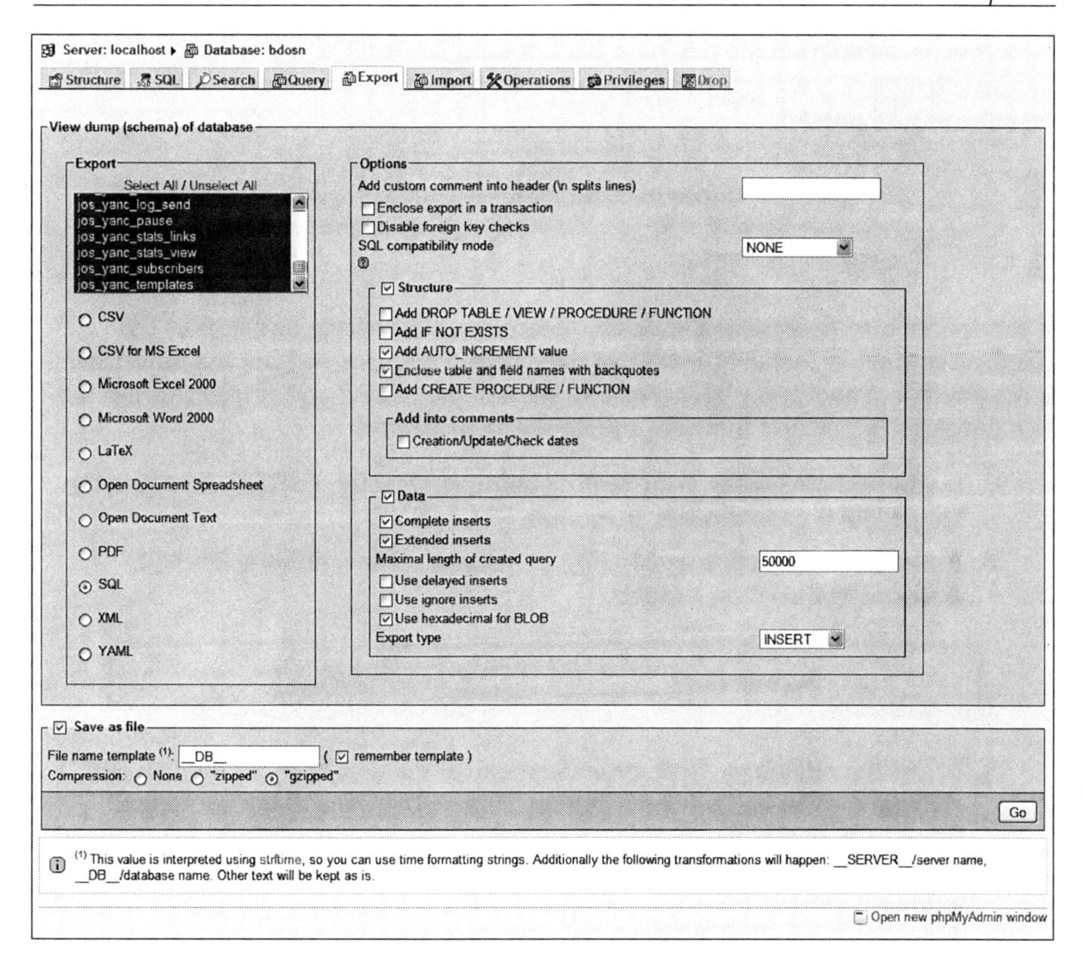

3. In the **Export** section click on **Select All** and **SQL**.
4. In the **Structure** section, check **Structure, Add AUTO_INCREMENT value**, and **Enclose table and field names with backquotes**.
5. In the **Data** section, check **Data, Complete inserts, Extended inserts**, and **Use hexadecimal for BLOB**.
6. Check the **Save as File** option. In the **File name template** type **__DB__** (that is, two underscores placed before and after DB), and check **gzipped** in the **Compression** field.
7. Click on the **Go** button to export the database structure and data.
8. After a few seconds, your browser will ask you to save the file or open it with some application. Select the option to save the file on your computer. The file will be saved as `bdosn.sql.gz`.

Now, we have exported the database file from phpMyAdmin. If you have not installed phpMyAdmin, or prefer to use command line, then use **mysqldump** command.

For more information on using the **mysqldump** program, consult MySQL Reference Manual at `http://dev.mysql.com/doc/refman/5.1/en/mysqldump.html`.

It is now our turn to recreate the database on our online server and import the database content to that database from the dump file `bdosn.sql.gz`. As most Linux hosts provide cPanel and phpMyAdmin, we will use cPanel and phpMyAdmin for this purpose. To perform this task, follow the steps below:

9. Login to cPanel using your hosting account. Usually, the URL for cPanel is `http://www.yourdomain.com:2082`.
10. From the cPanel, click on **MySQL Databases**. This will bring **MySQL Account Maintenance** screen:

New Database: [ ] [Create Database]

11. In the **New database** field, type the name of the database, say **bdosn**, and click on the **Create Database** button. This will create a database named **bdosn**. On shared hosting, generally, the user account name is also prefixed with this name. For example, for my server the database name becomes **suhreed_bdosn**:

Current Users:
suhreed_bdosn Delete
suhreed_borhan Delete

Username: [ ]
Password: [ ] [Create User]

12. In the **Current Users** section, you will see the available database user names. We will create another account for this new database. Type **bdosn** in the **Username** field and a password in the **Password** field. Then, click on the **Create User** button. Like the database name, a new user will be created with the username **suhreed_bdosn**:

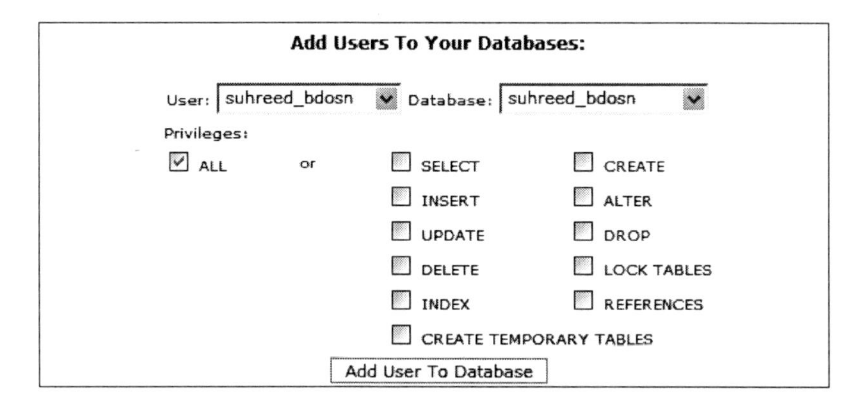

13. Now, it's time to assign permissions to this user so that this user can connect to the database and use it. In the **Add Users To Your Databases** section, select **suhreed_bdosn** from the **User** drop-down list, and **suhreed_bdosn** from the **Database** drop-down list. In the **Privileges** section, check **ALL** and click on the **Add User to Database** button.
14. Now, look at the bottom of the **MySQL Account Maintenance** screen and click on the **phpMyAdmin** link. This opens up **phpMyAdmin**.
15. In the **phpMyAdmin** window, click on the **suhreed_bdosn** database and then on the **Import** tab. That shows the import window:

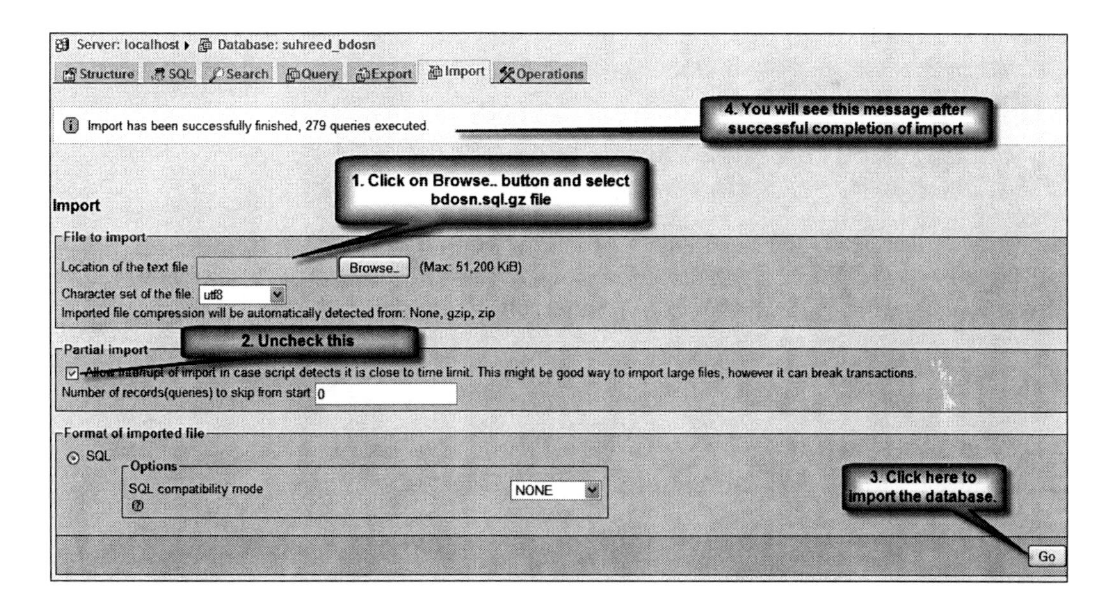

16. Click on the **Browse** button and select the database dump file, that is, bdosn.sql.gz. Uncheck **Allow interrupt of import in case of ...** , and finally click on the **Go** button.

Based on the content you have added to database, it may take some time to upload and execute. After finishing executing the query, it shows a message on the same window showing the number of queries executed to successfully import the dump file.

The database is now ready. You can see the tables to the left pane. Click one or two tables to see whether they resemble the tables on your local host. The next step will be to configure the Joomla! configuration file so that Joomla! can use this database.

Step 3: Reconfiguring Joomla! and VirtueMart

Once you have uploaded the Joomla! and VirtueMart site files, and recreated the database on online server, you need to reconfigure Joomla! so that it can use the new paths and database. As you know, Joomla!'s initial configuration for connecting to a database and paths are stored in the ./configuration.php file. When all of the files are uploaded, you can find it at the root of the directory, where you have uploaded all the files. For example, we have uploaded the files to the ./public_html/bdosn/ directory. Therefore, the path of configuration file will be ./public_html/bdosn/configuration.php.

You can open this configuration.php file from your local host, and then replace the one on the remote server. Open this file with your favorite text editor and find the following lines:

```
var $log_path = 'E:\\www\\bdosn\\logs';
var $tmp_path = 'E:\\www\\bdosn\\tmp';
```

As we have uploaded the files to the ./public_html/bdosn/ directory on our remote server, the path for logs and temporary files will be relative to this new directory. Therefore, change the above lines as follows:

```
var $log_path = './public_html/bdosn/logs';
var $tmp_path = './public_html/bdosn/tmp';
```

This is all about changing paths. Now, we can look into the database connection. Find the following lines in the configuration.php file:

```
var $dbtype = 'mysql';
var $host = 'localhost';
var $user = 'root';
var $db = 'bdosn';
var $dbprefix = 'jos_';
```

The first two lines will remain same, as our database type is still MySQL and the script can connect to the database using the **localhost** name. Here, we have used root user to connect to database, which does not contain any password. But on our active site, we have a different username and password for connecting to the database. Therefore, change the above lines as follows:

```
var $dbtype = 'mysql';
var $host = 'localhost';
var $user = 'suhreed_bdosn';
var $password = 'xyz***';
var $db = 'suhreed_bdosn';
var $dbprefix = 'jos_';
```

You may also like to recheck the settings for mail. Find the following lines in the `configuration.php` file:

```
var $mailer = 'smtp';
var $mailfrom = 'suhreedsarkar@gmail.com';
var $fromname = 'Bangladesh Open Source Network';
var $sendmail = '/usr/sbin/sendmail';
var $smtpauth = '0';
var $smtpuser = '';
var $smtppass = '';
var $smtphost = 'localhost';
```

You may like to use `sendmail` as the mailer, as it is available on your remote server. Therefore, change the highlighted lines (`$mailer` and `$sendmail`) as follows:

```
var $mailer = 'sendmail';
var $mailfrom = 'suhreedsarkar@gmail.com';
var $fromname = 'Bangladesh Open Source Network';
var $sendmail = '/usr/sbin/sendmail';
```

If you are using an SMTP server, then provide the SMTP server's fully qualified domain name, such as `mail.suhreedsarkar.com`, and credentials for authentication.

Once these changes have been made, save the file and upload it to your remote server, replacing the `configuration.php` file on the remote server, that is, `./public_html/bdosn/configuration.php`. Try connecting to your web site using the the appropriate URL (for our case, it is `http://www.suhreedsarkar.com/bdosn/`). If the database name, username, password, and paths are correct, the site will work fine.

Faster relocation using JoomlaPack

The site relocation, or transferring local site to remote web server, described earlier is easy, but time consuming. If you have tried it by this time, you know how much time it takes to upload the files. There are more than 8,000 files to upload for such a Joomla! site and VirtueMart shop. Uploading these files may take hours depending on the speed of your Internet connection. There is another way to make it faster, and that is using a third-party Joomla! component named JoomlaPack.

JoomlaPack is a free component for Joomla! which can be used for backing up and restoring Joomla! sites, as well as for relocating Joomla! sites to different servers. You can download JoomlaPack and its documentation at `http://joomlacode.org/gf/project/jpack/frs/`. You can install this component from the **Extensions | Install/Uninstall** screen of Joomla!'s administration panel.

On your local Joomla! and VirtueMart site, install JoomlaPack and go to **Components | JoomlaPack**. That shows the JoomlaPack control panel. Click on the **Backup Now** icon. It will start the **JoomlaPack:: Backup Now** screen:

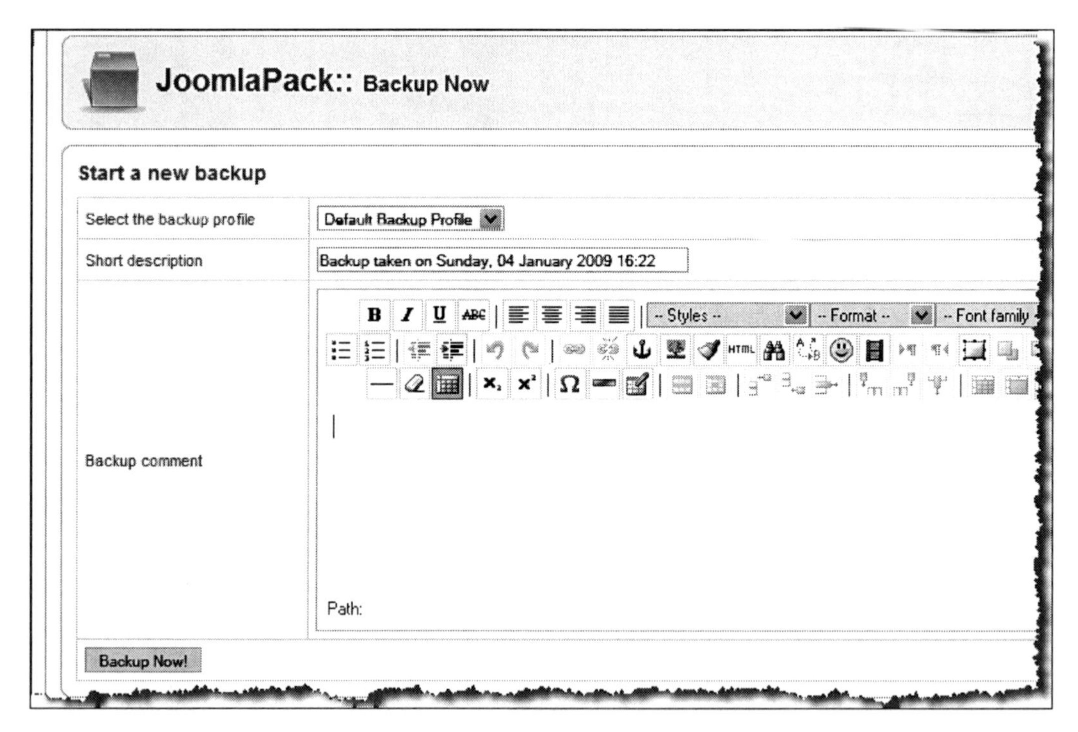

Enter the backup comments and click on the **Backup Now** button again. That will start backing up the database and files, and display the status. You must not navigate away from this page until the backup is finished:

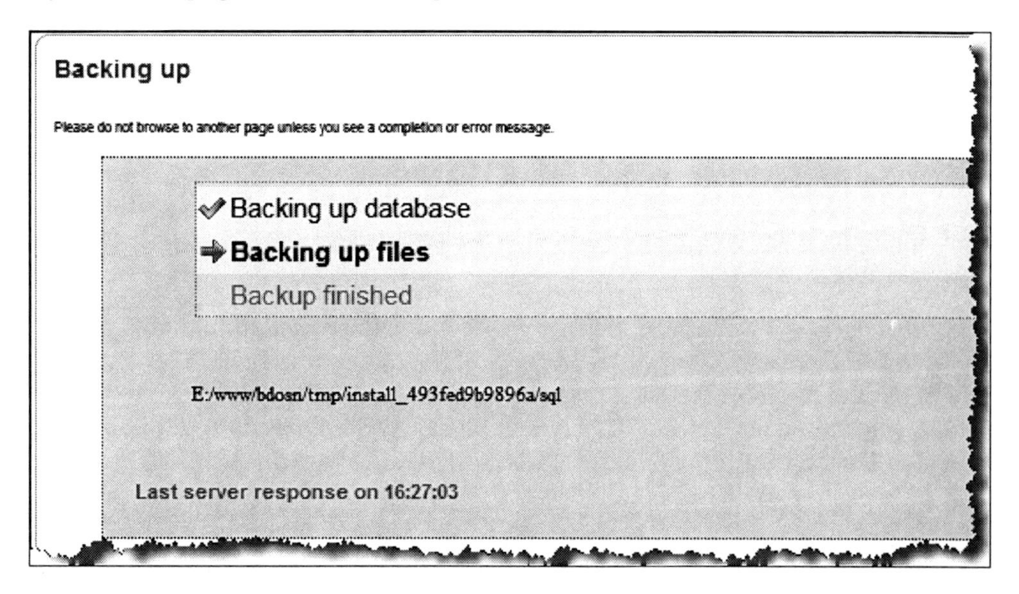

On successful completion of the backup, you can see the **Backup Completed Successfully** screen:

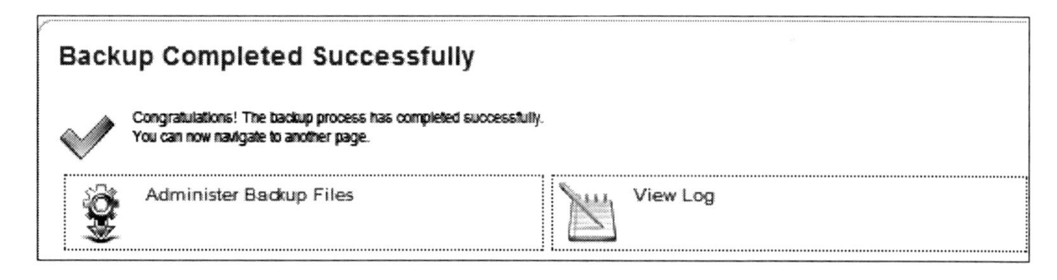

To view the backup files, click on the **Administer Backup Files**. That shows the list of backup files:

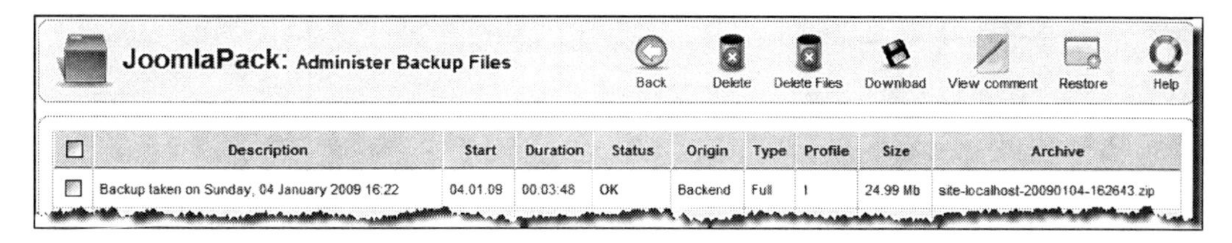

Select the latest backup file and click on the **Download** icon in the toolbar. That will download the backup file to your computer. Save the file in a convenient place. We will need this file again after some time.

While downloading JoomlaPack, also download the documentation and `kickstart-2.0.1.zip` file. Actually, this Kickstart file will do the magic for us during relocation. Now, we just need to upload the backup file (zipped) and the `kickstart.php` file to the remote web server's web root. For example, we have created a sub-domain `http://bdosn.suhreedsarkar.com` which will redirect to the `./public_html/bdosn/` directory. Therefore, we need to upload the downloaded backup file (something named as `_www_bdosn_administrator_component_....zip`) and `kickstart.php`.

When the files are completely uploaded, we can start the installation. Point your browser to the Kickstart file `http://bdosn.suhreedsarkar.com/kickstart.php`. This will initiate the **JoomlaPack Kickstart** wizard. First, select the backup archive from the drop-down list, select **AJAX (refreshless), Write Directly to Files,** and then click on the **Start** button. It will extract the files from the backup archive:

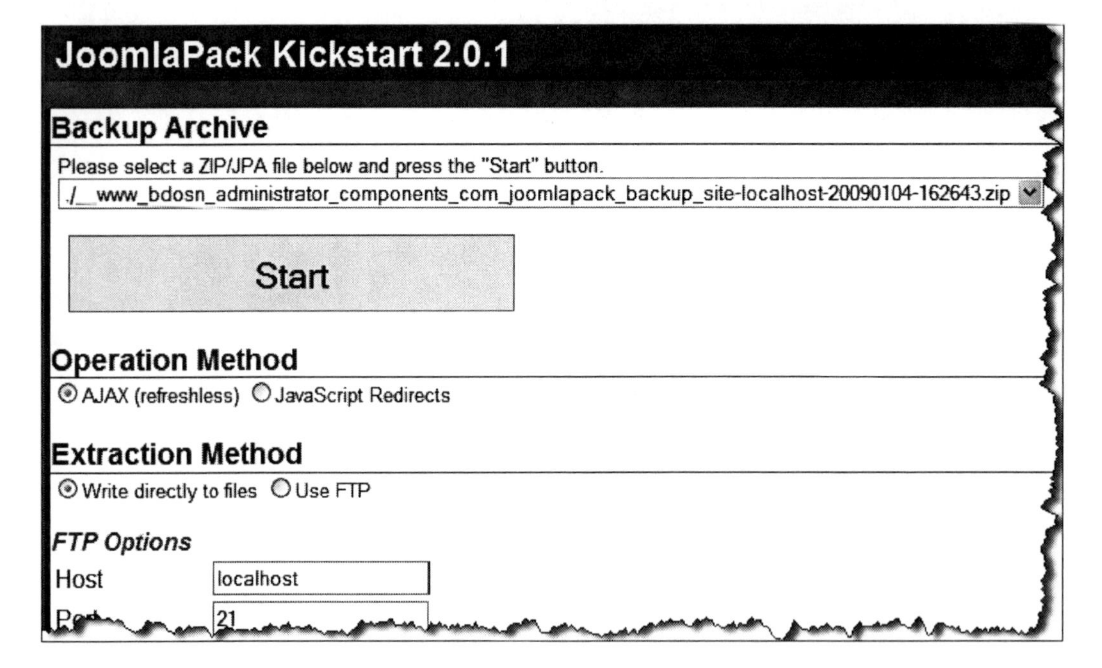

JoomlaPack Kickstart will show the file processing progress. After extracting all of the files from the zipped archive, it will display the page as shown in the screenshot below:

There are two links in this window. First, you click the upper link, which will launch JoomlaPack Installer 3 (JPI3). JPI3 is the Joomla! restoration wizard which looks similar to the Joomla! installation wizard:

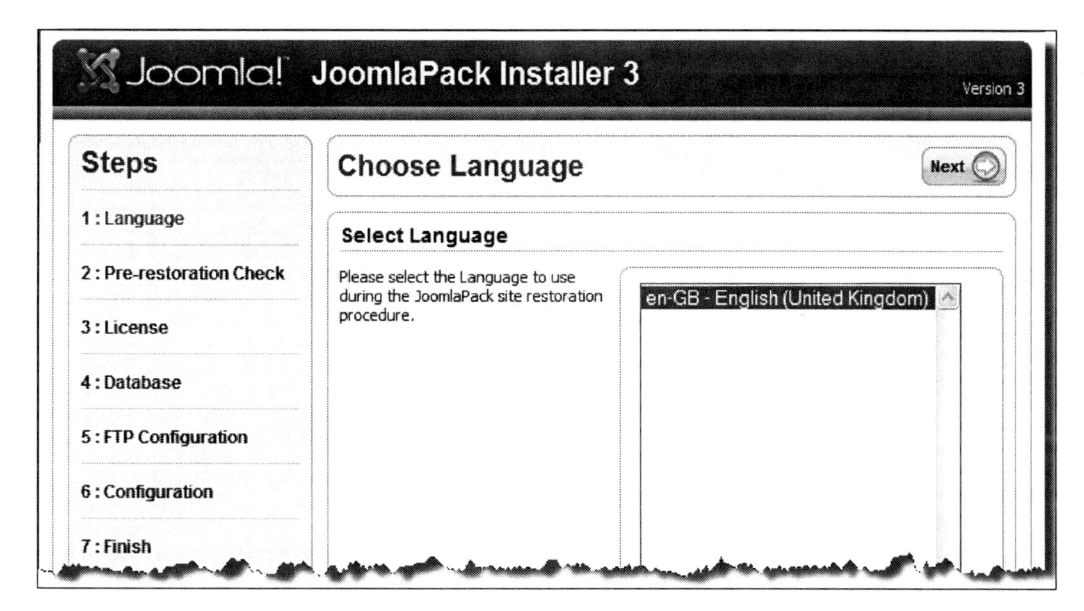

JoomlaPack Installer 3 has seven steps. At present, it only supports English (United Kingdom) as the language of the installer screens. Click on the **Next** button to proceed with restoration of our site. That brings the **Pre-Restoration Check** and displays information about the server environment. All of the variables need to be in green. Any setting the Joomla! restoration requirements will be highlighted in red color. Click on the **Next** button to proceed with the restoration. The **GNU General Public License** will be displayed. Read it, and click on the **Next** button to proceed. You will now see the **Database Configuration** screen, which is similar to database configuration screen used during Joomla! installation:

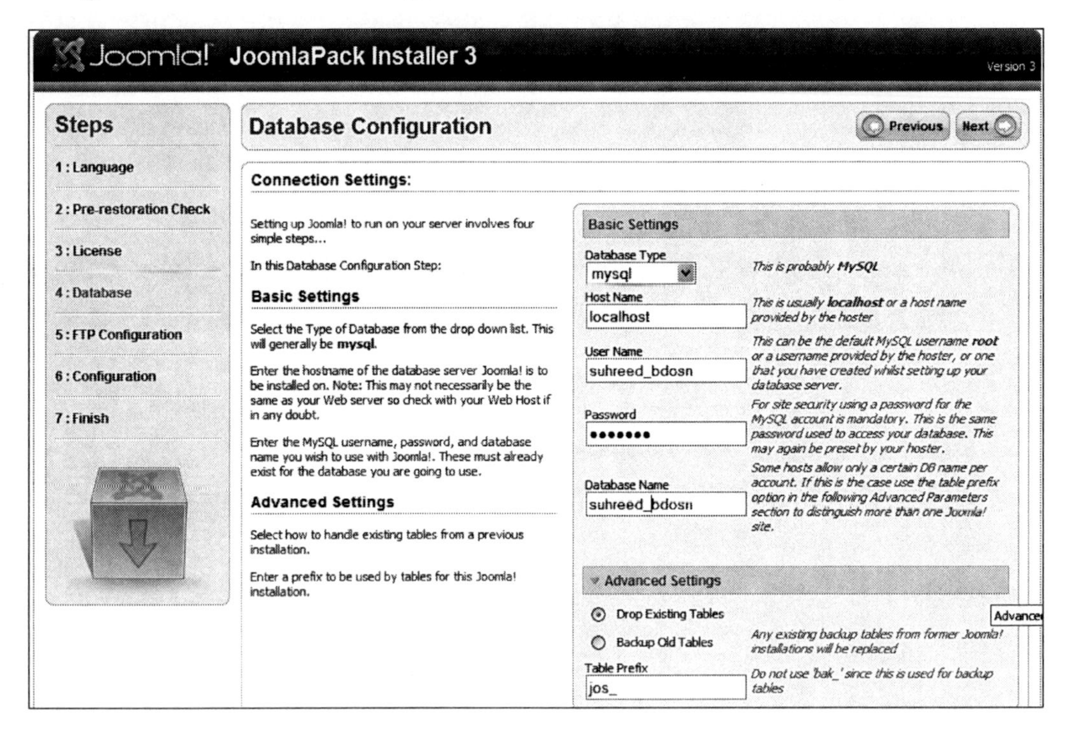

In this **Database Configuration** screen, type the hostname (**localhost**), database user name, password, and database name. As described earlier, you need to create the database user and assign the user permissions to the database. In the **Advanced Settings** section, you can select to backup the old tables or drop the existing tables from the database. You can also specify a table prefix in this section. When the database configuration information has been provided, click on the **Next** button to proceed. This will show the **Database Restoration** screen:

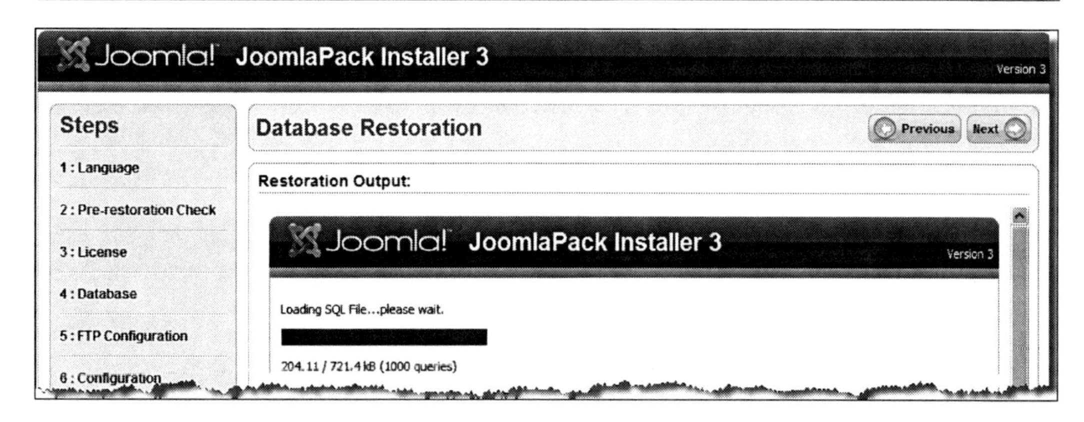

The **Database Restoration** screen will display restoration progress, and when done, it will congratulate you for a successful restoration. After receiving this message, click on the **Next** button. This will show the **FTP Configuration** screen. Select **No** and click on the **Next** button. You get the **Main Configuration** screen:

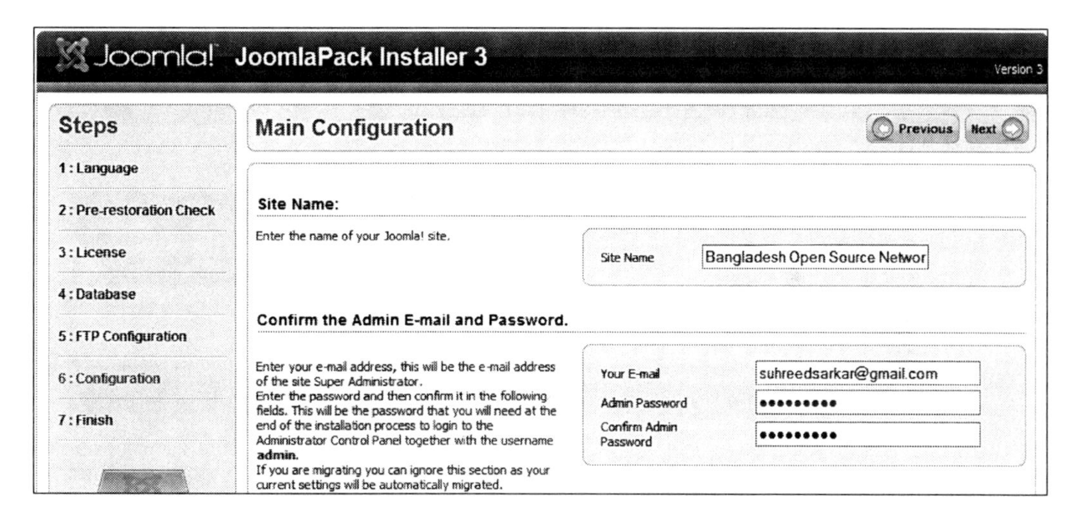

In the **Main Configuration** screen, provide the site name, your email address, administrative password, and confirm the administrative password. When these are given, click on the **Next** button. You will see the **Finish** screen. It instructs to delete the installation directory and browse either to the admin section or to the site's frontend.

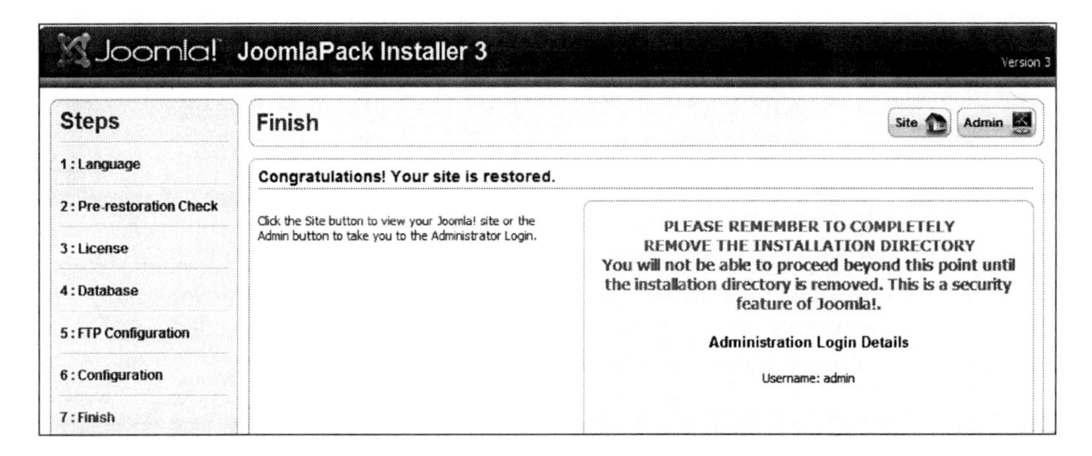

Before clicking on the **Site** or **Admin** button in the **Finish** screen, go back to the **Kickstart** window:

In this Kickstart window, click on the link as shown in the above screenshot. This will delete the `./installation` directory and configure the `.htaccess` file. You will get a message when these are finished. You are now done, and can browse to either the site or admin section. Our site is now online and fully functional.

The JoomlaPack installer can also work in automated mode. Please read the JoomlaPack manual for details on automated restoration and other information.

Backing up files and databases

Backing up your Joomla! site and VirtueMart store will be a regular maintenance task that you need to perform. The importance of backing up site files and your database is obvious. Any time there may be some disaster when the backups will save your work and shop. There are many ways to backup your site files and database. You can backup these either manually or by using some backup tools.

A manual backup consists of two parts: backing up the site files and backing up the database. You can back up the site files by transferring the files from the server to another remote server or local computer. An FTP client can help you do so. You can also backup the database through the **mysqldump** program or more conveniently from phpMyAdmin's web interface. Just create full export of all the database tables and store that `.sql` file in a safe place. In case of an emergency or disaster, you can again upload the files and recreate the database from the `.sql` file. However, the main constraint of backing up manually is that you need to spend more time for this.

As backing up files (and sometimes restoring from backups) will be a regular task, you can save a lot of time by using some backup extensions made for Joomla!. Some of these can generate automatic backups and for some you need manual interventions. We will learn about two backup and restoration utilities for Joomla!: JoomlaPack and LazyBackup.

Using JoomlaPack

By this time, you have learned about JoomlaPack. JoomlaPack was initially designed for backing up and restoring Joomla! site files and databases. It is powerful and we have already seen how it can be used for site relocation. In this section, we will look into some other features like creating scheduled backups.

Once downloaded from `http://joomlacode.org/gf/project/jpack/frs/` and installed in Joomla!, you can configure this component from **Components | JoomlaPack**:

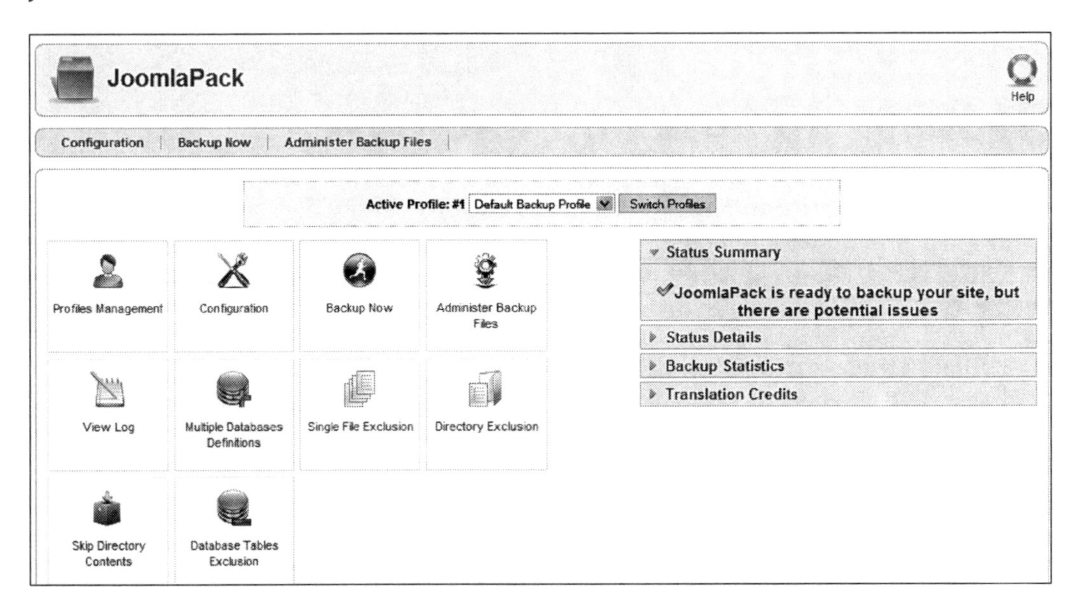

From the JoomlaPack control panel, you can define multiple profiles, configure JoomlaPack, configure exclusion of single file, a directory, or all contents in a directory. You can also configure exclusion of certain database tables. When these configurations are done, you can create a backup of your site files and database by clicking on the **Backup Now** button. In the next screen, you can give a title and comment for the backup archive and again click on the **Backup Now** button to start backing up files and database. In the next screen, you will see progress of the backup process, and when finished, you will be notified.

Once the backup is finished, you can see the backup archives by going to **Components | JoomlaPack | Administer Backup Files**. That screen lists the available backup sets. You can select one or multiple backup sets to delete or download. Selecting a backup set and clicking on the **Delete** button will delete the record of the backup and the backup archive file. The set will not be listed in this screen again. On the other hand, selecting a backup set and clicking on the **Backup Files** button deletes the backup archive but keeps the backup record in the database.

It is always recommended that you keep the backup set offline and away from the server. Therefore, after creating a backup set, select the set, and click on the **Download** icon in the toolbar. That will download the backup archive file, which can be used for restoration or relocation of the site later on:

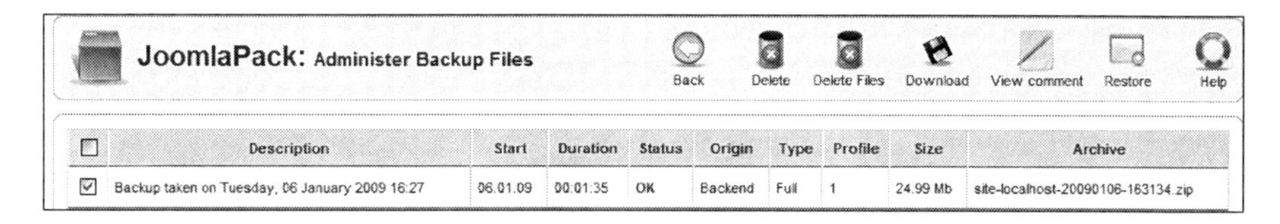

We have seen how to restore from the backup set using JoomlaPack Kickstart and the JoomlaPack Installer. Now, we will look into how to restore a backup from inside JoomlaPack. As you have noticed, in the **JoomlaPack: Administer Backup Files** screen, there is a **Restore** icon. You can start a restore by selecting a backup set and clicking on the **Restore** icon. That will generate a random password and advise you to write it down. Do as instructed. You will need this password during restoration from the backup archive:

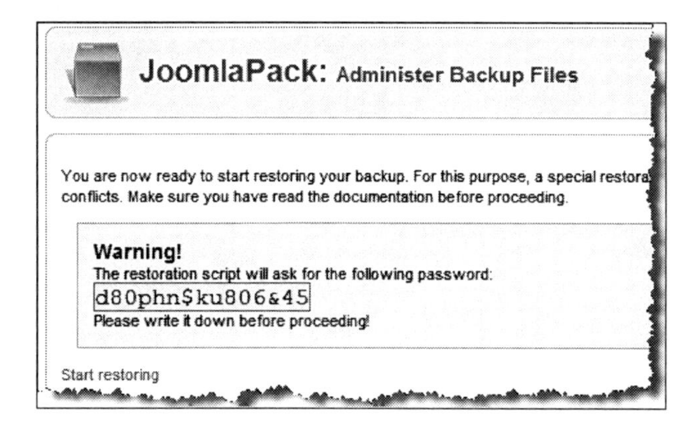

Once the password is written down, click on the **Start restoring** link to proceed with restoration. This will launch the **JoomlaPack Kickstart** and ask for the password. Type the password and click on the **Authenticate** button. This will bring up the **Kickstart** screen where you select the archive file and click on the **Start** button to begin restoration. The files from the archive will be extracted by Kickstart and then it will prompt you to click on the link, which will launch JoomlaPack Installer 3. The remaining steps are the same as described in the site relocation section earlier in this chapter.

By default, JoomlaPack backs up site files and databases. The backup archives generated through JoomlaPack are generally stored in the **backup** sub-directory under the components directory. However, you can change the location and some other important settings from **Components | JoomlaPack | Configuration**. For more information on JoomlaPack configuration and administration, please read the manual available on its site.

JoomlaPack can also perform unattended, timed backups, which are known as frontend backups. This frontend backup is actually running a script using your server's scheduling utility like **cron** for linux and unix hosts. If you are using linux hosting and cPanel, you can schedule the **cron** job by clicking on **Cron Jobs** icon in cPanel. The command to be run through **cron** will be as follows:

```
wget --max-redirect=1000 "http://www.yourserver.com/index2.php?option=
com_joomlapack&view=backup&key=yoursecretkey&format=raw"
```

The above command should be a single line and must contain the `--max-redirect=1000` option. You must provide a secret key in place of the text *yoursecretkey* shown in the above code. You will get this secret key when enabling the frontend backup from the **Components | JoomlaPack | Configuration** screen (seen below). In fact, you must first enable **Front-end Backup** from this screen, assign the secret key, and get the URL to be run by **wget**.

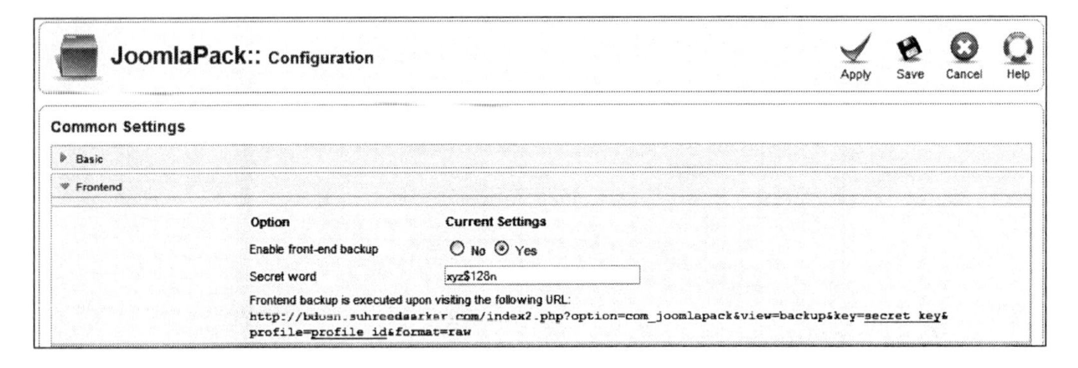

If you schedule **cron** to run at midnight, it will run every night at midnight and perform the backup.

Using LazyBackup

Another useful plugin for backing up a Joomla! database is LazyBackup. As the name implies, it is for lazy administrators who want to get their Joomla! database backed up without doing anything. You can download this plugin from `http://joomlacode.org/gf/project/resurrection/frs/`.

Once installed, you need to configure and enable this plugin. Go to **Extensions | Plugin Manager**, find **LazyBackup** and click on it. That will open up the **Plugin: [Change]** screen:

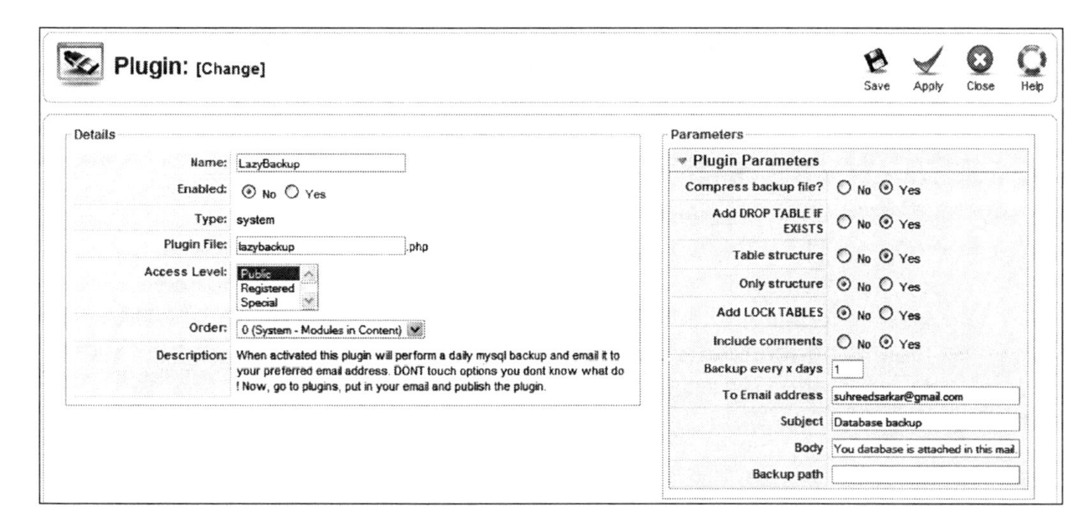

You need to check **Yes** in the **Enabled** field, and configure the parameters. For most of the fields, the default values are fine. However, you need to provide one or more email addresses (separated by commas) in **To Email address** field. The backups generated will be sent to these email addresses and will also be stored on the server. You can configure backup intervals by days. By default, the backup generated is stored in the `./media` directory on the server. However, you can specify a separate path for storing backups.

Remember that LazyBackup only backs up the Joomla! database, not the site files. Therefore, you need to backup the site files separately. Also note that the task performed by LazyBackup can also be done by JoomlaPack, except that JoomlaPack will not mail the backup file to specified email addresses. Only use this plugin when you cannot run JoomlaPack or some other sophisticated backup extension for Joomla!.

Auditing and hardening security

For any web application, security is of great importance, especially for applications like online shops. Joomla! has a track record of being secure, however, administrators still need to be vigilant. The administrators of any Joomla! web site should regularly audit its security and take necessary actions whenever needed. From time to time, the Joomla! community releases security patches and updates, which need to be applied to your site.

VirtueMart works within the security context of Joomla!, and security concerns related to Joomla! also apply to VirtueMart.

There are a few tools for auditing and hardening security in Joomla!. We are going to learn about Joomla! Tools Suite: JTS Components and JTS Snapshot, and GuardXT.

Joomla! tools suite

Joomla! Tools Suite: JTS Components and JTS Snapshot currently run on Joomla! 1.0.x and 1.5.x (legacy mode) and is available for download from `http://joomlacode.org/gf/project/jts/frs/`. This is designed to check pre- and post-installation Joomla! Health, Installation, and Security Audit (HISA). In fact, every Joomla! administrator should use this component to get an audit of their Joomla! installation and take necessary security measures as recommended by this component.

Once installed, you can run the Joomla! Tools Suite and see the overall results by going to **Components | Joomla Tools Suite | Joomla Tools Suite with Services**. You see the default **Home** tab where summary of the audit findings are displayed:

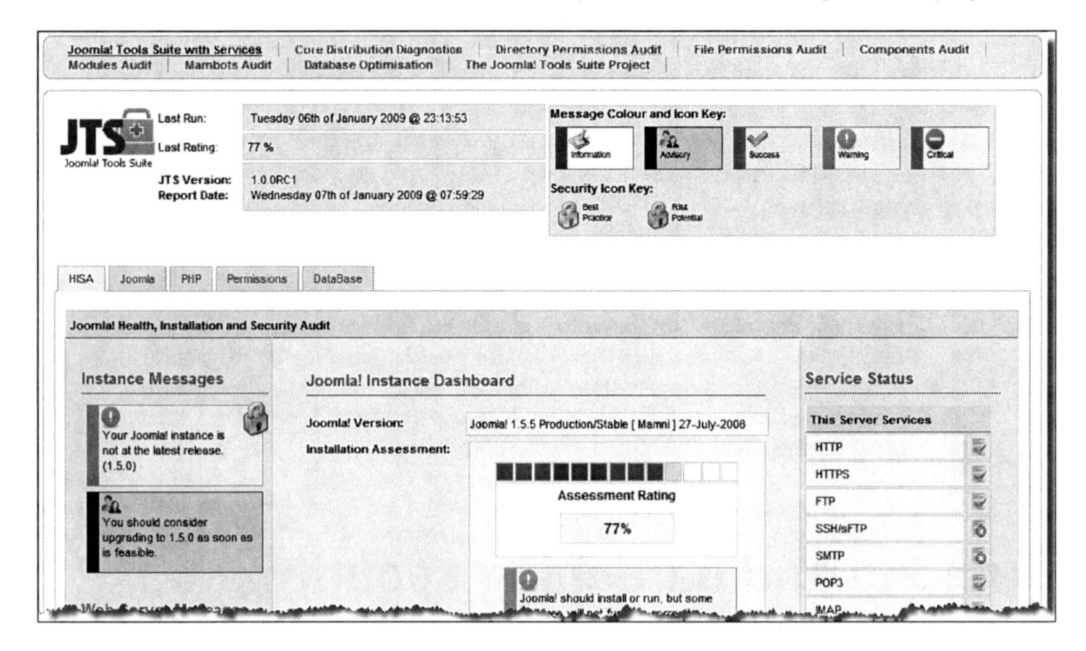

As you can see, the screen shows the summary, different types of warning in different colors, and also shows the overall assessment rating. It also shows the services running and ports open. You can move to other tabs and see detail assessment results. For example, the **Joomla** tab shows settings for Joomla! and their security impact:

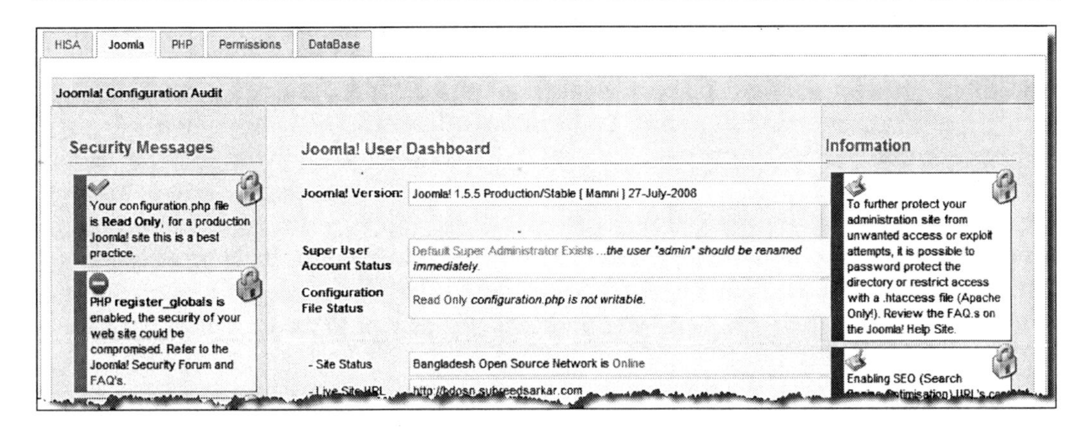

From the **PHP**, **Permissions**, and **Database** tabs, we can get more information about the PHP environment, permissions set on different files and folders, and the MySQL server environment including an integrity check for each table.

From the Joomla! Tools Suite site, you can also download Joomla! Tools Suite Snapshot (JTSSnap) module. Install the module and enable it in **cpanel** position. Once published, the module shows a summary of the security audit which can keep you vigilant about security:

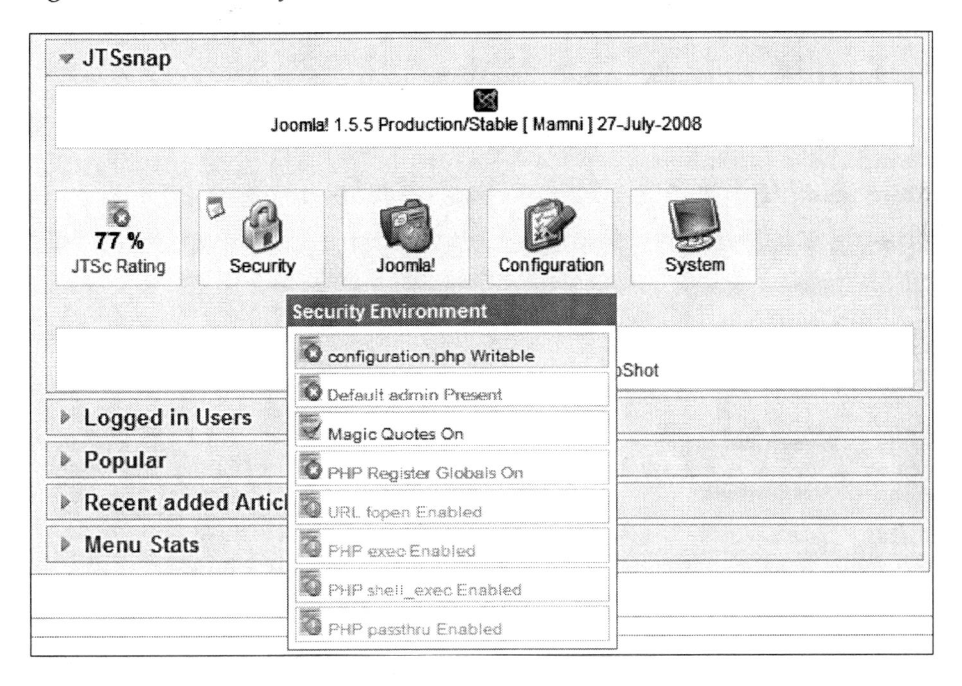

GuardXT

GuardXT is another Joomla! 1.5 native component, which is designed for Joomla! security auditing and configuration. You can download and install this free component from `http://jforms.mosmar.com/`. It does mostly what Joomla! Tools Set does, but it also provides some additional solutions. For example, Joomla Tools Set recommends that you should turn off `register_globals` directive. However, it may be difficult for you to do as you don't know how to do it, or have no access to the `php.ini` file as you are using shared hosting. In that case, GuardXT suggests you to create a local `php.ini` file, and with a wizard, helps you to create a `php.ini` file with recommended settings:

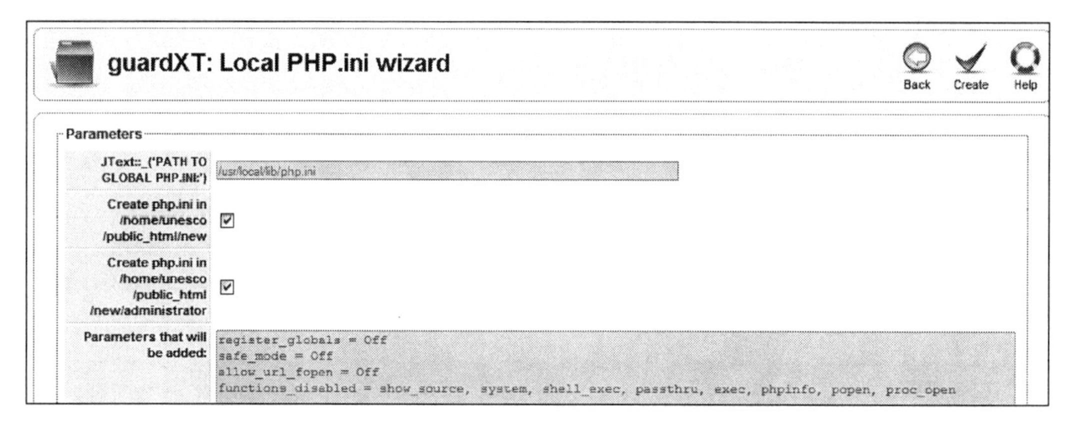

GuardXT also provides version information of the installed extensions and the latest versions available for those extensions. Like Joomla! Tools Suite, it also shows the inappropriate security settings and provides a way to correct them.

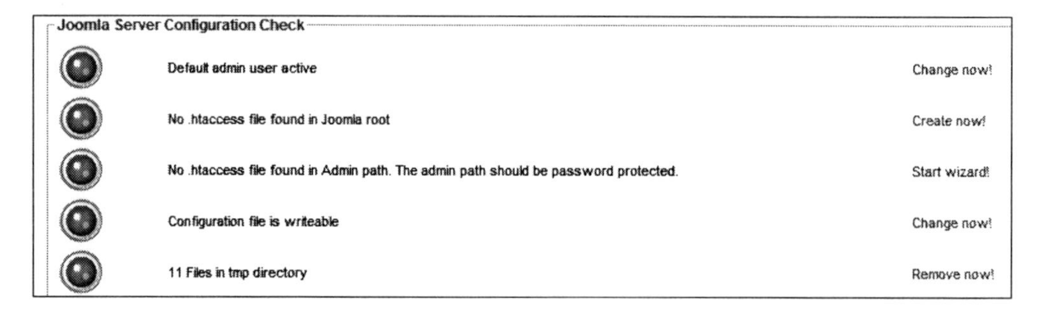

As you can see from the screenshot above, after running **Joomla Server Configuration Check**, it reported that the default Joomla! admin user is active. Clicking the **Change Now** link besides this warning, opens up the user edit screen from where you can rename or block the account. Similarly, you can create a `.htaccess` file with required directives, make the configuration file un-writable, and delete unnecessary files. This is the added benefit of using GuardXT over Joomla! Tools Suite.

Some tips about security

The Joomla! documentation site has many resources for security settings. You must check the security checklist at `http://docs.joomla.org/Category:Security_Checklist`. However, the following are some of the measures you should take to harden security of your Joomla! and VirtueMart installation:

- Just after completion of installation of Joomla!, delete the `./installation` directory completely. New Joomla! versions now make it mandatory to delete this directory because this can be a big threat to your site as people can point their browser to this directory and start installing Joomla!.
- Default the super administrator account in Joomla! named as **admin**. You cannot change this during installation, but after finishing the installation you should create another super administrator account with a different name and delete the default **admin** account, or rename the admin account to something else which is hard to guess.
- Disable `register_globals` directive. Keeping this directive **ON** is a security risk.
- Once necessary changes are made, make the `configuration.php` file read-only.

There are some more issues to be looked at to ensure security. Please read the Joomla! and VirtueMart documentation available online. There is another great book from Packt called *Joomla! Web Security*. You may also like reading that to know more about Joomla! security.

Common problems and troubleshooting

While running your Joomla! and VirtueMart site, it is not unlikely that you will face some problems at one stage or another. For reporting any problem and finding out a solution, you can always visit the Joomla! and VirtueMart forums. Both Joomla! and VirtueMart communities are active and supportive. You need to check the existing posts first, and if you find that solution to your problem is not already provided, you may ask for help. While posting on the forums, please try to be specific, describe the problem as accurately as possible. Providing the error messages and log files can expedite getting the solution from the community.

In general, we can divide the common problems into several categories, namely Joomla!-related problems, VirtueMart-related problems, PHP-related problems, and problems related to other third-party extensions.

Joomla!-related problems

The best place to search for solutions related to Joomla! problems is the Joomla! forum at `http://forum.joomla.org`. First, search the forum for the problem and solution. If you cannot find that a similar problem has been reported, register with the forum and post the problem on the forum. As the Joomla! community is very large, you may expect to get the solution quickly. The more descriptive and clearer your report problem, the greater your chances are to get the correct solution quickly.

The Joomla! forum has many sections, and it is convenient to browse the specific sections. For example, if you suspect that the problem on your Joomla! site is caused by a particular component, then visit the **Extensions | Components** section in the Joomla! forum.

Problems with installation of extensions

In Joomla! 1.5, you can install all extensions from one place, that is, **Extensions | Install/Uninstall**. However, in Joomla! 1.0.x, you need to select a different screen based on the type of extension you are going to install. Usually, that used to create a lot of trouble with installation of extensions as some of the administrators use to try installing modules from the component installation screen, and vice versa. Joomla! 1.5.x eliminates that confusion. However, you may still face some problems during the installation of an extension.

The following are some of the common errors that occur during the installation of an extension:

- You may get an error message saying that direct access to the directory is not possible. This mainly happens due to inappropriate permissions to the directory, or a Joomla! installation with inappropriate access rights. You can solve the problem by setting the appropriate permissions to the directory, especially, write permissions to the group in the component and template installation directories.
- For some extensions, you may be warned that the extension is written for an earlier version of Joomla! and you need to enable the **System - Legacy** plugin for working with this extension. This happens when you are trying to install an extension marked as '1.5 legacy mode'. You must enable the **System - Legacy** plugin from **Extensions | Plugin Manager** to run this type of extensions.

- While installing some extensions, you may be notified that another template, component, module, or extension is at that location. This happens if you have already installed that extension, or another extension in the same name exists. For solving the problem, first uninstall any previously installed extension, and then try installing the extension again. If you cannot uninstall that extension from Joomla!'s admin area, then login to cPanel and delete the respective folder (for example, `./administrator/components/com_links`) from the web server.
- For some extensions, you may get an error message saying that the XML setup file could not be found in the package. It may be due to the fact that the XML file is corrupt, missing, or does not exist at all. For verifying the package, open the zipped package file on your local computer and verify that the XML file exists and is in the correct name and format. You may also get this message when trying to install an extension which is solely designed for Joomla! 1.0.x.

As we can see, most of the installation problems are related to either insufficient permissions or inappropriate package files. You can easily avoid these by checking the appropriate version of package and permissions set to the directories.

SEF problems

Joomla! administrators often face some common errors after enabling search engine friendly URLs. When you enable SEF from the **Global Configuration** screen, Joomla! generates SEF URLs. However, when you choose to use `mod_rewrite`, the SEF may not work as you expected. This may happen due to the fact that you have not renamed the `htaccess.txt` file to `.htaccess`. When you choose to use `mod_rewrite`, you also need to use the `.htaccess` file which comes with the Joomla! installation package. You may also face problems even after renaming the `htaccess.txt` to `.htaccess`. In that case, you may need to check the `.htaccess` file. First, make sure that `RewriteEngine On` is there. Then, check the `RewriteBase` line. This line should reflect your Joomla! root directory. For example, if Joomla! is installed in the `./public_html/bdosn/` directory, then the `.htaccess` file should contain `RewriteBase ./public_html/bdosn/`.

VirtueMart-related problems

In addition to problems directly related to Joomla!, you may also find some problems with the VirtueMart component. The problems can be classified into some broader categories. The following sections describe some common problems which you may face with the VirtueMart extension.

Problem after relocation

After relocating the VirtueMart store from your localhost to remote host, you may find that the VirtueMart product images are not displayed. Even you cannot use the VirtueMart features like adding to cart and checking out. When you tried to click on a VirtueMart product link, it may redirect you to your local site. This happens if you do not change the site URLs in VirtueMart's configuration. To solve this problem, go to VirtueMart's administration panel and click on **Configuration**. Go to **Security** tab:

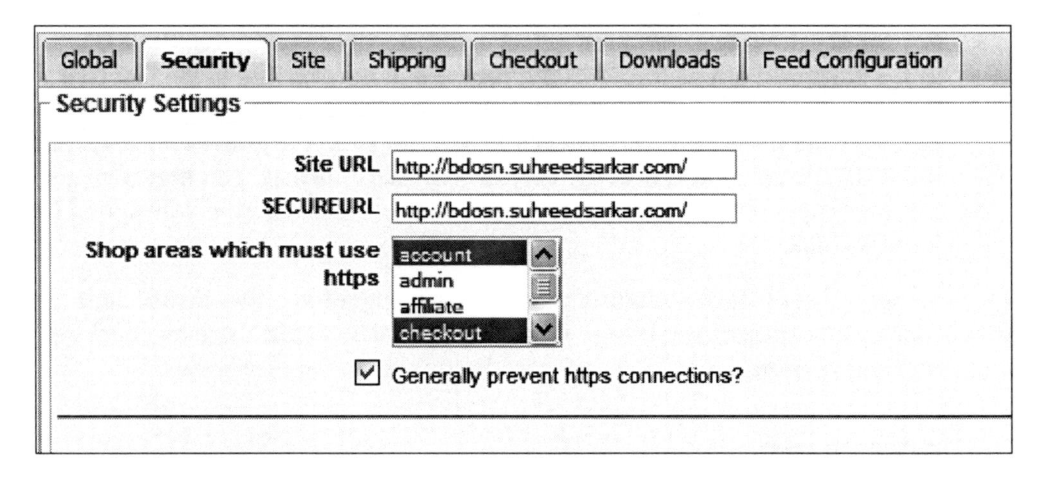

In the **Security Settings** section, you will find two fields: **Site URL**, and **SECUREURL**. Check the settings in these two fields. The values are probably for your localhost. Change these values to your shop's online server address, something like: `http://bdosn.suhreedsarkar.com/`.

Issues related to user registration

Sometimes you may find that users can register to your site but they are not available as customers in the VirtueMart store. This may happen mainly due to two settings: user registration settings in VirtueMart's configuration, and use of the **VirtueMart User Login** module. As we have seen, in the **VirtueMart | Configuration | Global | User Registration Settings** section, we can choose how users for VirtueMart will be created. If **No User Creation** is selected in the **User Registration Type** field, then you may not see the users registered in VirtueMart. On the other hand, if you use Joomla!'s built-in **Login Form** module, that will create a normal Joomla! account, but not a VirtueMart user account. When you are using VirtueMart, disable Joomla!'s **Login Form** and enable **VirtueMart Login Form**.

Showing latest products

While configuring the theme file for VirtueMart, we can specify it to show the featured products, latest products, and recent products on the shop's home page. However, the latest products are not displayed, even though you select it to display. This happens due to a bug in the `./administrator/components/com_virtuemart/classes/ps_product.php` file. In this file, you will find the following code block:

```
function latestProducts($random, $products) {
    return "";
}
```

As you understand, the code block will not show anything. Let us add some codes inside the block so that it selects the latest products from the catalog and displays the product snapshots for those products. Replace the entire code block with the following:

```
function latestProducts($random, $category_id) {
global $VM_LANG;
require_once( CLASSPATH . 'ps_product_attribute.php');
$ps_product_attribute = new ps_product_attribute();
$max_items = 4;
$db = new ps_DB;
$tpl = new $GLOBALS['VM_THEMECLASS']();
$category_id = null;
if($categories) {
     $category_id = vmRequest::getInt('category_id');
   }
$q  = "SELECT DISTINCT product_sku,#__{vm}_product.product_id,
product_name, product_s_desc,product_thumb_image, product_full_image,
product_in_stock, product_url FROM #__{vm}_product, #__{vm}_product_
category_xref, #__{vm}_category WHERE \n";
$q .= "(#__{vm}_product.product_parent_id='' OR #__{vm}_product.
product_parent_id='0') \n";
$q .= "AND #__{vm}_product.product_id=#__{vm}_product_category_xref.
product_i d \n";
$q .= "AND #__{vm}_category.category_id=#__{vm}_product_category_xref.
category_id \n";

if( !empty( $category_id ) ) {
        $q .= "AND #__{vm}_category.category_id='$category_id' ";
}
if( CHECK_STOCK && PSHOP_SHOW_OUT_OF_STOCK_PRODUCTS != "1") {
        $q .= " AND product_in_stock > 0 ";
```

```
}
$q .= "AND #__{vm}_product.product_publish='Y' ";
$q .= "ORDER BY #__{vm}_product.product_id DESC ";
$q .= "LIMIT 0, $max_items ";
$db->query($q);
if( $db->num_rows() > 0 ){
$i = 0;
$latest_products = array();
while($db->next_record() ){
   $flypage = $this->get_flypage($db->f("product_id"));
   $latest_products[$i]['product_sku'] = $db->f("product_sku");
   $latest_products[$i]['product_name'] = $db->f("product_name");
   $price = "";
if (_SHOW_PRICES == '1') {
// Show price, but without "including X% tax"
  $price = $this->show_price( $db->f("product_id"), false );
}
$latest_products[$i]['product_price'] = $price;
$latest_products[$i]['product_s_desc'] = $db->f("product_s_desc");
$latest_products[$i]['product_url'] = $db->f("product_url");
$latest_products[$i]['product_thumb'] = $db->f("product_thumb_image");
$latest_products[$i]['product_full_image']= $db->f("product_full_
image");
$latest_products[$i]['product_id'] = $db->f("product_id");
  $latest_products[$i]['flypage'] = $flypage;
  $latest_products[$i]['form_addtocart'] = "";
  if (USE_AS_CATALOGUE != '1' && $price != ""
    && !stristr( $price, $VM_LANG->_('PHPSHOP_PRODUCT_CALL') )
    && !$this->product_has_attributes( $db->f('product_id'), true )
    && $tpl->get_cfg( 'showAddtocartButtonOnProductList' ) ) {
     $tpl->set( 'i', $i );
     $tpl->set( 'product_id', $db->f('product_id') );
     $tpl->set( 'ps_product_attribute', $ps_product_attribute );
     $tpl->set( 'product_in_stock', $db->f('product_in_stock'));
    $latest_products[$i]['form_addtocart'] = $tpl->fetch( 'browse/
includes/addtocart_form.tpl.php' );
    $latest_products[$i]['has_addtocart'] = true;
   }
   $i++;
  }
  $tpl->set( 'latest_products', $latest_products );
  return $tpl->fetch( 'common/latestProducts.tpl.php');
  }
}
```

In addition to this block, save the `ps_product.php` file. Now, the Latest Products will be displayed on the shop's home page.

Issues related to vendors

While configuring the VirtueMart shop, you have learned that the vendor feature of VirtueMart is still immature and will hopefully be developed soon. The shop owners who try to add other vendors know that it supports only one vendor as they cannot change the vendor. Actually, there is a bug in the SQL query which prevents updating vendor information and associating the vendor to a product. You can easily solve this problem by editing the `./administrator/components/com_virtuemart/classes/ps_product.php` file. In this file, at around line # 503, you will get the following line of code:

```
$db->buildQuery( 'UPDATE', '#__{vm}_product', $fields,
'WHERE    product_id='. (int)$d["product_id"] . ' AND vendor_id=' .
  (int)$old_vendor_id );
```

As you can see, while updating the query, it also tries to insert the old vendor id. This prevents changing the vendors for a product. We can correct this by replacing the above line of code with the following:

```
$db->buildQuery( 'UPDATE', '#__{vm}_product', $fields,
  'WHERE product_id='. (int)$d["product_id"]);
```

Once this change is made to the `ps_product.php` file and saved, you can change the vendor for a product from the product update page in the VirtueMart administration panel.

Issues related to VirtueMart SEF

As we saw earlier, the default SEF feature of Joomla! does not work with VirtueMart as expected. For a work around with this, we suggested using third-party SEF extension such as *sh404SEF*. The component works fine with VirtueMart and multilingual contents including the Joom!Fish extension. However, you need to remember that while enabling the *sh404SEF* component, you must keep the Joomla! core SEF disabled. You can also use *sh404SEF* with or without **mod_rewrite** (`.htaccess` file). Without using **mod_rewrite**, *sh404SEF* will generate SEF URLs which contain `index.php`.

When you use **mod_rewrite**, the URLs do not contain `index.php`. However, using **mod_rewrite** needs some understanding for **.htaccess** file. For using **mod_rewrite** with *sh404SEF*, please consult the documentation available with the component. It describes where you can activate **mod_rewrite** mode and what changes you need to do in the `.htaccess` file.

When you publish **mod_virtuemart**, you can mouse over the link **List All Products**. Clicking on this link shows a listing of all the products available in the store. When you enable *sh404SEF*, you may find that the SEF URL for this link became `http://yourdomain.com/view-all-products-in-shop.html?category=`. As you can see, the URL is not fully SEF, the last portion, `?category=`, is unexpected. This happened due to some bug in the `mod_virtuemart` file. Open `./modules/mod_virtuemart/mod_virtuemart.php` file and go to line #102. You will see the following lines:

```
<a href="<?php $sess->purl($mm_action_url."index.php?
   page=shop.browse&category=") ?>">
   <?php echo $VM_LANG->_('PHPSHOP_LIST_ALL_PRODUCTS') ?>
</a>
```

Note the word `purl` in the code above. Don't think that it's a typo. In fact, it is a web service. PURL means Persistent Uniform Resources Locator. You may learn details about PURL at `http://www.purl.org`.

The error is in the highlighted line above. Let us correct the highlighted line so that it looks like the following:

```
<a href="<?php $sess->purl($mm_action_url."index.php?page=shop.
browse") ?>">
```

Save the file and refresh the home page of your site. Now, the SEF URL for this link becomes perfect, you see `http://yourdomain.com/view-all-products-in-shop.html`.

Another problem in VirtueMart and *sh404SEF* use is that **PDF**, **Print**, and **Email** buttons for the products do not work. This can be solved by editing the `./administrator/ components/com_virtuemart/classes/htmlTools.class.php` file. First, find the following at around line #961:

```
$link .= '&amp;pop=1';
```

Change it to:

```
$link .= '&amp;pop=1';
$link = $mosConfig_live_site."/".$link; /* sh40sef FIX */
```

Find the following at around line #981:

```
$link = $sess->url( 'index2.php?page=shop.recommend&amp;product_id=
'.$product_id.'&amp;pop=1'.(vmIsJoomla('1.5') ? '&amp;tmpl=component'
: '') );
```

Change it to:

```
$link = $mosConfig_live_site.'/index2.php?option=com_virtuemart&
   page=shop.recommend&product_id='.$product_id.'&pop=1'.
   (vmIsJoomla('1.5') ? '&amp;tmpl=component' : ''); /* sh404sef FIX
*/
```

Find the following at around line #997:

```
$query_string = str_replace( 'only_page=1', 'only_page=0',
vmAmpReplace(vmGet($_SERVER,'QUERY_STRING')) );

$link = 'index2.php?'.$query_string.'&amp;pop=1'.(vmIsJoomla('1.5') ?
'&amp;tmpl=component' : '');
```

Change it to:

```
$query_string = ""; /* sh404sef FIX */
foreach($_GET as $opt=>$val) {
      $query_string .= $opt."=".$val."&";
  }
$query_string = str_replace( 'only_page=1', 'only_page=0',
  $query_string);
$link = $mosConfig_live_site.'/index2.php?pop=1&'.$query_string; /*
   sh404sef FIX */
```

With all of these fixes in the `htmlTools.class.php` file, the pdf, print, and email buttons on VirtueMart product pages will work fine.

Issues related to multilingual contents in VirtueMart

As we are using Joomla! and VirtueMart's language files, as well as Joom!Fish for content translation, there may be some problem during translation and showing the translated content. When translating the language files, both for Joomla! and VirtueMart, be careful about missing quotation marks. Whenever you see a `T_STRING` error for a language file, check for such missing quotation marks or special characters.

For Joom!Fish, the translations should work fine. However, you should know about the basic principles of its working. Virtually all content (whatever stored in the database) can be translated through Joom!Fish. Joom!Fish allows you to translate the content through importing content elements. Content elements for Joom!Fish are defined through XML files. The structure of the content, element XML files are straight forward. First, it starts with an XML tag, then the name, author, version, and description will be there. The main section is the `<reference> </reference>` section, under which we refer to the table through `<table name="" > </table>` tag. Table's name must be the name of the table used in database, except the prefix, `jos_`.

Then inside table, we must define the fields which should be translated. For example, we want to create the content elements for VirtueMart vendors. The table used to store vendor information is `jos_vm_vendor`. Therefore, a content-element definition file will be as follows:

```
<?xml version="1.0" ?>
<joomfish type="contentelement">
 <name>VirtueMart Store Information</name>
 <author>Suhreed Sarkar</author>
 <version>2.0</version>
 <description>Definition for VirtueMart component (Store Information)
   </description>
 <reference>
  <table name="vm_vendor">
     <field type="referenceid" name="vendor_id"
           translate="0">ID</field>
     <field type="titletext" name="vendor_store_name"
           translate="1">Store Name</field>
     <field type="text" name="contact_last_name"
           translate="1">Contact Last Name</field>
     <field type="text" name="contact_first_name"
           translate="1">Contact First Name</field>
     <field type="text" name="contact_title" translate="1">
           Contact Title</field>
     <field type="htmltext" name="vendor_store_desc"
           translate="1">Description</field>
     <field type="text" name="vendor_address_1" translate="1">
           Address Line 1</field>
     <field type="text" name="vendor_address_2" translate="1">
           Address Line 2</field>
     <field type="text" name="vendor_city" translate="1">City</field>
     <field type="text" name="vendor_country"
           translate="1">Country</field>
     <field type="htmltext" name="vendor_terms_of_service"
           translate="1">Terms of service</field>
  </table>
 </reference>
</joomfish>
```

This file should be saved as `vm_vendor.xml`. The naming of the filename should be as per the referenced table. As this file refers to the `vm_vendor` table, therefore, its name should be `vm_vendor.xml`. In fact, there is a similar file named `vm_store_info.xml`, but that does not work as the name of the file and the name of the table differs.

For more information on writing content-element definition files, you can consult the Joom!Fish manual available at `http://www.joomfish.net/en/ documentation/developer-docs/30-creation-of-content-elements`.

You should remember another point about Joom!Fish. Whenever you want to use Joom!Fish for translating the contents of a table, the SQL queries should be formed in a way, that it always select the primary key (`vendor_id`) and do not use a table alias. As we are dealing with vendors, the queries for vendor functions are in the `./administrator/components/com_virtuemart/classes/ps_vendor.php` file. Open the file and find the following query (line #413):

```
if ($vendor_id) {
 $q = "SELECT vendor_name FROM #__{vm}_vendor WHERE vendor_id
   ='$vendor_id'";
  } elseif ($product_id) {
   $q  = "SELECT vendor_name FROM #__{vm}_product, #__{vm}_vendor ";
   $q .= "WHERE product_id = '$product_id' ";
   $q .= "AND #__{vm}_product.vendor_id = #__{vm}_vendor.vendor_id ";
   } else {
    /* ERROR: No arguments were specified. */
   return 0;
}
```

Now, change the above block as follows:

```
if ($vendor_id) {
   $q = "SELECT vendor_id, vendor_name FROM #__{vm}_vendor
     WHERE vendor_id = '$vendor_id'";
   } elseif ($product_id) {
   $q  = "SELECT vendor_id, vendor_name FROM #__{vm}_product,
     #__{vm}_vendor ";
   $q .= "WHERE product_id = '$product_id' ";
   $q .= "AND #__{vm}_product.vendor_id = #__{vm}_vendor.vendor_id ";
} else {
   /* ERROR: No arguments were specified. */
   return 0;
}
```

We have now added `vendor_id` in the query. Like this code block, find other queries in the `ps_vendor.php` file and add the `vendor_id` field in the SQL queries. When you have changed the queries and saved the file, you can proceed to installing the content elements and translating the vendor information through Joom!Fish's translator interface.

Summary

In this final chapter, we have seen how to relocate the finished site from a local development server to an online production server. We have used JoomlaPack to successfully relocate the files and database, and have also learned how to use JoomlaPack's backup and restore features. You have also learned about other methods of backing up site files and database.

Later in the chapter, we looked at ways for auditing and hardening the security of a Joomla! and VirtueMart site. You have learned about the use of Joomla! Tools Suite and GuardXT. Both are excellent tools for security auditing and fixing the problems.

In the last part of the chapter, you have seen how common problems for a Joomla! and VirtueMart site can be solved. In general, the best way for getting support is to consult the respective component's forum. However, sometimes a solution may come from other places as well. In this chapter, we have illustrated how some common problems related to Joomla! and VirtueMart can be solved.

With this chapter, the book ends. And you have built a Joomla! and VirtueMart shop. Have good luck and good fortune with your shop!

A
Configuration Options

There are a lot of payment and shipping modules for VirtueMart. These modules have specific configuration options that need to be set. In Chapter 3 of this book, we saw how to configure some important payment and shipping modules. In this appendix, we are going to see the configuration options for other shipping and payment modules for VirtueMart.

Configuring shipping modules

As you saw in Chapter 3 of this book, there are many bundled shipping modules. An administrator can enable all of the modules or only a few. However, it is necessary to learn how to configure all of these modules. In the following sections, we will see the configuration options for these shipping modules. Remember, you configure the shipping modules from the **Store | Shipping Module List** screen in VirtueMart's administration panel.

Australia Post

Enable and configure this module if you are going to use Australian Post shipping facilities. For configuring this module, click on the **Configure Ship Method** link below **auspost**. This will show the configuration options for the **auspost** module. It has two fields to configure:

- **Packing and Handling Fee**: Add your packing and handling fee for this shipping method. This will be added to the charges applied by Australian Post. Shipping charges for Australian Post will be returned from their server when the customer selects this shipping method.
- **Tax Class**: Select a tax class for this shipping method.

Canada Post

For using Canada Post as a shipper, you need to have a Canada Post merchant ID and configure this module accordingly. The following information needs to be configured for the Canada Post shipping module:

- **Canada Post Merchant ID**: This is the merchant ID you get when you register yourself with Canada Post. For more information on getting a merchant ID at Canada Post, please visit `http://www.canadapost.ca`.
- **Canada Post Server IP**: You need to provide the Canada Post server IP. The default setting is fine for the time being, however, you need to check it with Canada Post.
- **Canada Post Server Port**: The default port for connecting to the Canada Post server is 30000. Again, you need to check it with Canada Post as this may change.
- **Canada Post Federal Tax Amount**: Please specify the federal tax amount, which will be applicable for all shipping through Canada Post.
- **Canada Post Provincial Tax Amount**: Please specify the provincial tax rate, if any, which will be applicable for all shipping through Canada Post.
- **Arrival Date Description**: In this box, please provide your message to the customers about the expected arrival date of the shipped products. For example, you may add *Your shipping order will be delivered within 4 working days*.
- **Handling Charge Description**: A brief explanation about the handling charge may be provided in this text box.

DHL

DHL is one of the popular world-wide courier services and you may be willing to use this as your shipping method. For configuring the DHL shipping method, you need to provide the following information:

- **DHL ID**: This is the DHL ID you get when you register with DHL as a merchant. For more information about becoming a DHL merchant, please visit their web site `http://www.dhl.com/`.
- **DHL Password**: This is the password you get from DHL, once you have registered with them. This should be kept secret.
- **Domestic DHL Shipping Key**: DHL provides a separate access key for domestic shipping. Type that access key in this box.
- **International DHL Shipping Key**: Like the domestic shipping access key, DHL also provides a separate access key for international shipping.

- **DHL Account Number**: This is the DHL account number what you get after registration.
- **Too Late to Ship at (24h format)**: This is the time after when it is too late to ship the product on the same day. Specify the time in 24 hour format, such as 1600 instead of 04:00 PM.
- **Use Test Mode**: Before attempting to actually ship through DHL, you need to test the settings. First, configure this module with the required information and select **Yes** in this drop-down list. When you find that the test shipping is working fine, only then should you change its value to **No**.
- **Enable Express Shipping Method**: If you enable the express shipping method, then orders placed by customers can also be shipped using the express method. However, before enabling this method, first check the rates with DHL, as this method costs more.
- **Enable Next Afternoon Shipping Method:** Similar to the express method, this can be enabled if you want customers to choose express delivery where the product will be delivered the next afternoon.
- **Enable Second Day Shipping Method**: Select **Yes** if you want to enable this shipping method. However, first check the rates for this shipping method.
- **Enable Ground Shipping Method**: This shipping method may be enabled as it is often preferred by the customers and it costs much lower than other express methods.
- **Enable Express 10:30am Shipping Method:** This is another express method, for which rates should be checked. If you think customers would like to use it, only then should you enable this method.
- **Enable Express Saturday Shipping Method (Fridays only)**: For orders placed on Friday, express shipping can be attained through this method. Be sure to check the rates before enabling this.
- **Enable International Express Shipping Method**: International customers may like to get their product delivered quickly. Therefore, enabling this will be a good choice.
- **Domestic Package Type**: Select the package type that will be used for domestic shipping. You can either select **Letter/envelop** or **Package**.
- **International Package Type**: Select what type of packaging will be used for international shipping. You can choose **Letter/Envelop**, **DHL packaging**, or **Your Packaging**. If you select **DHL Packaging**, DHL will provide the packaging for the shipped products.

- **Shipping Contents Description (for Intl.)**: For international shipping, you often need to describe what is being shipped. A common statement about the product shipped can be specified here. For example, if you are selling mostly books, then type *Books and Printed Matters* in this field.
- **Weight of packaging**: Specify a packaging weight, which will be added to you product's weight. If the product's weight include the packaging weight, then type **0** in this field.
- **Shopper Group to Use for Duty Values (for Intl.)**: You can create a special shopper group who will use international shipping and get a special price discount. If you don't want to use that group, keep it blank.
- **Additional Protection Type**: You can enable additional protection from this drop-down list. Select **Asset Protection** to insure the products. If you don't need additional protection, then select **Not Required**.
- **Shopper Group to Use for Insurance Values**: You may create a special shopper group for which insurance values will be stored. The name of that shopper groups should be specified here. Keep it blank to not use such group.
- **Default Domestic Insurance Rate**: This is DHL's default domestic insurance rate. This amount is a flat rate and only for the entire package.
- **Default International Insurance Rate (per pound)**: This is DHL's default insurance rate for international shipping. This rate is per pound, which means heavier packages will have more fees for insurance.
- **Tax Class**: The tax class that will be used for this shipping method.
- **Handling Fee**: Specify a fixed amount which will be charged as a handling fee for each shipment.

FedExdc

This shipping module is for using FedEx world-wide courier services for shipping your store's products. You need to have an account with FedEx, and only then will you be able to configure this shipping method module. The following information needs to be given:

- **FedEx Account Number**: This is the account number you get after registering with FedEx.
- **FedEx Meter Number**: This access key is also provided to you only after registering with FedEx.
- **FedEx Server Address**: This address will be needed to get rates and exchange orders. Please check with the FedEx about the exact URL for the server.

- **Tax Class**: Select a tax class which will be used for this shipping method.
- **Handling Fees**: Add a handling fee for each shipment through this method.
- **Allowed Services:** From the list of FedEx services, select the services which you want to offer to your customers. The services you select here will be available to the customers during their checkout and shipping method selection step.
- **Signature Option**: Specify how the product will be delivered. You can choose **Deliver without signature**, **Indirect signature**, **Direct signature**, or **Adult signature**.
- **Rate Display Order**: Select how the rates will be displayed on the shipping method selection step (in ascending or descending order).

Flex

This shipping module is named Flex, which means flexible shipping method. In fact, this method is straightforward as it applies a flat shipping rate and proportional rate after the base amount. The following are the configuration options for this shipping module:

- **Charge flat shipping rate to this amount**: This is the amount of order, up to which flat rate shipping charge will be applied.
- **Minimum Shipping Charge**: Specify the minimum shipping charge, which will be applied up to the order amount specified in the field before.
- **Percentage to charge if total sale is over base**: If the order amount is over the base amount specified earlier, the shipping charge will increase proportionately. Type that proportion (percent) in this field, for example, 7.
- **Fixed Handling Charge**: As usual, for each shipment, you may charge a fixed handling fee.
- **Tax Class**: Select the tax class which will be applicable for this shipping method.

Intershipper

Intershipper gives you the opportunity to use five of the most popular shippers: DHL, UPS, FedEx, US Postal, and AirBorne. Configure this module as follows:

- **InterShipper Username**: This is the username you get when you register with Intershipper service. Check with `http://www.intershipper.com` for more information on their services and registration.

- **InterShipper password**: This is your InterShipper password to access InterShipper services.
- **InterShipper Email**: This is the email address you used to registered with InterShipper. This is required because all correspondents with you will be through this address.
- **Carrier 1 - Invoice - Account Number**: Select a carrier name from the drop down list, then select **Yes** or **No** in the **Invoice** column. If you want an invoice, then select **Yes** , otherwise **No**. In the account number column, you can specify the account name for that carrier. For example, you have an account with DHL that can be mentioned here. This will help you avail their special offers.

  In the same way, select other carriers, and specify whether you need an invoice or not, and the account information with that carrier (optional).
- **Classes of Service**: From the checkboxes, select the services you want to make available to your customers. Services listed here are: **1st Day**, **2nd Day**, **3rd Day**, and **Ground**.

Shipvalue

Shipvalue is a shipping method where shipping rates are calculated based on the value of the order. You can specify shipping charges based on several order value ranges. As seen in the following screenshot, you can configure ten rates, and the tax class for this shipping method:

Shipping Module Configuration: shipvalue.php

Order total value 1:	20.00	Shipping charge 1:	2.95
Order total value 2:	50.00	Shipping charge 2:	4.70
Order total value 3:	70.00	Shipping charge 3:	5.50
Order total value 4:	10000.00	Shipping charge 4:	0
Order total value 5:		Shipping charge 5:	
Order total value 6:		Shipping charge 6:	
Order total value 7:		Shipping charge 7:	
Order total value 8:		Shipping charge 8:	
Order total value 9:		Shipping charge 9:	
Order total value 10:		Shipping charge 10:	
Tax Class	2 (8.25%)		

Standard shipping module

The standard shipping module is your own way of shipping products to customers. When you are using this shipping module, you can create your own shippers and shipping rates to different countries and areas with different package sizes. For using this module, you need to follow the steps below:

1. First, you need to define the shippers you are going to use. You can define shippers from **Shipping | Create Shipper**.
2. When shippers have been created, you can add the shipping rates. This can be done through **Shipping | Create a Shipping Rate**. In creating a shipping rate, you need to provide the following information:
    - **Shipping Rate description**: A descriptive name for the shipping rate.
    - **List Order**: In which order the rate will be displayed.
    - **Shipper**: Select a shipper by which you want to ship the product.
    - **Country**: Select the country or countries for which you are defining the shipping rate.
    - **ZIP range start**: For a large country, you may also specify the area by ZIP range start.
    - **ZIP range end**: For a large country, you can specify a portion of the country by specifying ZIP range start and ZIP range end.
    - **Lowest weight** and **Highest weight:** You can specify the lowest and highest weight for which the shipping rate will be applicable.
    - **Fee**: Specify the fee for shipping the products to the locations specified above and the weight range included.
    - **Handling Fee**: As usual, add a fixed handling fee for every shipment.
    - **Currency**: Select the currency in which the fee will be calculated.

3. You can create as many rates you may need. When all of the rates are created, you can see the list of these rates from **Shipping | Shipping Rates** list:

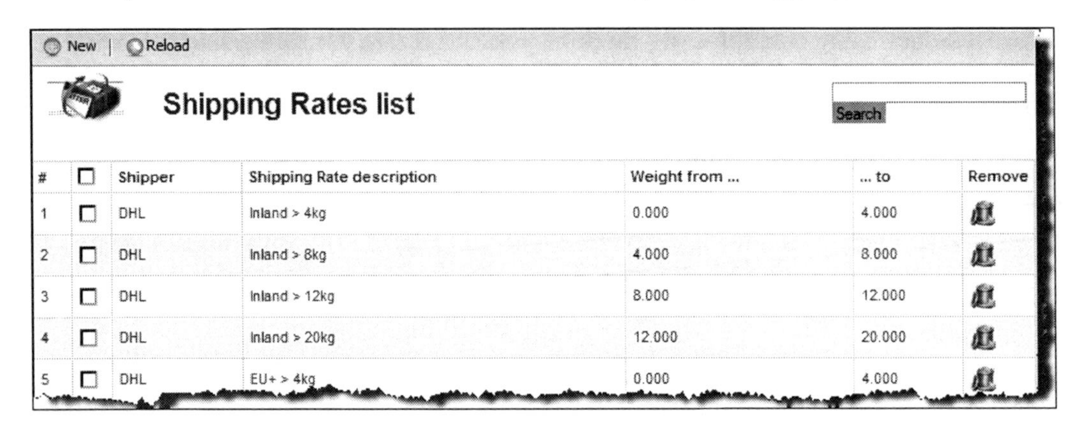

#		Shipper	Shipping Rate description	Weight from ...	... to	Remove
1		DHL	Inland > 4kg	0.000	4.000	
2		DHL	Inland > 8kg	4.000	8.000	
3		DHL	Inland > 12kg	8.000	12.000	
4		DHL	Inland > 20kg	12.000	20.000	
5		DHL	EU+ > 4kg	0.000	4.000	

UPS

United Postal Service is another renowned shipper which can be used with VirtueMart. You need to configure the following options for this shipping module:

- **UPS access code**: This is the access code you get when registering with UPS.
- **UPS user id**: This is your user ID for your UPS account.
- **UPS password**: You need this password to access to your UPS account.
- **UPS pickup method**: Select a pickup method for UPS shipping. This is actually the method for giving your package to UPS. Select one of the options available here: Daily Pickup, Customer Counter, One Time Pickup, On Call Air Pickup, Letter Center, and Air Service Center.
- **UPS Packaging?**: Select what type of packaging you want to use for products shipped through UPS. There are several options provided by UPS, you may choose one or none. Packaging options are: Unknown, UPS Letter, Package, UPS Tube, UPS Pack, UPS Express Box, UPS 25kg Box, UPS 10kg Box. You may see more details about these packaging types by visiting `http://www.ups.com`.
- **Residential Delivery?**: There are two types of delivery, Residential (RES) and Commercial (COM). Charges for these two types are different. Select the type which you want to use. If you choose **Commercial (COM)** delivery, then products will be delivered only during normal office hours.
- **Handling Fee**: Like other shipping methods, you may add a handling fee here.
- **Tax Class**: Select a tax class which will be applied for this shipping method.
- **Ship From Zip Code**: You may enter a zip code here to override the zip code provided by the vendor.

- **Show Delivery Days Quote?**: Check this box if you want to show the days when the product will be delivered.
- **Show Delivery ETA Quote?**: Check this box if you want to show the estimated time of arrival when placing the order.
- **Show Delivery Warning?**: Check this box if you want to show any warnings regarding delivery through UPS.
- **Select Authorized Shipping Methods**: From the list of shipping methods, select the methods which you want to make available to your customers. When enabling these methods, you can also add fuel surcharge as percent. For details of the shipping methods listed in this section, please visit the UPS web site at `http://www.ups.com`.

Before configuring this shipping method module, you should be familiar with the terms and best shipping methods.

USPS

United States Postal Service (USPS) is another popular shipping provider which can be used with online shops. The USPS provides a number of service options and shipping rates. You can learn more details about their services, rates, and terms and conditions at `http://www.usps.com`. In VirtueMart, you need to provide the following information for configuring the USPS shipping module:

- **USPS shipping username**: You get a username for USPS service after registering on their web site.
- **USPS shipping password**: This is the secret password which you need to login to your USPS account.
- **USPS shipping server**: Specify the default USPS shipping server address from where the shipping rate quotes will be retrieved. Consult USPS for getting the correct address.
- **USPS shipping path**: This is the path relative to the shipping server where the shipping API resides. You will get the correct address from USPS.
- **USPS Package Size**: Select a package size. There are three sizes for USPS: Regular, Large, and Oversize.
- **Tax Class**: Select a tax class to be used for this shipping method.
- **Your Handling fee for this shipping method**: Like the other shipping methods, you can add a fixed handling fee for each shipment.

- **Percent to pad weight for shipping package. (Include %)**: Specify a padding weight, in percent, to allow the shipping weight to expand including the package weight. The default padding is 15%, which seems to be adequate for most of the shops.
- **Your International per pound rate for USPS shipments**: You can specify a per pound rate for international shipping through USPS.
- **Your International Handling fee for USPS shipments**: Specify a handling fee for international shipments via USPS.
- **Machinable Packages?**: Select **Yes** if your packages can be processed through machines.
- **Show Delivery Days Quote?**: Select **Yes** if you want to show the number of days required for delivery on the shipping rate quotation page.
- **Domestic Shipping Options**: This section allows the domestic shipping options to be made available to your customers. There are around eleven options, such as USPS Express Mail, USPS Media Mail, and so on.
- **International Shipping Options**: From this section, select the options which you want to make available to your customers for international shipping.

To learn more about the types of shipments, rates, and other terms of service, please visit the USPS web site at `http://www.usps.com`.

Configuring payment modules

In Chapter 3, we saw how to configure different payment modules for VirtueMart. There, we could not discuss the configuration options for all of the payment modules. Therefore, in the following sections, we will look at the detail configuration options which were not covered in Chapter 3. As you can recall, the payment modules can be configured from each payment module's edit screen. You can see the list of payment modules by going to VirtueMart's control panel and selecting **Store | List Payment Modules**.

2Checkout

2Checkout is a popular web-form based payment module. If you have a merchant account at 2Checkout.com, you can activate this payment module in VirtueMart. This is an HTML-form based payment module, and uses the **ps_twocheckout** class for its business logic. Besides setting a shopper group, discount type, minimum and maximum discount amount, you need to set the following specific information for the 2Checkout payment module (from **Configuration** tab):

- **2Checkout.com Seller/Vendor ID**: It's obvious that you'll get a seller or vendor ID and you need to put that ID in this field.
- **2Checkout.com Secret Word**: This is the password for the seller or vendor ID you received from 2Checkout.
- **Order Status for successful transactions**: Select an order status for successful transactions. As this is an online payment processing service, you can select Confirmed for successful transactions.
- **Order Status for failed transactions**: Select an order status which will be set upon a failed transaction. The default setting is Cancelled, and you may set it to Pending.
- **Merchant Notifications**: Select Yes if you want to be notified of every transactions through 2Checkout.
- **Test mode?**: Before using the 2Checkout payment processing module for a production site, you need to test the settings to ensure they are working as you expected. Select Yes to set it to test mode. There will be no actual transactions in this mode. When you find the results satisfactory, set it to No. At this point, actual transactions will start.
- **Extra Info**: This box contains some extra code for working with 2Checkout. Usually, you don't need to change anything here. Be careful about changing anything in this box.

For creating an account, or to know more about the services offered by 2Checkout, please visit their site at `http://www.2checkout.com`.

Credit card (eProcessingNetwork)

This is another module for online credit card processing using eProcessingNetwork. This module uses the `ps_epn` class for business logic, and can support all major credit card types. In the Configuration tab, you need to provide the following information related to the eProcessingNetwork module:

- **Test mode?**: Select Yes to enable test mode. Once testing is successful, switch it to No.
- **eProcessingNetwork.com Login ID**: This is the login ID you get after registering with eProcessingNetwork.
- **eProcessingNetwork.com Transaction Key**: This is the transaction key for the eProcessingNetwork.
- **Request/Capture Credit Card Code Value (CVV2/CVC2/CID)**: Select Yes to capture CVV2/CVC2/CID to verify credit cards.
- **Recurring Billings?**: Select Yes if you want to use this payment processor for recurring billing.

- **Authentication Type**: This is the authentication type used by ePProcessingNetwork. You can select AUTH_CAPTURE or AUTH_ONLY from the list. In the first option, authentication information will be captured by this module. For the second option, only authentication will be done without storing authentication information.
- **Order Status for successful transactions**: Select the order status to be set after a successful transaction through this method. As it is online payment gateway, the order status may be set to Confirmed upon a successful transaction.
- **Order Status for failed transactions**: Select the order status for failed transactions. It may be Pending or Cancelled.
- **Payment Extra Info**: This section may contain some custom code for displaying extra information.

For detailed information on eProcessingNetwork and its services, please visit their web site at `http://www.eprocessingnetwork.com`.

Credit card (PayMeNow)

PayMeNow is another online payment processor, which can process credit card information submitted by customers. This payment module uses the **ps_paymenow** class for its business logic. You need to configure the following fields specific to PayMeNow in the **Configuration** tab:

- **PayMeNow ID**: This is the ID you get after creating a merchant account with the PayMeNow service.
- **Request/Capture Credit Card Code Value (CVV2/CVC2/CID)**: Select Yes to capture CVV2/CVC2/CID to verify credit cards.
- **Order Status for successful transactions**: Select the order status to be set after a successful transaction through this method. As it is online payment gateway, the order status may be set to Confirmed upon a successful transaction.
- **Order Status for failed transactions**: Select the order status for failed transactions. It may be Pending or Cancelled.
- **Payment Extra Info**: This section may contain some custom code for displaying extra information.

For creating an account and to know more about PayMeNow, please visit their web site at `http://www.paymenow.com`.

eCheck.net

eCheck.net is service provided by Authorize.net, by which customers can pay through electronic checks. In fact, it is an electronic payment through a Bank debit method. This payment module is configured as a bank debit type and uses the **ps_echeck** class for its business logic. You need to configure the following options for this payment module:

- **Test mode?**: Like other payment modules, this can be set to Yes to test the settings. Once the test is successful, set it to No.
- **eCheck.net Login ID**: You get this Login ID after creating a merchant account for eCheck.net service.
- **eCheck.net Transaction Key**: You get the transaction key from your merchant account for eCheck.net service. You can view or update the transaction key by clicking on the Show/Change the Transaction Key button.
- **Recurring Billings?**: Select Yes if you want to receive recurring bills through this payment method.
- **eCheck.net Transaction Type**: This is the authentication type to be used for this module. You can select AUTH_CAPTURE or AUTH_ONLY from the list. In the first option, authentication information will be captured by this module, but for the second option, only authentication will be done without storing authentication information.
- **Payment Extra Info**: This section may contain some custom code for displaying extra information.

For creating an account for eCheck.net or to know details about the service, please visit `http://echeck.net/solutions/merchantsolutions/merchantservices/echeck/`.

eWay

eWay is an online payment processor and supports major credit cards. This module uses the **ps_eway** class for its business logic. You need to configure the following settings for this module to work:

- **eWay Login ID**: You get this Login ID after creating a merchant account for eWay service.
- **Request/Capture Credit Card Code Value (CVV2/CVC2/CID)**: Select Yes to capture CVV2/CVC2/CID to verify credit cards.

- **Order Status for successful transactions**: Select the order status to be set after a successful transaction through this method. As it is online payment gateway, the order status may be set to Confirmed upon a successful transaction.
- **Order Status for failed transactions**: Select the order status for failed transactions. It may be Pending or Cancelled.
- **Test mode?**: Like other payment modules, this can be set to Yes to test the settings. Once the test is successful, set it to No.
- **Payment Extra Info**: This section may contain some custom code for displaying extra information.

For creating an account and know more details about eWay services, please visit `http://www.eway.com.au`.

iTransact

iTransact is another online payment processor. This module uses the **ps_itransact** class for its business logic, and is configured as an HTML-form based payment type. The form that will be displayed for processing payment through this gateway is specified by the custom code provided in the **Payment Extra Info** field on the **Configuration** tab. No other information is needed. For more information on iTransact and its services, please visit `http://itransact.com`.

noChex

noChex is another online payment processor gateway. However, like PayPal, this module uses HTML-form based processing. This module uses the **ps_nochex** class as its business logic. The form definition is specified in the **Payment Extra Info** field on Configuration tab. In addition to this, you also need to provide your email address which was used for creating your noChex account. For more information on noChex services, please visit `http://nochex.com`.

PayMate

PayMate is another online payment processor gateway located in Australia. This payment module is also HTML form-based and form codes are provided in the **Payment Extra Info** field on the **Configuration** tab. In addition to this, you need to provide your PayMate customer identification code in the **PayMate Username** field. For more information about PayMate and their services, please visit `http://www.paymate.com`.

VeriSign Payflow pro

VeriSign PayFlow Pro (now known as PayPal PayFlow Pro) is a premium payment processing service. This module uses an online payment processor, and its business logic is defined in the **payflow_pro** class. The unique configuration options for this module are:

- **VeriSign processing Partner ID**: You will get this Partner ID when registering through an authorized VeriSign reseller. Provide that partner ID in this field.
- **Merchant Login / Vendor Name**: This is the merchant account name or vendor name. When you create an account for this service, you get this name.
- **User Name**: This may be the merchant login name or username for logging into the account.
- **Password**: Provide the password for logging into your merchant account for PayFlow service.

Some other fields for this service are similar to the other modules. For more information on VeriSign PayFlow Pro service, please visit `http://www.paypal.com`.

WorldPay

WorldPay is another online payment processing gateway where major credit cards are supported. The WorldPay payment module for VirtueMart is HTML form-based. Form definition is given in the **Payment Extra Info** field on the **Configuration** tab. In addition to this, you need to specify your WorldPay Installation ID, which you get after signing up with WorldPay. To know more about WorldPay, please visit `http://www.worldpay.com`.

B

Resources for Joomla! and VirtueMart

As discussed in the main text of this book, we will be developing the Joomla! site and VirtueMart shop on a local computer first, and then upload it to an online web server. We have also referred to many web sites for collecting resources for Joomla! and VirtueMart. There are hundreds of sites from where you can get extensions, templates, tutorials, and support for Joomla!. Similarly, some sites are also dedicated to providing resources for VirtueMart including extensions to VirtueMart, tutorials, and support. In this appendix, we will learn how to set up WAMP server on your local computer to get a development environment and the places for searching resources for Joomla! and VirtueMart.

Setting up the WAMP server

You need Apache, MySQL, and PHP for running Joomla!. You can use a hosting server for hosting your Joomla! site and VirtueMart shop. However, at the time of building the shop, it is recommended that you do that in a development environment. If you are using a Windows PC, you can use one of the Apache, MySQL, and PHP packages. Here, we are going to discuss how you can setup and configure WAMP on your Windows computer.

Step 1: Getting the WAMP Server. WAMP server gives you Apache, MySQL, and PHP. Point your browser to `http://www.wampserver.com` and download the latest version of WAMP server.

Step 2: Installing the WAMP Server. Once WAMP server is downloaded to your computer, double-click on the installation file. It will be installed, by default, on `C:\wamp`. Under that, there will be a `www` directory, which is known as web directory. This implies whatever web applications you want to run should be put inside this folder (for our case, it is `e:\www`).

Step 3: Running the WAMP Server. You can configure your WAMP server to run when Windows starts. Alternatively, you can run it as and when needed. You can start WAMP server from **Start | All Programs | WampServer | Start WampServer**. When the WAMP server starts, you see the WAMP server icon in the system tray. Click on that icon, and you get WAMPserver menu:

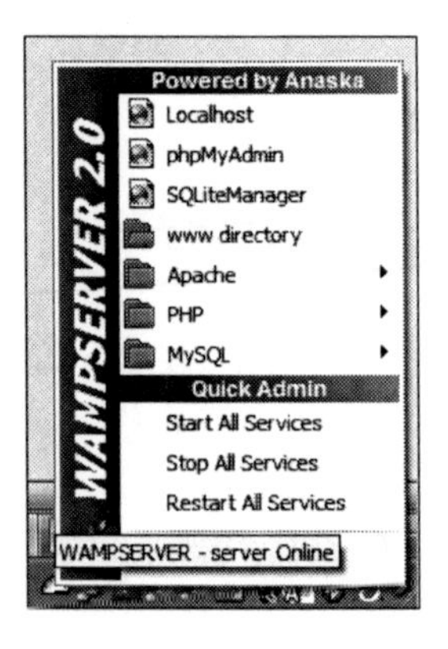

For starting all services (Apache, MySQL, and PHP), click on **Start All Services**. For configuring PHP, go to **PHP**. You can create databases through **phpMyAdmin**. To see the default page in the web root, click on the **Localhost** link, or type `http://localhost/` in your browser's address bar. It will display a page like this:

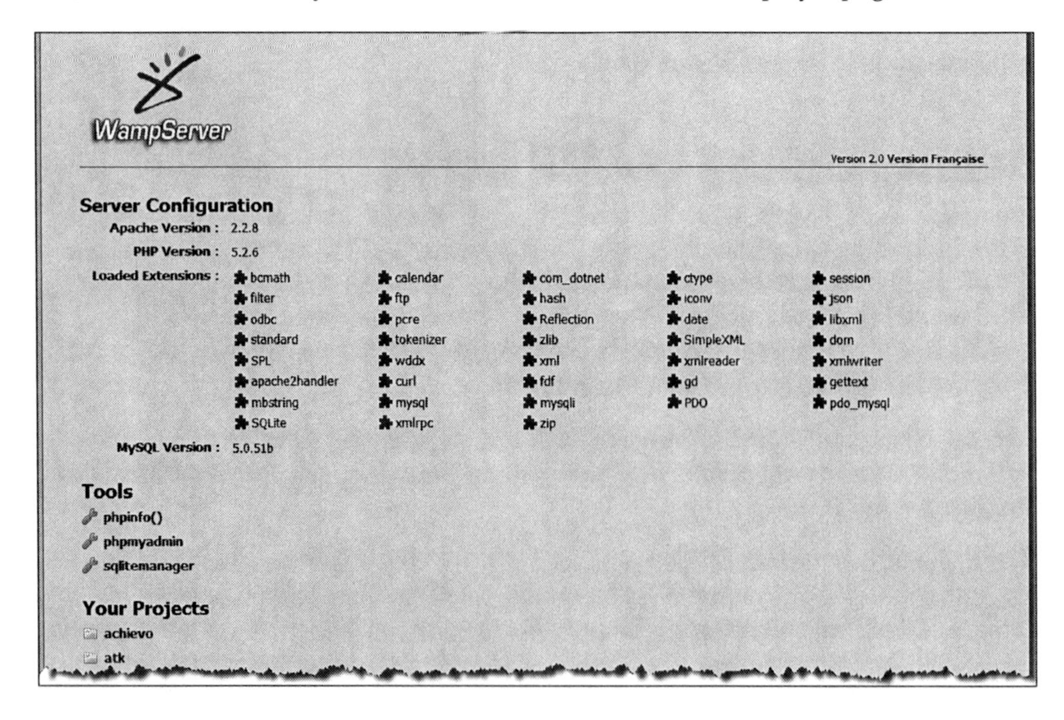

If it works fine, you are done! Your WAMP server is working. So, get ready for the next step!

Step 4: Getting the Joomla! installation package. It is now your turn to get a Joomla! installation package, by which you will install Joomla! on your local computer. Open your browser, and type `http://www.joomla.org` in the address bar. You will see the Joomla! home page. On the right-side, there is download link for the latest release. Click on this link to download the latest release of Joomla!. It comes as a `.zip` or `.tgz` archive.

Step 5: Installing Joomla! on your local computer. Once you have downloaded the installation package for Joomla!, follow the steps described in Chapter 2 for installing Joomla! on the local computer.

Resources for Joomla!

As indicated earlier, there are hundreds of sites which provide resources for Joomla!. With the increasing popularity of Joomla!, new sites are coming into operation and providing new services. The following are some of the sites you should search for Joomla! resources:

- **Joomla! Home page** (`http://www.joomla.org`): This is the first place you should check while searching for Joomla! resources. This site provides updates on Joomla! development and news relevant to Joomla!. This also serves as entry point to the Joomla! extensions directory, download site, support site, and documentation site.
- **Joomla! Forum** (`http://forum.joomla.org`): Joomla! forum is an indispensable resource for any Joomla! site builder. When you find a problem on your site, and suspect that it might be related to Joomla!, first search the forum. The forum is divided into several sections. You may also concentrate on the VirtueMart extension section for finding solution to Joomla! and VirtueMart.
- **Joomla! Extensions Directory** (`http://extensions.joomla.org`): Many of the extensions mentioned in this book are available from this extension directory. Check this directory regularly to find updates to the extensions you are using for your site.
- **JoomlaCode** (`http://joomlacode.org`)**:** This is a software repository for Joomla!. Developers can build and host their Joomla! extensions on this server. Almost all of the popular Joomla! extensions can be found here. The extensions listed in the Joomla! extensions directory are often downloaded from the `joomlacode.org` server.

- **Joomla! Documentation** (`http://docs.joomla.org`): This is Joomla!'s official documentation site. Start reading the available documents on this site before beginning to build your first Joomla! site.
- **Joomla! Developer** (`http://dev.joomla.org`): This site is for Joomla! developers. If you are interested in knowing about Joomla! development and want to join Joomla! developer team, this will be the best place to start.
- **Best of Joomla** (`http://www.bestofjoomla.com`): This site can be a good place to start searching for Joomla! templates, extensions, and other resources. This site aggregates information from other Joomla! sites and provides categorized listing of templates, extensions, and tutorials.
- **Joomla Tutorials** (`http://www.joomlatutorials.com`): This site provides some useful tutorials for building Joomla!-based web sites. The video tutorials section can greatly help beginners.
- **Joomla24** (`http://www.joomla24.com`): This is a vast base for searching free Joomla! templates.
- **Joom!Fish** (`www.joomfish.net`): The homepage for the Joom!Fish extension. It has updated documentation and an active forum. Consult these when facing problem with multilingual content created with Joom!Fish.
- **extensions.Siliana.com** (`http://extensions.siliana.com`): You get *sh404SEF* extension from this site. For updated releases of *sh404SEF*, visit this site. Consult the forum, if you are having problems with *sh404SEF*.

Resources for VirtueMart

There are many resources available online which can be used while building a Joomla! site and VirtueMart shop. The following list shows some of the web sites which might help you understand VirtueMart and receive support from the online community:

- **VirtueMart Homepage** (`http://virtuemart.net`): Visit the VirtueMart homepage frequently to know about developments, and next releases or security warnings.
- **VirtueMart Forum** (`http://forum.virtuemart.net`): The best place to search for a solution. Even when you are not bogged down with some problem, visit this site and read the posts. That will make you aware about the potential problems and help you solve them when they occur.
- **VirtueMart Extensions Directory** (`http://extensions.virtuemart.net`): This directory lists extensions specifically designed for VirtueMart.

- **VirtueMart Templates** (`http://www.virtuemarttemplates.net/`): This site contains some templates and themes designed for VirtueMart.
- **Powered By VirtueMart** (`http://www.poweredbyvirtuemart.com/`): This site lists some professionally designed templates and themes for VirtueMart. This site also lists some video tutorials for VirtueMart.
- **VJ Templates** (`http://www.vjtemplates.com`): This site contains some VirtueMart themes and Joomla! templates specially designed to be used with VirtueMart.

As new resources are being added daily, it is a good idea to regularly search for updated resources available for VirtueMart. You can use Google and other search engines with the keywords 'Joomla Virtuemart' to get sites relevant to Joomla! and VirtueMart. The **Links** section at `http://www.virtuemart.net` also provides links to additional VirtueMart resources.

Index

Symbols

A

B

C

D

E

F

G

H

I

J

L

M

N

O

P

R

S

T

U

V

W

Y

Z

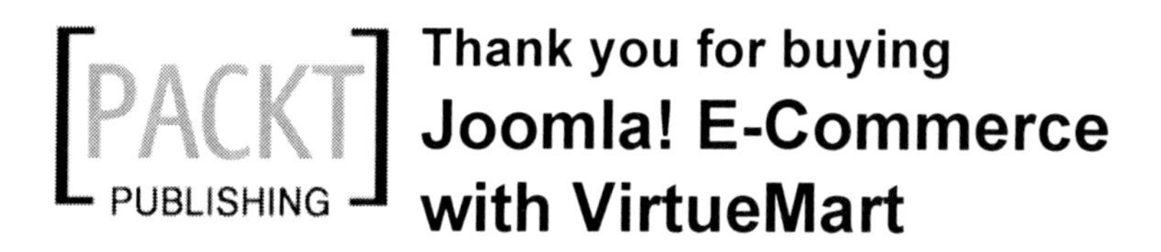

Packt Open Source Project Royalties

When we sell a book written on an Open Source project, we pay a royalty directly to that project. Therefore by purchasing Joomla! E-Commerce with VirtueMart, Packt will have given some of the money received to the Joomla! Project.

In the long term, we see ourselves and you—customers and readers of our books—as part of the Open Source ecosystem, providing sustainable revenue for the projects we publish on. Our aim at Packt is to establish publishing royalties as an essential part of the service and support a business model that sustains Open Source.

If you're working with an Open Source project that you would like us to publish on, and subsequently pay royalties to, please get in touch with us.

Writing for Packt

We welcome all inquiries from people who are interested in authoring. Book proposals should be sent to `authors@packtpub.com`. If your book idea is still at an early stage and you would like to discuss it first before writing a formal book proposal, contact us; one of our commissioning editors will get in touch with you.

We're not just looking for published authors; if you have strong technical skills but no writing experience, our experienced editors can help you develop a writing career, or simply get some additional reward for your expertise.

About Packt Publishing

Packt, pronounced 'packed', published its first book "Mastering phpMyAdmin for Effective MySQL Management" in April 2004 and subsequently continued to specialize in publishing highly focused books on specific technologies and solutions.

Our books and publications share the experiences of your fellow IT professionals in adapting and customizing today's systems, applications, and frameworks. Our solution-based books give you the knowledge and power to customize the software and technologies you're using to get the job done. Packt books are more specific and less general than the IT books you have seen in the past. Our unique business model allows us to bring you more focused information, giving you more of what you need to know, and less of what you don't.

Packt is a modern, yet unique publishing company, which focuses on producing quality, cutting-edge books for communities of developers, administrators, and newbies alike. For more information, please visit our website: `www.PacktPub.com`.

Joomla! Web Security

ISBN: 978-1-847194-88-6 Paperback: 248 pages

Secure your Joomla! website from common security threats with this easy-to-use guide

1. Learn how to secure your Joomla! websites
2. Real-world tools to protect against hacks on your site
3. Implement disaster recovery features
4. Set up SSL on your site
5. Covers Joomla! 1.0 as well as 1.5

Joomla! Accessibility

ISBN: 978-1-847194-08-4 Paperback: 160 pages

A quick guide to creating accessible websites with Joomla!

1. Understand what accessibility really means and why it's important
2. Ensure that content editors and writers publish accessible articles
3. Create accessible Joomla! Templates
4. Understand Assistive Technology (AT) and the needs of people with disabilities

Please check **www.PacktPub.com** for information on our titles

Printed in the United Kingdom by
Lightning Source UK Ltd., Milton Keynes
140633UK00001B/77/P